Law of the Sea: Neglected Issues

Law of the Sea: Neglected Issues

Proceedings

Law of the Sea Institute
Twelfth Annual Conference

Co-sponsored by the
Institute of International Law
of the University of Utrecht

October 23–26, 1978
The Hague, The Netherlands

Edited by
John King Gamble, Jr.

FINANCIAL SUPPORT
OF
THE LAW OF THE SEA INSTITUTE

THIS CONFERENCE HAS BEEN MADE POSSIBLE BY THE GENEROSITY OF THE FOLLOWING CONTRIBUTORS WHOSE SUPPORT IS GRATEFULLY ACKNOWLEDGED:

Stevin Baggeren B.V.

Bos Kalis Westminster Group N.V.

Exxon Corporation

Faculty of Law, University of Utrecht

Hawaii State Marine Affairs Coordinator

Imperial Oil Limited

Institute of International Law
of the University of Utrecht

J. Ray McDermott and Company, Inc.

Ministry of Economic Affairs, the Netherlands

Ministry of Education, the Netherlands

Ministry of Foreign Affairs, the Netherlands

Ministry of Transport and Public Works, the Netherlands

Mobil Oil Corporation

Ocean Minerals Company

Research Corporation of the University of Hawaii

Shell Oil Company

Shell Nederland B.V.

Smit Internationale N.V.

The Law of the Sea Institute is a project sponsored in part by the University of Hawaii Sea Grant College Program under Institutional Grant No. 04-8-M01-178 from NOAA, Office of Sea Grant, U.S. Department of Commerce.

Sea Grant Miscellaneous Report
UNIHI-SEAGRANT-CR-7901

CONTENTS

FOREWORD, *John King Gamble, Jr.* ix

OPENING ADDRESS, *D. S. Tuijnman* xi

PART I - STAGE-SETTING SESSION 1

NEGLECTED ISSUES AT THE THIRD UNITED NATIONS LAW OF THE SEA CONFERENCE, *Robert L. Friedheim and Robert E. Bowen* 2

COMMENTARY, *David A. Ross* 40
Edward Miles 41
Albert W. Koers 43
Leo J. Bouchez 44
H. Gary Knight 46
John P. Craven 47
Isabella Diederiks-Verschoor 48

DISCUSSION AND QUESTIONS 49

PART II - NON-NODULE RESOURCES OF THE DEEP SEA-BED

RESOURCES OF THE DEEP SEA OTHER THAN MANGANESE NODULES, *David A. Ross* 54

LEGAL PROBLEMS RELATING TO THE EXTRACTION OF RESOURCES OF THE DEEP SEA OTHER THAN MANGANESE NODULES, *Thomas A. Clingan, Jr.* 69

COMMENTARY, *Judith Kildow* 86
David L. Larson 89
Paul Fye 94

DISCUSSION AND QUESTIONS 95

PART III - AIR SPACE AND THE LAW OF THE SEA 119

INTRODUCTORY REMARKS BY SESSION PROGRAM CHAIRWOMAN, *Isabella Diederiks-Verschoor* 120

UNILATERAL CLAIMS FOR THE USE OF OCEAN AIRSPACE, *Carl Q. Christol* 122

AIR SPACE OVER EXTENDED JURISDICTIONAL ZONES, *Paul P. Heller* 135

COMMENTARY, *K. Hailbronner* 154

DISCUSSION AND QUESTIONS 159

PART IV - PROBLEMS OF POLAR REGIONS 163

INTRODUCTORY REMARKS BY SESSION CHAIRMAN, *Edward Miles* 164

THE CONTINENTAL SHELF - ISSUES IN THE "EASTERN" ARCTIC OCEAN, *Willy Østreng* 165

THE "NORTH AMERICAN" ARCTIC OCEAN, *Donat Pharand* 183

REGIMES FOR LIVING AND MINERAL RESOURCES IN THE ANTARCTIC, *Finn Sollie* 193

LEGAL ISSUES REGARDING TOWING OF ICEBERGS, *Curt Epperson* 209

DISCUSSION AND QUESTIONS 240

PART V - CHANGING REGIME FOR SHIPPING 245

INTRODUCTORY REMARKS BY SESSION CHAIRMAN, *Leo J. Bouchez* 246

THE "FREEDOM" OF OCEAN SHIPPING AND COMMERCIAL VIABILITY, *Edgar Gold* 248

COMMENTARY, *Menso de Jong* 259
Mr. Gezelius 262

DISCUSSION AND QUESTIONS 264

PART VI - ENERGY SOURCES FROM THE OCEANS 269

INTRODUCTORY REMARKS BY PROGRAM CHAIRMAN, *John P. Craven* 270

INTERNATIONAL REGULATION OF OCEAN FLOATING ENERGY PLATFORMS, *Kent M. Keith* 275

THE RELATION OF OCEAN ENERGY TO OCEAN FOOD, *John E. Bardach* 297

OIL STORAGE IN LAID-UP TANKERS: THE JAPANESE PLAN, *Yoshihiko Miwa* 311

COMMENTARY, *E. D. Brown* 317

DISCUSSION AND QUESTIONS 323

PART VII - MILITARY ISSUES IN THE LAW OF THE SEA 325

INTRODUCTORY REMARKS BY PROGRAM CHAIRMAN, *H. Gary Knight* 326

MILITARY IMPLICATIONS OF THE CHANGING LAW OF THE SEA, *Kenneth Booth* 328

COMMENTARY, *Frank Fraser* 398
Shannon D. Cramer 404
Michael MccGwire 408

DISCUSSION AND QUESTIONS 416

PART VIII - SEA-USE PLANNING IN THE NORTH SEA 423

INTRODUCTORY REMARKS BY PROGRAM CHAIRMAN, *Albert W. Koers* 424

NEED FOR SEA-USE PLANNING IN THE NORTH SEA, *D. Eisma* 425

SEA-USE PLANNING IN THE NORTH SEA: THE LEGAL FRAMEWORK, *E. D. Brown* 436

COMMENTARY, *O. Wattne* 481
D. Tromp 485
John M. Armstrong 488

DISCUSSION AND QUESTIONS 494

PART IX - CONCLUDING SESSION 501

REMARKS BY CONFERENCE PROGRAM CHAIRMAN, *John King Gamble, Jr.* 502

COMMENTARY, *Barry Buzan* 503
Douglas M. Johnston 509

DISCUSSION AND QUESTIONS 514

BANQUET ADDRESS, *Jens Evensen* 526

PARTICIPANTS LIST 537

FOREWORD

This volume contains the proceedings of the 12th annual conference of the Law of the Sea Institute held in The Hague the Netherlands, October 23-26, 1978. It was my pleasure to serve as program chairman for the conference.

It is abundantly clear from the contents of this volume that scores of people worked hard to make the conference a success. It is they with whom principal credit for a successful meeting and proceedings should rest.

Every Law of the Sea Institute Conference depends heavily upon support from the Institute's staff, Director, and Executive Board. I am extremely grateful to them for all their assistance.

This conference represented a new direction for the Law of the Sea Institute since it was the first conference held outside of the United States. The conference would have been impossible were it not for the strong support of numerous agencies and individuals in the Netherlands. Among all those who assisted with the conference, special appreciation and thanks are due Professor Albert Koers and Ms. Ninke van Keulen.

The Law of the Sea Institute has endeavored to produce the published proceedings relatively quickly after the conclusion of the conference. The need for rapid publication coupled with problems attendant with producing a book from an essentially oral conference introduces errors of omission and commission. Responsibility for these rests entirely with me.

John King Gamble, Jr.
The Behrend College
The Pennsylvania State University
Erie, Pennsylvania
February 23, 1979

OPENING ADDRESS

D. S. Tuijnman
Minister of Transport and Public Works
The Netherlands

Ladies and gentlemen,

On behalf of the government of the Netherlands I would like to welcome you to our country. The Hall of Knights which will house your conference has been the stage for numerous important events in the history of the state of the Netherlands. Likewise, I hope that this hall will mark an important occasion in the history of international law and in particular the law of the sea. For several reasons the Netherland has been heavily involved with the law of the sea. Our geographical position stimulated a very early and keen interest in the development of the law of the sea. By their very nature small countries have great interest in rules which assure orderly relations between nations. When most of the communications are effected by sea, a law of the sea is of paramount importance for a viable national economy. The legends of the flying Dutchman may have diverted your attention, but the principle of the freedom of navigation has long provided the background for the Dutch commercial economy. Still, talking history, I have to admit that the developments in the realm of the law of the sea were stimulated more by the work of Grotius than by the miracles of Hans Brinker, the little Dutch boy in a fairy tale who prevented flooding by closing the hole in a dyke with his finger.

Since I have the privilege of addressing such a learned assembly of persons who occupy themselves with the law of the sea, I would like to present to you some issues which in my opinion are highly relevant for the development of the law of the sea.

The sea which is the object of our concern may be viewed from several angles. Firstly, the sea may be used as a means of transportation. Secondly, the sea provides humanity with natural resources, oil, gas and minerals. Thirdly, the sea supplies man with food. Finally the sea is, however much we may regret so, employed to dump all kinds of waste.

As the Minister of Transport I am primarily interested in the sea as means of transportation. Other important elements of my ministerial responsibility are the management of the waterways and the protection of the marine environment.

Of old the sea has been employed by ships to carry persons, goods or arms. Until recently this has been the only communication function of the sea. In this century new ways of communication started using the sea or the airspace above the sea: pipelines, telecommunication cables, and airplanes. It is not only the historical environment in which we find ourselves here today that inspires me to expand some ideas on the oldest means of communication, shipping. It is also the urgency of some of the problems which are connected with modern shipping.

The past thirty years have shown a tremendous change in shipping. Most of these regulations have been developed internationally in the Inter-Governmental Maritime Consultative Organization (IMCO). They are embodied in international conventions such as the Safety of Life at Sea Convention and the Oil Pollution Prevention Convention.

Making rules alone does not improve the safety at sea and the protection of the marine environment. The implementation of international rules by the individual nations and observation of these rules by their ships is essential. For this purpose the implementation and observation of international measures should be general and on a worldwide basis. Unfortunately this is seldom the case. Regional action may to some extent alleviate the problems which general and worldwide implementation and observation pose.

Regional action may take the form of concerted action by coastal states in a given region to force other states and their ships to observe the international rules. The recent North Sea Memorandum concluded this year here in The Hague constitutes a good example of concerted regional action. In the "Memorandum of Understanding between certain Maritime Authorities on the Maintenance of Standards on Merchant Ships," as it is officially designated, the eight participating authorities take it upon themselves to maintain the general surveillance in their ports of standards laid down in IMCO and ILO conventions and resolutions. In the future the possibilities for coastal states to apply rules for protection of the marine environment and to take measures for their enforcement will be extended, when the new law of the sea will be accepted.

I have the impression that many governments content themselves with the adoption of international measures, but as experience has shown they do not precipitate with their implementation. Thus, for example, in the course of the last decade several amendments to the Safety of Life at Sea Convention have been adopted by IMCO but none has ever come into force. Such amendments did not obtain the required number of ratifications.

Similarly, many important recommendations for the safety at sea or the protection of the environment have been adopted unanimously by the Assembly of IMCO, but a worldwide or even a regional implementation never took place. A conspicuous example is the recommendation containing the Code for the Construction and Equipment of Ships Carrying Dangerous Chemicals in Bulk which was adopted by IMCO in 1971. The recommendation was a reaction to international concern about the growing number of tankers carrying a still increasing variety of chemicals.

Notwithstanding the adoption and implementation of safety measures, the risk of casualties or even calamities remains. The updating and strengthening of international safety and marine protection regulations proceeds too slowly to match the developments in shipping. Furthermore, the rules and regulations for navigation are drafted so as to provide an internationally acceptable minimum of safety and environment protection.

Such rules and regulations do not measure up to the needs of dense traffic areas. These areas often require stricter measures. The Amoco Cadiz disaster off Brittany's coast has diminished the number of supporters of an all too rigorous application of the sacrosanct principle of freedom of navigation of yesteryear. Presently the international world is blooming with activities to develop more stringent safety and environmental protection rules.

Apart from international action, national action can be taken to further safety at sea and the protection of the marine environment. In this respect it is important that individual nations effectively <u>exercise</u> the powers granted to them by international conventions. Thus, for instance, the national powers laid down in the International Convention Relating to Intervention on the High Seas in Cases of Oil Pollution Casualties of 1969 permit in my opinion effective national measures. It amazes me to hear countries calling for international action to combat marine pollution while they apply simultaneously a restrictive interpretation to existing relevant international law.

There are other means for individual nations to protect their coasts and coastal waters. One way to do this by enforcing international regulations. I think that there should be more inspection in ports to ensure that ships comply with minimum technical, safety and labor standards. Surveillance of the coastal waters should be organized for tracing violations of traffic rules or marine pollution prevention regulations. Plans should be made and an organization should be established to coordinate the combating of pollution.

Of course, possibilities for national action would be enhanced by the extension of the territorial sea beyond three nautical miles. Finally, I would like to mention two phenomena which constitute the main causes of marine casualties. These phenomena also aggravate marine casualties, thereby occasionally leading to an outright disaster.

These two phenomena are:

1. The absence of international minimum standards for crew qualifications and the composition of the crew.

2. Mismanagement of ships consisting of wrong judgments and decisions, and bad maintenance of the ships.

I would like to emphasize that a very large portion of casualties and pollution incidents is caused by human errors. These errors are not all due to lack of seamanship or quality of the responsible officers, but are sometimes the result of "economic" pressure or faulty shore operations.

Modern ships' operations are managed for a large part from the shore. The shipowner and shore operator exercise the actual control of the ship. Yet national and international law do not account for this. Traditionally, the law reserves the exercise of the control of the ship for the captain. The law holds the captain of the ship in most cases responsible for all the operations of the ship. National and international law should reflect the new situation. Presently discussions in international fora take place to determine whether and to what extent adaptation of the law is desirable.

I consider it urgent that the shipowner pay much greater attention to improving management and operation of his ships. One of the elements of good management consists of adequate manning. More attention should be paid to the selection of a well qualified crew in more sophisticated ships.

There is a need for studies and concerted action by shipowners together with governments and unions to come to internationally recognized manning rules.

Ladies and gentlemen. The safety of life at sea and the protection of marine environment are of a great importance to mankind. Therefore, I enjoyed the occasion to talk about these matters. I thank you very much for your attention and wish you a very successful conference.

PART I

STAGE-SETTING SESSION

NEGLECTED ISSUES AT THE THIRD UNITED NATIONS LAW OF THE SEA CONFERENCE[1]

Robert L. Friedheim and Robert E. Bowen
Institute for Marine and Coastal Studies
University of Southern California
Los Angeles, California

Despite what appears to be a melancholy task assigned us--to organize a discussion of neglect--we are honored to lead off a conference on the law of the sea in the homeland of the acknowledged father of the law of the sea. What is remarkable is how long the ideas of Hugh DeGroot, or, as the world knows him, Hugo Grotius, have survived. 370 years after the publication of his Mare Liberum we are still debating concepts Grotius would recognize. While we will contend that defining neglect is a difficult task, contemporary advocates of Grotius' ideas would find it easy. They could merely point to the idea of freedom of the seas as the major problem of neglect in the contemporary law of the sea. This is a theme that is bound to be reiterated frequently during the four days of our meetings.

The Purpose of the Paper

We have been told that what we are about is presenting the stage-setting paper. It particularly behooves us. therefore, to be clear about our purpose. There is a wide range of options. Should we act as Impressarios or Shauspieldirectors? As directors, should we order or align our colleagues who will follow us on the podium? If the authoritarian tone of command implied by that role falls upon the reluctant ears of colleagues, then perhaps they will accept the milder idea of our "guiding" their efforts in a common direction? In other words, should we at least coordinate the separate substantive panels so that a common purpose is served? Assuming that stage-setting is the purpose of this paper, however, could allow us to slip past a function often reserved for a beginning paper: to introduce who and what will follow. Often such an introductory paper introduces by making a tour d' horizon. Sometimes the best way to mark the boundary of the work of a number of scholars is not actually to walk the territory enclosed but rather to state the rules by which fences have been implanted. This can be done by providing a conceptual framework and/or defining the terms of

---

[1]This work is a result of research sponsored by the NOAA Office of Sea Grant, Department of Commerce, under grant #04-7-158-44113. The U.S. Government is authorized to produce and distribute reprints for governmental purposes notwithstanding and copyright notation that may appear hereon.

reference. If all or too many of these purposes are not fulfilled, we, as well as those diplomats whose conduct we examine, will be guilty of neglect.

Rather than choose one objective, we hope this paper will be able to achieve multiple, if closely related, objectives. We do expect to introduce, set the scene, and provide some guidance for subsequent sessions. We believe strongly that a synergistic effect can be achieved if the substantive panels are interrelated by a specific attempt at coordination. Rather than attempt to write everyone else's paper for him, however, we hope to define the terms of reference and establish the framework that will tie together the individual panels. If this is done, our concerns about our neglect should be minimal.

The Nature of Neglect

The first term of reference that must be defined is neglect itself. According to the Webster *Third International Dictionary* neglect means "to give little or no attention or respect to." The dictionary definition does not give the word a pejorative meaning or connotation. The English word neglect is derived from a Latin root, the word *neglegere*. A direct translation of the Latin would come out "not to choose."

However, many present usages of the English word "neglect" give it a pejorative connotation. "Neglect implies failure to give full or proper attention to some one or something that has a claim on one's attention." Indeed, if we fail to pay proper attention and the subject or person has a claim on us for attention it would be appropriate to apply one of a large number of candidate synonyms to such behavior. These would include: slight, disregard, carelessness, thoughtlessness, dereliction, supineness, laxity, slackness, evasion, or mere inattention. Those who engage in neglect of the type for which it is inappropriate to refer to them pejoratively are often referred to as neglecters, triflers, procrastinators, wastrels, slackers, or Micawbers. Since neglect as failure to give proper attention to requires action by the neglecter or slacker, there is also a list of appropriate pejorative verbs such as let slip, lose sight of, ignore, wink at, connive at, or leave in the lurch. If, by now, you are indignant at neglecters, please keep in mind Thucydides' words, "Everybody fancies that his own neglect will do no harm."

Neglect and the Law of the Sea Conference

We believe that it is useful to preserve the distinction between neglect as a lack of choosing certain options and neglect as a failure to do one's duty. If we choose to treat certain issues or problems that could have been addressed at the U.N. Law of the Sea Conference (UNCLOS) but were not, we should raise a set of considerations very different from those which we would derive if we choose to view those issues as problems that were consciously and heedlessly disregarded. In fact, we expect to do both. This will be our basic approach throughout this paper.

We will examine first those issues neglected because they were completely or partially ignored at UNCLOS III. We will make no judgments concerning whether the issues should have been addressed. Rather, we shall attempt to develop a framework for subsequent analysis by our colleagues for these acts of omission. Within this approach we shall try to sketch some ways of answering three subordinate questions. First, what are the reasons for these issues being addressed not at all or only marginally at UNCLOS III? Second, what are the linkages, if any, between the seven issues that are on the agenda of this LSI Conference and potentially might have been on the agenda of UNCLOS? Third, what are the linkages, if any, between the issues unaddressed or only partially addressed at UNCLOS III with those that have been addressed?

Neglect as a failure to pay proper attention to, will be examined in a subsequent section. Neglect as dereliction will be broken down into six subordinate categories: 1) the issues that should have been addressed; 2) the national interests that should have been taken into account; 3) the regional management needs or group preferences that might have been better served; 4) the particularistic ocean management notions already being enforced by states but not considered in UNCLOS that should have been considered; 5) the conceptual frameworks or principles that were not derived before specific legal obligations were developed; and, 6) the bargaining opportunities and their associated costs that were missed. Despite the formidable list of alternative analytic categories under which any analyst could flay the diplomats who have worked so intensively in Caracas, New York and Geneva, we intend to extend to them the maximum amount of charity possible. While it was desirable for some bargaining groups to have a large number of issues on the agenda to promote trade-offs, there was never a hope that all issues in the law of the sea could be dealt with simultaneously or that all states invited to the largest multilateral decision conference ever held could be satisfied uniformly by the outcome of the deliberations. We shall not claim that all relevant issues could have been dealt with simultaneously or that all interested parties could have been perfectly satisfied with the outcome.

Nevertheless to pursue seriously the idea that UNCLOS III by omission or commission failed to deal with some problems it should have addressed and solved is to require that we make normative judgments. These are always difficult. Frequently one person's neglect is another person's compromise or trade-off. Yet, while we must recognize that a normative judgment is being expressed in every aspect of the analysis contained in the second part of this paper, we shall try to avoid making our points merely an example of Morley's "the too neglected list of good causes lost."

Neglect As Issues Unaddressed

Why Were The Unaddressed Issues Unaddressed?

Neglect as System Overload

We cannot begin an examination of why certain subjects were not put on the UNCLOS agenda or why certain items on it might have received cursory treatment according to critics, without reiterating our belief that it is conceited to believe that UNCLOS could have been a totally encompassing ocean legislative assembly or its outcomes could be all things to all people. As it is, the "system" is obviously overloaded, and from the beginning of the current 11-12 year effort to redo the law of the sea, has stood in danger of being almost critically weighted down. There have been too many participants, too many items on the agenda, too many irreconcilable interests that must be satisfied for a collectivized solution, and too many different functions that must be served simultaneously; for example, finding appropriate rules for actual present and probable future ocean uses, contributing to a New International Economic Order, raising capital funds for distribution to Third World countries, reducing tension and friction and leading to world peace, etc.

Serious questions have been raised by some critics, from the time of Dr. Pardo's speech in 1967, that called into question whether conference diplomacy as we have come to know it could have succeeded (that is, written a widely acceptable comprehensive treaty) in an expeditious manner in a bargaining arena which has so many built-in attributes that lead to inertia. Friedheim for one was skeptical that the proceedings of a conference operating under parliamentary rules would be rapid in concluding its deliberations, fair to the widest variety of interests, and would result in a technically sound set of rules for the management of ocean space (Friedheim, 1974). It was clear from the beginning that some issues must be "neglected," and some interests ignored, if the conference were not to be in continuous session from 1973 to infinity. Since the conference process is political, it was highly probable that the general criteria for what would be included, what excluded, what emphasized, that deemphasized would be political. That is, matters included and emphasized would be those issues most highly salient to those states and bargaining groups that have the most bargaining leverage in the context of a UN Conference (the Group of 77, the states among the Group of 77 for whom ocean issues are highly salient, and the major ocean-using states without whose cooperation most new ocean management schemes probably would not work). Conversely, not included or deemphasized would be those issues most highly salient to those states and bargaining groups that have the least bargaining leverage in the context of a UN Conference (the geographically disadvantaged, the distant-water states that would have preferred the freedom of the seas conceptual framework from which the detailed rules could be derived, the states with limited ocean interests whose failure to cooperate could not cripple most new ocean management measures). This is not to say that the former will be satisfied and the latter dissatisfied with the outcome of the negotiations, but merely that they generally had more or less control of the input or agenda-setting.

A Typology of UNCLOS Neglect

The previous paragraph argues that choosing the formal and informal agendas was not a random process. But it only states the most general criteria. We will show that there might have been other more explicit criteria for choice, at least for the seven issues being considered by this Conference. Whether these are the real reasons for neglect or merely the rationalizations heard in the UN halls when these subjects were broached is beyond our powers to say. Below we have divided our seven issues into three reasons for neglect.[2]

FIGURE 1

A Typology of UNCLOS Neglect

Reasons for Neglect	Issues
Too little known to consider as subject of regulation or management	· Non-nodule resource recovery · Energy Resources beyond 200mi EEZ/ margin
Issue too delicate or political	· Polar Regions · Military Uses
UNCLOS Inappropriate Forum	· North Sea · Airspace · Navigation

[2]The categories are not mutually exclusive; e.g., it can be argued that UNCLOS is not an inappropriate forum for discussion of Arctic problems since it is purely a regional issue. We treat them as exclusive only to save time.

One of the great problems of our age is the inability of social systems to manage the changes brought about by the explosion of the fundamental knowledge and the extraordinary leaps in technology. Although a variety of supposed non-nodule resources is included in the deep seabed regime (Article 133 of the Informal Composite Negotiating Text), it can be argued that we know too little as yet about the fundamental facts concerning the nature, origins, and potential uses of non-nodule resources of the deep oceans to try to regulate in detail at this time any future attempt to harvest these resources. While we know that many fundamental ocean processes generate energy (the physical ability to do work) (Thirring, 1958) in the form of wind, waves, currents, tides, salinity and thermal gradient differences, we know little about how to harness them.[3] An important consequence of the lack of fundamental knowledge and the fact that exploitative engineering systems, if they are in the pipeline at all, are in the earliest development stages, is that we have too few tools to anticipate the impact of attempts to use new ocean areas or resources. Unless we have some better means of measuring probable impacts on a complex system with multiple opportunities for substitution responses, it will be very difficult to forecast what the consequences will be to the world political or economic system of "exotic" non-nodule uses or exploitation of deep ocean areas and resources. Today we are very conscious of the need to avoid unintended social, political or economic consequences of new knowledge, but it cannot be said that we are certain how. Small may be beautiful, but it is a large hungry world, and many are not yet convinced this is the answer (Schumacher, 1973).

Answers purportedly will come when we develop an appropriate technology forecasting methodology. In the United States the current movement of technology assessment has produced useful specific analyses, but has not yet developed a solid methodological base (Cetron, 1969; Jantch, 1967; Wilmot & Slingerland, 1977). Perhaps we do not anticipate new issues arising out of new knowledge or technology because there is a failure of imagination or training. Indeed there are few John Cravens who have training in both science and social science, as well as the imagination to grasp future possibilities.

When stating we know too little about a future possibility, we stand on the horns of a dilemma. On one sharp peak we face the danger of an arrogant modern belief in human perfectability; i.e., if we had the appropriate knowledge we could find and

---

[3]For a useful introduction to ocean energy possibilities; see: <u>Oceanus</u> XXII (Summer 1974). It is reprinted along with much other useful material: U.S. House of Representatives, Committee on Science and Technology. <u>Energy From the Ocean</u>, 95th Cong., 2d Sess., April, 1978.

impose the perfect solution on the problem. On the other peak is the universal conservative preference of many of us to do nothing unless imminent disaster is staring us in the face. We cannot ignore the problems or possible consequences of energy extraction from the oceans, or non-nodule resource recovery, but we must become both smarter and humbler in attacking these subjects in due course.

For a sample of one, we submitted a list of our seven issues to our colleague Arvid Pardo for his opinion on how he should sort or categorize the issues. He immediately picked out problems of polar regions and military uses of the oceans as issues that would be neglected at UNCLOS because they are too overtly political, or too delicate. Since our sample of one was not the man in the street, we should listen carefully. What we believe Dr. Pardo means is that the major interested parties are: 1) not willing to negotiate at all on some of these subjects; 2) willing to negotiate only superficially and not make fundamental alterations in present arrangements on others; and 3) willing to negotiate some aspects of these issues in other bargaining arenas where the weight of opinion of states outside the club, the region, or treaty adherents will be felt less.

Polar issues might well be seen as delicate by the interested parties. It is clear that regarding the northern polar regions most of the countries that border on the Arctic prefer their own unilateral solutions to the problems arising from anticipated or increased use or would encourage, at most, a regional set of agreements among the interested adjacent states. Claims to special pollution zones and other functional rights by adjacent states, sectors, or other sovereign-like nations, do not encourage a belief that outside parties would gain much by participation in such negotiations. Moreover, these formal claims and the more numerous informal arguments are usually based on statements as to the uniqueness of the area or the special impact use practices that could normally be tolerated in more temperate areas could have upon a fragile Arctic ecosystem. All of these claims point to the fact that outsiders' participation in the making of Arctic decisions is not encouraged by the adjacent states (Meconchie and Reid, 1977; International Canada, 1970; Bilder, 1970; Beesley, 1971-72; Butler, 1971; Olenicoff, 1972). This is not to imply that the adjacent states have been able to handle their problems in the Arctic in routine fashion. Indeed the imbroglio over the voyage of the Manhattan in 1969-70 was a low point in US-Canadian relations. Currently relations between Norway and the Soviet Union are strained concerning claims to the Barents Sea area, Spitzbergen, and a mystery surrounding Soviet ship movements in the area (Apple, August 4, 1978; Apple, August 6, 1978). But except to justify domestic acts, the regional states have little incentive for serious multilateral negotiations of Arctic problems.

The Antarctic is another matter. Because of the Antarctic Treaty of 1959 with its thirteen consultative parties and six other adherents, many of whom are not states geographically contiguous to the Antarctic Ocean, the problems of the Antarctic are inherently multilateral. Nevertheless, there is little propensity to negotiate Antarctic problems in a larger arena than the Treaty group (although there may be a possibility of adding Canada and West Germany to the group). But interest in Antarctic problems and opportunities cannot be confined as easily to the club as Arctic problems could be confined mostly to the contiguous states. Middle East states who might sponsor programs to exploit Antarctic icebergs as sources of fresh water are not members of the club. There are estimates and rumors of vast biological resources in the waters around the Antarctic land mass and even more fabulous estimates and rumors of mineral and energy wealth on and in the frozen land mass ("Antarctica", 1974; Auburn, 1978; Bakus, Garlin, & Buchanan, 1978; Final Environmental Impact Statement, 1978; Green, 1977; Kaczynski, 1978; Ludwigson, 1978; Mitchell, 1977; "Moratorium", 1977). The treaty only "freezes" exclusive territorial claims. The agreement worked out recently at the Ninth Meeting of the Consultative Group concerning the conservation of krill is open to all those who choose to exploit the resource. Thus, we still have a situation of open entry. As far as we know the entrepreneurs who are now in the discussion or even planning stages of schemes to tow icebergs to the Middle East or California, do not expect to "pay" for the resource they will be removing from the region. Open entry problems will probably make difficult the working out of any future regime at the Tenth Meeting of the Consultative Group concerning exploitation of the energy and mineral wealth. If the rumors of wealth prove even partly true, the situation could be potentially explosive in the next several years. The treaty can be renegotiated by 1991. In the meantime, the consultative parties are trying to keep the lid on and work out arrangements before the deadline. Serious discussions at UNCLOS could have "blown the lid off" and doubtless were resisted. Thus, while the subject is at present considered by the interested parties, non-negotiable in a context larger than the consultative structure, most of them are aware that it will be very difficult to confine the future regime of Antarctica to the present consultative group.

Military issues have indeed been negotiated at UNCLOS but overall they are among the class of issues that have been dealt with only superficially. It was obvious from the beginning that if the conference chose to make overt fundamental alterations in the right of the so-called "blue-water" navies to move their fleet units virtually where they please beyond a relatively narrow territorial sea, their political masters would choose not to negotiate seriously on other issues. In other words, the major naval states signaled early that they considered military movement rights so salient that they would sacrifice other issues to get as much of a reaffirmation or at least the least restriction on traditional movement right as possible. As a result, the majority of "have not" states (in terms of size and capacity of navies, as well as by other measures) were provided a most important bargaining ploy. It was in their interest to make maximum noises to threaten blue-water navy rights early on in UNCLOS to induce a willingness of the well-to-do blue-water navy states to compromise on issues the less well-to-do considered salient. For the most part it worked for both sides. There are relatively mild extensions of territorial seas and coastal rights to regulate military transit through straits as well as no extravagant statements of archipelago rights that could restrict navies operating in archipelagic waters. On the other hand, most blue-water navy states acquiesced in general ocean enclosure. At the rare times when it appeared that an important state was seriously going to back an attempt to regulate navies directly on issues other than transit (we will discuss later the indirect regulatory effects on the military of general ocean enclosure), quiet but firm messages were sent to indicate that such a restriction could upset delicate compromises. This was the fate of a Mexican proposal to restrict the right of states to construct military installations on their own seabeds. This is the probable fate of any conference attempt at adding direct restrictions to the still relatively free uses of the sea by navies. Most states know that for the most part they cannot gain by agreement what they lack the physical capability for, i.e., to exclude foreign naval vessels from engaging in a whole range of coercive activities not too distant from their coasts. They are even more aware that if they seriously pursue enclosure efforts with direct impacts on navies, they will lose much of their bargaining leverage. But some states may be well aware of the possible long-run impact on military rights of general ocean enclosure and believe they can successfully pursue the goal of restricting the rights of blue-water navies by indirection. We will deal with this problem in a subsequent section.

Our third major category for explaining why certain subjects were "neglected" by UNCLOS is that the United Nations Conference system is an inappropriate forum for the particular problem under discussion. It may be inappropriate per se for the class of problem, or there may be another forum that is more appropriate.

Many of the states bordering on the North Sea could argue that North Sea use planning should be dealt with in a regional, and not a universal, forum. With congestion problems arising from the growing number of oil rigs, with externalities being produced by oil platform accidents, use conflicts arising from competition for space between oil drillers, merchant marines, fishermen and navies, there are many reasons to plan the uses of the North Sea. It can be argued that the problem should be dealt with on a regional level because the basic issues that had universal impact have already been settled. The major issue was who has jurisdiction over the seabed and therefore who should regulate its uses and the consequences of its use. The seabed was divided up between the United Kingdom, Norway, Denmark and The Netherlands in 1964 on the basis of the 1958 Continental Shelf Convention. After a dispute was settled by the International Court of Justice in 1969, the Federal Republic of Germany joined the others with proprietary interests. However, not all interested parties are coastal states. Others use the North Sea for transit into the Baltic Sea and for North-South transit off the European coast. It has been reported that the Soviet Union is unhappy with coastal state responsibility for congesting Russian lines of transportation and communication, and coastal state plans to use the oil rigs for defense purposes. On the other hand, "buzzing" of rigs has been experienced and the coastal states have expressed concern over the security of their oil sources in times of conflict ("Europe," 1975; Blundy & Dawe, 1975; Kessler, March 1976; Kessler, June 1976). But even if it is possible to reduce or exclude non-coastal states from decision-making concerning the North Sea, there is still another question--who will be the appropriate regional decision-making body: the bordering states, including Norway, or the European Economic Community (EEC), which does not include Norway? It has been reported that North Sea issues--oil and fish in particular--were among those that most influenced the vote to keep Norway out of the EEC. While there is no effective Community control of offshore oil and gas exploration or production, the Community does claim that continental shelf activities fall within the scope of its regulatory powers (Janis, 1975).

Those who wish to explain why aviation and marine transportation problems were not dealt with at UNCLOS with the seriousness they deserve would undoubtedly acknowledge the importance of those problem areas but point to the fact that universally based specialized organizations exist to deal with these matters with technical expertise that is not available at UNCLOS. In short, IMCO (Inter-Governmental Maritime Consultative Organization) and ICAO (International Civil Aviation Organization) are the appropriate fora for the detailed regulatory adjustments necessary to carrying out the consequences of the general allocation decisions being made at UNCLOS. UNCLOS simply is not equipped to resolve the technical and detailed problems of arranging future use patterns for aircraft flying over and ships navigating upon the enlarged territorial seas and economic zones as well as the shrunken open sea.

Linkages Between the Unaddressed Issues

All but one subject among the neglected issues can be viewed by economic and political criteria as allocation questions, and by legal criteria as jurisdictional questions. In other words the neglected issues concern who gets what, who will manage what has been acquired, and by what principles or conceptual framework. How to deal with deep-sea minerals, airspace use, the Arctic and Antarctic, ocean energy, shipping and the North Sea involves solutions to allocation and jurisdiction questions.

In all of the questions that we must deal with there is an assumption of scarcity. If the ocean and its resources are infinite, we need not move away from the rules posited by Grotius. If there is enough for all, then it makes sense to have open entry to the areas or their resources. Instead, today we are more and more conscious that there is only so much territory and so many resources out there. Moreover, we frequently treat these problems as if they are real-world applications of a zero-sum game; i.e., the gains and losses are additive, and what one party gains the other loses. While the "real" world is far more complex than the game table, with many extenuating and mitigating factors that vary the uniformity of the zero-sum solution, we believe that underlying the attitudes of many nation-states today is the belief that what value they do not capture will go to others. Further, we believe this will affect the way they view the issues we examine today.

Allocation problems are not a new class of problems for economic or political analysts. Microeconomics concentrates upon how resources are allocated, and the phrase we alluded to before (Who Gets What) is borrowed from the title of one of the most distinguished political analyses of our time (Lasswell, 1936). Thus, we have much empirical analytic experience and a body of theory to bring to our analysis of ocean allocation problems. The theory has already helped clarify the allocation problems of ocean fisheries and, to a lesser extent, ocean mining (Christy and Scott, 1965; Eckert, 1979; Gordon, 1954; Scott, 1955). We do not need a new or different conceptual framework to attempt to deal with polar issues, energy, shipping, air rights, and non-nodule deep sea minerals.

There has been a very discernable trend in our time in the ocean allocation decisions made. Even those who ardently fought the trend recognize that the world is in the midst of a vast enclosure movement. Whether by unilateral national action or by a future UNCLOS treaty which will in good part ratify national enclosure actions, all observers today must concede that the coastal states of the world are arrogating to themselves at least allocation and regulatory rights over the economic zones off their coasts out to 200 miles or perhaps the end of the continental margin. Most of the issues on our menu for the next several days have been and are being importantly affected by this trend in either of two ways. First are those issues where the basic decision to enclose has been made, or at least attempted, and the concerned parties are grappling with the details relating to the implementation of enclosure. This would include the problems of allocation and management of minerals and energy problems within 200 miles of the coast or end of the margin, air space over national territory, the Arctic, coastal shipping activities, and the uses of the North Sea. The uncertainties here relate to how to apply and enforce enclosure claims so that practices are more efficient and perhaps (though not true in many cases) more just. While we generally know where we are going, as two of the participants in the conference have put it, here there are "opportunities for imaginative action" (Ross and Miles, 1978).

In the second category are those issues that must be decided in the absence of enclosure. Here the basic question is whether national enclosure, central enclosure (making people of the world the rights holder with a universal organization as their agent), or open entry will be the regime framework. One of the reasons that the negotiations in the First Committee of UNCLOS have proved so difficult is because the solution to the basic conceptual question is still being debated fiercely simultaneous with the negotiations on implementing details. We suspect that if an agreement on the basic framework is worked out, the details could quickly be resolved. Instead, the states with the capability to do the first generation of deep-sea mining are attempting to recoup in negotiations on details a battle they could not win if they continued to focus on the general framework for the regime. Other minerals presumably would come under the same regime as deep-sea manganese nodules if Article 133 of the Informal Composite Negotiating Text becomes international law. But there is uncertainty as to whether energy generated from wind, waves, currents, temperature gradients, biomasses in the water column, or air-sea interface would also come under a central enclosure regime because of Article 135's guarantee of freedom of the seas. On the other hand Article 133 does mention "water," "steam," and "hot water" as resources of the area. If clarification of these questions is not forthcoming in the remaining negotiations, a serious jurisdictional problem may face those who would wish to promote ocean energy schemes. But the basic regime question has not been resolved. Obviously, basic regime questions also must be faced in the case of Antarctica and in the case of ocean navigation beyond 200 miles.

By now perceptive readers should be asking, "Did they forget ocean national defense?" No, we did not. We believe that the use of naval power to defend the interests of the states of the world in the uses of the oceans and its resources is very little connected to the enclosure movement or to problems of allocating rights. (It is an outlier.) This is curious, because Alfred Thayer Mahan, the 19th century American naval officer, quoted as guru on the role of navies by virtually all writers justifying the existence of blue-water navies, emphasizes that one of the chief functions of a navy was to protect the right of a state to use the seas. Command of the sea to secure a nation's trade and access to resources was an important part of Mahan's doctrine (Mahan, 1890; Rosinski, 1977; Turner, 1960). It is still frequently invoked today. But there is very little evidence that it is really considered a major function of navies with the capacity for sustained high-sea combat in ocean areas distant from their own coasts. The foreword to the latest edition of Jane's Fighting Ships is a prime example of this sort of ritualistic invocation. After stating that "a state that is dependent on the sea for its being, on sea transport, on fisheries and on all that lies beneath the surface must view the whole scope of that dependence with objectivity" because "he who depends upon the sea may also die should it be denied him," Captain J. N. Moore then proceeds to devote only 150 words of an approximately 9000 word analysis (1.6%) to naval activities designed to protect states' ocean interests (Moore, 1978)[4]. The same pattern was evident in the writings of the Commander-in-Chief of the Soviet Navy. In the final essay in the now famous series of articles in the Soviet naval journal Morskoi Sbornik, Admiral of the Fleet Sergei G. Gorshkov addressed the "problems in mastering the world ocean." After a technically good description of modern problems of ocean allocation, the subject was dropped when he discussed the problems of a modern navy.[5]

Major navies have had a great deal of influence on the posture their states have adopted in the UNCLOS conference but very few of their efforts have been devoted to activities that would support their states' present and future uses of the sea. There is little in their strategic doctrine, missions assigned to fleet units, or in funding decisions that would indicate that protection of ocean uses was an important function, even for the most obviously traditional and still most important of those uses, marine transportation and trade. There are few examples in

---

[4]For a similar expression of concern that naval leaders assume that a ritual invocation of past strategic thought serves as substitute for rethinking the problems of naval strategy in the light of present world political conditions see: Etzold, Thomas H. Seapower: our tarnished treasure. Washington Post, September 18, 1978, p. A23.

[5]Gorshkov, Sergei G. Red Star Rising at Sea. Annapolis: United States Naval Institute, 1974, pp. 123-135. There has been considerable debate among specialists as to: 1) whether "The Problems of the World Ocean" chapter is anomolous and 2) whether the Soviets, when they use the phrase "command of the sea," are really invoking the Mahanian notion. See the essays in MccGwire, Michael (Ed.), Soviet Naval Developments, New York: Praeger, 1973; MccGwire, Michael (Ed.), Soviet Naval Policy, New York: Praeger, 1975; MccGwire, Michael, Soviet Naval Influence, New York: Praeger, 1977.

modern times of major navies being employed to succor their ocean-using civilian compatriots.[6] In the wake of the Arab oil embargo, there has been much discussion of developing sea control ships to secure U.S. lines of communication to the Persian Gulf in times of general war, but little has been done about it. This is not to argue that naval protection of major states' ocean use rights should indeed be a major function, comparable to strategic deterrence or general war fighting. Activities that are matters of concern to this audience under the jurisdiction of blue-water navies are seen by them as support functions for themselves or civilian agencies. They are involved in ocean research, pioneering of new ocean engineering techniques, management of Arctic and Antarctic programs, and patrolling of the North Sea. Reductions in ocean use rights brought about by either national or international enclosure could create inconveniences for them. But they need not fear a major reduction of the use rights from the present ICNT which could seriously imperil their main missions. Predictions that the impact of the ocean enclosures of the early 1970's would be minor have held up very well (Breckner, 1972).

What blue-water navies fear are not the immediate, measurable reductions of rights but rather the slow erosion of their rights over time as the regime changes. Since these are difficult to predict with precision, naval decision-makers tend to rely upon worst-case models to guide them. Several years ago there was some debate among ocean specialists as to what "Craven's Law" meant. Perhaps Dr. Craven can give us an authoritative answer but if memory serves, it was defined as the tendency of jurisdiction to move from seabed to water column. If that is correct, it is only part of what the military feared was "creeping jurisdiction," the worst case. For them, creeping jurisdiction means a more generalized, albeit relatively

---

[6] In a little known incident in 1969 the Soviets used a threat of naval force against Ghana to press for the release of some fishing vessels held in port. However, since they were seized by Ghana for alleged gun running and not illegal fishing even this incident cannot be cited as use of a threat of force to protect traditional ocean rights. It also might be argued that the U.S. naval and marine rescue effort to get Cambodia to release the crew of the vessel Mayaguez was an example of using force to protect the right to use the ocean. We would contend that the Mayaguez would not have been in proximity to the Cambodian coast but for the Indochina war. We contend that the U.S. rescue effort is more properly viewed as one of the last U.S. coercive efforts in that war. For a thorough analysis of Soviet use of its navy for political purposes see: Dismukes, Bradford N. and McConnell, James M., Soviet Naval Diplomacy (forthcoming).

gradual, transformation of specific functional jurisdiction to generalized sovereign control. In that worst case the ability of blue-water navies as we know them to perform their stated missions could be seriously hampered. It is this longer-run fear--not any short-run, measurable impact--that has impelled blue-water navies to play as strong a role in their national delegations as they have.

Before moving on, we should note that "brown-water," or coastal and riverine navies not having the same assets and firepower as blue-water navies, also have different missions. They are, for the most part, more defensive in their orientation, and protection of the recently acquired rights of their states within 200 miles off shore is likely to be among the most important of their missions. Some militarily and politically "interesting" problems may arise, since technological change has favored those navies on a buying spree to acquire small, fast patrol vessels armed with missiles.

Linkages between Addressed and Unaddressed Issues

Most of the issues that we might point to as not being decided at all or only superficially at UNCLOS are linked to issues that UNCLOS and its predecessor organizations have struggled with for eleven years. The unaddressed issues are linked together by being mostly allocation problems, and they are linked to the addressed issues which are also predominantly allocation problems. As we have seen, we have an array of analytic tools to deal with these problems if we chose to treat each of these problems separately, according to the framework of the several social science disciplines. But, we face another important task in our conference; i.e., if addressed and unaddressed issues are linked, we believe we can safely assume that they will have impacts upon each other. We need an approach to estimating the scope and intensity of those impacts. There has been considerable recent literature on flows of international systems (Rosenau, 1969; Rosenau, 1973). Inevitably there are also, at a lower level, impacts of issues on each other. We must try to capture some of these in our discussions. Below we will suggest some ways of looking at these patterns. They are mere suggestions intended to further discussion, not findings of a thorough study.

The relationship between issues can be mutual and equal. Each issue would have approximately the same impact on the other as the other issue has upon it. This relationship can be plotted:

FIGURE 2

Linkages: Symmetrical Relationship

Probably more common is a situation of asymmetry where one issue has more influence upon the other than the reverse. There are two subsets of this relationship that may fit our problem. The first is where the addressed issues influence the unaddressed issues:

FIGURE 3

Linkage: Addressed Issues Dominant

Article 133 of the ICNT deals with a variety of mineral resources, including manganese nodules, but not by name. We can consider manganese nodule exploitation beyond 200 miles (approximately) as an addressed issue. Because there is no precise geographic description of the "area," many of the exploitation schemes to take energy from the water column or from surface winds are unaddressed issues. It is our guess, however, that management plans for such efforts will be heavily influenced by the management scheme for nodules addressed in the ICNT.

The second asymmetrical situation is where unaddressed issues "drive" the addressed issues:

FIGURE 4

Linkage: Unaddressed Issues Dominant

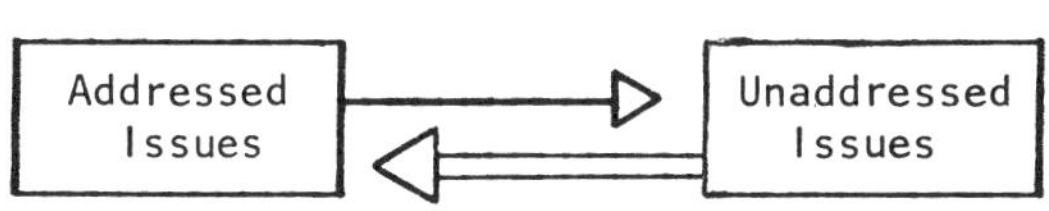

The obvious example is where the unaddressed military issues influenced the acceptance by the major ocean-using states of the national enclosures out to 200 miles.

Too often specialists attempt to pull the subject of their study out of its appropriate context. To avoid this, we also must consider in our deliberations unidentified issues that may not be directly ocean-related, or only partially ocean-related, but have an impact upon UNCLOS decision-making. Many ocean decisions are often heavily influences by non-ocean considerations:

FIGURE 5

<u>Linkage: Trilateral Relationship</u>

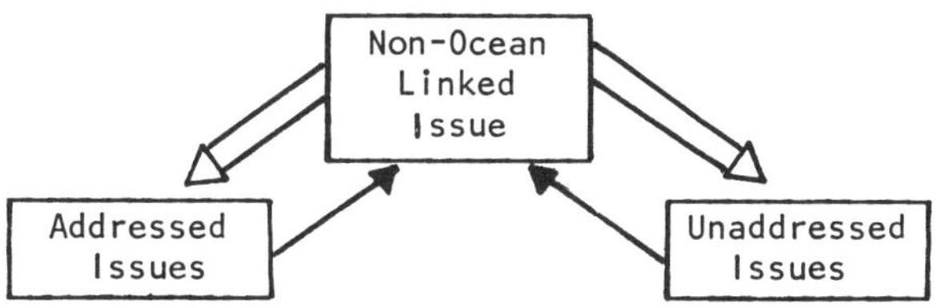

There are many examples of non-ocean issues that are linked to the outcome of both addressed or unaddressed direct ocean issues. Among them is the question of the aspirations of the developing countries to create, via bargaining in the UN system, a "new international economic order" (NIEO) that they consider more just, which would apply to ocean (addressed and unaddressed) and non-ocean issues uniformly. Another example is the decisions on oil pricing of the Organization of Petroleum Exporting Countries (OPEC). They are bound to have an important influence upon the allocation and management decisions concerning ocean energy inside and outside 200 miles. Two further subsets of the impact of non-ocean issues are possible where there is a disproportionate influence of non-ocean issues on either the addressed or non-addressed ocean issues. But, we will leave it to our colleagues to see if there are UNCLOS examples that fit these models.

The previous models we introduced have implicit within them an assumption of causality. The heavy arrow shows a larger impact imposed upon the receiving units by the sending unit. Many of our issue relationships may be well described by such a model, but we also ought to consider the situation where the issues are so intertwined as to form a completely interpenetrated relationship. Such relationships would be best shown graphically by an intersection of sets. For example, the relationship of nodule mining from the seabed beyond 200 miles with energy extraction from the water column beyond 200 miles:

FIGURE 6

Linkage: Interpenetrated Relationship

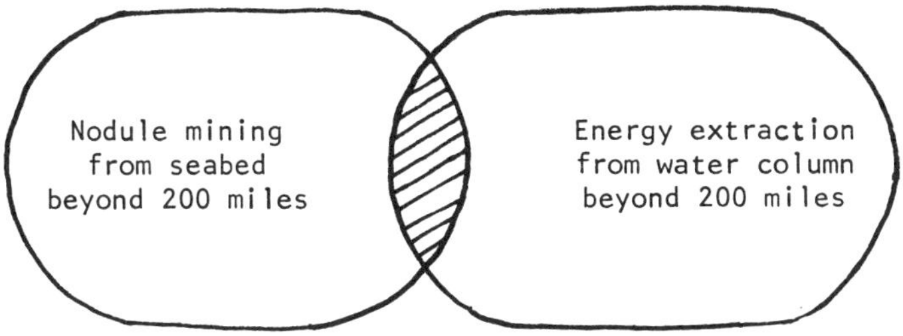

The interesting problems are in the shaded areas. For a trilateral relationship it is not difficult to imagine the problem we plot below:

FIGURE 7

Linkage: Trilateral Interpenetrated Relationship

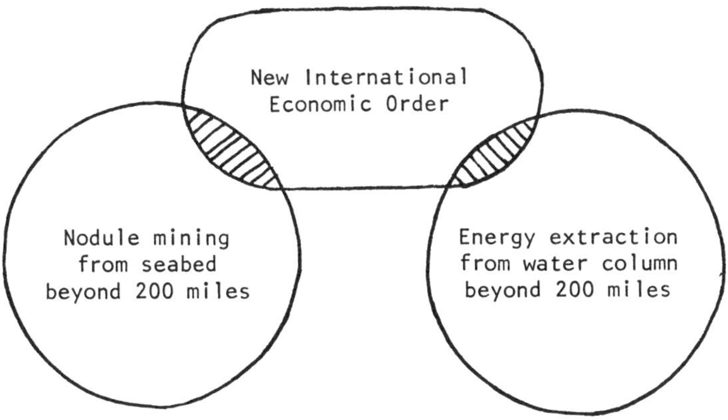

Although we do not believe that it is fair to excoriate the delegates to UNCLOS for not dealing with the future problems of energy from the deep ocean in the light of what they did do on nodule mining and in the light of the NIEO, there are many issues where we should remind ourselves where the delegates neglected their duty. Let us get on to them.

Neglect as Dereliction: What Have the Delegates to UNCLOS III Ignored, Winked at, or Lost Sight of?

It is inevitable that the exaggerated hopes for "success" of UNCLOS III will be dashed even if a treaty emerges. For years too many commentators as well as delegates glowingly reported that the conference could succeed in producing something that would be all things to all people. Moreover, they repeatedly promised that a draft treaty would be produced after just one more negotiating session. While these dashed hopes are not entirely the fault of the delegates, it is they as well as the "system," who put us where we are today. At the moment it appears they must answer for a document, the single negotiating test and the modifications under discussion at the rump four week session in New York during the summer of 1978. There are serious disputes concerning all parts. The First Committee draft on a regime to govern the exploitation of seabed minerals is hotly disputed by developed states who have the capability to mine. The Second Committee draft which, in good part, ratifies the national enclosures of nearshore areas out to 200 miles or the end of the margin, is viewed as prejudicial to the interests of the geographically disadvantaged states. The Third Committee draft is seen by many as not doing the necessary work to control major ocean pollution while doing too much to hinder ocean science.

If we take seriously the idea that many of these deficiencies are a result of neglect as failure of the delegates to give full or proper attention to matters that had a claim upon their attention, we will spend the next four days in merely listing their sins. In order to proceed we must sample, and doubtless we, ourselves, will neglect many worthy candidates. Our sample will be eclectic. Where it is possible to view major problems of neglect only with qualitative data, we will do so. Where we can be more systematic because of the availability of quantitative methods, we will do so. The quantitative data and forecasting models are derived from the Law of the Sea Forecasting Project conducted for a number of years by Friedheim and Kadane. The models were specially designed to analyze the negotiations of UN-type conferences.[7] The data are a content analysis of the statements of delegates, indicating their state's policy preference from 1967-75. We still believe it to be valid for analysis because we captured the basic preference of states during that period. Virtually all changes in national positions since 1975 were incremental adjustments to the stated positions of states rather than jump shifts that radically altered their positions.

[7]A short description of the methodology is available from the authors: Institute for Marine & Coastal Studies, University of Southern California, Los Angeles, CA 90007 USA.

Neglected Issues

Many among us will consider the seven major issues with which this conference is concerned as issues that have been neglected through carelessness or deliberate evasion. We offer them as such for your consideration with the caveat that not all specialists or experts would agree that although "neglected," they should have received more actual attention. For certain issues, such as navigation, some of us may agree with William Burke that it is a good thing that the delegates tampered little with rules that have worked so well in managing ocean transportation (Burke, 1977). On other issues, it may be advantageous for the world that not much attention was lavished upon them because examination of the facts of the situation would indicate that such issues contain few foreseeable problems of public policy. This may be the case for resources of the deep sea other than manganese nodules about which our colleague David Ross writes, "aside from the hot brines of the Red Sea, there will be no mining of deep sea minerals (exclusive of manganese nodules)...in the near future, if ever" (Ross, draft). No mining, no impacts, no reason to pay attention.

But there are more obvious existing problems where the impacts can be measured and where the delegates were culpable for their inattention. Most important among them is the question of how the international community should attempt to control pollution of the marine ecosystem from human activities on land. Suggestions made initially by Japan during the UN Seabed Committee plenary meetings held during July and August 1972 and by other nations since concerning the importance of controlling man-made material pollution of the marine environment regardless of source have been largely ignored by the Conference. Approximately two-thirds of the oil in the oceans results from river runoff, municipal waste, urban runoff, industrial waste, and coastal oil refineries (National Academy of Science, 1975). Virtually all of the halogenated hydrocarbons (DDT and PCB), heavy metals, sewage and fertilizers and radionuclides that find their way into the oceans originate from human activity on land (Goldberg & Menzel, 1975; Thacher and Meith-Avin, forthcoming, 1978). Two articles of the ICNT (208, 214) urge states to pass appropriate laws, to harmonize their policies regionally and to cooperate with competent international organizations, but do not tell them what laws, based upon what principles, will solve the problem. In short, these are pious hopes and not a solution. We call this neglect.[8]

[8] Samuel R. Levering would not agree with us. See: "The Oceans as an Avenue Towards World Peace," Issue Paper prepared for NACOA's Workshop on Reorganization, September 1978, p. 5.

Islands, because they are surrounded by water, are inherently ocean policy problems. Advocates of treating island problems in a more rigorous manner are capable of presenting numerous arguments in support of their position. Island nations are, when considered as a group, much more resource poor than other nations, are more underdeveloped and have less experience in operating independently within the international political arena. Although there has been considerable debate within UNCLOS halls on the subject of islands, their status, their special needs, the subject has been deemphasized since 1974. One article on the subject in the ICNT (121) that provides a bare bones legal description of islands could be viewed by some as neglect.

If you believe the efforts of coastal states and the International Whaling Commission (IWC) are leading toward the successful survival of marine mammals and their proper conservation and use, you would not agree that UNCLOS has neglected the subject of marine mammals in the two articles which cover the subject (65, 120). Article 65 turns over management of marine mammals to the coastal states within their economic zones, and to the IWC beyond. If you believe that the extension of national jurisdiction will allow some coastal states to decimate the stocks within 200 miles, or that the IWC moves too slowly and ineffectively because it is dominated by the whaling states, you might agree that UNCLOS disregarded an issue that could be resolved properly only through a general ocean treaty.

Those who believe that what is scientifically or technologically feasible today has a high probability of becoming the technological reality that will shape tomorrow must be unhappy that the delegates neglected to be forward-looking. Earlier we touched upon the difficulty of regulation where probable impacts of development of new knowledge are hard to measure. But there has been so much discussion, and a reasonable amount of research and development money spent upon superports, offshore thermal energy conversion units (OTEC's), floating cities, and open-ocean mariculture that it was possible for the delegates to consider some of the problems these potential exploitation schemes present for regulation. OTEC's are neither vessels nor fixed structures and could not sensibly be managed by the rules developed for ships or structures (Washom & Nilles, 1977). Floating cities probably could not easily be subsumed under Articles 60 or 82 because if they float they are not an artificial island. Whether they are "installations" or "structures" is not clear in the ICNT.

Unfortunately, the list goes on. Why did the delegates not pursue a solution to the problem of nuclear testing in, on, and under the ocean? Why were there no further efforts at ocean arms control at UNCLOS after the treaty to ban nuclear weapons on the seabed? If ocean terrorism becomes a problem, the ICNT gives no guidance toward a solution. If coastal states have the right to regulate on-site scientific research in their exclusive economic zone, why do they not have a right to regulate the gathering of the same knowledge by satellites? If we continue, we are afraid we will have a complete catalog of Morley's "too neglected list of good causes lost."

Neglected Interests

Another way to examine the concept of neglect is to offer some analysis not of what issues have been neglected but rather of whose interests have been neglected most consistently during the course of deliberations. We are not suggesting that neglect as used here means that these nations have not had an adequate forum through which their views may become known. Nor do we believe that the level of neglect is necessarily high enough for a nation to refuse to accept a specific section of a text. Indeed, through the many iterations of the bargaining process many of these countries may have grudgingly come to accept the substantive outcome identified in the draft even though they would still prefer other wording. Rather, our purpose here is to identify states whose basic preferences are not being met in a significant fashion by the Informal Composite Negotiating Text or the modifications discussed at the latest session.

The identification of neglected interests was again carried out by an analysis of data collected by Friedheim in the Law of the Sea Forecasting Project. Specifically, it consisted of an examination of the direction cosines calculated in the vote maximization model developed for the project by Kadane. The purpose of the direction cosines is to offer an indication of the amount of resistence each country has to accepting the various provisions of a given package of issues.[8] The "given" package we used was the ICNT. We used the provisions of the ICNT on 14 major issue areas to determine how "acceptable" that document was to 29 states. Only differences between the set package and national preferences that were greater than .1 were noted. Figure 8 is revealing.

As one would clearly expect, the more "conservative" ocean states are the ones who feel most often neglected; the Soviet Union, Great Britain, Austria, and the United States are easily identifiable here. The Soviet preferences for a very narrow coastal zone with relatively free access has consistently been a minority position, and draft texts have never defined a position in accord with their expressed preferences. Additionally, as is the case with many other states, the pollution question is

---

[8]For a fuller description of the formulas used to calculate the direction cosines along with a discussion of the vote maximization model, contact the authors.

	Exploiters of Internat'l Area?	Prod. Controls	Dist. of Money	Terr. Sea. Delimit.	Transit thru Straits	Econ. Zone Delimit.	Econ. Zone-Ltd. or Exclusive	Nav. Rights in Econ. Zone	Fish. Zone Delimit.	Foreign Access to Coastal Fishe.	Vessel Source Poll. Standards	Poll. Enforce. in Econ. Zone	Sci. Res. beyond Nat'l Jurisdiction	Sci. Res. in Econ. Zone
AUSTRALIA											X		X	
AUSTRIA							X	X					X	
BOLIVIA								X						
BRAZEL					X			X	X					X
CANADA											X		X	
CHILE					X			X			X		X	
CHINA					X	X		X					X	
FIJI						X				X			X	
FRANCE	X										X		X	
FED. REP. OF GERMANY											X		X	
INDIA								X			X		X	
INDONESIA						X							X	
JAMAICA								X			X		X	
JAPAN	X										X		X	
MALDIVE ISLAND								X	X		X		X	X
MEXICO								X		X	X		X	
NETHERLANDS							X							
NEW ZEALAND											X		X	
NIGERIA						X		X			X		X	
NORWAY											X		X	
PERU					X			X			X		X	
PHILIPPINES					X	X							X	
SRI LANKA						X		X			X		X	
UGANDA								X						
USSR							X	X			X		X	X
UNITED KINGDOM	X	X									X		X	
UNITED STATES		X									X		X	
YUGOSLAVIA					X			X					X	X
ZAMBIA								X						

FIGURE 8

Non-Acceptability of ICNT Provisions to 29 Major States

another issue in which the Soviet position has not been defined by a majority. The various alternatives to the questions surrounding who will exploit the international area identify a clear example of neglect for France, Japan, and the United Kingdome. Their preferences, shared by others, for a regulatory licensing system have been stressed often, but their arguments have not convinced large numbers of other states. It is also not surprising to note the strong disagreement with existing provisions manifested by such nations as Austria, Bolivia, and Uganda over the question of geographically disadvantaged states' access to coastal waters. Existing articles would make access to the highly productive coastal zone very difficult for any save the coastal state, a position totally unacceptable to these nations. As we will suggest later, the neglect of the interests of these and other nations over this issue could well be a rather key point for the Conference.

As noted earlier, the question of pollution enforcement in the economic zone is an area considered neglected by a number of important conference participants. The United States, United Kingdom, Japan, France, Federal Republic of Germany, Canada, and others are not completely agreed to the pollution enforcement standards identified in the ICNT. The disagreement, in its various phases, is long-standing and oft-articulated. With such strong opposition, it is not surprising to note that the debate surrounding this issue has taken up so much of the Conference's time recently.

It would, however, be both unjust and untrue to suggest that it has been only the more developed, conservative states that have had their positions neglected by the majority. As the chart indicates, some key members of the Group of 77 have defined national positions more than slightly out-of-step with the Conference as a whole. Chile, Peru, Brazil, and China have all been quite vocal concerning their desire for national sovereignty for a broad coastal zone, a position not likely to be accepted by the Conference as a whole.

Neglected Groups

Along with neglect of the preferred positions of nation states, we can also engage in an analysis of the neglect of the interests of various selected regional caucusing and interest groups. Some of these groups have met and attempted to form common bargaining positions; others merely share one or more interests. Using the same issues identified earlier, we offer an analysis of group and regional neglect, once again based on data collected during the earlier Friedheim research effort. Central to this analysis was an identification of national positions based on statements made by official national representatives. These preferred positions were coded and scaled for each nation and a group mean was calculated. This mean was then compared to the median position for all states on that issue, treated here as the probable outcome, and these data were used to create Figure 9.

The results offered by Figure 9 are in some ways, not surprisingly, similar to those identified earlier for national neglect. Eastern Europe and the European Economic Community are clearly not terribly happy with the basic direction of the Conference on these issues. Based on their known preferences, neither group finds strong attraction for the Conference's treatment of the international area exploitation question and the EEC, with several members being fairly vocal, finds that its basic position on the question of production controls has not been terribly influential in the direction of the Conference on this matter. Again, the question of pollution enforcement regulations is one which the preferred positions of both the EEC and Eastern Europe are still some distance from the median positions of the other Conference states.

To restate, we are suggesting not that these group preferences will preclude members of the EEC or Eastern European countries from accepting the relevant articles of the ICNT or any other draft treaty, but rather that given their stated basic preferences they would clearly prefer different provisions in a treaty.

If one examines the WEO group, which includes Western Europe and "other" nations such as Australia, New Zealand and the United States, it is interesting to note the moderating influence of nations not included in EEC membership on the WEO position. Whereas member states of the EEC were some distance away from the probable preferred outcome on eleven of the issues we have analyzed, with the additions of the "other" states, the number of issues in which the average preferred position of the WEO membership is significantly different from the median is zero. This is, it would appear, a clear and interesting example of the potential influence of cross-cutting pressures within a regional caucusing group. What is key to such an analysis is a comparative examination of the means of the two groups and of the standard deviations of the scaled preferences of the groups. What results is that the EEC, with a much smaller standard deviation, is a much more cohesive group than is the more diverse WEO. Large diverse groups like the WEO, if they are able to define a common preference at all, are, by the nature of such a process, able to define a position identified only as a least common denominator. Such a position is clearly going to leave some member states at least partially discontented over a range of issues. It is the level and importance of that internal disagreement that offers the analyst a most difficult task.

FIGURE 9

Group Mean Preferences Compared to Probably Outcome

	Exploiters of Internat'l Area?	Prod. Controls	Dist. of Revenue	Dec.-Making in Coun.	Terr. Sea Delimit.	Transit thru Straits	Econ. Zone Delimit.	Econ. Zone-Ltd. or Exclusive	Nav. Rights in Econ. Zone	Fish. Zone Delimit.	Foreign Access to Coastal Fishe.	Vessel Source Poll. Standards	Poll. Enforce. in Econ. Zone	Sci. Res. beyond Nat'l Jurisdiction	Sci. Res. in Econ. Zone
AFRICA						X									
ARAB						X								X	
ASIA						X									
COASTAL STATES					X	X		X	X						
COASTAL ARCHIPELAGOS				X					X			X			X
DISTANT FISHING	X			X						X		X			X
EASTERN EUROPE	X			X		X	X	X		X	X		X	X	X
EEC	X	X			X		X	X		X	X	X	X	X	X
GROUP OF 77															
LAND-LOCKED STATES					X		X	X						X	X
LATIN AMERICA					X	X		X							
MAJOR MERCHANT MARINE												X	X	X	X
SCANDINAVIA									X				X	X	X
SHELF-LOCKED STATES							X			X	X				
OCEAN ARCHIPELAGOS	X	X			X				X			X			
WESTERN EUROPE AND OTHERS															
YAOUND CONFERENCE STATES					X	X		X							

The kind of discontent manifested by the EEC in the WEO case is also a factor that has to be taken into account when one engages in an analysis of the Group of 77. As Figure 9 indicates, there are no issues over which the member states of the Group of 77 (now numbering 119) taken as a whole are discontent. In our analytic terms they are no great distance from the probable preferred outcome. However, it is clear that the geographically disadvantaged states among the Group of 77 have expressed positions not nearly as close to the group mean as the rest. Some of those issues, such as foreign-state access to the coastal zone and separate questions of land-locked/shelf-locked states rights, are central priorities to these nations. If the Conference defines provisions on these issues that are too far removed from the preferences of these states, it is questionable whether their continued support of the Group of 77 caucusing group can be assumed.

Additionally, particularly on the issue of the legal definition of the coastal zone, the Latin American group has been unsuccessfully vocal in its attempt to define sovereignty for the zone, a view not shared by the Conference or the Group of 77 as a whole. Our preference data alone are insufficient to forecast action. Thus, we do not know if the Latin American group will choose drastic action if their preferences are not acknowledged in a more tangible fashion. But our data do demonstrate a slightly less unified front for the Latin Americans than is sometimes assumed.

Particularistic Ocean Management or Allocation Notions

Since the purpose of UNCLOS is to create a universally applicable set of rules to govern the uses of the oceans, it would be unfair to expect that the delegates would be able to accommodate each state's claim that because of special circumstances it required some special rules written into the treaty. Nevertheless, there have been a number of particularistic ocean allocation or management notions that have received some attention over the years. How these would influence the implementation of a potential general ocean law treaty or in turn be influenced by the implementation of a potential ocean law treaty is a relevant subject of concern.

Analytic problems abound if we discuss these particularistic allocation and management notions. It is difficult to know how seriously to take ideas such as historic bays, closed seas, sector principles, special security zones, and "natural prolongation" theories. Some are the laws of certain countries. Others are official claims. More are bargaining demands. Still others are obsolete laws not enforced. Certain of them are merely the ideas of private scholars, although some of these are "floated" on behalf of governments to test reactions.

There were many reasons why delegates to UNCLOS from delegations that were strongly pro or con on many of these notions "neglected" them. Many delegations who favored one or more of the concepts doubtless feared that a specific rejection of their favored particularistic idea would weaken its standing before future courts or in future bargaining. States that would disavow such notions no doubt hope that the future general law of the sea treaty can be used to argue that these particularistic notions, because they were not mentioned in the treaty, have no standing in international law. How much, if any, these ideas were discussed at UNCLOS, or their relationship to the substantively associated provisions of the single text, is a mystery only to be revealed when a legislative history of the law of the sea negotiations is completed. Then we may know whether all or most of these particularistic demands upon the system were neglected by UNCLOS.

Conceptual Framework

The process by which a new law of the sea treaty is being negotiated with its compromises and trade-offs tends to divert some observers from examining a persistent problem of social process. There are those who believe that to have a consistent regime it is necessary to have a consistent well developed conceptual framework. Opponents are more existential. They believe that the regime emerges from the process of making decisions.

Supporters of the importance of conceptual frameworks believe that its purpose is to guide action. If such a framework does not exist or if it is not used, then, these critics claim, the product of law-making will be an undigestable melange of contradictory, conflicting, and unmanageable specific regulations. Among others, Arvid Pardo feels the lack of adherence to a conceptual framework in the making of the LOS Treaty dooms the work of the delegates to virtual uselessness (Pardo, forthcoming, 1979). This failure results largely from neglect of the importance of a conceptual framework.

Pardo's notion of the common heritage of mankind (not the current ritualistic invocation of the term) is a 20th century version of Kantian idealism (Pardo, 1975). For those who have "right reason" it is an excellent framework for guiding the making of a legal regime. However, it is not without rivals. At least two others have also been injected into the UNCLOS proceedings with their proponents claiming that even where they have affected specific provisions, they have been neglected in relation to their influence on the negotiations as a whole. Market economics has been expounded as the appropriate framework by the delegates from some developed states. At the other end of the political spectrum are theories of national patrimony espoused primarily by Latin American states.

Proponents of the view that conceptual frameworks emerge from human interaction would be less insistent that their importance has been neglected at UNCLOS. For them a conceptual framework is a rationalization after the fact of the interactions of human beings. If the trends in human behavior are in a consistent historical direction, then a conceptual framework emerges. Our question at this workshop is whether sufficient decisions of this sort have been made to discern whether a "new" conceptual framework has emerged. If it has, and we do not identify it, it would be our neglect, not the delegates.

Bargaining Opportunities

The final manner in which we will examine the concept of neglect is an attempt to identify the bargaining opportunities either missed or ignored by the majority of participants at the Conference. We will engage, again by use of Friedheim and Kadane's vote maximization model, in a comparative analysis of a number of the various draft treaties, proposals, and national and regional positions, to try to reach some greater understanding of the rate and strength of the bargaining progress made by the delegates during the course of the Conference.

The model used allowed us to gain insight into the preferences of each participating state for one package of issues over another in a forced vote situation. The analyst can then determine how many states prefer and marginally prefer one package over another.[9] Critical to this model is the assumption that countries indicating a preference for one package over another are forced to choose their more preferred package over their less preferred package. Questions such as further amendments or abstentions are not taken into account here.

Initially, we compared the three negotiating texts with one another. According to our analysis, the Revised Single Negotiating Text (RSNT) and the Informal Composite Negotiating Text (ICNT) were both more acceptable to a greater number of states

---

[9]The vote maximization technique used in this analysis involves the following steps. First, we make a determination of the amount of resistance each country has to accepting each of the components of the package. Second, we combine these resistance measures for all countries over all issues in the package to determine a policy direction measure. These combined measures, like the components of each package, define an array of numbers that constitute the change that the model recommends be made to the respective components so as to create a new package more acceptable than the initial one to the Conference as a whole. The technique then allows for a determination of the number of states preferring one packaging over another, in a forced vote situation.

than was the Conference's initial attempt at a draft text, the Informal Single Negotiating Text (ISNT). This is a positive indication of the bargaining progress. However, neither the RSNT nor the ICNT was able to garner close to a two-thirds majority, in this forced vote situation. If the comparison is restricted to the two later texts, it is interesting to note that the RSNT is at least marginally preferred by a greater number of states than is the latest attempt by the Conference, the ICNT. This is a rather key point, for it is an indication that the great amount of work put into making the RSNT a more generally acceptable document was not very successful. In our terms, the work in preparation of the ICNT seems to have neglected the bargaining opportunities offered by the RSNT. Importantly, however, in neither case does any of the Conference states, based on their basic preferences, identify a strong preference for either draft text.

Let us shift the analysis and force a comparison between the U.S. position and the two latest texts. We have chosen to use the U.S. position in this comparison for several reasons: the United States has defined a fairly strong leadership role among the major ocean users. It has, perhaps until recently, been working actively at reaching consensus for a treaty; and, it has made a fair number of rather key concessions during the course of the deliberations. We, therefore, felt that a treaty comparison with the U.S. positions may well be insightful.

If the comparison is between the U.S. position as it stood in 1975 and the two latest texts, it is interesting to note that it is the U.S. position that is preferred by a greater number of states; and, in the case of the ICNT, the U.S. 1975 position is able to gain either strong or marginal support of a two-thirds majority of the participating states.

If the input to the model is redefined to include a comparison of the present U.S. position and the last two drafts, the U.S. position is again preferred by a larger number of participating nations than either the RSNT or the ICNT. When the forced choice is between the U.S. 1978 position and the ICNT, the U.S. is able to define a two-thirds majority of states that strongly prefer its position while the strong supporters of the ICNT number less than 10% of the Conference participants. In this case the U.S. position is preferred by an admittedly disparate coalition of states obviously wanting very different things. This group is composed primarily of the traditionally conservative maritime states such as a number of the members of the European Economic Community and the Eastern European caucusing group. However, strong additional support is offered by key blue-water fishing states, such as Japan, and by a number of important geographically disadvantaged states, such as Nepal, Austria, Bolivia, and Uganda. The key to this support seems to center around the question of national control over the coastal zone. The geographically disadvantaged states perceive the attempt by the coastal states to reduce or prevent access to the coastal zone as a decision that will have direct negative effects on their economies, and one that strikes at the core of their marine-related concerns. There are 29 land-locked nations at the Conference and an additional 27 nations that are shelf-locked. Clearly, these nations comprise a large proportion of the nations attending the Conference and as the analysis indicates, a group whose preferences can be key if the disadvantaged states can grasp this opportunity. We must restate, however, that we have been measuring preference and not action. There is no way for us to know whether or not they will neglect their opportunities, just as there is no way for us to determine the level of cohesiveness that will be manifested by the Group of 77.

The importance of these issues is substantiated by a comparison of the U.S. position and that of the Group of 77 caucusing group. If one compares their positions as they stood in 1975 in a forced vote situation, the U.S. position is preferred by close to a two-thirds majority of states. If the comparison is based on the position identified in 1978, the U.S. position is again preferred by the largest number of states, a number, in this case, that reaches beyond the level of a two-thirds majority. Again, the key here is the support offered by several geographically disadvantaged states along with a number of distant water fishing states. The question of whether or not the Group of 77 can maintain a sufficient level of solidarity and avoid the abandonment of a large number of land-locked/shelf-locked states is clearly a central factor in the Conference proceedings.

What is suggested here is not that the Conference should, or could, adopt the current U.S. position as the central input to a new draft treaty, but rather that if the Conference is going to reach consensus it should recognize not only that there are still a number of states whose basic preferences are still some distance from being met, but also that, at least in the case of the geographically disadvantaged states, the level of that disagreement could well be a major deterrent to the adoption of a treaty.

We believe that the greatest neglect the Conference could commit would be not to pick up the key bargaining opportunities that could lead the participants closer to agreement. The main purpose of the techniques we have been utilizing here is to attempt to point out the general structure of a treaty that would be acceptable to a greater number of participating nations than would some other text. We do not claim to be able to identify or advise on details but we do feel we can point to fundamental directions where basic compromises must be made for consensus to be reached. We feel that it is possible to arrive at the general shape of a draft treaty that would be more popular than the existing documents produced by the Conference.

We will attempt to model one of the two possible decision processes that may be used in creating decisions for UNCLOS. The first is the traditional article (and amendments to all or part) by article voting, then voting on the draft of the committee's text as a whole. This would allow us to look at, first, the issue by issue preferences of states as well as the trade-offs that go into a committee (a subsystem) decision. The second is to simulate a vote on the grand package of all the major issues that would be voted upon only once. This is realistic in that it attempts to show what might happen if there is an attempt to preserve the consensus decision system so far employed. Because of time we will present our analysis only of the latter possible decision situation.

There are some basic assumptions that should be introduced here. The model is based on the concept of one-nation, one-vote, which is, we recognize, an idea that has both assets and liabilities. The assets are that it does not forget quiet or weak voices. Statements made by all participating nations during the entire course of the deliberations are coded and recorded and can be included in subsequent analysis. Its liability is that it makes no attempt to identify a measure for the supposed disproportionate political power of major states. The liability notwithstanding, we feel the model can correctly identify, based on national preferences, both the direction and degree of change necessary for successful treaty bargaining. However, we do recognize that the positions identified by the model may not have substantive meaning and in some extreme cases may be substantively absurd. In this case it is left to the analyst to exercise judgment.

Using these techniques, we developed Figure 10 which identifies the basic structure of a more generally acceptable treaty and the general direction and distance in which the Conference must move to define such a document.

On the key issues debated by Committee I the changes in the ICNT suggested by the model are not large, but they may be radical. As most negotiators are quick to point out it is the smallest of changes that is often the hardest fought. On the questions most central to the exploitation of the area, the preferred provisions are ones in which the language would be softened slightly to accommodate to a greater degree the needs of the major ocean users.

The Committee II negotiations offer other problems. On the question of the delimitation of the territorial sea, the model suggests that the Conference should try to accommodate to a greater degree the needs of the 200 mile club. While these seem

FIGURE 10: Outline of Model Draft Treaty

ISSUE	PREFERRED PROVISION	NECESSARY CHANGE
Who shall exploit the international area	Dual system	Soften language slightly to accommodate major ocean users
Production controls	Moderately stringent controls	Soften language to accommodate major ocean users
Distribution of revenue	Facilitate general economic development/LDC preference	No change
Decision-making in council	3/4 majority for passage	No change
Territorial sea delimitation	12 mile territorial sea	Greater acknowledgement of the needs of the 200 mile club
Transit through straits	Transit passage	Adjust slightly toward more coastal state control
Fishing zone delimitation	200 miles	No change
Economic zone delimitaiton	200 miles or to edge of margin	Adjust language to soften coastal state control
Access to the economic zone	Coastal state authorize activities in the zone; accommodate other users	Adjust substantially to accommodate other users
Navigation rights in the economic zone	Free navigation	Stiffen language to accommodate coastal state
Foreign access to coastal fisheries	Coastal state authorize activities: accommodate other users	Adjust substantially to accommodate other users
Vessel source pollution standards	Coastal state jurisdiction based on international standards	Adjust toward slightly less coastal control
Pollution enforcement in the economic zone	Coastal state enforcement and residual competence	Adjust to accommodate other users
Scientific research beyond national jurisdiction	State right to conduct research; comply with international standards	Adjust toward compliance with international standards
Scientific research in the economic zone	Coastal consent for research; consent normally given	Adjust toward more explicit description of consent criteria

to be provisions accepted by those nations interested in a 200 mile sovereign coastal zone, we stress again that what we are identifying is what nations prefer. The Conference's dealings with the questions of access to the coastal zone, as identified earlier, are going to have to move more toward greater access of non-coastal state users if a greater number of state preferences are to be met. Again, as stated earlier, this does appear to be an area of some importance but we have no way to foresee how well states will be able to organize their forces with regards to these issues. It may well be that the relatively quiet voices of the geographically disadvantaged will remain silent.

The Committee III debate is one that, again, may not require substantial shifts, but, still, some adjustment of the present text is in order. This is particularly true of the pollution issues. To move closer to a consensus position on these issues would require that provisions be drafted that would define a greater relaxation of coastal control over coastal pollution problems. With regards to scientific research, the Conference could come closer to the preferences of a greater number of states if the provisions regulating scientific research were adjusted to include wording indicating that research should comply with some set of international standards.

Whether the delegates understand what it will take not to neglect the opportunity that exists to arrive at a treaty acceptable to the largest number of state parties, we cannot forecast. But as critics we must ask whether the entire law of the sea treaty effort has been worthwhile. We could, of course, attempt to answer such a question with a deeply felt personal "gut" reaction. Or, we could ask, was the result of the time, money, and effort used better on the attempt to create a comprehensive treaty or could they have been better employed elsewhere? The concept we put forward here is that of "opportunity cost." The direct financial costs of UNCLOS have been high to get where we are. There is a rumor in the U.N. halls that it costs $2 million a day for the UNCLOS meetings. This includes the expenses of the member governments who had to send delegates to the meetings in Caracas, New York, and Geneva, and the U.N. that had to provide halls, translators, documents and other services. If the negotiations go to nine sessions (also a current rumor), and the preliminary Ad Hoc and Permanent Seabed Committee sessions (discounted at $1 million a day because the delegations were smaller, etc.) are included, a rough estimate of the total cost of UNCLOS is $1.25-$1.50 billion. It is a legitimate question for some delegates to ask--if the developing member states kept the assets they used for UNCLOS in their treasuries and the developed donated their costs to the developing, would not a new international economic order be further along than it might get through UNCLOS decisions? This judgment can be made even if a treaty is achieved. But this is only one aspect of the opportunity cost problems. Another aspect is whether the world would have engaged in more collective violence in the enforcement of the enclosure claims that have been, in good part, legitimized by the discussions and bargaining of UNCLOS. The costs of adjusting claims as we enclose the more valuable portions of the world's oceans are costs we cannot overlook. We believe that the cost of engaging in the partisan mutual adjustment of ocean claims were not excessively high, even at $1.25-$1.50 billion,whether or not a treaty is signed (Lindblom, 1965; Friedheim, 1975). UNCLOS as a whole has performed a very useful function even at the costs we can attribute to it. We would be negligent if we did not point that out.

REFERENCES

Antarctica: world hunger for oil spurs security council review. Science, May 17, 1974, pp. 776-778.

Apple, R. W., Jr. Mysterious Soviet ship movements worry and puzzle Norwegians. New York Times, August 4, 1978.

Apple, R. W., Jr. Soviet and Norway seen in Arctic waters. New York Times, August 6, 1978.

Auburn, F. M. United States Antarctic policy. Marine Technology Society Journal, Feburary-March, 1978, pp. 31-36.

Bakus, Gerald J., Garling, Wendy, and Buchanan, John E. Final report: The Antarctic krill resource: prospect for commercial exploitation. Tetra Tech Report TE-903, February, 1978.

Beesley, J. Alan. Rights and responsibilities of arctic coastal states: the Canadian view. Journal of Maritime Law and Commerce, 1971-72, 3, 1-12.

Bilder, Richard. The Canadian Arctic Waters Pollution Prevention Act: New Stresses on the Law of the Sea. Michigan Law Review, 1970, 69, 1-54.

Blundy, David and Dawe, Tony. Fears grow over oil and sea gas defenses. The Times (London), May 11, 1975, p. 3.

Breckner, Norman V., et al. The Navy and the Common Sea. Washington: Government Printing Office for the Office of Naval Research, 1972, p. 212.

Burke, William T. Who goes where, when and how: international law of the sea for transportation. International Organization, Spring, 1977, 31 (2), 288.

Butler, William E. Soviet Arctic and the Northeast Passage. The Nautilus Papers No. 2, June 1971.

Cetron, Marvin J. Technological Forecasting. New York: Gordon & Breach, 1969.

Christy, Francis T., Jr. and Scott, Anthony. The Common Wealth in Ocean Resources. Baltimore: John Hopkins Press, 1965.

Eckert, Ross. The Enclosure of Ocean Resources. Stanford: Hoover Institution Press, forthcoming, 1979.

Europe fears growing Soviet submarine fleet poses future threat to North Sea oil supply. Wall Street Journal, June 11, 1975, p. 32.

Final Environmental Impact Statement for a Possible Regime for Conservation of Antarctic Living Marine Resources. Department of State, June, 1978.

Friedheim, Robert L. A law of the sea conference - who needs it? In Rogert G. Wirsing (Ed.), International Relations and the Future of Ocean Space. Columbia: University of South Carolina Press, 1974, pp. 46-62.

Friedheim, Robert. Toward a treaty for the oceans. In Don Walsh (Ed.), The Law of the Sea: Issues in Ocean Research Management. New York: Praeger, 1975.

Friedheim, Robert L. and Pardo, Arvid. The law of the sea conference and the future of the oceans. In Robert L. Friedheim (Ed.), The Oceans: A Citizen's Guide. New York: Marcel Dekker, forthcoming, 1979.

Goldberg, Edward D. and Menzel, David. Oceanic Pollution. In J. L. Hargrove (Ed.), Who Protects the Ocean?. St. Paul: West, 1975, pp. 37-62.

Gordon, H. Scott. The economic theory of a common property resource: the fishery. Journal of Political Economy, April, 1955, 63, 116-124.

Green, Katherine A. Role of Krill in the Antarctic Marine Ecosystem. Final Report to the Department of State, Division of Ocean Affairs, Contract 1722-720248, December, 1977.

International Canada, April, 1970, 1(4), 79-86.

Janis, Mark W. The roles of regional law of the sea. San Diego Law Review, April, 1975, 12(3), 561.

Jantch, Erich. Technological Forecasting in Perspective. Paris: OECD, 1967.

Kaczynski, Woldzimierz. Economic importance of the Antarctic Marine Living Resources. Norfish, Institute for Marine Studies, University of Washington, April, 1978.

Kessler, J. Christian. Potential threats to offshore structures. Technical Report No. 2, produced under ONR Contract #N-0014-68-0091-0023, March, 1976.

Kessler, J. Christian. Legal issues in protecting offshore structures. Professional Paper No. 147. Center for Naval Analyses, June, 1976.

Lasswell, Harold. Politics: Who Gets What, When, How. New York: McGraw-Hill, 1936.

Lindblom, Charles. The Intelligence of Democracy: Decision-Making Through Mutual Adjustment. New York: Free Press, 1965.

Ludwigson, John. Bring home the iceberg. Ocean World, January, 1978, pp. 29-33.

Mahan, Alfred Thayer. The Influence of Seapower on History, 1660-1783. Boston: Little, Brown, 1890.

Meconchie, Roger D. and Reid, Robert S. Canadian foreign policy and international straits. In Barbara Johnson and Mark W. Zacher (Eds.), Canadian Foreign Policy and the Law of the Sea. Vancouver: University of British Columbia Press, 1977, pp. 167-178.

Mitchell, Barbara. Antarctica: a special case? New Scientist, January 13, 1977.

Moore, J. N. (Ed.). Janes' Fighting Ships 1978-79. New York: Franklin Watts, 1978. (forward to Janes; reprinted in Seapower, August, 1978, pp. 23-31.)

Moratorium set on Antarctic oil in October meeting. Science, November 18, 1977, pp. 709-712.

National Academy of Science. Petroleum in the Marine Environment. Washington: author, 1975.

Olenicoff, S. M. Territorial Waters in the Arctic: The Soviet Position. A report prepared for Advanced Research Projects Agency, No. 189-1. Santa Monica: Rand, 1972.

Pardo, Arvid. The Common Heritage. Valetta: Malta University Press, 1975.

Rosenau, James N. (Ed.). Linkage Politics. New York: Free Press, 1969.

Rosenau, James N. Theorizing across systems: linkage politics revisited. In Jonathan Wilkenfeld (Ed.), Conflict Behavior and Linkage Politics. New York: McKay, 1973.

Rosinski, Herbert (Ed.) with an introduction by B. Mitchell Simpson III. The Development of Naval Thought. Newport, Rhode Island: Naval War College Press, 1977.

Ross, David A. Resources of the deep sea other than manganese nodules. Draft, p. 22.

Ross, D. A. and Miles, E. Editorial: The importance of marine affairs. Science, July 28, 1978, p. 305.

Schumacher, E. F. Small is Beautiful: Economics as if People Mattered. New York: Harper & Row (Perennial Library), 1973.

Thacher, Peter S. and Meith-Avin, Nikki. The oceans: health and prognosis. Ocean Yearbook 1. Chicago: University of Chicago Press, forthcoming, 1978, pp. 293-339.

Thirring, Han. Energy for Man: From Windmills to Nuclear Power. New York: Harper & Row (Colophon Books), 1958, p. 15.

Turner, Gordon B. Classic and modern strategic doctrines. In Gordon B. Turner and Richard D. Challener (Eds.), National Security in the Nuclear Age. New York: Praeger, 1960, pp. 20-21.

Washom, Byron J. and Nilles, Jack M. Incentives for the Commercialization of Ocean Thermal Energy Conversion Technology (OTEC). A Report to the National Science Foundation, Research Applied to National Needs. Los Angeles: Office of Interdisciplinary Program Development, University of Southern California, 1977, p. V30-31.

Wilmot, Philip D. and Slingerland, Art. Technology Assessment and the Oceans. Boulder: Westview, 1977.

COMMENTARY

David A. Ross
Woods Hole Oceanographic Institution

As a practicing marine scientist, I think I would have preferred to see some other things left out of the law of the sea negotiations. In particular, I think I would have liked scientific research left out because it looks like there will be an extension of coastal state control over marine science out to at least 200 nautical miles. This will present considerable problems for marine science research.

I think one could easily also argue that the knowledge obtained from marine scientific research probably is one of the motivating factors for us in actually having a law of the sea conference in the first place. The session that we are going to have this afternoon concerns some potential resources of the deep sea other than manganese nodules. Although I feel that many of these resources may never be mined, with some exceptions, the volume of this deep sea material is so immense that their actual low value often is neglected. Because of this, it is conceivable that a regime could be established for these supposed resources. If this were to happen, I could also visualize additional further losses for marine science.

For example, if you remember Articles 143 and 151 in the present ICNT concerning "the Area," there are items mentioned that could be interpreted as putting controls or restrictions on marine scientific research. Article 151 says that the "Authority shall carry out marine science research concerning the Area and its resources and may enter into contracts for that purpose." It also says the "Authority shall promote and encourage the conduct of marine science in the Area, harmonize and coordinate such research, and arrange for the effective dissemination of the results thereof." The words "harmonize and coordinate research in the Area" scare me quite a bit.

Perhaps I am being too pessimistic. Perhaps an optimistic view would be to say that the Authority will indeed fund marine science research. Or perhaps another view is that there are going to be 150 new funding agencies that want to fund marine science research, i.e., the states that now have interest in their own large areas.

COMMENTARY

Edward Miles
Institute for Marine Studies
University of Washington

This is a very provocative paper, and I do not have the time to raise all the questions which I would like to raise. So I shall save some for a private discussion with the authors over the appropriate beverage. There are, however, some points that I do wish to make.

First, concerning typology of UNCLOS neglect, the authors argue that both those issues which have been dealt with in the Conference and those issues which have been neglected are allocation issues. So we must find some explanation for what determined those issues that the Conference chose to deal with and those they chose to neglect. I find the typology offered unsatisfactory because the categories are not mutually exclusive.

The authors give us three reasons. First, there are those issues on which too little is known for them to be considered the subject of regulation or management. Secondly, there are those issues that are too delicate or political. And thirdly, there are those for which UNCLOS is considered the inappropriate forum. But I do not think that the latter two are separate types. I think they can be collapsed into a single category, combined by two variables. That is, when the issues are of high salience and, at the same time, when they affect a restricted number of players directly, then claims are made that they are either too delicate or political or that UNCLOS is the inappropriate forum because they are too delicate or political. So I think some revision is necessary there.

In the case of the polar regions, which I have been given to understand by the chairman I should refer to, these issues illustrate the point quite clearly. We have long-standing issues of high salience in both the Artic and Antarctic of interest to a very small number of players, the Arctic being of high strategic significance, the Antarctic so far not being so. In addition, the Arctic has quite considerable resource implications. The change in the ocean regime plus advancing technology are the two variables that precipitate the instability in the polar regions at this time.

As far as the Arctic is concerned, there is the question of the economic zone and the continental margin as related to Norway versus the Soviet Union, and Canada and the U.S. The question of scientific research between Canada, the U.S.S.R. and the United States is another problem. The new missile technologies, particularly the strike range of the submarine-based deterrent, increases the value of the Arctic to the Soviet Union and increases their concern about U.S. studies with respect to sound propagation in the Arctic Ocean.

With respect to the Antarctic, we have the situation of the new ocean regime affecting the claims of the potential claimant states. Will they seek to extend to 200 miles? What are the possibilities of exploiting both living and non-living resources? For the Japanese, the Soviets and others, living resources of the Southern Ocean are important as a result of their having been displaced elsewhere in the world through enactment of 200 mile zones.

So it does seem to me that both the Arctic and the Antarctic have not been included in the law of the sea negotiations because these issues are of very high salience plus the fact that they are of interest to a restricted number of players in a direct sense.

Now, the claim has been made that the Antarctic resources ought to be treated in the same fashion as the seabed beyond national jurisdiction. This claim was made in a number of places, most particularly by Sri Lanka at the meeting of Heads of State of Non-Aligned Countries in Colombo a couple of years ago. But is quite clear to me that the performance of the Law of the Sea Conference does not provide a useful example for dealing with Antarctic resources.

Contrary to the authors, I am prepared to come to the defense of the Conference. You know, in the words of Senator Patrick Moynihan, neglect is okay if it is benign. I think that the problem with the Law of the Sea Conference is that it took on much too much and did not neglect enough. So I would not say that they ought to be blamed for not dealing effectively with land-based pollution, for instance. There is nothing the Conference could have done about land-based pollution, looking at the problem itself. I do not think they ought to be blamed for neglecting the whaling issue either, no matter what the United States suggests (somewhat misguidedly in my view). I do not think there is anything the Conference could have done about the whaling issue at all. We could go down the list that the authors present and in each case make a case that the Conference did the right thing by neglecting that particular issue.

With respect to the calculations of preferred positions, even though the caveat was made that these are preferred positions, not actions, I think the direction of that analysis is misleading. It is no good to say that "two-thirds of the Conference potentially preferred the U.S. position on most issues." I think it may, in fact, be the other way around, i.e., that the United States has been induced to accept the positions advocated by most countries in order to buy things in which they claim they are most interested.

Additionally, it is not particularly useful to focus on the individual preferences of individual delegations. What is missing is another matrix which shows the trade-offs, the packages, and the two major subpackages, one in Committee I, one in Committee II, and the relationships between them because the preferences change when you look at them in the context of that matrix. So I think the matrix presented here by the authors is misleading.

Finally, there is the interesting table where the authors courageously stick their necks out to indicate what change in direction is required in order to get a treaty. Fourteen changes of direction are indicated and I disagree with 50 percent of those. We do not have time to go into them in detail. But if people were to do what you say, I think we would be worse off.

COMMENTARY

Albert W. Koers
Institute of International Law
of the University of Utrecht

I should like to address very briefly the question of why we have in this conference a session on Sea-Use Planning in the North Sea. Part of the answer you will find in Professor Friedheims's and Mr. Bowen's paper, but I would like to add a few very brief comments.

First, we felt that at this first LSI conference in Europe we should give some special emphasis to a question that is of particular concern to us here in Europe. However, that question should, of course, not be irrelevant to other regions of the world's oceans. Sea-use planning is, I think, such an issue. If you consider the ever-increasing utilization of the seas and of their resources, the problem of the interaction between the various forms of utilization is constantly gaining in importance. This implies that planning in relation to the various forms of utilization as a whole becomes indispensable. In the past, freedom of action, freedom of the high seas could prevail. Nowadays (and I borrow from Professor Brown's paper which you will hear on Thursday) "what is done in or under the seas should be done by design in accordance with a positive and cohesive approach based on forward projection."

Second, sea-use planning is a neglected issue not only in the United Nations Conference but also elsewhere. Certainly, national governments have a great deal of experience with planning in relation to individual activities, individual forms of sea utilization such as shipping, fishing, oil and gas exploration. However, a comprehensive approach in relation to all activities in a given area is still only a concept, and not a clearly defined concept at that.

Internationally, sea-use planning is even more of a neglected issue. The United Nations Conference on the Law of the Sea takes essentially an activity-by-activity approach; it gives little attention to the interaction between various utilizations of the sea. A provision like Article 87, paragraph 2 of the ICNT which states that the various freedoms of the high seas have to be exercised "with due consideration for the interests of other states" may be sound in principle but is inadequate in dealing with all the specific practical problems that arise in a heavily used sea area.

There is one additional element I should like to mention. International law has developed, and continues to develop, to a very large extent in response to immediate problems and pressures. For example, it took a Torrey Canyon incident to bring us new rules on pollution. Therefore, planning on an international level may place requirements on international law for which it is not adequately equipped.

To sum up, sea-use planning in the North Sea is a necessity, but not yet a reality. To develop it will require creative thinking, nationally but perhaps even more so internationally. We have included this session on sea-use planning in an attempt to make a small contribution to this kind of thinking.

COMMENTARY

Leo J. Bouchez
Institute of International Law
of the University of Utrecht

I wish to make some comments on the changing regime for shipping. Freedom of navigation, one of the traditional freedoms of the high seas, has been dealt with at length both directly and indirectly at the aforementioned conference. New concepts with respect to freedom of navigation have been submitted, such as the right of transit passage through international straits and the right of archipelagic sea lane passage through the waters of archipelago states in order to guarantee freedom of navigation.

In addition the concept of the exclusive economic zone has been tailored so far in such a manner as to protect freedom of navigation against creeping jurisdiction of coastal states. In light of these observations, it does not seem justified to refer categorically to freedom of navigation as an issue neglected at the Third Law of the Sea Conference.

The aforementioned aspects of freedom of navigation have a bearing on the question of where and under what conditions ships of all states may navigate freely. A completely different question (which has not been discussed at the Third Law of the Sea Conference) is whether the traditional freedom of navigation in the sense of freedom to transport ocean-borne cargo can still be upheld. Before elaborating this issue a little further it deserves consideration that from the economic point of view ocean navigation as a means of transport is of paramount importance, since according to recent information about 80% of world trade is carried out by sea. This makes clear that the words of the Roman admiral Sextus Pompei "navigare necesse est" which, incidentally, is also the motto of Rotterdam harbor, are still most relevant. It is understandable that within the context of the traditional approach as regards the transport of ocean-borne cargo by far the larger part of such transport has been carried out by those who possess the necessary experience, technological know-how and financial resources. Accordingly ocean transport has been controlled for a long period of time by ships from the Western world (including flags of convenience). However, this situation has changed recently because of the rapid increase of the merchant fleets of the East Bloc countries.

In addition, the control of the means of ocean transport by the industrialized countries has been criticized severely and repeatedly by the developing countries during the last decade. In this connection reference should be made, for example, to the objections raised by the developing countries against the liner conferences as they presently exist under the laissez-faire approach. These objections are: (i) the conferences which have a bearing on their trade are dominated by shipping lines of developed nations; (ii) they are not in a position to affect the freight rates and the nature of the services provided by the liner conference which do not correspond to their particular needs and interests; and (iii) the level of freight rates and adequate services are of critical interest for their export earnings.

The criticism of the laissez-faire approach by the developing countries, in particular at the UNCTAD shipping meetings in the beginning of the 1970's, finally resulted in the Geneva Code of Conduct for Liner Conferences of August 6th, 1974. According to this Code of Conduct, the traditional system of free competition relating to a substantial part of ocean-borne cargo will be replaced by an extensive regulation of market allocation. Although the new system seriously interferes with the policy and practice of the shipping lines of industrialized states, it is likely to contribute to the promotion of the interests of developing countries. I wish to submit that, as with respect to other uses of the sea such as the exploitation of the natural resources, the developing countries are no longer satisfied with a merely passive role in so far as ocean transport is concerned.

I finally hope that our working sessions on Tuesday may contribute to possible solutions of the juridical problem of freedom of ocean transport.

COMMENTARY

H. Gary Knight
Louisiana State University

On page twelve of the Friedheim-Bowen paper, there is the following statement: "We believe that the use of naval power to defend the interests of the states of the world in the uses of the ocean and its resources is very little connected to the enclosure movement or to problems of allocating rights." By exercise of great restraint, I am not going to respond to that personally. Like John Gamble, I have retained several very able people to discharge my responsibilities, and you will hear those very able people Wednesday afternoon. I think the statement that the Friedheim-Bowen paper makes will be the focus of that debate.

My own view is that I do not think military issues have been neglected at the Law of the Sea Conference. Through such subtle techniques as deliberate ambiguity, it has in a fashion been the dominant issue at the Law of the Sea Conference. What has been neglected is public analysis of these issues. A very few individuals, with great diligence, have been able to ferret out from publicly available sources the facts concerning the military situation underlying law of the sea positions taken by various nations. One of the high points of this analytic process occurred five or six years ago at another annual conference of The Law of the Sea Institute in a paper prepared by Dr. John Knauss, one of the initiators and guiding lights of this Institute.

Dr. Knauss' analysis of the military issues of the law of the sea was at that time so well done that a United States admiral attending the session took the floor to comment that he was delighted to have a copy of Dr. Knauss' paper to distribute to all of the individuals on his staff. As a result of recent hijackings, American diplomats and military personnel had been forbidden to carry classified information when traveling by aircraft. Dr. Knauss, the admiral noted, had resolved that problem. His staff could simply carry Dr. Knauss' paper with them from then on.

It was a brilliantly done effort. I think that you are in store for a similar high point Wednesday afternoon in this difficult process of analyzing the military issues and the law of the sea. On the plane trip over, I read the principal paper prepared for the session by Professor Ken Booth. It is extremely stimulating and thought-provoking.

We have on the Wednesday afternoon panel Professor Michael MccGwire from Dalhousie University in Canada. Those of you who know Mike know that it does not take a great deal of stimulation to get Mike to elaborate on his views. I think Ken's paper will provoke Mike considerably.

We also have two representatives of military institutions, Admiral Fraser, representing the Indian Navy, and Admiral Cramer representing the United States Navy. Each will comment on Ken Booth's paper and on the comments made in the Friedheim-Bowen paper in the context of those two nations' (India and the United States) quite disparate interests in the military aspects of law of the sea.

COMMENTARY

John P. Craven
University of Hawaii

Let me take this opportunity to say a word about the energy from the oceans and as it relates to the excellent paper that Bob Friedheim and Mr. Bowen have presented.

Energy from the oceans has two parts, one very much not neglected, namely the oil resources of the ocean (and that has been the major subject of concern in all of the continental shelf negotiations). The other aspect has to do with energy sources from the ocean that we have not yet exploited, some of the unusual aspects of energy from the ocean. And the authors are quite right to say that this has been a neglected issue because of lack of knowledge.

But I might point out that it might have profited from a little more neglect because in point of fact there is one sweeping statement in the latest text of the U.N. Conference which, when talking about the jurisdictional responsibilities in the 200 mile zone, grants responsibility to the coastal state for devices which extract energy from the ocean. While the exact meaning of this statement may have been clear to some, the term itself is large, sweeping, and all-encompassing. So much so, in fact, that not only does it take into account such future energy items from the ocean as ocean energy extraction, but it sweeps back into antiquity and includes by the very nature of its description all sailboats and sailing ships that have ever plowed the seas.

COMMENTARY

Isabella Diederiks-Verschoor
Institute of International Law
of the University of Utrecht

Introducing the subject "Airspace and the Law of the Sea," I would like to emphasize that the problems regarding the regime of the airspace above the exclusive economic zone have been sorely neglected indeed, as Professor Friedheim and Mr. Bowen also observed in their papers. In the conventions on the law of the sea of 1958, especially in Conventions on the High Seas, the Territorial Seas, and the Continental Shelf, air law has followed the rules established for the law of the sea for some specific subjects, for instance, the right of hot pursuit.

But the basis for legal rules regarding aviation is formed by the Convention on International Aviation, known as the Chicago Convention of 1944. As a basic principle in aviation, we must consider that each state has complete and exclusive sovereignty over the airspace above its territory. The technical aspects of the Chicago Convention are elaborated it its 17 annexes. These annexes are in force only when they are incorporated into national law. Nevertheless, the standards of Annex 2 establishing the rules of the air for aircraft flying over the territory of a state, over territorial waters, or over the high seas are for safety reasons considered as <u>jus cogens</u>. Neither the Chicago Convention nor Annex 12, the annex dealing with rules of the high seas, gives a definition of the term "high seas." However, the establishment of an economic zone of 200 nautical miles beyond and adjacent to the territorial water raises the problem, to what extent the coastal state can control overflight and set its own regulations to apply to aircraft. The Informal Composite Negotiating Text makes it clear that the controlling state cannot claim sovereignty over overflight, but questions of control are not settled.

As Dr. Heller observes rightly in his recent article "Zeitschrift für Luftrecht" (1978, page 15 and following) "exclusive jurisdiction" as expressed in paragraph 2 of Article 60 of the Informal Composite Negotiating Text proposed at the third Conference on the Law of the Sea, must be distinguished from sovereign rights, which the coastal state may exercise.

We are happy that it was possible to engage such excellent experts as Professor Christol, Dr. Heller, and Dr. Hailbronner to tell you about the problems and pitfalls that this neglected subject may cause.

DISCUSSION AND QUESTIONS

H. H. M. SONDAAL: Mr. Chairman, I have heard and I was struck by the statement that resources in the deep sea-bed constitute an issue that has correctly been neglected. The reason why this issue has been rightly neglected is said to be the fact that we do not know much about those resources. I wonder whether this kind of thinking should not have been used in respect to manganese nodules, because one of the main reasons the negotiations in Committee I of the Law of the Sea Conference are tedious and difficult is that the facts are not sufficiently known. In so far as they are known, they are held by a few companies; they are propriatory. For that reason, negotiations in the Committee I are ruled by fear in the sense that you do not know what you are giving and you do not know what you are getting.

That poses as far as I am concerned a very important question as to international negotiations as such. The question being, when do you start to negotiate? When you know nothing, so you can freely make rules or when you know something so you can make really good rules? That is a very important question and I think that maybe we could address that question somewhat later.

EDWARD MILES: Since there is time, I would like to come back to the point raised by Mr. Sondaal if I may, because it is a very important question. I am not sure we have that much choice about when we begin to negotiate given the system as it exists. You remember, of course, way back in 1968 Arvid Pardo's speech and the suggestion somehow that there was a cornucopia at the bottom of the oceans. This was pursued by others, in particular the United States, for very curious reasons, especially the attempt at making trade-offs between what the U.S. and the U.S.S.R. wanted with respect to the territorial sea and straits used for international navigation and what they perceived as ways of paying for this.

Then we have the peculiarities of the Caracas session and what I view again as the very misguided attempt of the U.S. delegation, pushed by the Treasury, to negotiate a horrendously detailed series of conditions because of the lack of trust. Now, if you have a situation in which there is great uncertainty about the technical/operational dimensions of the resource and the information, as you point out, is held by companies, not governments, it is a bit absurd to negotiate this stuff purely in nation-state terms when the major players are not nation-states.

In such a situation, one runs the risk of fueling the negotiation process to the extent that it responds not to the dynamics of the external world ("reality") but to its own internal dynamics which are quite separate. So we end up in the rather absurd situation that the Conference may fail on the basis of the sea-bed negotiations. We have pushed these resources to a position out of all relationship to their real value. I do not see, really, that given the nature of the system we are dealing with we have much of a choice. So I shudder about the Antarctic.

ELIZABETH YOUNG: I want to make a few remarks. One, first I want to express the extraordinary gratification that I feel to find sea-use planning, a phrase and concept that came to me in a dream in early 1970, finally making it in the international world. Thank you very much, Dr. Koers, for making it possible.

For my second point, I want to take Mr. Bowen up on one of his statements. He referred to the Soviet preference for "narrow coastal zones." This is, of course, the case in other people's coastal zones, but only in other people's. The Soviet Union in fact claims "internal seas," the regime of "historic seas," in all the four major Arctic seas. No one knows where its territorial waters begin, let alone end, on their way toward the North Pole. The Soviet Union attempts to claim "regional seas" status for both the Baltic and the Black Sea and of course does not recognize either "free transit through straits" in its own territorial seas or "innocent passage" for warships or even for ordinary merchant shipping.

ROBERT FRIEDHEIM: We did address that issue very generally in the paper in the section on what we call particularistic management notions. There we touched upon many of the things that Elizabeth Young mentioned. Because of the length of the paper we did not attempt to relate them to what is being negotiated in the law of the sea negotiations. There is no way that those particularistic claims could have been brought into the UNCLOS negotiations without creating total chaos. But for us scholars taking a look at the impact later, if we have a treaty that results from the law of the sea negotiations, is important. In particular we will need to estimate how the provisions of an UNCLOS treaty will be enforced by states that have been enforcing many of these particularistic claims and management notions.

ROBERT FRIEDHEIM: In the first place, I hope most of you recognize the fact that in being asked to write an organizing paper, we were asked to organize a large amount of material. We were not asked to merely express our personal opinions. We were provided a set of issues drawn up by others which were supposedly neglected. I had no choice over them. I tried to deal with them as honestly as I could. But the fact is I do not always feel that the kinds of things I pointed out as potentially neglected issues are neglected issues. I hope in all cases the issues we pointed to as neglected issues are legitimate subjects of debate and discussion. We attempted in the paper to indicate the range of these issues and some of the criteria critics would use in characterizing those issues as "neglected."

The criteria were not always the criteria that I or Bob Bowen believed in. Many indeed were not. And for the most part, I would agree with many of the comments that were made about issues that should have been neglected. My preferences can be seen in my past writings. We were acting as lightning rods. We do not always believe our long list of neglected issues as neglected.

Let me touch briefly on the kind of modeling we were doing. One of the values of trying to model a problem is that sometimes the models will reveal things which you do not ordinarily see. You do not ordinarily see them because very often the problems are too complex to deal with simply, if you like to use the term, by the seat of your pants. One very nice thing about the models of the sort we have developed is that they have no emotions and they have no personal commitments and involvements.

I respect Ed Miles' position on a number of these things. And as we have indicated, we used the United States in one part of our analysis as a bench mark against which to test positions of others. I agree fully with Ed that the United States has come a long way since these negotiations started in 1967-68. Thus the United States' position is not static and care should be exercised in using it as a bench mark. We believe we did use appropriate care. We think despite U.S. bargaining movement that it was proper to use the 1975 U.S. position as a bench mark because overall U.S. negotiators have retreated from these positions slowly.

Secondly, Ed is quite right that you are going to get some very different forecasted outcomes if you base your forecasts on committee by committee decisions rather than as a decision of the whole body. The models that we showed you today were based upon a decision by the whole body. We did this mainly in order to keep our paper to reasonable or at least not completely unreasonable length. If you make the opposite, or committee by committee decision assumption, you will get very different results. We have done such work elsewhere and have gotten very different results.

The model that we showed you makes a very explicit assumption that there is a trade-off among all major issues simultaneously. The model also makes the assumption that each of these issues is weighted by nation-states according to the salience of each of these issues to them. We, the analysts, did not apply a subjective weighting factor.

I am surprised that Ed was really very mild, even about that, because what we did was to provide in our presentation (without any explicit editorial comment on our part) enough information for our critics to make a judgment from our presentation, that we were saying that a comprehensive law of the sea treaty adopted by consensus or near consensus may be impossible to adopt. Indeed, we may be saying that. At the least we were saying that if you try to account for all the major preferred positions of states that it does not look as if the world will get a substantively satisfying treaty, at least not one that satisfies all the major states on all the major issues. Moreover, unless there are some critical changes in national positions on key issues, I do not see how the world will get such a treaty.

PART II

NON-NODULE RESOURCES OF THE DEEP SEA-BED

RESOURCES OF THE DEEP SEA OTHER THAN MANGANESE NODULES[1]

David A. Ross
Woods Hole Oceanographic Institution
Woods Hole, Massachusetts

Introduction

During the Law of the Sea (LOS) negotiations, discussion of deep sea[2] resources has centered essentially on manganese nodules. This is an appropriate decision since manganese nodules, and their contained elements, have the most immediate potential as a marine mineral resource in the region outside of pending national jurisdiction. The objective of this paper is to describe some of the "other possible resources" of the deep sea--but I wish to emphasize that few of these "other possible resources" are economically meaningful at this time and most may never be.

Before starting, some definitions are appropriate. A resource simply means a supply of something, be it food, minerals or water. Resources such as food or forests are considered to be renewable resources since their supply can be replenished by photosynthesis or other processes. Mineral deposits, on the other hand, are generally considered to be nonrenewable resources since their supply decreases as the material is used. Resources also can be subdivided on the basis of economics. In general, the term "resources" is applied to a supply that can be worked or produced at a price somewhat higher than presently prevailing. A marginal or paramarginal resource is one that is recoverable at one to one and a half times the prevailing price (McKelvey and Wang, 1969), whereas a submarginal resource requires higher costs. A reserve is a known deposit that can be

---

[1]Support for writing this paper came from the Office of Sea Grant, Department of Commerce under Grant 04-8-M01-149 and a contract with the Office of Naval Research, but the comments are the responsibility of the author. I thank Drs. K. O. Emery and Paul M. Fye for reviewing the manuscript. Woods Hole Oceanographic Institution Contribution No. 4241.

[2]"Deep sea" is used here to define that region beyond the limits of national jurisdiction based on present LOS negotiations or, in other words, the region outside of the exclusive economic zone (EEZ). In this paper it includes both the water and the sea floor although the latter is emphasized. The continental rise is not included in the deep sea as most, if not all, of the continental rise will probably be included within the EEZ.

developed under present technological and economic conditions. These terms are obviously not very precise. What is a resource today may become a reserve tomorrow. However, this is not generally the case for deep sea mineral resources.

One other important point is necessary as an introduction. That is the generally voiced concern that we - the world - are rapidly running out of mineral resources. The earth itself, as well as sea water, contains an immense and essentially inexhaustible supply of minerals. An example often quoted is that one cubic kilometer of average crustal rock contains 200,000,000 tons of aluminum; 100,000,000 tons of iron; 800,000 tons of zinc, etc. (Brooks and Andrews, 1974). Likewise, sea water contains vast amounts of different elements such as over 3 billion tons of uranium and copper, 500 million tons of silver and as much as 10 million tons of gold (or about 2.5 kg for each person on earth). This is not to imply that crustal rocks or sea water will be our future source of these minerals but rather to show that an immense supply exists. For example, considering gold, its average concentration in sea water ranges from 0.000004 to 0.000006 ml/l or about 50 pounds per cubic mile of water. The value of the gold in a ton of sea water, however, is only one thousandth of a penny. The two major mineral resources that are in danger of being exhausted are oil and gas. Oil and gas are chemical compounds formed by biochemical processes requiring time periods in the order of millions of years for formation.

Resources of the Deep Sea Water Column

The deep sea, for the purposes of this paper, can be divided into two regimes, the water column and the sea-bed (including the sediment and rocks below the sea bed). Although the latter is the principal subject of this manuscript, some comment about the resources of the former is appropriate. Three particular types of resources are possible from the deep sea water column. The first is the water itself and, in particular, using glaciers or icebergs as a source of fresh water. This subject has received considerable recent publicity due to interest by the Saudi Arabian Government in such a project. It is possible to move icebergs with existing technology; however, there are big unknowns such as cost, how long it will take, and whether ice can be moved from Antarctica to the Middle East before it melts. Conventional thinking would indicate that the idea is unreasonable, but it should be emphasized that over 80% of the world's fresh water supply is in the form of ice; the volume of the ice is equivalent to more than 200 years of rainfall. Moving icebergs to areas like New Zealand or Australia, where water is also needed (and thus not having to cross the equator) may be more feasible and practical.

The second possible resource from the deep sea water column is biological resources. The biological potential of the open ocean as shown by Ryther and others is generally very small. This is mainly due to the "unmixed nature" of the surface waters which prevents nutrients at depth from being returned to the surface waters and re-introduced into the biological cycle. Most estimates are that about 99% of the commercial biological resources of the ocean are to be found in coastal and upwelling regions (generally not in deep sea areas). One major exception to this is the Antarctic region where the west-wind drift causes a strong vertical mixing of the water column and the replenishment of the surface nutrient supply. A principal result of this is an apparently large resource of krill, a shrimp-like organism, in this region. The actual amount available of this high protein resource is unknown, but estimates of potential yearly catches of 200 million tons (about three times all other fish caught) have been made. Krill, at this time, should not be considered as a solution to the world's food problem as several problems exist, including the understanding of its ecology within the Antarctic food chain, difficulties in processing the catch, and fishing in the Antarctic including both technological and legal complexities.

The third resource of the deep sea water column could be its use as an area for innovative thermal energy conversion (OTEC) systems (Figure 1) or for other systems such as capturing wind or wave energy. This subject is treated elsewhere in the symposium and need not be examined further here.

Before considering the resources of the sea bed and underlying rocks of the deep sea, a few words about the state of our knowledge of this region is appropriate. During the last two decades we have learned much about the evolution of the sea floor; these discoveries have come from a collection of routine geophysical and geological observations made over many years. The observations can be incorporated into a single, unifying concept called sea-floor spreading, or plate tectonics. To reach this level of understanding marine scientific research in all parts of the ocean was necessary. Ironically, it is this type of research, having basic scientific goals, that stands a good chance of being most restricted because of the law of the sea negotiations.

Resources of the Deep Sea Bed

The sea-floor spreading concept has shown us that the ocean and the continents are composed of a number of large and small plates that move relative to each other (Figure 2). In general, three types of movement between plates are possible; the effects of the movement are seen mainly at the plate boundaries. In some areas one plate is thrust or collides against another, and in this instance if one plate is composed of heavier oceanic material it will generally be thrust under a lighter continental plate. These areas, called convergence

OCEAN THERMAL ENERGY CONVERSION (OTEC)

Oceans are constantly collecting massive amounts of solar radiation and storing it as heat energy. A gigantic heat engine – such as diagrammed here – uses the warm surface water as the heat source, and the cold water from the depths as a heat sink. The warm water vaporizes a liquid, such as ammonia. Like steam, this gaseous, pressurized ammonia drives turbine-generators. The ammonia then is condensed to its liquid form by the cold ocean water, and this closed cycle continues. When fully developed, an OTEC heat engine is expected to supply significant amounts of electric power at competitive prices.

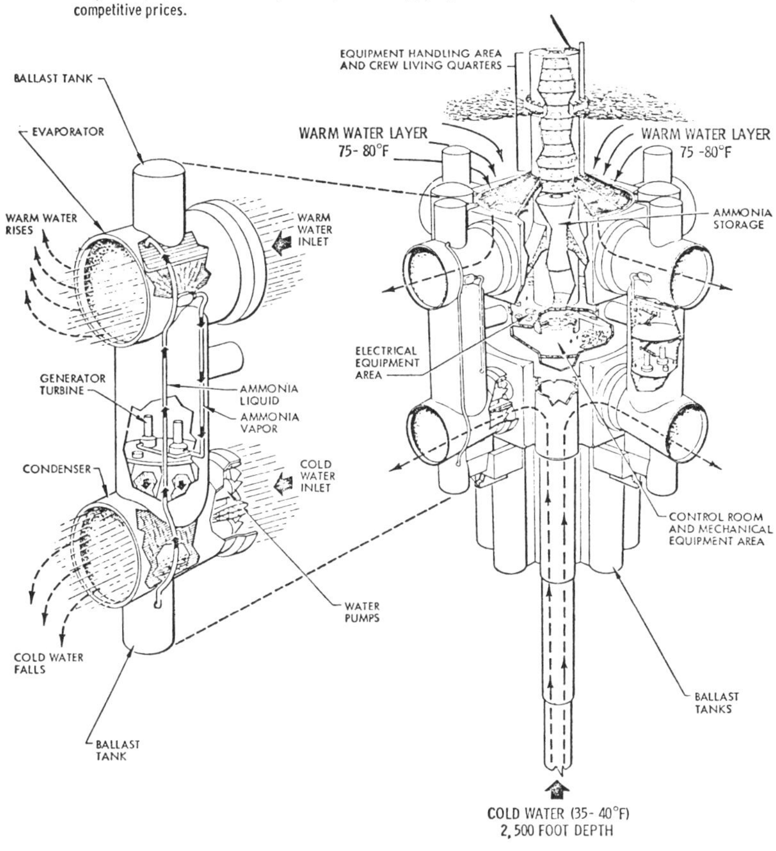

FIGURE 1

A MODEL OF AN OCEAN THERMAL ENERGY CONVERSION SYSTEM.
Figure courtesy Lockheed Missiles and Space Company

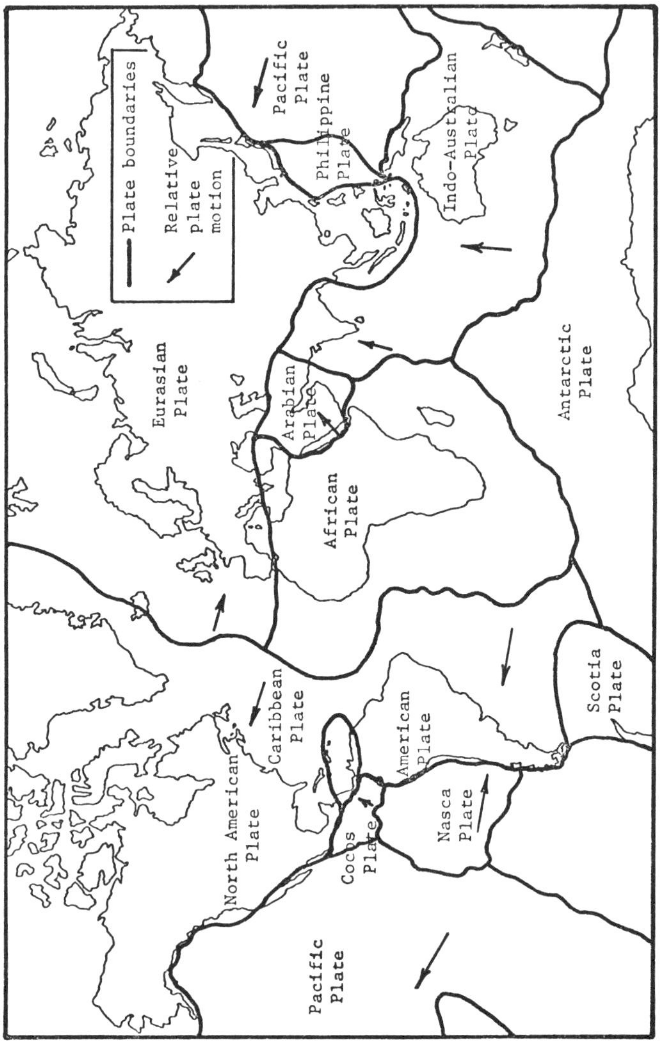

Figure 2

The major plates of the world. Some of the larger ones can be subdivided into smaller plates and in some classifications as many as twenty-six plates are possible. The plates have thicknesses in the order of 100-200 km. From Ross, 1979.

zones, often result in deep sea trenches (Figure 3). When plates of the same composition (i.e., two oceanic or two continental plates) collide, a mountain range may result (if the plates are continental) as when the Indian plate collided with the Asian forming the Himalayas. If both plates are oceanic an island arc system may form.

In some regions plates may be moving away from each other (called divergence zones or spreading centers) and new sea floor (volcanic rock) forms in the resulting gap. With time the initial volcanic rock moves away from the spreading center and is covered by a veneer of sediment; but new volcanic rock will continue to form on the spreading center. An example of a divergence zone is the Mid-Atlantic Ridge or the central part of the Red Sea. The third possible type of movement occurs when two plates slide by each other creating a shear zone or a zone of translation. An example of this is the San Andreas Fault in California or the Jordan Rift Valley in Israel. These three types of movement--convergence, divergence and translation--occur at plate boundaries (one plate can have all three types), while within the plate seismic and tectonic activity is usually minimal and the sea floor may have quietly existed and evolved for literally hundreds of millions of years. Plate boundaries, as well as the interior portions of the plates, may have economic potential although the mechanisms and resulting deposits are considerably different for each region. As a plate evolves certain geological events may occur and control the resulting mineral deposits. The one we have heard most about is manganese deposits. These deposits form in the interior portions of plates, isolated from sources of other sediment. Nodules grow extremely slowly, at a rate of about one atomic layer a day, and can easily be buried or diluted by other sediments.

On portions of a plate that are near land and have a large sediment supply, a thick continental rise may form that could have oil or gas potential. This will not occur if a trench or convergence zone is present along the coast since it will trap the sediments and eventually move them under the continent (see Figure 3). Nevertheless, continental rises are outside of the geographic area of discussion for this paper.

The resources of the deep sea bed and below, exclusive of manganese nodules, can be categorized into two major groups: first, the sediments themselves, and second, zones of mineralization occurring at areas of divergence and certain unique heavy-metal rich muds. The deep sea does not have significant oil and gas potential for two major reasons. First, the total sediment accumulation is too thin and second, the actual rate of deposition is too slow. The slow rate of sedimentation (a few cm or less per thousand years) ensures that organic material from settling plant and animal material will remain on

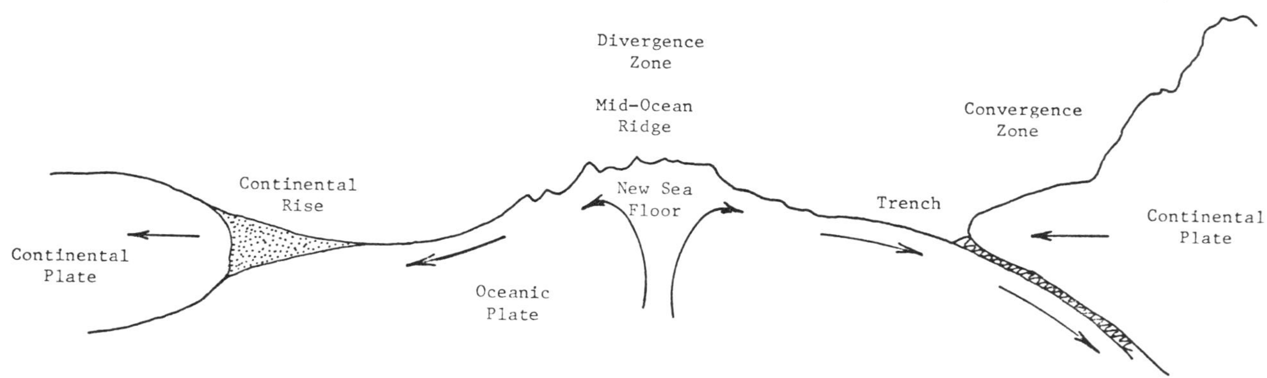

FIGURE 3

Schematic view of an oceanic and two continental plates. Note the convergence zone on the right of the figure where the ocean plate is being thrust under a continental plate, whereas on the left side of the figure both the oceanic and continental plates are moving (arrows indicate direction of movement) in the same direction and a continental rise has formed rather than a trench.

the sea floor surface long enough to be oxidized and thus will not be converted into petroleum. If the sedimentation rate were high, the organic matter could be preserved by burial. The sediments themselves generally are microscopic particles and shells that usually do not produce sufficient reservoir or source beds for petroleum accumulation. In addition, the resulting thin sediment layer (a few hundred meters or so), because of the low deposition rate, will not be adequate to produce the heat necessary for the important geochemical reactions that form oil and gas.

Deep Sea Sediments

Deep sea sediments can be divided into two basic groups: red or brown clay and oozes (mainly shells of planktonic organisms). The dominance of one or another is a function of their sedimentation rate. Brown clays have extremely low sedimentation rates on the order of a few millimeters per thousand years; whereas oozes accumulate at the rate of a few centimeters per thousand years or an order of magnitude faster than the brown clays. Under areas of high biological activity, the settling shells (oozes) will generally dilute any brown clay deposit.

Brown clay deposits cover an area of about 100 million square kilometers of the sea floor. Assuming an average thickness of 200 meters, they have a volume of about 20 million cubic kilometers. Their weight would be about 10^{16} tons with about 5×10^8 tons being deposited yearly. Chemical analyses of the brown clays show as much as 9% aluminum, 6% iron, and smaller amounts of copper, nickel, cobalt and titanium. Some of these metals are more enriched in brown clay than in rocks mined on land, and thus it is logical to think that brown clays on the sea floor might eventually also be mined. Mero (1969) has estimated that brown clays contain enough aluminum and copper that, if they could be economically mined, there would be a supply that would last over one million years at present rate of consumption. The "if" is a big one, for among the major problems are recovery from depths of 5,000m or more far from land and considerable difficulties in refining the fine-grained material.

The oozes are of two main types, calcareous oozes or siliceous oozes, determined by whether they are composed mainly of shells made of calcium carbonate or shells made of siliceous material. Collectively, oozes exceed brown clays in areal extent, although the two are not mutually exclusive. It is a question of which dominates; this is influenced by near-surface oceanographic conditions that determine the growth of the organisms and the depth of water, since calcium carbonate tends to dissolve below depths of 5,000 meters.

Calcareous oozes may cover as much as 50% of the ocean floor and can contain carbonate contents as high as 95%. At these concentrations they could be used as a source of lime for cement. As in the case of brown clays, the volume of this material is awesome and if ever mined, could supply lime at an amount equal to several million years of consumption. On a carbonate-free basis, carbonate oozes are enriched in iron and manganese (up to 25-30% iron and 7-9% manganese); other elements--such as copper, chromium, arsenic, zinc, cadmium, and vanadium--are also abundant. Siliceous oozes (which cover almost 40×10^6 km^2) could be mined for their silica content which can be used for insulation and soil conditioners.

One specific potential clay resource from the deep sea is zeolite, a mineral of which phillipsite is the most common form. This mineral apparently forms on the ocean floor from the decomposition of volcanic glass. Phillipsite is extremely common in the Pacific and may be one of the most abundant minerals on the earth's surface, it could be a source of potash and used for fertilizer.

The oozes and muds must be considered only as potential resources based on present-day needs and the technological difficulties of mining them, and are presently worth little more than the overlying water. Even so, numerous people have been impressed by their vast extent and have suggested that they could become important potential resources in the near future. There are some aspects of this that are especially appealing. One is that their rate of accumulation, which although amazingly small, extends over such a large area that the net rate of accumulation of several elements is considerably higher than the present rate of their consumption on land. For some elements, such as nickel, copper, cobalt, manganese and some rare earths, contents are higher in deep-sea sediments than in igneous rocks. This does not necessarily mean that deep-sea sediments can be mined, but rather that such deep-sea deposits, when found on land and improved by enrichment processes such as weathering, could be a resource. It is easy to be swayed by the large numbers and volume of these deep-sea sediments, but they are similar to the values of igneous rocks and gold in sea water that I mentioned earlier and which probably never can be of economic value.

Zones of Mineralization

The second major type of economic deposit in the deep sea is principally associated with zones of divergence (where the sea floor is spreading and new ocean floor is being created). Basically two major processes could form mineral deposits. The first is due to the actual emplacement of the volcanic rock that forms the new sea floor. The second results from chemical reactions between the volcanic rock and sea water (generally called hydrothermal reactions.

First, I shall consider the volcanic rocks of the sea floor which are mainly basalts. Basaltic rocks (a range of types are possible) when compared to the principal igneous rocks on land (granites) have relatively high amounts of magnesium, iron and calcium but relatively low amounts of silicon, potassium and sodium (Table 1). Ocean basalts contain valuable elements such as chromium, copper, nickel and plutonium similar to basalts on land, but the rocks themselves do not have much potential as a resource unless some form of enrichment (weathering, etc.) occurs that would concentrate some of the various elements. In general, the rocks of the sea floor are not competitive with those of land where enrichment processes are more common and recovery is much easier. Actually most of the important mineral deposits on land are found or formed from rocks not common to the deep sea.

It is conceivable that, during slow cooling of basaltic magma within the earth, different mineral crystals settle out by gravity so that layers or sequences of distinctive minerals may form within the rock, and could have economic value. There would be major difficulties, however, with detecting such a deposit and making the necessary assay of its value in particular since gravitational settling will not occur at the ocean surface but deep below it. If a similar event occurred on land, erosion could expose such a deposit. One possible exception could be where large scale crustal movements have exposed or elevated such layers, but so far few of these exposures have been found. One example of such deep sea regions now incorporated into a continent may be the Sudbury, Canada deposits of copper and nickel.

A different type of deposit can form from the chemical reactions between sea water and basaltic rock. Such reactions can cause alteration (metamorphism) of the rock sometimes forming copper or other mineral deposits. The faulted nature of many oceanic ridges (principal divergence zones of the ocean) may permit sea water to penetrate to considerable depths (and be heated) into the basalts. Again, however, the possibility of finding such deposits below the sea floor is difficult. Actually, the potential resources of the oceanic ridge areas really are not well known. Although the ridge system extends through all oceans (indeed it is the world's largest mountain system) we have little direct observations from it except where it comes to the surface as oceanic islands such as Iceland.

The second type of process in the deep sea that could form deposits results from the fact that heated sea water has the capability to leach certain elements from basalt or other rocks or sediment. These hydrothermal waters can pick up certain

TABLE 1

MAJOR, AVERAGE ELEMENTAL (AS OXIDES) COMPOSITION OF OCEANIC AND CONTINENTAL ROCKS[1]

	Average Oceanic Rocks	Average Continental Rocks
SiO_2	50.0	61.9
TiO_2	1.4	0.8
Al_2O_3	16.9	15.6
Fe_2O_3	2.3	2.6
FeO	6.4	3.9
MnO	0.2	0.1
MgO	7.0	3.1
CaO	12.6	5.7
Na_2O	2.6	3.1
K_2O	0.4	2.9
P_2O_5	0.2	0.3

[1]Data from Ronov and Yareshevshy (1969).

metals from the basalts (such as iron, manganese, copper, zinc, etc.) and deposit them elsewhere (such as in the pathways where the water moves) usually as sulfides. They may also precipitate mineral phases on the sea floor when the hydrothermal solutions come in contact with the overlying sea water. In this case they usually form oxides. The Troodos Massif of Cyprus (a large copper deposit) is an example of an ancient hydrothermal deposit that has been thrust up above sea water. The hydrothermal water may also sufficiently alter the basalt so that it could have potential as a resource.

The best example of hydrothermal activity on the sea floor that is producing a mineral deposit is the hot brine area of the Red Sea. The so-called Red Sea metalliferous muds will probably be mined before the end of the 1980s. This deposit, found essentially by chance, is situated along the central part of the Red Sea. In certain areas hot salty waters (hydrothermal solutions) containing enrichments of heavy metals are escaping from the sea floor and accumulating in small pools on the bottom. The process is similar to hot springs or geysers on land. More recently similar activity has been found in all oceans and most dramatically in the Galapagos region of the Pacific where it has given rise to a unique fauna that is feeding from these waters. These areas of hydrothermal activity have the potential to form deposits of economic value, if the conditions are right. So far only one such "right" deposit has been found--in the Red Sea--and it is of value to discuss it briefly, even though it falls within the EEZ of Saudi Arabia and Sudan.

The Red Sea is a zone of divergence--the Saudi Arabian Peninsula and Africa are slowly (about 1-2 cm/year) moving apart. The movement has formed a deep axial valley composed of new sea floor. Within several areas in the valley submarine discharge of hot salty water (salinities up to 257 $^{o}/_{oo}$ or 25.7% and temperatures of over 60°C) has accumulated (water depths are of the order of 2,000m). This accumulation aspect appears to be unique to the Red Sea and results from the fact that the sediments buried beneath the flank of the sea contain salt deposits that have been leached by the migrating fluids and thus the fluids have increased in density. The hot water, when it reaches the sea floor, is thus denser than sea water and remains there rather than being dispersed as it appears to be doing in other oceans. Salt deposits, similar to the Red Sea, are not expected in open areas of the ocean. The fluids, once in the depressions of the Red Sea, then react with the overlying sea water producing sediments enriched in many heavy metals. Over ten of these pools have been found, but the Atlantis II Deep, covering an area of over 70 square kilometers, and situated about equidistant between Saudi Arabia and Sudan, seems to have the best immediate potential. The _in situ_ value of the top 10 meters of its deposits exceeds two billion dollars (some estimates are over 4 billion dollars). The two adjacent countries (Sudan and Saudi Arabia) have negotiated an agreement to develop these and other similar Red Sea deposits. It is not obvious, however, that even such a concentration of elements (Table 2) such as found in the Atlantis II Deep is actually economic. Problems of retrieval and refining are still unsolved. The Atlantis II sediments are worth about $50/1000 kg (or about a ton) and are relatively more enriched in many of the metals found in deep sea sediments (for example, the Atlantis II sediments contain 30 times more copper than brown clays).

It does not, at present, seem probable that such high concentrations of metals similar to the Red Sea are present along other zones of divergence (Mid-Atlantic Ridge, East Pacific Rise, Mid-Indian Ridge) or buried along the flanks of the ridge. Many of the sediments of ocean ridges, however, have enrichments of iron, copper, manganese, nickel, lead, chromium, cobalt, and other elements. These concentrations are generally far from economic but higher concentrations may exist locally. There have been some indications of such local concentrations. For example, small veins of copper have been found in basalt rock below 400m of sediment on the Ninety East Ridge in the Indian Ocean and in sediment underlying the continental rise off New York. Manganese oxide accumulations (not nodules) have been found on parts of the Mid-Atlantic Ridge that appear to accumulate at a relatively high rate compared to nodules. In spite of these examples no known methods exist for adequate exploration and exploitation of mineral resources on the divergent portion of the sea floor. It is clear, however, that heat (therefore water movement) is coming from certain areas along the ridges and that there are chemical alterations of rocks due to these hydrothermal fluids. Further exploration, using research submersibles and other equipment, is necessary before the possibility of such deposits can be more realistically evaluated.

Mineral deposits also may occur along the convergent parts of plates due to mineralizing solutions coming from the melting of downthrusted plates. These resources, however, will generally fall within the proposed EEZ and are outside the range of discussion of this paper. Examples of such deposits are the sulphide deposits of Kuroko, Japan and the Philippines.

Conclusions

The prime, non-manganese nodule, potential mineral resources of the deep sea are brown clays and carbonate oozes from sedimentation and zones of mineralization resulting from the cooling of volcanic rock and the activity of hydrothermal solutions. It is essentially impossible at this time to place a value on these deposits for many reasons, in particular since the cost of recovery from oceanic depths (5,000m or more), combined with the costs of exploration, transportation and refining, is unknown. The difficulty of finding deposits in zones of mineralization is awesome since many of these deposits, if

TABLE 2

GROSS VALUE OF METALS IN UPPER 10 METERS OF SEDIMENTS COLLECTED FROM ATLANTIS II DEEP BASED ON 1967 METAL PRICES (ADAPTED FROM BISCHOFF AND MANHEIM, 1969)

Metal	Average Assay (%)	Tons	Value ($)
Zinc	3.4	2,900,000	$ 860,000,000
Copper	1.3	1,060,000	1,270,000,000
Lead	0.1	80,000	20,000,000
Silver	0.0054	4,500	280,000,000
Gold	0.0000005	45	50,000,000
TOTAL			$2,480,000,000

indeed they are there, would be below the sea floor and be covered by sediments and perhaps rocks. Weathering and erosional processes, which in many instances improve mineral deposits on land, are not common under the ocean. Further research could lead to the discovery of some resources, but, aside from the hot brine areas of the Red Sea, no mining of deep sea minerals (exclusive of manganese nodules), should be anticipated in the near future, if ever.

REFERENCES

Bischoff, J. L. and Manheim, F. T. Economic potential of the Red Sea heavy metal deposits. In Degens, E. T. and Ross, D. A. (Eds.), Hot Brines and Recent Heavy Metal Deposits in the Red Sea: A Geochemical and Geophysical Account. Springer Verlag, 1969, p. 535-541.

Brooks, D. B. and Andrews, P. W. Mineral resources, economic growth and world population. Science, 1974, 185(4145), 13-19.

Emery, K. O. and Skinner, B. J. Mineral deposits of the deep ocean floor. Marine Mining, 1977, 1(1/2), 1-71.

Mero, J. L. Minerals of the Ocean. In Firth, F. E. (Ed.), Encyclopedia of Marine Resources. van Nostrand Reinhold Company, 1969, p. 404-411.

Ronov, A. B. and Yareshevsky, A. A. Chemical composition of the earth's crust. In Hart, P. J. (Ed.), The Earth's Crust and Upper Mantle. American Geophysical Union, Geophysical Monograph, 1969, 13, 37-57.

Ross, D. A. The Uses and Opportunities of the Ocean. Springer Verlag, 1979.

Skinner, B. J. and Turekian, K. K. Man and the Ocean. Prentice-Hall, Inc., 1973.

LEGAL PROBLEMS RELATING TO THE EXTRACTION OF RESOURCES OF THE DEEP SEA OTHER THAN MANGANESE NODULES

Thomas A. Clingan, Jr.
Professor of Law
University of Miami School of Law
Coral Gables, Florida

David Ross, in his concise exposition regarding the resources of the deep sea other than manganese nodules has concluded, as many others have long suspected, that aside from the hot brine areas of the Red Sea, no real ocean mining should be anticipated for other than manganese nodules.[1]

I certainly accept that judgment. However, for the sake of this discussion, I shall, with his permission, set it aside and ask the "But, what if..." questions. While this may seem to be an exercise in futility, I believe it can still serve some useful purpose. First, it may shed some light on the degree to which, if at all, the Third United Nations Law of the Sea Conference (UNCLOS) is providing for future unanticipated uses of the oceans. Second, it might put some further focus upon the legal restraints (and corresponding economic burdens) which will have to be faced in a "go,no-go" decision regarding planning of activities of a marginal nature in the deep seas. Thus, I shall assume the possibility of <u>some</u> living or non-living resources being extractable by man from areas outside of the limits of national jurisdiction, and concentrate on the legal issues that come to mind.

There are two kinds of problems involved: jurisdictional and substantive. Restated, the questions are: (a) how large is the area beyond national jurisdiction; and (b) what is the nature of the legal restraints operating in that area? In responding to these questions, I shall consider not only my own view of the existing state of international law, but also the position reflected in the existing language of the Informal Composite Negotiating Text (ICNT).[2]

---

[1]The views expressed herein are purely those of the author and do not reflect the position of the U.S. government.

[2]A/CONF.62/WP.10. July 15, 1977. For the purposes of simplifying the discussion in this paper, the ICNT will be referenced as it now stands without reference to possible emerging texts. For those details, the reader is referred to "Reports of the Committees and Negotiating Groups on

The Jurisdictional Question

The question of jurisdiction is a threshhold one for it defines the areas in which resources might be located and sets the legal competence to regulate their extraction. These resources could fall either inside or outside coastal state jurisdiction, depending upon which formula is used in drawing the line that separates the coastal state from the international area. If they are outside coastal state jurisdiction, they would be extracted from locations within what the ICNT refers to as "the Area." Under the text's terms, there is only a vague reference to the scope of the Area (ICNT, Art. 134), but in a previous iteration (RSNT), the area was defined as "the seabed and ocean floor and subsoil thereof beyond the limits of national jurisdiction"(RSNT, Part I, Art. 2).

National jurisdiction extends seaward from the coastal state's land mass in two basic ways. The first is through the establishment of special zones of national jurisdiction, measured from the baseline from which the breadth of the territorial sea is measured; the second is through the concept of the continental shelf.

Under existing international law, the question of the size of the area beyond national jurisdiction is extremely unclear. If one is to define the area as that extending beyond the territorial sea, one must then examine the law with respect to the breadth of that jurisdictional zone. On this subject, the 1958 Geneva Convention is unclear[3], and obviously it was not possible to agree on a breadth either then or, subsequently, in 1960 at a conference convened for that sole purpose (Dean, 1960, p. 751). While the United States continued to claim a three mile limit following the 1960 attempt, more than half the states in the world now claim 12 nautical miles, or more (Limits in the Seas, No. 36), and several claim as many as 200. The present version of the ICNT contains the 12 mile figure (ICNT, Art. 3). That number seems to have widespread support as part of an overall acceptable negotiating package, with only the hard-line

---

negotiations at the Seventh Session contained in a single document both for the purposes of record and for the convenience of delegations," May 19, 1978, and to reports of chairmen from the summer session in New York, when they should become available.

[3]Convention on the Territorial Sea and the Contiguous Zone, U.N.T.S., <u>516</u>, p. 205; U.S.T., <u>15</u>, p. 1606, T.I.A.S. 5639, in force Sept. 10, 1964. Articles 1 and 2 accord with the adjacent state sovereignty over the waters, seabed and airspace. Due to disagreement, however, no breadth of the territorial sea was specified.

territorialists holding out.[4] Thus, the area beyond the territorial sea, under existing law, depends upon one's view of the international limit, if any, receiving widespread approval in state practice, and that is hard to say.

If "the Area" is defined as that portion of the seabed beyond the limits of the continental shelf, which certainly extends beyond most nations' territorial sea claims, the definitional problems are just as severe. The normally-accepted definition of the outer limits of the continental shelf (with which we have all struggled at one time or another) is that found in the 1958 Geneva Convention on the Continental Shelf (U.N.T.S., _499_, p. 311):

> Article 1.
>
> For the purpose of these articles, the term 'continental shelf' is used as referring (a) to the seabed and subsoil of the submarine areas adjacent to the coast but outside the area of the territorial sea, to a depth of 200 metres or, beyond that limit, to where the depth of the superjacent waters admits of the exploitation of the natural resources of the said areas; (b) to the seabed and subsoil of similar submarine areas adjacent to the coasts of islands.

Obviously, this politically masterful manipulation of depth, adjacency, and exploitability is of little help in adding precision to an outer shelf limit. Since the coastal state has _exclusive_ jurisdiction (whether it exercises it or not) over the exploitation of the living and non-living resources of the shelf out to that limit, delimitation of the area beyond is difficult and largely subjective in the sense that the coastal state will make the necessary decisions subject to challenge by the international community at large.

Moving from existing law, if one looks to the ICNT as reflective of new trends which, in some cases may even be representative of customary international law, there are two concepts which have a direct bearing upon the problem. They are the "exclusive economic zone" and, once again, the continental shelf.

---

[4]This is reflected, for example, in a proposed new article by Ecuador which reads: "National legislation enacted, prior to the adoption of the Present Convention, with respect to zones extending beyond 12 nautical miles may continue to be applied to the extent that it does not affect the rights and obligations of all states in accordance with the present convention." C.2/Informal Meeting/29, dated May 3, 1978.

The ICNT provides that the exclusive economic zone is an area, beyond and adjacent to the territorial sea, where the coastal state has (Art. 56)

> Sovereign rights for the purpose of exploring and exploiting, conserving and managing the natural resources, whether living or non-living, of the sea-bed and subsoil and the superjacent waters, and with regard to other activities for the economic exploitation and exploration of the zone, such as the production of energy from the water, currents and winds.

This zone is an optional one, to be established at the will of the coastal state, which may not exceed 200 nautical miles from the baseline from which the breadth of the territorial sea is measured. If one chooses the outer limit of this zone as the legal dividing line between coastal state jurisdiction and an international area beyond, then, of course, the area to which we are addressing ourselves would include all of the seabed, regardless of depth, beyond 200 nautical miles. This has been estimated to be 288.04×10^6 sq. km. (Economic Significance, 1973).

However, we might still wish to consider the impact of the existence of a continental shelf beyond 200 nautical miles. While this area might not be significant in terms of overall statistics, it represents extensions of national jurisdiction of great political and economic importance to some states. The definition of the ICNT differs from that in the Geneva Convention. It is as follows (ICNT, Art. 76):

> The continental shelf of a coastal state comprises the sea-bed and subsoil of the submarine areas that extend beyond its territorial sea throughout the natural prolongation of its land territory to the outer edge of the continental margin, or to a distance of 200 nautical miles from the baselines from which the breadth of the territorial sea is measured where the outer edge of the continental margin does not extend up to that distance.

The question is raised here concerning the meaning of "natural prolongation," a term used by the ICJ in the North Sea Cases (1969). Obviously, it could be very broadly construed. If it is interpreted to include the "last grain of sand" of the continental rise, then vast portions of the seabed could be subjected to national jurisdiction, leaving little of value to the international community other than nodules. For this reason, the Conference is struggling with several alternative formulae to achieve a more precise delimitation, but which also must be politically acceptable. Such a formula would have to produce a legal definition of the continental shelf broad enough to satisfy the broad margin states who feel that they already have acquired rights to the entire margin, as well as the developing countries in the Conference seeking to maximize as much as realistically possible the "common heritage of mankind."

The first such proposal is the so-called "Irish formula." This formula is backed by or agreed to by most of the broad margin countries. It provides that coastal state jurisdiction would be restricted to the natural prolongation of the continental land mass (a) to a distance based upon the thickness of sedimentary rocks, or (b) to a fixed distance from the foot of the continental slope.[5] A second proposal, by the Soviet Union, would limit the margin at a point defined by geological or geomorphological data, but not to exceed 100 nautical miles beyond the economic zone.[6] The third, a position taken by the Arab Group, would make the legal limit of the margin coterminus with the 200 mile limit of the economic zone.[7] Obviously, this latter formula would maximize the size of "the Area," and hence the amount of non-manganese nodule resources available to the international community and subject to the jurisdiction of the International Seabeds Authority. This formula would thus internationalize some quantities of oil and gas as well as other shelf mineral resources. One estimate has suggested that as much as 284 billion barrels of oil and equivalent gas could be involved (Weeks, 1976), although his estimates are considered by some to be generally high. The Arab formula has been rejected by states having broad margins; thus, the choice is narrowed to Article 76 of the ICNT as written or a text defining the margin with greater precision. As between the Irish or

---

[5]Submitted in an informal document to Negotiating Group 6, established by the plenary of the Eighth Session of the Law of the Sea Conference. This suggestion also included a provision for a boundary review commission, but this part of the proposal has not been subject to much discussion.

[6]The Soviet proposal would depend, for the drawing of limits, upon a structure adequate to support the extraction of minerals. In that sense, it could, in certain areas, exceed the 1% limitation of the Irish formula. A study has been requested by the Conference president that would illustrate how this limit would look vis-a-vis other proposals. During the Seventh Session, however, the representative of the IOC reported that it had not yet been possible to derive an interpretation of the Soviet formula with sufficient precision to complete the study.

[7]This formal position of the Arab States is the only bloc position on the limits of the shelf. It is expected that, individually, various Arab States have some flexibility should they be released from the bloc position. Of these, only Iraq has indicated a preference for the Soviet formula.

Soviet texts, states disagree which takes more from the common heritage and which will better accommodate the interests involved, with the odds seemingly against the Soviets.

I would like to diverge slightly to make one point here, though it is not directly relevant to the main theme. There is at present a negotiating "stand-off" between proponents of the Soviet and Irish formulae. Although the vast majority of states has accepted the Irish formula as the most likely compromise, the eastern bloc countries stand firmly behind the USSR draft. Should this confrontation remain unresolved, a likely outcome would be the retention of Article 76 as it is, since the Chairman of Committee Two might be compelled to take the position that there was no agreement to any amendment to that article, and that neither the Irish nor Soviet proposals rejected the basic concept of jurisdiction over the margin. The broad scope of interpretation permitted by Article 76 would have serious implications for the conduct of marine scientific research because much research would then be under tight coastal state control. Correspondingly, of course, Article 76 would eliminate any possibility of a limit short of the full geological extent of the margin.

Where the shelf extends beyond 200 nautical miles, coastal state resource jurisdiction would be increased. A recent study conducted by the UNCLOS Secretariate illustrates the various jurisdictional areas suggested by various limits. A map (A/CONF.62/C.2/L.98/Add.1) produced shows substantial shelf extension beyond 200 nautical miles near the Australian continent, around certain Indian Ocean and east coast African countries, western Africa, eastern South America, Canada, and parts of the northeastern Atlantic. The political questions posed by the map and addressed by the various formulae is the degree to which these extensions should be included within coastal state jurisdiction. The question takes on different significance according to the breadth of states' margins and attitudes with respect to the accommodation of the common heritage.[8]

[8] In response to objections that the Irish formula deprived developing landlocked and geographically disadvantaged states of a portion of the common heritage, the U.S. proposed a system of revenue sharing which is now found in ICNT Article 82. A variation on the system was proposed by the Seychelles during the last negotiating session which would increase the percentage of revenues available, stimulating one of the first substantive discussions on the issue. There is, however, a widely held view that revenue sharing beyond 200 miles is an essential part of any agreement on the continental shelf issue.

The Substantive Matter - Existing Law

Assuming that the limits of national jurisdiction eventually will be sorted out, and the size and content of the area thus established, what substantive rules should be applied?

Because the work of the U.N. with respect to the law of the sea began before there were realistic expectations of taking anything at all out of the deep seabeds, or the water column above them, the focus in the negotiations fell, quite naturally, not upon existing law but upon the creation of appropriate machinery for regulating the extraction process at some future time when such an event became economically and technically feasible. Few envisaged the length of the negotiations or the rapid advance of technology. Thus, the negotiations in UNCLOS III proceeded along predictable lines. But when the United States Congress recently decided to press ahead with unilateral legislation to enable the mining process to begin, the issue of existing law was necessarily engaged. The threat of imminent action brought reaction and counter-reaction to the Eighth Session of the Law of the Sea Conference.

At the final plenary of the last summer session, the Group of 77, through its Chairman Satya Nandan of Fiji, denounced unilateral legislation on the initiative of any state. He said, in part:

> The Group of 77 rejects the entire basis for such legislation - in particular the premise that the right to engage in mining of the resources of the seabed beyond the limits of national jurisdiction is a legal freedom of the high seas. There is no practice, much less custom in the legal sense, of actual exploitation. Nor is there a general treaty authorizing the exploitation of the seabed. The Declaration of Principles embodied in Resolution 2749 (XXV) expressly excludes the unfounded argument of pretending an extension of high seas freedom to the seabeds and subjects the exploration and exploitation of the seabed to the international regime to be established.[9]

It is the Declaration of Principles, adopted without dissent, that the Group of 77 finds to be controlling. According to them, it confirms the legal consequence that unilateral legislation is incompatible with the common understanding of nations.

---

[9]Preliminary copy, Statement Declaring the Position of the Group of 77 on Unilateral Legislation Affecting the Resources of the Deep Seabed, September 15, 1978.

It is no answer, they explain, to claim that General Assembly resolutions are not binding, because the Declaration of Principles was a "solemn declaration" that the resources of the seabed are the common heritage of mankind and cannot be unilaterally appropriated.

The statement of the 77 was reinforced by several interventions on the part of the individual states, including one by the Soviet Union branding the action as "illegal."

Ambassador Elliot L. Richardson, head of the delegation, responded on the part of the U.S. He said:

> Legal restraints may be imposed on national action beyond the limits of the jurisdiction of any state only by their inclusion in rules of international law. With respect to seabed mining we are unaware of any such restraints other than those that apply generally to the high seas and the exercise of high seas freedoms, including the prohibition on sovereignty claims, the exclusive jurisdiction of states over their ships and nationals, and the duty to have reasonable regard for other high seas users. States will become subject to additional restraints when they adhere to a treaty that establishes an international authority to manage and oversee seabed mining. They will then have voluntarily accepted the alteration of those freedoms in the broader interest of creating a stable legal regime for the use and management of the world's oceans and their resources.[10]

With respect to the point raised concerning the Declaration of Principles, Richardson acknowledged the widespread support enjoyed by them, but said that the proclamation of such resources as the "common heritage" did not in any way prohibit access to them. In fact, he implied, retardation of ocean mining would not be in anyone's interest, developed or developing.

Prior history of this question suggests that at least some scholars view the use of the seabed and water columns as controlled by the general regime for the high seas (Laylin, 1972; Knight, 1978, p. 536; Thompson-Flores, 1978, p. 40). Colombos (1967, p. 67), for example, has written "...it's (the seabed's) legal status is the same as that of the water of the open sea above it." If that is a proper interpretation of the existing state of the law, then without a treaty, presumably these are

---

[10]Statement by Ambassador Elliot L. Richardson, Special Representative of the President for the Law of the Sea Conference to the Plenary Meeting, September 15, 1978.

the same rules that would apply. Since the Declaration of Principles was not intended to create an interim mining regime, but merely a backdrop against which international negotiations could continue, the freedom to mine would be the rule of the day. This would apply not only to manganese nodules, but to any extractable resources of the seabed, subsoil, or water column.

In the commentary to Article 27 of its draft, the high seas article, the International Law Commission pointed out that the list of freedoms contained in the 1958 Convention is not restrictive. It made reference to the sea bed and subsoil as follows:

> The Commission has not made specific mention of the freedom to explore or exploit the subsoil of the high seas. It considered that apart from the case of the exploitation or exploration of the soil or subsoil of a continental shelf...such exploitation had not yet assumed practical importance to justify special regulation.[11]

This language is found in the paragraph dealing with other freedoms than those specifically referred to in Article 2 of the Convention. This would, taken with the language, imply that high seas mining continues as a freedom until other regulation is justified. Such other regulation could only, as Richardson has said, come through the agreement of nations, presumably through the Law of the Sea Conference.

It should be explained that, at least with regard to the mining of nodules (if not all submerged minerals), there is a valid fisheries analogy. With regard to unilateral action concerning fisheries, Lauterpacht (1950, p. 376) wrote as follows:

> ...unilateral acts such as the Proclamation of the United States of 1945 in the matter of fisheries although amounting in some way to a claim to exercise jurisdiction on the high seas in areas in which fishery rights have hitherto been exercised only by citizens of the United States, may not necessarily be inconsistent with a rational interpretation of the principle of the freedom of the seas so long as its primary object is not the exclusion of nationals of foreign states.

---

[11]Report of the International Law Commission Covering the work of its Eighth Session, U.N. Gen. Ass. Off. Rec., 11th Sess., Supp. No. 9 (A/3159), pp. 23, 24; II Yearbook of the International Law Commission, 1956, pp. 253, 278.

While factual distinctions could be made, the importance of Lauterpacht's analysis for purposes of our discussion is his allusion to the degree to which the exercise of a right beyond national limits interferes with or represents an exclusion of nationals of foreign states. There is no such exclusion, of course, in the case of non-site specific mining legislation. Thus, one can conclude that with respect to nodules, in situ minerals other than nodules, and suspended minerals in the water column, existing law would permit extraction on a non-exclusive basis.

Now, with respect to the living resources of the high seas, under existing rules of international law, states are free to capture fish at least beyond any national 200 mile limit (Convention on the High Seas, Art. 2) subject to the agreement of the state of origin in the case of anadromous species. Two hundred mile fishing zones have been declared by a number of states, including the United States (Fisheries Management, 1976) in which the coastal state exercises conservation and management powers. Such action is consistent with the principles set forth by the ICJ in the case of U.K. v. Iceland[12] and is also consistent with the practice of states and trends in the Law of the Sea Conference.[13] Beyond the 200 mile limit, the generally accepted principles of the freedoms of the high seas apply, with some conservation obligations imposed upon parties to the 1958 Convention on Fishing and special obligations for highly migratory species.

The subject of high seas fishing of krill in the Antarctic is a unique subject deserving some attention, but that subject is being treated by on-going negotiations seeking to set up a special conservation regime. Since this subject is presumably to be covered by another panel at this meeting, it will not be discussed here.

Likewise, the placement of installations for the extraction of energy from the oceans will be covered elsewhere; thus it will here be sufficient to point out that the placement of floating or semi-submersible platforms on a non-exclusive basis beyond national jurisdiction would be an exercise of high seas freedoms. Other legal questions that would have to be addressed with respect to such platforms would include criminal and civil jurisdiction over personnel on manned stations particularly in those cases where the "flag" of the installation does not coincide with the nationality of the workers.

---

[12]Fisheries Jurisdiction Cases, I.C.J. 3, 197, 1974.

[13]See ICNT, Part V, Exclusive Economic Zone provisions.

The Substantive Matter - The ICNT

As previously explained, in this section the existing text of the ICNT will be referenced, although it must be pointed out that there are a large number of highly unsatisfactory provisions in the ICNT as it is viewed by a number of countries. Thus, substantial change should be expected. The exercise here is for the purpose of illuminating problem areas which will have to be dealt with in some satisfactory manner.

First, let us identify the resources of the area covered by the ICNT. Resources, according to the ICNT, means mineral resources in situ (ICNT, Art. 133(b)). These include the following categories:

(i) Liquid or gaseous substances such as petroleum, gas, condensate, helium, nitrogen, carbon dioxide, water, steam, hot water, and also sulphur and salts extracted in liquid form in solution;

(ii) Useful minerals occurring on the surface of the seabed or at depths of less than three metres beneath the surface and also concretions of phosphorites and other minerals;

(iii) Solid minerals in the ocean floor at depths of more than three metres from the surface;

(iv) Ore-bearing silt and brine (ICNT, Art. 133(c)).

Living resources of the high seas are governed separately by the provisions of Part VII, Section 2 of the ICNT. They will be referred to subsequently.

The principle underlying the ICNT is that no state shall claim or exercise sovereignty or sovereign rights over any part of the area or its resources (ICNT, Art. 137). All rights to resources of the area are vested in "mankind as a whole" (ICNT, Art. 137(2)) raising questions with respect to how an entrepreneur gains and transfers title to them. The ICNT, in form, purports to establish a dual-access, or parallel system whereby activities in the area shall be carried out on behalf of the International Seabed Authority by its operating arm, the Enterprise, or in association with the Authority by states parties, or state entities, or persons natural or juridical which possess the nationality of states parties, through contractual arrangements (ICNT, Art. 151(2)). The modalities of the extraction of resources are extremely complicated under the terms of the ICNT. No effort will be made to analyze them in detail here. Rather, a few of the more serious problem areas will be suggested.

First, there is a serious question in the minds of the industrialized states with regard to just how "dual" the system really is. In many respects, the text appears to establish a parallel system in name only. Duality implies balance, and in context it suggests that there should be equal opportunity for competition on a free and open basis between the Enterprise and entities of states parties or a state enterprise itself. But many provisions of the text would seem to offset this generally desirable principle. Since the Authority's powers would apply to all resources of the area, as defined, the system would govern the resources under discussion.

Activities of the area are to be carried out either by the Enterprise or in "association with" the Authority in accordance with the provisions set forth in an annex to the treaty. This annex[14] consists of a complex of highly technical, virtually incomprehensible series of requirements concerning the qualification of applicants and the precise manner in which contracts shall be negotiated. The totality of the system would raise genuine questions concerning assurance to access and tenure of investment.

In addition, the text could be read to make technology transfer a condition of access by contractors[15], providing the Enterprise with an important competitive "equalizer" in the extraction of minerals, an equalizer not generally shared in international contracting in general where technology is available through the market system, but in an atmosphere where bargaining for that technology is done with both parties on an equal footing.

Next, the text can also be read to give the Authority the power to mandate joint ventures (ICNT, Annex Para. 5(g), 5(i)) which may not be the best way in all circumstances for dealing with marginal ocean endeavors. It also provides for a wide and potentially damaging range of financial burdens to be paid as the price for conducting operations (ICNT, Annex Para. 7). In this sense, once again, there has been a distinct failure to comprehend the possibility of other extraction activities than those related to nodules, and the marginal nature of such operations.

---

[14]ICNT, Annex II. This annex deals with the basic conditions of exploration and exploitation. It contains details with respect to the qualifications and selection of applicants, financial terms, and rules, regulations and procedures of the Authority.

[15]ICNT. Annex Paragraph 5(j) (iv) requires the contractor to make technology available to the Enterprise on "fair and reasonable terms."

There would be an artificial limit set on the production of nodules and other resources (ICNT, Art. 150). But in the case of these other resources, the text is totally open-ended, permitting the Authority to regulate production "under such conditions and applying such methods as may be appropriate" (ICNT, Art. 150(g) (C)).

Another potential difficulty is found in the system of governance of the Authority. At the present time there are no sufficient assurances that the legitimate interests of ocean mineral extractors, to say nothing of consumer interests, would be taken into account adequately in the decision-making process.[16] In fact, under the present text, the important decisions could be made by those having the least interest in the benefits that might flow from ocean mining. Finally, there is no assurance that a dual or parallel system, even if fairly constituted, could survive a 20 year review period established by the ICNT. The text now reads in a way that it becomes mandatory that a purely unitary system under the Authority would be established at the end of that period.[17]

The above discussion overlooks many things. It is not an attempt to make a detailed review of ocean mining provisions, but merely to highlight a few and to raise, by inference, the prospect that such provisions create problems of an even higher order of magnitude if we are discussing mining of a much more marginal nature than the extraction of manganese nodules. It overlooks, for the sake of brevity, provisions of the text dealing with pollution control, settlement of disputes, and marine scientific research. It is not, of course, that these are considered unimportant. They would have to be factored into the business decisions to be made. It also overlooks the fact that some progress has been made in improving the texts over the last year. Those improvements, reflected in the reports of the chairmen of the various negotiating groups (supra footnote 2) have not been discussed here because they are not yet mature enough to be included in a revised text, and because they may be too small to achieve a consensus. The short litany of woes with regard to deep seabed mining, I trust, is adequate, however, to discourage any possible interest that might remain with regard to mining other than nodules after Dave Ross finished with his analysis.

Let me just turn for a moment to the question of living resources. The ICNT includes freedom of fishing as one of the

---

[16]See, generally, the composition, functions, and voting provisions for the council and assembly contained in Part XI, Section 5 of the ICNT.

[17]This would be the operative effect of the Review Conference provided for in ICNT 153.

freedoms of the high seas[18] (as did its forebearer, the Geneva Convention), subject to provisions that would require states to cooperate in arrangements for the conservation of stocks that redesigned to achieve the maximum sustainable yield as qualified by relevant economic factors, including the special requirements of developing countries, and taking into account fishing patterns, the interdependence of stocks and any generally recommended subregional, regional or global minimum standards (ICNT, Art. 119). These are the same standards imposed upon coastal states within their own economic zone. States are called upon to cooperate as appropriate through regional or subregional fisheries organizations (ICNT, Art. 118). Once again, special arrangements are called for in the case of anadromous[19] and highly migratory species.[20] Other than these, there are no high seas fishing limitations. Article 120 provides that Article 65 applies to the conservation of marine mammals on the high seas. Article 65 states that the convention in no way restricts the right of a coastal state or international organization to prohibit, or limit the exploitation of these mammals, and that states should cooperate either directly or through appropriate international organizations with a view to their protection and management. During the immediately preceding phase of negotiations, an initiative was undertaken by one country which had as its objective to make clear that the Article 61 conservation standards are the minimum standards that are to be applied by the coastal state or international organization when regulating these stocks. Other clarifications were also sought. It is to be expected that this initiative will carry over to the Eighth Session of the Conference. Should these changes be acceptable, it would be clear that emphasis with regard to the regulation, study, and management of marine mammals would tilt in the direction of conservations.

Conclusion

The obvious conclusion with regard to legal restraints on the mining of hard minerals other than manganese nodules from the area beyond national jurisdiction is that they would be overwhelming. While the Conference struggles on with the problem of how to make the complexities over manganese nodule

---

[19]ICNT, Art. 66 deals with the questions of anadromous stocks. By its provisions, it permits certain fishing on the high seas (in this context, meaning beyond the economic zone) where otherwise there would be economic dislocation for a state other than the state of origin. To that extent, there is a special provision for "high seas" salmon fishing.

[20]Article 64 of the ICNT calls for cooperation for the management of tuna throughout their migratory range, both within and without the economic zone.

mining more amenable, what chance do the miners who seek the less valuable resources have of surviving? This is only partially the result of a Conference failure to focus on the broader questions. It is the direct function of the emergence of a system, indeed a philosophy, that is basically unsupportable in the form that is emerging. The amount of detailed regulation being developed for an industry that is yet unproved and basically unknown is staggering. A general realization of the problems of workability of the system in the Law of the Sea Conference is reflected in the provision calling for a review and re-evaluation of the system after a period of operation to permit adjustment of measures that have proved themselves to be unworthy in day-to-day operation. Unfortunately, as previously mentioned, that provision has other serious problems. In fact the ICNT _in toto_ has so many problems with regard to mining that one wonders how the remaining work can be accomplished in any kind of realistic time frame.

With regard to new uses of the seabeds, one should scan the entire ICNT to look at the kinds of institutional models that are available with a view to seeing if other institutions could be applied. This springs from the feeling one has that less formal arrangements should be required for the governance of resources so marginal and speculative, something a great deal simpler.

One such model is found in the article dealing with highly migratory species.[21] It calls for cooperation of states directly or through appropriate international organizations for the conservation of highly migratory species, both within and beyond the exclusive economic zone. Where there is no existing organization, coastal and other states whose nationals harvest the fish have a legal obligation to cooperate in the establishment of such an organization and participate in its work. This, of course, is not directly translatable to deep seabed mining. First of all, the HMS organization would be regional rather than global and it would not deal with the question of interim measures to be applied pending the creation of a workable international organization. The point is that early tuna negotiations, like the seabeds negotiation, tended to bog down in the great quantity of detail concerning membership, voting arrangements, quotas, licensing, enforcement and fees. At some point, however, it was noted that it would probably be impossible to achieve agreement, given the many diverse national interests involved, on this kind of detail in a highly political forum where a large number of states neither had real interest in nor understanding of the problems of the regional management of tuna. At that point it was understood that this kind of detail is best left to be worked out by the international

[21] Id.

organization itself whose membership presumably would be made up of the most interested states. This could be done at the formative state of the organization, or at some subsequent time.

When we speak of minerals other than manganese nodules, beyond national jurisdiction, why not restrict oneself to a basic charter consisting of:

(a) the institutional features of the future organization, including a balanced system for taking decisions;

(b) reasonable guarantees of access and assurances for a workable parallel system; and

(c) good working system for the settlement of disputes?

Perhaps one would want to develop this with other features as well. But the point is that the bulk of the detail could be left out of the body of the treaty subject to being negotiated in the interim period either by the seabed institution itself or a committee formed specially for that purpose. The suggestion begs the question, of course, whether such an approach should be limited only to those minerals referred to in this general presentation.

No summary conclusions need be addressed with respect to living resources, except, once more, to note the special problems relating to the living resources of the Antarctic area, which in my view require special handling, and are receiving that attention. With respect to the legal status of the hot brines, it has already been indicated that they would fall within the jurisdiction of one or more coastal states.

REFERENCES

Colombos. International Law of the Sea, 6th ed. 1967.

Convention on Fishing and Conservation of the Living Resources of the High Seas. U.N.T.S., 559, p. 285; U.S.T., 17, p. 138; T.I.A.S. No. 5969; in force March 20, 1966.

Convention on the High Seas, Article 2. U.N.T.S., 450, p. 82; U.S.T., 13, p. 2312; T.I.A.S. No. 5200; in force Sept. 30, 1962.

Dean. The second Geneva conference on the law of the sea: the fight for freedom of the seas. AJIL, 1960, 54, p. 751.

Economic Significance, In Terms of Sea-Bed Mineral Resources of the Various Limits Proposed for National Jurisdiction. Report of the Secretary General, U.N. Doc. A/AC.138/47 and Corr. 1, June 4, 1973.

Fisheries Management and Conservation Act of 1976. *U.S.C.*, *16*, S1801.

ICNT (Informal Composite Negotiating Text)

Knight. *The Law of the Sea: Cases, Documents and Readings.* 1978 ed.

Lauterpach. Sovereignty over submarine areas. *Brit. Yb. Int'l L.*, 1950, *27*.

Laylin. Seabed mining beyond the limits of national jurisdiction. *Proceedings of the Seventh Annual Meeting, Law of the Sea Institute.* 1972.

Limits in the Seas: National Claims to Maritime Jurisdictions, No. 3. Office of the Geographer, Bureau of Intelligence and Research, Department of State.

North Sea Continental Shelf Cases. I.C.J. 3, 1969.

RSNT (Revised Single Negotiating Text)

Thompson-Flores. In *Proceedings of the Seventh Annual Meeting, Law of the Sea Institute.* 1972.

U.N.T.S., *499*, p. 311; *U.S.T.*, *15*, p. 471; T.I.A.S. No. 5578; in force June 10, 1964.

Weeks. *Petroleum Resources Potential of the Continental Margins.* 1976.

COMMENTARY

Judith Kildow
Massachusetts Institute of Technology

I would like to respond first to the statement from the gentlemen from the Netherlands this morning, who wondered about the question of even debating something in the U.N. negotiations about which we knew very little. I thought about that awhile and I came up with the best analogy I could because I think I tend to agree with the implications of this statement. My analogy goes back into the history of my own country, the United States, with which I am most familiar. It has to do with my forebears and the development of the Constitution for the United States.

Had they debated the details of the Constitution in Philadelphia to the extent that the U.N. representatives are debating the sea-bed regime for manganese nodules, our Constitution probability would not have been written.

I tried to think of an analogy that was hotly debated in the Constitutional Convention, and the Commerce Clause seemed appropriate. The differences between the North and the South over their perceptions of the way commerce should be carried out were not of an equitable nature. Wisely, the framers of the Constitution generalized and did not create tariff schedules in detail of how interstate commerce should be carried out but, rather, said that the commerce should be carried out in a way that was equitable to all the states.

If only we could apply that principle to the so-called type of constitution that they are trying to work out in the U.N. negotiations, I think we would get much further. Our Constitution, up to now, has stood somewhat of a test of time in that it is general enough to apply to things that we could not predict.

My contention is that we cannot begin to predict the implications of deep sea mining. I do not think the industry is keeping that much from the public. Information regarding the technology has been selectively withheld due to competition, and that is a very normal way of proceeding in the part of the world where private enterprise competition tends to be a way of life.

I think as far as the value of the resource, you can debate it in vain. I do not think there is anyone who really knows the value of that resource, or the implications of long-term mining on the deep seabed. To try to negotiate a text with the degree of detail and regulation that is being negotiated will only prove to be irrelevant and, perhaps, a great impediment to the whole international community. I think many of the results from these debates have been misconceptions, myths, and misunderstandings.

I would like to elaborate about some of those myths and misunderstandings. First of all, if one listened to the comments of some of the negotiators, one would think that innovation and discovery magically spring forth from the minds of people in corporations. There have been many studies on how innovation occurs, how discovery has occurred, what the relationship is between technological innovation and discovery, the relationship between technological innovation, scientific discovery and economic development and growth.

We seem to ignore all of these things we have learned in these negotiations. Innovation and technological innovation do not <u>just</u> occur. They occur under certain kinds of conditions. The conditions under which they occur are being highly neglected in negotiations. If one reads the latest text for the proposed regime, one would think the objective was to inhibit, not facilitate, resource development. The conditions of the text further impede technological innovation and scientific discovery through a system of disincentives.

The case of manganese nodules, although that is not the resource we are supposed to discuss, should be looked at in view of all that has been said today on this panel regarding the potential resources that at a later time could be extracted from the seabed. Manganese nodules became interesting because they became accessible at competitive costs. Their discovery lay dormant for about 100 years before anybody decided to do anything about it. Technology emerged in the 1960's made their harvesting possible. There was an evolution of technological development, due to a lot of other economic incentives in industry development, which made it possible to get access to the nodules.

Once access was possible, we understood a little bit about the value of those nodules. It gave some industries incentive to spend a fair amount of money, more than $100,000,000 in some cases and a proposed $700,000,000 or more down the road, to look into the possibility of building the equipment to mine and market this resource. That didn't just happen. They saw that it was an economically feasible thing to do and that the marketplace could allow it.

Somehow, the second myth that I think occurs in these negotiations is the separation of political objectives and economic realities ignoring the world marketplace for the goal of obtaining political objectives, which appears to be the case, will only inhibit deep sea mining. The various industries are not a captive audience. If they cannot go out to the deep sea bed, they have investment alternatives. Their stockholders will say, "Don't spend the money that way, we will go to land or other resources or other things. We will develop innovative technologies on land", which they are doing. New processes for extracting copper and drilling into the ground avoid the costs and environmental damage of mining it in the old ways.

There are a lot of alternatives available other than the deep sea-bed. But these are land alternatives, perhaps, or these are even foreign policy or domestic policy alternatives. The deep sea-bed could be at least temporarily by-passed if things proceed the way they are. The investments are not immutable. They can be used in other ways. I think this would be an unfortunate situation because if the alternatives are pursued, the benefits will accrue to the same nationals that have gotten the benefits before and the more disadvantaged countries negotiating in the U.N. will lose out again. It will be a long time before not only nodules, the manganese nodules that we hear so much about, but any of the other potential resources on the sea bed, will ever be exploited.

It should be noted that the exploitation of the nodules is really minor relative to land mining which is a much bigger business. Placing inhibitions and uncertainties along the way will only discourage the industry, and will inhibit the synergistic effects that might come from going to the deep sea-bed. Permitting industry under more general conditions to begin doing the mining would provide a learning process about the deep sea-bed, an area we do not yet know very much about. We are just beginning to implement scientific programs to help us better understand that part of the oceans.

David Ross alluded to the sea floor spreading, plate tectonic theories, that were proven not long ago. When the Glomar Challenger was able to do its coring and the technology permitted such access to that information, it created a revolution in our scientific information, which created the basis for a much larger revolution. That knowledge gave scientists the capability to predict, to some extent now, where resources may be and learn much more about the formation of resources on our planet.

That came about from science and technology feeding each other. Without scientific discovery and technological innovation as mutually supporting systems, that might not have occurred. What I am suggesting is that if we highly inhibit work on the sea floor, the way we are through the current negotiations, we will not know as much. It will take much longer to learn about the sea floor and whatever potential resources are there; it will be a long time before benefits accrue to the rest of the world.

COMMENTARY

David L. Larson
Department of Political Science
University of New Hampshire

For the purposes of discussion, I would start with some of the definitions which David Ross sets forth in his paper.

First, he suggests that few of the "other possible resources" of the deep sea, aside from manganese nodules, "are economically meaningful at this time, and most may never be." I think that this assertion is open to question, in view of increasing demands for oil, gas and selected minerals, and in view of rapid technological developments for mining or exploiting the deep seabed.

Second, he suggests that a "resource in a simple sense means a supply of something be it food, minerals or water." This definition seems to be much too restrictive, and does not include the notion that a resource is also "something that lies ready for use," (Grolnick, 1970) such as the ocean dumping of radioactive wastes.

As early as 1969 it was estimated that the worldwide value of minerals from the sea and seabed, broadly defined, was $7,070 million in 1969 dollars. Of that amount, $6,100 million was the value of oil and gas (UNESC, E/4973, 1971).

In calendar year 1977, the value of offshore oil and gas production (3.911 bbl. and 9.54 tr.cu.ft.) was estimated at $60,258 million, which is a ten-fold increase in just eight years. About eighty percent of this dollar increase is due to the quadrupling of oil prices by OPEC in 1974 and inflation, whereas about twenty percent of this dollar increase is due to a real increase in both the demand and supply of offshore oil and gas (_Oil and Gas Journal_, 1977).

As recently as the summer of 1977, H.D. Hedberg, J.D. Moody and R.M. Hedberg estimated that there is probably "as much geologically prospective acreage for petroleum under the oceans beyond the (continental) shelf edge as on the shelves." Oil and gas geologists tend to be optimistic, by nature, but the Hedbergs and Moody set forth some impressive data produced by the Joides Deep Sea Drilling Program and the International Phase of Ocean Drilling.

If there are significant oil and gas reserves on the continental margins, the small ocean basins and the central ocean region, and if the technology can be developed to retrieve this oil and gas, these deep sea regions may produce as much oil and gas as the continental shelf (Hedberg, Moody and Hedberg, 1977). The production of oil and gas on the continental shelf in 1977 was eighteen percent of total world production, and according to the National Petroleum Council in 1975, "world offshore proved reserves amounted to 135 billion barrels of oil and 491 trillion cubic feet of gas, some 20% of the world's total proved reserves" (Time Magazine, October 16, 1978). Assuming that the technology can and will be developed to retrieve this oil and gas, that would be an economically meaningful resource.

Therefore, on the basis of these preliminary surveys and the emerging technology, it seems much too early to dismiss the potential resources of oil and gas on the deep seabed, and premature to discount the possibility of technological retrieval systems that are economically viable.

The problem of dumping radioactive wastes in the deep sea and into the deep seabed is a relatively new aspect of ocean pollution, and potentially the most dangerous. Between 1946 and 1970, the United States Atomic Energy Commission "licensed the dumping of more than 86,000 containers of low-level wastes, totalling 94,000 curies into the Atlantic (80,000) and Pacific (14,000) Oceans" (Deese, 1977, p. 51). Between 1951 and 1966 Britain dumped about 45,000 curies of low-level radioactive waste in the North Atlantic, and from 1967 to 1976, the European Nuclear Energy Agency dumped about 300,000 curies of low-level and medium level wastes in the North Atlantic at a site located about 1,000 km. west of mainland Europe (46° - 15' N and 17° - 25' W). The United States proposed to establish a radioactive waste dump in the center of the Gulf of Mexico in 1959, but after protest by Mexico this plan was dropped, and since 1971 all United States radioactive waste material has been stored on land at three main sites: Hanford, Washington; Oak Ridge, Tennessee; and Snake River, Idaho, with a fourth under consideration near Alamagordo, New Mexico.

The First International Workshop on Seabed Disposal of High-Level Radioactive Wastes was held at Woods Hole in February 1976, and sponsored by the European Nuclear Energy Agency and the American Energy Research and Development Agency. A second workshop was scheduled for late 1977, and David Ross might report on the results. However, it was reported that these workshops were to be largely a "scientific and technical effort to map a potential international program for the investigation and assessment of seabed disposal."[1]

---

[1] The reports of these workshops were not available at the time of writing this paper.

Given the pressures to find some alternative to land based disposal of radioactive waste material, known as the "not in my backyard" syndrome, this has led to a search for the "least valuable piece of real estate on this planet" which is geologically stable (Frosch, 1977). This pressure and the search has naturally focused on the deep seabed. The problem is:

1. to locate an environment which will be isolated from man for at least a million years;

2. to locate an environment which is geologically and oceanically stable.

These criteria have narrowed the search down to the mid-plate gyres (MPG's), which are near the centers of the lithospheric plates and the mid-ocean gyres.

The basic reason for this concern is that the maximum permissable level of REMS (6×10^7 million electron watts per gram of tissue) for an average human being in one single dose is about 250. And, it is estimated that one metric ton of high-level radioactive waste from a light-water reactor ten years after removal from the reactor is about 1.7 billion times the whole-body exposure level of REMS permitted by the Nuclear Regulatory Commission (Heath, 1977). However, as yet the science on what the impact of the 440,000 curies (3.7×10^{10} disintegrations per second - about 1 gram of radium) dumped in the North Atlantic alone is still negligible.

The volume of radioactive waste generated globally each year is difficult to estimate, partially because it includes both civilian and military uses. However, it is estimated that the free world has a 15,000 metric ton capacity for processing radioactive wastes, which is not near the needed capacity.

At the present time, the only international regulation that we have on dumping radioactive wastes in the deep sea is the Convention on the Prevention of Marine Pollution by Dumping of Wastes and Other Matter, signed in 1972 and in force since 1976 with twenty-nine ratifications. However, this Convention does not provide adequate protection against low level and medium level radioactive wastes, since Annex 1, Item 6, only prohibits the dumping of:

> High level radioactive wastes or other high-level radioactive matter...as unsuitable for dumping at sea.

And there is no explicit prohibition against the dumping of radioactive wastes in Article 211 of the Informal Composite Negotiating Text, although there is a general exhortation in Paragraph 1 that:

> States shall establish national laws and regulations to prevent, reduce and control pollution of the marine environment from dumping.

Therefore, it is still legally permissable to dump low level and medium level radioactive wastes in the deep sea or seabed, and that prospect has become an increasingly attractive alternative to the land based producers of radioactive wastes. Clearly some remedial legislation is needed in this area. However, until such time as there is better knowledge about the technology of radioactive waste disposal, and the appropriate locations, if any, to dispose of such wastes in the deep seabed, nation-states ought to refrain from dumping such wastes in the deep sea.

The need for greater and better knowledge about the resources and uses of the deep sea and seabed seems to be paramount, before any effective international legal regime can be developed.

The 1970's were designated as the International Decade for Ocean Exploration by United Nations General Assembly Resolution 2467D (XXIII) in 1968, and after an auspicious start this global research program has slowly ground to a halt. Part of the reason seems to have been a fear by many nation-states (Group of 77) that the United States was pre-empting the knowledge gained, and would thereby enhance its technological advantage. Part of the reason may have been due to unspecified fears in regard to the national security of the coastal states (Soviet Union). All of which were reflected in the Third United Nations Conference on the Law of the Sea, and in the draft articles of the ICNT pertaining to the exploration and exploitation of the deep seabed (the Area) and marine scientific research.

In conclusion I would strongly urge the resumption of research activity under the aegis of the International Decade for Ocean Exploration, and a modification of restrictive articles in the ICNT pertaining to research in the deep sea and the deep seabed (especially Article 133, Use of Terms, and Article 143, Marine Scientific Research).

REFERENCES

Deese, David A. Seabed emplacement and political reality. Oceanus, 1977, 20(1).

Frosch, Robert A. Disposing of high-level radioactive waste. Oceanus, 1977, 20(1).

Grolnick, David B. Webster's New World Dictionary, 2nd College Edition. Englewood Cliffs, NJ: Prentice-Hall, 1970.

Heath, G. Ross. Barriers to radioactive waste migration. Oceanus, 1977 20(1).

Hedberg, H.D., Moody, J.D., and Hedberg, R.M. The Oil and Gas Journal, November 28, 1977.

Oil and Gas Journal, November 28, 1977, p. 92.

Time Magazine, October 16, 1978.

UNESC (United Nations Economic and Social Council). The Sea: Mineral Resources of the Sea, E/4973, April 26, 1971.

COMMENTARY

Paul Fye
Woods Hole Oceanographic Institution

This is a most impressive gathering, in an awe-inspiring, even intimidating setting. I would congratulate the arrangements committee for the arrangements they have made and the privilege that we have in being here. I have nothing significant enough to say in these sacred halls.

This assembly is a clear indication that the law of the sea is alive, even though not very well. Dr. Ross, in his excellent paper, has shown that, in addition to manganese nodules, there are enormous amounts of resources, mud, rocks, water, energy, and krill in the deep sea. But these resources are so thinly distributed that they are worthless, or more correctly, economically impractical to harvest.

Ambassador Clingan, in his equally excellent paper, has demonstrated that even if they were of value, the legal entanglements might block their potential use.

My comment, I guess, is more political than scientific, although science is where I belong. I would point out that it may be fortunate if no one gets the idea that the "inexhaustible wealth of the sea" goes beyond the nodules. Ed Miles referred to the Arvid Pardo cornucopia which suggests that ocean scientists who pointed out the great wealth of the sea (and I may have been one of them) have done us a great disservice. Perhaps if lawyers and the diplomats had not been misled by visions of quick riches from the ocean, the Law of the Sea Conference might have been much shorter and the world would not have witnessed the greatest land grab in its history by the coastal states.

Thus, one could argue that if a conception of great additional resources in the deep sea becomes prevalent, this could result in the extension of coastal or maritime jurisdiction even farther and an indefinite extension of the Law of the Sea Conference _ad infinitum_, _ad nauseum_.

But, perhaps, I am too skeptical. I do conclude, along with our two principal speakers, that the resources of the deep sea, other than manganese nodules and perhaps krill, are too dilute to be of interest to us other than as scientific information.

So, perhaps we are fortunate if these remain neglected issues. Dave Ross, Ed Miles and others have emphasized the importance of not restricting scientific research even further. I would regard the extension of international restrictions on science in the deep sea as a calamity for the world and, perhaps, I could illustrate by reverting to my proper role as a scientist by a story to which Dave Ross has alluded.

When the Woods Hole Research Submarine Alvin visited the Riff Valley between Ecuador and the Galapagos Islands, only geologists and geochemists were members of the scientific party. As many of you have heard or have read the story in the October 1977 issue of the National Geographic Magazine, the big surprise of the expedition was the astounding discovery of very prolific life in five oases in what was otherwise a marine desert. In one oasis there were giant clams, a foot across, a species which normally grows to perhaps one-sixth that size; in another, giant tube worms, 25 to 34 cm. long and two or three cm. in diameter. Normally that worm is almost invisible. In another oasis, mussels were 25 cm. long. Octopi, crabs, and other animals were also found.

This new, unexpected scientific discovery was at a depth of 3,000 meters, where there is complete darkness and hence, no chance of any photosynthetic action. Nor could this life be supported as life on the bottom of the ocean normally is by falling debris from the surface.

I would not claim that this new and exciting discovery has economic value or is economically significant, but it is a new basis for life on the bottom of the ocean. Further, I would point out that these oases occur at a distance of about 200 miles from the Galapagos and 200 miles from Ecuador and, thus, if restrictions on scientific research were extended or a jurisdictional dispute in this area had occurred, we probably would never have gone there and this discovery may have been delayed for many years.

DISCUSSION AND QUESTIONS

RODERICK OGLEY: I hastened to come to this Conference, drawn by the prospect of non-nodule resources of the deep ocean floor. I am a bit bewildered to conclude that there aren't any that are worth economic attention. But, perhaps, I could make some comment on the trend of the discussion with regard to the regime for the deep ocean floor.

I am delighted to note, from both a representative of the United States delegation and other speakers on the panel, that there seems to be a new attractiveness in the idea of simplicity in negotiations of what used to be part one of the various texts. It was, after all, the United States delegation at Caracas, in the person of Leigh Ratiner, who insisted that the Conference should turn its attention to establishing detailed basic conditions of exploitation.

It has been the developed states that have consistently insisted that the financial obligations of contractors should be written into the Convention. It seems to me that now, at last, we may be getting a more hopeful sign of successful negotiations if we are reaching a point where the developed states are saying, let us establish a structure of the international authority in which we have confidence that our interests will not be overridden. Then let us give that authority or that structure the discretion to manage the mining of manganese nodules and any other resources of the deep ocean floor that may survive the skepticism of Professor Ross.

What is the alternative? It seems too easy to me, as a non-lawyer, to assert that ocean mining is a freedom of the seas. If it is, it is very unlike any other freedom in that it involves taking over large areas of the ocean floor for long periods of time and, presumably, restricting the freedom of other miners to come within any specified range of the first mine.

It also, of course, involves interference with other uses of the sea. Therefore, I would hope that the attempt to create a regime based on the doctrine of the freedom of the seas is merely evidence of an understandable exasperation of developed states with the slowness of negotiations and does not represent a seriously entertained prospect for the legal basis or political basis of this kind of mining.

THOMAS CLINGAN: I would like to say, first of all, what I should have said in the beginning and emphasize that I am not appearing here as a representative of the government of the United States but rather as a professor of law from the University of Miami. My views are my own and not those of the United States government.

Having said that, I certainly agree that, looking back in history, some of the complexities in the texts were the result of proposals made by the United States government early in the process.

My remarks today were directed at the kinds of resources that David Ross was speaking of, i.e., resources of the deep sea-bed, other than manganese nodules. I was proposing simplification only in that sense.

When you get into a much more marginal operation, such as that which we are discussing, such burdens as those applicable to nodules would be intolerable. Therefore, simplification would be required.

I had not really heard the suggestion that the same approach might be extended to nodules. I think it is an interesting thought and one that we might ponder.

With regard to taking over large areas for long periods of time, I certainly agree with your comment. That is why I stressed the quotation with regard to fisheries from Lauterpacht that says that freedom of the seas is exercised only so long as it does not result in the kind of interference that you are suggesting. So it would seem to me that an operation under the freedom of seas doctrine would have to be conducted in such a way that it would not result in long term, large scale interference.

As I understand what the industry is proposing, it wouldn't be so site-intensive as to amount to such unreasonable interference. The 1958 conventions do, of course, permit some interference, but no unreasonable interference with freedom on the part of other individuals. At any event, I certainly hope that we won't have to wind up going the "freedom of the seas" route and that we can have an agreed rational regime, on a global scale, to which we can all adhere.

DANIEL S. CHEEVER: My question is directed to Dr. Kildow. Can the resources already invested really be directed in other ways without great loss? While I have no certain basis for quarrelling with this proposition, I wonder what we should conclude from it.

Perhaps she is leaving that to us. Are we to urge restraint, for example, on the industrialized maritime powers and urge them not to start sea-bed mining without international agreement? Should the industrialized powers restrain themselves from taking unilateral action to mine the sea bed on an interim basis? Or, are we to conclude, perhaps, that the 77 should be a little less doctrinaire? Actually, both sides are doctrinaire and a bit stiff, as I have suggested in a recent journal article. Sea-bed mining isn't so important to either side as to warrant their jeopardizing the overall benefits both will receive in the short run if a comprehensive ocean treaty comes into force.

It would be well worthwhile, as I think one of the speakers said, if we could limit and postpone sea-bed activity for the time being and simply incorporate the common heritage principle in the proposed treaty.

JUDITH KILDOW: In the first place, I think that the general issues of the sea-bed should be included in the text of the treaty, but I think that the details which are dependent on market conditions and other things that are relatively unknown, cannot be considered within the context and framework of the law of the sea negotiations, and should be separated.

Until that time when only those with truly a vested interest in mining the nodules can sit down and discuss the economic and market conditions of land-based and sea-based mining, I do not think that much will happen. I think that the firms will take alternative investment opportunities.

Certainly the technology has been developed to some extent and investments made. We cannot deny that. However, some of it may be used for other kinds of work, until it is time to mine the deep sea-beds. But the losses aren't nearly as great as some of you may think. The IRS codes in the U.S. have provisions for investment losses. Most American companies that have invested in the consortia for manganese nodules are major multinational corporations. They most certainly can take some losses. In fact, losses can often be an advantage for tax purposes. I don't think they will be that badly hurt by it if they have to delay for ten years. In fact, I have heard several of the heads of some of the companies involved in the consortia say we plan to delay for five to ten years. We don't see anything in it for us now. The markets for nickel and copper are down. They will be back up in six or seven years. They can take their losses on the tax side.

So, I will repeat. The ones who get hurt are those who might benefit from the mining of an area in which the international revenues, whatever they may ultimately be, could be equitably allocated.

DAVID ROSS: I would like to comment on Professor Larson's remarks. He is, in part, correct. I did read his paper and I saw the errors of his ways. I did not change my definition but tried to clarify it for him. But the point is very important and I would like to belabor it a little more, if I may.

The deep sea, as I defined it here and as I defined it in my paper, excludes the area under national jurisdiction. As I said very clearly, it also excludes the continental rise. If you look at the ocean as a geologist or a geophysicist does, the geomorphic provinces that you see as you proceed seaward are very clear and very distinct. First you have the continental shelf, then you have the continental slope, then you have the continental rise and then you have the abyssal plains and then you have the oceanic ridge and then it starts again going over to the other side of the ocean.

What I said is that the deep sea region includes the abyssal plains and the ocean ridges. It does not include the rise. It does not include the continental margin. Now the term continental margin also seems to be confusing. For geologists (who defined the term) it includes the shelf, slope, and the rise.

Now, the reason for this confusion, the reason why it is important, refers to the statements that Professor Larson made. He quoted the article by Hedberg et al. and the three authors of that article are emminent petroleum geologists and colleagues of mine. Actually, I have no quarrel with what they said; it is Professor Larson's interpretation that causes the problem.

He said there is potential "beyond the shelves." Now, what they (Hedberg et al.) meant is the shelves in the geological sense. I am afraid Professor Larson meant the shelves in the sense it is said in the ICNT, which includes the shelf, the slope, and the continental rise. Hedberg, et al. were referring to the continental slope and the continental rise, which clearly is not the area of the deep sea as I defined it.

Now, they also included marginal seas, and almost all marginal seas will fall under national jurisdiction. This point is very important, as I will come to in a second. They also said, in the article, as Professor Larson correctly mentioned, that many of the holes that have been drilled in the ocean have shown organic matter contents above 0.5%. I would offer Professor Larson a shovel and suggest that he walk from the Netherlands to the tip of Italy, and anywhere he can, to stick that shovel in the ground. I assure him that most times he will come up with sediment that will contain 0.5% organic material or more. In any case, 0.5% organic matter does not insure oil.

Professor Larson mentioned that there was one oil and gas field shown in the deep sea. Indeed, that is correct. It was in the Gulf of Mexico (a marginal sea), an area where considerable oil and gas has already been found. However, almost all of the Gulf would fall into an EEZ when and if they are adopted.

The reason why I am emphasizing this is because I personally feel that it would be a shame if we went away thinking that the oil and gas potential in the deep sea, as I originally defined it, and as I defined it in my talk, is considerable or is, in fact, even significant. This will confuse the issue, delay negotiations, extend jurisdiction, cause all kinds of problems, some of which Dr. Fye has mentioned.

On the other hand, I should indicate that oil and gas is ubiquitous. You find it everywhere but that is not the point. You have to find it in amounts that can be worthwhile. That does not seem to have the slightest chance of being possible in the abyssal plains or the oceanic ridges, i.e., the deep sea of the ocean.

So, I would hope that Professor Larson, perhaps, might want to go back and get the facts correct.

I would like to make one more point. The previous gentleman referred to my statements as indicating skepticism about the resources of the deep sea. Perhaps that is an appropriate word.

I had quite a hand in the discovery of the Red Sea mineral deposits. I probably could have spent my entire scientific career working on the Red Sea mineral deposits, if I chose to. So in that respect finding potential mineral resources can be very rewarding. But when I say there are no mineral resources present in the deep sea, I am trying to be factual, not skeptical. There is a difference.

DAVID LARSON: I have to say, first of all, that I am not a geologist, I am a political scientist. I accept your geological definitions but I think that the point you made in your paper here, which gets to Tom Clingan's paper, is national jurisdiction. The definition of national jurisdiction is not geological but political and legal. I think that the question as to what falls within national jurisdiction and what does not fall within national jurisdiction, unfortunately, may bear little or no relationship to geologic formations. I think this is one of the points made by Hedberg, Moody and Hedberg.

Secondly, I anticipated your response in regard to Hedberg, Moody and Hedberg, so I xeroxed their article and brought it with me. Unless I misunderstand what they are saying, they are saying two things here. First, continental margins look like the most promising areas for oil and gas, if the continental shelf or the economic zone is the outer limit of national jurisdiction, i.e., the margin, the slope, and the rise are the most promising.

But, second, they also point out what they define as small ocean basins. Small ocean basins may or may not be within the 200 mile zone, but they are suggesting in the article that many of them are beyond 200 nautical miles. These small ocean basins have some promise of oil and gas in them as well.

So what they conclude, and I am reading, that Hedberg and Moody think that there may be "sizeable oil accumulations in the deep off shore." They previously defined the deep off shore as being beyond the continental slope. But, you know there is ambiguity here. Does this include the rise or not?

So, I am just using their article as part of the basis for discussion because it caught my eye. As you say, I have been told that these are reputable marine geologists.

DAVID ROSS: I don't want to make this a private dialogue but I feel I must respond.

As you said, beyond the slope is the continental rise, which indeed may be the most significant province for oil and gas. The definition I gave puts it (the continental rise) within national jurisdiction.

Concerning your point about marginal seas, some parts of marginal seas are outside of national jurisdiction, as defined in the present ICNT. For example, a small part of the Gulf of Mexico and a small part of the Bering Sea, but it is a very small area.

TULLIO TREVES: I will try to make a few observations on the legal regime of the non-nodule resources of the sea-beds, on which we have heard the illuminating report of Professor Clingan. I will concentrate on Law of the Sea Conference and on the ICNT.

If we look at the ICNT, we see that the general principles on the regime of the international sea-bed area deal with all resources, while the detailed rules are conceived only for nodules. What perhaps is not as much recognized, is that these detailed rules cover, indeed, most of the ground.

To take a few examples, all the financial provisions, which have been discussed in Conference this year, are conceived and drafted with the nodule industry in mind. The composition and decision-making procedures of the Authority's main organ, the Council, are debated with reference to categories related to production and consumption of minerals contained in the sea-bed polymetallic nodules.

Another main item in the negotiation, the rules on the limitation of sea-bed mineral production, is considered in the ICNT, as well as in all proposals, in terms of the metals (actually, or one of them, nickel) contained in nodules. Of course, this last point is so evident that the ICNT had to include here a specific rule on non-nodule minerals. This is Article 151,1(g)C, which gives competence to the Authority to regulate production of non-nodule minerals.

This being the situation, where most of the provisions we have deal with nodules, and where, after all, as Dr. Ross has indicated today, beyond nodules, the sea-bed does not hold valuable minerals that, for the time being, can be economically mined, why should we not think of a convention only on nodules?

I do not underrate the political difficulties that could arise in achieving this goal. I feel nonetheless that, if we want to be wise, we should avoid the danger of having the mineral resources different from those contained in nodules regulated by a set of provisions conceived and drafted for an industry whose character is as peculiar as that of the nodule industry. These resources should be out of the tangles of the rules that have been elaborated to date, and which will have to be elaborated in the follow-up of the Convention, with specific reference to nodules.

For these reasons, I think (and I would like to know what Professor Clingan thinks about this) that the Conference should try to clean up the ICNT in order to specify that the whole text deals with nodules and that whenever other minerals will come to the fore, specific negotiations will have to be started. The basis for such negotiations should be the Declaration of Principles on the Seabeds of 1970. This is more than enough for problems which belong to the domain of what is not yet economically feasible and, thus, legally relevant.

THOMAS CLINGAN: You have raised an issue that I did not directly address in my paper; but I think it is one that should be raised at this point.

One of the reasons that I made reference to the complexities of the rules and regulations is because I think it really is unclear as to whether or not they could be applied to non-nodule resources.

Now, I would certainly agree with you that I would rather see the text cleaned up to apply only to nodules rather than leaving ambiguity about the other issues. So I didn't address that and perhaps should have and I appreciate your calling my attention to it. I was simply assuming, I suppose, that minerals other than nodules were going to stay in the text and went on from there to say if that is the case then I think we ought to simplify the regime for them.

GORDON CHRISTENSON: I noted a bit of disparity between our keynote papers this morning and some of the discussion this afternoon. If I might take off from the point that Judy Kildow made, it is that as we increase in our intensity of analysis we move toward our great desire for certitude. To define all those unexamined areas where there are questions that need resolution we may have converted ourselves via the Law of the Sea Conference into a continuing assembly, a continuing parliamentary assembly. We may have promoted ourselves into positions of staff and counsel to that assembly, backed by great wealth as that continues with 1.5 billion dollars already having been expended. Who knows what untold riches can come our way if this continues?

In contrast with that, if I might be so flip as to suggest what one of our American compatriots, a humorist, a satirist by the name of Will Rogers, said about Calvin Coolidge, "He don't say much but when he does he don't say much."

Apropos of my earlier point, the tendency of the analysts to move toward certainty could lead us to saying less and less of certitude about more and more of nothing. Apropos, again, of our generative capacities, that is our capacities not for distributive justice of what we have or think we have or don't have, in advance, we might concern ourselves with the more dynamic process of change, of wealth creation.

Thus, in a more serious vein, I should like to suggest that we are confusing, in the Law of the Sea Conference, three different kinds of questions. The first and what we began with in this effort when I was part of one aspect of it back in 1967 is really a constitutive process, the allocation of jurisdiction and the overwhelming concern of who decides and how and how that decision process is fairly done.

Only secondarily do we move into the normative or the second level legal order of norms or rules that is legislative. But, strangely, it seems that we have added even a third process, which is a regulatory scheme based upon a fight about economic assumptions and markets that we don't really understand. It just occurred to me that part of the clarity of thinking through some of these questions might be to keep in mind, as we are proceeding on the deep sea-bed authority and all of the horrendous regulations that have been proposed before we know anything about what resources or markets are available, that part of it is constitutive, part of it is legislative, and part of it is regulatory.

It seems to me we are trying to do those functions all at once. If we could, at least in our own thinking, keep those functions straight, we might have made a bit of contribution.

JORGE VARGAS: I have three questions. If I remember correctly, some time ago, there was a scientific dispute trying to determine whether lobsters, for instance, were animals connected with the continental shelf or if they were swimming animals. This problem provoked a very heated dispute between Brazil and France.

I also recall that some decades ago, the scientific literature in the area of geology asserted that oil could not be found in the submarine continental shelf.

What I would like to find out is what is the basis that Dr. Ross has to qualify or define krill as a resource from the deep sea-bed; being a marine geologist, I think Dr. Ross should have some scientific evidence to assert that. As far as I know, krill is more, according to marine biologists, a surface kind of resource, not a deep-sea resource.

My second question is to Professor Clingan. I was very interested in his presentation concerning the legal regime of the high seas. With all the authors he mentioned, I was wondering whether at this moment the doctrine of the freedom of the seas is still valid or to what extent it has been affected by the work undertaken by the Third Law of the Sea Conference? Is there any place where you can draw a line between the *lex lata* for instance, and *de lege ferenda* in connection with the high seas? Are there any impacts, for instance, that the establishment of 200-mile zones on a global basis has produced in the doctrine of the high seas? I would like to hear about that.

The third question is to Dr. Fye. I wonder whether the oceanographic vessel off the coast of Ecuador had Ecuadorian scientists aboard when those giant shells were discovered?

DAVID ROSS: Concerning the krill, perhaps I was speaking too fast. What I believed I said and I hope I said, krill is indeed an animal of the water column and not of the sea floor. So, you are indeed correct in what you said.

THOMAS CLINGAN: I am glad to report to you that Hugo Grotius is alive and well in the Netherlands. I do believe there still is validity to the high seas doctrine. I don't think that you can take a 300 year old doctrine and cast it aside, except upon the consent of the international community and I don't think we have reached that point yet.

The doctrine, of course, will take on different colorations depending upon what you are talking about at what point in time. If you are talking about the area beyond the economic zone, there is no question that the high seas doctrine exists and it is normatively about the same that it has been in the past. If you are talking about the area within the economic zone, I believe that, qualitatively, it is exactly the same as it was. What we are achieving with regard to the economic zone is a more careful elaboration of rules so that each of the parties, both coastal states and other states, who would be operating in this area, would know precisely what the rules are, how people should respond and how they should act, in terms of navigation, and in terms of resource and energy extraction. All these things are being more carefully and more clearly spelled out than ever before. I happen to think that is a very good development but it certainly doesn't change my judgment on the qualitative nature of the superadjacent waters.

PAUL FYE: Dr. Vargas, I don't actually know whether or not there were Ecuadorian scientists on that expedition. It is our practice, and has been for many years, to invite scientists from the nearby coastal state to be on board with us when we are working.

That particular expedition had scientists from, if I remember correctly, 16 different institutions. I just don't know, in that instance, whether there was someone from Ecuador on board or not.

DAVID ROSS: I believe there were none, but you raise a very interesting point I would like to comment on.

Many of my colleagues, when we do scientific projects anywhere, would like to invite foreign scientists to participate, and often do. Even without the law of the sea, I could honestly say we probably don't invite enough. It is not sufficient to take one or two foreign scientists when you are working off their waters. For example, it would be nice to take them on other expeditions so they can gain additional knowledge and benefits from what is being done elsewhere.

It would be nice if some international organization could arrange a mechanism so that scientists who go to sea would know how to find foreigners who might want to participate and how to contact them. I had always hoped that TEMA of the Intergovernmental Oceanographic Commission could serve this mechanism. Regardless of what happens concerning scientific research, I think it is a necessity for the oceanographically developed countries to extend their knowledge, their technology and their opportunities to scientists from oceanographically less developed countries.

GARY KNIGHT: I would like to respond, if I may, although I am not a panelist, by way of elaborating for a second on Tom Clingan's reply to Jorge Vargas. I think Jorge raises an extremely important question, particularly should the Conference fail to agree on a sea-bed mining regime and should the law develop henceforth on a basis of state practice or customary law.

Jorge's question, essentially, is accepting, arguendo, that we have a high seas regime applicable to the sea bed; have not the current negotiations and discussions altered that? I think he would probably accept the fact that we start with existing law -- Grotius' Law if you will. To displace one law you must have another law -- not another idea but another law.

In international law there are two ways we can secure such

a new law: treaty or customary law development. We do not have a treaty, that is clear. So the question is "has what has gone on in the Conference produced a new rule of customary law re-characterizing the resources of the deep sea bed?" I would suggest that this has not happened, for the simple reason that resolutions of the U.N. General Assembly do not constitute law. Now I would qualify that slightly because I know Jorge would respond, being a student of Myres McDougal, that expressions of great unanimity by the members of the international community create community expectations, which may be the genesis of, if not indeed evidence of, new rules of customary law. The only reply I can make to that is that the negotiating record (and much of it is off the record) would indicate that when the "Principles Resolution," which is what we are talking about, was adopted by such an overwhelming majority, it was so adopted after careful rewording and negotiation and the inclusion of deliberate ambiguities in such number as to make it acceptable to a large number of states so that the negotiations could move from elaboration of principles to the nuts and bolts of putting a treaty together.

I think that this deliberate ambiguity in the use of the phrase "common heritage of mankind" as used in the "Principles Resolution" takes away from its efficacy as a law-creating device because all legal systems require specificity before they will enforce laws.

PATRICIA BIRNIE: I am reminded by some of the remarks I have heard this afternoon of the cartoon I saw in The New Yorker a year or so ago, which showed what must surely have been the board room of a multinational company, with the chairman saying, "Gentlemen, what we are about to do may not be legal but it is defensible." I think we are in danger of getting into this field.

I want to comment on the remarks of Professors Kildow and Clingan. Professor Kildow was urging us in the direction of leaving the management of exploitation of both manganese nodules and any other resources that may eventually be exploited on the deep sea-bed to those states which have an interest in them. Professor Clingan said something rather similar but also said that he thought that the solutions to this might be better found in other articles of the ICNT, in particular the article on the management of highly migratory species.

I would like to draw attention to the article following that, which deals with marine mammals and remind you of the results of leaving the management and development of whale species to those states which have an interest in their exploitation and to the fact that the International Commission which manages this particular resource (admittedly a living and not a non-living resource) at many meetings has been subject to criticism by the United States delegate, among others, to the effect that it was a great pity that this particular organization was for many years left to those who had an interest in the resources. If only more states that didn't have commercial interest had joined or would now join it, there might be more rational and effective management policies.

THOMAS CLINGAN: I think we are not far apart at all. The difference is that I should have been clearer in defining what I meant by interest. When I said one was interest in conserving resources, I was not thinking of the IWC comparison because that is not what I have in mind at all.

What I was thinking was more along the lines of the, let's say, American Tropical Tuna Commission, which consists not only of those coastal states that have an interest in conserving the resource but those coastal states that fish them as well. Both sides are represented. The IWC experience, I think, has proved that you cannot manage a resource by shutting out people that are involved on both sides of the resource question.

What you must do is to extablish a forum to bring them together. To go back to the migratory problem, if you do not bring those states fishing the species into the organization, then they will stay outside the area and fish. That is not what is wanted. That is neither conservation nor management. You must bring all the interested parties into the process. Once you get them in and get them committed to a set of regulations and rules that both sides can live with, then you have them. Otherwise you have chaos in the management of the resource. That is what I was suggesting.

JUDITH KILDOW: I think that we aren't that far apart because I think you misinterpreted what I said and perhaps it needs more clarification. When I was talking about leaving the details to those with the most interest, I wasn't talking of just the mining industry. It is a two-edged sword. There are consumers and then there are the producers.

The producers are the mining and associated industries, the producers of the resource. The consumers are equally important and have equally been taken into consideration in the discussions that I was referring to with regard to detail. Consumers are even more important, in fact, than the producers in that they create the markets for these minerals and without them, there is no minerals industry.

There are many interested parties. There are countries who are net producers and net consumers, who have the greatest interest. They represent both the developed and developing world.

My suggestion was that rather than dealing with 154 states with varying degrees of interest, that we try to deal, at first, at least, with this next level of detail, with the states with the most vested interest in consuming as well as producing.

So I am not saying that the companies should be left to their own devices. I am saying that the consumers and the producers should have a larger part in this. In fact, one of the positive outcomes of the discussions that have gone on is that the producers and the consumers are finally getting together to try to come to some resolution.

THOMAS CLINGAN: I did not go into this in much detail in the paper, but what I was suggesting was that for resources other than nodules, we look at the functional arrangement by which those resources should or could be managed and eliminate some of the detail in order to reduce the burden on marginal operations.

I was <u>not</u> suggesting that what one ought to do is make a committee of three and then go home and think that we have done our job. This goes back to what Gordon said earlier about separating the normative and regulatory functions. What I am saying is we exercise the normative functions with regard to these resources, these marginal resources and then, if we can incorporate them into a treaty, then perhaps we all know there is going to be quite a considerable period of time before the treaty goes into force. During that period of time, it might be broken down into two phases.

First would be a phase where the regulations themselves could be developed to fulfill these normative functions, either by the international authority itself or by a special committee set up for that purpose. Second, there could be a provisional period of operation under these regulations to see whether they work or not before states get to the point of ratification.

BARRY BUZAN: I would just like to ask David Ross if he would elaborate a little bit on hot brines. The last time I looked at this literature, which I admit was a couple of years ago, the speculation was that these may be found in places other than the Red Sea. Are these now categorically eliminated? Is this a special case of the Red Sea? Or are these things likely to appear on other mid-ocean rifts?

DAVID ROSS: The mechanism that forms these brines can occur in other oceanic ridge areas just like in the Red Sea. What makes the Red Sea unique is the salt deposits on the flanks of the ridge. When the circulating waters go through or near the salt ridges their density will be increased. When the water reaches the sea floor, it is denser than normal sea water. Therefore, it stays there and minerals have a chance to precipitate out of solution into the depression. It does not look like salt deposits of this type form in the open ocean. Therefore, when this mechanism occurs along the Middle Atlantic Ridge, the East Pacific Rise or in the Indian Ocean and it does happen, the water, because of its high temperature, and without an increase in density, will dissipate almost immediately. This is what we have seen in the region of the Galapagos that Dr. Fye mentioned.

What happens then is that the waters quickly dissipate and mix with the overlying sea water because they are less dense than sea water. The result is that some minerals still will precipitate out but the concentrations, although anomalous and although scientifically interesting, are usually two to three orders of magnitude less than that found in the Red Sea area. So the process can happen in many places, but it needs special conditions to form a significant deposit.

LEWIS ALEXANDER: There was a term which was used for small ocean basins. The more I thought about it the worse I felt.

As part of the enclosure movement, which is sometimes misreferred to as Craven's Law, we go out to 200 miles off any coast. Beyond that, we go out on the continental margin perhaps to the last grain of sand. Now we have small ocean basins that may have oil in them too. So, Bob Smith and I were sitting here trying to figure out what might be the small ocean basins that were not already included in the 200 mile zone or in the continental margins. We have not found very many but, again, we are breaking up the high seas into still another subdivision over which some types of control might be extended.

We came up with the Arabian Sea, the Philippine Sea, and the Tasman Sea; a few of these seas are tremendous. They are almost oceans. It scares me to think we are now going to start talking about "small ocean basins" separating them from the rest of the high seas and including them also in the enclosure motion.

DAVID ROSS: I think you raise a valid point. I believe these authors mean marginal seas when they say small ocean basins. This would include areas like the Gulf of California, the Red Sea, the Gulf of Mexico, the Bering Sea, and perhaps even the North Sea. Marginal seas are those seas that are partially separated from the main ocean basin.

DAVID LARSON: I would just merely add to the definition--the Hedbergs and Moody also say, or call them "restricted seas." I think this is analogous to what you were defining in terms of restricted seas, they are closed or semi-enclosed seas.

JEAN-PIERRE BEURIER: I have a question about biological resources. The stocks of the international zone are generally not ready for our immediate consumption, and especially the krill that you mentioned.

So, the best way to manage these resources of the open sea is to leave them to their natural predators; krill are good for whales, just as grass is good for cows.

Don't you think we should first of all organize a real management of sea cattle and international fisheries - which implies stopping the killing of whales - instead of trying to preserve the grass of the sea, even if it is legally shared between nations.

Biological resources as a whole belong to fisheries law (a part of LOS III) and should not be considered as a part of neglected issues.

DAVID ROSS: I could not argue at all with the points you raise. I think they are very valid.

To perhaps emphasize what you say, let me make another point about krill. You may be aware some people have suggested that if it is properly treated you can make it into a paste that tastes like shrimp. If that is indeed true and indeed there are 200,000,000 tons of krill that can be obtained each year, I predict that there is going to be a severe world shortage of crackers in the near future.

EDGAR GOLD: I have a general question on scientific research. In recent years, as the Conference has been progressing, the scientific research debate has been worrying me more and more. Perhaps I am confused about it but Dr. Fye's remarks seemed to indicate that my worries were well founded. This morning, in Dr. Ross' statement there appeared an indication of the fear of future restrictions on scientific research and an acceptance of the slogan that "what is good for science must be good for the world." Now we have Dr. Fye who uses the rather attractive illustration of previously undiscovered two foot clams and 25 cm. mussels to tell us that jurisdictional disputes would, in future, probably preclude such research.

Perhaps I am simplistic but I read this as an implicit threat from the scientific community. I know that the scientific community has been fiercely defending the so-called freedom of scientific research. At the same time I also know that the world will need to know much more about the oceans and will need the scientists to broaden this knowledge. However, I am wondering whether Dr. Fye and Dr. Ross could not tell us that the scientific community, or the "scientific industry" -- I think that term must be used -- is not also quite capable of competing on an equal basis with other oceanic uses, although given that it will have to alter its approach somewhat. In other words, what I am asking is why this threat of withdrawal of oceanic scientific research? Is this not the sort of confrontative brinksmanship we least need at this particular stage in the Law of the Sea Conference?

DAVID ROSS: I find your points very interesting. I will try to answer for at least myself and, hopefully, for some of my scientific colleagues.

I think what will happen, or what could happen, is that we get into a scenario where a scientist planning a marine expedition may have to change his program because of difficulties from the LOS. For example, in planning an expedition you have to get a ship to some part of the world. You have to raise money for this expedition. You have to get people to participate. It will be difficult to do some of this because of the complexities in the ICNT. You have to provide certain information, for example, you have to say exactly where you will be working long before you even know there will be an expedition. You have to provide later corrections to this information and, indeed, the corrections themselves can be used as a basis for denying permission.

You have to obtain money from a funding agency, but why should a funding agency commit itself when they don't know if you will get permission to do the research? Well, perhaps you can get a letter or some sort of document from a foreign country but this may not happen.

The point is that the scientist now faces a complex situation based on considerable unpredictability. He is not sure if he can make the expedition work. Some scientists will be more successful than others. But I suspect that most will not be able to do this.

A scientist is under strong pressure, for example, when his institution wants him to obtain research money, to publish papers. The tendency may well be to turn towards an area of research where some predictability exists. I suspect in the case of my country, the United States, more research will occur in our own exclusive economic zone (if we establish one). By working in a U.S. zone, the scientist is certain to be able to publish his results. Remember, it is still not clear in the ICNT that the scientist will be able to publish his results. He will probably also find it easier to secure funding to work in U.S. waters. Likewise, he will find that it is easier to get his colleagues to participate and get permission for the work.

Now, the sad thing about this, as you well know, is that it is the boundary or edge of the ocean where all the interesting things happen, where most pollution, for example, gets into the ocean. So what I could conceive of happening is that individual countries, particularly the countries that are competent in marine science, will start looking more towards their own waters.

I don't believe that marine science will stop. I suspect ten years from now it will still be an exciting field but each country could be working more within its own waters and those countries that are now knowledgeable about marine science will be even more knowledgeable about marine science in the future; countries that know little about marine science will continue to know little. The marine science knowledge gap will widen.

I think that this is the threat. In other words, why get involved in a situation, as a scientist, where such a high degree of unpredictability exists that your work could be jeopardized. I would hope that my colleagues see this as perhaps an opportunity. But I think before this can happen, it would be most beneficial if some items in the ICNT could be clarified.

In doing so, I don't think the coastal state has to give up one bit of its control, although I think it should make the mechanisms of doing research a little easier.

If I may belabor this a little bit more, it is also my opinion that many marine scientists, and I suspect yourself included, enjoy working in foreign waters with foreign people and working on these problems. Indeed, it certainly increases the excitement of the field of marine science.

PAUL FYE: I was merely going to point out that in spite of Dave Ross' story about the miniscule brains of marine scientists they are still people and they react just like other people. As Dave just indicated, if it gets too complicated to go one place, scientists will simply go elsewhere. It is a big ocean. It is not a threat at all.

I have no illusions whatsoever that scientists have the clout to make an effective threat. We do not attempt brinkmanship or we would have no influence whatsoever. The way we do science has changed enormously already and will continue to change. Oceanographers must learn to live with these changes. There is no question about it.

When I first went to sea as a scientist, it was quite a long time ago, my predecessor, the Director of the Woods Hole Oceanographic Institution, gave me a letter which said that I was a bona fide oceanographer (he was stretching the truth since I had never been to sea before), so I could present this to government officials for entry into their waters. It worked beautifully. We even got a fancy reception in the governor's palace.

Now, we know that is not the way you get clearance today. It has changed enormously. It will continue to change. We are trying to learn to live with these changes.

But there was no implied threat such as: "If you don't agree to us, we will go somewhere else." It is just the practicalities that Dave has already enumerated. Oceanography will continue. Scientists will still go to sea. But they will go to sea where it is possible to go and where it is less complex. It is just a statement of what I believe to be the truth of the matter. It is in no way a threat of any kind. There is nobody we could threaten if we wanted to.

THOMAS CLINGAN: I am just interested in your choice of words on confrontation politics.

There isn't any real confrontation on science in the Conference any more, as you know. The United States delegation tabled some amendments to the scientific articles last session, but we don't view them as being a confrontation. At one point in the Conference, we felt that there was fairly widespread agreement on the political realities of the marine scientific situation. Somehow or another, that agreement did not find its way into the ICNT. The U.S. amendments are designed to clarify what really was agreed upon. It has been a cooperative effort to try to work out these clarifying kinds of changes that we are presenting. I agree entirely with David that we don't think this has any impact whatsoever on the coastal state control that is reflected in the basic marine scientific research regime as it appears in the ICNT.

ELIZABETH YOUNG: Dr. Ross is obviously right about the plight of the scientists and his gloomy scenario is very plausible, but I think that we need to look at the other side and try to envisage why it is that governments worldwide are suspicious of marine scientists of one kind or another. Let us remember Howard Hughes going to sea in theory to pick up nodules; it turned out to be the CIA looking for a submarine.

Now in point of fact many countries don't want either Howard Hughes or the CIA messing about, as they see it, on their sea-bed. They are suspicious. Can one say that they are completely wrong?

I think the difficulty is just this - the pure scientist has very great difficulty in proving his purity. How is he going to set about it? Now, frankly, I don't think it should be beyond the wit of the international scientific community to set about this. Can they not unite, the scientists who want to go into the sea, and bring out all this information that the world is certainly in need of? Can there not be a body, perhaps an Academia Marina, which should be genuinely international, genuinely civil, and genuinely pure?

DAVID ROSS: In my opinion, you have a very valid point. Let's even extend it a little bit further. Almost any knowledge you obtain from the ocean can have military or political usefulness. It is an awful thing to have to admit but it is probably true. How do we indicate that we, as scientists, are really pure and above this? Well, one way is that if you work with a country in its waters, make sure that they are well represented. I had an expedition on the Nile Delta with Egyptians. I took five Egyptians aboard, I bought a copying machine and everything was copied. Everytime I used a computer, I made two copies. Every sample I took I split and gave half to them.

Concerning the idea of having scientists unite, my experience with scientists suggests that it might be easier to get lawyers to unite.

Your response, which I just had a feeling might happen, shows that you understand the problem. I would go a step further and say that if we did unite, whom would we talk to? Would they really listen?

We could talk to each other, as you said, but that would not get us any hearing in the United Nations. The idea is good. I would love to see it happen, and I would pay my dues but I am not too optimistic that it would work.

JUDITH KILDOW: I would just like to make two comments. I have worked with the scientists a little bit on scientific research issues before. They do talk to each other, believe me, in multiple fora.

Unfortunately, scientists from certain countries must represent their governments and not their profession and unfortunately in many countries that are involved in this discussion, there aren't even marine scientists to talk to. That is my first comment. They have tried. They have tried the IOC. They have tried SCORE, which is the scientists. They have tried all fora. So I really must say that they haven't succeeded.

A long time ago the phrase "knowledge is power" became the phrase of much of the developing and disadvantaged world. The fact that a scientist, no matter how benign, comes in and gathers information in their coastal waters, worries them just because somehow that knowledge filters down into application and, obviously, some form of economic or whatever power they want to define.

The problem is the publication issue, which I think David alluded to, and I think needs a little bit more elaboration. Most of real oceanographic science is done from an academic institution where, as David elaborated very well, scientists publish for their survival. That is not a joke.

To publish information about whatever one finds in the coastal waters of a nation is somewhat of a threat because of the proprietary nature of the information. Many coastal states are not very happy for all coastal states and other states to know about what is in their coastal waters. So publication is definitely a major problem. And it is, perhaps, one of the principal reasons the scientists have not found an audience to listen to them.

PAUL FYE: I am surprised no one has commented on Professor Larson's point about nuclear wastes. It is a very interesting question and certainly can be considered one way to make use of the oceans.

I heard a lot last night about Craven's ocean and it's possible he thinks of the ocean as his front yard. I must confess I tend to think of the oceans as my backyard, but I don't subscribe to the theory that you can't put anything in it. It is one of the places for useful disposal of all kinds of waste products resulting from life on earth. It is a natural sink which nature has provided. This is the essential reason the ocean is salty.

I do wish and hope that before we use the oceans for disposal of waste products, we will know what we are doing. There are a billion gallons of sewage that come out of the New York metropolitan area every day going into the oceans. If we were more intelligent about it, we might find ways of using the nutrients in those sewage products in a beneficial way.

There is a lot of talk about the heat waste from nuclear plants being harmful. I hate to think of heat in any form being a waste. If we have the wit, as you said, we should be able to make use of such energy.

On the nuclear wastes, the proposal which was discussed at the Woods Hole Conference which you referred to, was not really to put these wastes in the oceans at all. It was rather to plant them far beneath the bottom of the ocean.

I do recognize the fact, however, if we are going to make use of nuclear power (and I submit that we are) then a very urgent question is where to put the nuclear wastes. We know this could be one of the greatest hazards that mankind produces for future generations.

I would agree, even as an oceanographer, that one of the places that ought to be considered along with others in determining where it would do the least potential harm, could be in the oceans. Now, whether that is beneficial to mankind or not is a matter of balancing the pluses and minuses in the use of nuclear energy and the use of the oceans.

DAVID LARSON: Last summer, when Dave Ross contacted me about participating on this panel, I confessed I didn't know a great deal. So I started digging in, with the aid of some colleagues who are physicists, geologists and so on; and this issue of radioactive wastes surfaced. We began to move in on it.

But one of the things which came up very quickly in the research was that there is a decided difference of opinion in the so-called scientific community as to the danger. I found two distinct groups: one saying no, we think we have this radioactive waste disposal safely under control, the technology is developing where we can handle it; and the other saying absolutely not.

The ones who say they have it under control argue in this way. The deep sea-bed will take radioactive wastes. We will solidify them. We will vitrify them in the form of glass, which is a fairly stable mass, almost insoluble, and then we will bury it deep in the sea-bed. The figures used here are anywhere from 3 to 400 meters in the sea-bed, depending upon content and depth of the sediment of the sea-bed where they want to drop it. The notion is that after it is buried in the deep sea-bed that, yes, it will generate radioactivity, but that the encasing plus the sediment will absorb most of the heat and the radioactivity. That is one school of thought. That tends to be the U.S. Department of Energy.

Whereas, on the other hand, the people whom I would classify as the civilian scientists, meaning the non-governmental scientists, expressed deep reservations and concerns. It was they who really articulated their concern about the 440,000 curies that we already have deposited in the North Atlantic. They think the potential hazard there, not simply for human existence, human life, but for animal life and sea life in general, is enormous. They expressed the concern that there has not yet been, to the best of their knowledge, any coordinated, concerted research, either in the government of the United States or outside of the government, as to radioactive waste disposal in the deep sea-bed.

DAVID ROSS: I would like to make a few comments. Some of you may have heard a remark made by a famous ecologist many years ago - there is no free lunch. If you are going to use nuclear power, you are going to have nuclear waste and you are going to have to do something with it. One mechanism is to convert it to something else, but this technique hasn't yet been developed.

I am not too enthusiastic myself about seeing nuclear waste disposed of in the deep ocean but, if that is the safest place, and it is a big if, then it certainly should be given strong consideration.

Among some of the advantages of putting nuclear waste in the ocean is that you at least have it separated from us by water, rather than by the atmosphere. The wastes will also be trapped by deep sea sediments and the sediments of the deep sea are highly impermeable.

So admittedly, all the data are not in, and hopefully no conclusions are yet made. There are some arguments to support the deep sea position, and there are good arguments against the deep sea position. When a decision is made, hopefully it will be made by reputable people, regardless of where they are employed, who will consider all possibilities.

DAVID LARSON: I would like to question Dave about a related matter. Apparently some people think these convergent zones of the tectonic plates where there is a subduction, one plate going underneath another, such as off Peru, Chile, Ecuador, that you drop all the radioactive waste down in there and it will be slowly ground underneath the earth's crust and go back into the magma. Could you comment on that?

DAVID ROSS: It would be my pleasure. You are, indeed, correct, as you stated it. It will slowly be ground below the earth's crust. And ground means like you said, it is going to be destroyed, consumed, broken up, but there is considerable possibility of leakage. We don't know exactly what pathway the material will take. In most cases it probably will be plastered against the side of the continent.

At best, 25 million years later, it will reappear in a mountain range. We could probably accept that. At worst, the containers will have a considerable potential for being destroyed introducing the material into the environment.

If it works, 25 million years from now our mountain ranges will glow at night. But it will make navigation easier. It is an interesting idea. The question is can the material survive the trip? I would suggest, at this stage of our knowledge, that it is not as good a possibility as the deep sea.

PART III

AIR SPACE
AND THE LAW OF THE SEA

INTRODUCTORY REMARKS BY SESSION PROGRAM CHAIRWOMAN

Isabella Diederiks-Verschoor
Institute of International Law of the University of Utrecht

First of all, it is my pleasure to introduce the members of my panel. Our first participant is Professor Carl Christol, Professor of International Law and Political Science, University of Southern California. Professor Christol is a former holder of the Stockton Chair of International Law at the United States Naval War College, a former president of the American Bar International Institute of Space Law, a member of the advisory panel of international law of the United States Department of State from 1970-75, and Board of Editors of the International Lawyer, American Bar Association.

Our second participant is Dr. Heller, a lecturer in law at the University of Auckland, New Zealand. He is a graduate doctor of laws in Vienna, Austria, and holds the master of laws at the McGill University, Montreal. After practicing as a solicitor in Austria, he joined the New Zealand civil service and became the head of the Air Transport and External Relations Section of the Civil Aviation Administration. In 1952-53 he was a member of the Institute of International Air Law, McGill University. And from 1961-67, Dr. Heller was Financial Secretary and Administrator of Civil Aviation in Western Samoa. Since retirement from government service, he has lectured at Auckland University since 1968 in air and space law and in comparative law.

Following papers by Professor Christol and Dr. Heller will be a commentary by Dr. Hailbronner. He is the assistant of the vice-president of the Constitutional Court at Frankfurt, Germany, and affiliated with the Max Planck Institute in Heidelberg. He was recently nominated as professor in international law and European law at the University of Constanz.

I very much appreciate the fact that this conference has created another opportunity for cooperation between maritime law and air law. Recently, a tendency has developed not only for cooperation between maritime law and air law, for instance concerning rescue operations, but also between maritime law and space law, as for example the establishment of the Convention on the International Maritime Satellite Organization created in September of 1976. This is a special organization to implement and operate the international maritime satellite communication system. The organization must be certain its work conforms to generally recognized principles and rules of international law including the proper provision of the United Nations Charter, to multilateral agreements regarding exploration and exploitation of space and the 1958 Geneva Conventions on the Law of the Sea. The convention states that provisions should be made for the benefit of ships of all nations.

UNILATERAL CLAIMS FOR THE USE OF OCEAN AIRSPACE

Carl Q. Christol
University of Southern California
Los Angeles, California

The emerging international law of the sea will influence the transit of aircraft in ocean airspace. This assessment seeks to portray emerging trends respecting the present and future use of such airspace.

Certain complex social forces will condition expectations relating to the use of such airspace. Among such forces are the continuing discoveries and innovations of science and technology, the increasing needs to facilitate the long-distance movement of individuals and their goods, comparative financial costs for such services, on-going concerns for national security, and the constant demand for the discovery and use of natural resources. Air traffic continues to increase as man engages in a more intensive exploitation of the ocean's living resources, the oil and gas lying beneath the territorial waters, contiguous zones, and continental shelves, and the gathering in the future of the manganese nodules and other resources lying within the "Area" proposed in the Informal Composite Negotiating Text of the United Nations Third Conference on the Law of the Sea (ICNT, 1977). Affecting each of the identified forces, and there are many other such influences, is the fact of the rapidity of change, the quantum jumps which are the scientific and possibly political hallmark of the 20th century.

Rational policies respecting the use of ocean space require that decision makers take into account such complex social forces. When decision-makers employ existing international institutions and identify the extent to which they are controlled by such forces, they are then able to apply values or interests identified by them to the formulation of political-legal claims. Out of this mix of complex social forces, institutions, and values, will it be possible to arrive at meaningful political decisions? Such decisions can be clothed in the fabric of the law. Such decisions can then become the foundation for subsequent modifications as the elements of this particular mix engage in their natural cleansing and refining processes. When a process such as this is effective it allows for the realization of community decisions based on acceptable (sometimes minimal) community wants and needs.

Included within the complex social forces is the awareness that the natural resources of the universe are often finite, and even when infinite there is a frequent claim of priority of use. The resource debate, which forms a part of the rich-poor stand-off now dominating international negotiations, most often surfaces in connection with tangible materials. This need not be the case, as is seen in the examples of eagerly sought after radio frequency allocations and the present claims of eight equatorial states to sovereign rights in the spatial area occupied by geostationary orbiting space objects when situated at some 22,300 miles above the surface of the earth.

The resource dispute centers on the ultimate beneficiary of the resources of the universe, the rich nations that possess the scientific and technological edge or the poor and developing states which represent the bulk of humanity. In the past, land and ocean resources have been placed in the framework of global resources and have been accepted as relevant elements of global resource policy formation. It is suggested here that ocean airspace should also be considered to be a global resource, and that the resource should be the area occupied by airspace, as well as the winds identified as a source for the production of energy pursuant to Article 56 of the ICNT.[1]

If the ocean airspace is accepted as a natural resource it becomes possible to comprehend prospective rights and duties of states within the context of the ICNT. Treating ocean airspace as an area also makes it possible to make comparisons with other geographical areas identified in the ICNT, such as territorial waters, contiguous zones, straits, archipelagic waters, exclusive economic zones, continental shelves, and high seas. In particular it allows for a more precise assessment of the claims advanced by states as they have sought to protect their varying interests in the conference negotiations.

Oda, in commenting on the formulation of policy by states interested in fishing opportunities, has noted many of the less-developed states took a short-term view of their respective interests. He has asked "Who will benefit most out of the present marine resources expansion of coastal and offshore zones?" His response was: "It is quite ironical to note that it is the advanced nations with vast coastal lines which take advantage of the demands of the eager developing nations" (Oda, 1977, p. 176). The same question can be asked regarding the claims of states relating to the use of the ocean airspace resource.

ICNT Provisions Relating to the Use of Ocean Airspace

Claims relating to the use of ocean airspace have found their maximum assertion in the 1977 ICNT, as well as in the

[1]The text does not specify whether such winds are considered to be situated just above surface levels or if they occupy all of airspace.

continuing negotiations at the Third UN Conference on the Law of the Sea. However, as will be noted below, there are historic claims relating to the permissible uses of ocean airspace that have not received the direct attention of the negotiators.

At this point it is desirable to identify in short form the provisions of the ICNT that relate to aerial transit through ocean airspace in those spatial areas specifically identified in the Text. A reading of relevant textual provisions leaves one with the feeling that the expression "free as the air" has lost some of its conventional wisdom. Such a reading fortifies the preceding observation that the concept of a resource is being continually expanded and that ocean airspace is not a major exception. In short, conference participants treating ocean airspace as a resource are engaged in arriving at a decision as to their authority in such areas. Important rights and duties are contemplated.

Critical Text terms are "sovereignty," employed in Article 2, 34--where "jurisdiction" is also used--49, 135, 137, 213, and 223; "sovereign rights" employed in Articles 56--where the term "jurisdiction" is also used--, 77--using the expression "exclusive sovereign rights--, 78, and 137--referring to both sovereignty and sovereign rights; "control" in Article 33; "Right of Transit Passage" in Articles 38 and 29; "Right of Archipelagic Sea Lanes Passage" in Article 53; and "Freedom of Overflight" in Articles 58, 86, and 87. Several of the articles are referenced explicitly in other articles. Others are directly associated with each other. Since the Text makes no attempt at providing definitions of these concepts, one is obliged to look at the principles of international law for guidance in their use. To the extent that the ICNT does not make provision for the use of ocean airspace it may also be assumed that existing customary or treaty international law will remain applicable.

It is noteworthy that four of the concepts--sovereignty, sovereign rights, control and jurisdiction--accord authority to states to prohibit or to regulate the conduct of other states, including their natural and juridical persons. One exception exists in Article 78 which prohibits the exercise by a state of sovereign rights in the airspace above the waters superjacent to a continental shelf, when such continental shelf lies below the high seas.[2] Three of the concepts--right of transit passage, right of archipelagic sea lanes, and freedom of overflight--facilitate transit in ocean airspace resource areas.

---

[2]The Article reads: "The rights of the coastal State over the continental shelf do not affect the legal status of the superjacent waters or of the air space above those waters."

These provisions, constituting a meaningful, if not particularly tidy mosaic, seek to serve several purposes. The eager developing nations, along with their advanced counterparts, have sought to extend their national authority ever farther from their respective shorelines. Perceiving ocean airspace as a valuable natural resource states have opted for one of several theoretical positions. Thus, to the extent that the national authority granting provisions mentioned above finds acceptance in the final Text, there will be an acceptance of exclusive national interests in given areas. However, to the extent that the other identified articles allow for specific uses, there is an acceptance of world community interests. These provisions and interests relate specifically to freedom of aerial transit. Whether in the last analysis respective claims will be exclusive, i.e., serving purported national interests, or will be inclusive, i.e., serving purported world community interests, will depend on the practical implementation of the respective provisions of the final Text.

In addition to the resource and freedom of transit aspects of the foregoing provisions of the Text, there remain important issues having to do with such matters as security considerations, pollution of the resources, and scientific research in the resource area. The use of the Antarctic area will also have to be taken into account.

Assessment of Specific Claims Relating to the Use of Ocean Airspace

Many interesting problems are presented as to the need on the part of aircraft to be freely mobile while at the same time subject to uniform area controls of the kind found in ICAO's "Rules of the Air." Related to this are latent concerns on the part of states of destination for their national security. Thus, states may wish to establish spatial points in the ocean airspace designed not so much to maintain protections against unsafe or nonstandardized aircraft as to offer additional hopes of national security. Such spatial positions may be located miles seaward from coastlines in the expectation that the identification of foreign aircraft at such distances may enhance the security of the affected state. More specifically, the question exists as to whether there is anything in the proposed Text, or in the provisions of the December 7, 1944 Chicago Convention,[3] that would prevent a coastal state from asserting national standards respecting transit that occurs either over the high seas; over exclusive economic zones; or both; and whether a coastal state might impose different procedures, for example, above the high seas that incoming aircraft would be

[3]Convention on International Civil Aviation, 3 Bevans 944, 1947.

expected to conform to within the contiguous zone, territorial waters, or other sovereign airspace of the destination state. In assessing such an issue, it is anticipated that different values and responses would be applicable to security considerations, as opposed to research, pollution, and Antarctic situations. Thus, transit related to security considerations will be examined first.

The ICNT and Security Considerations in Ocean Airspace

A state may consider it necessary to impose limitations on access to its sovereign areas; such limitations may extend into ocean airspace situated seaward from such areas. Two illustrations will offer clarity. In the first instance two states may be separated by a narrow stretch of the high seas as well as the 188 mile EEZ. In the second instance two states may be separated by a very wide stretch of the high seas, as in the case of Europe and the Americas or the Americas and Asia, as well as by relevant EEZs. Until the advent of the EEZ concept there was no thought that a coastal state might not for special security reasons exercise contiguous zone "control" of the kind contemplated in Article 33 of the ICNT.

Because of the general claims of states to expanded areas of sovereignty, sovereign rights, jurisdiction, or control reflected in the expression "creeping jurisdiction" in recent years, concerns have been expressed during the Conference negotiations as to the legal rights and duties associated with the EEZ concept. The meaning of this concept must be assessed in connection with exclusive claims to fishery resources and the positions now taken by a number of states that they are entitled to assert and maintain 200-mile fisheries conservation and management zones. Such claims have raised doubts as to the rights of coastal states to exercise exclusive rights over surface transit through such waters and to aerial overflights above such waters.

The issue was posed: Can the fisheries situation be treated alone, or is there a need to treat surface and overflight situations in the same legal context as fisheries? This issue now appears to be resolved through the proposed establishment of a "specific legal regime of the exclusive economic zone" in which a coastal state will possess limited "sovereign rights," "jurisdiction" in specific matters, and "other rights and duties" as provided for in the proposed convention. The closest that the grant of sovereign rights comes to the use of ocean airspace is set forth in Article 56 1. (a), which establishes such rights with regard to "other activities for the economic exploitation and exploration of the zone, such as the production of energy from the water, currents and winds." In assessing this right of the coastal state it should be recalled that paragraph 2 of Article 56 requires the coastal state to "have due regard to the rights and duties of other states." This language does not create sovereignty or sovereign rights for coastal states in the airspace superjacent to EEZ waters. Neither does it, by providing a new boundary between traditional high seas and the new EEZ, prevent coastal states or more distant states from establishing security conditions relating to the uses of the airspace above the several EEZs or the intervening airspace above the high seas separating the EEZs. Thus, in terms of applications it seems reasonable that if a coastal state were to use its sovereign rights to explore and exploit energy-producing winds at a height normally used by aircraft engaged in overflight, and if this exploitative activity were to require the establishment of wind-energy exploitation zones or areas that the use of spatial areas would nonetheless have to be accommodated to the rights of other states to have access to and to engage in overflight in such zones. The users of such spatial areas for the exploitation of this resource could be required to provide assurances that such energy-producing areas were not being used in a manner to pose security risks to a concerned state. Such assurances could take the form of aerial reconnaissance overflights through such energy zones 'by non-sovereign rights' states. It would also be possible for a state having concern that access to its territory might come through the energy-producing areas to require suitable identification of transiting aircraft flying in the direction of the concerned state.

Rights involving national security take precedence over economic rights. In commenting on the provisions in the ICNT relating to the wind-energy resource, Oxman has noted that the 1977 draft provision on economic exploitation and exploration of the zone had been moved from the exclusive rights and jurisdiction category and "combined with rights over natural resources in the 'sovereign rights' category. In the context of the other changes made, this emphasizes the point that the zone is an 'economic' one in concept; the sovereign rights are economic rights" (Oxman, 1978). Following his assessment of the quantity and quality of rights in the EEZ, Oxman concluded that "the new texts apply the relevant bodies of law directly to specified geographic areas in specified ways. . .An aircraft flying over the economic zone is not within the national jurisdiction of the coastal State" (Oxman, 1978, p. 174).

This being the case the potentially accessed state may look to its right to protect national security by facilitating identification and possible modification of the course of incoming aircraft. This national right would have application to aircraft seeking access without regard to its being above the high seas, the EEZ, contiguous zones, or territorial waters. Since the past practice of states asserting such security zones has been to require identification one hour's flying time outside of national territory, it is unlikely that the economic emphasis on a 188 mile EEZ will affect the greater distance.

Aerial safety is also a factor in the establishment of identification zones. Following the enactment of the Fishery Conservation and Management Act of April 3, 1976 in the United States (P.L. 94-265, 16 USC 1801), which is in agreement with Article 57 of the ICNT dealing with the breadth of the EEZ, the United States has made provision for detailed surveillance of fishing activities taking place within the fishery conservation zone identified in section 101 of the statute. Five areas for U.S. Coast Guard Aircraft patrols have been identified with the resultant additional burden on the areas available for overflight (Office of Technology Assessment, 1977).

States also wish to be able to have close approach to other states for reconnaissance purposes, even though there is no plan to have access to a foreign destination. As a result of disarmament and arms control agreements states seek to verify compliance through national technical means of verification, which means include aircraft operating in ocean airspace. All these uses add to the congestion of ocean airspace. Thus, in addition to the ICAO Rules of the Air, states have established procedures to effect national control respecting foreign aircraft in ocean airspace. In 1950 the United States by Executive Order No. 10197 established a plan to exercise security control over aircraft in flight (15 Fed. Reg. 9180, 1950). The order established an Air Defense Identification Zone (ADIZ) which placed restrictions on the freedom of passage of aircraft situated above the high seas and demanded compliance on the part of all foreign aircraft flying in the delimited zones. Canada soon followed with its CADIZ on May 12, 1951 (Department of Transport, 1951).

While ADIZ and CADIZ regulations are essentially the same, the Canadian provision adds to the U.S. requirement that approaching aircraft having the intention of landing, and departing aircraft, must provide identification and location reports. The Canadian plan requires such information additionally from aircraft not flying to Canada but which pass through the Canadian zone while en route to another destination (Head, 1964; Columbia Law Review, 1961; Whiteman, 1968).

Security needs of states have also resulted in the establishment of airspace areas adjacent to coasts identified as "restricted areas." An illustration is the Libyan Arab Republic's establishment of such an area defined as the airspace within a radius of 100 nautical miles from Tripoli.[4] In March, 1973, a United States military C-130 aircraft entered this area,

[4] Digest of United States Practice in International Law, 1973, p. 302 (1974).

but in so doing remained outside the 12-mile territorial waters claimed by Libya. Following a protest to the U.N. by Libya, the United States stated to the Security Council that "the aircraft in question was in flight far outside the 12-mile territorial waters claimed by the Libyan Arab Republic and therefore in international air space. This unarmed aircraft was nevertheless intercepted and fired upon by aircraft of the Libyan Arab Republic Air Force.[5] In identifying the U.S. position concerning "Libya's so-called 'restricted area'" it was stated:

> The establishment by the Libyan Government of this 'restricted area' within a radius of 100 nautical miles from Tripoli is inconsistent with the Convention on International Civil Aviation, to which the Libyan Arab Republic is a party, and with generally recognized principles of international law...[6]

Another incident occurred between these states in January, 1975. Libya, acting on the basis that U.S. military aircraft had infringed the 12 mile territorial water boundary, declared its intention to "proceed with the measures it deems necessary in this regard and which would guarantee its duty and right to protect its land, air space, and sea waters."[7] The United States replied that the U.S. aircraft were "over international waters, in keeping with the longstanding United States position of freedom of flight in such areas. Such flights in no way constitute a threat against any sovereign nation."[8] Thus, the United States retained the distinction between the duty to provide information upon entry into its ADIZ as contrasted with the unacceptability of a state's establishing a prohibited zone located above the free high seas.

It should be noted that the Libyan concept of restricted areas would have extended its claims beyond territorial waters and would have placed such areas under its control on a permanent basis. Thus, Libya was not engaged in making claims to a temporary exclusive use in non-contiguous areas of the ocean airspace. A temporary use would have been a different legal matter (McDougal and Schlei, 1955; Margolis, 1955, p. 629).

Failure to respond to demands for identification and location have, as observed as recently as 1978 in the instance of an off-course commercial passenger plane in the airspace of the Soviet Union, produced serious consequences. The Soviet

---

[5] Digest of United States Practice in International Law, 1973, p. 302 (1974).

[6] Ibid, p. 303.

[7] Digest of United States Practice in International Law, 1975, p. 451 (1976).

[8] Ibid.

response reinforces the fact that states will retain their security rights in connection with territorial overflight, as well as access flights in other areas, if there is a basis for having legitimate concern. The recent Soviet response finds counterparts in earlier experience (Lissitzyn, 1953). While the Soviets overreacted to the presence of this particular aircraft and in fact placed unreasonable limitations on its transit, nonetheless the case identified the need to obtain a suitable compromise between valid security concerns and the need to allow for reasonable transit even in the event of technical violations.

Support for imposing limitations on transit, in addition to the factor of security, includes the maritime analogy of a requirement that a ship show its flag in the event of uncertainty or the right of a state to engage in summary action respecting pirates and to a lesser extent for those using the oceans for the slave trade. In recent years restrictions on national conduct have received approval so that the sea is not open to use wholly without limitation. Examples include limitations on scientific inquiry, on practices injurious to the environment, and on unrestricted mining of the seabed. These illustrations, although constituting limits on the wholly free use of the surface of the ocean or to the deep seabed, also have applicability to ocean airspace. The mere carving of an EEZ out of previously high seas areas has not reduced the powers of coastal states to engage in protective measures in areas beyond the sovereign areas of states. The problem is to be able to identify whether the state is in fact threatened.

The ICNT and Pollution of the Marine Environment

In the area of pollution, coastal states are free to impose constraints upon conduct that would allow airspace--according to Article 213 of the proposed Convention "atmosphere"--to pollute the marine environment. By this Article states are required to take national action affecting airspace under their sovereignty with regard to aircraft flying their flag to "prevent, reduce and control pollution of the marine environment from or through the atmosphere" (Article 213.1). Such national regulatory action would affect areas beyond the limits of national sovereignty.

In the United States it is expected that concerns for offshore prejudices to security and to environmental needs will continue to provide support for policies of protection. Thus, when the United States adopted in 1976 the Fishery Conservation and Management Act, whereby it extended jurisdiction relating to fishery resources, it made clear a national policy "to maintain without change the existing territorial or other ocean jurisdiction of the United States for all purposes..." (Article 213.1, Section 2 (c)). Although this language related only to ocean--as opposed to ocean airspace--jurisdiction, the fact that very broad terms such as "other" and "for all purposes" are set out in the policy provisions of the statute indicates that if the issue were as to the continued viability of the ADIZ policy it is entirely probable that relevant legislation relating to maintaining this security posture would be as broadly stated.

The United States also has adopted legislation in the anti-pollution field whereby pollutant discharge is prescribed out to 200 miles from the coastline (Clean Water Act, 1977). However, the 1977 text imposes a more limited role upon the area in which states can secure the implementation of anti-pollution measures. Thus, part XII of the ICNT dealing with the protection and preservation of the marine environment, and in particular Articles 213 and 223 dealing with national legislation, including enforcement provisions, relating to pollution from or through the atmosphere, "significantly delimits the scope of coastal state enforcement jurisdiction with respect to national environmental standards in the territorial sea and exclusive economic zone" (International Law Association, 1978). This resulted from opposing positions on the part of environmental interests that wished to grant to states extended powers over pollution-causing events and by shipping interests who feared that such wide-ranging and spatially broad areas would impose significant limits on freedom of navigation. This resulted in a compromise contained in the 1977 Text. Coastal states may establish and enforce national standards regarding discharges of pollutants in territorial waters but not in the EEZ. Further, coastal states may not fix standards for construction, design, equipment and manning criteria for vessels. But, to appease the environmental point of view, the Text allows port state jurisdiction over pollutants whereby coastal states may establish environmental standards relating to the constuction, design, equipment, and manning of such vessels as a condition of port entry. These provisions run contrary to the establishment of coastal state standards for fisheries running out to 200 miles and to the even more extended authority that a state may exercise with respect to ADIZ security concerns. While a state may not impose pollution controls on aircraft of foreign states beyond the airspace under the sovereignty of the state, a coastal state can impose such limitations on national aircraft wherever they may be (ICNT, Article 213).

Transit Passage and the Right of Archipelagic Sea Lanes Passage

Although the guarantees and assurances contained in the ICNT on these matters introduce new concepts into the law of the sea and the law of ocean airspace, it is reasonably clear that all parties can expect to benefit from their provisions. They provide the benefits of uniformity of rules and the right of access needed by aircraft engaged in international transit. They provide the security and environmental protections needed by subjacent states. The bargains were fully negotiated. Since all parties have derived benefits--for the moment only prospective--from the protection of their respective interests, it is not likely that new claims will emerge in this area.

Antarctica

The terms of the Antarctic Treaty of December 1, 1959[9] contain rather special rights and duties relating to ocean areas adjacent to the continent and aerial flights. Moreover, the Treaty is the province of specifically affected states. Its special terms for the designated area, to the extent that they provide for behavior other than that found in the ICNT, would take precedence over the latter. Provisions of the agreement that have relevance are set out in Article VI and VII. Thus, Article VI provides that international law will apply to the high seas within the area. Article VII provides for freedom of access at all times to any or all of the areas, which would include the high seas areas. Article VII 4. provides that "Aerial observation may be carried out at any time over any or all areas of Antarctica by any of the contracting parties having the right to designate observers." Only states parties to the agreement are entitled to appoint observers. Whether non-parties will assert claims to engage in aerial observation remains to be seen. The search for new resources in the area may induce non-signatories to assert claims to Antarctic riches (Mitchell, 1977). Further, the agreement did not effect a definition of the territorial waters of the continent, thus leaving the extent of high seas uncertain. Over time it may be necessary for the 12 parties to the Antarctic Treaty to adjust its provisions to those treaty terms coming from the U.N. Conference on the Law of the Sea.

Conclusion

The terms of the ICNT, particularly through the identification of the EEZ, have caused a sudden flurry of concern relating to international legal rights in ocean airspace. This has been resolved favorably so far by allowing for the free transit of aircraft in such areas, for special rights of the kind established for fisheries have not been extended to ocean airspace. By establishing the EEZ, the prior freedom to catch fish in the high seas is restricted when such fish are to be found in the EEZ. But, with respect to aerial transit through ocean airspace, there is still freedom of transit without regard to the legal condition assigned to high seas or EEZ. Clearly, an aircraft within the ocean airspace above the EEZ is within neither the sovereign territory nor the national

[9]12 UST 794, TIAS 4780. It entered into force for the United States on June 23, 1961.

jurisdiction of the coastal state. Nonetheless, for security reasons a coastal state may impose notice requirements on aircraft transiting such ocean airspace, and--provided that it does not impose permanent limitations on the use of such airspace, as attempted by Libya in its ordinance on restricted zones--may have occasional exclusive uses of such ocean airspace. In this sense the work of the Conference supports the adage that the more things change the more they remain the same.

The bargains struck with regard to transit rights and the right of archipelagic sea lanes passage established important legal provisions. It is expected that they will be well received and respected, since they give assurances to the states territorially proximate to such areas that their environmental needs will be protected while allowing mobility for international air transit. Uniformity of conduct has been identified; benefits will result from the existence of common standards.

The parties to the Antarctic Treaty will have to coordinate its terms with those to be found in the final work product of the Conference on the Law of the Sea. Their respective claims against each other may be as worthy of attention as those of the eager developing nations and the more advanced states in the historic ocean-air conference still in session.

REFERENCES

Clean Water Act of 1977, P.L. 95-217, 91 State. 1567, Section 58a.

Columbia Law Review. Legal Aspects of Reconnaissance in Air and Outer Space. Columbia Law Review, 1961, 61, 1086.

Department of Transport. Information Circular No. 0/19/51. Director of Air Services, Civil Aviation Division.

Head, I. L. ADIZ, International Law, and Contiguous Airspace. Alberta Law Review, 1964, 3, 184.

ICNT (Informal Composite Negotiating Text). U.N. Doc. A/Conf. 62/WP.10, July 15, 1977.

International Law Association. Report of Committee on Law of the Sea. American Branch of the International Law Association, 1977-1978, p. 100.

Lissitzyn, O. J. The Treatment of Aerial Intruders in Recent Practice and International Law. American Journal of International Law, October, 1953, 47, 559.

Margolis. The Hydrogen Bomb Experiments and International Law. Yale Law Journal, 1955, 64, 648.

McDougal, M. S. and Schlei, N. The Hydrogen Bomb Tests in Perspective: Lawful Measures for Security. Yale Law Journal, 1955, 64, 648.

Mitchell, Barbara. Resources in Antarctica, Potential for Conflict. Marine Policy, April, 1977, p. 91.

Oda, S. Contemporary Issues of the Law of the Sea. Marine Technology and Law, Proceedings of the 2nd International Ocean Symposium, 1977, p. 176.

Office of Technology Assessment. Establishing a 200-Mile Fisheries Zone. Office of Technology Assessment, Congress of the United States, 1977, pp. 32-36.

Oxman, B. H. The Third United Nations Conference on the Law of the Sea: The 1977 New York Session. American Journal of International Law, January, 1978, 72, 68.

Whiteman, M. M. Digest of International Law, 1968, 9, 321.

AIR SPACE OVER EXTENDED JURISDICTIONAL ZONES

Paul P. Heller
Honorary Lecturer
Faculty of Law
University of Auckland, New Zealand

This paper has been written by a teacher of air law for discussion at the 12th Annual Conference of the Law of the Sea Institute of a particular problem involving both the law of the sea and the law of the air. For the specialists in the law of the sea the paper has to include an outline of the air law background; but, as the paper may also come to the attention of lawyers mainly interested in air law, and with little knowledge of the work of the Third United Nations Conference on the Law of the Sea, it must also refer to certain provisions of the Informal Composite Negotiating Text (ICNT) which was published at the end of the sixth session of this Conference in July 1977.[1] The results and documents of the seventh session (March to May and August to September 1978) have not been available to the writer, nor has he had access to more than a few of the many books, articles and working papers dealing with the law of the sea, its development prior to and after 1958, and, in particular, with the proceedings of the Conference.

Rules of the Air

In order to prevent collisions in the overcrowded parts of the world, sea, road and air traffic require uniform regulation within states, and on a supranational level in respect of activities extending beyond national boundaries. These technical regulations must keep in step with the development of technical knowledge and experience. This requires a method of adopting and amending technical regulations which eliminates time-consuming formalities to the greatest possible extent.

In the field of international civil aviation, technical regulations were kept apart from the main body of the International Convention for the Regulation of Aerial Navigation (Paris 1919), and from the main body of the Convention on International Civil Aviation (Chicago 1944), to which they are attached as "Annexes." The Paris Convention (as amended) provided that its provisions are completed by Annexes "which shall have the same effect and shall come into force at the same time as the Convention itself." But it provided for a different procedure for

---

[1]United Nations, Third Conference on the Law of the Sea, A/Conf. 62/WP.10 15 July 1977, with Corrections 1 and 2.

approving amendments to the annexes (which were binding on contracting states), from the procedure for amending the articles of the Convention. Any modification of the annexes could be made by the International Commission for Air Navigation when such modification was approved by three-fourths of the total votes of the states represented at the session of the Commission and two-thirds of the total possible votes which could be cast if all the states were represented at such session. Modifications of the articles of the Convention itself, on the other hand, could only be examined by the Commission and could be proposed for adoption by contracting states if it were approved by at least two-thirds of the total possible votes. All such proposed modifications of the articles of the Convention (but not of provisions of the annexes) required formal adoption by the contracting states.

Under the Chicago Convention (Article 37) contracting states undertook to collaborate in securing "the highest practicable degree of uniformity in regulations, standards, procedures and organization in relation to aircraft, personnel, airways and auxiliary services in all matters in which such uniformity will facilitate and improve air navigation. To this end the International Civil Aviation Organization (ICAO) shall adopt and amend from time to time, as may be necessary, international standards and recommend practices and procedures..." Contrary to the annexes to the Paris Convention, neither the international standards contained in annexes, nor, of course, the recommended practices are binding on contracting states. The obligation of contracting states is confined to collaboration in securing the highest practicable degree of uniformity in regulations, standards, procedures and organization (Article 37) and to notification of the differences between a state's practice and that established by a standard (Article 38).

The only exception from this rule is set out in Article 12 of the Chicago Convention, reading as follows:

> <u>RULES OF THE AIR</u>
>
> Each contracting State undertakes to adopt measures to insure that every aircraft flying over or manoeuvring within its territory and that every aircraft carrying its nationality marks, wherever such aircraft may be, shall comply with the rules and regulations relating to the flight and manoeuvre of aircraft there in force. Each contracting State undertakes to keep its own regulations in these respects uniform, to the greatest possible extent, with those established from time to time under this Convention. <u>Over the high seas, the rules in force shall be those established under this Convention</u>. Each contracting State undertakes to insure the prosecution of all persons violating the regulations applicable.

The "rules of the air" in the title of this article are described in its text as the rules relating to the "flight and manoeuvre of aircraft." They are the equivalent to "marine traffic " or "safety or navigation rules" in the movement of ships on water (for example, in Article 42(1) (a) of the ICNT) and to "rules of the road" in the Geneva Convention on Road Traffic (1949). The reference in Article 12 to rules "established under this Convention" means the international standards, recommended practices and procedures adopted by ICAO under Article 37 of the Chicago Convention and designated as annexes to the Chicago Convention.

Under these provisions of the Chicago Convention, ICAO has up to now adopted 17 annexes, among them Annex 2, published as "International Standards - Rules of the Air." In adopting this annex, the Council of ICAO resolved that the annex constitutes rules relating to the flight and manoeuvre of aircraft within the meaning of Article 12 of the Convention. The Council added in its resolution the following words: Over the high seas, therefore, these rules apply without exception[2] (Buergenthal, 1969; Carroz, 1959, p. 158; Drion, 1957, p. 323). That means that if a state desires to register with ICAO its departure from any standard adopted in Annex 2, it can do so only in respect of its own or foreign aircraft when flying over its own territory, but not in respect of its own aircraft when flying over the high seas.

In interpreting Article 12, the question has been asked whether it is for the Council of ICAO, when adopting an annex, to pronounce that it establishes rules relating to the flight and manoeuvre of aircraft within the meaning of Article 12 which apply over the high seas without exception (Buergenthal, 1969, pp. 82-83; Carroz, 1959, pp. 168-170). Buergenthal reported that in the Council debate preceding the adoption of Annex 2 some Council members considered that "Article 12 applied to any rules relating to the flight and manoeuvre of aircraft regardless of the Annex in which these rules were established."

Another annex (No. 11) contains international standards and recommended practices for air traffic services, applying in those parts of the air space under the jurisdiction of a state wherein air traffic services are provided, and also where a state accepts responsibility for providing such services over the high seas or in air space of undetermined sovereignty. Chapter 2 of this Annex provides that a state accepting such responsibility may apply the standards and recommended practices in a manner consistent with that adopted for air space under its own jurisdiction. That means that the state may register with ICAO departures from standards in Annex 11 in respect of aircraft flying over the high seas.

---

[2]Annex 2, paragraph 2.1.1, note 1.

When Annex 11 was before ICAO for adoption, it was realized that some standards did constitute rules relating to flight and manoeuvre of aircraft. Quoting from Carroz (1959, pp. 162, 170-171) and Buergenthal (1969, pp. 83-85)[3] the United Kingdom representative inquired "whether there was any reason why the Air Traffic Services standards should not be mandatory over the high seas." The Chief of the ICAO Legal Bureau replied that "a careful study of the Convention had convinced the Legal Bureau... that 'the rules and regulations relating to flight and manoeuvre of aircraft' were any rules that the Council designated as such and were not limited to the Rules of the Air as set out in Annex 2." The United States representative suggested that if the rules of Annex 11 were made mandatory over the high seas they "might deter a State from supplying a much needed service in these areas since...this service might have to be provided in accordance with rules differing in some respects from those applicable in its own territory."

The Chairman of the Air Navigation Commission of ICAO stated that his Commission "was opposed to making the rules of Annex 11 mandatory over the high seas because of the technical problems that would result whenever a State providing air traffic services decided to deviate from Annex 11. Such a State would then 'have two sets of air traffic services regulations--one applicable to (the) air space of its own territory, the other to the air space over the high seas...'" The Council finally decided against making the rules of Annex 11 mandatory over the high seas.

Carroz (1959) concluded that in the last resort the states concerned determine the rules covered by Annex 11 which are to be applied over the high seas. Insofar as these rules relate to the flight and manoeuvre of aircraft, he thought it is questionable whether such a procedure is in conformity with Article 12. Buergenthal (1959) held that "the existence side-by-side of two different sets of rules cannot but cause confusion and create air navigation hazards."

In conclusion of these short notes on the ICAO machinery for establishing international air traffic rules over sea and land, it can be stated that there has been some uncertainty and argument as to which standards established by ICAO, apart from Annex 2, are mandatory over the high seas, and in respect of which member states of ICAO may register deviations. But there has, at least, been no argument as to the geographical area of water (high seas as against territorial sea) in respect of which deviations may or may not be filed.

---

[3]As a copy of the original ICAO documents was not available to the author, he had to rely on the references to documents by Carroz (1959) and Buergenthal (1969).

The Right to Fly According to Air Law

In order to ascertain the rules of international law about flying of aircraft through the oceanic air space to and from the territory of a state, one has to look through the codifications of international air law and also through the proposed ICNT. No rules have yet been drafted about the movements of spacecraft (which are not considered to be "aircraft") through the air space on their way to and from outer space.

The Chicago Convention mentions in Article 2 the "territorial waters" which together with the land areas under the sovereignty of a state are deemed to form its territory. The only other reference to the "high seas" is in Article 12 of this Convention, which has already been referred to. Chapter II (Articles 5 to 16) of this Convention deals with the flight over the territory of contracting states by non-scheduled aircraft and scheduled international air services (see the definitions of "air service," "international air service," "airline" and "stop for non-traffic purposes" in Article 96). As already stated, the term "territory" includes the territorial waters.

These provisions of the Convention are supplemented by two other multilateral international conventions agreed upon at Chicago in 1944, viz, the International Air Services Transit Agreement and the International Air Transport Agreement under which each contracting state grants to the other contracting states the freedom (or privilege) to fly across its territory (which here again includes its territorial waters). Reference can also be made to the Multilateral Agreement on Commercial Rights of Non-Scheduled Air Services in Europe, signed in Paris in 1956, and to thousands of bilateral air transport agreements.

The requirement for the multilateral or bilateral grant of transit-rights through the air space above the territorial sea of a state other than the state of registration of the aircraft or of the airline can be explained by the fact that the rules of international air law do not provide for a right of innocent passage by aircraft of one state through the air space over the territorial sea of another state on its way to or from an aerodrome in this or in another state. This is, of course, different from the provisions of Articles 17-26 ICNT dealing with innocent passage of ships through the territorial sea (which right does not include the launching, landing or taking on board of any aircraft).

Provisions of the ICNT About Air Space, Aircraft and Flying

A. High Seas

The provisions of Part VII of the ICNT apply to all parts of the sea that are not included in the exclusive economic zone, in the territorial sea or in the internal waters of a state, or in the archipelagic waters of an archipelagic state (Article 86). According to Article 87, all states, coastal and land locked, may exercise, *inter alia*, the freedom of overflight and the freedom to construct artificial islands and other installations permitted under international law. No state may validly purport to subject any part of the high seas to its sovereignty (Article 89). Other provisions of this part which have application to flying deal with the duty to provide search and rescue services regarding safety on and over the sea (Article 98), repression of piracy (Articles 100 to 107), the exercise of the right of visits (Article 110) and of the right of hot pursuit (Article 111).

I suggest that it is not beyond doubt as to whether the provision of Article 109 about unauthorized broadcasting from the high seas applies only to broadcasting from vessels on the high seas, or also to broadcasting from aircraft flying over the high seas.

The formulation of a set of principles to govern direct broadcasting by satellite is still being considered by the United Nations Committee on the Peaceful Uses of Outer Space.

B. Territorial Sea

The sovereignty of a coastal state extends to the air space over the territorial sea which may be exercised according to the proposed Convention and to other rules of international law (Article 2). Only ships, not aircraft, have a right of innocent passage through (or over) the territorial sea, but according to Article 18 ships may stop and anchor in the territorial sea *inter alia* for the purpose of rendering assistance to aircraft in danger or distress; passage is not innocent if a ship engages in the territorial sea in the launching, landing or taking on board of any aircraft (Article 19).

C. Straits

In straits which are used for international navigation between one area of the high seas or an exclusive economic zone and another area of the high seas or an exclusive economic zone, aircraft enjoy the right of transit passage which is the exercise of the freedom of overflight solely for the purpose of continuous and expeditious transit between the two areas mentioned, or for the purpose of entering, leaving or returning from a state bordering the strait, subject to the conditions of entry to the state (Article 38).

The juridical status of waters forming straits used for international navigation will not affect the exercise by the states bordering the straits of their sovereignty or jurisdiction over their air space (Article 34). Special duties of aircraft during their passage through the air space over a strait are set out in Article 39; this article includes the very significant provision that aircraft in transit over straits *must* observe the rules of the air established by ICAO, and must at all times monitor the radio frequency assigned by the appropriate internationally designated air traffic control authority or the appropriate international distress radio frequency. The wording of this special reference to Annex 2 to the Chicago Convention clarifies the mandatory character of the "Rules of the Air" as established by ICAO (without allowing states to register differences). The significance of this special provision will be discussed later. States bordering straits must not hamper transit passage and must give appropriate publicity to any danger to overflight over the strait of which they have knowledge (Article 44).

D. Archipelagic Waters

The sovereignty of an archipelagic state extends to the air space over the archipelagic waters (Article 49). The archipelagic state may designate sea lanes and air routes thereabove, and all aircraft enjoy the right of passage in such air routes in the normal mode solely for the purpose of continuous, expeditious and unobstructed transit between one part of the high seas or an exclusive economic zone and another part of the high seas or an exclusive economic zone. Such air routes traverse the archipelagic waters and the adjacent territorial sea and include all normal passage routes used as routes for international overflight through the archipelagic waters. Aircraft in archipelagic sea lanes passage shall not deviate more than 25 nautical miles either side of the axis lines defining the sea lanes, but if an archipelagic state does not designate air routes the right of archipelagic sea lanes passage may be exercised through the routes normally used for international navigation (Article 53). The provision of Article 39 about the observation of Annex 2 to the Chicago Convention applies also to aircraft during their flight in archipelagic sea lane passages (Article 54).

E. Continental Shelf

The rights of the coastal state over the continental shelf do not affect the legal status of the superjacent waters and of the air space above those waters (Article 78).

F. The "Area"

The "Area," as defined in Article 1, means the sea bed and ocean floor and subsoil thereof beyond the limits of national jurisdiction. The provisions of Part XI of the ICNT will not affect the legal status of the waters superjacent to the Area or that of the air space above those waters (Article 135). No state may claim or exercise sovereignty or sovereign rights over any part of the Area or its resources (Article 137).

G. Freedom of Transit for Land-Locked States

In order to exercise their rights provided for in the Convention, land-locked states are to enjoy freedom of transit through the territories of transit states by "all means of transport" (Article 125). But according to the definition in Article 124 "means of transport" means: railway rolling stock, sea-, lake- and river-craft and road vehicles--but not aircraft. I suppose "all means of transport" in Article 125 means all means enumerated in Article 124, otherwise, the provisions of Part X of the ICNT would have to be coordinated with the provisions of the various international aviation conventions and agreements providing for transit flight by aircraft.

H. Exclusive Economic Zone (EEZ)

This is an area beyond and adjacent to the territorial sea (Article 55) the breadth of which must not extend beyond 200 nautical miles from the baselines from which the breadth of the territorial sea is measured (Article 57). While other parts of the sea and the air space above have a "juridical status" (territorial sea - Article 2; waters forming straits - Article 34; archipelagic waters - Article 49), the EEZ has a "specific legal regime" (Article 55), established in Part V of the ICNT, "under which the rights and jurisdictions of the coastal State and the rights and freedoms of other States are governed by the relevant provisions of the present Convention."

Before describing the respective rights and duties of the coastal state and of other states respectively in and over the EEZ, the following quotation from McDougal and Burke (1962, pp. 82, 610-611) may assist in understanding the use of the terms "sovereignty" and "jurisdiction" in the statement that,

> no State may subject any part of the high seas to its sovereignty; hence no State may exercise jurisdiction over any such stretch of water:
>
> Much of this confusion appears to derive from a failure to distinguish between claims to all that comprehensive and continuous competence which is summed up as 'sovereignty' and claims to exercise only the occasional and limited competence over certain particular events which is commonly called 'jurisdiction'. The fact that world public order denies 'sovereignty' over certain ocean areas to any single State does not mean that it denies to States competence to apply their authority to certain particular events, such as the activities of vessels and aircraft whether national or foreign. Conversely, the fact that States are authorised to exercise some such authority upon the high seas over navigation, fishing, flying, cable-laying and so on, does not mean

> that they are authorised to exercise such authority at all times and at all places, under all conditions, without any interference from similar uses by others and without regard for the consequences of their ocean uses upon others. The competence conferred upon States by 'freedom of the seas' is not an absolute competence, but a relative, shared competence which can survive only if it is exercised in accommodation with the similar competence of others.

The rights and jurisdiction of the coastal state in the EEZ are set out in Article 56:

> (a) sovereign rights, to be exercised only "for the purpose of exploring and exploiting, conserving and managing the natural resources, whether living or non-living, of the sea-bed and subsoil and the superjacent waters, and with regard to other activities for the economic exploitation and exploration of the zone, such as the production of energy from the water, currents and winds;
>
> (b) jurisdiction as provided for in the relevant provisions of the present Convention with regard to:
>
> (i) the establishment and use of artificial islands, installations and structures;
>
> (ii) marine scientific research;
>
> (iii) the preservation of the marine environment;
>
> (c) other rights and duties provided for in the present Convention.

The coastal state must have due regard for the rights and duties of other states (Article 56) who, in turn, must have due regard for the rights and duties of the coastal state and must comply with the laws and regulations established by the coastal state in accordance with the provisions of this Convention and other rules of international law insofar as they are not incompatible with Part V of the ICNT (Article 58). The same article grants all states with reference to Article 87 the freedom of overflight in the EEZ. This cross-reference from Part V (EEZ) to Part VII (High Seas) is an indication of the "specific legal regime" of the EEZ which has been regarded by some "as *sui generis*, distinct from the high seas," by others "as a part of the high seas subject to certain coastal state rights and jurisdiction" (Clingan, 1977, p. 541; Fleischer, 1977, p. 567; Oxman, 1978, p. 57).

The ICNT does not define in general terms the exact legal status of the EEZ. It does not form part of the high seas

(Article 86), though aircraft are to enjoy the freedom of overflight over the EEZ as they enjoy it over the high seas (Articles 58 and 87). No state may claim sovereignty over the high seas (Article 89), but the sovereignty of the coastal state extends to the air space over the territorial sea. In the EEZ, the coastal state has only limited sovereign rights for the economic exploration and exploitation of the zone, and certain jurisdiction and other rights (Article 56). Though indirect reference to the air space above the EEZ has been made by reference to "overflight" in Article 57, the ICNT fails to grant to the coastal state jurisdiction in the air space above the EEZ.

Civil Aviation Jurisdiction of the Coastal State Above the EEZ

Rules of the Air

Oxman (1978, p. 74) considered that "(w)hether the 200-mile line is juridically significant depends on the purpose for which the question is asked. If one is discussing navigation, by and large, it is not. If one is discussing fishing, it is." With due respect, I cannot agree with the statement that the 200 mile line is insignificant as regards flying over the EEZ.

When dealing with other parts of the sea, the lawyers drafting the ICNT have considered the question what navigational rules (for aircraft the term "Rules of the Air" has been and ought to be used) should apply. Aircraft in transit over straits *must* under Article 39 observe the Rules of the Air established by ICAO (Annex 2 of the Chicago Convention) without distinguishing whether the air space used in transit over the strait is above the territorial sea of the states bordering the strait or above the high seas. As Article 39 is worded, the Rules of the Air (Annex 2) are mandatory, as if all the waters forming the strait were high sea. Notwithstanding the mandatory application of Annex 2, areas of internal waters within a strait and the status of the waters beyond the territorial seas of states bordering the straits as exclusive economic zones or high seas will not otherwise be affected (Article 35).

The same problem was again considered in Part IV of the ICNT dealing with archipelagic states whose sovereignty extends over the archipelagic waters, regardless of their depth of distance from the coast, and to the air space over these waters (Article 49). Aircraft exercising the right of archipelagic air route passage fly through the air space over archipelagic waters (being another part of the sea which was not considered when drafting the Chicago Convention and Annex 2) and the adjacent territorial sea (Article 53).

It was, consequently, realized that the ICNT should provide a ruling on the question as to whether archipelagic states may or may not file differences from Annex 2 (Rules of the Air) in respect of the archipelagic air route passages over the territorial sea adjacent to the archipelagic waters (Article 53).

This problem has, however, not been taken care of or has not been clarified beyond reasonable doubt, when drafting Part V of the ICNT. Let us consider the case of an aircraft approaching a coastal state by flying first over an area of the high seas for which the coastal state has accepted responsibility for the provision of air traffic services. While over the high seas, the aircraft must comply with the Rules of the Air as adopted by ICAO in Annex 2 to the Chicago Convention, and the air traffic authorities of the coastal state must guide the aircraft in accordance with these rules and the rules of Annex 11. When the aircraft crosses the 200-mile line, it enters a "grey area." Neither Article 12 of the Chicago Convention, nor Annex 2, nor the present draft rules of the ICNT, provides any clear guidance whether the original Annex 2 as adopted by ICAO or Annex 2 as amended following deviations registered with ICAO by the coastal state should apply, if the coastal state considers the EEZ to be "sui generis." Further on, when the aircraft crosses the 12-mile line and enters the air space over the territorial sea, another change of Rules of the Air may take place in accordance with any deviations from the original text of Annex 2 registered by the coastal state.

A factual and legal situation as described above explains and supports the statements referred to earlier in this paper which were made at the Air Navigation Commission and the Council of ICAO when considering Annexes 2 and 11 about the existence of different sets of rules causing confusion and creating air navigation hazards.

Apart from "Rules of the Air," a pilot must comply with the civil aviation regulations applying in the territory over which he is flying, and in the absence of such regulations with those of the country of registration. Unless the coastal state is granted civil aviation jurisdiction in the EEZ, different regulations may be applied to aircraft flying simultaneously and possibly in some proximity over the EEZ. Under these circumstances it should not be left to states to make individual decisions on the question as to whether the EEZ is sui generis, distinct from the high seas and consequently not covered by the reference to the high seas in Article 12 of the Chicago Convention, or whether it is part of the high seas. It depends on this decision whether Annex 2 applies as established by ICAO, or is subject to the departures filed with ICAO under Article 38 of the Chicago Convention.

The great difficulties in drafting the specific legal regime for the EEZ must be realized. Oxman (1978, p. 74), when referring to the considerable progress made in producing the ICNT, added: "None of this is to suggest that the text could not do with improvement."

The problem ought to be considered by the Conference on the Law of the Sea together with legal and technical (Air Traffic Control) experts from the International Civil Aviation Organization. One possible solution would be a statement in Part V of the ICNT (similar to Article 54 in Part IV) that paragraph (3) of Article 39 should apply, mutatis mutandis, to aircraft exercising the freedom of overflight over an EEZ. This would create uniformity in the Rules of the Air for aircraft of all states flying over the EEZ, but would still leave, as at present, states who had registered with ICAO deviations from Annex 2 of ICAO and who provide air traffic services over the high seas having to administer two sets of standards, one applicable in the air space above their own territories, the other above the EEZ. This solution would place the boundary between the area where the Rules of the Air as established by ICAO apply, and the area where Annex 2 subject to the deviations as filed by the coastal state applies, at the boundary between the coastal state's territorial sea and the adjoining EEZ.

This would be a somewhat similar situation of extending navigational rules beyond the high seas proper as they apply in shipping. According to Rule 1, paragraph (a) of the International Regulations for preventing Collisions at Sea, approved at a Conference in London in 1972, these rules apply "to all vessels upon the high seas and in all waters connected therewith navigable by seagoing vessels." These rules apply, consequently, also in the territorial sea as far as it is connected with the high seas and navigable by seagoing vessels; exemptions may be made only "for roadsteads, harbors, rivers, lakes, or inland waterways connected with the high seas and navigable by seagoing vessels" (Rule 1, paragraph (b)). This solution would give recognition to the view that the EEZ is part of the high seas.

A second solution in line with a sui generis status of the EEZ would require amendments of Article 56 and Article 60 of the ICNT. A provision to be added to Article 56 would say that aircraft in transit over the EEZ or flying between the coastal state and a point within the EEZ must observe the Rules of the Air established by the International Civil Aviation Organization[4] and all the regulations applying to operation and navigation, as they apply in the coastal state; and Article 60(2) would grant to the coastal state further jurisdiction with regard to civil aviation regulation on artificial islands, installations and structures. This solution would restrict the area where the Rules of the Air as established by ICAO apply, and where aircraft must comply with the rules of the state of their registration, to the high seas proper, not including the EEZ.

---

[4]Subject to any directions registered by the coastal state.

The third (and escapist) solution would be to rely on the provision of Article 59 of the ICNT and to have the conflict, if and when it arises, resolved on the basis of equity and in the light of all the relevant circumstances.

It is suggested that it would be preferable, if politically possible, to make a decision whether to adopt the first or second solution, by way of an amendment of the ICNT prior to the finalization of its text, than to leave it to action under the "resolution of conflicts" clause of Article 59. The general decision to be made during the Law of the Sea Conference would have to be made, in the same way as a future special decision under Article 59, "on the basis of equity and in the light of all the relevant circumstances, taking into account the respective importance of the interests involved to the parties as well as to the international community as a whole."

As a subject for further discussion among lawyers and air traffic experts, the author suggests that his second solution, i.e., the extension of the civil aviation rules of the coastal state, be given first consideration. Such an extension of control by the coastal state beyond the original limit of the territorial sea of three miles has been the trend of development over many years. We have seen the extension of the breadth of the territorial sea, the establishment of fisheries limits, the extension of jurisdiction to prevent pollution and to apply to the continental shelf (Burke, 1975, p. 27; Gutteridge, 1974, pp. 197-202).

The control of the air space even beyond the contiguous zone was advocated by Martial (1952, pp. 256-257, 259) as follows:[5]

> ...in countries or regions where air circulation is extensive, where because of the proximity of large industrial centres there is intensive air traffic, it is possible that further regulation by the subjacent State will be necessary, because of the speed of planes, to exercise some control over approaching aircraft before they enter the territorial air space or even the contiguous air space. This would permit air control officers to give directional orders to incoming planes and thus prevent the danger of collision.

He also referred to the Air Defence Identification Zones which were established by the United States in 1950 and by Canada in

[5]A further extension of the coastal state's control beyond its territorial sea has been sanctioned under Note 2 to paragraph 2.1.2 of Annex 11 as follows: "...a contracting State accepting the responsibility for providing air traffic services over the high seas...may apply the Standards and Recommended Practices in a manner consistent with that adopted for air space under its jurisdiction."

1951 under which these countries assumed jurisdiction for security purposes in the air space over large areas of the high seas adjoining their territories.

The existence of Annex 2 to the Convention on International Civil Aviation, of the standards established by ICAO, and of the provision of Article 12 of the Chicago Convention has not escaped some writers on the law of the sea; but, as far as I am aware, and again referring to the fact that only a limited range of literature was available to me in preparing this paper, none has mentioned the provision of Article 38 of the Chicago Convention which permits states to file with ICAO deviations from the standards except for flights of their aircraft over the high seas (Burke, 1975, pp. 8, 14; McDougal and Burke, 1962, pp. 785, 1080).

Primarily in the interest of safety of air traffic, the Rules of the Air, and the rules applying to operation and navigation of the coastal state, should be the same as those applying in the air space over the territory of the coastal state; for inward flights from the moment an aircraft crosses the boundary between the high seas and the coastal state's EEZ, and for outward flights until the aircraft crosses the boundary between the coastal state's EEZ and the high seas. Only this solution will prevent the danger of collisions of aircraft of different nationalities flying over the coastal state's EEZ applying not only Rules of the Air and other regulations different from those established by the coastal state, but also different rules according to each aircraft's nationality.

Aircraft Movements in the EEZ[6]

Up to now this paper has dealt with the flight of aircraft through the air space over the EEZ. But now the question has to be faced what law applies, or should apply, to aircraft operations into and from airports established within the EEZ on artificial islands, roadsteads, installations, structures and ships. According to Soons (1974, p. 3), the term "artificial island" refers to constructions which have been created by the dumping of natural substances like sand, rocks and gravel; the term "installation" refers to constructions resting upon the seafloor by means of piles or tubes driven into the bottom, and to concrete structures. They are established, and are required, as aids to fishing, for submarine exploration and exploitation, and for scientific investigations. Where aircraft, in particular helicopters, are required for transportation or investigation purposes, artificial islands, installations and ships form the basis for establishing airports within the EEZ. Lawrence (1975, p. 577) reported on the section of oceans as potential sites for offshore airports.

---

[6]The term "movement" is used in its aviation-technical meaning as referring to aircraft landings and take-offs.

In addition to the Rules of the Air and the standards applying to the provision of air traffic services, the pilot in charge of an aircraft must comply, when flying, including landing and taking off, with detailed operational rules issued by the state of nationality of his aircraft, or of any other state in the territory of which his aircraft is operating. There is no mandatory uniformity under the Chicago Convention for operational standards applicable over the high seas (or the EEZ), nor is there mandatory uniformity for the standards applicable to aerodromes to be established within the EEZ, and for authorizing the use of certain locations within the EEZ as aerodromes (including helipads).

The ICNT provides only inadequate answers to the problem. For roadsteads extending beyond the outer limit of the territorial sea, Article 12 provides that they are under certain circumstances included in the territorial sea. The landing and take-off of a helicopter on the outer end of a roadstead may, consequently, be subject to the civil aviation legislation of the coastal state. This extension of sovereignty into the EEZ has not been applied to artificial islands, installations and structures. It appears to be doubtful (and consequently should be clarified) whether the right granted to the coastal state in Article 60(1) to regulate the operation and use of artificial islands, installations and structures includes the right to regulate and exercise jurisdiction with regard to aviation, because of the reference to particular governmental interests (customs, fiscal, health, safety, immigration) only in Article 60(2).

Conflicting views have been expressed prior to the drafting of the ICNT in the legal literature. Soons (1974, p. 22) held that "a State may only exercise jurisdiction over activities on such structures when (a) the activities are conducted by nationals of that State, and (b) the activities affect certain legal interests of that State." He suggested that when

> a State itself or a State-Owned enterprise constructs and operates an artificial island or installation the link with that particular State is so strong that it can be considered as having exclusive competence to regulate all activities conducted thereon...In the case of facilities constructed just outside the territorial sea, or on the continental shelf in general, one could take the view that the interests of the coastal State are always, by their mere occurrence, affected by the activities on the facility. Partly on these considerations the Netherlands based its much-discussed North Sea Installations Act of 1964, by which it extended its jurisdiction over all the installations on the Netherland's continental shelf. The correctness of this view will not be dealt with here; suffice it to say that the imperfections of the present system make

it clear that it is highly desirable to include provisions on this issue in the new treaty on the law of the sea to be concluded.[7]

There has been no alternative for coastal states but to extend by unilateral legislative action their civil aviation jurisdiction (this paper does not deal with other legislative problems) beyond the outward boundary of the territorial sea to be exercised as regards aviation operations to, from and on artificial islands, installations and structures in the EEZ[8] (Knight, 1973, p. 382, 386-387; Lawrence, 1975, p. 58).

Walker (1973, p. 662) recommended the establishment of

> an international regime encompassing artificial islands... Such a regime should recognise that the coastal State has inherent, paramount economic and security interests in the seas appurtenant to its coast and is best able to promote and protect these interests and should thus have primary jurisdiction to construct and control activities on artificial islands within an area encompassing some distance seaward, which would be set by agreement among nations. The coastal State's jurisdiction within this area should not be exclusive: there should be international machinery, perhaps a special commission, to ensure that the freedom of the seas is preserved...This should be an expressly limited extension of coastal State authority.

Koers (1974, p. 229) proposed unilateral extension of the jurisdiction of the state on whose continental shelf an island would be located.

Schwenk (1976, p. 234) discussed in some detail the problems created and the solutions adopted in the Federal Republic of Germany with regard to aviation activities to and from ships and drilling platforms. He considered that the statutory requirement for approval of aerodromes situated within German territory does not apply to landing places on ships or drilling platforms, but aircraft require approval for take-offs and landings under a provision of German law. Though this provision is meant to apply only within German territory, it should, by way of analogy, be extended to apply also to take-offs and landings from and on ships and drilling platforms situated in an area outside the jurisdiction of any other State.

---

[7]For further reference to the legislation passed by the Dutch government see Lawrence (1975) and Knight (1973).

[8]As advocated by Knight (1973), Lawrence (1975) considered that airports built upon the high seas would occupy a considerable area of ocean space and the air space over and around the oceanic airport would necessarily be subjected to control, which would violate the freedom to fly over the high seas.

Summary and Conclusions

The area of the high seas bordering the territorial sea, the air space above and the seabed below, have become of increasing national importance and concern for coastal states, because of:

(a) their interest in exploring, exploiting and preserving the resources of this area in the light of an overall decrease of resources available to an increasing world population;

(b) their interest in providing safe flightpath to and from their territories for an increasing air traffic;

(c) their interest in ensuring that unwelcome aircraft are identified some distance from their shores and kept away.

The increase in the price of oil and technical advances made it economically sound and technically feasible to drill for oil from deep sea platforms established beyond the territorial sea. These platforms are being supplied primarily from helicopters flying from and to the coastal state, thus further increasing air traffic. In addition, aircraft have been and will increasingly be used to control fishing in the EEZ.

The codification of a new and more comprehensive law of the sea must be coordinated with a reconsideration of certain aspects of air law. The Chicago Convention on International Civil Aviation of 1944 and its Annexes deal with flying in the air space above a state's territory (including the territorial waters) and through the air space above the high seas; but there are, as yet, no rules of international air law dealing specifically with flying through the air space above the EEZ, and with flying between a coastal state, artificial or floating islands (including ships) and installations and structures established in the sea beyond the territorial waters. All these facts demand, in the interest of safety, an examination of the question whether the existing rules controlling the increased aviation activities in the air space above the EEZ are adequate.

The substantial increase in air traffic and its control demand uniform Rules of the Air; this uniformity has been assured by the Chicago Convention for air traffic over the high seas, but not over the EEZ, unless it were clearly and unequivocally established and agreed in air and sea law that the EEZ is not a zone *sui generis*, but covered by the term "high seas." The dangers arising from lack of uniformity of the Rules of the Air were recognized when Article 12 of the Chicago Convention and Annex 2 were drafted, and again when Annex 11 dealing with air traffic control services was under consideration.

The possible inadequacy of this paper, and the reason for it, were explained in the introductory note; though I suggest that the increase in flying over the EEZ in order to provide transportation services for drilling and other platofrms, and to control fishing activities of other countries would provide a strong argument for the _sui generis_ status of the EEZ and for extending the coastal state's Rules of the Air over the EEZ, I consider that this is a decision depending substantially on advice from air traffic experts.

But it is for lawyers to draw attention to possible dangers to air traffic and possible disputes between states which could eventuate unless certain provisions of the ICNT are clarified and coordinated with air law. Whether this is possible is not a legal or technical, but a political problem.

REFERENCES

Buergenthal. _Lawmaking in the International Civil Aviation Organization_, 1969.

Burke. _Contemporary Law of the Sea: Transportation, Communication and Flight_, Occasional Paper No. 29. Law of the Sea Institute, University of Rhode Island, 1975.

Carroz. International legislation on air navigation over the high seas. _Journal of Air Law and Commerce_, 1959, _26_.

Clingan. Emerging law of the sea: the economic zone dilemma. _San Diego Law Review_, 1977, _14_.

Drion. The Council of ICAO as international legislator over the high seas. In _Studi in onore di Anonio Ambrosini_, 1957.

Fleischer. The right to a 200-mile exclusive economic zone or a special fishery zone. _San Diego Law Review_, 1977, _14_.

Gutteridge. Beyond the three mile limit: recent developments affecting the law of the sea. _The Virginia Journal of International Law_, 1974, _14_.

Knight. International legal aspects of deep draft harbour facilities. _The Journal of Maritime Law and Commerce_, 1973, _4_.

Koers. Artificial islands in the North Sea. In Gamble and Pontecorvo (Eds.), _Law of the Sea: The Emerging Regime of Oceans_, 1974.

Lawrence. Superports, airports and other fixed installations on the high seas. Journal of Maritime Law and Commerce, 1975, 6.

Martial. State control of the air space over the territorial sea and the contiguous zone. Canadian Bar Review, 1952, 30.

McDougal and Burke. The Public Order of the Oceans. Yale University Press, 1962.

Oxman. The Third United Nations Conference on the Law of the Sea: the 1977 New York session. American Journal of International Law, 1978, 72.

Schwenk. Die Anwendung luftrechtlicher Vorschriften bei Flugen von und nach Schiffen und Bohrinseln. Zeitschrfit fur Luft und Weltraumrecht, 1976, 25.

Soons. Artificial Islands and Installations in International Law, Occasional Paper No. 22. Law of the Sea Institute, University of Rhode Island, 1974.

Walker. Jurisdictional problems created by artificial islands. San Diego Law Review, 1973, 10.

COMMENTARY

K. Hailbronner
Max Planck Institute
Federal Republic of Germany

It is perhaps not accidentally that the traditional customary law concept of the freedom of the airspace over the high seas is not mentioned in the paper of Professor Christol. Professor Christol starts with the basic concept of the airspace above the ocean as a global resource. Consequently, this concept leads him to an evaluation of conflicting interests. Professor Christol's basic approach for the present and future use of airspace is that certain complex social forces have to be taken into account to facilitate the long distance movement of individuals and concerns for national security and the demand for the discovery and use of natural resources. I would like, however, to comment with respect to some of his conclusions concerning the emerging trends with respect to the use of ocean airspace.

Professor Christol comes to the conclusion that an aircraft within the airspace above the EEC, although it is not within the national jurisdiction of the coastal state, may be subject to security requirements. A coastal state may even have, provided that it does not impose permanent limitations on the use of such airspace, occasional exclusive uses of such ocean airspace.

This reflects probably an adequate evaluation of the conflicting interests at stake and can, therefore, be regarded as a sound basis for the aerial regime of the ocean. Allow me, however, to put forward some questions and doubts with regard to the emerging trends.

On the other hand, there is the concept of the Chicago Convention that the airspace above the high seas is free. And I would like to remind you in this context that freedom of the airspace is not limited to a right of overflight only. It is really much more. It is an establishment of a free area not subject to any national restrictions with regard to airspace. Here in the Netherlands, a country that has traditionally upheld very strongly the concept of the freedom of the airspace, I believe that this traditional customary rule of international law is a requirement that we should not give up very easily.

On the other hand, there are national interests such as security considerations, pollution and scientific research in the ocean airspace. Generally, I believe there is an increasing tendency for industrialized and developing countries to unduly extend national sovereign rights.

Let me deal first with security considerations, especially identification requirements, filing of flight plans, and similar conditions like Professor Christol mentioned especially with regard to air defense identification. Of course, there can be no objections raised against the exercise of control necessary to prevent infringement of national customs, physical immigration, and sanitary regulations such as is contemplated in Article 33 of the Informal Composite Negotiating Text. These rights are, however, explicitly limited to 24 nautical miles according to Article 33 of the Text. I think this is with good reason since otherwise there would be the danger of "creeping jurisdiction."

The security requirements, in effect, may be the beginning of subjecting part of the ocean airspace to national jurisdiction. In fact, from a legal point of view, I do not see such a big difference between a restricted area and certain security requirements in the airspace above the ocean. After all, according to these regulations transit is only allowed if certain requirements are fulfilled. There are no criteria for judging what are reasonable limitations of flight in such zones. Of course, it depends very much on the kind of security requirements. I suggest, however, that we should not be too quick to recognize alleged security interests which in fact may endanger the freedom of flight.

I would like to remind you also in this respect of the problem of straying aircraft. Security requirements tend to be enforced. The risk of an aircraft having to comply with several different identification and security requirements should not be overlooked. I wonder about the situation of an aircraft captain who is flying through several different economic zones having to comply with all kinds of security requirements. I cannot really judge, but I wonder if this too might not unduly hamper the safety of aviation.

My second point is pollution control. Again, one could hardly dare to argue against pollution control by coastal states. There is hardly one day where there is not a big oil tanker breaking into pieces causing enormous damage. Of course, there is also the problem of pollution to the marine environment by aircraft. That is why states are not only allowed but obliged under Article 213 of the Informal Composite Negotiating Text to check pollution with respect to aircraft flying under the flag or in the airspace under their sovereignty. This provision, however, does not allow part of the ocean airspace and especially over the EEC to be subjected to national antipollution legislation, including environmental standards. I agree, however, with Professor Christol that this does not exclude pollution control as a condition of port entry.

Again, this limitation of jurisdiction seems to be an indication that the jurisdictional rights that are granted by the Informal Composite Negotiating Text are rather limited for specific purposes. The concept of the exclusive economic zone does not mean an extension of sovereignty as Professor Christol pointed out. We should not accept a quasi-jurisdiction by coastal states over the airspace above their economic zones.

Let me add a few comments with regard to the report of Dr. Heller. Again, we are faced with the same problem, freedom of the air versus security and safety considerations, particularly with regard to the rules of the air applicable and also with regard to the freedom of overflight. The main problem of airspace over extended jurisdictional zones results, as Dr. Heller pointed out, from the fact that the Chicago Convention distinguishes only between airspace over a state's territory including its territorial waters and airspace over the high seas. The Law of the Sea Conference introduces new areas with a mixed concept of sovereign but not unlimited rights. This is especially true with regard to the exclusive economic zone.

There are two types of questions which we have to face. The first refers to the freedom of flight over the high seas. As I pointed out already, the establishment of jurisdictional zones may endanger the existing pattern of international air traffic. In principle, there is no right of innocent passage by aircraft of one state through the airspace of another state. Of course, there are provisions, as you know, in the Informal Composite Negotiating Text relating to the freedom of navigation and overflight, such as Article 58 with regard to the exclusive economic zone. I suggest, however, that it is not completely irrelevant if the freedom of overflight is granted on the basis of principally unlimited sovereign rights of the coastal state or as an expression of the traditional freedom of airspace over the high seas.

In the first case, it is up to the coastal state to regulate the freedom of overflight by its national laws. The recognition of the freedom of overflight does not necessarily mean that a state must not make the overflight of its economic zone dependent on certain requirements such as previous permission. I am afraid, again, that the danger of excessive restrictions of the freedom of flight cannot be ruled out altogether by the recognition of a right of overflight. This is why I am rather inclined to argue in favor of the economic zone as part of the high seas with regard to the airspace rather than a special area not covered by the Chicago Convention.

I think this can be justified by two arguments. The economic zone is limited to certain specific jurisdictional purposes and certain sovereign rights to be exercised for these specific purposes like exploring and exploiting. I suggest that such a concept cannot be enlarged to sovereign rights over the airspace. Secondly, the Informal Composite Negotiating Text makes clear with regard to archipelagic waters that the sovereignty extends to the airspace above. There is no similar provision for the EEZ.

The question of sovereignty arises also in respect of the rules of the air applicable in the airspace over the EEZ. According to Article 12 of the Chicago Convention, the rules relating to the flight and maneuver of aircraft apply without exception. No state may register its departure from standards adopted in Annex 2 concerning flights of aircraft over the high seas.

Dr. Heller came to the conclusion that it is very doubtful if these rules apply also to aircraft flying in the EEZ. He proposes two possible solutions. The first is to give recognition to the view that the EEZ is part of the high seas. The second would restrict the area where the rules of the air as established by the ICAO apply to the high seas proper, not including the EEZ. The difference between the solutions seems to be that in the first case the rules of the air are obligatory, while in the second case the coastal state may register departure of these rules and submit the aircraft to its jurisdiction.

Dr. Heller seems to tend to the second solution. While I agree with him insofar as this solution reflects a recent trend to extend the control by the coastal state beyond the limit of the territorial sea, I do not think it advisable to extend the jurisdiction of the coastal state *in toto* over the airspace of the EEZ. Article 12 makes sure that the rules relating to flight and maneuver of aircraft over the high seas are uniform. Generally speaking, these rules reflect a minimum standard of safety which are not always achieved in national civil aviation legislation. The evident advantages of such a regime seem to be the reason why the Informal Composite Negotiating Text declares the rules of the air obligatory even with regard to transit flight through straits or archipelagic waters.

In my opinion, this is a very strong argument for the view that flights through the economic zone are also subject to the regime of Article 12 of the Chicago Convention. We cannot, however, overlook the fact that a coastal state has limited sovereign rights and jurisdiction in the EEZ. As far as the use of these rights is concerned, the coastal state must have a right to extend its civil aviation jurisdiction to the EEZ. This implies the flying and landing of helicopters to platforms within the EEZ as well as certain safety requirements concerning installations, artificial islands, and structures in the EEZ.

I do not believe, however, that there is a right to extend the civil aviation jurisdiction *in toto* to the EEZ. I realize, however, that this might cause new problems with regard to different sets of rules applicable; and I agree insofar with Dr. Heller too that in the last resort we would have to seek the advice from air traffic experts in deciding this question.

DISCUSSION AND QUESTIONS

CARL CHRISTOL: Under the general heading of trends, I think that it is undoubtedly true that nations are going to assert ever more concern for and exclusive control over resources. Of course, I am most sympathetic to the problems of mankind as identified in a number of international resolutions. And I am also very sympathetic to the notion of the common heritage of mankind as it finds itself also in a number of international resolutions and in the Text. I have a feeling that this objective is a worthy one. And when the time comes to distribute the benefits of resources such resources should be distributed equitably and fairly on the basis of these very important concepts.

I think, however, that one should not accept the proposition that states may in effect impose a veto upon the exercise of the use of and exploitation of such resources at the present time. I think that over time we are going to see demands on the part of those that have the scientific and technological capability to use these resources with the expectation that at a future time when the political climate is suited there may be a more equitable distribution and division of such resources. And I am thinking of this not only in terms of ocean airspace but also in terms of very tangible things such as the mining of asteroids in outer space, the use of orbital positions in the geostationary orbit, and the capture, for example, of solar energy at a geostationary orbital level and the transmission of this to earth. So I think the trend for the moment is for those that have the scientific and technological capability to engage in the exploitation of resources wherever they may be.

Going on to the matter of the importance of aerial transit, of course, I am totally supportive of what you said, Dr. Hailbronner. I think it should be subject to uniform rules; and I think that the aircraft should be as mobile as possible. So I think we have no great difference in our values on that particular point. The issue, of course, is how this is to be accomplished. This then brings me to your other comments on security concerns and on pollution and also the limitations that you refer to as set forth in Article 33 of the Text relating to the contiguous zone. I would be quite supportive of a need not to impose limitations upon the state's control of customs, fiscal matters, immigration, or sanitary regulations within national territory or the territorial sea.

But I think that these controls which a state may possess in this 24 mile zone must be distinguished from the security considerations that I was talking about which would go further out. Once an enemy bomber, for example, if the backfire type, is 24 miles out, it is a little too late to do anything reasonably important to destroy its possible hostile significance. There is, therefore, a need I think to require identification at zones further out.

Furthermore, I think that the security considerations which I mentioned earlier do have merit. I do not think that they would necessarily impede the transit of aircraft for commercial purposes that you and I accept as terribly important and as a part of an acceptable way of life. I do think that from time to time it may be necessary at distances out above the high seas or out above the economic zones to impose constraints or limitations upon aircraft that may not have that commercial objective in mind. So I think that this may be a limitation on the use of the airspace resource. Claims for security in such areas can be rendered somewhat the equivalent of "creeping jurisdiction," but I do not regard it as that because, in my opinion, a limited occasional use rather than a prohibited zone of the kind that the Libyan government put into operation is permissible under existing law.

Finally, on the matter of pollution, I think that the Text is quite clear here that the state can impose pollution requirements upon its own national aircraft wherever that aircraft may be. It may not impose these constraints upon foreign aircraft above the high seas under the terms of the Text. However, one can imagine a situation involving a foreign airline of country X that consistently puts a lot of pollutants into the air when it comes into a destination state. And it does so not only above the territorial waters but out, say, in the contiguous zone or out above the economic zone. It would be perfectly permissible for the various countries involved here to simply terminate under the terms of the bilateral agreements the relationship between these two countries until the polluting state and its aircraft would conform, not by reason of the Text but rather by reason of a new bilateral agreement, to the needs of the destination state so that the airspace would not be polluted.

We spent a lot of time yesterday talking about the problems of marine biologists andothers interested in examining in a scientific way the flora and the fauna of the sea. I think it should be noted in passing that there is a very important need for those interested in identifying the purity of air, the kinds of pollutants that get into the air, to have opportunities to engage in this kind of research the world over. Some of us have been concerned, for example, about pollution of the ozone layer. Others are concerned about scientific data that are acquired only through the use of some extremely sensitive technical and chemical apparatus and instruments. I think we have got to assure ourselves that this kind of research can also proceed just as it is important for those in the field of marine biology to engage in their scientific research.

JOHN ARMSTRONG: I enjoyed thoroughly the comments of the three gentlemen on the airspace problem. All of your comments were primarily focused on the question of transit and aircraft movement primarily, and perhaps that is proper. I am wondering whether or not the question of weather modification in the ocean airspace is something that deserves more attention. Perhaps it is a little further away in real application, but I think it is an important problem. It certainly deals with the manipulation of the airspace and the dynamic characteristics. Is that a separate subject of discussion here? I know it occurs in the airspace, and I am wondering if there is any comment on that.

CARL CHRISTOL: Let me respond very briefly to that. It is certainly an extremely relevant point. The problem of weather modification and certainly the fuels used by high-flying jet aircraft and space objects, as well as aerosols which find their way up to the ozone level, all have an immediate and important impact upon the quality of the atmosphere and, therefore, may influence weather conditions. I am sure that this is a subject that probably, on my part at least, should have received a little more treatment.

But it is clear that there are major concerns as to the kinds of fuels that are being used. When a space shuttle goes into operation and is employed every three weeks or once a month, there is going to be an awful lot of special fuel used; this may have a very substantial impact upon the quality of the airspace. This is one of the reasons I wanted to make it clear a moment ago that there is a need to have equipment and instruments in place to identify the changes so one would actually know how dangerous (if dangerous is the word) the situation may be.

Now I have made a study of the use of space objects and the fuel employed there. I came away from that study with a feeling that this does not pose at the present time a major concern for the amount of ozone in the ozone layer. And of course as we all know, if the ozone is reduced, this allows the sunlight to come through in greater amounts and imposes an environmental hazard.

JOHN ARMSTRONG: Let me just clarify my question. I was referring primarily to <u>intentional</u> ocean airspace weather modification rather than passive. That was the subject of my comment, in the context that such weather modification actions could have effect on coastal states, and would require policy considerations to deal with the effects of ocean airspace weather modification.

ISABELLA DIEDERIKS-VERSCHOOR: I regret very much that there is no opportunity for more questions, but I hope that any questions you still have can be settled in private conversations.

I should like to thank Professor Christol, Dr. Heller, and Dr. Hailbronner for their very valuable contributions. I would like to thank the Law of the Sea Institute for having inserted the subject of air law in the sessions of this conference, and I thank you all for your attention.

PART IV

PROBLEMS OF POLAR REGIONS

INTRODUCTORY REMARKS BY SESSION PROGRAM CHAIRMAN

Edward Miles
University of Washington

Good afternoon ladies and gentlemen. The topic of this session is "Problems of Polar Regions." We have two papers each on the Arctic and the Antarctic. We shall begin with the Arctic and consider the implications of changes in the law of the sea for the "European" and "North American" sub-regions. The European paper will be delivered by Mr. Willy Østreng, Director of the Fridtjof Nansen Foundation, Polhøgda, Norway. The North American paper will be delivered by Professor Donat Pharand of the Faculty of Civil Law, University of Ottawa. Professor Pharand is the author of the authoritative book, the _International Law of the Arctic_.

With respect to the Antarctic, the first paper will be delivered by Dr. Finn Sollie, also of the Fridtjof Nansen Foundation. He will evaluate some of the current trends and future prospects affecting development of regimes to govern exploitation of living and non-living resources in the region. I owe Dr. Sollie a special debt of gratitude. I had originally asked Dr. Brian Roberts of the Scott Polar Research Institute in Cambridge, U.K. to come to talk to us, but late this summer Dr. Roberts unfortunately became very ill and cannot be with us today. Dr. Sollie very graciously agreed to step in for Dr. Roberts even though he is now in The Hague via Tokyo!

The last paper will be delivered by Mr. Curt Epperson on the policy issues raised by proposals to tow icebergs from the Antarctic. Mr. Epperson is a graduate student in the Law and Marine Affairs Program at the School of Law, University of Washington.

THE CONTINENTAL SHELF - ISSUES IN THE "EASTERN" ARCTIC OCEAN. IMPLICATIONS OF UNCLOS III, WITH SPECIAL REFERENCE TO THE INFORMAL COMPOSITE NEGOTIATING TEXT (ICNT)

Willy Østreng
The Fridtjof Nansen Foundation at Polhøgda

At the Ditchley Conference on the Arctic Ocean in May 1971, J. A. Beesley declared that "the term 'Arctic sovereignty'... suffers from an inherent imprecision which has been aggravated by misuse. Indeed, the very term the 'Arctic' is itself used and understood in different ways in different contexts, thus compounding the confusion surrounding the notion of Arctic sovereignty" (Beesley, 1971, p. 1). This is undoubtedly a correct observation, the question of sovereignty in the Arctic Ocean being a very special one, and to some extent incapable of exact definition, owing primarily to the status in international law of the sea ice. Some 80 to 90 percent of the surface of the Arctic Ocean is permanently frozen over and consequently this is the only one of the oceans of the world which in theory can be traversed on foot. The Eskimos use the ice, among other things, as a substratum for moving home, for hunting and trapping, and for transport, while the super powers use it to provide landing strips for aircraft, and as a platform for scientific research. This has resulted in a certain measure of confusion. Should the ice be regarded as "Arctic Ocean water" (which, in fact, is what it is) or as "Arctic Ocean territory" (which is what it is from any practical point of view). The problem of the Arctic Ocean, in terms of international law, has therefore aptly been described as "...the Arctic Ocean has the characteristics of both land and sea, and yet is totally unlike both" (Olenicoff, 1972, p. 2).

Several of the islands in the Arctic Ocean also possess a special status, even though their sovereignty is not subject to any doubt or international disagreement. For long the harsh climate and inhospitable conditions made colonization of the islands in the Arctic Ocean a matter of difficulty, and for this reason the requirement of <u>effective occupation</u> could only partially be satisfied. It was on this basis that Denmark obtained sovereignty over Greenland, thanks to a flexible interpretation of the need for effective occupation, while the disputed sector principle was applied to the islands to the north of the Canadian and Soviet arctic coast. The question of Svalbard's sovereignty was settled on the basis of a treaty.

Soviet international law experts claim that the sector principle, which up till now has been in force for the islands north of the Euro-Asian continent, can also be applied to national acquisition of the rest of the sector, ocean and ice included (Olenicoff, 1972; Pharand, 1973). It is further maintained in Soviet government quarters that the Svalbard regime, as defined in the Svalbard Treaty of February 9, 1920, must be made to apply to adjacent ocean and continental shelf areas. In other words, the prospects envisaged in this connection suggest that the legal principles for governing land areas can be applied in their entirety to ocean and seabed areas. This serves to emphasize further the very special nature of the problem of sovereignty in the Arctic Ocean.

The aim of this paper is to look more closely at this problem in connection with (a) the Norwegian/Soviet negotiations on the boundary between the two countries' continental shelf and fisheries jurisdiction areas in the Barents Sea, and (b) the Norwegian/Soviet dispute as to whether the continental shelf around Svalbard is to be governed in accordance with the international law on continental shelves or in accordance with the provisions of the Svalbard Treaty. Each of these questions will then be considered in the light of developments at UNCLOS III.

Negotiations on Partition of the Continental Shelf in the Barents Sea

The large continental shelf, some 5 million square kilometers in extent, north of the Euro-Asian continent, is to be divided in three places between four of the five arctic nations: in the extreme east between the USA and the Soviet Union, in the Barents Sea between Norway and the Soviet Union, and in the Greenland Sea between Norway and Denmark. As yet, only negotiations between Norway and the Soviet Union have been initiated.

Already in 1967 the Norwegian Government broached the question of a partition of the continental shelf in the Barents Sea with the Soviet Union. These negotiations have continued on and off ever since 1974, although without the prospect of an immediate solution. Both parties to the negotiations have endorsed the 1958 Continental Shelf Convention and both invoke Article 6 as a basis for negotiation. The problem in this connection is that the parties are invoking different sections of Article 6, Norway maintaining that the median line should constitute a point of departure for negotiation, while the Soviet Union favors a dividing line "justified by special circumstances." According to the Soviet Union, the dividing line should coincide with the sector-line; that is to say, it should be drawn along longitude 32°04'35" East. This line was drawn when the Soviet Government in 1956 issued its Sector Decree, which asserts sovereignty over all islands (discovered and undiscovered) between 32°or'35" East and 168°49'30" West (see Figure 1).

FIGURE 1

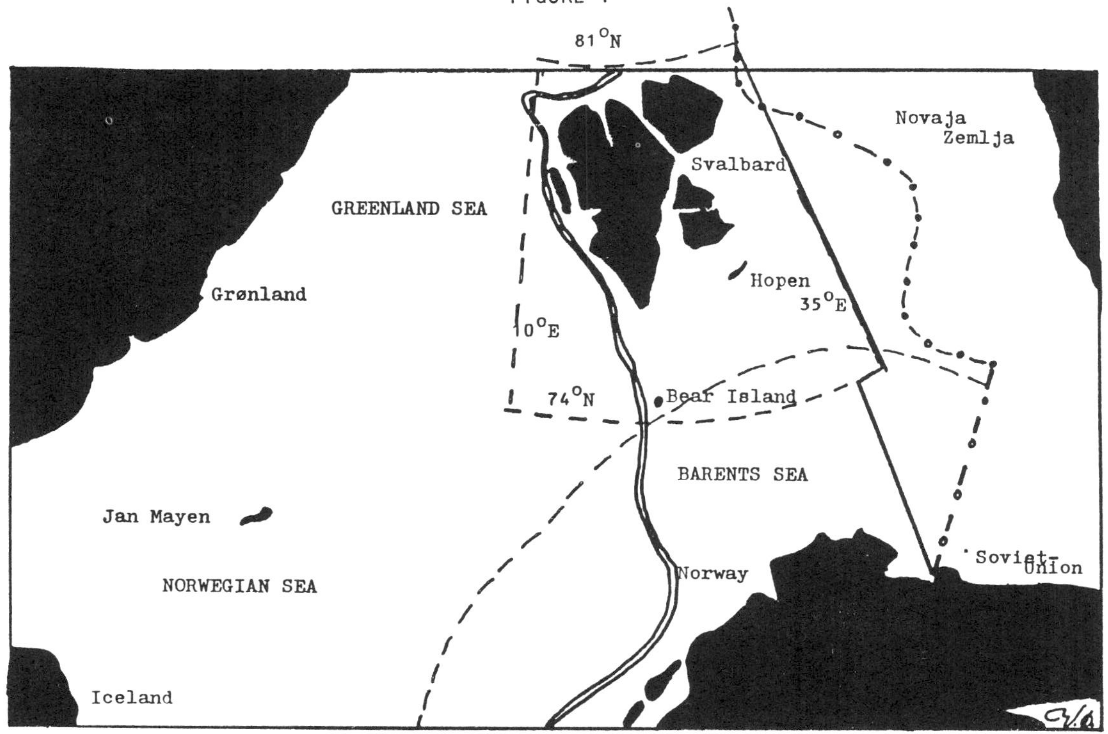

------ 200 n.m economic zone
______ the sector-line
-·-·-· the equidistance-line
▬▬ shelf edge

The ocean between the median line and the sector line covers an area of about 155,000 square kilometers, i.e., an area larger than the Norwegian North Sea continental shelf (approximately 144,000 square kilometers) and somewhat less than one-half of Norway's land area. It comprises rich fishing banks, is a potential source of oilfields, and is situated in the very middle of the strategically important and sensitive Barents Sea.[1] The partition and development of this area is consequently of considerable interest to both parties.

Negotiating Positions

The Soviet Union:

The Soviet Union invokes "special circumstances," in a very wide sense of the word, as the basis for establishing a boundary. The list of circumstances has gradually assumed considerable proportions. Not only does it include the sector claim, but also takes into account economic, demographic, security-political, and other aspects in this region. While the contents of the list have not been published in detail, it is nonetheless sufficiently well known for various interesting features to emerge.

Among other things the Soviets appear to invoke two types of special circumstances. One category comprises what might be called arctic legal arguments, which are based on the physical and climatic peculiarties of the region. The sector claim is one example of this. S. M. Olenicoff (1972) has expressed this as follows: "Because of its inscrutable character, and the fact that until several decades ago it was an unexplored, blank spot on most maps, the first territorial aspirations in the Arctic Ocean took the form of 'sector claims.'"

The other main category of circumstances is what might be called general practical considerations, in the sense that they are not specially characteristic of the Arctic, but may be applied to any region whatsoever. The population density in the area is one example of this.

Even though the Soviet Union bases its claims on two main types of circumstances, the tendency nevertheless appears to be for the Soviets in the course of the negotiations to attribute increasing significance to the sector principle. In view of this development we need to look a little more closely at the

---

[1] For a more thorough discussion of the strategic and economic significance of the Barents Sea area see Kim Traavik & Willy Østreng: Security and ocean law. Norway and the Soviet Union in the Barents Sea. In Ocean Development and International Law Journal, 1977, 4(4), pp. 343-367.

background and contents of the sector claim. When the Soviet Union promulgated its Sector Decree in 1926, the claim to sovereignty only comprised the islands, not the ocean, nor the ice, nor the continental shelf within the sector. Islands already under the sovereignty of other countries, such as Svalbard, were also exempt from the claim. This is still the situation. For this reason the sea and ice areas outside territorial waters must be regarded as open sea.

Leading Soviet experts on international law, such as V. L. Lakhtin, S. A. Bergvinov, E. A. Korovin, S. S. Sigrist, and others, have on the other hand maintained in lengthy theses that grounds exist for extending the sector claim to include (a) the waters between the islands; (b) the waters between the islands and the mainland; (c) the pack-ice and the ice-islands; (d) the remainder of the area within the sector and (e) the airspace over the entire sector (Olenicoff, 1972). S. S. Sigrist has expressed this in the following words: "In the spirit of the 1926 Decree we must maintain that the whole region from the Soviet mainland to the Pole is Soviet possession even if it is just as difficult to go there as to climb the summits of the Caucasian, Ural, Atlantian or other mountains the Soviet ownership of which has never been disputed" (Olenicoff, 1972, p. 9).

These views, many of which were put forward during the Stalin area, represent deeply-held official Soviet policy. Official Soviet maps, in fact, show the sector lines as boundaries for "Soviet arctic areas." In their negotiations with Norway, they have even gone a step further than their own international law experts, by maintaining that the continental shelf to the east of the sector line should also be considered a Soviet possession. In 1977 Deputy Foreign Minister Zemskov declared, according to the Norwegian press, that Norway should not delude herself into believing that the Supreme Soviet would accept a solution in the Barents Sea involving any deviation from the sector line (Klassekampen, 1976).

There are many possible reasons why the Soviet Union would appear to insist uncompromisingly on the sector line. In leading political quarters in Norway it has been flatly stated that the Soviets base their sector claim primarily on arguments involving security.[2] There is no way of knowing whether this is true or not. On the other hand, it is an indisputable fact that the Soviets have very considerable military-strategic interests in the area. The Kola Peninsula, for example, is the

---

[2]One subscriber to this particular point of view is Mr. Nils Utsi, a member of Parliament and a main spokesman of the ruling Labour Party in defense matters. See Dagbladet, December 8, 1976.

home port of <u>the Northern Fleet</u>, without doubt the largest of the four Soviet fleets, with a total of 167 submarines, including 70 percent of the Soviet Union's strategic submarines and all the new and highly advanced Delta-class submarines. The Kola Peninsula, moreover, is the home port of 223 surface vessels, including the anti-submarine aircraft carrier "Kiev" (<u>Military Balance</u>, 1977-78). Clearly, the need to ensure that these naval units enjoy freedom of manoeuvre in the Barents Sea and access to the North Atlantic has a very high priority. For this reason, with the close defense of the Kola base in mind, it would be desirable for the Soviet Union to extend the dividing line as far west into the Barents Sea as possible. In this connection the sector line is probably the westernmost boundary that the Kremlin feels it can reasonably invoke. Additionally, the geological conditions for an oil strike on the continental shelf in the easternmost areas of the Barents Sea appear to be promising. Even though for the moment the Soviet Union is the world's major oil producer, there are reasons to suggest that the Soviets are also interested in these potential resources, in view of the fact that the growth in the Soviet petroleum production has slumped from 16 percent in the first half of the 1960's to 7 percent today. At the same time the consumption of and need for this raw material have increased. For this reason a number of experts are of the opinion that in the 1980's the Soviet Union will have to depend on imports, unless fresh sources are discovered. In this connection, the Barents and Kara Seas have attracted the attention of Soviet geologists. The matter is important because it is assumed that more than half of the Soviet Union's total potential reserves of gas are to be found on this continental shelf, while one of the attractions of the Barents Sea is that the Gulf Stream helps to reduce the problems of freezing up that would be encountered in offshore drilling operations (Johansen, 1977; Kjølberg, 1977). Dividing the continental shelf on the basis of the sector line would consequently leave Norway with the least attractive share.

Norway rejects the sector principle on the grounds that its use is highly controversial in international law. Apart from the Soviet Union, only Canada maintains this principle as the basis for a territorial claim in the Arctic. The USA and Denmark likewise reject the principle. Moreover, according to the official Soviet view, the Sector Degree applies exclusively to islands, not to ocean and continental shelf. The Norwegian view consequently is that it cannot be invoked in this case. Furthermore, Norway maintains that the term "special circumstances," in accordance with the Hague Tribunal, refers to geographical factors, such as the configuration of the coastline, the existence of islands, and so forth. For this reason the economic, demographic, and security-political aspects of the area have no relevance in international law. It is throughout characteristic of the Norwegian approach to these negotiations that it is based on established international law (the Geneva Convention). This implies rejecting a division of the continental shelf in the Barents Sea in accordance with special international law principles. On the other hand, the Norwegian Government has made it clear that it is prepared to arrive at a compromise in these negotiations.

Implications of the ICNT

The belief is widely held that the importance of the median line principle as a boundary criterion has declined in the course of UNCLOS III. Article 83 of ICNT states: "The delimitation of the continental shelf between adjacent...states shall be effected by agreement in accordance with equitable principles, employing, where appropriate, the median or equidistance line, and taking into account all relevant circumstances." The median line principle is here clearly subordinate to equitable principles and to the requirement to pay due regard to all relevant circumstances. It is reasonable to assume that the Soviets should invoke this development and that the Soviet negotiating position has as a result gained in strength vis-a-vis the Norwegian one. It might perhaps be more accurate to say that in the course of negotiations Norway's position vis-a-vis the Soviet Union has been weakened. On the other hand, the median line principle is the only specific criterion mentioned in the ICNT. Norway will consequently still be in a position to invoke the median line as a dividing line, and as a basis for negotiation, without in any way abandoning her position in international law.

Whether this development in the sphere of the law of the sea will exercise any decisive influence on the outcome of the present negotiations is doubtful. The Soviet reluctance to accept the Norwegian standpoint over a period of eleven years would appear to indicate that they are firmly committed to the sector line, no matter what may be laid down in current law of the sea. In this case, national interests and not legal principles appear to constitute the decisive factor. The progress of the Law of the Sea Conference, on the other hand, may serve to safeguard Soviet interests. The equitable principle (Article 83 of ICNT) appears to admit of the possibility that arctic environmental conditions may be taken into consideration in cases where this would be natural. This principle also facilitates an extended interpretation of the term "special circumstances." For this reason developments in the Conference on the Law of the Sea may result in the Soviet Union being still more strongly committed to the sector line.

Article 83 could also make it easier for the Norwegian Government to maintain its willingness to compromise. However, it is hardly likely that the government, in view of Norwegian public opinion and its own established opposition to the sector principle, could accept the sector line as a final dividing line. For this reason in Norway, too, political considerations will have a bearing on the extent to which one is prepared to compromise. In view of this, the result of the negotiations is hardly likely to depend on developments at UNCLOS III, but on the political willingness of the two parties to reach some agreement.

Status of the Continental Shelf Round Svalbard

In international law the continental shelf is regarded as an extension of the land territory of the coastal state. It follows from this that the coastal state also exercises rights on the continental shelf. A state's rights, on the other hand, are not as exclusive on the continental shelf as they are on land territory. In accordance with the Geneva Convention, coastal states exercise supreme rights on exploration of the continental shelf and exploitation of its natural resources. The main principle, in other words, is that the rights of the coastal state on the continental shelf derive from its sovereignty over land territory, but that sovereign rights on the continental shelf differ from those on land.

As far as Svalbard is concerned, however, the question has been raised whether the special status on land incorporated in the treaty provisions should not also be applied uncurtailed to continental shelf areas beyond territorial waters. Or, to put it more concretely, are these shelf areas to enjoy a status in accordance with the provisions of the Geneva Convention or according to the provisions of the Svalbard Treaty of February 9, 1920? The problem in this connection is that international law nowhere states clearly what sovereignty is to apply to sea and continental shelf areas adjacent to land territory subject to special sovereignty. The reason for this is most probably that the question, with the possible exception of the Antarctic,[3] does not arise anywhere else but at Svalbard.

The status of Svalbard is unique and has been defined in the Svalbard Treaty of February 9, 1920. According to Article 1 of this treaty, Norway is granted "full and unrestricted sovereignty" over Svalbard on certain conditions. The Norwegian state, for example, may not exercise sole rights to the economic resources of the islands. These may be exploited by nationals of other signatory states on an equal footing with Norwegians. This obligation to grant equality of treatment applies primarily to fishing, trapping, and all sorts of maritime, mining, industrial, and commercial activity. The treaty also restricts the rights of Norwegian authorities to tax any activity carried out in Svalbard. Tax revenue can only be

---

[3]The shelf problem in Antarctica is well discussed by Kim Traavik: Antarktis og den internasjonale havbunnorganisasjon, in Internasjonal Politikk, No. 4, 1977.

spent in the archipelago; taxes can only be levied to the extent conditions warrant this. In other words, Norway cannot by virtue of her title to sovereignty, supplement the Norwegian state treasury with tax revenue levied in Svalbard and earmark it for use on the Norwegian mainland. The Norwegian state is also obliged to ensure that no naval bases or fortifications are set up in the islands "which may never be used for warlike purposes" (Article 9). Svalbard is, in fact, demilitarized (Østreng, 1978).

In the opinion of Norwegian authorities, these restrictions on sovereignty cannot be given extended interpretation. They are final and apply only to the areas explicitly mentioned in the treaty. This means that Norway has been granted the role of sovereign legislator, administrator, and executor of law and order in all other areas (White Paper No. 39).

The continental shelf and the sea beyond territorial waters are not mentioned in the Svalbard Treaty. The only reference to the sea is to be found in Articles 2 and 3, where territorial waters are mentioned in connection with fishing and maritime interests. In 1971 Norwegian territorial waters around Svalbard were established at four nautical miles, bringing them into line with the rest of the country. In the Norwegian view, restrictions on sovereignty as laid down in the Svalbard Treaty do not consequently apply outside the four-mile limit. In this area the continental shelf is subject to Norwegian sovereignty in accordance with the provisions of the Continental Shelf Convention of 1958. According to this Convention, the coastal state exercises sovereign rights over exploration and exploitation insofar as it is technically possible to exploit natural resources. Exploiting resources at a depth of 500 meters is entirely feasible today; the average depth in the Barents Sea is 229 meters, with maximum depths of about 500 meters. In the Norwegian view this means that Norway has sovereignty over an uninterrupted continental shelf running from the coast of Finnmark to the deep waters of the Arctic Ocean. Nor has this view ever been questioned whether the Svalbard Treaty regime (first and foremost the principle of equality of treatment and the provision on limited right of taxation) should not apply as well to the sea and continental shelf areas around the islands. Norway rejects this view, with reference to her interpretation of the Svalbard Treaty and the Geneva Convention; whereas, the Soviet Union already in 1970 maintained that this was the case. A number of western countries, including the USA and Great Britain, have reserved the right to return to this question.

It is not officially known what legal arguments the Soviets use to controvert the Norwegian view of the continental shelf. For that reason it is impossible here and now to set the respective arguments against one another. Despite this, the contrast between the two views does suggest that the following question of principle still remains unanswered, i.e., are continental shelf areas adjacent to land areas enjoying a special status to be ruled according to other laws and regulations than those presently in operation for continental shelves generally (Geneva Convention)? In principle, three main types of solution present themselves:

1. The regime of the land area can be applied in its entirety to the continental shelf;

2. The existing continental shelf law can be applied;

3. A solution that is midway between 1 and 2 above, involving both current shelf law and portions of the rules applying to the land, can be applied.

Of the above alternatives, Norway has opted for number 2; whereas, it is somewhat uncertain whether the Soviet Union has chosen the first or third alternative. As a matter of principle, the Soviets appear to hold the opinion that the regime on land is also to apply to the continental shelf and the sea. On the other hand, they appear essentially to invoke the treaty provisions on equality of treatment, the right of access, and conditions for taxation, whereas the demilitarization clause is excluded. If, on the other hand, they hold to the first alternative, then this means that this clause, too, may have some bearing on the exploitation of the continental shelf. Even though Article 9 primarily aims to prevent the construction of naval bases and fortifications, it is also stated that the area must not be used "for warlike purposes." There is, however, no doubt that the Soviet Union makes more use of these waters for naval purposes than any other power. It would, therefore, be doubtful whether the Soviet Union would stand to gain if the first alternative were used as a solution.[4] If this argument is correct, it appears that the Soviets apply the third alternative. And yet there is nothing which would initially suggest that Article 9 is less applicable to these waters than, for example, the principle of equal treatment. From this point of view it would be unreasonable to expect that only provisions of benefit to other nationals should apply, while those that involve disadvantages should be excluded. In this connection, the Soviet Union would appear to have some problem in supporting its argument.

---

[4]For a more thorough discussion of this aspect see: Finn Sollie & Willy Østreng: Betydningen av Svalbardtraktatens art. 9 i relasjon til den militær-strategiskr utvikling i Barentshav- Svalbard-området in Internasjonal Pilitikk, No. 4, 1977.

Nor is it by any means certain that the political implications of applying an exclusive part of the Svalbard regime to the continental shelf would serve Soviet interests, since the Soviet view means that companies from a total of 41 signatory states are entitled to the same rights to search for and exploit deposits on the continental shelf in this area. Not only would this mean that the Soviet Union's share of these resources would be a modest one, but free access would make it extremely difficult for Norway to control developments and prevent an "unchecked" race for resources. A free-for-all would create conditions of tension and disorder in an area where both parties would appear to be best served by the preservation of order. This has been pointed out inter alia by Norway's foreign minister, Knut Frydenlund.[5] In view of this, one wonders whether Soviet resistance to the Norwegian attitude to the question of the continental shelf may not be of a tactical nature, based primarily on interest in negotiations on a dividing line. The hypothesis is that the Soviets are anxious to obtain a package deal in which the Soviet Union would waive its resistance to the Norwegian continental shelf view in return for Norway accepting a dividing line closely approximating the sector line.[6] From the Soviet point of view a solution of this kind might have several advantages. In the first place, they would achieve a division of the continental shelf in the Barents Sea closely approximating the one they have worked hard to achieve for eleven years. Secondly, Norway, who for years has demonstrated an understanding of Soviet security interests in the area, would be in a position to supervise any foreign presence on the continental shelf around Svalbard. The Svalbard Treaty allows nationals of signatory states unrestricted access to search for resources. Only by governing this continental shelf in accordance with the provisions of the Geneva Convention will Norway be in a position to limit access and regulate this presence. When all is said and done, an arrangement of this kind would, of necessity, appear more desirable to the Soviet Union than a more or less unregulated western presence in the Soviet's most important naval sphere. The Norwegian authorities have also made it clear that prospecting for oil in northern waters would be subject to stringent state control (Frydenlund, 1977, p. 2).

---

[5]This has been stressed by Foreign Minister Knut Frydenlund on several occasions. See for instance his speech on The Significance of the Northern Area in Norwegian Foreign Policy, in UD-informasjon No. 30, 1977.

[6]This viewpoint has been put forward by the director of the International Office of the Norwegian Labour Union (LO) Kaare Sandegren. See Kaare Sandegren: Om Norges sikkerhet og havrettspolitikken, in Treholt, Dahl, Hysvær, Nes (eds.): Norges Havretts- og resurs-politikk, Oslo 1976, pp. 182-183.

On the other hand, lumping together areas of dispute in this way would mean that the Norwegian government would be obliged to abandon its policy of refusing to accept a package solution to all outstanding issues of dispute between the countries in the North (Sollie, 1976; Østreng, 1977). At the moment there is little to suggest that a reappraisal of this policy is contemplated in Norwegian quarters.

On the other hand, it is by no means certain that the Soviet Union would want a package solution to all outstanding questions. It would be very easy to argue the opposite. As long as the questions at issue remain unsolved, the parties--particularly Norway--whose overriding aim is to preserve tranquility and stability in the area, will need consultations and negotiations in order to avoid any episodes likely to engender tension. This will help to achieve a bilateralization of conditions and of developments, and enable the Soviet Union to exercise some influence on developments on the "Norwegian" side of the Barents Sea as well. Taking the long-term view, the possibility cannot be ruled out that force and not international law will gradually define the boundary lines and control of the continental shelf in the area. A development of this kind will only benefit the stronger party.

It need not necessarily be assumed, of course, that developments in the Barents Sea will benefit only Soviet interests and take place on Soviet terms. The Soviet Union, too, is dependent on reduced tension in the area. One of the reasons for this is the Soviet Union's expressed interest in continued promotion of detente between East and West, as well as its local defense interests. Any escalation of the level of conflict in the region would undoubtedly affect the maintenance of these interests. Unsolved questions of international law could easily provide a basis for conflict and tension. In view of this, it would, therefore, be in the interest of the Soviet Union, on a long-term basis, to exercise restraint and endeavor to arrive at a final solution in the Barents Sea. What assistance can the parties involved expect to get from UNCLOS III?

The Implications of the Development of the Law of the Sea at UNCLOS III

Article 76 of ICNT states that "the continental shelf of a coastal state comprises the sea-bed and subsoil of the submarine areas that extend beyond its territorial sea throughout the natural prolongation of its land territory to the outer edge of the continental margin, or to a distance of 200 nautical miles from the base lines from which the breadth of the territorial sea is measured where the outer edge of the continental margin does not extend up to that distance." Should this proposal be incorporated in a future treaty of the law of the sea, it would support the Norwegian view that Norway exercises sovereignty over an uninterrupted continental shelf stretching from North Norway past Svalbard to the continental margin of the Arctic Ocean. But there is no knowing whether the margin criterion will win the day at the Law of the Sea Conference. Among the inland states, geographically disadvantaged states, and the African countries in particular, considerable resistance to the margin solution has been noted, and a corresponding support for the 200 nautical mile limit. The distance criterion is also supported by the Soviet Union, which favors a 300 nautical mile limit. There is consequently no excluding the possibility that the margin solution, supported inter alia by Norway, will be rejected even though the probability of this happening is slight.

If the extent of the continental shelf in the future is exclusively based on the 200 mile criterion, then this means that the continental shelf, measured from the Norwegian mainland and running north, will not extend as far as Svalbard, which is situated some 355 nautical miles north of North Norway. In that event the Svalbard continental shelf will be measured from the archipelago itself. However, a solution of this kind would, according to the Norwegian authorities, not alter the fact that Norway exercises sovereignty over the continental shelf in accordance with the provisions of the Continental Shelf Convention of 1958. This is because the restrictions on sovereignty embodied in the Svalbard Treaty do not apply to the continental shelf, and because Article 1 of the treaty grants Norway "full and absolute sovereignty" in areas not restricted by the treaty. This means that, according to the Norwegian view, the result of the Law of the Sea Conference will not affect the substance of Norwegian authority over the continental shelf around Svalbard, but only the manner in which Norway acquires it.

No matter what criterion UNCLOS finally chooses for defining the limits of the continental shelf, this choice will have no decisive bearing on the question of the sort of regime that is to apply to the continental shelf areas abutting territory enjoying a special status. This question cannot be solved unless it is explicitly made the subject of negotiation.

Since the Svalbard Treaty itself lays down no procedure far apart from UNCLOS for the solution of disputed interpretations, three alternative solutions are in principle available: (1) the parties involved would submit the question for arbitration to the International Tribunal at The Hague; (2) a special Svalbard conference would be convened between the states which have adhered to the Svalbard Treaty; or (3) political settlements between the parties would be reached.

If The Hague alternative is to provide a solution, this presupposes that Norway and the Soviet Union agree to submit the matter to the tribunal and that both are prepared to accept its recommendations. The Soviet Union, generally speaking, is skeptical of The Hague Tribunal as an organ capable of solving international conflicts. Besides, in view of the Soviet possibility of bilateralizing the situation in the area, it is doubtful whether they would be prepared to entrust the initiative and the solution to an outside organ. Its findings might run counter to Soviet interests, and for this reason, on a short-term basis, it is hardly feasible to assume that the Hague Tribunal presents any feasible alternative.

Convening a Svalbard conference would also be tantamount to entrusting the initiative to an outside organ. This would, therefore, be subject to the same objections as could be raised against The Hague alternative. But there are other problems, too, involved in a Svalbard conference. It is, for example, inconceivable that a conference of this kind would be able to contribute to any solution, unless this had the support and approval of the Soviet Union. Solutions unfavorable to the parties most closely concerned in the area would in themselves create tension and promote conflict. This is also true of relations to Norway, whose principal aim in the area is to contribute to preservation of stability and tranquility. Norway faces the additional uncertainty of whether her western allies would support her interpretation of the continental shelf. In this event, their reservation could naturally find expression in a policy counter to Norwegian interests. Furthermore, it may be doubted whether a conference of these dimensions (so far forty-one states have adhered to the Svalbard Treaty) would be a suitable forum for solving a problem as complex as this. The experience provided by conference diplomacy of this kind in the 1970's, including UNCLOS, makes this highly unlikely. In the light of this, it is hardly probable that Norway and the Soviet Union would consider it in their interests to convoke a new Svalbard conference.

The remaining alternative--a political solution arrived at between the two countries--is the one which at the moment appears most likely. This is, furthermore, an alternative which the Soviets would appear to prefer, and which provides a basis for a bilateralization of the question. There are grounds for assuming that the Norwegian authorities are on their guard against undue bilateralization in the area. In Svalbard Soviet attempts of this nature have been categorically rejected. Nonetheless, at the moment it would seem that consultations and negotiations, aimed at arriving at a solution, would appear most probable. The problem, however, is undoubtedly a complicated one. Foreign Minister Knut Frydenlund has repeatedly emphasized that Norway's "...freedom of action in the East depends on her links with the West" (Frydenlund, 1977, p. 2). In order to secure this freedom of action it is in Norway's interest to ensure that any Norwegian-Soviet solutions do not conflict with the interests of western countries in the region.

When all is said and done, several western countries have expressed reluctance to accept the Norwegian continental shelf view. Furthermore, contacts with western powers help to give credibility to the Norwegian handling of this question in the eyes of the Soviet Union. In this way, considerations for the West constitute both a precondition for, and a complicating factor in, the endeavors to arrive at a settlement between Norway and the Soviet Union. This is clearly one of the reasons why Norway has consulted the USA and Great Britain on the subject of the northern regions on several occasions subsequent to 1975.

Several of the objections raised against the above-mentioned alternatives could also apply to UNCLOS. Furthermore, it might be pointed out that the purpose of the Conference on the Law of the Sea is to develop a new system of laws governing the sea, and not to solve specific problems connected therewith. On the other hand, it might be argued that a solution in the Svalbard case might also have some bearing on future regulation of the continental shelf around the Antarctic. But even this argument is not necessarily airtight. The question of the continental shelf around the Antarctic, for example, can be referred to the Consultative Meetings in connection with the Antarctic Treaty of 1959, in which case the question of the status of the continental shelf around Svalbard would once again be so special that it would be more difficult to include it on the agenda for UNCLOS.

My purpose in presenting these observations is to shed some light on a number of the problems that must be faced in finding a solution to unique problems of the law of the sea. It still remains to be seen whether any attempt will be made to utilize the fora I have mentioned, and whether they can produce any results. No matter what alternative is chosen, problems are bound to arise.

The Basic Problem in Resume and Perspective

The questions of the status of the continental shelf around Svalbard and of the division of the continental shelf in the Barents Sea affect in varying degrees the same basic problem of international law, viz., to what extent legal principles governing land territory (in this connection, the sector principle and the Svalbard Treaty) can be applied to seabed areas? For the moment, no clarification of this question exists in principle. However, what is so striking is the dissimilarity and not the similarity of the two problem areas. While the sector principle is in dispute, the Svalbard Treaty is an integral part of established international law. The importance of the basic problem to a solution of the two questions is also different. As far as the continental shelf around Svalbard is concerned, the basic problem is the only problem; whereas in negotiations on a dividing line, it constitutes only a limited part.

In invoking the sector principle in their negotiations with Norway, the Soviets are implicitly invoking the very special physical and climatic features of the region as a legal argument. The underlying problem in this connection is that adjustments carried out on the basis of international law in ice covered seas often demand solutions that reflect the physical peculiarities of the area. Rules of law applied to ice-free sea will not always prove practicable or possible in the Arctic Ocean. Recognition of this fact was, for example, to some extent responsible for the adoption by the Canadian Government in 1970 of their Arctic Waters Pollution Prevention Act, which provided the warranty for establishment of a special environmental protection zone of 100 nautical miles north of the Canadian Arctic. The demand for protection of the vulnerable ecological system in the north was also one of the motives for the introduction by the Soviet Union in the early 1970's of special rules for the prevention of pollution in their Arctic areas.

Acceptance of this, on the other hand, does not mean that any general standard of law of the sea is automatically unsuitable in this region. Several of the arctic states, including the Soviet Union, have established 200 mile fishing zones in the Arctic Ocean, citing general practice as their justification. From this point of view the main problem consists of deciding what conditions must be present in order to be able to invoke the application of special law of the sea solutions adapted to the physical conditions of the Arctic Ocean, and which of these would have to be present for the application of existing law of the sea.

This question poses special problems in those parts of the Arctic Ocean which may be said to combine the peculiarities of ice covered and ice free sea. The Barents Sea is a region of this kind. Thanks to the Gulf Stream large areas of the Barents Sea are free from ice and navigable year round. Most of the surface of the sea, on the other hand, is covered by ice. In years of particularly bad icing conditions the belt of drift ice may extend as far south as Bear Island, covering practically 70 percent of the surface. In this connection, we should do well to remember Beesley's statement: "The very term 'Arctic' is itself used and understood in different ways in different contexts, thus compounding the confusion surrounding the notion of arctic sovereignty." The Soviet Union itself appears to recognize the semi-arctic status of the Barents Sea by citing general practical considerations to support its claim, to draw the dividing line along the sector line.

Arctic legal arguments, on the other hand, are not explicitly invoked when the Soviet Union disputes the Norwegian continental shelf view, maintaining that the status of Svalbard (the Svalbard regime) cannot be applied totally to the continental shelf around the islands. The basic problem in this connection is that no clear answer exists to the question of whether continental shelf areas adjacent to uniquely regulated land areas are to be subject to the same rules and regulations as terra firma. No land areas in the world are administered in the same way as Svalbard, for which reason the problem may appear to be of limited interest. On the other hand, the relevance of this problem to the Antarctic cannot be dismissed offhandedly.

The problems posed in this paper are regional in their nature. This does not mean that a solution might not have political interest and spinoffs beyond the region itself. The continued development in a military-strategic and politically sensitive area such as the Barents Sea may be of considerable significance to East-West relations. For this reason several states may be interested in a solution of the problems at issue between Norway and the Soviet Union in this area. To the extent that the parties concerned live up to their declared aim to promote continued detente between the blocs, they will also have to show proper restraint and compliance in solving outstanding problems. If this were done, various negotiating fora from binational to global may prove practical, even though we should bear in mind that all of these are beset with certain weaknesses qua adjudicating bodies, UNCLOS included.

REFERENCES

Beesley, J. A. Rights and responsibilities of Arctic coastal states: the Canadian view. Speech at the Ditchley Conference on the Arctic Ocean, May 1971, p. 1.

Frydenlund, Knut. The significance of the Northern Area in Norwegian Foreign Policy. UD-informasjon No. 30, 1977.

Johansen, Jahn Otto. Sovjetisk olje- og gass-politikk. Internasjonal Politikk, 1977, 2.

Kjølberg, Anders. Oljen i Arktis, Muligheter, Problemer og utfordringer. Internasjonal Politikk, 1977, 4.

Klassekampen, September 10, 1976.

Military Balance 1977-78, Norwegian edition. Norwegian Atlantic Committee. pp. 78-82.

Olenicoff, S. M. Territorial waters in the Arctic: the Soviet position. R-907-ARPA, July 1972, Santa Monica, p. 2.

Østreng, Willy. Politics in High Latitudes. The Svalbard Archipelago. London: Ch. Hurst & Co., 1978.

Pharand, Donat. The Law of the Sea of the Arctic, with Special Reference to Canada. Ottawa. 1973.

White Paper No. 39, 1974-75, concerning Svalbard.

THE IMPLICATIONS OF CHANGES IN THE LAW OF THE SEA FOR THE 'NORTH AMERICAN' ARCTIC OCEAN

Donat Pharand
University of Ottawa
Canada

1. Continental Shelf and Economic Zone

Under this first heading, I shall address myself to both the lateral delimitation as well as the seaward limit of the continental shelf and the economic zone.

(a) Lateral Delimitation

Starting at the boundary between Alaska and the Yukon, the question arises as to whether the equidistance line will be considered appropriate and equitable, in spite of certain circumstances which might be considered "special" or, at least, "relevant." These circumstances might be the concavity of the Yukon coast, the use of the 141st meridian in the 1867 cession treaty from Russia to the United States to establish the eastern boundary of Alaska, and Canada's subsequent use of that meridian.

Because of the concavity of the Yukon coast and the slight convexity of the Alaskan coast, the equidistance line is pulled toward the east appreciably, thus resulting in a more favorable delimitation of the shelf for the United States. On the basis of the North Sea Case of 1969, as well as the Arbitration Case between France and the United Kingdom in the English Channel of 1977 where geography was held to be more important than geology, Canada might argue for a modification of the equidistance line.

Canada could conceivably rely on the 1867 treaty, which incorporated the description of the eastern boundary of Alaska found in the 1825 treaty between Great Britain and Russia. The boundary was there described as following the 141st meridian in its prolongation up to the Frozen Ocean. A study of those two treaties reveals, however, that it could hardly have been the intention of the parties to extend the boundary beyond the coast. It is evident that meridians were used as convenient geographical limits to demarcate the land possessions being dealt with, and there is no indication that the parties contemplated any part of the Arctic Ocean or the continental shelf to be included. In my opinion, it could not be used as a possible legal basis for the sector theory, as was advanced by the Soviet jurist Lakhtine in the 1930's.

In spite of the above, it might be possible for Canada to argue that it has used the 141st meridian to such an extent and for a number of external purposes that such use should be taken into account as a "special" or, at least, as a "relevant" circumstance, in the determination of the lateral delimitation of the continental shelf. In particular, Canada can point to the fact that it has used that line for the issuance of oil and gas permits since 1965 and for the definition of "Arctic waters" in its Arctic anti-pollution legislation of 1970. That same definition was then incorporated in the Ocean Dumping Control Act of 1975. More recently, in 1977, Canada established an exclusive fishing zone of 200 miles in the Arctic and again used the 141st meridian to define the zone.

As for the delimitation of the continental shelf and economic zone in the Bering Sea between the United States and the Soviet Union, the 1825 treaty can hardly be invoked to use the 168th meridian (more precisely the meridian 168° 49' 30" of longitude used by the Soviet Union in its 1926 decree to claim the islands north of its coast) for the same reason already mentioned with respect to the 1867 treaty, namely that parties could not have had in mind anything else but land possessions since the concept of the continental shelf was still unknown.

As for the continental shelf delimitation between Franz Josef Land of the Soviet Union and Svalbard of Norway, you have heard a full treatment of that question by Willy Østreng and, as you have learned, the question is not yet settled. On this side of Svalbard, I do not know whether Norway and Denmark have started negotiations for the delimitation of the shelf between Greenland and Svalbard. In the Lincoln Sea, the delimitation of the continental shelf between Greenland and Ellesmere Island has not yet been completed. I believe that talks have been held between Denmark and Canada and, presumably, the equidistance line will be the general basis of delimitation.

(b) Seaward Limit

The second aspect of the question of delimitation relates to the seaward limit of the continental shelf in the Arctic Basin. If you were to take 200 miles as being the limit, it would not quite cover all of the continental shelf. But, if you use a 300 mile limit, which the Soviet Union is apparently proposing at the Law of the Sea Conference, it would give the Soviet Union all of its continental shelf and, for that matter, the same result would obtain for the other Arctic states as well. In any event, regardless of the extent of the seaward limit, there will be something left in the middle as an international area.

2. Legal Regime of the International Area

The question now arises as to what is going to happen to the resources, if any, to be found in this international area. There are no manganese nodules there, but we have heard yesterday that you have other resources to be found in the water column of the oceans. However, as I understood, those resources are not worth very much presently or in the foreseeable future. In any case, they would not be commercially significant. Nevertheless, there is a question as to the geological nature of the Lomonosov Ridge, which might be a split off the outer edge of the continental shelf to the east and is within the international area. It has not been determined with certainty, however, if this is in fact a shelf fragment and, during my visit to the Soviet Union a couple of years ago, I tried to obtain more information on that, since the Soviet Union has done a lot of scientific research in the Arctic Basin, but without success. If this undersea mountain or ridge, cutting across the Arctic Basin, is in fact a fragment of the shelf, then there might be a chance of a certain oil and gas potential. Should there be, in fact, commercially exploitable resources in this central area of the Arctic Basin, the further question arises as to whether the International Authority, evisaged by the Law of the Sea Conference, would have jurisdiction over that international area as it would in any other ocean. The Arctic Ocean being a comparatively small one and virtually enclosed by the territory of the five Arctic states, including the two super powers, the closest cooperation of those bordering states would be necessary for the Authority to function effectively. In such an event, it might be found advisable to have a regional arrangement between the International Authority and the five Arctic states which would provide for a delegation of powers to those states to exploit the international area on behalf of the Authority.

3. Protection of the Marine Environment

It has been felt for some time by Arctic states, particularly Canada, that special preventive measures must be taken to protect the marine environment of the Arctic against damage from oil spills arising from navigation or exploitation. Although oil would not disintegrate easily in those frozen waters, cleaning-up operations would be nearly impossible since oil has a tendency to make its way under the ice. In addition, because of the two major current movements in the Arctic Ocean, an oil slick would spread to great distances and, in all likelihood, would affect most, if not all, of the bordering states. In these circumstances, Canada adopted special anti-pollution legislation in 1970, the Arctic Waters Pollution Prevention Act, enabling it to take certain protective measures up to 100 miles from its coast, in the event of a situation threatening its marine environment. Since then, a special provision

(Article 235) has been inserted in the ICNT, produced by the Law of the Sea Conference, entitled "ice-covered areas." This applies to the Arctic environment, although the Arctic is not specifically mentioned. It enables coastal states to not only establish but also enforce laws and regulations for the prevention, reduction and control of pollution from vessels in ice-covered areas within the 200 miles of their exclusive economic zone.

The question might well be asked if this provision could be used as a starting point for the development of a special legal regime for the protection of the Arctic environment. Such a regime could be agreed upon by special regional agreement among the Arctic states, and could find its legal basis not only in Article 235 already mentioned but also in another provision of the ICNT applicable to semi-enclosed seas. Indeed Article 123 provides that states bordering enclosed or semi-enclosed seas should cooperate with one another to coordinate their activities with respect to the living resources of the sea, scientific research and the preservation of the marine environment. Through such an agreement, it would be possible to establish a special legal regime for the protection of this specially delicate and fragile marine environment, and this would be done within the general framework of the new Law of the Sea Convention.

4. Legal Status of the Arctic Ocean

It has been asked occasionally whether the general principle of the freedom of the seas is applicable to the Arctic Ocean. The main reason for the question is the fact that the greater part of that ocean is covered with ice throughout the year and, consequently, surface navigation is restricted and sometimes impossible. However, the Arctic states, particularly the Soviet Union, have developed a considerable capability of navigation and it would seem that as the need arises the development increases. The Soviet Union is using the Northern Sea Route quite regularly, for at least three or four months a year, and it has recently extended its shipping operations in the western sector of the Sea Route to some eight or nine months. It now has three nuclear-powered icebreakers and, in August 1977, the *Arktika* became the first surface vessel to reach the North Pole, slashing its way through the ice without too much difficulty.

In addition to this limited possibility of surface navigation, one must not forget that the presence of ice does not interfere with sub-surface navigation. We know that, in the late 1950's and early 60's, the United States made a number of experimental submarine crossings. One can surmise that there is the odd submarine making the occasional crossing today. It is not impossible, for instance, to think that a submarine might come from the other side of the Arctic Ocean, down through Lincoln Sea and Robeson Channel between Greenland and Ellesmere Island. A submarine could conceivably, although not likely, come within the Canadian Arctic Archipelago.

Having regard to this possibility of navigation, I am inclined to the view that the general principle of the freedom of the seas ought to apply to the Arctic Ocean, at least to the extent that such application is possible. This, of course, is my own personal view, as a free academic, and does not necessarily coincide with the view of the Canadian government.

5. Scientific Research from Ice Islands

Another freedom of the seas which has been exercised to a considerable extent in the Arctic, for the last thirty years or so, is scientific research. This has been done on huge fragments of ice shelves which have detached themselves from Ellesmere Island and have been used as floating research stations, both by the United States and the Soviet Union. The United States has used only five or six so far, Ice Island T-3 having been operated for the longest period of time. You might recall the Escamilla Case, arising out of a shooting incident which took place on that ice island in July 1970, when it was located at approximately 185 miles north of the Canadian Arctic Archipelago and which raised a slight question of jurisdiction. As for the Soviet Union, it has been maintaining two or three drifting stations in the Arctic Ocean every year since the early 1950's and it presently has three of them in operation, the last one being NP-24.

The drift of those ice islands depends mainly on the current and the general movement of ice flows in the Arctic Ocean. There are two major drifts, one in the western sector which follows a clockwise movement, and the other, a transpolar drift which crosses the Arctic Ocean in an easterly direction and terminates in the Greenland Sea. As you can readily see from the map accompanying an article published by Professor Treshnikov in 1977 (Map No. 1), the Soviet Union has covered most of the Arctic Ocean in its scientific research operations. You will note in particular that those drifting stations pay no attention to any sector theory or limits of national jurisdiction. For instance, in 1959, NP-7 headed south through Robeson Channel and, in April 1961, was spotted by an RCAF plane off the east coast of Baffin Island. Naturally, the ice island was no longer inhabited but there were still three weather buildings on it. In 1977, NP-22 drifted considerably within the 200-mile zone, off the Canadian Arctic Archipelago, and questions were asked in the House of Commons as to the presence of the research station of the Soviet Union in that zone.

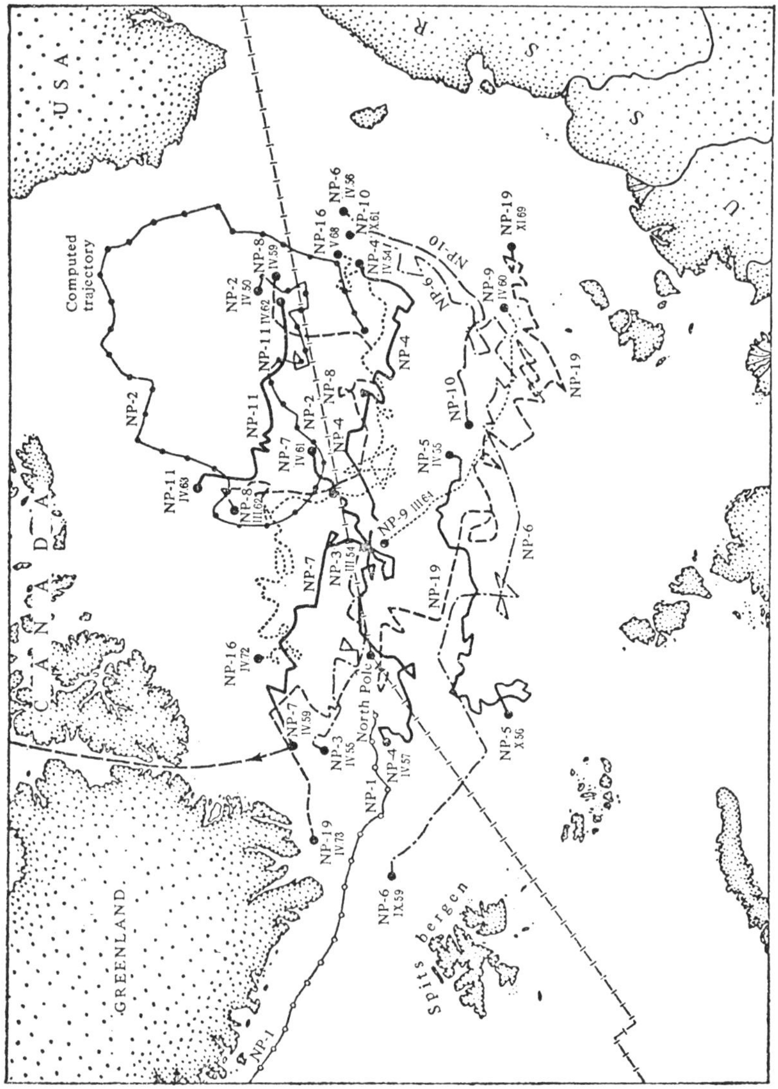

Drift of some North Pole scientific research stations over the period 1937–73.

MAP NO. 1

Soviet Ice Islands in the Arctic Ocean

Treshnikov, A.F., et al. Results of Oceanological Investigations by the North Pole Drifting Stations. Polar Geography, 1977, 1, p. 37.

Indeed, the question does arise as to what jurisdiction, if any, the coastal state may exercise over the activities being performed on those ice islands when they come within its exclusive economic zone and exclusive fishing zone or in the waters above its continental shelf. It seems to me that the provisions of the 1958 Continental Shelf Convention would apply, as well as the relevant provisions of the ICNT, if and when the latter comes into force. In addition, insofar as Canada and the Soviet Union are concerned, there is a General Exchanges Agreement which provides for the cooperation between the two states in the scientific, technical, cultural and related fields and, more significantly, envisions the exchange of scientific information. It would seem, therefore, that Canada might be able to use this additional legal basis to exercise some form of supervision over the activities being carried out in the waters adjacent to its Arctic coast.

6. Waters of the Canadian Arctic Archipelago

The reason for mentioning this question is that the Canadian Arctic Archipelago does not seem to fit well in the two categories of archipelagos provided for in the ICNT. On the one hand, it is not quite a fringe of islands along a coast, in the sense of the Anglo-Norwegian Fisheries Case of 1951 and now embodied in the 1958 Territorial Sea Convention and in the ICNT. On the other hand, it does not form an Archipelagic state, as envisaged by the ICNT and as in the case of Indonesia and the Philippines. In other words, it is neither a coastal archipelago, in the sense of a fringe of islands along a coast, nor an oceanic or out-lying archipelago as envisaged by the ICNT. It might be more accurately described as an off-lying archipelago, in that it lies off the northern coast of Canada and is a projection of that coast.

Canada has not yet drawn straight baselines around this archipelago for the purpose of delimiting its territorial waters. This does not mean, of course, that the waters within the archipelago are not already Canadian internal waters, since Canada might well be in a position to make proof of an historic title to those waters. If this is the case, then there is no reason why Canada could not simply draw straight baselines around the archipelago, since this would not have the effect of changing the legal status of the waters. If those waters are not internal waters already, a question then does arise and it affects the status of the Northwest Passage.

7. The Northwest Passage

You will note on Map No. 2 that there are four main routes through the Northwest Passage, joining Baffin Bay with the Beaufort Sea. We are concerned here with the two northernmost routes, one following Parry Channel as far as Banks Island,

MAP NO. 2

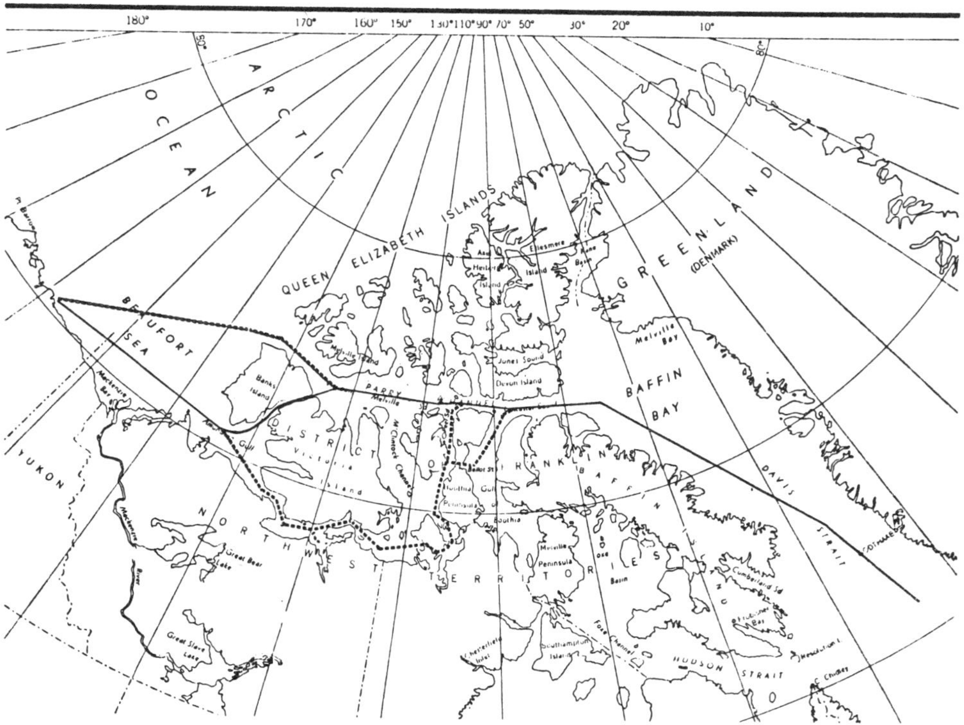

MAIN ROUTES OF THE NORTHWEST PASSAGE

crossing Lancaster Sound, Barrow Strait, Viscount Melville Sound and Prince of Wales Strait on the east side of Banks Island. The other route follows the Parry Channel throughout, including M'Clure Strait. This is the route which the _Manhattan_ attempted to follow in 1969 but, as you know, it had to turn back half way in M'Clure Strait because of the presence of polar ice, in spite of the help of the Canadian icebreaker _Macdonald_, and go through the narrow Prince of Wales Strait instead. This meant that the _Manhattan_ had to traverse Canadian territorial waters, even if Canada still claimed only three miles and presuming that those waters were not historic internal waters. As you know, Canada extended its territorial waters from three to twelve miles the following year, so that any foreign ship would have to go through waters whose legal status would be at least territorial, if not internal, between Lowther and Young Islands in Barrow Strait where the passage is only fifteen miles in width. On the other side of the pole, in the Northeast Passage, the situation is roughly the same, in that the Northern Sea Route includes the Vilkitsky Straits, both of which are less than twenty-four miles in width, one being twenty-two and one half and the other eleven miles wide.

The question now arises whether the Northwest Passage and the Northern Sea Route are affected by the ICNT provisions relating to international straits. So far, both of those passages have been used strictly for national or exploratory purposes. More specifically, there has never been any international commercial navigation on either side of the pole. However, with the exploitation of natural resources in the Arctic regions being envisaged, it is quite possible that both of those sea routes, in particular the Northwest Passage, might be used in future for international navigation. If so, the question of the exact legal status of this passage might arise. Unfortunately, the provisions of the ICNT are not more helpful than those of the 1958 Territorial Sea Convention, in that they do not give any definition of an international strait. In other words, we do not know the exact nature and degree of use required before a strait becomes one "used for international navigation."

Presumably, of course, what is envisioned is commercial navigation in the ordinary sense and would not include submarine navigation, so that Canada, for instance, would not wake up one of these mornings and be told that, although unknown to it, its Northwest Passage had been used for submarine navigation for a number of years and, therefore, had become international in nature. The only precedent which exists so far to help us define an international strait is the _Corfu Channel Case_ of 1949. In that case, the International Court of Justice took into account the fact that close to 3,000 ships of seven different nationalities had put in at the Port of Corfu over a period of twenty-one months. It concluded that the Corfu

Channel was a strait used for international navigation. More specifically, the Court stated that, although the volume of traffic was not the sole test, it was still necessary to show that the strait in question had been "a useful route for international maritime traffic."

If a similar question were to arise with respect to either the Northwest Passage or the Northern Sea Route, naturally one would have to take into account that those straits lie in more remote and less accessible regions than the Corfu Channel, in determining their legal status.

TRENDS AND PROSPECTS FOR REGIMES FOR LIVING AND MINERAL RESOURCES IN THE ANTARCTIC

Finn Sollie
Fridtjof Nansen Foundation
Norway

In moving the discussion to the problems of the Antarctic, one finds a situation that is literally poles apart from that of the Arctic. Over and beyond the geographical differences, which are fundamental, the legal and political circumstances of the Antarctic are entirely different from conditions in the northern polar region. Furthermore, the Antarctic Treaty provides a very special legal-political framework for the management and solution of the problems of the southern polar region.

In the following, I shall run quickly through some of the main issues in the development of the Antarctic Treaty system and point to some of its main principles and achievements. Next, I shall say a few words about potential resources in Antarctica and their possible exploitation before indicating steps that have been taken to assess the need for and need to work toward establishing a regime for the exploration and potential exploitation of mineral resources and for the marine living resources of the Antarctic region. In this context I shall try also to evaluate the prospects for the future development.

The Antarctic Treaty is an international agreement of fairly long standing that was concluded in 1959.[1] The need for a special treaty for the Antarctic arose from the uncertain legal

---

[1]On May 2, 1958, the United States invited the governments of Argentina, Australia, Belgium, Chile, France, Japan, New Zealand, Norway, South Africa, the Soviet Union and the United Kingdom to participate in a conference to negotiate "a treaty which would have the following peaceful purposes:

A. Freedom of scientific investigation throughout Antarctica by citizens, organizations, and governments of all countries; and a continuation of the international scientific cooperation which is being carried out so successfully during the current International Geophysical Year.
B. International agreement to ensure that Antarctica be used for peaceful purposes only.
C. Any other peaceful purposes not inconsistent with the Charter of the United Nations."

Participation was limited to states which had active scientific

status of Antarctica. During the first half of the century a number of states, seven in all, had claimed sovereign territorial rights on the Antarctic Continent.[2] The claims, however, have not been generally recognized internationally and consequently have an uncertain standing. It is particularly important that the claims were not accepted by the United States, which had long played an important role in Antarctic activities. Nor have the claims been recognized by the Soviet Union. Significantly, the Soviet Union and the United States are responsible for the larger part by far of scientific activities and operations in Antarctica.

A basic reason for national claims to jurisdiction over Antarctic territories was the wish to secure control of known and potential natural resources. It was a question of control of the coastline and of the islands beyond which Antarctic whaling and, before that, sealing had developed.[3] The first claim, which was made by the United Kingdom, was made shortly after the full development of modern Antarctic whaling had begun. All together, some 80% of the Antarctic continent had been claimed before the Second World War, that is, during the heyday of Antarctic whaling. Three claims overlap; two of these were made during the Second World War. Those were the claims made by Chile and Argentina, which overlap in part both with each other and with the previous claim made by the United Kingdom and known as the Falkland sector. The United States, which before and after the war had definitely conducted the most extensive scientific exploration of Antarctica, has not formally claimed any part of the Antarctica continent. However,

---

programs in Antarctica during the International Geophysical Year (1957-58). After an intensive series of preparatory meetings in 1958-59, the Antarctic Conference convened in Washington on October 15, 1959. Negotiations were completed and the Treaty signed on December 1, 1959.

[2]Claims have been made by the United Kingdom (1908), New Zealand (1923), France (1924), Australia (1933), Norway (1939), Chile (1940) and Argentina (1942).

[3]Early problems began in 1904, when a Norwegian whaler operating under Argentine registry established a whaling station at South Georgia and a British naval vessel forced him to lower the flag of registry which he had put up at the station. In 1906, the British Government promulgated "The Whale Fishery Ordinance for the Falkland Islands" and in 1908, the British claim was formalized and extended to include all islands and lands south of 50°S, between 20°W and 80°W. The claim originally included even the tip of South America and in 1917 was adjusted in response to protests from Chile and Argentina.

several hundred notes of a private nature claiming territory for the United States were dropped in Antarctica in 1939.[4]

One may, of course, wonder why the United States did not formally claim territory in Antarctica. Both principle[5] and political expediency would appear to be involved. The United States obviously would not be willing to fully recognize the claims made by other states and by making a claim of its own the United States would in fact have recognized the right of other states to claim territory on the southern continent.[6] By making a claim of its own a state will in fact accept the very principle of claimability; a national claim to one part implies a recognition of the right of other states to claim other parts. That again implies an exclusion of national pretentions in those other parts where other states may be sovereign. Thus a claim for less than the whole continent does have the disadvantage of limiting the area of operations. Furthermore, if new claims were to be made at a late stage, the result would be conflict with prior claimants of the same territory. I think that a similar line of reasoning may explain why the Soviet Union has not claimed territory in Antarctica.

To get away from, or rather to get around the problem of national territories in Antarctica, the United States in 1948 suggested to the seven claimant states that a joint solution in the form of a multiple condominium should be formed for Antarctica. Under that proposal the United States together with the seven claimants should have responsibility for the region and establish a joint commission for control of Antarctica and

---

[4]On his third expedition to Antarctica (1939-41) Richard Byrd acting on the basis of an understanding with President Roosevelt, left claim notes to secure a potential future claim by the U.S. government.

[5]In 1924 the U.S. position was stated by the Secretary of State, Charles Evans Hughes: "It is the opinion of this department that the discovery of lands unknown to civilization, even when coupled with the formal taking of possession, does not support a valid claim of sovereignty unless the discovery is followed by actual settlement of the discovered country."

[6]Because of the early U.S. opinion that actual settlement was the only valid base for a claim, other states could claim the best part of Antarctica before the U.S. policy could be reconsidered. Thus, if the U.S. were to revert to a claims policy, the claim must either be limited to the relatively small and unattractive sector that was left, or a claim must be made for territory already claimed by others - primarily by Great Britain and Commonwealth nations (Australia and New Zealand). Neither alternative would appear to be attractive to the U.S.

regulation of operations and activities there. However, the seven claimant states rejected the principle of condominium. Another result of the U.S. proposal was a protest from the Soviet Union, pointing out that the Soviet Union would not accept or recognize any decision on a future regime for Antarctica made without its participation.

Nevertheless, where political initiative failed, scientific cooperation succeeded. In preparation for the International Geophysical Year (1957-58) an informal agreement was reached between the scientists of several nations to the effect that in making use of free access to and freedom of scientific research in Antarctica, their activities should not in any way affect claims made by states for territorial rights or the attitude of any state to these claims. In other words, it should be possible to carry out scientific research on the Antarctic Continent and on the ice shelves without any hindrance and with no prejudice to claims made or to positions in regard to these claims. Subsequently, this was to be one of the main principles that nothing in the Treaty nor activities while the Treaty is in force shall prejudice previously asserted claims or the position of states with regard to those claims. Also, no new claims can be made while the Treaty is in force.

The Treaty, as I have said, was completed in 1959. It embodies a series of basic principles that make it a unique instrument for international cooperation. Principle number one is that Antarctica should be used for peaceful purposes only. In this connection, measures of a military nature, including fortifications and military bases, are prohibited. Moreover, the Antarctic Treaty explicitly prohibits nuclear explosions and thus stands as the first international test ban agreement. In this connection the Treaty also established free and full rights of inspection.[7] As a second principle, it is laid down that there should be freedom of scientific investigation and that international cooperation toward that end shall continue along the lines established during the International Geophysical Year. That included the continued operation of SCAR, the Scientific Committee on Antarctic Research, which had been established in connection with the IGY program. SCAR, a scientific and non-governmental group, has retained its role as a cooperative and coordinating international agency for scientific operations in Antarctica. It cooperates informally but closely

[7]Under the Treaty's inspection clause (Article VII), each Consultative Party to the Treaty is entitled to inspect "all areas of Antarctica, including all stations, installations and equipment within those areas, and all ships and aircrafts at points of discharging or embarking cargoes and personnel in Antarctica..."

with the Antarctic Treaty nations through national Antarctic committees in the respective countries.[8]

Furthermore, it was established in the Treaty that there should be free exchange, indeed obligatory exchange, of information about the plans for, and the results of the scientific programs and operations in Antarctica.[9] Under the system, there is complete freedom of access for scientific research in Antarctica. Also, under the Treaty "every encouragement shall be given to the establishment of cooperative working relations" with other international organizations and agencies with a scientific or technical interest in Antarctica. Close relations have been established with several of the U.N. family of agencies, such as WMO, the World Meteorological Organization.

Most importantly, under the Treaty an apparatus for follow up of the principles of the Treaty was established in the so-called consultative meetings. In other words, in the Antarctic system there is not only a Treaty regulating or setting principles for certain kinds of activity, but also an established machinery in the form of regular meetings between the parties[10]

---

[8] Because SCAR is a scientific and non-governmental body, only scientific criteria will qualify for participation in SCAR. There is no requirement that the host or home country be a party to the Antarctic Treaty nor indeed does partnership in the Treaty per se qualify one for membership in SCAR. Scientific activity is the only pass-key to that organization.

[9] According to Article III of the Treaty, "In order to promote international cooperation in scientific investigation in Antarctica...

(a) information regarding plans for scientific programs in Antarctica shall be exchanged to permit maximum economy and efficiency of operations;

(b) scientific personnel shall be exchanged in Antarctica between expeditions and stations;

(c) scientific observations and results from Antarctica shall be exchanged and made freely available."

Also, in connection with the inspection clause in Article VII, the parties "shall give...notice in advance of

(a) all expeditions to and within Antarctica, on the part of its ships and nationals, and all expeditions to Antarctica organized in or proceeding from its territory;

(b) all stations in Antarctica occupied by its nationals; and

(c) any military personnel or equipment intended to be introduced by it into Antarctica subject to the conditions prescribed in Paragraph 2 of Article I of the present Treaty."

[10] The original twelve signatories to the Antarctic Treaty are permanently represented at Antarctic Treaty Consultative

to discuss matters of common interest and to adopt recommendations[11] for measures in furtherance of the principles of the Treaty. These consultative meetings are held every second year, and so far have adopted 123 recommendations "in furtherance of the principles and objectives of the Treaty." While most of the recommendations are of a procedural nature, some of the measures definitely have a substantive or material content, such as the so-called Agreed Measures for the Conservation of Antarctic Fauna and Flora. Preservation and conservation of living resources in Antarctica is listed in the Treaty as one of the matters of special interest to and responsibility for the parties (Article IX, 1 (f)) and the parties have on the whole demonstrated special concern for these matters through a series of protective measures.

In the recommendation procedure, the parties have what might be called an early, international legislative procedure for inter alia the protection of the new environment in this physically vulnerable and politically disputed area.[12]

Meetings. Acceding parties are entitled to take part "during such time as that Contracting Party demonstrates its interest in Antarctica by conducting substantial scientific activity there" (Article IX, 2). Poland at the Ninth Consultative Meeting (London 1977) was the first acceding party to gain status as a consultative party.

[11]Recommendations adopted by Consultative Meetings, as the name indicates, are mere recommendations to the governments. They become effective if and when approved by all parties with consultative status. Thus, the unanimity rule does apply to such measures. However, under the rules of procedure, adoption of recommendations at Consultative Meetings requires a unanimous vote and consequently it is a rare event indeed that an adopted recommendation is not subsequently approved. One such event occurred with Recommendation III-VIII on "Agreed Measures for the Conservation of Antarctic Fauna and Flora" (1964), which was expected to run into formal obstacles in some governments. For this reason an additional recommendation (Recommendation III-IX (1964) was adopted to the end that "these Agreed Measures as far as possible be considered as guidelines in this interim period." This second recommendation was quickly approved.

[12]In some instances the Consultative Parties may find it more appropriate to use forms other than recommendations. Thus, in the case of seals, a separate Convention for the Conservation of Antarctic Seals was negotiated in 1972. First, however, a recommendation was adopted in 1964 (Recommendation III-XI) for voluntary restrictions and in 1977 Recommendation IV-21 established "Interim Guide Lines for the Voluntary Regulation of Antarctic Pelagic Sealing." An advantage of the convention form--and a reason why it was chosen for seals--is that third parties may join the convention without acceding to the Treaty.

As a result in part of the freedom of access and scientific research, and of the availability of information, research has revealed a potential in Antarctica that may encourage exploration of resources. Such exploration goes beyond purely scientific research, and may turn into a determined search for potential resources that may be retrieved and developed economically. In this way scientific research in Antarctica which has been carried out under the principles of the Antarctic Treaty has opened the pathway towards possible economic exploitation of the area. For this reason, it has become necessary to look into the need for establishing also rules and regulations pertaining to the economic exploitation of the resources that might exist.

Just like any other continent, Antarctica can be presumed to contain vital raw materials in somewhat equal proportions, that is, in proportion to occurrences in other parts of the world. Research has revealed that such materials of various kinds are present in Antarctica.[13] A wide variety of minerals which are commercially developed in other continents are known to be present in Antarctica. Many are known only by traces, but some, including iron and coal, are known in deposits. Furthermore, indications are that Antarctica will also hold deposits of petroleum or hydrocarbons either as gas or in the form of oil. Exploratory drilling for geological information on the Antarctic Continental Shelf in the Ross Sea has revealed traces of natural gas.[14] Although the traces are not sufficient to merit speculation about deposits of commercial value, the indications are there and some "guestimates" have been made about potential quantities of gas or oil.[15]

---

[13] It must be remembered, however, that the Antarctic ice sheet restricts potential exploration to only a few and small parts of the continent. Even in these relatively small areas present knowledge is sketchy and incomplete. Vast efforts are required to improve knowledge about mineral resources in Antarctica.

[14] In 1972 the American research vessel <u>Glomar Challenger</u> found traces of methane and ethane in shallow holes drilled into sediments in the Ross Sea. Such finds are fairly normal in sedimentary rocks and present no evidence of exploitable hydrocarbons. Nevertheless, the event has generated interest in further exploration.

[15] Figures for "recoverable resources" have been widely reported by the press at 45 billion barrels of oil and 115 trillion cubic feet of gas. The U.S. Geological Survey has been cited as source of the "estimate." Most geologists will point out that the calculation may be interesting as an intellectual exercise, but figures are by no means supported by available data.

At present, prospects for developing resources that may be found in Antarctica are fairly dim, although optimists do exist. It will be readily understood that conditions for exploiting resources in Antarctica are not exactly the best. In other words, Antarctic mineral resources may be regarded as rather marginal. Even if tremendous deposits of hydrocarbons or high grade iron ore should be found, the problems of developing these resources are such that a highly sophisticated and developed technology will be required. Such technology must be developed at immense cost. The work itself would be extremely costly; the transportation of bulk materials to the markets of the world would also incur rather heavy costs.[16]

For these reasons, the conclusion that has been made by informed opinion is that the outlook for actual development of mineral resources in Antarctica cannot be regarded as positive during this century, and probably not for a long time in the next century. The only possible exception may be oil on the continental shelf, which attracts most attention at this stage. Oil prospects, of course, are greatly affected by price developments in the international energy market. However, even with great increases in oil prices oil development in Antarctica is a long-term prospect. Development lead times for technical reasons will be long, 10 to 20 years, and before that political as well as environmental problems must be solved.

Marine living resources, on the other hand, offer quite good prospects. On an average, fish caught within the Antarctic region today is no more than a few hundred thousand tons per year at best.[17] That is not much and it is believed that this catch can be expanded. More important, however, is krill, which I understand has already been mentioned at this conference. I can only repeat that according to preliminary estimates it may be possible to catch up to 70 and possible as much as one hundred million tons of krill per year without exhausting the supply. When we remember that the total international catch of fish in recent years has been 70 million tons, we may see here a possible solution to the international food problem, at least as far as marine animal proteins are concerned.

---

[16] Other difficult and costly problems include such things as provision of energy and water at mining sites and, of course, labor in distant and barren lands with no established communities, communications and social amenities.

[17] Statistics on catches in Antarctic fishing areas are uncertain and incomplete. In a recent statement the FAO Committee on Fisheries could say no more than that "fish catches, mostly by the U.S.S.R., are thought to have exceeded 100,000 tons in recent years." (FAO/COFI/78/7, March 1978).

Again, however, we have various difficulties. One is the difficulty of developing the technology required; this development is underway, but it is costly and can only be carried out by advanced fishing nations. Even with improved technology and more advanced methods, krill fisheries in such distant waters will be a capital intensive, high technology operation. This means, of course, that the cost of the product will be fairly high. Other problems relate to the processing of krill and the development of marketable products. The range is wide, from fish meal for animal feed to luxury products with snob appeal. To become a mass product for human consumption, krill must be made into new and palatable products with a wide market appeal. Apart from the cost involved, that development will require quite considerable changes in international eating habits and that, at best, will take time. On the whole, therefore, we have good reason to doubt that 50 to 70 or 100 million tons of krill will be caught within this century or indeed within the next.

Nonetheless, there is enough optimism about the use of these resources to cause concern about the possible effects of such activities. Some of these effects can be felt even at low levels of activity and generally are of two main kinds. One general effect of even low level economic activity in Antarctica would be that it would raise questions about jurisdiction and authority to regulate such activities. That again would raise the question of sovereignty, which has not been solved, but merely delayed by the Antarctic Treaty.[18]

The other major problem is that extensive exploration and exploitation of resources might affect the Antarctic environment. For these reasons, the Antarctic Treaty Consultative Parties have deemed it essential to seek a solution and to establish a regime for mineral resources and for marine living resources.

The question of economic exploitation of Antarctica was very carefully kept out of the Antarctic Treaty itself. The question was brought up during the negotiations of the Treaty in 1958 and 1959, but it quickly became apparent that many of the parties were not at that time willing to accept any provisions regulating such activity. Claimant states might consider such

---

[18]In a formal sense, the sovereignty question is a non-issue by virtue of the Treaty provision (Article IV) that neither the Treaty nor acts and activities while the Treaty is in force shall prejudice or affect claims or the position of parties in regard to claims. In every practical sense, the problem remains an issue despite the moratorium and if no way is found around it, the issue must be faced head on in the resources problem.

provisions an infringement of their sovereign rights and therefore a cause for not agreeing to the Treaty. Hence, matters of exploration and exploitation and commercial use of Antarctica were kept out of the Treaty. For this reason, too, parties at first were hesitant to take up the problem when it became apparent that commercial exploration might become a real issue. The question was first brought up informally at the Sixth Consultative Meeting in Tokyo in 1970. It was not included on the agenda but was informally discussed by delegates. It was then taken up at the Seventh Consultative Meeting in Wellington, New Zealand in 1972. On this occasion it was agreed among the parties that there was a need to study further the problem of mineral resources and effects of exploration upon the Treaty and upon the environment in Antarctica.[19] Subsequently, the subject of mineral resources has been discussed at every Consultative Meeting and at each meeting a new step has been made toward an ultimate regime.

To help discussion on the subject, the Nansen Foundation held an informal meeting of experts in 1973. Even at that time, it was apparent that governments were hesitant to commit themselves to full and open discussion of the issue of commercial exploration and exploitation. Hence, it was felt that an informal meeting where experts were invited in their personal capacity and could speak without binding their government might help the process of discussion and study along. The informal meeting produced a report on legal issues as well as technical and economic issues relating to mineral resources in Antarctica.[20] This report contributed to the debate among the parties, which continued at the Eighth Consultative Meeting is Oslo in 1975.[21]

---

[19]Recommendation VII-6 asked that "the subject 'Antarctic Resources - Effects of Mineral Exploration' be carefully studied and included on the Agenda of the Eighth Consultative Meeting."

[20]Antarctic Resources, Report from the Informal Meeting of Experts 30 May - 9 June 1973, The Fridtjof Nansen Foundation at Polhøgda.

[21]The Oslo Meeting witnessed the first full and formal debate of the urgency of the minerals issue and of ways of meeting the problem. Under Recommendation VIII-14 from the Oslo meeting, it was agreed that the question of mineral exploration and exploitation be fully studied in all its aspects in relation to the Treaty and be the subject of consultation among them with a view to convening a special preparatory meeting during 1976. The recommendation also advised study of the environmental implications of mineral resource activities and invited SCAR to "make an assessment on the basis of available information of the possible impact on the environment," as well as to consider the need for further scientific programs. The SCAR report was to play an important role in discussions at the Ninth Consultative Meeting.

Next, a special preparatory meeting was arranged in Paris in 1976 for extensive discussion of both the technical issues involved and the legal and political problems relating to mineral resources.[22]

At the subsequent Ninth Consultative Meeting in London in 1977, technical experts for the first time were formally included in the delegations of the various parties for discussion at the consultative meeting to include technical as well as the legal and the political problems involved. The Ninth Consultative Meeting demonstrated determination to push towards establishing a regime. Several preliminary proposals already have been discussed by the parties; these questions will be discussed at the Tenth Consultative Meeting in the United States in 1979. Before that, special preparatory meetings will be held on technical issues and on legal issues. In other words, we see among the parties to the Treaty a progressive process in which they have made their intention clear to establish among themselves a regime governing the economic exploration and exploitation of the potential resources in Antarctica.

The question of marine living resources was first brought up only in 1975 at the Eighth Consultative Meeting in Oslo. In retrospect it appears odd that some parties at first were hesitant to take action. However, at the Oslo meeting it was agreed that there was an urgency to the situation and that one would have to press towards establishing a regime for the Antarctic region.[23] Discussions continued at the Ninth

---

[22]The report of the Paris Special Preparatory Meeting covered both technical and legal-political issues and became the basis for continued discussions at the Ninth Consultative Meeting. The Paris meeting proposed the following broad principles which were subsequently included in Recommendation IX-1:

"(i) the Consultative Parties will continue to play an active and responsible role in dealing with the question of mineral resources in Antarctica;

(ii) the Antarctic Treaty must be maintained in its entirety;

(iii) protection of the unique Antarctic environment and of its dependent ecosystems should be a basic consideration;

(iv) the Consultative Parties, in dealing with the question of mineral resources in Antarctica, should not prejudice the interests of all mankind in Antarctica."

[23]Recommendation VIII-10 called for further study of marine living resources and also invited SCAR to continue its work in the field and to call "as soon as practicable, a meeting to discuss current work and report on programmes for the study and conservation of Antarctic marine living resources." SCAR and SCOR (Scientific Committee on Ocean Research) jointly organized a meeting in 1976 and have made a number of

Consultative Meeting in London, where it was decided that an effort should be made to establish a new regime governing marine living resources in Antarctica before the end of 1978.[24] A special meeting on marine living resources, begun in Australia in February of this year, has continued with a new session in Buenos Aires, and a third session in the United States this fall. The purpose is to prepare a definitive document to regulate the marine living resources and their conservation. Success before the deadline is uncertain, but the effort *is* being made. The proposal prepared through these special meetings will be submitted to a special conference. At this conference non-parties to the Antarctic Treaty may be invited to take part in the negotiations and join the final convention.[26] The marine living resources issue, in other words, will be dealt with in much the same way as was the sealing question which in 1972 resulted in a special convention on the protection of Antarctic seals.

In regard to Antarctic living resources then, we see that the parties to the Antarctic Treaty act with determination to develop a regime. In this case it is evident that the regime should be adopted through a special convention and that it should be open for outside participants. In regard to the mineral resources, this has not yet been decided.

Other international organizations have shown some interest in Antarctic resources. This is particularly true for FAO where the Committee on Fisheries takes special interest in the resource potential of the southern seas and has proposed that a research and development program be set up for the use of these resources for the benefit of all mankind. It is quite clear

---

recommendations, including an expanded research program for Biological Investigation of Marine Antarctic Systems and Stocks (BIOMASS). SCAR/SCOR reports have provided essential material for continued discussions among the parties.

[24]Recommendation IX-2, Section III, 1: "A definitive regime for the Conservation of Antarctic Marine Living Resources should be concluded before the end of 1978." The recommendation also included measures regarding scientific research, including support for the BIOMASS program, and interim guidelines for the conservation of resources.

[25]We now know that the deadline could not be met and that the concluding session planned to be held in Canberra in late 1978 had to be postponed.

[26]According to Recommendation IX-2, the current special meeting shall "decide on participation in such a meeting by States other than Consultative Parties which are actively engaged in research and exploitation of Antarctic Marine Living Recources..."

that the Antarctic Treaty parties are not happy about the FAO approach. They have tried to dissuade FAO from adopting too extensive a development program for the southern seas by pointing to the special responsibility of the Antarctic Treaty parties in areas south of 60°[27] and pointing also to the need for special expertise in Antarctic matters to handle these questions.

In this connection the Antarctic Treaty parties have pointed out that they have taken a number of important and effective steps toward the conservation of the resources and that they hope FAO will have a role in the context of that regime. The, should we say, unhappiness of Treaty parties when other international organizations take separate initiatives in Antarctic affairs is often apparent. It is reflected in their frequent emphasis of their special responsibilities and parties have informally stressed the need for other agencies to refrain from premature action while the Antarctic Treaty parties themselves are actively working to develop necessary regimes.

The development of typical resource regimes for Antarctica, for mineral or living resources, will begin a new era in the region. Obviously, adoption of rules and regulations for economic activity such as resource exploration and exploitation does raise a series of difficult problems both within the Treaty context and between the Treaty parties and outside parties. Negotiations so far have demonstrated that it is difficult for the parties to the Antarctic Treaty to find a clue toward a solution of the sovereignty issue. Some states with claims stand on their claims, while other states do not recognize claims. Somehow a way must be found through or around the sovereignty issue in order to get an agreed regime. If there is no way around the sovereignty issue, the issue itself will have to be opened. In that case, the question of the attitude of the nonclaimant states to the claims and of their right to present claims of their own will have to be faced fully. Various suggestions might be made toward an agreed compromise, including elements, for instance, of the Svalbard Treaty of 1920. That Treaty recognizes Norway's sovereignty in the Svalbard (Spitsbergen) Archipelago[28], but grants to the subjects

---

[27] FAO/COFI proposals apply to areas south of 45°S with no southern limit, whereas the Antarctic Treaty Area extends north to 60°S. Defining lines of demarkation between waters under national jurisdiction, under special treaty jurisdiction and under general international law is one of the most difficult and potentially controversial issues involved in establishing the marine resources regime.

[28] Under the Treaty "The High Contracting Parties undertake to recognize, subject to the stipulations of the present Treaty, the full and absolute sovereignty of Norway over the Archipelago of Spitsbergen..." (Article 1).

of all Treaty parties an equal right of access and equal rights of exploring and exploiting natural resources in the Svalbard region.[29] Such a system might be imagined also in Antarctica, where an equal access clause could be extended to include economic activities, and where taxation should only be used in favor of the Antarctic region and not for the benefit of those claiming jurisdiction. Such a solution, however, will raise opposition at least from some of the parties, particularly those that are close to Antarctica. I mention them specifically because Latin American parties to the Treaty (Argentina and Chile) and Australia find it more necessary perhaps than any of the other states to point to the importance of recognition of their full national, sovereign rights. Other states, including Norway and the United Kingdom (and New Zealand) appear to be more flexible on this score, and may be prepared to compromise in favor of a joint solution within the framework of the Antarctic Treaty. If that would be enough to satisfy the nonclaimant states and, particularly, all non-member states, is a different question.

This is where you have the second set of serious difficulties. In addition to internal problems between the Antarctic Treaty parties on the one hand, problems also may arise between the Treaty parties and nonparties on the other. Development in regard to these problems may be strongly affected by the outcome of the Law of the Sea Conference. Antarctic resources are discussed primarily in the context of continental shelf and fisheries development. The final result of the Law of the Sea Conference obviously may be expected to have an impact upon the legal and the political status of Antarctic ocean space. You can imagine two types of effect here. First of all, if the underdeveloped countries of the world do not get from the Law of the Sea Conference that degree of benefit which they expect from an international seabed regime, we may assume that these states will want to move into any new field that might be exploited to benefit their interest. Antarctica today is the only remaining major resource area in the world apart from the deep seabed that could be impounded for the benefit of the underdeveloped countries.

---

[29] Thus, "Ships and nationals of all the High Contracting Parties shall enjoy equally the rights of fishing and hunting" (Article 2) and "subject to the observance of local laws and regulations, they may carry out there without impediment all maritime, industrial, mining and commercial operations on a footing of absolute equality..." (Article 3). Furthermore, "Taxes, dues and duties levied shall be devoted exclusively to the said territories and shall not exceed what is required for the object in view..." (Article 8).

Even if an effective international seabed authority is established, problems may evolve both because success may sharpen the appetite and because there will be a question of defining the limit between the potential Antarctic regime and an international regime. Should the 60°S limit of the Antarctic Treaty apply even though that would withhold vast areas of high seas from the international authority? If so, what does it mean when the Treaty itself says that it applies to all areas south of 60°S but without prejudice to international rights on the high seas within that area?[30] Or should one introduce national 200-mile economic zones in Antarctica, such as some states are considering, or a "collective Antarctic Treaty Zone"?

I should like to conclude my remarks by pointing to the opposing tendencies that are evolving here. On the one hand, the Treaty parties themselves are pressing forward with determination to reach a solution among themselves. While striving to act without prejudice to the interests of all mankind in Antarctica, the Consultative Parties nevertheless want to present the world with a fait accompli in a regime for minerals and for marine living resources. The parties do this in recognition of their own special responsibility for Antarctica; and they do it in an effort to preserve what they see as a paramount interest, that of protecting the Antarctic environment and its ecosystems against excessive and unwise use. But of course in doing this they also want to benefit their own interests.

On the other hand, there is an international community that so far has been passive in regard to the Antarctic region, but that may soon find it necessary or convenient to take up the Antarctic issue in a different forum than that of the Consultative Parties. In one sense, then, there is a race for time where Antarctic Treaty parties may feel pressed to act more deliberately and with necessary speed to adopt a regime before it is too late, before the question is brought into a different forum. Parties outside the Antarctic Treaty may push exactly for that in an effort to have a say in the distribution of hoped-for riches of Antarctic resources.

Open conflict between these two trends, I submit, will not benefit either the solution or Antarctica itself. It will

---

[30]Under Article VI of the Antarctic Treaty "The provisions of the present Treaty shall apply to the area south of 60° South Latitude, including ice shelves, but nothing in the present Treaty shall prejudice or in any way affect the rights, or the exercise of the rights, of any State under international law with regard to the high seas within that area."

definitely take both wisdom and statesmanship within the Antarctic Treaty context to establish a wise regime that takes into account broad international needs and requirements for resources and the interests of both the claimant states and the rather exclusive group of states that is active in Antarctica. At present it seems that the Antarctic Treaty approach is gaining support. Consultative Parties to the Treaty are acting more deliberately and with greater success in handling the formerly "untouchable" problems of economic exploitation and resource regimes. Significantly too, other countries with an interest in Antarctic resources that until now have not participated in the Antarctic Treaty Consultative Group are now joining in. Already, Poland has acquired consultative status; additional countries have acceded to the Antarctic Treaty.[31] There is little doubt that they do so primarily because they have an interest in the marine living resources in Antarctic waters. This means, then, that the Antarctic Treaty system now includes most of the states with a capability for Antarctic operations. I find it very difficult to believe that any solution to the Antarctic resources problem in the form of a regime adopted in any other forum than the Antarctic Consultative Group can be carried out with success unless, of course, the Consultative Parties are fully agreed to moving negotiations into a different forum and approve the final result.

---

[31] The following states have acceded to the Treaty: Poland (1961, consultative status 1977), Czechoslovakia (1962), Denmark (1965), Netherlands (1967), Romania (1971), German Democratic Republic (1974), Brazil (1975), Federal Republic of Germany (1978).

INTERNATIONAL LEGAL ISSUES REGARDING TOWING OF ICEBERGS AND ENVIRONMENTAL EFFECTS OF ICEBERG EXPLOITATION

Curt Epperson
University of Washington
Seattle, Washington

Introduction

This article examines some of the legal issues which may arise if exploitation of Antarctic icebergs is begun. The purpose of this article is to examine questions of passage arising from towing of icebergs through areas subject to national jurisdiction and legal issues arising from possible environmental harm.

This article is an edited version of a much longer paper. However, those issues which are not discussed here have been the subject of analysis at other times and places. For the readers' convenience some citations to those other materials are here included in Appendix I.

I. Proposals to Transport Icebergs

The idea of towing icebergs from Antarctica to various dry areas of the world has been around since the 1950's, at least. John Isaacs of Scripps Institute, La Jolla, seems to have been the first to make a scientifically based proposal, although it was not published until 1961 (Isaacs, 1961). The idea of towing icebergs was discussed simplistically in other publications during the 1950's (Burt, 1956, p. 2). During the late 1960's and continuing to the present, interest in towing icebergs has grown, and recently several detailed, technical proposals have been published explaining problems which iceberg moving schemes will encounter and offering some solutions. For the purpose of this paper, it is not necessary to examine all of these schemes (Al-Faisal, 1978; Benedict, 1978; Job, 1978; Davis, 1978; Fuhs, 1978; El-Hares, 1978). But for purposes of a general understanding and because some legal questions could arise as a result of movement problems, I will summarize a couple of the first detailed proposals (Weeks and Campbell, 1973, p. 207; Hult and Ostrander, 1973).

A. Weeks-Campbell Proposal

The Weeks-Campbell Proposal considers the problem in four main parts. The first deals with the location of a supply of large tabular icebergs and concludes that the Antarctic ice shelves create a wide choice of sizes of tabular icebergs.[1] Tabular icebergs are ideal for towing because they are flat on top and will likely prove to be more stable under tow (Allaire, 1973, p. 21).

Weeks and Campbell then discuss problems associated with movement of icebergs. They calculate towing force requirements by examining the drag of different size icebergs and show that form-drag will be very high. Some advantage can be gained by either choosing more "ship-shape" icebergs or by undertaking some shaping operations. They calculate that a towing velocity of between .25m/s - .5 m/s (=½ -1 knot) will be sufficient to allow maneuverability under adverse conditions, while keeping at a minimum the drag increase which occurs as velocity increases. (Drag is proportional to velocity.)

Weeks-Campbell calculations on the amount of towing force needed show that no single tug currently in existence has the amount of power required to tow huge icebergs. (Towing small icebergs may be possible with existing tugs, but the smaller the iceberg the less fresh water left after melting loss.) However, they conclude that a super tug could be built with a power plant sufficient to do the job. The power plant would be similar to those proposed for large icebreaking tankers. Furthermore, they note that the U.S.S. Enterprise has 50% more power than the amount they calculate is necessary. Such a tug could tow an iceberg 230 m. wide with a length of 920 m. (509 x $10^7 m^3$ of ice).

Melting in transit is the third main point of the analysis. Here, Weeks and Campbell have an extensive discussion which looks at water temperatures, trajectories (routes to Australia and Chile), and towing times. They conclude that "if a large enough iceberg could be towed, large volumes of ice could still be delivered, even considering the melting losses (Weeks and Campbell, 1973, p. 218).

The fourth part of the analysis is concerned with an estimate of economic feasibility. The approximate costs of constructing and operating a tug are stated; costs of iceberg water are compared with desalinated and irrigation water. The data

---

[1]The only source of large tabular icebergs in the Arctic is the Ward Ice Shelf in Greenland. However, production of icebergs there is erratic, and very few of those which are produced exit into the Greenland Sea where they are accessible. Tabular icebergs begin as snowfall, which over time becomes packed down into ice. The ice moves plastically down the slope of the continent toward the sea, where large icebergs eventually calve off and float out to sea.

indicate that for deliveries to Australia or the Atacamba desert, iceberg exploitation for fresh water is economically competitive.

Weeks and Campbell conclude by looking at their previous analysis stating that it could be greatly improved. There is a need for more information, perhaps based upon some experimentation. Environmental effects need greater study, as do methods of processing the iceberg once it reaches its destination. Weeks and Campbell refer to their study as a "first approximation" which, although not an "adequate look," yields results "which are very exciting."

B. Hult-Ostrander Proposal

The Hult-Ostrander study takes a broader approach to the idea, not limiting its analysis to iceberg use in the Southern Hemisphere. The study begins with an explanation of current water shortage problems in the Southwest United States and later deals with iceberg use in the U.S., Africa, the Middle East, and Australia.

Hult and Ostrander propose towing trains of icebergs. They also discuss wrapping these huge icebergs with sheets of plastic to reduce melting.[2]

Hult and Ostrander calculate that at low speeds in high latitudes the coriolis force will be from the dominant resistance. The effects of this force can be calculated, but it introduces a factor which previously has been unimportant in ocean transportation (El-Hares, 1978). The exact effect is unknown as is the effect of waves and winds, and these are areas which need further investigation. Hult and Ostrander examine the use of icebergs in the context of the Southwest U.S. concluding that iceberg water would be a valuable augmentation for existing supplies (see also Hult, 1974).

The Hult-Ostrander proposal contains technical data and analysis on ice accumulation and loss in the Antarctic, controlling melting of icebergs, costs of moving icebergs, transport calculations and models, and water flow around a submerged moving body. The actual calculations are not important for the

---

[2]This idea of wrapping an iceberg to reduce melting is very important, although it may seem silly. Wrapping an iceberg would reduce melt loss enough to make feasible the towing of much smaller icebergs. This in turn means that existing ships might have the power required to do the towing. See M. Al-Faisal, Water Supply and Weather Modifications Through the Use of Transported Icebergs from the Antarctic. Desalination, 1977, 20, p. 415.

purposes of a legal analysis. What is important is that Hult and Ostrander, like Weeks and Campbell, are able to show technological and economic feasibility. Additionally, it seems certain that continued technological advances will make iceberg exploitation less costly. For example, a method has been devised to calculate iceberg volume from photographs (Farmer, 1977, p. 83), and the Earth Resources Technology Satellite provides a good method of locating suitable icebergs (Hult and Ostrander, 1973).

C. Participant Nations

Because iceberg exploitation will be extremely costly and profitability uncertain, there are likely to be only a few nations which attempt exploitation. Potential exploitation by the U.S. is mentioned by Hult and Ostrander, since there is a great need for more water in the arid Southwest. However, those needs may be satisfied by interbasin diversions, e.g., taking Columbia River water through pipes to California. Even given the opposition in the Pacific Northwest to such a plan, it seems more likely than a major iceberg exploitation scheme.

Weeks and Campbell focus their proposal on possible use in Chile (Atacamba Desert) and Australia. Those areas are attractive for iceberg exploitation not only because of the need for more fresh water, but also because of their proximity to Antarctica. Not only are they much closer than other arid regions of the world, but the ocean currents favor transport to Australia and Chile. However, in the case of Chile, it seems very unlikely that a country with triple digit inflation will take on a high risk, high technology, high cost venture like iceberg exploitation until economic stability is achieved. When that goal is reached Chile may engage in iceberg exploitation, although Chile will experience special costs due to the necessity of pumping the water over the coastal mountain range. This economic stability consideration does not apply to Australia. Iceberg exploitation may, in the near future, provide a way to irrigate large portions of Australia.

South Africa, also in an advantageous geographic position, perhaps could use the water for agriculture in its arid regions. But current political instability casts doubt that any such huge project will be mounted in the near future.

Saudi Arabia is the remaining most likely participant. The interest of that nation must be judged in the context of the immediate future, i.e., within 4-8 years. The need for fresh water is increasingly desperate[3]. The geographic problem is the

[3]Prince Mohammed Al-Faisal, Instigator of the First International Conference on Iceberg Utilization, held October 2-6, 1977, at Iowa State University, and formerly the head of Saudi

major obstacle; it seems likely that some sort of protection to inhibit melting must be devised for the iceberg.[4] In any event, the interest of Saudi Arabia must be taken seriously, given the vast financial resources available. The only other source of fresh water is through desalinization. Thus, the problem is to devise a way to deliver and prepare for use iceberg water at less cost than desalinized water. Given all the unquantified variables which could greatly increase or decrease costs (for example, the radical increase in fuel costs, which would affect on Saudi Arabia in the form of opportunity costs), it seems likely that the actual costs of iceberg exploitation will not be known until it is studied much more, or perhaps tried. It may be that Saudi Arabia intends just such an experiment.

II. Claims with Respect to Movement of Icebergs

A. Claims to Access

1. Territorial Sea

There are several water areas over which coastal states have varying degrees of authority. In areas where icebergs are towed near land, this authority may have an impact on iceberg exploitation. The first area to be examined is the territorial sea. (The internal waters are not discussed, since it is unlikely icebergs will be towed through any internal waters, and coastal state authority is absolute in any event.)

a. 1958 Convention on the Territorial Sea and Contiguous Zone

Coastal state authority in the territorial sea is very broad, but an important limitation on that authority is the right of innocent passage. That doctrine seeks to balance the interests of the coastal state (for example, security and prevention of activities which might have an adverse effect on the land areas nearby) against the general community interests (promotion of transportation and trade). The 1958 Convention provides that "the coastal state must not hamper innocent passage through the territorial sea"(Convention on Territorial Sea, Article 15). The party towing an iceberg will claim passage through the territorial sea as a right under the doctrine of innocent passage.

Arabia's water desalination program, told an Iowa T.V. audience that his country would spend $15 billion on desalination by 1981, and not have enough drinking water by 1985. Science, 1977, 198, pp. 274, 276.

[4]Wilford Weeks has said if you tried to drag an unprotected iceberg to Arabia or Southern California, "you would end up with nothing but a towline." Science, 1977, 198, p. 275.

The first claim that a coastal state may make to support a denial of passage by a ship towing an iceberg is that innocent passage is a right which only pertains to vessels, and since an iceberg is not a vessel, there is no right of innocent passage. Although this argument may be technically correct (the 1958 Convention specifically says "ships of all states...") (Convention on Territorial Sea, Article 14) it has little other validity. Since coastal state authority is predicated upon the notion of balancing coastal state and community interests, the right of innocent passage should not depend upon a technicality such as this.

In looking at Article 14(4) one sees that it defines innocent passage in a way which leaves a great deal of discretion in the coastal state, i.e., "passage is innocent so long as not prejudicial to the peace, good order, or security of the coastal state."

Based upon this language, arguments which a coastal state might pose as a justification for denying passage to icebergs under tow are: (1) the potential disruption of other traffic caused by the slow-moving tug with its iceberg; (2) the potential hazard from an iceberg grounding or breaking up, i.e., calving off smaller icebergs; and (3) the potential disruption of coastal fisheries caused either by thermal pollution or the presence of fresh water from melting. These are all unknown elements which might cause a coastal state to assert passage is detrimental to its "peace, good order, or security." Under the 1958 Convention, such arguments by the coastal state might be valid, since the Convention provisions are obviously ambiguous.

The final impact that the territorial sea authority of a coastal state may have on iceberg towing relates to the power of the coastal state to promulgate regulations pertaining to navigation (McDougal and Burke, 1962, p. 301) and pollution.[5] Under the 1958 Convention, it is not clear if non-compliance with such regulations renders passage non-innocent, but the question is largely irrelevant. If a potential violator knows of the regulations and knows its vessels will be subject to detention or arrest, it will probably choose not to enter the territorial sea. The result is the same as if innocent passage had been denied.

---

[5]In this regard the 1958 Convention is not clear. It refers to the Authority to enforce "sanitary" regulations out to the limits of the contiguous zone, i.e., 12 miles. The practice of states is to prescribe pollution regulations for the territorial sea and contiguous zone and over wider areas in some situations (for example, the 1970 Canadian Arctic Waters Pollution Prevention Act).

b. Informal Composite Negotiating Text

The ICNT Provisions on the territorial sea and the right of innocent passage are quite clear. Under terms of the ICNT, there is no question that the coastal state can regulate pollution.[6] Furthermore, the ICNT provides that passage is not innocent if it involves "any act of willful and serious pollution, contrary to the present convention" (Article 19). Of course, there is some question as to what constitutes "serious" pollution, but given the nature of coastal state control in the territorial sea, i.e., sovereign control subject only to the rather limited right of innocent passage,[7] the coastal state may very well be able to define thermal pollution from icebergs as serious, in the absence of any data to the contrary.

It appears that under the ICNT, the coastal state may proscribe passage of icebergs through its territorial sea by classifying it as non-innocent or regulate such passage under its power to regulate navigation and pollution. The latter powers are limited by Article 24, which says the coastal state shall not impose requirements "which have the practical effect of denying or impairing the right of innocent passage." But here again, it is unclear what that clause means, since regulations may have practical effects which differ greatly from one ship to another. A logical interpretation would seem to dictate that where the use is extraordinary or unusual, regulations which apply to other uses, and are reasonable in that regard, might proscribe the extraordinary or unusual use.

2. Exclusive Economic Zone

We see from the discussion above that there is a variety of arguments a state could use to prevent passage of icebergs

---

[6]ICNT (Informal Composite Negotiating Text), Third U.N. Conference on the Law of the Sea, N. Y. Session, May 23-July 15, 1977, at Article 21.

"1. The coastal state may make laws and regulations...in respect of...

f. the preservation of the environment of the coastal state and the prevention, reduction and control of pollution thereof;"

See also, Article 212(3)

"coastal states may, in the exercise of their sovereignty within their territorial sea, establish national laws and regulations for the prevention, reduction, and control of marine pollution from vessels."

[7]For a discussion of the coastal states' sovereignty over the territorial sea, see D. P. O'Connell, The juridical nature of the territorial sea, British Y.B. International Law, 1971, 45, pp. 303, 357-361.

through its territorial sea. However, the practical effect of this may be minimal. The icebergs which are large enough to be exploited economically also require depths of at least 500 feet. Thus with only a few exceptions (perhaps only where a state claims a 200 mile territorial sea) tugs towing icebergs will not traverse territorial seas.

Even though territorial seas may be avoided along most potential routes, it is more difficult to avoid passage through 200 mile exclusive economic zones. Admittedly, the exact provisions of national legislation establishing an EEZ may vary from state to state, and so in specific situations national legislation should be closely scrutinized. Here, we will analyze the provisions of the ICNT, on the assumption that it is an expression of customary international law, at least insofar as transit through the zone is concerned.

The first point to make is that coastal state interests in the EEZ are less broad than in the territorial sea. Specifically, coastal state interest in protecting its security and sovereignty, requiring authority over a 200 mile zone adjacent to its territorial sea, is not as strong. Given this, good policy dictates that the coastal state exercise less authority in the EEZ than it does in the territorial sea (Burke, pp. 267, 282). This is especially true when one recognizes that community interests in freedom of navigation are much greater in the EEZ, since avoidance of such broad zones is more difficult, and therefore potentially more costly, than avoidance of transit through a territorial sea.

Under the ICNT, the EEZ is not a part of the high seas (Article 86), and, therefore, high seas freedoms are not all applicable in the EEZ. But neither is the EEZ sovereign state territory. According to Article 56, the coastal state has "sovereign rights for the purpose of exploring and exploiting... the natural resources." But, even given this relatively limited degree of coastal state authority, the ICNT seems to make the rights of navigation in the zone subservient to the coastal state rights. Article 58(1) states,

> In the exclusive economic zone, all states, whether coastal or land-locked, enjoy, <u>subject to the relevant provisions of the present convention</u>, the freedoms referred to in Article 87 of navigation and overflight and the laying of submarine cables and pipelines, and other internationally lawful uses of the sea related to these freedoms...

The right to navigation is further restricted by Article 58(3) which states,

> In exercising their rights and performing their duties under the present convention in the exclusive economic zone, states shall have due regard to the rights and duties of the coastal state and shall comply with the laws and regulations established by the coastal state in accordance with the provisions of this Convention and other rules of international law...

Obviously the coastal state may prescribe some regulations, and such ability to regulate implies some competence to enforce (Burke, p. 285). But since Article 58 provides for freedom of navigation, it seems the coastal state may not prohibit transit as a punishment for violation of whatever regulations it establishes.

At this point, it must be recognized that the nature of coastal state regulations which might affect iceberg transport is unknown. Under customary international law there does not appear to be coastal state authority to regulate pollution outside the territorial sea and contiguous zone. However, the ICNT in Article 56 gives the coastal state jurisdiction to preserve the marine environment. That jurisdiction must be exercised in accordance with other provisions of the ICNT, specifically, Article 212 which provides,

> ...coastal states, for the purpose of enforcement as provided for in section 6 of this Part of the present Convention, may in respect of their economic zones establish laws and regulations for the prevention, reduction and control of pollution from vessels <u>conforming to and giving effect to generally accepted international rules and standards established through the competent international organization or general diplomatic conference</u>.

It is clear that this article gives very little competence to the coastal state to regulate vessel source pollution in the EEZ.[8] There is no coastal state prescriptive competence separate from prescriptions arising from international organizations or diplomatic conferences (Burke, p. 286). Although Article 212 provides for slightly greater coastal state competence in "special areas," even that is limited by provisions requiring appropriate consultations through the competent international organization which must in effect give its approval to any pollution control regulations for the "special area."

---

[8]Note that this provision applies only to <u>vessel</u> source pollution. Therefore, if a country restricts entry into its territorial sea on the grounds that icebergs aren't vessels and therefore can't undertake innocent passage, that country may find difficulty in later asserting control over thermal or fresh water pollution by the iceberg.

To reiterate, the ICNT gives the coastal state very little authority to regulate pollution in the EEZ, and at present there will be little impact on iceberg towing. The coastal state must conform to international law, and there is at present no customary international law relating specifically to the types of pollution which an iceberg might cause, i.e., thermal pollution or fresh water pollution. However, the development of customery international law regarding exclusive economic zones is moving along outside of the confines of UNCLOS III. It may be that there will soon be a recognition of coastal state authority to regulate pollution within the economic zone, as a part of its well-established authority to regulate and conserve fisheries. Furthermore, although in the past the focus of international conventions has concentrated on pollution of the sea by oil[9] and by dumping,[10] attention is now shifting to pollution of many varieties. The 1973 IMCO Convention for the Prevention of Pollution by Ships[11] (not in force) directs its attention to prevention of pollution by oil, noxious liquids, harmful substances, and ship sewage or garbage. None of these provides a basis in international law for coastal state regulation of iceberg passage through its EEZ, but this discussion illustrates how customary international law is developing. If it could be shown that icebergs had an adverse effect on fisheries within the EEZ[12], we should expect coastal states and international organizations[13] to begin regulating iceberg passage.

---

[9]See the International Convention for the Prevention of Pollution of the Sea by Oil, UST, 3, p. 2989; TIAS 4900; amended in 1962, UST, 17, p. 1523; TIAS 6109; amended in 1969, TIAS 8505 (not in force) and in 1971 (not in force).

[10]Convention on the Prevention of Marine Pollution by the Dumping of Wastes at Sea, UST, 26, p. 2403; TIAS 8165.

[11]IMCO Doc. MP/conf/SP.35; Int'l Legal Materials, 1973, 12, p. 1319, opened for signature 1-15-74.

[12]For example, the thermal or salinity gradients caused by icebergs may have an effect on fish, although it isn't clear if they would be attracted, repulsed, or otherwise affected. See R. Love, The Chemical Biology of Fishes, 1970, pp. 187, 209.

[13]For an example of comprehensive regulations which would encompass iceberg transport see Canada, Fiji, Ghana, Guyana, Iceland, India, Iran, New Zealand, Phillipines, and Spain: draft articles on a zonal approach to the preservation of the marine environment. Presented to the Third U.N. Conf. on the Law of the Sea, U.N. Doc. A/conf.62/L6 (1974).

B. Accommodation with Other High Seas Users

1. Customary International Law and Freedom of Navigation

The first point to be made here is the obvious one, i.e., the towing of icebergs in areas outside national jurisdiction will be undertaken as a right under the principle of freedom of navigation on the high seas.[14] For our purposes here, it is sufficient to define the high seas as the area which is outside the exclusive control of any state. That definition as a general statement may be inadequate, but since the issue here is not which areas are under state control, the definition will suffice.

The freedom of the high seas is something of a fiction, since states are not free to do whatever they please. "In past practice, the freedom of the seas has meant that each state was free to use the oceans in accommodation with other uses, not that each state was given a license to engage in any activity irrespective of effects upon the interests of others" (McDougal and Burke, 1962, p. 81). Given that restriction, what uses of the high seas are permissible? In situations where one use may conflict with another, the question can only be answered by examining and balancing values. Some exclusive use of the high seas has been recognized. (For example, nations have at times closed off an area of the high seas for weapons testing (Whiteman, Digest Int'l Law, 1965).) However, the general policy goal of maximizing production and distribution of values should be recalled when we balance conflicting uses.

The reason for this discussion is to lay some background as regards what high seas uses come under the doctrine of "freedom of the seas." There is some possibility that long, slow moving trains of icebergs will interfere with existing transportation on the high seas. However, that potential interference should not disqualify the transport of icebergs from residing under the umbrella of freedom of navigation. Given technological advances making possible many more uses of the high seas, uses which may prove extremely valuable to mankind, it would be folly to adopt an approach which unnecessarily prohibited or discouraged new uses. Assuming that iceberg towing will probably result in little interference with present uses, and given that such interference need never rise to the level of exclusive use of a given area, it would be incorrect to

---

[14] "Broadly speaking, one may say that the freedom of navigation is to serve maritime traffic in the widest sense." Butler, The freedom of navigation under international law. J. Int'l. & Comp. Law, 1976, 6, pp. 107, 108.

argue that iceberg towing is not permissible under customary international law and bad policy to argue that it ought not be allowed. Potential interference caused by slow-moving iceberg trains could be minimized by careful route selection. It may be necessary to avoid certain areas,[15] but this should not present a major obstacle to transport operations.

2. 1958 Convention on the High Seas

So far this discussion has attempted to look at the customary international law relating to freedom of the high seas. There are, however, specific treaty provisions regarding the matter. The 1958 Convention on the High Seas (UST 13, p. 2312, TIAS 5200) lists some freedoms of the high seas in Article 2, but it is arguable whether this list is complete (McDougal & Burke, 1962, pp. 753-763). In any event, the freedom of navigation is expressly recognized, although not defined. This means that iceberg transport is a legitimate use of the high seas, either as a new use, included in the general doctrine of freedom of the seas, or as an aspect of the long recognized freedom of navigation. The former argument is dependent upon the concept of reasonableness implicit in the 1958 treaty on the high seas.[16] The latter argument is dependent upon analogy to other presently conducted activities (for example, towing of barges). One might argue that the increased size of the object under tow makes iceberg transport non-analogous to the mere towing of barges. However, that argument tends more to show that iceberg transport should be required to comply with more strict rules of the road to ensure safety (perhaps special lights or other gear) and not that freedom of navigation does not apply. If such an argument can be used to show freedom of navigation is inapplicable, it also seems that operation of ultra-large crude carriers (which are many times larger than tankers of just 10 years ago) cannot be conducted as part of the freedom of navigation. Such an assertion is at least far-fetched, if not ridiculous.

---

[15]See Regulation 8, Chapter V, of the Int'l Convention for the Safety of Life at Sea, UST, 16, p. 185; TIAS 5780.

[16]McDougal & Burke assert a principle of reasonableness "may be inferred from the special references to certain uses of the high seas which might adversely affect other uses. In paragraph 5 the Commission listed a variety of uses which 'adversely' affect other uses and expressly stated they were permissible activities or exercises of authority. In sum, the Commission seems to have affirmed, implicitly and awkwardly, that the sea is open to use for every purpose, subject to the limitations of the requirement of reasonableness in relation to other users." (McDougal & Burke, 1962, p. 761)

3. Informal Composite Negotiating Text

It appears that iceberg transport is an allowable use of the high seas under customary international law and under the provisions of the 1958 Convention (which to a large extent simply set out in treaty form customary law). However, there still remains the ICNT. An examination of its provisions relating to the high seas is necessary to determine if those provisions deviate from the 1958 Convention or the customary principle. Such an examination reveals that the ICNT contains no significant and relevant changes--there is no new issue to analyze. Article 87 of the ICNT contains a non-exclusive list of high seas freedoms, which must be exercised with "due consideration for the interests of other states." This language is far too general to constitute a meaningful restriction and presents no new legal obstacles to iceberg transport.

Even if there are no international legal principles which prohibit iceberg transport on the high seas, it is arguable that the actual conduct of the activity should be subject to special safety regulations.[17] Transport of icebergs on the high seas may pose unique hazards to other shipping. For example, smaller icebergs may calve off and float away from the iceberg under tow (Robe, Maier, Kollmeyer, 1977, p. 505), or an iceberg may become grounded and immobile. Such grounding would result in what is essentially an island, in an area where there was not an island previously. Therefore, it would not be shown on charts and could constitute a significant hazard to navigation. A small iceberg resulting from calving could also constitute a navigational hazard, particularly if such calving occurred in tropical waters where there is normally no expectation of encountering icebergs.

The special hazards which may accompany iceberg transport give rise to some interesting questions of liability. For example, is a towing party liable for damages which result from collision with a small iceberg which calved off a large iceberg under tow? Does the answer depend upon whether the accident

---

[17] It is assumed that, at the least, established international safety regulations will apply to icebergs under tow. These would include such things as lights and other necessary safety equipment. See IMCO, The Activities of the Inter-Governmental Maritime Consultive Organization in Relation to Shipping and Related Matters (1974); also, the 1950 International Convention for the Safety of Life at Sea, UST, _16_, p. 185, TIAS 5780; The 1972 Convention on the International Regulations for Preventing Collisions at Sea, London, Oct. 20, 1972, reported in _IV New Directions in the Law of the Sea_, 505, by S. Fay, R. Churchill, M. Nordquist (Eds.), 1973.

occurs in an area where icebergs are normally found, or in a tropical area? The general admiralty principle which will apply is that liability is based upon fault (Gilmore and Black, 1975). But in this context, what constitutes fault? For example, is a party not at fault if it takes reasonable precautions to prevent grounding or calving? Perhaps strict liability should apply to iceberg towing. If so, will there be limits on liability? These questions are obviously very complicated and would properly be subject to an in-depth analysis. Such an analysis will not be undertaken here because of the complexity and variety of the issues. The issues are mentioned because many future problems may be avoided by present recognition of potential hazards. As a general proposition, it is safe to say that reasonable precautions may serve to prevent accidents and, if such occur, reduce liability.

C. Potential Environmental Hazards from Iceberg Exploitation Activities

Opposition to iceberg exploitation may arise from private groups or states on the basis of concern over possible adverse environmental effects. Included among these is the possibility of damage to the marine environment by pollution. For our purposes marine pollution can be defined as

> Introduction by man, directly or indirectly, of substances or energy into the marine environment (including estuaries) resulting in such deleterious effects as harm to living resources, hazard to human health, hindrance to marine activities including fishing, impairment of quality for use of sea water and reduction of amenities.[18]

Adoption of this harm-oriented definition of pollution requires that one examine an activity to determine what harmful effects it might manifest on the marine environment. In the case of iceberg exploitation activities, this is at best a speculative task. The discussion which follows is not an extensive review of all harmful effects which iceberg exploitation may have on the environment. It is only intended to suggest that there may be some environmental damage. This possibility requires an analysis of international environmental law.

---

[18]Comprehensive Outline of the scope of the long-term and expanded programme of Oceanic exploration and research, as approved by the IOC, Sept. 1969, Part I.3. (UNESCO/IOC, Summary Report of Sixth Session, Sept. 2-13, 1969, Annex IV at 12. U.N. Doc. SC/MD/19 (June 1, 1970).

1. Environmental Hazards in General

To begin with, there will be some cooling of sea water surrounding the iceberg, both during transit and at the destination. The extent to which this cooling will take place is unclear, primarily because a strong incentive exists to reduce the effect as much as possible.[19] This is because the greater the insulation around the iceberg the less loss there will be due to melting, with consequent gains in economic feasibility.[20] Given this incentive, there is good reason to believe this cooling effect will be kept to a minimum. However, to the extent that it does take place, there could be some harm to the marine ecosystem. Many marine organisms can survive only within specific temperature ranges; cooling or heating the water may result in such effects as reduced reproductive rates, slowed growth, or death.[21] However, in the past scientific concern has focused primarily upon the effects of thermal pollution in the form of heat discharge (which is still regarded as a local, not an international, problem), so further study of this cooling effect is needed (Davis, 1972, p. 305; Bader, Roessler, Thorhaug, 1972, p. 425).

Another possible environmental effect is contamination of the salt water around the iceberg by fresh water. This effect is like the cooling discussed above in that it is a result of the melting process. As with cooling, this effect may be insignificant because of the strong incentive to inhibit melting as much as possible. Again, in the absence of studies specifically dealing with this problem, any attempt to define possible harmful effects is speculative. There are studies showing that

---

[19]The most discussed method by which this would be accomplished involves wrapping the entire iceberg in plastic at the beginning of the towing operation. See Prince M. Al-Faisal, supra Footnote 2.

[20]Note that in this respect, iceberg exploitation differs radically from other activities which cause pollution as a by-product. In this situation, the cost of pollution is automatically internalized, and the cost to the polluter may be much greater than the cost to the general community.

[21]It may be possible to increase growth rates and reproduction of fish by controlled artificial warming of cold waters by thermal effluents (see J. W. Hedgpeth and J. J. Gonor, aspects of the potential effect of thermal lateration of marine and estuarine benthos in F. L. Parker (Ed.) Biological Aspects of Thermal Pollution, Nashville, Tennessee: Vanderbilt University Press, 1969, p. 80. See also J. A. Mihursky on possible constructive uses of thermal additions to estuaries. Bio Science, 1967, 17, p. 698. Given the above, it may follow that artificial cooling will result in slowed growth of some marine life.

reduced salinity increases mortality among some species of coral,[22] but this information may be irrelevant when we consider the fact that icebergs suitable for exploitation will draw 500-1000 feet of water.[23] Most corals must be much closer to the surface to get sufficient light to live. Additionally, there is research showing mortality in corals resulting from increased salinity (Johannes, 1972, p. 369). Effluents from desalination plants (the source of fresh water which iceberg exploitation may supplant) are characterized by high salinity levels. This leads to the conclusion that in areas where icebergs may result in coral mortality, the effect of a likely substitute source of fresh water, i.e., desalination, may be similar. However, which source of fresh water creates less hazard to coral is not presently known.

The last potential environmental effect which will be examined is really not just a single effect, but a group of things which may or may not happen. For convenience we can label these under the category of climate or weather modification effect.[24] While these are more speculative than the

---

[22]"Fresh water is thus clearly a pollutant when introduced into the reef environment through man's carelessness." R. E. Johannes, coral reefs and pollution. In M. Ruivo (Ed.) Marine Pollution and Sea Life, Fishing Books LTD, London, 1972, pp. 364, 367.

[23]There is an interesting sidelight to the problem of pollution from icebergs. If an iceberg operation is conducted in such a way as to cause a great deal of cooling in surrounding waters, or a decrease in salinity, it will be because the iceberg is floating unwrapped, perhaps waiting to be cut up and towed into shallow waters. However, because the fresh melt water is less dense than salt water, melt from the iceberg will rise from the bottom, along the sides of the iceberg. This effect has been calculated and the resulting conclusions are that a melting iceberg will produce significant upwelling of nutrient-rich bottom water to the surface. More study of this is needed to determine to what extent this advantageous effect might offset possible other adverse effects. See S. Neshyba, upwelling by icebergs, Nature, 1977, 267, p. 507.

[24]"The distinction between weather modification and climate modification also should be made clear. Weather modification activities attempt to produce transient effects on localized weather systems for immediate or short-term results. Climate modification is still a potential development for the future; such activities would attempt to make relatively long-term or lasting changes in climate. Although mankind may be modifying climates inadvertantly through industrial or technological activity, human induced climate changes have not been documented satisfactorily and cannot yet be manipulated for beneficial results." L. D. Wood, weather modification activities, Nat. Res. Lawyer, 1970, pp. 367, 368.

things discussed above, they are also potentially the most hazardous and may form the basis for vehement opposition to iceberg exploitation from the international community in general. Even though these highly speculative effects are so unlikely as to be barely worth consideration, they are worthy of mention, if for no other reason than to point out the virtual impossibility of occurrence. (This will be particularly true if iceberg exploitation under U.S. sponsorship is undertaken and an environmental impact statement is required, as it surely will be (National Environmental Policy Act, 1969)).

The first aspect of this problem is to look at possible global climatic effects resulting from removal of icebergs from Antarctica.[25] Knowledge about Antarctica's role in determining world climate is recent and incomplete. The polar ice is known to act as an insulator of the water from the air, which reduces heat exchange both in winter and summer.[26] Theoretically, if enough icebergs were removed from the Antarctic, there could be an effect on the heat exchange and thereby an effect on the global climate.

The likelihood of this effect is remote, to say the least. The number of icebergs which will be removed to satisfy demand for fresh water will be very small in relation to the total number of Antarctic icebergs.[27] Furthermore, the water area

---

[25] Although the effects are discussed here as potential hazards, their likelihood is extremely remote. The need for fresh water and the capacity to move it from Antarctica to other places in the world is infinitesimal when compared to the amount of water stored in the form of Antarctic ice. Initial Antarctic iceberg exploitation will be comparable to removing a handful of sand from an ocean beach.

[26] "...(T)he extent of ice on the ocean regulates heat exchange between ocean and atmosphere and influences the pattern of net atmospheric cooling, thereby influencing the thermal forcing of the dynamic system." J. L. Fletcher, polar ice and global climate machine, Science and Public Affairs, Bulletin of the Atomic Scientist, 1970, 26, pp. 40-41.

[27] Although the number of icebergs in Antarctica is not known, estimates have been made regarding the amount of fresh water contained in a huge tabular iceberg, and the amount is staggering. The U.S. Navy has been tracking an iceberg in Antarctic waters for the past 10 years (fearful that it might enter shipping lanes). The iceberg is 45 miles long and 25 miles wide (about the size of Rhode Island). Its depth is estimated at 750-1000 feet. This is, of course, far beyond towable size, but this iceberg contains enough fresh water to supply all of California's needs for 1,100 years! Aviation Week and Space Technology, 106, p. 42, April 25, 1977.

covered by those icebergs is slight when compared to the total area of the Antarctic pack ice, which provides the bulk of the insulation mentioned above.[28]

Another climatic effect with interesting implications is deep ocean currents. Cold water from the Antarctic flows off the continental shelf and moves north (at up to 3 miles/day) along the ocean bottom.[29] The exact impact which this has on ocean currents (and thereby on global climate) is unknown, but removal of too much Antarctic ice might have an effect on this phenomenon. Again, however, it seems unlikely that much ice will ever be removed.[30]

Given the discussion above, it is apparent that actual removal of icebergs from the Antarctic at least for the foreseeable future will have no perceivable climate or weather modification effects. But the presence of icebergs in arid regions of the world could easily have noticeable weather modification effects. Creation of fog and a lowering of regional temperatures are the most obvious examples.[31] Although the impact of these changes will increase as an exploitation program grows, it seems likely that local weather modification will be noticeable at a relatively low level of activity, and not dependent upon attainment of a much higher level of future activity. This potential local weather modification, along with the potential pollution discussed above, mandates some examination of international environmental law.

---

[28]The Antarctic ice pack during winter is 1½ times the area of the continent and 1/5 its winter area during the summer. Fletcher, supra footnote 25.

[29]Although water is unique among compounds in that it expands and becomes less dense when frozen, it contracts while being cooled until it reaches about 4 degrees centigrade. This increased density results in cold Antarctic water flowing down the Antarctic Continental Shelf, creating deep ocean currents which reach into the North Atlantic and North Pacific oceans.

[30]The role that icebergs play regarding the deep ocean currents is unknown. They probably contribute to the cooling of the water around them, but the deep ocean currents are not composed of fresh iceberg water, but rather cooled salt water. The fresh water rises to the surface.

[31]Prince M. Al-Faisal suggests modifying Saudi Arabia's weather by lowering the temperature. He asserts that a 200 million ton iceberg could cool by 5 degrees centigrade a "mass of air equal to the one that would flow within 110 m. from the ground at 1m/sec. on a 10 km wide front for five months." Supra footnote 2 at 421.

2. International Environmental Law

a. Treaties and Conventions on International Environmental Law

International law concerning pollution and modification of the ocean environment is just beginning to develop. The area, since it has been one of concern for a relatively short time, will be subject to further development in the near future.[32] The view for hundreds of years was that the oceans were so vast and man's activities so limited that the impact of those activities was negligible. Obviously, this is no longer true. The doctrine of freedom of the seas, insofar as it embellishes freedom to pollute subject only to flag state jurisdiction, is inadequate as a result of modern technology and new ocean uses.

This discussion is not intended to be a detailed analysis of international environmental law generally, but rather an examination of international environmental law as it may impact on iceberg exploitation. There are no international treaties or conventions which directly apply to iceberg exploitation. Article 1 of the 1958 Convention on Fishing and Conservation of the Living Resources of the High Seas (UST, 17, p. 138, TIAS 5969) imposes a general duty upon states to conserve living resources of the high seas. That Convention, however, is concerned with fishing activities; although it can be interpreted to prohibit a use which destroys fishery resources on a wide scale, it should not be interpreted as prohibiting new ocean uses which may or may not have a slight impact on living resources.

Article 25 of the 1958 Convention on the High Seas requires state cooperation to prevent pollution of the high seas by radioactive materials or other harmful agents. However, once again, this very general language should not be read as a prohibition of an activity such as iceberg exploitation. Rather, the language in both these conventions can be accurately interpreted as evidence of international concern regarding pollution of the oceans and recognition that cooperation between states is necessary to avoid destruction of marine resources. States which are parties to these conventions and which engage in iceberg exploitation can satisfy their treaty obligations by undertaking to limit adverse environmental effects as much as possible through the use of technology and cooperation.

---

[32]The real impetus toward development of international principles regarding the ocean environment has paralleled the growing world concern over the environment in general, i.e., growing and gaining momentum for approximately the past 20 years.

Given the above concern, the focus of international law has been on the greatest perceived threat to the marine environment, oil pollution.[33] But the agreements reached deal with oil pollution exclusively and do not apply to iceberg exploitation.

As a general statement, it is safe to say that international conventional law is lacking insofar as regulation of substances other than oil and radioactive materials is concerned (Waldichuk, 1977, pp. 269, 289-290). Part of the gap is filled by the Convention for the Prevention of Marine Pollution by Dumping of Wastes and Other Matter and the International Convention for the Prevention of Pollution from Ships. The former of these agreements does not apply to iceberg exploitation since "dumping" is defined in Article 3 as "deliberate disposal...from vessels, aircraft, platforms or other man-made structures."

The Pollution from Ships agreement (Article 2) seeks to regulate discharge from ships of any harmful substance. A harmful substance is anything which may harm living resources in the sea. A ship is a "vessel of any type whatsoever operating in the marine environment and includes...fixed or floating platforms." The issue is whether or not an iceberg is a vessel. Earlier in this paper it was argued that for purposes of innocent passage an iceberg was not a vessel (although given the policy considerations behind the concept of innocent passage icebergs should not be disqualified on that technicality). Here the policy (and the detailed regulations) of the Convention for Prevention of Pollution from Ships shows that its provisions are designed and intended to apply to man-made platforms.

Even if one concludes that the Convention for the Prevention of Pollution from Ships applies to icebergs, its provisions restricting discharges will not be applicable. Annex II of the Convention sets out the regulations for the control of pollution by noxious liquid substances in bulk, but the liquid discharged by an iceberg will be clear fresh water, and such is categorized in Appendix III as a non-harmful discharge. As such, the discharge of iceberg water is not subject to the Annex II regulations.

Other annexes of the Convention would seem applicable only if there are persons stationed upon the iceberg. In such a

---

[33]See the Int'l Convention for the Prevention of Pollution of the Sea by Oil, supra footnote 9; The Int'l Convention Relating to Intervention on the High Seas in Cases of Oil Pollution Casualties, UST, 26, p. 765; TIAS 8068 (1969); and the Int'l Convention on the Establishment of an Int'l Fund for Compensation for Oil Pollution Damage, Int'l Legal Materials, 1972, 11, p. 284.

situation, Annex IV (which is applicable only if an iceberg is defined as a ship or perhaps part of a ship while being towed) requires sewage treatment or a holding tank (Reg. 3). Annex V regulates the disposal of garbage. (For example, disposal of plastics is prohibited by Reg. 3.) Food wastes may be disposed of only after they have been ground up (Reg. 4).

The point of the above discussion is that there is no international treaty or convention which directly applies to iceberg exploitation. The nearest thing to a regulatory document (The Convention for Prevention of Pollution from Ships) is not clearly applicable and not yet in force.

This is not to say, however, that there are no international principles which might serve as the basis for opposition to iceberg exploitation. Customary international law regarding environmental protection is in the developmental stages. This development may proceed by way of judicial decisions, unilateral national action (for example, the Canadian Arctic Waters Pollution Prevention Act),[34] and/or international conferences and subsequent declarations of principles.

b. Judicial Decisions on International Environmental Law

In the area of transnational environmental harm, declarations of principles are the crux of the developing law. There is, however, one arbitration decision (Trail Smelter Arbitration, UNRIAA, 1905, 3)[35] which is important in this area and which established the now generally accepted principle that a nation may not use or permit the use of its territory in a way which causes serious transnational injury. This rule imposes responsibility on the government even if the injurious activities are under private management.[36] If iceberg exploitation causes environmental damage which harms another state's interests (or the interests of a private group), claims for compensation or abatement of the activity might be asserted on the basis of the above principle. For example, if icebergs

---

[34] Supra footnote 5.

[35] History and Opinion reprinted at Am. J. Int'l L., 1941, 35, p. 684.

[36] See Bleicher, an overview of international environmental regulation, Ecol. L.Q., 1972, 2, p. 1 and L. K. Caldwell, concepts in development of international environmental policies, Natural Res. J., 1973, 13, p. 190. Note that in Trail Smeltor, the harm occurred in the sovereign territory of the United States. This makes it at least arguable that Trail Smeltor is not applicable where harm occurs on the high seas.

en route to Saudi Arabia are moored on the high seas of the Gulf of Aden or the Arabian Sea and harm occurs to fisheries of the region, parties harvesting those resources will certainly object and assert a claim for compensation.

The question of to whom a harmed party may complain is important in this context. In Trail Smelter, supra, the activity took place in Canada and the harm occurred in the U.S. The parties submitted themselves to the jurisdiction of an arbitration body and agreed to abide by its decision.

There are a variety of hypothetical situations where an agreement analogous to that reached between the U.S. and Canada would be advantageous. For example, iceberg towing activities might harm high seas fisheries which a coastal state exploits but has no jurisdiction over. Or perhaps harm will occur within a coastal state's jurisdiction from iceberg towing on the high seas, e.g., disruption of fish migration patterns.

If no Trail Smelter-type arbitration agreement is reached, the injured nation or any other injured party is in a difficult situation. If the complainant is a sovereign government and it and the offending nation agree to jurisdiction, an action can be brought in the International Court of Justice. Barring that, the complainant could bring an action in the courts of the offending nation. There seems little likelihood an action could be brought in the courts of the complainant nation, since there would be no jurisdiction over the offending party. Underlying all this is the issue of sovereign immunity, which may or may not be a defense.

The point of this discussion is not to pose all the possible hypothetical situations but rather to point out that fora for relief (although limited) are available to a harmed party. The facts of a particular case will determine the forum in which relief can be obtained; the particular facts will determine applicable law. For example, if harmful activity occurs within the jurisdiction of a state, it can bring an action in its own courts and apply its own law. If the activity occurs on the high seas, the flag state will have jurisdiction and its internal law and general international law will apply. Additionally, the impartiality of the courts will vary; in some situations it may be very difficult for a complainant to get an adjudication from an impartial court.

c. Unilateral National Legislation

The second area of customary international law mentioned was unilateral national legislation. The unilateral measures which affect iceberg exploitation are assertions of authority over high seas. These assertions may take the form of pollution control zones or economic zones. However, because routes for iceberg transport are not yet known (they will depend heavily on such things as depth, currents, and prevailing wind direction), no attempt will be made to examine particular national legislation. Suffice it to say that when various potential routes are considered, the impact of national environmental protection laws must be weighed.

d. Declarations of Principles from International Conferences

This brings us to declarations of principles issued by international conferences. In the area of environmental law, the most important set of principles is contained in the Report of the United Nations Conference on the Human Environment.[37] Although this conference was not capable of producing declarations which can be characterized as binding in international law, the conference and its declaration of principles are still important.[38] At the conference Canada contended that at least one of the principles (Principle 21) was in accordance with existing international law (Goldie, 1975, p. 107). The best view is that the principles of the Stockholm Conference provide a starting point for the development of international and transnational environmental law.

Even though the Stockholm principles are not binding on states, it is likely they would not be overlooked by the parties to a dispute over the legality of iceberg exploitation activities which cause some environmental harm.

Principle 6 prohibits the discharge of heat in "quantities or concentrations which exceed the capacity of the environment to render them harmless." Assuming thermal discharge from icebergs is harmful, this principle requires states to "take all possible steps" (Principle 7) to prevent pollution of the seas

[37] Stockholm, June 5-16, 1972, U.N. Doc. A/conf.48/14/Rev.1.

[38] "Recommendations and declarations issued either by intergovernmental organizations or by international conferences generally have no binding force. They constitute what is called "soft law," i.e., rules which have to be considered as law insofar as they fix norms with which states should comply, but which cannot be enforced in the traditional meaning of the term." A. L. Kiss, Survey of Current Developments in International Environmental Law, International Union for Conservation of Nature and Natural Resources, Switzerland, 1976, p. 23.

[39] The Secretary-General characterized the conference as "the first attempt to give expression to an international consensus on the environmental ethic." Secretary-General, An Action Plan for the Human Environment, U.N. Doc. A/conf.48/5 at 6.

by harmful substances, and Principle 21 mandates that states "ensure that activities within their jurisdiction or control do not cause damage to the environment of other states or to areas beyond the limits of national jurisdiction." This principle establishes protection of the environment as a primary duty of states. It is this principle which Canada considers an expression of customary international law.[40]

Even though these declarations are at best "soft law," commentators agree that international customary law is shifting toward increased responsibility for environmental protection and liability for damage to the "commons."[41] The need for international action to protect the environment is more widely recognized than in the past; although international control is not likely in the near future, the groundwork is being laid. "(I)nvestigation and control of marine pollution...is a matter on which international action on both a regional and global scale is now becoming urgent.[42]

If it is shown that iceberg exploitation will have harmful environmental effects, either by thermal or saline pollution, or by causing climatic changes, this trend toward greater environmental protection is likely to manifest itself in the form of opposition based upon the principles set out above. But because those principles cannot yet be seen as expressions of international law, the resolution of any dispute will to a large extent depend upon political and economic power. The

---

[40] See also, Charter of Economic Rights and Duties of States (resolution of the General Assembly on Dec. 13, 1974, Res. #3281 XXIX). Article 30: "The protection, preservation and the enhancement of the environment for the present and future generations is the responsibility of all states. All states shall endeavor to establish their own environmental and developmental policies in conformity with such responsibility." See also, The Declarations Concerning the Problems of the Sea Issued by the Carribbean Countries at Santo Domingo, June 9, 1972, 1973 ILM 893 "The International responsibility of physical or juridical persons for damaging the marine environment is recognized."

[41] It is often argued that the Corfu Channel Case (1949) ICJ 22, established the liability of a state when it knowingly allowed its territory to be used contrary to the rights of other states. But that was by no means an environmental case, so the argument is somewhat weak when used in the context of international environmental law. See also Kiss, *supra* footnote 38.

[42] Statement by the Secretary-General (U.N. Doc. E/4487, April 24, 1968, para. 278).

resolution of any dispute will clearly be another step in the development of international environmental law.

e. Informal Composite Negotiating Text

The ICNT has provisions in Part XXII (Articles 193-235) dealing with the Protection and Preservation of the Marine Environment. However, that part is so poorly drafted that analysis in a specific context is an enormous task. Part XII is at best convoluted. Article 194 establishes a general duty to "protect and preserve the marine environment." Article 195 requires of states "the best practicable means at their disposal and in accordance with their capabilities" and "all necessary measures to ensure that activities under their jurisdiction or control are so conducted that they do not cause damage by pollution to other states and their environment." No indication is given as to what constitutes "best practicable means" or "all necessary measures" or "states and their environment."

Without accompanying definitions or further elaborations, these clauses are too ambiguous to be effective. For example, what measures are in accordance with a state's capabilities? To apply a specific context, is a different standard of environmental protection to be applied to a U.S. iceberg exploitation scheme than is applied to an Australian or Saudi Arabian scheme? Should this difference be based upon different economic and technological capabilities or perhaps different socio-political capabilities? For example, if a particular political system is capable of greater control over private enterprise, is that factor to be taken into account?

The general duty enunciated in Article 194 receives no support or clarification in Articles 205-207, concerning monitoring and environmental assessment. Article 205 requires states to evaluate, "the risks or effects of pollution on the marine environment." Article 206 requires those studies to be published or made available to organizations. Article 207 requires nations to assess "potential effects of activities on the marine environment and communicate reports of the results of such assessments in the manner provided in Article 206." This assessment must only be made "as far as practicable" and only when states have reasonable grounds for expecting that planned activities under their jurisdiction or control may cause substantial pollution of, or significant and harmful changes to, the marine environment."

These articles could have served to enhance the Article 194 duty simply by expressly prohibiting activities when the environmental assessment substantiated the potential for "substantial pollution of or significant and harmful changes to, the marine environment." However, there is no such prohibition in Articles 205-207. This failure to prohibit leaves the question of whether states may go ahead with damaging activities after the assessment is done. If the intent of the assessment is to provide an indication of when prohibition is required, Article 207 should have so stated. The implication is that the assessment need not lead to any prohibition or abatement of an activity.

There is one more article of the ICNT which could conceivably prohibit or limit iceberg exploitation. Article 197 requires all nations to "prevent, reduce and control pollution of the marine environment resulting from the use of technologies under their jurisdiction or control..." This article appears to create a greater duty on states to protect the marine environment wherever "technologies" are involved. But the text does not reveal what the term "technologies" includes. All uses of the ocean involve some technology; so if the normal meaning of the word is meant, all ocean uses are covered. In any event, it is unclear if this Article establishes a duty greater than that in Articles 194 and 195, since 197(2) says, "This article shall not affect the application of the present convention regarding the prevention, reduction and control of pollution of the marine environment."

3. Possible Weather Modification Effects

Thus far in this section the focus has been on general environmental harm occurring in areas outside of any national jurisdiction (with the exception of the Trail Smelter discussion). There is at least some basis upon which one can argue for either damages or abatement of an activity. However, at the beginning of this section, weather modification effects were mentioned; now they will be examined in more detail.

The global climatic changes which were mentioned as a result of iceberg harvest are so unlikely as to deserve no further attention. The problems of proof are too overpowering. But the creation of fog in the region where an iceberg is moored, along with the consequent lowering of the temperature, are both likely.[43] To the extent that these effects take place outside areas of national jurisdiction, the principles discussed above will apply. But to the extent that icebergs are used to modify the weather within a nation's own territory, not all of those principles are applicable. Principles 6 and 21 of the Stockholm Convention[44] seem applicable, as is the general duty of a state not to use its national territory in such a way as to harm other states. But the issue here is not really primary

---

[43] Supra footnote 2.

[44] Supra footnote 37.

or secondary effects of pollution, but rather effects which causally speaking may be much further removed. Causal relationships will likely be much more difficult to prove.[45] For example, what will be the effect on nations surrounding Saudi Arabia if instead of desert that nation is at least partially transformed into farmland?

In addition to these problems of proof, the argument that principles such as 6 and 21[46] do not apply to national weather modification is strong. Its strength is derived from the fact that other nations are currently engaged in weather modification activities (Battan, 1977, p. 4; Hearing before Subcommittee, 1972) and that such activities are currently accepted. Therefore, the only sure principle that exists in this regard is the duty of a state not to use its national territory in such a way as to harm other states, and the resultant obligation to pay reparations for damages.

Any conclusions to be drawn from the above discussion must result from a careful balancing. The gains that may be realized from successful exploitation of icebergs are great. But the adverse environmental effects, although localized, may be major. Every attempt should be made to avoid such harm. But what is first needed is a better prediction of potential environmental effects. This could take the form of an environmental impact statement (Goldie, 1973, p. 256) or some other comprehensive interdisciplinary study. The crucial point is that although iceberg exploitation will be conducted as a high seas freedom, developing international law is closing in on the "freedom to pollute." Although the support for a claim to proscribe an activity based upon environmental harm is currently weak, there is good reason to recommend that iceberg exploitation activities be conducted with an eye toward limiting potential environmental harm.

---

[45] One definition of weather modification itself mirrors these difficulties. "The subjects of weather and climate modification are concerned with any artificially produced changes in the composition, behavior, or dynamics of the atmosphere. Such changes may or may not be predictable, their production may be deliberate or inadvertent, they may be transient or permanent, and they may be manifested on any scale from the micro climate of plants to the macrodynamics of the worldwide atmospheric circulation." Committee on Atmospheric Sciences, National Academy of Sciences, National Research Council, Weather and Climate Modification, Problems and Prospects (Pub. No. 1350, 1966).

[46] Supra footnote 37.

Conclusion

Engineers and scientists have discussed the technological possibility of using Antarctic icebergs as a source of fresh water. Although problems exist, it seems that they are not insolvable. Economic feasibility, i.e., cost competitiveness, is the large unanswered question. This paper has shown that although there is potential for legal disputes, there is no single issue which will prevent iceberg exploitation. The greatest danger posed is the potential environmental harm, particularly the possibility of damage to fisheries.

Those potential effects need more study. It may be that some damage to fisheries could be allowed, if the result is greater overall production of food via increased agriculture. Attempts should be made to gauge accurately all benefits and balance all interests before an iceberg exploitation project is undertaken. Such an examination may reveal costs which make the project clearly uneconomic. However, an in-depth analysis may reveal benefits which make the project easily cost competitive with other sources of fresh water. For example, icebergs might be used in conjunction with Ocean Thermal Energy Conversion facilities, thus providing a way to melt the icebergs. Additionally, a method may be found to use the upwelling potential of icebergs and still capture melted water. Even more theoretical is the possibility of using the salinity differential around the iceberg to generate electricity.

The point of this discussion is to show that although the idea of towing icebergs sounds fanciful, a little imagination may show ways to make a full-scale project economically feasible. The indications are that exploitation of icebergs will take place. The questions which remain to be answered are how soon and for what combination of purposes.

REFERENCES

Al-Faisal, HRH Mohammed. Feasibility of using paddle-wheels for the propulsion of icebergs. In A. Husseiny (Ed.), Proceedings of the First International Conference on Iceberg Utilization. New York: Pergamon Press, 1978.

Al-Faisal, M. Water supply and weather modifications through the use of transported icebergs from the Antarctic. Desalination, 1977, 20.

Allaire, P. E. Stability of simply shaped icebergs. J. Can. Petroleum Technology, 1972, 11.

Battan, L. J. Weather modification in the Soviet Union. Bulletin of the American Meteorological Society, 1977, 58.

Benedict, C. P. A new iceberg towing system. In A. Husseiny (Ed.), Proceedings of the First International Conference on Iceberg Utilization. New York: Pergamon Press, 1978.

Burke. Who goes where, when and how: international law of the sea for transportation. Int'l Org., 1977, 31.

Burt, J. C. Iceberg water for California. Science Digest, 1956, 39.

Convention on the High Seas. U.S.T., 13, TIAS 5200.

Convention on the Prevention of Marine Pollution by the Dumping of Wastes at Sea. U.S.T., 26, TIAS 8165.

Convention on the Territorial Sea and Contiguous Zone. U.S.T., 15, TIAS 5639.

Davis, J. D. Osmotic propulsion of icebergs. In A. Husseiny (Ed.), Proceedings of the First International Conference on Iceberg Utilization. New York: Pergamon Press, 1978.

El-Hares, H. Considerations about the cariolis effects on icebergs towed for fresh water production. In A. Husseiny (Ed.), Proceedings of the First International Conference on Iceberg Utilization. New York: Pergamon Press, 1978.

Farmer, L. D. Photogrammetric determination of iceberg volumes. Photogrammetric E. R., 1977, 43.

Fuhs, A. E. Self-propelled icebergs. In A. Husseiny (Ed.), Proceedings of the First International Conference on Iceberg Utilization. New York: Pergamon Press, 1978.

Gilmore and Black. The Law of Admiralty, 2nd Ed. Foundation Press, 1975.

Goldie, L.F.E. International impact reports and the conservation of the ocean environment. Nat. Res. J., 1973, 13.

Goldie, L.F.E. International maritime environmental law today: an appraisal. In J. L. Hargrove (Ed.), Who Protects the Ocean. St. Paul, Minn.: West Publishing, 1975.

Hearings before the Subcommittee on Oceans and International Environment of the Senate Foreign Relations Committee, 92nd Cong., 2nd Sess., 1972.

Hult, J. L. Water Rights and Assessments (Proposals involving Antarctic icebergs for the Colorado River Basin, California, Mexico, and other arid lands). Rand Report #P-5271, 1974.

Hult, J. L. and Ostrander, N. C. Antarctic Icebergs as a Global Fresh Water Resource. Rand Report #R-1255-NSF, 1973.

Hult, J. L. and Ostrander, N. C. Applicability of ERTS for Surveying Iceberg Resources. Rand Report #R-1354, 1973.

ICNT (Informal Composite Negotiating Text), Third U.N. Conference on the Law of the Sea. New York Session, May 23-July 15, 1977.

Int'l Convention for the Safety of Life at Sea. U.S.T., 16, TIAS 5780.

Isaacs, John. The Sea, LIFE Nature Library, TIME, Inc. New York, 1961.

Jab, J. G. High efficiency iceberg propulsion systems. In A. Husseiny (Ed.), Proceedings of the First International Conference on Iceberg Utilization. New York: Pergamon Press, 1978.

Love, R. The Chemical Biology of Fishes. 1970.

McDougal & Burke. The Public Order of the Oceans. Yale Press, 1962.

National Environmental Policy Act. U.S.C., 1969, 42.

O'Connell, D. P. The juridical nature of the territorial sea. British Y.B. International Law, 1971, 45.

Robe, R. O. Maier, D. C., Kollmeyer, R. C. Iceberg deterioration. _Nature_, 1977, _267_.

Waldichuk, M. Control of marine pollution: an essay review. _ODIL_, 1977, _4_.

Weeks, W. F. and Campbell, W. S. Icebergs as a fresh-water source: an appraisal. _Journal of Glaciology_, 1973, _12_.

Appendix 1

For a detailed look at Antarctic Mineral Resource potential see:

Mineral Resources of Antarctica, compiled and edited by N. A. Wright and P. L. Williams, in U. S. Antarctic Policy, Hearings before the Subcommittee on Oceans and International Environment of the Senate Committee on Foreign Relations, 94th Cong., 1st Sess., 1975.

For information on the Antarctic Treaty, 12 U.S.T. 794: TIAS 4780; 42 U.N.T.S. 71, see:

Taubenfeld, H. J. A treaty for Antarctica. _Int'l Conciliation_, 1961, _531_, pp. 245, 278.

Hannessian, J. _The Antarctic Treaty_. 1959.

Int'l and Comp. L. Q., 1960, _9_, pp. 436, 456.

Hayton, R. D. The Antarctic settlement of 1959. _Am. J. Int'l Law_, 1960, _54_, pp. 349, 359.

For discussions of the question of sovereignty over portions of Antarctica see:

Richardson. New Zealand's Claim in the Antarctic. _N. Zealand L. J._, 1957, _33_, p. 38.

Toma, P. A. Soviet attitude towards the acquisition of territorial sovereignty in the Antarctic. _Am. J. Int'l L._, 1956, _50_, p. 611.

Chichvarini, V. A. _Theoretical Problems of Conservation of Antarctic Resources Under Int'l Law_, U. S. Department of Commerce Joint Publications Research Service, 1973.

Bernhardt, J. P. Sovereignty in Antarctica. _Calif. W. Int'l L. J._, 1975, _5_, pp. 297, 305.

DISCUSSION AND QUESTIONS

DAVID ROSS: I, of course, enjoyed that idea about towing icebergs and I think it is a lot of fun like you said. Perhaps next time you discuss it you might want to modify the concept a slight bit, which I think would make everything much easier, especially the legal aspects. Visualize towing an iceberg below the surface, not on the surface, and putting a little bendable mast on it. Since ice, as you know, will float with much of it below the surface, it should not be so hard to sink it a little bit more. And if you did that, since ocean water becomes much colder with depth, the melting problem could be minimized considerably. The fresh water pollution problem also will not be so bad since the fresh water would almost immediately dissipate as it floated up. But the best thing would, of course, be the legal aspects. Now, here is what you do with that berg being towed below the surface. Every time you come into someone's exclusive economic zone, you push a little button and up comes that mast, and you say it is really a submarine. Now you can claim innocent passage. Most of the problems would be solved. As you said, to paraphrase you, I am not a lawyer.

LEWIS ALEXANDER: I have a question for Donat Pharand, but I want to say one word about the icebergs, too. I think in the first place that Curt should have changed the title and borrowed from Eugene O'Neill, calling it "The Iceberg Cometh." The other point is that if the iceberg is going to be drawing 200 meters of water you are not going to get very close to Saudi Arabia. And indeed if you did send some frogmen down to chip off a bit at the bottom, you are then going to have the problem of transit passage of icebergs through straits; I do not think the ICNT has yet said anything about this.

But so far as the story goes about possibly closing off the Canadian Archipelago with straight lines, I was wondering under which of the ICNT articles this would be done. If you close them off as an archipelago as Indonesia has, you would have to have archipelagic sealanes through it; if you use the argument that this is a fringe of islands in the immediate area of the coast, I think it might be hard to prove that they are really a fringe. Or would they represent a special cirumstance; in which case, this would be the reason for doing it?

DONAT PHARAND: Well, I am very pleased that you raised the question. I have asked myself exactly the same question over the years and I have really never been able to answer it. It is obvious, of course, and I think I have indicated this very briefly in my remarks, that the Canadian Arctic archipelago could hardly be considered as a fringe of islands along a coast in exactly the same sense as it was used to describe the Norwegian "skjaergaard."

The second possibility is to consider it as an archipelagic state kind of archipelago, as that of Indonesia, as you say. If you did, look at the legal results. As you know, the sea-lane passage, which for all intents and purposes is the same as transit passage, would apply. This would mean the right of passage for all ships, including warships and submarines in their "normal mode" of passage. This was inserted in the ICNT provisions at two places, both with respect to the transit passage and the sealanes passage for that very purpose, that is to cover submerged submarine passage. This, of course, might not be so obvious to the foreign service advisor some 25 years from now. But it is very obvious to us, any one of us who has been following the Conference for the last six or seven years. So my answer to your question is: I don't really know the answer. I think the possibility, however, exists for Canada to make a special case in the same way as Norway did in 1951.

If you take a close look at the Court's judgment in the Fisheries Case, you will notice that the Court emphasized throughout its reasoning the special physical reality of the situation, and that physical reality happened to be a fringe of islands along the coast. It seems to me that the decision could still be invoked in order to justify those baselines. What I am saying to you, in effect, is that if I had to advise the Canadian government to find a proper legal basis for the drawing of those strait baselines, I would say, don't rely on the Territorial Sea Convention, of which, in any event, you are not a party, and rely instead on the Norwegian Fisheries Case. That would be my answer to your question.

RAINER LAGONI: I have two questions about the Antarctic. I appreciate very much that Mr. Sollie is here; and I would like to ask him whether the common heritage principle would apply to the Antarctic Treaty area.

My second question is, whether the regime of the continental shelf applies to the Antarctic. We know that the average depth of the waters above the continental shelf of Antarctica is far below that which you normally have elsewhere; it is about 500 meters, if I am right.

FINN SOLLIE: If I could answer the second question first. The Geneva Continental Shelf Convention provides that the continental shelf to 200 meters or so far as resources can be retrieved, belongs to the coastal state. Presuming, then, that either the treaty parties collectively or the individual claimant states can be said to have control over the coastline, the shelf provision will apply provided you can get something up from 500 meters depth. Today that is not really difficult. And as a matter of fact, I think some states, including Chile and Argentina, have already tried to apply the treaty to the Antarctic. I have heard no protests against that, so we might also assume that the regime has been accepted.

The parties to the Antarctic Treaty apparently believe the common heritage does not apply completely! In the opinion of the claimant, it states it is part of their national territory. In the opinion of the treaty parties generally, apparently, they feel that the Antarctic Treaty consultative parties have a special responsibility that it is not part of the generally considered common heritage. This does not mean that the parties do not feel a special responsibility to make the resources and benefits from Antarctica generally available.

Obviously, the argument may be one of crocodile tears, because they are also aware that unless they make concessions to the international community, it will be more difficult to have the international community accept a special regime.

BARBARA MITCHELL: I have one question and two comments. First, the question. Why are signatories of a scientific agreement, only three of whom are seriously fishing for living resources in the Southern Ocean, better qualified to elaborate a resource management framework than the fisheries committee of FAO?

Moving on to the comments, you told us that the living resource management convention negotiated by Antarctic Treaty parties would be open to outside participants. I think it is worth bringing out that participants other than signatories of the Antarctic Treaty will only be allowed in at the very last stage in the negotiations, when the broad outlines of the arrangements will have been decided upon.

It is also worth bringing out that special rights will be reserved on a permanent basis to the <u>initial</u> signatories of the living resource convention. That is not just the Antarctic Treaty parties but all those who participate in the definitive meeting in January of 1979 or June, if it is postponed. That is to say that any country that starts fishing for krill any later than mid-1979 will be denied the same rights as the initial signatories, in decisions of the future commission.

As to my second comment, you talked about the progress that is being made by the Antarctic Treaty parties in drawing up management arrangements for living resources and mineral resources in Antarctica. I think it is fair to say that we must reserve our judgment as to whether treaty parties are right in doing so until we see what kind of arrangements they produce. In other words, it is not just the speed with which they proceed which is important; in fact, one could almost talk about indecent haste. As we understand it, the living resource arrangements that are emerging are very deficient from an environmental point of view. For example, there is likely to be a provision for consensus voting on conservation measures, which will make it very difficult indeed to set any catch limits on a year by year basis. Secondly, it is very unlikely that there will be any interim measures. We know how long conventions take to be ratified and to come into force and for the machinery to actually come into operation.

FINN SOLLIE: I merely refer to what is the considered opinion of the treaty parties themselves.

As for the various comments, I find them very much to the point and exactly this issue of whether outsiders should be allowed in, at what point they should be allowed in. We have, however, to be aware that when you are negotiating an international agreement you always have to look for the best possible solution. Some may feel the best possible solution would have been participation by outsiders. I must point out, however, that it is better to be represented at the final conference before the convention is adopted, than only to be invited to join the convention after it has been adopted.

A weakness of the present text is that there are no entry measures. We all are agreed, I think, that it is a weakness that the convention, if and when adopted, will not apply immediately. However, the parties have already agreed through their recommendation adopted in London to adopt interim guidelines for their own behavior in Antarctic waters and to try to impress upon non-parties to the treaty the need to follow these same guidelines when they operate in Antarctic waters. This is not ideal again, but at least it is something.

HIDEO TAKABAYASHI: Dr. Østreng speaks about the problems of the Arctic Ocean, especially the demarcation problems of shelves between two countries. I think you did not address the principle of natural prolongation of land territory into the sea. If we confine the problem to Arctic regions, I think, both the sector doctrine and the principle of natural prolongation will bring similar results as to the lateral boundary of continental shelves. My question is very simple. Do you think that the principle of natural prolongation will have any effect on the claims of the sector doctrine?

WILLY ØSTRENG: As a matter of fact, the theory of prolongation is one of the justifications used by the Soviet Russians to apply the sector principle. So, consequently, the linkage between the sector principle and the theory of prolongation is close.

FINN SOLLIE: I think in this connection we should point out that the continental shelf dividing line negotiations between Norway and the Soviet Union are the only negotiations so far where the question of sector or not sector is at issue. In these negotiations, the Soviets have not directly claimed the sector principle as applicable. They have pointed out that the dividing line between Norway and the Soviet Union on the northern continental shelf is a question subject to special considerations. There are special circumstances that will lead to the median line principle not being applicable. The Soviets pointed to the sector principle, not to the principle as such but to their sector decree of 1926, as one of the special circumstances justifying a line other than the median line in this region. This is only one of the special circumstances mentioned.

In other words, we have the impression that the Soviets, although indications point toward a sector line on their part, might see fit to claim more than the sector.

DONAT PHARAND: If I could just add a comment. I think one could say that Canada in respect to its delimitation in the Beaufort Sea could adopt a similar position, not relying on the sector theory I personally do not like to call it a principle; it is simply a theory which cannot serve as a legal basis to claim sovereignty. Canada could invoke one leg of the sector, that is the 141st meridian, and point to the use which it has already made of that line and ask that this historical line be considered a special circumstance. Personally, I would be inclined to think that there might be some merit in that kind of an approach, whereas I would see no merit in using the sector theory as such.

PART V

CHANGING REGIME FOR SHIPPING

INTRODUCTORY REMARKS BY SESSION PROGRAM CHAIRMAN

Leo J. Bouchez
Institute of International Law
University of Utrecht

First of all I wish to introduce Professor Edgar Gold who will present a paper on the freedom of ocean shipping and commercial viability. Dr. Gold is Professor of Maritime Law at Dalhousie University, Halifax, Canada.

In addition, I wish to introduce Mr. Gezelius, Managing Director of the Dutch Shipowners Company Incotrans in Rotterdam and Mr. de Jong, Research Associate of the Netherlands Maritime Institute in Rotterdam.

First, we shall address the question of the risks of pollution caused by ships. In this connection two aspects of shipping deserve special consideration:

A. Internationally, criteria have to be set and applied with respect to shipbuilding, in particular insofar as certain types of ships, such as tankers and other ships transporting dangerous cargos are concerned.

B. In order to avoid pollution of the sea caused by collisions, groundings, and similar incidents, specific regulations have to be applied with respect to safety of traffic, such as inter alia shipping routes and traffic separation schemes.

In these two fields, IMCO has been most active and has made important contributions during the last decade.

The aforementioned regulations will unavoidably affect the commercial viability of shipping. Nevertheless, it is difficult to uphold the view that such regulations would be ipso facto contrary to freedom of navigation. The necessity of coping with the increasing density of maritime traffic and the technological changes in shipbuilding rather than intending to restrict the freedom of navigation unnecessarily is the main reason for these regulations.

A completely different question, which directly affects the commercial viability of ocean navigation, is whether the traditional freedom of transportation should be upheld as an essential element of freedom of navigation or whether the traditional laissez-faire approach should be replaced by an extensive regulation of market allocation as, for example, is embodied in the Geneva Code of Conduct for Liner Conferences. This would mean a serious restriction of the economic freedom of navigation.

As I stated earlier, the developing countries are no longer satisfied with a passive role so far as ocean navigation is concerned any more than they are satisfied with traditional patterns of natural resource exploitation.

THE 'FREEDOM' OF OCEAN SHIPPING AND COMMERCIAL VIABILITY: MYTHS AND REALITIES IN THE AFTERMATH OF UNCLOS III

Edgar Gold
Dalhousie University
Halifax, Nova Scotia
Canada

Preface

At an annual meeting of the Law of the Sea Institute held in its original home in Rhode Island just over two years ago, I was a commentator on a panel which discussed problems relating to navigation at UNCLOS III. At that time, I stated that it would take more than a law of the sea conference to stop shipping. By way of illustration, I said (in retrospect, rather rashly) that during my sea-going career, I had worked for shipowners who would unhesitatingly take a 120,000 ton tanker up the mountain to Kabul, Afghanistan, as long as it would have made money. When John Gamble was kind enough to honor me by this invitation to give this paper, I received the distinct feeling that he wanted me to prove that proposition. I am not going to do it! In any case, yesterday we were told of the possibility of sending garbage rockets toward the sun; we have heard from Mr. Epperson about towing iceberg trains from the Southern Ocean to Saudi Arabia. Obviously, it is far less difficult to take a large ship up a mountain.

I. Introduction

There is probably little doubt that UNCLOS III which, with its staggering agenda, is attempting to draft a new law of the sea affecting most users of the oceans, has neglected one of the most traditional of these, namely ocean shipping. There is no question that shipping is truly one of the neglected areas at UNCLOS III. In almost abstract terms the Conference has been discussing questions related to ships' use of ocean space, such as transit and passage rights, as well as the controls coastal states may exert over shipping in order to preserve their marine environment. The term 'abstract' is used because it seems, at times, that these discussions see ships sailing from point A to point B for the sake of making the trip rather than in the pursuit of economic activities which are the very basis of their existence. Certainly the question of commercial viability is rarely raised and if it is, then only as a rather shrill defense of the maritime states' status quo.

The problem is that ocean transportation in its virtual absence from the Conference has become a victim of its own history. Despite the fact that ocean use and ocean use regulation are both interlinked within the same marine system, something which the scientists have been telling us for years, in terms of law the commercial transportation function of ships has become separated from ships' use of ocean space. As a result the stage has now been reached -- or is actually being perfected at UNCLOS III -- that while ships are being governed by laws relating to their commercial activities (either through the laws of their flag state or international private maritime law rules), their actual passage on the ocean may be determined by another set of laws which may well disregard the commercial function of the ship. Of course, the spatial extensions of coastal state jurisdictions have brought, and will continue to bring, this contradiction to a head.

The purpose of this presentation is to attempt to quickly trace the antecedents of this contradiction, to analyze its present status, and then venture a rapid glance at the future of the world shipping industry in the aftermath of UNCLOS III.

2. The Separate Development of Maritime Law and Policy

The present dilemma the international shipping industry finds itself in at UNCLOS III (as well as in other fora) is due to the fact that it has become a victim of its own history. The law of the sea as we know it, or the law relating to the use of ocean space, or the public international law of the sea, is of relatively recent vintage when compared to the law governing the commercial function of ships. This is the private maritime law, admiralty law, shipping law or whatever it may confusingly be called, which has existed for millennia. We know that some of the earliest law known to man was shipping law because men were sailors long before they did most other things. Even the great Roman law simply codified pre-existing rules which had been compiled from earlier customary Mediterranean commercial practice. Law related to the use of ocean space was not a pressing concern despite Roman protestations that the sea is open to everyone, according to Vulpian, and, like the air, common to all mankind according to Celsus. We must remember that these were gratuitous statements as the political reality was that Rome controlled most of the known world and its oceans at that time and had little need to consider dominion over the ocean in a jurisdictional sense.

The world was then plunged into what historians call the Dark Ages for almost a thousand years. Whatever sea existed ceased to operate. In a perverse sense it can be said that the Norman and Saracen pirates, who ravaged commercial shipping during this era, enjoyed the most lengthy period of freedom of the sea in its history! However, despite this prolonged period of darkness the commercial law was further developed by the city states of the Mediterranean and the new commercial interests on the western and northern seaboard of Europe. The further refinement and codification of this law has given us the basis for most of the shipping law we use today throughout the world. However, the growth of the Mediterranean city states and the Iberian 'superpowers' also gave us the beginnings of the real law of the sea as we know it. It should not be forgotten that Mediterranean coastal state expansionism into ocean space and the Iberian wish to dominate the the oceans was motivated almost entirely by commercial ambitions. Hugo Grotius' essay Mare Liberum was written as a plea to allow the fledgling commercial and maritime power of the newly created United Provinces of the Netherlands access to the commercial riches of the East Indies. The Portugese wanted to keep the Dutch out by restricting their shipping from trading in the area. Grotius was hired to defend the Dutch trading right. His impassioned plea has not only become a part of the history of the international law of the sea, but is also frequently used out of context. Much later in 1637, the great Grotius having long completed his maxim opus De jure Belli ac Pacis, even went so far as to dismiss the earlier work as a young man's book written out of fierce passion for his fatherland. And yet, as we all know, it was this chapter alone which caught the emotional imagination of the world. The 'freedom of navigation' became part of the 'freedom of the seas' which henceforth would become an accepted principle of the international law of the sea. The Dutch East Indies dispute, however, set a pattern which has frequently repeated itself throughout history.

It is generally suggested that the 'freedom of navigation' was not a policy favored by the powerful states and consequently imposed by them on the weaker ones, but that, on the contrary, it was a principle for which the latter had to fight bitterly against the major maritime powers in order to achieve its recognition and implementation. Such a suggestion fits, of course, neatly within the general framework of "oceanic equality" of which the principle itself is always considered to be a vital part. However, seen in its historical framework a different aspect appears which shows the powerful states giving up something which they no longer wanted or needed anyway. They could gain much more by supporting universal oceanic freedom. The opening of the world had made real colonial and commercial power possible and ocean transportation was the only means to achieve it. Suddenly everyone appeared to benefit from shipping; the freest use of the oceans appeared to be a natural conclusion. For example, from the late 18th and early 19th centuries onwards, Great Britain, the leading maritime state, pursued and consolidated its oceanic ambitions on a world-wide scale, fully exploiting the new freedom of the seas which she had found unacceptable less than three generations earlier.

Most, if not all, maritime states followed suit. Maritime power was what the world required during the next 150 years and maritime power demanded freedom of navigation.

Obviously this change from coastal power to sea power, in its widest sense, required a whole range of legal norms specifically designed for the new spatial requirements of ocean use. Prior to the Grotian period ocean use by ships had been subordinate to the commercial function of the ship itself. By the 19th century a separation had occurred. The major maritime powers had formulated new maritime policies based, of course, on commercial prerogatives, but which had created a new area of dominance in the "public" or jurisdictional aspect of ocean use. The more traditional "private" or commercial aspect of navigation was thus sidelined. Henceforth the "public" law would concern itself with rules relating to ocean space such as the high seas and marginal seas and would be the responsibility of government departments dealing with foreign affairs and external relations with other states. On the other hand, "private" maritime law and practice would become more and more the responsibility of those with direct interest in the commercial aspects of shipping with a vaguely defined chain of responsibility ultimately passing to a sector of government dealing with trade, commerce and colonial affairs. Quite naturally the two areas drifted apart and soon even their real purposes were separate. The public law aspect of ocean use now provided a service to the political aspirations of oceanic jurisdiction. The traditional private law component was expected to (quite self-sufficiently) interpret the economic and commercial aspects of ocean transportation. Of course, this neat division has probably never existed when one views the political and historical processes which have influenced ocean uses. There has hardly ever been a political or jurisdictional aspect in the law of the sea which has not had its effect on the commercial and economic use of the sea. The reverse is equally true.

Interestingly enough the private shipping interests were, probably right up to UNCLOS III, quite happy with their lot. They had reaped the benefit of a protective public law system and were allowed to get on with their commercial aspirations basically unhindered by international law or national regulation. They formed powerful and influential organizations such as Shipowners and Maritime Law Associations at the national level, and the International Chamber of Shipping and the Comité Maritime International (CMI) at the international level. Within such groupings their members and member states prospered as they consulted with each other on methods to achieve greater uniformity on commercial rules or on specific, but invariably private, maritime law problems. They kept their group relatively small, even today the CMI has under 40 members, and were able to achieve broad consensus at periodic gatherings of like-minded similar interest groups of shipowners, maritime lawyers, underwriters, shippers, shipbuilders, forwarders, etc. They survived two shattering world wars which destroyed their fleets but from which they rebounded with renewed vigor and increased the world fleet which would double and triple in a few decades. The development of international shipping, and the private law which governed it, during this whole period was simply phenomenal and contributed directly to the full development and prosperity of the industrialized world. On the technical front, shipping adapted to the change from sail to steam; from coal-fired to oil-fired propulsion and developed the tankship when petroleum became the world's primary energy source. Commercial and legal transactions were governed by a smooth network of customary rules which had as its base several millennia of trading practice and which were now codified, to a great extent, in widely accepted international "private" law conventions. The only flaw in an otherwise perfect picture was the fact that, as always, prosperity and self-sufficiency appears to breed a certain inability or reluctance to project and perceive changes in the international political scene. This resulted in an industry, almost completely isolated from the public or political aspect of ocean use, that genuinely believed in the slogan "what is good for shipping must be good for the world." The industry came to believe it was immune to interference and change. Three law of the sea conferences from 1930 to 1960, dealing with jurisdictional aspects of the public law of the sea, should have been clear warning signals. But even these conferences viewed any changes to the accepted tenets of the law of the sea as abrogations of the freedom of the seas principle, and even a modest demand by coastal states for a wider territorial sea and contiguous zone failed.

However, certainly by 1958, these debates had become politicized and the "freedom of navigation" was defended for reasons quite far removed from those originally promulgated by Grotius. The commercial aspect of ocean use had by 1958 become only one of several ocean uses all forced to compete for consideration from a very rapidly changing political world. In other words, the "freedom of the sea" was being defended by states that considered such a defense as a convenient tactic for protecting other oceanic interests and aspirations. The commercial component of the "freedom of navigation" was hardly considered as it must have been quite clear in 1958 and 1960 (and is probably so now) that the coastal state claims, even if they could be considered as abrogations of the freedom of the sea, were certainly not abrogating the "freedom of navigation." However, just in case they were, the concepts of innocent passage, and later, transit rights, came into being. On the high seas, jurisdiction over merchant ships was strictly limited to the flag state.

However, by the 1960's we were witnessing the "rise of the coastal state in the law of the sea" caused to a great extent by the failure of the major maritime states to face up realistically to the changing political scene which demanded some relatively modest changes in a law of the sea which had become inadequate for the drastically expanded world of the late 1950's and 1960's. Sight had been lost of what the freedom of navigation, or even that of the sea, had been established for in the first place. Ocean use had become a political question debated in terms of a public international law which was now far removed from the commercial content of private maritime law which was now discussed at very different fora and usually by different people.

3. The Expansion of Ocean Use Since World War II

The vast political changes resulting from the international and national dislocations of World War II affected ocean use and ocean law as much as anything else. In the "public" law of the sea, unsettled jurisdictional questions left over from the 1930's would now be further complicated by a great number of new actors in the "drama of the oceans." When the 1930 Hague Codification Conference met, 38 states comprised the totality of oceanic interests. At UNCLOS I and II this had increased to 88 states, most of whom were coastal states in every sense of the word. Their numbers were further swelled due to the great rush of independence in Africa and Asia which resulted in many new states with maritime ambitions or, at least, perceptions.

In the "private" field of shipping there were also considerable changes during this period. The establishment of IMCO, a specialized agency of the United Nations to deal with matters relating to international shipping, had been resisted quite tenaciously by the major maritime states that feared such an agency would have regulatory powers that might be used to hurt or alter the established pattern of shipping practice. As we know, the IMCO Convention took a decade to enter into force despite the fact that the organization's terms of reference gave it only advisory and consultative powers. Because of the practices of the shipping states in the organization, coastal states very quickly regarded it as a "shipowners' club"; it gained acceptance only slowly and by carrying out excellent and necessary work, particularly in the field of maritime safety, which had been neglected by the shipping industry. When many of the newly independent states commenced to join IMCO they found, however, that the organization was still dominated by the maritime states; this domination was difficult to break.

The marine pollution debate ushered in by the *Torrey Canyon* incident in 1967, gave IMCO the much-needed additional leverage to represent international public interest in ocean transportation. The period of environmental concern which followed would also present the shipping industry with one of its most difficult challenges. Marine pollution was the undesirable and, usually undesired, by-product of the ocean transportation process. It straddled aspects of both "public" as well as "private" marine law and policy. However, in an almost last-ditch stand, the maritime states vigorously resisted coastal state demands on both fronts. On the public side, any attempt by coastal states to enforce more rigid regulations in coastal waters was termed an abrogation of the "freedom of navigation." This resulted in international rules at numerous conferences being reduced to the lowest common denominator usually not acceptable to coastal states. In private law the question was one of liability and compensation resulting in haggling over what to pay when, to whom and by whom, in the case of a pollution incident. The two areas of law were thus united in defending an almost indefensible status quo but in little else. Clear and forward-looking maritime policy had not been formulated. If it had it was defensive at best. At the same time, the IMCO battle, for example, need not have been fought. A little forthcoming compromise could easily have won the day for the maritime states. Instead they became more and more tainted as intransigents which would hurt them in other fora.

The great North-South developmental debate was bound to include shipping. Already at the first UNCTAD in Geneva in 1964, the question of shipping was raised and, after very strong protests by the developed states, placed on the agenda. For the developing states:

> The economic and commercial aspects of shipping were almost virgin territory at the time of the Geneva Conference, a forbidden land to which neither international organizations nor developing countries had easy access. On the international scene it was one of several untouched strongholds of anachronistic private enterprise and its credo of laissez-faire, with liner conferences enjoying oligopolistic privileges. Generally, data was scarce and there was a dearth of published materials on the economics of ocean transport. This was primarily due to the secrecy which shrouded the practices of liner conferences, price fixing and costs. The absence of reliable figures prevented developing countries from fully substantiating their grievances and suspicions about certain shipping practices. (Gosovic, <u>UNCTAD: Conflict and Compromise</u> (1972))

As a result, and after considerable debate, UNCTAD's shipping division was founded and would henceforth become the champion of the developing world in shipping matters. However, even here the division of the two maritime laws created problems. UNCTAD had no mandate, nor did it seek it, to look at questions of public law and policy relating to the use of ocean space. Yet UNCTAD in its search for greater equity in shipping matters had to deal with the same maritime states which were defending their status quo at IMCO or the Law of the Sea Conference and face the same resistance only expressed in different terminology. Nevertheless UNCTAD confined itself to private maritime law which, in the view of developing states, had been basically compiled by the traditional shipping states and was thus unduly favorable to such states. We are at present just before UNCTAD V and since UNCTAD I the Conference has come a long way in its difficult quest for a more equitable division of the world's resources. Shipping is considered to be one such resource; during the past sessions of the Conference much progress has been made to allow greater access to world shipping for developing states. To be fair, it must be stated that the developed states were also faced by considerable difficulties in this forum. They were asked to give what they could not. The history of ocean transportation had seen to it that an intensely private industry had been created over which governments had, certainly in many countries, relatively little control. The members of delegations from the developed states thus were often chosen from the industry itself and could hardly be expected to hand over much of what was theirs to protect. Thus "public" and "private" marine law and policy was again uncoordinated. The maritime states were, once again, seen by both coastal and developing states at their intransigent worst.

4. UNCLOS III: Global Ocean Conference without Shipping

From this background it would obviously have been surprising if the Third Law of the Sea Conference had concerned itself in any detail with ocean shipping. The private aspects of shipping were now quite far removed from international consideration and debated instead in fora such as IMCO and UNCTAD and, to a lesser extent, at the non-governmental CMI level. The antecedents of the latest Conference commenced by Pardo's brilliant initiative were at first strictly related to the seabed. The inability of the United Nations to confine itself to that subject, due to much of the unfinished business in the law of the sea, resulted in the whole public area being opened up for discussion. However, shipping, the most traditional use of the oceans, was most noticeably absent from the agenda of a conference which set out to re-codify all aspects of the law of the sea and would soon become a global law of the sea reform movement with all the commensurate difficulties.

Shipping appeared only in three areas at the Conference. The Second Committee discussed questions relating to the traditionally thorny issue of marginal seas jurisdiction. A relatively satisfactory regime relating to transit rights and innocent passage of ships in spatial zones under control or quasi-control of coastal and island states was slowly worked out. However, here again, the debate was in the form of the defense of and attack on the principle of the "freedom of the seas." The maritime states would paint coastal state expansionism in the darkest color of "anti-Grotian" sentiment and intention; some coastal states would rattle the brittle skeleton of "creeping jurisdiction" in their cupboards. In reality the "freedom of navigation" was hardly ever at issue. Free transit, right of free tansit, or free passage are all expressions used interchangeably to delineate the basic rights under the principle of free navigation on the seas. There has been little, if any, attempt made to assert that such a right is not a part of the very principle of "freedom of the seas." Yet free transit for international shipping should simply have been viewed as something quite separate from the spatial concern of territorial seas and their breadth whatever it may be. If so viewed, then the functional character of this navigational right would remain quite secure regardless of any new widths of territorial seas or economic zones. Unfortunately, this functionality was hardly ever considered at the Conference. Transit right appears to be well established in international law and appears in little danger to have changed in principle from the rule as expressed by Grotius to be: "lands, rivers and any part of the sea that has become subject to ownership of a people ought to be open to those who, for legitimate reasons, have need to cross over them."

The second area related to shipping on UNCLOS III's agenda concerned a variety of articles relating to rules governing vessels on the high seas. There has been some updating, but few changes from the 1958 Convention are apparent. The "genuine link" which had to be established between the flag state and the ship is still required despite the fact that the futility of attempting to establish such a link has been universally accepted, and that the rather murky reasons behind this so-called theory of international maritime law has been conclusively and decisively discredited. Many of these high seas articles are a strange collection of technical rules and customary norms. One could easily question their utility or place in a global ocean treaty. Quite obviously they now fit much more within IMCO's sphere of interest.

Finally, the Conference, in its Third Committee, concerns itself with ship-generated marine pollution. To the credit of that Committee, after much painstaking work, a consensus appears to be close, but what problem had to be overcome! The continuing struggle between coastal and maritime states concerning marine pollution, so familiar to IMCO, had to be endlessly repeated at UNCLOS III. Once again, the battleground would have to be the principle of the "freedom of the sea" rather than the community interest of reducing marine pollution to its lowest common denominator. Coastal state regulation was seen as direct interference with legitimate shipping patterns and the "crazy patchwork-quilt" of differing national legislation was often put forward as an extreme argument by the maritime states. Yet everyone accepted the fact that the environmental problems could best be solved by internationally accepted measures, except that the maritime states had shown, at IMCO and in the CMI liability meetings, that such measures would be reduced to the lowest common denominators, whereas coastal states demanded somewhat higher standards. The result of this endless and totally unnecessary debate is a less than acceptable consensus as reflected in the ICNT and its latest refinements. Much of the language is torturous and many of the measures are unenforceable. Thus coastal states will still go ahead and implement their own rules but for safety's sake and not to interfere with shipping, except with such shipping that is so substandard, in terms of safety, that it would not be allowed into any state's coastal waters. As a result, there will be changes in coastal waters for ship use. New regulatory patterns will be established, including special tanker zones, traffic separation systems and eventually many compulsory pilotage areas. Rather than affecting the commercial viability of shipping such new measures will assist it, just as air traffic regulation assists aviation. On the other hand, if these new regulations will drive sub-standard vessels from the seas or will up-grade standards, the commercial viability of such shipping will be adversely affected. And so it should be. In other words, for ocean shipping, UNCLOS III is basically a political and rhetorical issue.

5. The Future of International Shipping in the Aftermath of UNCLOS III

It is fitting by way of conclusion to cast a rapid glance ahead and look at the future of international shipping in the aftermath of the Law of the Sea Conference. I have been quite critical of the shipping industry which we know, admire and understand. It has become the victim of its own history; its difficult position today is exacerbated by a lack of clearly defined and comprehensive policy. What is needed at this stage is a massive build-up of the industry's international research capability at all levels of international intercourse in order to share ocean transportation more equitably. It is not enough to "lobby" for privileged position and status quo retention. At the same time we must remember that Professor Edward Miles has taught all of us that the modern law of the sea is so much more perception than policy. It is the perception of the shipping industry as well as its uncertain mentors, the major maritime states with their own perceptions, that will have to change and new policy will follow easily.

Nevertheless, if ocean shipping is in any substantial way hampered by anything which UNCLOS III will produce (which is doubtful), then the blame will rest squarely on the inflexibility and intransigence of the international shipping industry rather than on the 'enclosure movement' of the Conference itself. The industry has shown itself as an anachronism wishing to protect a no longer defensible privileged position at any price in almost every forum, whether it is on questions of safety and environmental protection at IMCO, commercial equity at UNCTAD, or general law of the sea questions at UNCLOS III. This position does little justice to an industry which since pre-history has been renowned for its viability, flexibility and adaptability to change. There is little, if any, evidence that the outcome of UNCLOS III will seriously affect the commercial viability of international ocean transportation. The 'enclosure movement' of the Conference will obviously affect shipping routes and dictate departure from some traditional and accepted practices, but there is also little evidence whatever that even the most 'territorialist expansionist' coastal states seek to drive shipping away. The benefits of international seaborne trade need little emphasis. Interference with trade benefits no one. At the same time, shipping will have to contend with a more regulatory atmosphere at all operative levels in a more regulated world. This will be one of the prices to be paid in the late 20th century in a search for greater equity in all aspects of ocean law and policy. Because of the rather shortsighted attitude of the international shipping industry some of these changes will be imposed on it when, in reality, it had ample opportunity to have been a viable part of these changes. However, the industry missed this opportunity and will have to adapt to these changes at a time when it faces other serious challenges in economic terms brought about, to some extent, by the oversupply of shipping and, of course, the rise of East bloc, third world and flag of convenience shipping which, in turn, is simply providing the answers to questions which the traditional shipping industry has not been able or willing to give. Nevertheless, history gives us ample evidence that ocean shipping will survive these economic and political, as well as legal, challenges in the latter part of the 20th century as it has done in previous complex situations. It will also survive UNCLOS III and its inevitable many successors.

COMMENTARY

Menso de Jong
Netherlands Maritime Institute

Mr. Gold's lecture on ocean shipping has given me the impression that there exists a large conspiracy among shipowners and that even the lawyers cannot beat that conspiracy. You will no doubt agree with me that Mr. Gold is to be complimented for his courage to say these words and to attack the traditional maritime countries here in this country, in the middle of the lion's den. Fortunately, Mr. Gold has assured us that Grotius is not going to turn over in his grave. His _Mare Liberum_ was a young man's first job and later dismissed by him.

Returning to Mr. Gold's attack on the traditional maritime countries, I understand that Mr. Gold sees these countries fighting to maintain the status quo in maritime matters and to prevent any progress in international organizations such as IMCO, UNCTAD and UNCLOS. Mr. Gold has hardly substantiated these charges. We have to be satisfied with his remark that the traditional countries are not supplying the answers to the difficult questions of new maritime laws. Instead, we are told that the East bloc, Third World, and flags of convenience are providing the answers needed. But we are also left in the dark as to what replies these flags are giving.

In my opinion the Third World is advocating the use of cargo reservation. The East bloc practices cargo reservation already, but has added hidden forms of subsidy. Is, therefore, the goal of shipping to have subsidized state fleets, carrying 50% of their nation's trade in oil, iron ore, liner cargoes, etc.? The flags of convenience are also providing an answer. Their message is that a profit can still be made in shipping, as long as costs and tax levels are low and as long as there is a free market in the carrying of cargoes.

The different flags which are supposed to give this important gathering the required answers are, in my opinion, giving different answers. One favors the regulated market, the other a free market in shipping. Mr. Gold has not guided you regarding the future course to be followed. Is it surprising that the traditional maritime countries are still studying the problems as well?

One could remark, however, that these problems have little connection with the law of the sea as discussed at UNCLOS. The problem of either a regulated or free market for the carrying of cargo is trade laws which are being dealt with at

UNCTAD. UNCTAD is not concerned with freedom of navigation; it has never suggested restricting freedom of navigation. Instead, UNCTAD proposes to restrict the shipper's freedom of choice. He may no longer be at liberty to select a vessel. In view of the restrictions of shippers' freedom of choice, the strength of liner conferences may increase. UNCTAD proposes, therefore, to give governments more regulatory powers over liner conferences. The European maritime countries are presently considering whether a European policy can be drafted to unify the protagonists and antagonists of the proposed UNCTAD code of conduct.

IMCO is indeed being considered as an organization of the traditional maritime countries. I cannot agree with Mr. Gold that these countries are endeavoring to maintain the status quo with IMCO. To the contrary, IMCO is undoubtedly one of the success stories of the United Nations. The major task of IMCO could be described as making traffic laws to apply at sea. These laws are aimed at preventing collisions, pollution and other calamities. Not only has IMCO a record of successful lawmaking, it has also restricted freedom of navigation more than any other organization. Mr. Gold has complained that UNCLOS is left outside the shipping scene and he suggests that this might be the result of a conspiracy by maritime countries and their shipowners.

As I explained, the shipowners and maritime countries already have to deal with IMCO and UNCTAD, respectively, for their traffic and trade laws. Why should they need to have another body to draft such laws? It can only delay the making of a new world wide shipping policy if two international organizations are dealing with the same problems. As far as shipping is concerned, UNCLOS is involved with the laws which apply to shipping in the territorial waters and the economic zones. The international shipping community was alarmed when UNCLOS started to aim at granting coastal states the right to apply their own maritime traffic laws to these waters.

With land transport we see that many countries are trying to harmonize their national traffic laws to arrive at an agreed to international traffic law. At sea, such internationally agreed to laws already exist. It would have been a step backward if these were to be replaced by national laws in international shipping straits and other sea areas close to land.

The traditional maritime countries and their shipowners would prefer to apply existing international laws to shipping in coastal waters which are regularly used by shipping. This does not mean that there is nothing left for UNCLOS to consider as far as shipping is concerned. To the contrary, there are a few neglected issues. The most important is perhaps that UNCLOS has been insufficiently concerned about the rights of shipping in territorial waters and economic zones. UNCLOS has been too much engaged, regarding the rights of coastal states.

To illustrate this, I would like to ask whether UNCLOS considers it a duty for coastal states to provide for salvage and life saving equipment and to provide for ports of refuge? Do they have a duty to provide charts and to provide navigationally safe routes? Can a Master be subject to "hot" pursuit if he picks up some refugees in distress while navigating an international strait?

Enforcement of IMCO's traffic laws and UNCTAD's trade laws is largely left to national governments. Many governments are not prepared to transfer part of their law enforcement powers to an international body. In this respect, UNCLOS is encouraged by most traditional maritime countries in its endeavors to set up an international organization to deal with disputes between governments.

COMMENTARY

Mr. Gezelius
Dutch Shipowners Company
Rotterdam

I must also compliment Mr. Gold, because I think he was successful in attacking shipping in all sorts of fields. I feel in some respects his remarks were dangerous. The only consolation was that, apparently, I was very prosperous.

Regrettably, I must paint a less prosperous picture of shipowners. They are not all conservative with many privileges and heaps of money to protect their own interests. Since UNCLOS has been looked at and elaborated now during ten years, it might be interesting to examine what the shipowners have been doing during these ten years.

In 1968, we transported 8,370 billion ton miles. In 1978, we will have transported about 17,700 billion ton miles. That is a doubling in ten years. It is not our cargo; it is your cargo.

What has happened more during this decade? Flexible liner vessels have gradually been replaced by less flexible and more expensive container vessels. In other facets of shipping, we have seen an increase in size. Huge investments have been made in modernized vessels with related equipment such as containers and terminals. This reduced flexibility means an increased risk-taking for the shipowner. Not until all major ports in the world are containerized will flexibility return. The new vessels which replace six to eight conventional vessels are running on very tight schedules. Conventional liner vessels spend 40-60% of their time in port, handling about one hundred tons per hour. Contrastingly, container vessels spend about 20% of their time in the port handling 250 tons per hour.

The investments in modern containerized vessels and huge bulk and tank vessels have also led to an increased number of consortia, perhaps particularly in the liner trade, where shipowners from various countries join forces in order to offer the market a competitive service.

In the West, we have seen an increased competition from Community countries that offer rates that are not considered commercially justifiable. We have seen an increasing protectionism in shipping. In some countries this may be understandable because many shipowners are fighting for their survival and need assistance from their governments. Whereas, in other countries, the establishment of shipping companies is done for political rather than commercial reasons. The profitability of shipping declined. At least in Europe, we see the need for a maritime policy.

These observations will hopefully have given you the impression that shipping is an industry undergoing dramatic development. You may question what role the shipowner plays in this development. The answer is that he participates in all facets of this development. Increasingly, shipowners are participating in the political discussion leading to the development of a maritime policy which I just mentioned.

Coming back to the freedom of ocean shipping, it may be considered inflexible to advocate the continuation of this basic principle of freedom. I agree that this concept may be used in various contexts but the general idea, at least as I see it, when referring to freedom of the seas is to underline the importance of a continued liberal base for future shipping development. If we abandon this basic principle, we may see a development similar to what we have in aviation, with strictly regulated terms based on certain bilateral agreements. As I see it, the developments in shipping do not justify such a drastic change. We must protect ourselves from any unnecessary restriction of the flexibility that is essential for continued development. When we talk about freedom in shipping, it also means freedom of choice for you, the shippers, the owners of cargo. In shipping, flexibility necessitates uniformity. If we get different rules in different countries, this will have a negative influence on development. Uniformity is more necessary today than ever before. Delaying one of today's vessels is equivalent to delaying six or eight vessels ten years ago. Shipowners are not against laws and regulations; on the contrary, we see the value in laws but such laws should always be adopted internationally. We should try to avoid bilateral or unilateral regulations.

Shipowners are definitely prepared and will continue to participate in discussions; we have also participated in the UNCLOS discussions. But I hope that shipowners will continue to insist on advocating efficiency on a self-regulating basis. Good law must combine stability with modern technological and operational developments.

DISCUSSION AND QUESTIONS

EDGAR GOLD: Thank you very much, Mr. Chairman. I felt that the commentators on my presentation were well chosen and, to a certain extent, augmented some of the points which I tried to make. In particular, Mr. Gezelius' views of the economic difficulties in which the shipping industry finds itself in are of great interest. Of course, we could debate this problem for a considerable time. The problem is caused by an over-supply of shipping capacity which has forced the industry to chase fewer cargoes with too many ships causing a considerable loss both to individual states as well as to individual shipowners. At the same time the problem was seen by many marine economists a long time ago. The shipping slump is something which was entirely forecastable and is a part of the international economic and cyclical shipping pattern. Some shipowners saw this; many did not. That is why we have Mr. Miwa telling us tomorrow how to use tankers to store oil.

I thought that I made it clear that IMCO certainly is a success story considering its very modest terms of reference. At yesterday's opening ceremony of this Conference, Mr. Tuijnman, the Netherlands Minister of Transport and Public Works, spoke about IMCO and its importance. He said that many more states must ratify IMCO conventions. However, the difficulty is that many states will not ratify these conventions because they are not considered to reflect adequately the very international standards which both Mr. Gezelius and Mr. de Jong seek. This makes it very difficult both for the shipping countries as well as coastal states. Finally, I was most impressed by the way in which the views of the industry were stated in terms which are most closely related to its concerns.

YOSHIHIKO MIWA: I am a newspaper reporter from Japan. I should like to ask Professor Gold's opinion about the recent activity of the Soviet Union's merchant marine in Pacific waters. Soviet shipping agents tend to offer their clients, shippers, extremely competitive rates of freight in order to obtain as much seaborne cargo as possible.

It seems that this trend has become more noticeable since this summer. Shipping companies in the free world can hardly compete with such a price offensive by a state-owned shipping company. Of course, this price offensive has inflicted serious damage on the Japanese shipping companies. May I have your comments on this problem?

EDGAR GOLD: Well, Mr. Miwa, I suppose I am no more qualified to speak on behalf of the Soviet Union that you are. Soviet maritime policy is fairly well known. As far as international shipping is concerned, the Soviet Union is certainly considered to be a maritime nation. The Chinese at various conferences usually say that the Soviet Union and "another super-power" wish to extend their "hegemony and undesirable ambitions on the Seven Seas." The build-up of the Soviet merchant fleet has certainly been very considerable, both in the liner and the tramping trades, and now also in the tanker and container trades. I know that is worrying the traditional shipping states.

I have some difficulty about the frequent questions raised relating to "commerciality" of Soviet shipping. It is very difficult to say that something which is not commercial for me may not be commercial for somebody else. To the best of my knowledge, many of the Soviet shipping routes are run on a fairly sound commercial basis, although not in the beginning. To get into a particular trade they cut freight rates. On occasions, such as the Far East/Australia Conferences, they have cut these by at least 60%. Obviously, it is very difficult to have a commercial success if you are undercutting somebody else by 60%. Nevertheless, that is the name of the game, which the international shipping industry has been practicing for centuries, although not necessarily with 60% cuts. The Soviet Union thus seems to use a commercial and a political combination to get into the shipping trades. At the same time, the Soviets have been accepted by several shipping conferences. It probably will not be very long until there will be an application made in Tokyo for companies like FESCO, the Soviet Far Eastern Shipping Company, to join the Far Eastern Conference Lines. That will be a very difficult decision for that particular Conference to make. They will have the difficult choice of either allowing participation or else being undercut. The decision will really be made by the shipper who will be faced with these low undercut rates. Will he remain loyal to his traditional conference line? I remember on the Australian trade during the Viet Nam war, when Soviet vessels were taking military equipment to Haiphong and then coming empty down to Australia to pick up wool cargoes. At that particular time Australia was at war as a participant in the Viet Nam conflagration; the Australian Government appealed to the wool exporters not to trade with the enemy. The exporters said: "yes, yes we do understand that, but 40%,...what can we do?"

One of the points which I thought Mr. Gezelius made extremely well is that international shipping is not only faced with new competition today. At the same time shipping is becoming more sophisticated and more expensive. The Soviets and the third world are benefiting from the technological research of the West and, at the same time, are also benefiting from some of the very practices which originated in the traditional shipping states.

MR. GEZELIUS: Consider the case of the North Atlantic where we see a number of so-called outsiders. They start and run their service for several years and then disappear. I think this is good for the business because they are competing on about equal terms. If they cannot run their business efficiently, they will leave the area. But the situation we fear is of a different type. The East Bloc countries, mainly for political reasons, run a service as long as they like. The end result of this trend may be that only government controlled shipping companies remain. I wonder whether that would be a satisfactory development.

MR. DE JONG: Some people propose planning and regulation to avoid the complications which have just been described. There is a lot of informed opinion which believes that the tremendous expansion of the Soviet fleet is a result of a planning mistake of the Soviet Union. There may not be all kinds of dark political arguments behind this expansion, just a planning mistake of a large country with big planning boards prone to regulation. Regulation and planning by governments might, therefore, not be the complete answer to shipping in this respect.

H.F.M. BERTELS: I would like to begin by thanking Mr. Gold for his very interesting words, especially the historical background he sketched. I have a feeling that the nearer we came to the present times, the more the picture he gave us was colored a bit too dark. In my experience, much has changed in the last decade or two regarding the ability of the shipping industry to be flexible and adaptive to new contingencies. This applies not only to the shipping industry, but also to countries and international organizations in this particular field. For instance, states participating in the Law of the Sea Conference cannot be divided into two categories, coastal states and maritime states. I know of almost no "pure" coastal states or "pure" maritime states. My country is seeking a proper balance between real interests in both fields, in the field of protection of the environment and freedom of shipping.

On various occasions Mr. Gold spoke of the outcome of the present negotiations as the lowest possible common denominator that was reached. I think this is inevitable. We are in a laborious process of adapting, of seeking solutions in an inevitably changing situation. And the best we can hope in many cases is that we reach such a lowest common denominator. I think that is inevitable and should not cause us much distress, for that too is part of the historical process.

LEO BOUCHEZ: I wish to raise a particular problem to Mr. Gezelius and Mr. De Jong. Supposing that the developing countries continue to insist on participating more actively in ocean transport, what will be the position of the shipowners?

In this connection I wish to refer to the more or less similar problem of active participation by the developing countries in the exploitation of the natural resources of the international seabed.

MR. GEZELIUS: If I understood the question correctly, you asked about the view of the shipowners if the developing countries want to have a finger in the pie, so to speak. I do not think shipowners have been against competition. They have been against a system of profit-sharing that is not justified by commercial needs.

LEO BOUCHEZ: It has been a long day and this is the time to terminate this session. However, I think we had a most interesting meeting, in particular because of the different views expressed by several speakers with respect to the economic aspects of ocean navigation.

Finally, I wish to thank again Professor Gold for his most stimulating and thought provoking paper. In addition, I am very glad that we had two experts familiar with shipping practice, Mr. Gezelius and Mr. De Jong, who have explained clearly some present-day economic aspects of ocean navigation. As we all know, ocean navigation is a fascinating but most complex problem, particularly for the Western world. I wish to thank you all for your contributions.

PART VI

ENERGY SOURCES FROM THE OCEANS

INTRODUCTORY REMARKS BY SESSION PROGRAM CHAIRMAN

John P. Craven
Law of the Sea Institute

This session deals with energy in the oceans. We shall have three papers by Mr. Keith, Dr. Bardach, Mr. Miwa; Dr. Brown will critique each of the three papers and my remarks.

To put this session in context, I will take the liberty of speaking in some detail about the "road map" of energy and the oceans. When examining this issue, we must realize that the chief and most important energy resource of the ocean at the present time is the oil on continental shelves. Indeed this has been a major non-neglected issue of the law of the sea conference. As a matter of fact, it has been so well attended that under either the Hedberg formula or the Irish formula, coastal states have jurisdiction over every last drop of oil and gas. There remains little, if any, in the areas beyond national jurisdiction.

But associated with offshore oil is the transportation and storage of oil. We can assume,that as far as this session is concerned, we have all but completed a discussion of shipping and transportation with respect to this law of the sea interaction; but we have not discussed the problem of storage at sea. Therefore, one of our papers this morning will relate to a specific storage scheme, one which we chose as an example because of its interesting interaction with the law of the sea and the problems that this will raise. That paper will be presented by Mr. Miwa.

After oil is delivered, it is then essentially applied and transduced, if you will. It is usually used for transportation purposes, for automobiles, for airplanes, or it is employed in power plants for generating electricity. In this generation of electricity, we come to the primary new resource use of the ocean, i.e., the cooling water, water used to cool power plants of all varieties. Few people really understand or appreciate the value of this resource. For most of us, when we think of energy we think of heat. In the discussions the last few days when people have been talking about energy they have been talking about the conservation of waste heat with the general notion that anything which is warmer than this room is capable of creating energy.

Those who have been involved in the energy-creation process are aware that energy is created by the difference in temperature, and that the efficiency with which this process generates is given by a simple formula, the Carnot efficiency, the maximum efficiency that can be achieved is T1 minus T2 divided by the absolute temperature. T1 is the hot source, the hot source whether it is produced by fossil fuel, coal, nuclear power, or by ocean thermal energy. T2 is the exhaust temperature, the temperature of heat rejection. It is obvious from this formula that the colder you get, the more energy you get. It is the difference in temperature that generates the energy. Cooling water, always a major problem in energy, is becoming a critical problem. Cooling in the past has been done by using rivers, streams and lakes. We now see that this is generating thermal pollution in these small bodies of water with the total amount of power generated limited by the availability of this very valuable land resource.

Cooling towers operate by evaporation in the ambient environment. Thus, cooling towers are not very cool; the efficiency of thermal power plants using cooling towers is very very poor compared to power plants located on the sea. It is for this reason we are seeing an increasing number of coastal power and floating power plants. These have been proposed. Designs for an offshore floating nuclear power plant have been completed by Westinghouse Corporation. There have been designs for offshore coal-fired power plants and for fossil fuel plants. Most of these floating plants are going to be within the economic zone, because the electricity they generate must be transmitted to the shore. Since many of them are going to generate power for industrial purposes, the industrial purpose might as well be located right at the power plant site. Thus, we might find that these floating power plants will become floating industries. Investors in these plants will then begin examining the law of the sea with a great deal of care, because they will want to locate these plants in the jurisdiction of greatest convenience. It is for these reasons that one of our major papers in this session will deal with legal problems associated with floating power plants and floating industrial plants.

We all recognize that there also will be changes in the source of T1, the hot source. There will be a shift from oil to coal. There will be shifts to other novel and unique forms of energy generation, not only because of economics, but because our society recognizes that it must develop alternate sources of energy. Significant political strength will derive from a multiplicity of energy sources.

Yesterday we heard an excellent paper on the towing of icebergs. Yet those of us who have read and digested the technical symposia on icebergs recognize that towing icebergs for fresh water is a perfectly feasible, relatively easy, straightforward engineering task. But, using icebergs as a component of ocean thermal energy or as energy for salt water differential is absurd. The reason is that ocean thermal energy requires huge volumes of continuously flowing cold water (T2). The iceberg, as large as it is, is a relatively small source of T2 water.

The primary new form of energy that we look at is solar energy, and indeed fossil fuel energy is solar energy. It is solar energy that was stored many millions of years ago by the sun growing things that later decayed, compressed, formed as sediments, crushed and fractured, and aggregated in structures where modern man could use them.

The primary problem with most solar energy is the fact that it is very low density. The energy density of the sun is barely enough to provide the light of the day along with a little warming. Thus, the principal problem for solar energy is finding integrating mechanisms, mechanisms that nature has created to integrate the energy of the sun. We see such mechanisms in the form of wind which is solar energy that has been integrated by movements of the atmosphere. Many see the value of wind power. Those who have examined it have determined that if the velocity is high, about 40 knots and continuous, then the energy that can be produced from wind power can be competitive with energy from other sources. Unfortunately, there are very few locales in the world where the velocity stays continually high at 40 knots.

In places like Hawaii--this is a plug for you to come to the future conferences at Honolulu--we have tradewinds which are quite constant but at about 15 or 20 knots. The only way you can get a velocity of 40 knots is to interpose a mountain with a pass so the winds accelerate to this higher velocity. So far as wind energy is concerned, it will be developed mainly in those peculiar geophysical configurations where there are continuous winds like the tradewinds which interact with mountainous terrain. Since there are very few mountains floating on the ocean, and since the construction of floating mountains high enough is not economically feasible, wind energy will not show up as an important component.

There are also the waves and the tides. The tides themselves are not uniformly distributed around the world; there are relatively few areas where the tides are of high enough amplitude to warrant this use of energy. Where they are of high enough amplitude, coastal states will no doubt exercise control.

I must make some critical remarks about waves. Waves have a very low energy density themselves; our technical colleagues from Japan have just completed building a ship, a rather large ship, quite a few thousand tons. They have taken it out and tested it in waves to generate about 175 kilowatts of electricity just as the computations indicated that it would. But the 175 kilowatts is barely enough to light up the sign on the ship indicating that this is an energy generating ship! Thus, we can expect that the energy density in waves and wave projects is so low, the capital investment required probably cannot be justified in the near future.

Ocean thermal energy has interesting potential. Nature has integrated the energy of the sun in the large tropical water masses on the surface; there is an abundant amount of T1, and just a few thousand feet below the surface is an abundant amount of T2. So the movement of these large masses of water will in and of itself consume very little energy. While the process is very inefficient in terms of the total energy involved in the flowing streams (about 9% of the energy would be extracted in the form), it is relatively easy to move this mass of energetic material through the plant.

Do not expect ocean thermal energy to show up in the very near future. When it does appear, do not expect it to show up as a process producing only energy, because it will not be economically justifiable on that basis. The ocean thermal energy process has the advantage of bringing up from the deep ocean water that is richer in nutrients than the surface water. Therefore, one could conceive of this as an artificial upwelling project as well as an ocean energy process. It is possible, perhaps probable, that a cycle called the open cycle process will be developed where fresh water will also be produced as a by-product of the process. The fresh water, the energy and the deep nutrients together may create an economically viable scheme. These developments will take place over a period of perhaps 25 years before a major total industrial operation based on the ocean temperature differential becomes attractive for capital investment. When that happens, we can expect to see these plants grazing in tropical waters and in the vicinity of islands and certainly in areas beyond national jurisdictions. The set of legal, environmental, and jurisdictional problems created is enormous.

But this is not the final source of solar energy. Throughout history we have been using solar energy in the form of the sun growing things. This has been the finest integrative mechanism for solar energy. Many of us tend to differentiate between food and fuel; but when one looks at the technology of food, it is clear that food is only a fuel for the machine called man. Given enough energy, one can produce enough food and vice versa. We would be remiss in discussing the problems of energy if we did not include the relationship between energy production and food production. A third paper will integrate not only the solar energy, but the substance of the technology so that we will have an insight to the relationship of energy and food and the ocean.

When and if we ever develop a fusion process, the fuel for fusion will be found in the ocean. I have been talking to my physicist friends about when fusion will come into being; they all say that they do not know. If they do not know, we cannot predict; so we will reserve that for our future conference.

THE INTERNATIONAL REGULATION OF OCEAN FLOATING ENERGY PLATFORMS

Kent M. Keith
Associate, Cades Schutte Fleming & Wright
Honolulu, Hawaii

The ocean is an important potential location for energy generation. This is due largely to ocean floating platform technology. Ocean floating platforms have been designed which can support any human activity which presently takes place on land.[1] An ocean floating platform could support the generation of many forms of energy: nuclear energy,[2] coal or oil-fired

---

[1] Craven, Present and future uses of floating platforms, Oceanus, 1975, 19(1), p. 67; Hansen, J. (Ed.), Open Sea Mariculture, 1974, pp. 299-333. Ocean floating platforms are widely used as oil-drilling rigs in the Gulf of Mexico and the North Sea. See Gerwick, Current projects in offshore structure development, Marine Technology and Law: Development of Hydrocarbon Resources and Offshore Structures, Proceedings of the 2nd International Ocean Symposium, Ocean Association of Japan, Tokyo, 1977, p. 109. Zapata Off-shore Company's Concord, for example, is a semi-submersible platform working in thousand-foot depths in the Gulf of Mexico. The Concord rises 23 stories above the waves, has a deck as large as a football field, and houses roughly 70 employees. Alexander, Offshore drilling is a world apart, Fortune, December 1976, p. 74. The Japanese built "Aquapolis," a prototype of the floating city of the future, for the International Ocean Exposition, Okinawa, Japan, in 1975. The "Aquapolis" is 100 m. square and 35 m. high weighs 16,000 tons and is capable of handling 2,000 visitors at a time.

[2] Offshore Power Systems, a joint venture of Westinghouse Electric Corporation and Tenneco, plans to build floating nuclear power plants on barges measuring 378 by 400 feet, 32 feet in draft, with the plant rising 177 feet above the barge. The barges will be anchored approximately 3 miles offshore in water which is between 45 and 70 feet in depth. The barges will be surrounded by a D-shaped breakwater designed to withstand 300 mph winds, 50-foot waves, and a collision with any supertanker afloat. Four 1,150 Mw floating reactors have been sold to an electric company in New Jersey. Initial plans called for the first two reactors to be moored by 1980. Selfridge, Floating nuclear power plants: a fleet on the horizon?, Environmental Law, 1976, 6, p. 791. A step forward for floating nuclear plants, Business Week, February 9, 1974, p. 57. Gwynne, Nuclear power going to sea, Technology Review, 1972, 75(2), p. 10.

energy,[3] wind energy (McGowan and Heronemus, 1975, p. 629; Wade, 1974, p. 1055; Putting the Wind, 1968, p. 760; Merriam, 1977, p. 29), ocean thermal energy (Avery, 1978, p. 9; Anderson and Anderson, 1966, p. 41; Claude, 1930, p. 1039), or wave energy (Wick and Schmitt, 1977, p. 16).

An ocean floating energy platform (hereafter "OFEP") may be positioned close to shore and feed power directly into municipal power grids.[4] Other OFEP's may roam some distance from the coast, transforming their energy into products such as ammonia which they can sell to coastal states.[5] OFEP's could also provide power for manganese nodule mining, mariculture, or other activities on the high seas.[6]

---

[3]A floating 100-MW coal-fired power plant has been designed by John P. Craven to match existing operational profiles, and where possible, the standard power plant arrangement, of conventional land-based power plants. The floating power plant would be 390 feet long and 340 feet wide, and would rest on three hulls which would be 390 feet wide, 750 feet long, and 90 feet deep. The coal would be brought to the plant by ship and carried aboard by slurry. Power would be transmitted to the shore by underwater cable. The plant would have ballast and buoyancy control and dynamic positioning capabilities. Craven, J., A Floating 100-MW Coal-Fired Power Plant, Marine Programs, University of Hawaii, 1975.

[4]This appears to be the most suitable of floating nuclear power plants and the floating coal-fired plant designed by Craven. Selfridge, *supra* footnote 2 at 797; Craven, *supra* footnote 3.

[5]While not delivering power directly, an OFEP could produce a product such as ammonia which now consumes land-based sources of energy. The electricity generated by an OFEP could be used to produce hydrogen by electrolyzing water and nitrogen from the air by liquefaction. The hydrogen and nitrogen can then be combined to form ammonia, which is liquefied and stored until transported to coastal states. It is estimated that tropical ocean thermal energy plants could supply all of the new ammonia demand in the United States by 1990. (Avery, 1978, p. 12)

[6]The cold water brought up by an ocean thermal energy plant may be rich in nutrients, and could support a major mariculture operation for food. The cold water could flow through ponds of algae, shellfish, shrimps, lobsters and seaweed before returning to the ocean. Othmer and Roels, Power, fresh water, and food from cold, deep sea water, *Science*, 1973, *182*, p. 121. For a complete discussion see Bardach, The relation of ocean energy to ocean food, *Proceedings*, 12th Annual Conference on the Law of the Sea Institute 1978.

An OTEC system may also be very promising for manganese nodule mining in the Pacific. The richest deposits of nickel,

Assuming that OFEP's come into existence, how will they be regulated by current and proposed provisions of the law of the sea? Initially, attempts may be made to regulate OFEP's by applying the traditional definitions of vessels, ships, structures, artificial islands, or independent states recognized under international law (Keith, 1977, p. 190). However, an OFEP could fit into more than one of these traditional categories, at the same time, or could change categories from time to time as its position or function changes. Appropriate international regulation is thus likely to require a new definition, perhaps one established by treaty. This paper will examine the traditional definitions, and then recommend a functional approach for an interim regulatory scheme.

Ocean Floating Energy Platforms as Ships or Vessels

Definition

OFEP's would qualify as vessels under U.S. law if they moved in transportation on water. The word "vessel" has been defined by United States statute to include "every description of water craft or other artificial contrivance used, or capable of being used, as a means of transportation on water."[7] The phrase "every description of water craft or other artificial contrivance" is broad enough to include the unusual design features and functions of an OFEP. OFEP's would be capable of being used as a means of transportation on water; some OFEP's may in fact roam offshore, producing ammonia or some other product and selling it to coastal states.

---

copper, and cobalt in the Pacific have been found in a belt running southwest of Hawaii to southeast of Hawaii, with coordinates of roughly 120 to 180° W. longitude and 5° to 15° N. latitude. State of Hawaii Department of Planning and Economic Development, Manganese Nodule Deposits in the Pacific, 1972, pp. 49-56. This belt coincides with a belt of ocean water with a prevailing surface temperature of 80° F., the optimum temperature for ocean thermal energy conversion. Avery, 1978, pp. 9-10. Because of the plumes of sediment which may result from discharges at the surface of a nodule mining operation, which could foul the OTEC intake system, as well as general congestion and differences in mobility between an OTEC platform and a mining platform, the OTEC platform could be positioned at a distance from the mining platform and provide energy by cable. With sufficient energy, the mining platform could also process the metals.

[7] 1 USC § 3. This definition was enacted as a rule of general construction and will apply to every federal statute unless that statute provides a different definition.

"Vessel" has been held by United States courts to include, among other things, barges, bathhouses, floating boarding houses or restaurants, houseboats, and pleasure barges.[8] In Offshore Co. v. Robison[9] the court held that a jack-up oil rig qualified as a vessel under the Jones Act.[10] The drilling rig had only a top deck and lower hull. It had no engines and was moved from location to location by tug. Once in position, hydraulic jacks lifted the platform 40-50 feet above water level. The court reviewed cases involving a submersible drilling barge, a lighter, a floating derrick, and dredges, and concluded that "under the Jones Act a vessel may mean something more than a means of transport on water."[11] If a platform which stands on legs on the ocean floor qualifies as a vessel even when it is stationary and resembles a tower, it is likely that floating energy platforms will also qualify. For purposes of the Jones Act, then, OFEP's are likely to be deemed vessels.

The word "vessel" includes the word "ship," and the two words are often used interchangeably in U.S. case law.[12] Thus, the specific attributes of a ship, as opposed to a vessel, are difficult to identify. In Pollock v. Cleveland Shipbuilding Co.[13] the shipbuilding company floated ships in front of Pollock's land while repairing them. The court had to define

---

[8]Woods Bros. Const. Co. v. Iowa Unemployment Comm'n, 229 Iowa 1171, 296 N.W. 346 (1941) (barge); The Public Bath No. 13, 61 F. 692 (1894) (Bathhouse); Petition of Kansas City Bridge Co., 19 F. Supp. 419 (1937) (floating boarding house); The Club Royale, 13 F. Supp. 123 (1935) (floating restaurant); The Ark, 17 F.2d 446 (1926) (houseboat); The City of Pittsburgh, 45 F. 699 (1891) (pleasure barge).

[9]Offshore Co. v. Robison, 226 F.2d 769 (1959).

[10]46 USC § 688. The Jones Act applies to seamen injured or killed in the course of employment. It was passed to provide seamen with the same rights to recover for negligence as they would have had if they had not been seamen. It has been interpreted to preserve the seaman's special rights to recover maintenance and cure and indemnify for unseaworthiness under general maritime law. Gilmore, G., and Black, C., The Law of Admiralty 328, 2nd ed., 1975.

[11]266 F.2d at p. 776.

[12]"In maritime law...in the absence of a compelling statutory definition, the terms ship and vessel are used interchangeably as synonymous terms, connoting a craft capable of being used for transportation on oceans, rivers, seas, and navigable waters." 1 Benedict on Admiralty, § 162 at 10-3, Release No. 17, 1974 (hereafter "Benedict").

[13]Pollock v. Cleveland Shipbuilding Co., 56 Ohio 655, 47 N.E. 582 (1897).

"ship" in order to establish whether the repair work involved a maritime contract. The court began by noting the definition provided from a treatise on admiralty: "'A ship' says Mr. Benedict in his work on admiralty (Section 215), 'is a locomotive machine adapted to transportation over rivers, seas, and oceans.'"[14] The court accepted this definition, but then broadened it to cover the case at hand. "In this sense," it said, "vessels moored by defendant, awaiting engines and boilers, were ships. They were machines upon the water, would float, and were capable of being moved and propelled on the water, and were so floating on the water, and intended as aid to commerce."[15] Benedict's definition[16] required a "locomotive machine," and this implies the power of a vessel to propel itself, a feature which would clearly distinguish a ship from a vessel such as a barge which must be towed. The court's definition, however, required only a machine "capable of being moved and propelled on the water," a definition which seems broad enough to include vessels which are towed as well as those which are self-propelled. By this standard, ocean floating energy platforms would qualify as ships.

The moment of birth and death of an OFEP ship may be difficult to determine under traditional definitions. When does an OFEP become a ship? Ships are generally launched into the water after christening, and are "born" when they touch water. As the Supreme Court said in Tucker v. Alexandroff:[17]

> A ship is born when she is launched, and she lives so long as her identity is preserved. Prior to her launching she is a mere congeries of wood and iron--an ordinary piece of personal property--as distinctly a land structure as a house, and subject only to mechanic's liens created by state law and enforceable in the state courts. In the baptism of launching she receives her name, and from the moment her keel touches the water she is transformed, and becomes a subject of admiralty jurisdiction. She acquires a personality of her own; becomes competent to contract, and is individually liable for her obligations, upon which she may sue in her name...She is capable too, of committing a tort, and is responsible in damages therefor.

---

[14] Id. at 584.

[15] Id.

[16] The current edition of Benedict on Admiralty (1974) defines "ship" by stating: "In common usage the word is applied generally to all larger vessels which are capable of self-propulsion either mechanically or by sails."

[17] Tucker v. Alexandroff, 183 U.S. 424 (1902).

Although the component parts of OFEP ships may be built on land, it is possible that the pontoons, columns, and buildings will actually be assembled in the water (Craven and Hanson, 1972, p. 33). A platform, then, may have no clear launching to indicate when it has become a ship.

The Supreme Court suggested a resolution to this issue in Thames Towboat Co. v. The Francis McDonald[18] which involved a ship which was launched as a hull by one company and towed to two other ship yards before being completed. The second ship yard sued under a maritime lien to recover for supplies furnished and repairs made while the ship was being completed. The court said that the settled rule was that a contract for the complete construction of a ship was nonmaritime, and not within the court's admiralty jurisdiction. The court distinguished Tucker by saying that it involved the detention of a foreign seaman, not a contract for ship construction. The court said:

> (T)he doctrine is now firmly established that contracts to construct entirely new ships are nonmaritime because not nearly enough related to any rights and duties pertaining to commerce and navigation.[19]

Benedict (1974) refers to Tucker as "The classic pronouncement as to the moment when a ship comes into being." However Benedict (1974, p. 10-6) cites Thames Towboat in saying:

> The fact that a structure is a vessel...does not necessarily attract admiralty jurisdiction in all cases having reference to her, for the law may, in respect of particular transactions, require other conditions to be fulfilled. For example, in matters of contract to furnish materials, work, and labor for the completion of a vessel, admiralty has no jurisdiction even after a vessel is launched while she is not yet sufficiently advanced to discharge the functions for which she was designed...In a case where a ship is launched but not completed, it is not that jurisdiction is barred in all cases of contract relating to her, but only in respect of a contract for the supply of materials, labor and work for completion of the vessel.

Under traditional definitions, then, a ship may be born for some purposes but not for others. For this reason, the most appropriate event for determining the birth of ocean floating platform ships may be neither the time of launching nor the time

---

[18] Thames Towboat Co. v. The Francis McDonald, 254 U.S. 242 (1920).

[19] Id. at 244.

of completion. Instead, it may be the time of registration of the OFEP as a ship.

The moment of death of an OFEP ship may be even harder to determine than its birth. A "dead ship" is a ship which is no longer in commerce and navigation. For example, in Hanna v. The Meteor,[20] the court found that the Meteor was completely withdrawn from navigation and commerce, was not used by the owners in the business of carrying cargo or passengers, had no crew, no machinery in operation, and no light, heat or power; the boilers were opened up and dry, the generators had been taken apart and preserved in grease; and it would have required a great deal of work to put the engineering part of the ship back into operation. The court therefore concluded that the Meteor was a dead ship.

Ocean floating platforms may provide a new twist to the "dead ship" definition. For example, the Hawaii floating city design (Craven and Hanson, 1972, p. 9) envisions pie-wedge shaped platforms which can join and disassemble as modules. One module might support a housing section, one might be a power plant, and one might be an office complex. Different ships could thus be linked together and then disassembled at will, depending on how many units of what kind were desired at what time. A registered ship with ten linked units which move and operate together could, over time, change all of its units and be an entirely different ship. In such a case the new ship may retain the original registration, or the original ship may be declared dead and new registration required. A result such as this might be avoided if each unit of the floating city registered individually as a ship. Avoiding one identity problem, however, might produce another. What would be the legal classification of that linkage of ten such registered ships, travelling and working as one unit for many years? It is also conceivable that engine units, for example, would register as ships while power generating units, for example, would not. It is not clear what status this mixture of ships and structures would have.

Thus, OFEP's would be classified as vessels under U.S. statutory and case law. OFEP's could also be classified as ships under U.S. case law, although the time of their birth and death may be difficult to determine. U.S. law, of course, is only an example of the kind of legal characterization which may achieve international recognition.

Regulation on the High Seas

If OFEP's fall within the definition of a ship, it is likely that they will seek to register as ships flying national

---

[20] Hanna v. The Meteor, 92 F. Supp. 530 (1950).

flags. This would give them legal status and rights under the law of the sea conventions currently in force. An OFEP could gain this status without subjecting itself to any major regulation. International regulation of ships depends on regulation by the flag state (Convention on the High Seas), flag-of-convenience states allow ships to register under their flags, pay minimal taxes, and then sail off into the high seas with little further contact with the flag state.[21] As a new kind of ship with unique problems and capabilities, OFEP's may seek, and flag-of-convenience states may offer, special registration terms which reflect their unique purposes and tonnage. The fact that an OFEP could largely escape regulation on the high seas would be significant if the OFEP ship intended to engage in commercial activities such as mariculture or sea bed mining. These activities would not be regulated under present conventions.

Regulation in the Territorial Sea and Contiguous Zone

Coastal states would have some powers in regard to OFEP ships which enter their territorial waters. Article 1 of the Convention on the Territorial Sea and the Contiguous Zone gives the coastal state sovereignty over its territorial sea, sovereignty which is modified by the right of innocent passage guaranteed under Article 14. Limitations on this right of innocent passage provide some basis for the regulation of OFEP ships. Under Article 16 "The coastal state may take the necessary steps in its territorial sea to prevent passage which is not innocent."[22] Passage which is not innocent is passage which is prejudicial to the peace, good order or security of the coastal state. A coastal state could thus assert control over an OFEP

---

[21] Article 5 of the Convention on the High Seas states that "There must exist a genuine link between the State and the ship; in particular, the State must effectively exercise its jurisdiction and control in administrative, technical, and social matters over ships flying its flag." A number of states, however, have chosen not to effectively exercise their jurisdiction and control. These flag states are known as "flags of convenience," and the convenience includes allowing the ownership and control of registered vessels by non-citizens, easy registration and transfer, the manning of ships by non-citizens, and low taxes or only registry fees and annual fees based on tonnage. Flags-of-convenience states typically do not have the power, governmental machinery, or interest required to enforce any international regulations regarding their registered ships. Jones, N., Flags of convenience in the Pacific 1-2, 1975, Working Paper No. 7, Sea Grant College Program, University of Hawaii.

[22] The coastal state is allowed other controls, in addition to the prevention of passage which is not innocent. Under Article 16, when ships are in the territorial sea on their way

ship by arguing that a very large, slow-moving OFEP disrupted "good order" in its territorial sea by interfering with coastal shipping, pleasure craft, fishing and other uses of the sea. If the OFEP ship broadcast unauthorized radio or television programs, it might be argued that it was prejudicial to "peace"; and if it obstructed the movement of military ships or blocked access to harbors of the coastal state used for military purposes, it might be argued that it was prejudicial to "security."

While registration as a ship could give an OFEP the right of innocent passage in territorial seas, few OFEP's may wish to exercise this right. OFEP's which operate close to shore, such as those designed to provide power directly to municipal systems, will be permanently positioned or positioned for long periods, and will probably not move any distance through the territorial sea. Other OFEP's will probably remain in deeper waters beyond the territorial sea. For example, ocean thermal energy conversion (OTEC) platforms could have pipes as deep as 3,000 feet, and thus would remain outside shallow territorial seas, using barges or tankers to transport their products to coastal markets.

---

to internal waters (landward of the territorial sea), "the coastal State shall also have the right to take the necessary steps to prevent any breach of the conditions to which admission of those ships to those waters is subject." OFEP's may seek admission to internal waters from the territorial sea in order to serve local power needs. Article 16 also allows the coastal state to "suspend temporarily in specified areas of its territorial sea the innocent passage of foreign ships if such suspension is essential for the protection of its security." This clause provides a method for temporarily banning all foreign ships, but it may not be a specific remedy for the problems imposed by ocean-floating platforms. Article 17 supports laws and regulations issued by the coastal state regarding navigation and transportation in the territorial sea, but under Article 18 the coastal state is not allowed to levy charges on foreign ships "by reason only of their passage through the territorial sea." Charges may be levied only "for specific services rendered to the ship." The coastal state thus cannot attempt to regulate OFEP ships by charging them for passage, although OFEP's might be a source of income from the sale of supplies and services rendered to them during their passage. The laws and regulations regarding navigation and transportation which can be issued under Article 17 are also modified by Article 15, which stipulates that "The coastal State must not hamper innocent passage through the territorial sea."

Current law of the sea negotiations

The Informal Composite Negotiating Text (ICNT A/CONF.62/WP.10) under consideration by the Third United Nations Conference on the Law of the Sea (UNCLOS III) provides in Article 21 that the coastal state can make laws and regulations in regard to the safety of navigation and regulation of marine traffic, but not in such a way as to "apply to the design, construction, manning or equipment of foreign ships" except when giving effect to generally accepted rules or standards. OFEP ships would be among the most unusually designed and constructed of all ships, but under this clause their design and construction could not be regulated. Under Article 22, the coastal state may require foreign ships to use certain sea lanes, but under Article 24 it may not "impose requirements on foreign ships which have the practical effect of denying or impairing the right of innocent passage." Special sea lanes may be designated for OFEP ships, but their innocent passage is still guaranteed.

The provisions in Part XI of the ICNT would give an International Sea-Bed Authority power to regulate resources on the high seas. The word "resources" is defined in Article 133 to mean "minerals"; minerals include water, steam, and hot water as well as metallic deposits such as manganese nodules. Thus, it appears that OFEP ships involved in nodule mining or ocean thermal energy conversion could be regulated by the Authority.

Conclusion

Under the conventions on the law of the sea as they now exist, OFEP's which qualify as ships may enjoy certain rights and escape some forms of regulation. Under the Convention on the Territorial Sea and the Contiguous Zone, OFEP ships could move through the territorial sea and the contiguous zone under the right of innocent passage, but few are likely to do so. OFEP's which register as ships are likely to be involved in mariculture or manganese nodule mining on the high seas, rather than near-shore power generation. If OFEP's were registered under a flag of convenience and positioned on the high seas, the Convention on the High Seas would provide no effective control over them. Under the proposed ICNT, OFEP ships involved in manganese nodule mining and ocean thermal energy conversion would be regulated.

Ocean Floating Energy Platforms as Structures

Definition

In Cope v. Vallette Dry-Dock Co.,[23] the United States Supreme Court agreed that the terms 'ships' and 'vessels' are

[23]Cope v. Vallette Dry-Dock Co., 119 U.S. 625, 30 L. Ed. 501, 7 S. Ct. 336 (1887).

used in a very broad sense, but observed that the fact that something floats on water does not make it a ship or vessel. The court went on to say: "We think no case can be found which would construe the terms (ship or vessel) to include a dry dock, a floating bridge, or meeting house, permanently moored or attached to a wharf."[24] This indicates that an OFEP which was permanently moored would not qualify as a ship or vessel. In later cases, however, lower courts have not focused on permanent mooring so much as the vessel's current function.

Hayford v. Doussony[25] involved a former U.S. gunboat which was refitted as "The Pirate Ship," an amusement or dance barge, docked at Canal Street in New Orleans. The Pirate Ship was attached to land by cables and clamps and a permanent gangway, and was connected to the shore by electric power lines and plumbing. The court said:

> The Pirate Ship was not used, or intended to be used, to carry freight or passengers from one place to another, was not an instrument of navigation or commerce, and performed no function that might not have been performed as well by a floating stage or platform permanently attached to the land.[26]

The Pirate Ship was deemed to have lost its character as a ship because it no longer functioned as one, even though it remained seaworthy and had in fact been towed to a different pier during litigation. A similar analysis is found in Cookmeyer v. Louisiana Dept. of Highways,[27] a case in which two barges were in use in a pontoon bridge attached to a pivot structure so they could swing aside from time to time to allow water craft to pass through. The court admitted the barges had been vessels, and could be used as vessels again in the future, but felt that the dispositive issue was the function and character of the barges at the time the litigation arose. Since the barges functioned as a bridge, and carried no passengers or cargo in navigation, they were a structure and not vessels.

A functional analysis led to a different result in Luna v. Star of India.[28] The Star of India was a three-masted bark launched in 1863 which was renovated and moored in North San

---

[24] Id. at 630.

[25] Hayford v. Doussony, 32 F.2d 605 (1929).

[26] Id.

[27] Cookmeyer v. Louisiana Dept. of Highways, 309 F. Supp. 881 (1970).

[28] Luna v. Star of India, 356 F. Supp. 59 (1973).

Diego Bay as a tourist attraction. The case arose when a visitor slipped and fell on board the Star. Earlier, the Maritime Museum Association, which maintained the Star, had presented evidence to the Coast Guard that the Star was permanently moored to the Embarcadero and was not intended to be used in the future as anything more than a floating museum. The Coast Guard's inspector had determined that the Star was "substantially a land structure" and therefore exempt from the usual inspection and navigation laws. The court, however, followed the 1 USC § 3 definition of a vessel as "every description of water craft or other artificial contrivance used, or capable of being used, as a means of transportation on water." The court found that, were the Star to slip from her moorings, "she would undoubtedly be capable of engaging in maritime transportation, if only as a towed craft."[29] Although historical curios were displayed on board the ship, the court found that "it is evident that the Star of India's primary function is to serve as a ship and only secondarily to house various historical curios."[30] It distinguished this case from the Hayford case discussed above, by noting that The Pirate Ship had been extensively modified to serve as an amusement and dance barge, which were non-maritime purposes.

Interpreting these cases gives rise to a general principle, which is that how a ship or vessel is currently being used is more important than how it is capable of being used. The courts decided that the barges in the pontoon bridge and the Pirate Ship were currently being used as structures, while the Star was currently being used as a ship. This functional analysis provides some support for the argument that OFEP's which stabilize their positions offshore should be defined as structures rather than ships or vessels. Again, these definitional distinctions under U.S. law are merely indicative of the kinds of distinctions which may evolve under international law.

Regulation by Coastal States

If OFEP's are defined as structures, they will have no rights under law of the sea conventions, and can be controlled and licensed within the territorial seas of coastal states. This control will be strengthened if current ICNT provisions are adopted.

The ICNT specifically addresses the question of the regulation of structures and installations in its provisions for an exclusive economic zone (EEZ). Under Article 56 the coastal state's rights over the EEZ would include the following:

---

[29] Id. at 66.
[30] Id.

(a) sovereign rights for the purpose of exploring and exploiting, conserving and managing the natural resources, whether living or non-living, of the sea-bed and subsoil and the superjacent waters, and with regard to other activities for the economic exploitation and exploration of the zone, such as the production of energy from the water, currents and winds;

(b) jurisdiction as provided for in the relevant provisions of the present convention with regard to: (i) the establishment and use of artificial islands, installations and structures...

OFEP's which operate on ocean thermal, wave or wind energy would clearly be regulated by this provision. Also, any OFEP which stabilized its position within the EEZ for any length of time would be likely to come under the scope of these provisions, since it could be classified as an artificial island, installation or structure. Under clause (b), if the OFEP were regarded as a structure, the coastal state would have jurisdiction with regard to its establishment and use. In addition, Article 60 provides that

1. In the exclusive economic zone, the coastal State shall have the exclusive right to construct and to authorize and regulate the construction, operation and use of:

   (a) Artificial islands;

   (b) Installations and structures for the purposes provided for in Article 56 and other economic purposes;

   (c) Installations and structures which may interfere with the exercise of the rights of the coastal State in the zone.

2. The coastal State shall have exclusive jurisdiction over such artificial islands, installations and structures, including jurisdiction with regard to customs, fiscal, health, safety and immigration regulations.

Article 60 further provides that due notice must be given of the construction of artificial islands, installations and structures; they may not be established where they will interfere with recognized sea lanes essential to international navigation; and coastal states may establish safety zones of up to 500 meters around them to ensure their safety and the safety of navigation.

Conclusion

It is likely that OFEP's will spend long periods of time or seek to be permanently positioned offshore in the territorial sea or EEZ. OFEP's which provide energy directly to coastal state power systems will necessarily be positioned only a few miles offshore. Even if the OFEP manufactures products instead of directly supplying energy, a position within 200 miles of the coastline would be convenient for purposes of resupply and repair, as well as rest and recreation for the crew. If the ICNT provisions are adopted, the coastal state would be able to control OFEP activities in the EEZ by exercising sovereign rights over the production of energy from water, winds, and currents, regulating the construction and use of OFEP's, and subjecting them to the full range of customs, immigration, fiscal, health, and safety regulations. Short of the adoption of such provisions, coastal state control would be strong but limited to sovereign rights over the territorial sea.

Ocean Floating Energy Platforms as New States

Definition

A state has been defined as "...(a) people permanently occupying a fixed territory (certam sedem), bound together by common laws, habits, and customs into one body politic, exercising, through the medium of an organized government, independent sovereignty and control over all persons and things within its boundaries..." (Moore, 1906, pp. 14-15). By this definition a state requires a body of people, a fixed territory, and a sovereign government. Of these basic elements of statehood, the most difficult concept for an ocean floating platform is that of fixed territory. The ocean floating platform would itself be a physical domain, but it would rest on another domain, the ocean. The solution to the question of territory may be to establish a horizontal property regime. The floating platform community could be granted territorial rights above the ocean surface, much as today's condominium apartment owners own living space ten stories above the ground. Floating platform communities may thus become condominium countries. Such city states would be unusual in character, but it has been said (Moore, 1906, pp. 14-15):

> It is a sound general principle...that international law has no concern with the form, character, or power of the constitution or government of a state, with the religion of its inhabitants, the extent of its domain, or the importance of its position and influence in the commonwealth of nations...Provided that the state possess a government capable of securing at home the

observance of rightful relations with other states, the demands of international law are satisfied.

An OFEP city state could be founded simply by building a floating energy platform, gathering a body of people to live on it, and organizing a government to run it. Whether the OFEP city truly becomes a state in international law depends on recognition by other states.[31] The granting of recognition is completely within the discretion of the recognizing state, which must also be a recognized state (Hackworth, 1940, p. 161) if the recognition is to be effective (Moore, 1906, p. 73). However, "Recognition is not necessarily express; it may be implied, as when a state enters into negotiations with the new state, sends its diplomatic agents, receives such agents officially, gives exequators to its consuls, forms with it conventional relations."[32]

Thus an OFEP city could set up its own sovereign government and then seek formal or implied recognition from other states as a means of securing sovereignty under international law. There is some evidence that entrepreneurial groups will attempt to do just that. In recent years, a number of attempts have been made to establish new states on reefs or shallows beyond the jurisdiction of coastal states.[33] There was no question in those cases that new states might be formed. The question was one of jurisdictional claims made by other states

---

[31] United States v. Carillo, 13 F. Supp. 121 (1935); Moore, 1906, pp. 14-15.

[32] Republic of China v. Merchants' Fire Assurance Corp. of New York, 30 F.2d 278 (1939); Moore, 1906, p. 73.

[33] Two groups made the attempt to build facilities on coral reefs 4-5 miles from Southeastern Florida, but were stopped by a federal court, which granted an injunction on the grounds that the reefs were within the territorial jurisdiction of the USA, construction activities were destroying irreplaceable natural resources, and a permit was required from the Secretary of the Army. United States v. Ray, 423 F.2d 16 (1970). Atlantis Development Corporation, a Bahamian corporation which intervened in the case, had planned to spend $250 million to establish a sovereign state on the coral reef, a state which would include radio and television stations, a post office, office buildings, stamp department, foreign offices, a government palace, congress, international bank and mint.

An attempt to found the new state of Abalonia was made 110 miles off the coast of San Diego on the Cortes Bank, a sea shallow which is rich in abalone and lobster. The state was to be built on a reinforced concrete ship, which was sunk in two fathoms of water. The mooring line broke, however, and the ship sank deeper. The Corps of Engineers declared that the

to the same reefs or shallows. As of this writing, a British court has upheld the independent status of the Royal Principality of Sealand, a one-family country established on a World War II anti-aircraft tower four miles beyond Britain's territorial sea.[34] A floating city could easily escape jurisdictional claims, because it need not rest on reefs, shallows, or any part of a continental shelf and could float beyond the jurisdiction of other states.[35]

Economic regulations

The birth of OFEP city states could be heavily regulated by coastal states; the tools of regulation would be those already familiar in international economic regulation. A wide variety of approvals and permits would be required to build and launch an OFEP city state. Imported materials would have to go through customs and currency exchange procedures. The people who assembled to form the new floating city state would be subject to immigration controls; those who built the floating city would be subject to labor controls. Local authorities might require the approval of a building site. A permit might be

---

ship was a hazard to navigation, and the federal government claimed jurisdiction to the area as part of the outer continental shelf. San Diego L. Rev., 1969, 6, p. 499. Another group, organized as Caribbean-Pacific Enterprises, Inc., erected two coral and chicken wire structures, planted two flags on the Minerva Reefs in the South Pacific, and declared the reefs to be the Republic of Minerva. The king of Tonga decided to claim the reefs himself, and a Tongan expedition tore down the flags. Dubois, Another Utopia?, Barron's, February 16, 1976, p. 9.

[34]The Royal Principality of Sealand consists of a platform 25 yards long and 10 yards wide, set atop two cement caissons. Roy Bates, a former British Army major, his wife and son occupied the tower in 1966 and declared independence in 1967. Sealand has issued 180 passports, printed postage stamps, and created a Sealand dollar. Negotiations with a group of German investors to build a $70 million hotel and gambling complex at Sealand recently failed. Sealand has survived a number of invasion attempts. "Emerging nations: Prince Valiant," Newsweek, August 28, 1978, p. 40; West, "He 'rules' over the world's smallest state off England," Honolulu Star Bulletin, September 2, 1978, p. B-16, col. 4.

[35]About 30 members of the Global Society, based in Venice, California, plan to build a concrete platform and establish a floating city state beyond the 12-mile limit. Members have called for the formation of global city states throughout the world, and have signed a Global Declaration of Independence. Bronson, "Establishing a new world," Oakland Tribune, October 31, 1976, p. 6-D.

required to tow the floating city across the coastal state's territorial sea, and so on. These direct controls would be ample to prevent the construction and launching of an OFEP city state should the coastal state wish to prevent it.

Even if OFEP city states succeed in getting launched from sympathetic coastal states, there is the question of their economic survival. OFEP's are serious contenders as new floating city states because they can make use of ocean energy not only for consumption by their citizens in their offices and homes but also to support major food production and industrial activity. OFEP's may derive energy from the wind, waves, and ocean thermal energy conversion, and they may fill some of their protein needs through mariculture and fishing operations. Commercial activities might include the mining of manganese nodules, mariculture, manufacture of ammonia, seasonal power generation for coastal states, or service as offshore recreation centers and gambling casinos.

Symbiotic relationships with developing coastal states are possible. The OFEP city state could buy raw materials from the developing nation, and manufacture and sell in return a number of goods which the developing nation needs. Floating only a few miles offshore, transportation costs would be low; the developing nation would not have to build major roadways to facilitate an industry. An OFEP city state might tie up offshore small nations during different seasons to provide additional energy to meet peak needs or support new industrial development. It is conceivable that a developing nation would set up and diplomatically recognize an OFEP city state designed to service its own particular needs. The OFEP city state might attract skilled professionals and immigrant laborers seeking new and better lifestyles under a government of their own choosing, economically tied but legally and geographically at arm's length from the developing nation or nations it serves. Professional skill, cheap labor, and the low cost of transporting goods over water could make OFEP city states economically viable in a symbiotic relationship with a coastal state.

This symbiotic relationship could be very stable politically. It is not likely that an OFEP city state would be seized or nationalized by a developing country. Its factories and assets would not be inside the land-based country, but out on the ocean. Its people would not be a local colony of foreigners but members of an independent state under international law. A large floating platform positioned on the high seas could be difficult to seize physically and could not be seized legally. This gives the OFEP city state strengths which a foreign enterprise does not normally have. Each party, the OFEP city state and the developing nation, would bargain from a balance of strength and need. The OFEP city state would need the developing nation to survive, but it could float off to another coastal state if a particular developing nation abused its trade regulation powers. The developing nation would be hurt if an entire industrial sector or source of power floated off into the horizon, but it could establish a new OFEP city state on the same basis. Neither party could demand too much without being faced with the prospect of having to start all over again and establish a new symbiotic relationship with another OFEP city state or developing nation.

If such coastal state-OFEP relationships are mutually advantageous, the economic regulation of OFEP city states would not be so harsh as to drive them out of existence. However, if symbiotic relationships are not formed, the power of coastal states to regulate trade would remain a major threat to the survival of OFEP city states once they are launched. If the OFEP city manufactured items, it would need to buy raw materials, and coastal state governments could bar exports to it; if it were involved in mining, manufacturing, or mariculture, it would need to export the finished product with coastal state governments placing tariffs on the product which would be high enough to make the product non-competitive.

Regulation by recognition

Even after an OFEP city state has been launched, has formed a government and declared independence, and has become economically viable, other states may attempt to regulate it by not granting diplomatic recognition and thereby keeping it in a state of limbo under international law. Opposition might be especially pronounced if the OFEP city state operated as a tax haven, abortion clinic, gambling casino, or center for private broadcasting. On the other hand, coastal states benefitting economically from their relationship with OFEP cities would probably grant recognition to OFEP city states which serviced their needs. Major military powers might recognize OFEP city states in return for treaty agreements granting them the right to refuel military ships, obtain hospital service for sailors, and install missiles and other war material there. Recognition can be implied rather than express and need not come from all the nations of the world to provide a minimum of status and diplomatic assurance of the rights of the OFEP city state. Nonrecognition by the majority of powers could cast a shadow over OFEP city states, but nonrecognition would be a weak tool of regulation.

Conclusion

Thereis agreement in principle that new states can be formed beyond the jurisdiction of existing states. An OFEP city may establish itself as a state by floating beyond coastal state jurisdiction, forming a government, and seeking the recognition of other states. Regulation by coastal states may make it difficult to build the OFEP city state and ensure that it is a viable economic activity once it is launched. Even if it becomes economically viable, such a state may not be granted diplomatic recognition by other states, thus preventing it from becoming a full-fledged member of the family of nations. However, it is possible that coastal states will help launch and then recognize new OFEP city states if they service coastal state needs. Close economic and political ties with coastal states may ensure the survival and international position of OFEP city states even without formal recognition.

Regulation of Ocean Floating Energy Platforms by Function

It is typical of both the law and human nature that new developments are met by an attempt to place them in old categories. Automobiles were merely "horseless carriages" until they began to transform urban society; submarines were "U-boats" until they transformed naval warfare. Similarly, ocean floating platforms will probably be structures, ships, or new states until they transform the use of ocean space and are placed in a category distinctly their own. In the transitional period, a functional analysis may evolve which relies upon but is not bound by the traditional definitions.

The functional approach was used by United Stated courts in deciding the status of The Pirate Ship, the barges in the bridge, and the Star of India discussed earlier. This functional approach may evolve of necessity, because OFEP's may change functions, while traditional definitions assume a single function which does not change. Rather than search for a legal definition which is appropriate to each kind of platform throughout its life, it may be best to apply the classification which is most appropriate to the function which the platform is carrying out at a particular time.

The advantages of the functional definition could be several. OFEP's could be required to obtain permits as structures, vessels, or ships, specifying the length of time they expect to function in that capacity, and subjecting themselves to the legal implications of each classification. This would establish their legal status and provide the coastal state with appropriate regulatory power over platforms as they change functions. An OFEP city state could either fall under the category of ship, vessel, or structure or seek recognition as an independent state and negotiate its own terms with coastal states. Thus, four categories would be sufficient for a coastal state regulatory scheme:

1. Structure. This category would include all OFEP's while they are being built, and all completed OFEP's which float in a fixed position for a year or more

within the territorial sea or EEZ (if the ICNT is adopted). This category would apply to OFEP vessels, ships, and city states if they took up fixed positions offshore for a year or more. Regulations would emphasize resource exploitation.

2. Vessel. This category would include OFEP's which take up fixed positions in the territorial sea or EEZ for more than 30 days but less than a year. This category would apply to OFEP structures, ships and city states if they moved frequently, taking up a new position every few months. The regulations would emphasize appropriate sea lanes and times for travel so as to minimize interference with other uses of the ocean.

3. Ship. This category would include OFEP's registered as ships and flying national flags. This category would apply to an OFEP city state which is registered as a ship and moves through the territorial sea or EEZ without taking up a position there for more than a month. While the status of an OFEP ship would remain unchallenged on the high seas, an OFEP ship would be treated as a vessel or structure in the territorial sea or EEZ if it did not move in transit but remained in a fixed position for more than 30 days. The regulations would emphasize the limits on innocent passage.

4. City State. This category would include all OFEP's which set up their own governments and declare independence. If a coastal state does not recognize the OFEP city state, it could regulate the city state as a structure, vessel, or ship. If recognition is granted, an exchange of letters or a bilateral treaty could establish the terms and conditions under which the OFEP city state remains in the territorial sea or EEZ.

Under this simple scheme, a platform being built would file as a structure; once built, it could continue that status or opt for the status of vessel, ship, or independent state. An OFEP could register as a ship, roam the oceans for a few years supporting deep ocean mining, and then return and file for status as a structure, taking up a position near shore and generating power into a local grid. An OFEP providing seasonal power could move from time to time as a vessel. An OFEP ship, vessel, or structure servicing the needs of a coastal state could develop a symbiotic relationship and declare itself a new state to negotiate the terms and conditions of its presence in the territorial sea or EEZ.

A functional approach would rely upon current law regarding states, ships, vessels, and structures, but would create a new regulatory scheme by applying current law in a far more flexible way. Such a scheme is suggested by the flexibility of admiralty law. As Benedict (1906, p. 10-2) says:

> It may happen that a structure may be a vessel or other appropriate maritime object for the purpose of the application of one rule of admiralty law and not for another; for example, a sea-plane in maritime peril can be the subject of a maritime salvage but may well not be a vessel within the meaning of the statutes limiting the liability of the owner for damage caused by it.
>
> Sometimes special provisions are enacted to regulate the operation of certain types of vessels, which while subject to a special statutory regime for certain purposes continue to be governed by the general law or other statutes for other purposes.

An international treaty could establish acceptable categories of ocean floating platforms and provide a framework for municipal licensing systems. The regulatory scheme of an initial treaty may be based upon application of the traditional definitions of state, ship, vessel, or structure. However, OFEP's are a new form of technology with multiple uses which make them substantially different from the single-purpose, single-use ships, vessels, and structures of the past. Thus, a treaty would be most helpful if it provided not only a declaration of policy and framework for regulation, but also a new definition of OFEP's based on their multiple uses.

REFERENCES

Anderson and Anderson. Thermal power from seawater. Mechanical Engineering, 1966, 88.

Avery. Ocean thermal energy--status and prospects. Marine Technology Society Journal, April-May 1978, 12(2).

Benedict on Admiralty, Release No. 17, 1974.

Claude. Power from the tropical seas. Mechanical Engineering, 1930, 52.

Convention on the High Seas, April 29, 1958, 2 UST 2312, TIAS No. 5200, 450 UNTS 82 (entered into force September 30, 1962).

Convention on the Territorial Sea and Contiguous Zone, April 29, 1958, 2 UST 1606, TIAS No. 5639, 516 UNTS 205 (entered into force September 10, 1964).

Craven, J. and Hanson, J. Hawaii's Floating City Development Program, 1972. First Annual Report, Fiscal Year 1972, University of Hawaii and the Oceanic Institute.

Hackworth, G. Digest of International Law, 1940, 1.

Keith. Floating cities: a new challenge for transnational law. Marine Policy, 1977, 1.

McGowan and Heronemus. Ocean thermal and wind power: alternative energy sources based on natural solar collection. Environmental Affairs, 1975, 4.

Merriam. Wind energy for human needs. Technology Review, January 1977.

Moore, J. A Digest of International Law, 1906, 1.

Putting the wind to work. Engineering, November 22, 1968, 206.

Wade. Windmills: the resurrection of an ancient energy technology. Science, June 7, 1974, 184.

Wicks and Schmitt. Prospects for renewable energy from the sea. Marine Technology Society Journal, 1977, 11(5&6).

THE RELATION OF OCEAN ENERGY TO OCEAN FOOD

John E. Bardach
The East-West Center
Honolulu, Hawaii

Introduction

Certain processes, man-made structures, or human activities in the sea related to energy transformations for power production can be or can be made to be beneficial for ocean-based food production. Conversely, they can be harmful to fisheries and/or aquaculture. In a number of instances, the relation is neutral; that is, the energy-related activity neither enhances nor depresses, actually or potentially, man's quest of deriving animal protein from the sea.

Discussion of these linkages from the vantage points of economics, biology, and technology will be easier keeping in mind the following properties of food production in the oceans:

1. The growth of aquatic organisms requires the input of nutrients and sunlight, as well as the medium of abundant water of a certain quality (salinity, temperature, etc.).

2. The limitations of biological production in a fishery or a mariculture operation are prominently food (or nutrients) and/or shelter (substrate). Seasonality and intensity of the input of solar energy are also important.

3. In both fisheries and aquaculture, what is eventually harvested has to be contained or "concentrated," this being the essence of fish catching as well as fish farming.

These facts provide the basis for a general evaluation of the various linkages between energy and food-related activities in the oceans. The evaluation is shown in the following table:

Energy Base	Operation or Structure	Relation to Food Production
Oil/gas	Rigs/wells	Positive--providing shelter, substrate. Negative--obstructing fishing operations. Also negative--if causing sporadic pollution.

Energy Base	Operation or Structure	Relation to Food Production
Oil/gas	Transportation (ships)	Neutral or negative--if sporadic spills occur. Also negative--if chronic pollution ensues.
Ocean Thermal Energy Conversion (OTEC)	Probably floating structure lifting deep, cold, nutrient-enriched water	Positive--can increase nutrients locally and concentrate fish. Or neutral to negative, if enrichment is to be avoided.
Nuclear fission	Uses ocean water for cooling of on-shore or floating power plants and emits heated waste water	Positive if waste heat is used to speed growth. Negative if heat reduces species diversity or causes fish kills. Also negative--leaks and spills may occur.
Nuclear fusion	Design characteristics not set	Probably same as for fission.
Tides/ currents	Plant-associated structures contain large masses of water that move in- and off-shore	Neutral to negative--as scouring by tidal current is possible; some positive effects may be related to water storage ("reservoirs").
Waves	Floating devices of as yet uncertain design	Neutral; if devices are large, positive effects could be like for floating platforms.

Oil Rigs and Fishery Management

Coral reefs owe their high diversity and biomass of fishes not only to the fact that photosynthesis occurs in the corals but also, prominently, to the fact that their three-dimensional structure provides substrate and shelter to predator and prey alike. Artificial reefs emulate the natural ones, at least in the latter property. In other words, the provision of structures, floating or attached, causes the promotion of fish concentrations around and under them. Oil rigs are artificial reefs of a kind; fish catches monitored in the vicinity of rigs have been found to be greater than in the open sea (Klima and Wickham, 1971).

It must be emphasized, however, that rigs do not increase biological production as such, except to a very minor extent if and where corals or algae attach themselves. Rigs can also obstruct currents, tending to retain plankton around them and thus afford some food to certain animals. Their prime value, however, lies in their being a "crowd stopper," as it were, for fish that may be netted but more likely can be caught by hook and line or in traps. These concentrations of fish may lead to slight increases in fertility, especially if currents around the platforms are slight and residues of fish metabolism are retained in the vicinity. These platforms can be a base for fishing with nightlighting. One may even envision the deployment of chemical attractants from them to further retain or concentrate predatory fish.

Several hundred tons of fish have been observed to mill around an oil rig. Assuming on the conservative side that only a hundred tons can be caught from every platform a year and that by 1990 there will be approximately 4,000 offshore production platforms of all kinds and sizes (Stone, 1975, reported that 2,900 of them were located in U.S. waters), at least 400,000 tons of fish could become available to fishermen who fish around all platforms. True, this tonnage is only two percent of higher-valued food fish catches (Bardach, 1977), but it is a catch for which no search is required, leading to fuel savings, and one which can be available even after the well is dry.

However, in U.S. waters, federal regulations specify that the platform be cut off 14 feet below the mudline and removed when an offshore field is depleted (Stone, 1975). The regulation was made to enable trawlers to resume using the grounds preempted by the oil rigs. Oil rigs often stand on soft bottom and in shrimping grounds at that. I know of no careful evaluation of the benefits of alternative management measures such as retaining some rigs even as markers for other submerged ones while reopening, by selective rig removal, the most productive former trawling grounds.

In addition to using rigs as fishing bases, an attempt has been made to culture high-priced marine food organisms on them. On the oil rig "Holly" in the Santa Barbara Channel in the U.S., environmental scientists of the Atlantic Richfield Company are now trying to rear abalone, one of the more expensive culturable sea delicacies. These herbivorous mollusks can be spawned in captivity, and once the young have been coaxed through a delicate period they are put in cages on the legs of the rigs and fed a slurry of algae (Siva, 1978). The method shows certain analogies to abalone culture developed in Japanese near-shore waters; the U.S. technique, however, tends to be more mechanized than the technique in the Far East.

Using oil rigs allows the culture operations to be placed in cleaner water than is now found closer to shore where competing uses of the land-water interface often restrict aquaculture. Obviously, aquatic farming will not be practiced on all rigs. Furthermore, such aquaculture may barely make a dent in the world's volume of cultured mollusks, but it does point to possibilities that are largely unused and deserve more study than they have received.

Oil Pollution

Even though the subject is treated voluminously elsewhere (Cowell, 1976), a realistic glance at the damage which oil spills can cause to fisheries should be included in this discussion. Data on such damage are still impressionistic, and assessment, in monetary terms, of the harm they do is difficult indeed. However, the data point to a number of likely facts: (1) seas with rocky shores are less vulnerable than those with sand or mud bottoms; (2) open-sea spills are less serious than near-shore ones; and (3) spills of refined oil products often taint the taste of sea foods. However, truly permanent economic damage to fisheries has not yet been ascribed to a spill (Cowell, 1976). A situation that may require special scrutiny is the planned stockpiling by Japan of oil on some twenty large carriers anchored in protected locations. No data exist on the effects of spilled liquid natural gas (LNG) on fishery resources, since no sea spill of LNG has yet occurred.

Effects of chronic oil pollution due to ship operations are now believed to be far the more serious, long-term depressants of fish production but occur synergistically with other human actions in the shore zone, such as agriculture and ports. Attempts are underway to assess all types of oil pollution through cooperative research under the aegis of several U.N. agencies (UNESCO, 1976). All that can be said to date is that it is difficult, if not impossible, to assess accurately the effect of chronic additions of oil to the water on the reduction in earnings of fishermen and aquaculturists.

Not to be taken as an excuse for relenting in measures against oil pollution, it is my impression, nevertheless, that no great permanent harm will have come to the biota of the world's seas specifically from chronic emissions and acute spills of oil or refined oil products by the time the last drop has been extracted from the world's oil wells. This impression is based, in the main, on three observations:

1. Cases of endemism notwithstanding, marine fish fauna are generally widespread; and after a localized kill, recolonization is the rule (Lagler, Bardach, Miller, and Passino, 1978).

2. Concentrations of oil residues are low and persistent fractions thereof are non-toxic.

3. These residues, being organic, are eventually decomposed by microbial action (Cowell, 1976).

Serious local harm may, of course, occur or an odd, perhaps cryptic, localized species could be eradicated or certain products of petro-chemical industries can be catastrophically harmful to plants and animals in the sea as well as on land, but this consideration far exceeds the confines of this paper.

Ocean Thermal Energy

The principle of OTEC (Ocean Thermal Energy Conversion) is simple: "Power is generated by using warm water at the surface of the tropical oceans in combination with the cold water available at the depth of half a mile to operate a heat engine" (Avery, 1978). The process that is presently favored by most engineers uses ammonia coolant, which is made to boil by warm, and to condense again by cold, water pumped up from 600 to 800 m. The temperature difference between deep and surface water in tropical seas of ca. 24°C occurs in a range which makes ammonia, or a substance with a similar boiling point, most suitable to generate vapor which drives a turbine. An alternative, open-cycle design which uses low pressure water vapor may have greater engineering difficulties to solve but has an additional, easy-to-obtain and potentially valuable by-product, namely fresh water. In either case, the small thermal differential available emphasizes the need for huge heat exchangers.

Therefore, OTEC plants are very sensitive to economies of scale and are best situated in near-equatorial regions where surface waters are warmest. At present, power costs of a 400 megawatt plant are approaching competitive status with coal and/or oil fired ones (Douglass, 1978). Bio-fouling, especially through bacterial slime, reduces heat transfer in heat exchangers, but various OTEC engineers anticipate that these problems can be overcome. It appears as if floating OTEC plants, even of smaller size will, under most conditions, be more economical to build than on-shore installations.

In connection with law of the sea, it is germane to note that some of these floating OTEC plants would be operating in the tropical open ocean, grazing, as it were, beyond 200 miles where they would encounter the greatest possible temperature differential between deep and surface waters (Avery, 1978). These plants would most likely produce ammonia from air and sea water; such ammonia would serve as a hydrogen carrier for a future power economy based on liquid hydrogen. Speculation about such OTEC grazers is based on the impossibility of power transmission by line over very large distances while taking advantage of using the best oceanographic conditions for OTEC power production. Such OTEC grazers would surely be of concern to the Third U.N. Conference on the Law of the Sea. The problems so generated would be similar in kind and dimension to those attendant with the mining of ocean minerals.

OTEC plants assume interest for aquaculture because the cold deep water which they use, and eventually discard, contains between 60 and 200 times the nitrate nitrogen and up to 20 times the phosphates of the surface water which also passes through the plant (Hirota, 1977); these comparative values vary somewhat regionally. Thus, theoretically, plant nutrients appear to be available relatively freely. Much theorizing and some experimentation have occurred concerning how these might be turned into food. It should also be noted that "rich" is a relative term when speaking of water; the water with which the People's Republic of China does aquaculture, using sewage and manure, and that which is used in experimental algae and oyster culture in diluted sewage in the U.S., are far more enriched and therefore more productive than deep ocean water.

High yields in aquaculture can be obtained through the culture of filter feeders (oysters, clams) with substantial inputs of labor and capital equipment. This indicates that an OTEC plant located on shore is more suitable for a combined power-aquaculture operation, mainly because the enriched water would not be diluted by the ocean surrounding the effluent. Such a plant would, however, have substantial land requirements for ponds and raceways. Laurence and Roels (1977) extrapolated from quasi-laboratory conditions geared to optimizing animal protein production that a 160 megawatt OTEC plant (Lockheed design) discharging 6.48×10^7 m^3 of water per day could produce 380,000 metric tons of clam meat a year from a water surface of 2,049 hectares. They experimented with 80 percent deep and 20 percent surface water in containers 4.88 m deep. The turnover rate of the water was slated to be $1\frac{1}{4}$ days. This tonnage of clam chowder ingredient is a staggering amount of high quality shellfish meat, especially if one notes that the 1976 world harvest of these and related mollusks (oysters and mussels not included) amounted to less than twice this weight (FAO, 1977).

It might appear that clam culture in enclosures facilitated by an OTEC plant was a bonanza, even to the extent of reconsidering priorities. In other words, should protein production perhaps not come first rather than power? To assess such a situation we must ask what the realistic prospects are of achieving such aquatic harvests from the waters which OTEC will spew out. First, extrapolations to an intensive aquaculture endeavor are dangerous. Nevertheless, practical yields from intensive sewage fish culture and/or intensive oyster and mussel farming have had best harvests of comparable magnitude for unit surfaces of illuminated water and/or flow-through volumes (Bardach, Ryther, and McLarney, 1972).

Perhaps the biggest obstacles to obtaining the animal protein yield projected by Laurence and Roels would be the following:

1. Adapting the OTEC design for optimal aquaculture use. (The clam growing experiments cited here used 80 percent deep and 20 percent surface water; such a mix for aquaculture in the output of an OTEC plant may not be obtainable without substantially raising the expenses of building the plant.)

2. The availability of several thousand hectares of suitable flat low-lying land or shallow protected water in the vicinity of the OTEC plant. (Only the water surface needed was mentioned; the entire installation will use still more area.) From a hydrographic vantage point, some suitable OTEC locations may exist near certain arid tropical shores, some of which may be flat. Only very few of them, the island of Hawaii being one and Puerto Rico perhaps another, might also develop large enough power needs for an economic OTEC plant unless it were planned to "export energy," for instance, as ammonia fertilizer.

3. Controlling in a cost-effective fashion, on the enormous scale necessary, composition of algae, parasites, predators, competitors and other bio-technical variables, including the securing of the clam seed to produce a high sustained aquacultural yield.

Of lesser, but not minimal, concern may be the dangers of eutrophication of near-shore waters from the effluents of the mollusk farm, since a substantial portion of the nitrogen and phosphorus metabolized by the clams would be excreted. True, consideration may be given to the addition of large-scale means of nutrient stripping through adding to clam culture the growing of valuable colloid producing red or brown algae, but this would produce additional massive requirements for low-lying flat land or shallow ocean waters.

It must also be pointed out that deep ocean water is low in concentrations of certain trace metals necessary for algal growth and high in concentrations of certain others. Even if growth of algae were not inhibited (North, 1977), there is the likelihood of accumulation of these metals in the flesh of the shellfish rendering them unfit for human consumption. Close examination of these possibilities on a pilot scale is clearly indicated.

The attainable production of a large OTEC aquafarm is likely to be lower than that envisioned by Laurence and Roels. However, before serious thought can be given to establishing it on the massive scale projected by these authors, there should be pilot experiments larger than hitherto undertaken, conducted uninterruptedly over two to three years. Careful evaluation would have to be made examining, among other things, the optimal depth of algae and/or shellfish containers--those in the experiments of Laurence and Roels far exceed in depth recommendations found elsewhere for optimal algal growth in sewage ponds (Oswald and Benemann, 1977). The deeper the ponds, incidentally, the greater the likelihood that additional pumping costs would be incurred, weakening one of the main economic advantages of shore-based OTEC aquaculture, namely free water delivered with a head. Only such measures would help establish at what scale this kind of animal protein production can become economical.[1] Dislocation of sea food prices would result from the potential dumping on the shellfish market of mollusks farmed in connection with OTEC plants, placing in jeopardy the rentability of large-scale OTEC plant-associated aquaculture. Thus, in an economic evaluation of large OTEC aquafarms, costs and benefits of alternatives such as further improving production of other forms of animal flesh must be considered.

One might look at floating OTEC plants if on-shore ones seem to have limitations for aquaculture. In such a discussion, it should be remembered that nature performs massive lifting operations of deep, nutrient-rich water, prominently in a few places on the globe, exemplified by the upwelling off the coasts of Peru and West Africa. These small portions of the sea (only around one-tenth of one percent of its total surface), not too far from shore, have produced between one-fourth and one-third of the world's total fish catch. The fishes--anchovies, sardines, and the like--are plankton filter feeders just like the mollusks mentioned earlier. To the extent that they are harvested, food for animals higher in the food chain, larger fishes and sea birds, is removed.

Comparisons between natural upwelling and the quasi-upwelling afforded by OTEC plants should permit some estimates of the fish these plants could produce. The Peru current transports between 17 and 19 million cubic meters per second horizontally away from the shore, with these water masses being continuously replaced from the deep (Wooster and Reid, 1963).

Sustainable anchovy harvest from this region off Chile and Peru of ca. 200,000 km^2 has been estimated as high as 11 million metric tons/year (Bathen, 1975), during periods of stable hydrographic conditions. This amounts to annual water requirements per ton of fish per year of about 40 million metric tons (m^3) of

---

[1]A small pilot installation of this kind to assess only the economics of deep water aquaculture is now slated to operate in Tahiti and another is being considered. Perrot, J.; personal communication; France-Aquaculture, Paris, France, August 24, 1978. Also, Grabbe, Eugene; personal communication; Department of Planning and Economic Development, State of Hawaii, Honolulu, Hawaii, September, 1978.

fertile water and an annual harvest of about 50 tons per average square kilometer. Using the above approximate figures and extrapolating from the flow calculated for a 1 MW OTEC pilot plant in Hawaii of about 29 million m^3 per year, as well as taking into account oceanographic investigations of the extent to which the fertilizing effects of the surface outflow of an OTEC plant can be felt (Bathen, 1975), a 400 Megawatt plant affecting between 7 and 10 km^2 of the ocean near Hawaii might give rise to between 300 and 500 tons of plankton-feeding fishes per year.

The range may, however, be even wider than that, due to uncertainties about the nature of the mixing process in the sea and the depth of the outfall plume. This depth affects the photosynthetic efficiency with which the algae will transform solar energy into biomass. The effluent of a floating OTEC plant is presently envisaged at a depth of about 40 m. The outgoing water would sink further to at least 70 m conditioned by temperature-determined specific gravity. Light at that level is already faint enough so that the nutrients in the effluent will be poorly utilized; algae blooms, as well as fish production, would be far less than if the effluent could be kept at the surface (Hirota, 1977).

It should also be mentioned that OTEC power plant platforms would certainly gather large fishes as do the oil platforms, even without the production of additional forage fishes. These aggregations might become mixed blessings when, as is not unlikely, periodic chemical antifouling treatments would cause massive fish-kills (Hirota, 1978).

The yields obtainable from simply gathering the bounty of the OTEC plume appear to be orders of magnitude below those obtainable from using it for aquatic farming on land. Why is this so? First, in gathering, as opposed to farming, no control is exercised over the many competitors for the nutrients, from protozoa to inedible small invertebrates; only a portion of the nutrients that go through algae find their way into fish. Second, capital and labor costs of the aquacultural installation are traded against those expended for gathering only. Third, fish are gathered in one case, whereas mollusks are grown in the other, the latter having supplied to them attachment or containment devices while they devote themselves incessantly to the filtering of algae grown in water of optimal quality. In economic, although not in physiologic, terms mollusks may be more efficient than most fishes at ultimate nutrient utilization.

If clues are taken from these facts and from harvest statistics of mollusks farmed in suspension culture under only broadly comparable conditions in the enriched bays near Vigo in Spain (where two to three hundred tons per hectare of mussel flesh can be obtained per year) (Bardach, Ryther, and McLarney, 1972), open-sea OTEC plants might be associated with submerged trellises for the rope or cage culture of site-suitable mollusk species. These could, theoretically, raise the total aquaculture yields from an OTEC plant by an order of magnitude or more over those obtainable by simply harvesting the schooling fishes that grow by themselves and thus lead to attaining from one floating OTEC plant thousands instead of hundreds of tons of usable animal protein per year. Such yields could only be obtained, however, if the nutrient-rich water were released close to the surface, well within the zone of photosynthesis. For this purpose, new aquacultural engineering devices would have to be developed. These would have to be tested in situ in connection with at least one plant permitting near-surface emission of nutrient-rich waste water for its better utilization by planktonic algae. Only then could the trade-off be assessed among a number of factors such as having fish with no inputs but for the catching, mollusks and other attached cultivars with likely high fixed and greater variable costs including those due to changes in power plant design. An investigation would also have to be made of the possible enhancement of internal biofouling through having structures in the sea near the plant outfall and of the effects on cultured or managed organisms of anti-bio-fouling materials or treatments.

Furthermore, it appears as if the simplest utilization of enhanced fertility through a floating OTEC plant, namely, a harvest of small schooling fishes, has other obstacles, such as efficient processing. Even a small barge cannery needs ten tons of fish per day for economic operation; a small fishmeal plant, perhaps also on a barge, needs to be fed a multiple of this amount to remain economical (Pigott, 1977). Only with a network of several floating OTEC plants of at least 100 MW, as envisaged by Avery (1978), might it become feasible, depending upon their distance from one another, to organize harvesting and processing the fish low on the food chain produced by the plants through properly sized factory ships with collecting vessels, or by locating floating OTEC plants near existing fishing grounds. Semi-intensive aquaculture using structures in the sea for both containment of the plume and attachment of cultivars seems more promising, but it cannot yet be evaluated for lack of models, let alone engineering specifications.

Nuclear Power Plants

Land-based nuclear power plants, located near the seashore and using ocean water for cooling, can, in theory, enhance the growth of cultured organisms. Heated waste water has been used experimentally to speed the growth of flat fishes in Scotland and of salmon in Sweden and to hasten the maturing of oysters in the northern United States, again on a pilot scale (Bardach, Ryther, and McLarney, 1972; Ryther, 1978). It is assumed, of course, that the effluents pass rigorous checks for contamination with nuclides conforming to the respective public health-oriented law. Even then, such use must be evaluated in the light of various constraints, the most potent of which is the fact that the supply of warm water is cut off when the plant shuts down. The results of such shut-downs are mass mortalities due to cold-shock in the aquafarms supplied by the heated waste water. Also, land and enclosed natural or man-made waters near nuclear plants are often too expensive for aquaculture.

Large floating nuclear plants have been envisaged even including the reprocessing of nuclear fuels. As presently envisaged, they would generate many thousands of Megawatts and temperatures which permit industrial processes on site (Murata, 1976). Japan's peculiar conditions of energy dependence, as well as the country's dense settlement patterns, make it likely that gigantic enterprises in the size range of 20 to 30 thousand Megawatt floating nuclear plants will be built in Japan's home waters, especially now that Japan's extended economic zone (EEZ) reaches out to 200 miles. In Japan, the technology of aquaculture is at a more sophisticated level than almost anywhere else, with endeavors under way among Japanese ocean engineers and mariculturists to develop massive aquaculture installations in their 200-mile EEZ. These are intended to produce sea food from home waters to make up for catches foregone by Japan through being excluded, fully or in part, from some former fishing grounds, now in the EEZs of other nations.

Also, deep nutrient-rich water is available close to Japan's Pacific shores. Using this water might be envisioned in combination with the very large floating nuclear plants. This might create the opportunity to build a floating OTEC plant in connection with a nuclear platform. Such an OTEC would have a higher efficiency than an ordinary one, due to the fact that it would use water from the nuclear plant which would be warmer than that found at the ocean surface. Incidentally, for the same reason, such floating, hybrid OTEC-nuclear power plants would no longer be restricted to the world's tropical regions (Goldstein, 1978). Also, since the enriched effluent would be warmed to surface temperature or higher, it would not sink; it could become the base for the production of fish or other aquatic foods in innovative high seas aquaculture developments.[2]

Obviously, such massive alterations of natural ocean conditions are very likely to generate a great many environmental

---

[2]The aforementioned ill effects of the shutdown of a nuclear plant on aquaculture is not likely to be serious here as one would envisage a rotation of such events in the ultra-large floating installation.

problems. It may be that some of them turn out to be so massively deleterious that they strongly mitigate against creating such floating energy islands. But without the speculations which are here just barely begun, it is impossible to determine how substantial the obstacles will be.

Conclusion

Oil rigs and OTEC plants have two characteristics in common: (1) using very high technology and (2) requiring massive investments. Thus, they are or will be owned by nations or by large corporations. Aquaculture that uses installations connected with either operation does not seem to be practical for small scale entrepreneurs. Whether or not their fish collecting and/or generating properties can be used by individual fishermen or fish farmers will depend on the location of the structures and the state of mechanization of the various harvesting fleets. Also to be considered are the mix of economic and social values resulting from the development of the aquacultural potential of these costly and massive ocean platforms. The alternative is capture of the new or newly gathered resource by the operator of the energy-related structure. One would then not be faced by problems of allocating a common property resource; such management is likely to be more efficient from a conservation point of view.

For most of the world's population, small to medium-scale energy generating devices and improvements in food production that work in a widespread manner are needed. It is a pity that neither energy generation from the sea nor the food production associated with it better fits this need.

All in all, it seems obvious that at present the prime purpose of the large engines and devices in the sea, as discussed here, is power generation. Food is a secondary priority because it is not yet as scarce as energy in the developed nations that possess high technologies. Nevertheless, studies are needed that would evaluate means of co-production of ocean energy and food, from both engineering and socio-economic vantage points. Such studies are also advocated by Laurence and Roels (1977) and by the Aquatic Food Sources Panel of the World Food and Nutrition Study of the U.S. National Academy of Sciences (Bardach, 1977). It is not known with what changes in the design of the power-generating structures costs fish or shellfish could be optimized. In view of the economies of scale noted for OTEC power, and hence of the costs of the installations, such assessments of compatibility of power and food production ought to be done from vantage points broader than those usually applied to sea foods, that is by considering a nation's entire range of food and energy policies.

REFERENCES

Avery, W. H. Ocean Thermal Energy - Status and Prospects. Marine Technol. Soc. Jour., 1978, 12(2), 9-16.

Bardach, J. Aquatic Food Sources. In Vol. I. Supporting Papers, World Food and Nutrition Study. Washington, DC: U.S. Nat. Acad. Sci., 1977, pp. 304-309.

Bardach, J. E., Ryther, J. H. and McLarney, W. O. Aquaculture. New York: Wiley-Interscience, 1972.

Bathen, K. H. A Further Evaluation of the Oceanographic Conditions Found off Keahole Point, Hawaii, and the Environmental Impact of Nearshore Ocean Thermal Energy Conversion Plants on Subtropical Hawaiian Waters. Prepared for Dept. of Planning and Economic Development, State of Hawaii, November, 1975 (mimeographed).

Cowell, E. B. Oil Pollution of the Sea. In Johnson, R. (Ed.). Marine Pollution. London: Academic Press, 1979, pp. 353-401.

Douglass, R. H. Progress and Prospects in Ocean Thermal Energy. Abstract of Papers, Circum-Pacific Energy and Mineral Resources Conference, Honolulu, HA, August, 1978.

FAO (U.N. Food and Agriculture Organization. FAO Yearbook of Fisheries Statistics, 1976. Rome: FAO, 1977, #42.

Goldstein, Mark, East-West Center, Honolulu, Hawaii. Personal communication, September, 1978.

Gulland, J. A. The Fish Resources of the Ocean. Rome: FAO, 1970.

Hirota, J., Dept. of Oceanography, University of Hawaii, Honolulu, Hawaii. Personal communication, September, 1978.

Hirota, Jed. Environmental Impact Assessment, "Ocean Thermal Energy Conversion, 1 MWe Early Ocean Test Platform." Interstate Electronics Corp. for U.S. Dept. Energy, Contr. #EG-77-C-06-1033.

Klima, E. F. and Wickham, D. A. Attraction of Coastal Pelagic Fishes with Artificial Structures. Trans. Amer. Fish Soc., 1977, 1, 86-99.

Lagler, K. F., Bardach, J. E., Miller, R. R. and Passino, D. R. M. Ichthyology, 2nd ed. New York: John Wiley & Sons, 1978, pp. 451-456.

Laurence, S. and Roels, O. A. Potential Mariculture Yield of Sea Thermal Power Plants. Part 2 - Food Chain Efficiency. In Ioup, G. E. (Ed.). Proc. 4th Annual Conf. Ocean Thermal Energy Conversion, OTEC. New Orleans: Univ. New Orleans, March, 1977, Section III, pp. 21-25.

Murata, H. The Status and Long Term Strategies of Nuclear Energy Development Programme in Japan. Tokyo, Japan: Japan Atomic Energy Research Institute, April, 1976.

North, W. J. Possibilities of Biomass from the Ocean; the Marine Farm Project. In Mitsui, A., Miyachi, S., San Pietro, A., and Tamura, S. (Eds.). Biological Solar Energy Conversion. New York: Academic Press, 1977.

Pigott, G., University of Washington, Seattle, Washington. Personal communication, August 31, 1977.

Ryther, J. H., Woods Hole Oceanographic Institution, Woods Hole, Massachusetts. Personal communication, September, 1978.

Siva, June, Atlantic Richfield Company, Box 2679 - T.A., Los Angeles, California. Personal communication, August, 1978.

Stone, R. B. Building Reefs for Better Fishing. Exxon USA, 1975 (Third Quarter), pp. 13-16.

UNESCO (United Nations Educational, Scientific, and Cultural Organization), Intergovernmental Oceanographic Commission. A Comprehensive Plan for the Global Investigation of Pollution in the Marine Environment and Baseline Study Guidelines. LOC Technical Series #14, Paris: UNESCO, 1976.

Wooster, W. S. and Reid, J. L. Eastern Boundary Currents. In Hill, M. N. (Ed.). The Sea, Vol. II. New York: Wiley-Interscience, 1963.

OIL STORAGE IN LAID-UP TANKERS: THE JAPANESE PLAN

Yoshihiko Miwa
Staff Reporter
Japan Industrial Journal

As one of the major consumers of oil, Japan has to import great quantities of crude oil, which, in turn, creates the problems of stockpile. Due to the difficulty of expanding on-shore oil-storage facilities, the Japanese government has decided to make use of laid-up tankers. This is neither a new use of the sea nor a neglected issue in the law of the sea, but is a new approach to an old issue that has emerged from the particular circumstances of Japan.

On July 4, 1978, the fifth meeting of the Ministerial Council for General Measures on Energy decided to start in September 1978 floating storage of crude oil in tankers as a temporary means to stock oil. The Ministry of International Trade and Industry (MITI) and the National Resources and Energy Agency (NREA), with one of its corporate subsidiaries, the Japan National Oil Corporation (JNOC, formerly Japan Petroleum Development Corporation - JPDC), were assigned to carry out the project in coordination with the Ministry of Transport (MT), the Maritime Security and Safety Agencies (MSA), and the Fisheries Agency (FA). In short, this is a unique and unprecedented scheme of the Japanese Government to store crude oil at its own cost.

On the part of the Japanese business community, the Japanese Shipowners' Association (JSA) and the Petroleum Association of Japan (PAJ) participate in this project in their capacity as representatives of ship-owners and of refining companies, respectively. Incidentally, JSA is a nationwide organization of owners and operators of vessels of 100 gross tons and over, while PAJ is organized by 37 refining companies.

Under the Government's program, JNOC is in charge of inviting bids for chartering tankers and for the purchase of crude oil. JNOC decided to charter 20 tankers of 200,000-250,000-DWT-VLCC-class from Japanese shipping companies for a period of two years. For safety reasons, all these tankers must be Japanese flag ships manned by Japanese crew, and this is why the so-called <u>shikumisen</u> (tie-in ships built in Japan specifically for use by foreign-registered Japanese maritime companies) have been excluded from consideration.

Under the present Japanese maritime regulations, all Japanese flag ships should undergo a periodic inspection in the dock every two years. A tanker is required to unload oil in its holds before the inspection. Therefore, JNOC cannot set the chartering period of tankers stowed with crude oil beyond two years.

JNOC also has decided to buy the Middle Eastern crude oil totalling five million kiloliters (one kiloliter is approximately 0.86 ton) from Japanese refining companies, on the condition that each successful bidder (seller) should buy back the full quantity at the market price after two years. The Middle Eastern Gulf is the only area where a large tanker such as a VLCC can expect a smooth loading of crude oil with fully equipped facilities. This is the reason why JNOC has decided to buy crude oil from the Middle East.

Based on the rate of consumption in 1977, a stockpile of five million kiloliters of crude oil is sufficient to supply Japan's demand for seven days. In other words, Japan's daily consumption of crude oil slightly exceeded 700,000 kiloliters in 1977. In fact, this program is regarded as a well-devised scheme, since it will help reduce Japan's controversial trade surplus by more than $400 million and serious tanker tonnage surplus as well, thereby serving two purposes.

The total amount of funds which JNOC financed to operate the entire project is $690 million (on the basis of ¥200 per $1.00); JNOC raised a $600 million private loan guaranteed by the Government. The remaining $90 million was appropriated from the Government's Oil Special Account.

Bidding for the purchase of crude oil and for chartering tankers was held twice respectively with the following results:

	Oil Purchase		Tanker Chartering	
September shipment	July 27	2½ m/kl	August 1	10 ships
October shipment	August 18	2½ m/kl	August 23	10 ships
Total		5 m/kl		20 ships

According to JNOC, nineteen refining and ten shipping companies have been successful in these two biddings, although the contract prices for each bid have not been made public. As a result, 20 tankers under contract have been grouped into two fleets comprising two groups of ten. The first fleet of ten tankers for the September shipment was instructed to drift in the designated area in the Pacific waters west of Iwo Jima. The second fleet is to remain anchored in Tachibana Bay off Nagasaki Prefecture in Western Japan.

Originally, a feasibility study of anchoring and drifting systems was jointly initiated by two organizations. One was a government organization founded in November 1977, under the name of the Tanker Oil Storage Operation Joint Committee. The other was the Tanker Oil Storage Technical Investigation Committee, which was a private organization jointly founded by PAJ, JSA, and JNOC in December 1977. Then in February 1978, the Japan Tanker Oil Storage Association (JTOSA) was formed with Chairman Kinzo Matsuo of Nippon Kokan (Japan's largest steel company) as its head. The Japan Association for Preventing Marine Accidents accepted an assignment of investigating the technical aspects of the two tanker storage methods.

For the management of these tankers, an operation agency was set up under JNOC in July 1978, to be called the Oil Storage Control Organization representing ten shipping companies. This company has been capitalized at ¥20,000,000 (roughly $100,000) and headed by Executive Director Hiroshi Hirai of the Mitsui O.S.K. Lines, who will control all aspects of the operation of these tankers on equal standards.

At the initial stage of planning, JSOJC studied the possibility of selecting a suitable bay in which all 20 tankers could anchor. Several places were considered in accordance with guidelines including that the anchoring areas must be semi-enclosed inlets where the heights of waves would not exceed one meter even in the worst weather. However, the inlets which satisfied such geographic and meteorologic conditions did not always satisfy the social and environmental conditions. In some cases, JNOC abandoned the idea of negotiating with the residents because of their deep-rooted antagonism against such a project.

Industrial facilities such as oil tanks in the vicinity of residential areas are regarded by the residents as potentially explosive and capable of causing environmental disruptions such as air or marine pollution. If the residents on the land are indifferent, the local fishermen tend to be intransigent whenever the use of the sea is at issue. In reality, the coastal areas along the entire Japanese archipelago are all narrow strips; the rest of the country is mountainous. These coastal areas are always densely populated. In many cases, both industrial complexes and residential districts are located side by side without clear distinction. Such a proximity of two different land-use districts often conflicts political interest between the residents of the region and the industries or the government. The use of the sea is not an exception.

In the selection of Tachibana Bay out of seven proposed inlets, JNOC gave up its initial goals of securing enough space for the anchorage of all 20 tankers together because of the anticipated difficulty of negotiating with the fishermen's union or the other parties concerned. Tachibana Bay is an ideal inlet in geographic and meteorologic terms. It is surrounded by hills on three sides and, only on the southwest, is open to the high seas. It is a natural "land-locked" harbor with calm seas throughout the year. But it is some 100 square kilometers in size; under the applicable regulations, only ten VLCC's can anchor in the Bay. Nevertheless, JNOC decided to use this inlet in appreciation of the Nagasaki Prefectural government's understanding attitude to accommodate this project. It may be noted that, whenever a central government agency has to negotiate with the fishermen's or farmers' union in a local area, it needs the strong assistance of the local government as an intermediary.

JNOC started formal negotiations with the Nagasaki Prefectural government on August 21, 1978, seeking its advice and assistance. In fact, there are 15 fishermen's cooperatives along the coast of this bay. With a total of 3,000 members, they are located in 15 towns and villages. A local newspaper reported that in 1977 the turnover of these 15 cooperatives totalled ¥6,970,000,000 (roughly $34,850,000) from an annual catch of about 20,000 tons. Sardines accounted for 65% of that haul. At the end of September 1978, JNOC was still engaged in intricate negotiations with the representatives of the 15 cooperatives. JNOC hopes to settle the compensation problems by the time the ten VLCC's for October shipment return from the Middle East to Tachibana Bay for anchorage.

The details of the compensation are that JNOC will pay ¥1,000,000,000 (roughly $5 million) to these 15 cooperatives annually in return for the use of the bay. In addition, ¥500,000,000 (roughly $2.5 million) will also be paid to the local autonomies as a grant-in-aid. The technical aspect of tanker anchoring has also been discussed in the negotiations, with a view to preventing maritime accidents. From an objective point of view, these terms of compensation are not at all unreasonable. However, the process of negotiation has not been as smooth as JNOC hoped at the beginning.

In the event that the negotiations are not finalized by the time the ten VLCC's return to Japan, these tankers will have to change their course and join the first fleet of ten VLCC's drifting in the designated Pacific waters. In this case, the drifting system can function as an alternative arrangement to the anchoring system.

In the selection of the drifting area on the high seas, JTOSA, JAPMA, and the other organizations concerned decided that the area should be situated away from the courses frequented by typhoons and other seasonal winds, routes of regular lines, the main course of the Japan Current and fishing grounds. The selection was made fairly in keeping with these guidelines, except for the involvement of the fishing grounds. Since Japanese fishermen have traditionally been active throughout the Pacific waters, it is always difficult to spot an area around the Japanese archipelago for any purpose without taking Japanese fishermen's activities into account.

The particular drifting area designated includes the traditional fishing grounds for a particular species, bonito and tuna, which are very important in the Japanese diet. JNOC was unable to reserve this area exclusively. The bonito fishing grounds spread all over the Pacific waters because of its migratory nature. The Confederation of National Fishermen's Cooperative Associations (CNFCA) claimed that the drifting tankers would disturb bonito fishing grounds. Negotiations were still underway at the end of September between JNOC and CNFCA for the settlement of this claim. It was believed that the negotiations would not drag on, because the fishermen's claims here were not as intricate as those in the case of Tachibana Bay.

In a recent development, the government decided in September, 1978, to build up an additional crude oil stockpile of two and one half million kiloliters in tankers, considering the popularity of such projects among the industries. Among others, recession-hit tanker owners welcomed this project. It is a fact that the tanker tonnage surplus has already reached serious proportions internationally. Japanese tanker owners have never found themselves in such a deteriorating situation. Under these circumstances, they have since 1977 appealed to the government to take urgent steps to cope with this problem. They believe this oil storage project is timely and has already begun to improve this situation.

As an instance of this, the world-scale by which the market price for the chartering-hire of tankers is measured has started to rise gradually ever since the inception of this project in July 1978. In June 1978, the world-scale had been hovering below 30 points. But it has reached nearly 40 points at the end of September 1978. An increase by ten points in world-scale proves a gain of about 75¢ per dead-weight ton in the chartering-hire of tankers. Tanker owners hold a strong view that this upward trend in world-scale has been mainly motivated by the present project in Japan.

OECD and the International Maritime Industry Forum (IMIF) are currently trying hard to find a way to cope with this international tanker surplus. If oil storage in tankers is also possible in other countries, it will surely help alleviate international tanker surplus. In this context, this project is worthy of close attention and intensive study.

Finally, it is necessary to look at the international legal problems which may arise under certain circumstances. In the case of the fleet anchored at Tachibana Bay, the tankers would not have to leave for the high seas, except when threatened by a typhoon or other emergencies. The other fleet drifting off Iwo Jima, however, has relatively higher potential to be exposed to law of the sea problems, because it will often find itself entirely outside of Japanese jurisdiction. As a matter of fact, between Iwo Jima and Okinawa there is a patch of no man's sea approximately 100 miles wide and 400 nautical miles long which is situated within Japan's 200-mile fishing zone and substantially overlaps with the designated tanker drifting area.

Specifically, two problems are conceivable. One is the conflict of interest with foreign fishing. Since both fleets will use waters fished predominantly by Japanese fishermen, such conflict is possible but not necessarily probable. The other would arise from the tankers as potential pollution hazards. In the case of the tankers drifting off Iwo Jima, however, the fact that the drifting area is situated on the seaward side of the Kuroshiho Current's route will almost safely protect the Japanese and foreign coasts from the damage of crude oil spillage. In the final analysis, however, it will be necessary to identify conceivable legal issues with reference to what UNCLOS III will eventually adopt as guidelines applicable to the situation.

COMMENTARY

E. D. Brown
University of Wales
Institute of Science and Technology

I think Dr. Craven mentioned earlier this morning that you will have to suffer me again tomorrow, so my remarks this morning will be suitably brief, and I hope this might give you an opportunity to respond to the very provocative papers we have had from members of the panel.

My approach to all three papers has been dictated by the theme of the conference, and I have asked myself whether UNCLOS III has in fact neglected to provide rules to regulate the uses of the ocean which have been talked about in these three papers, and, if so, what we must do about it.

Let me take first Mr. Miwa's paper on oil storage in laid up tankers. As you have heard, two types of locale have been considered for oil storage tankers. First, anchoring the tankers in Tachibana Bay; this would not seem to raise any novel problems as far as international law of the sea is concerned. I assume that this bay, described in the paper as a natural land-locked harbor of 100 square kilometers, is in internal waters, and even if it is partly in the territorial sea, there seems to be no reason why Japan should not anchor tankers in this way so long as it does not interfere with innocent passage through the territorial sea and steps are taken to ensure compliance with the rules of international law on oil pollution from vessels (for example, those laid down in Article 212 of the Informal Composite Negotiating Text).

The second proposal was that the ships would be "drifting" in a designated area of the Pacific west of Iwo Jima. Now, I am not entirely sure where this area lies in relation to Iwo Jima and Okinawa, but it would appear from the paper that it is partly within 200 miles of Japanese territory, and partly beyond 200 miles. So, I am assuming for the sake of argument that the drifting is taking place in two jurisdictional areas, the high seas and the exclusive economic zone.

Again, I do not entirely understand what drifting means in this context, so I have looked at three situations. If, first, drifting means that these vessels are not under power, and are freely drifting in the oceans, then this does present considerable problems in international law. I should have thought it was very likely indeed that such tankers would present a hazard to other shipping and possibly also to fishing. Although the free drifting of tankers is possibly a freedom of the high seas, it would not, I think, in these circumstances be a freedom of other states in exercising their freedoms.

It may be, however, that the intention is that the tankers should be under power but simply maintaining position or navigating within the area at very slow speeds. If so, subject to the usual "due regard" rule, this would seem to fall within the scope of the freedom of the high seas in the form of freedom of navigation.

Apart from providing employment for Japanese seamen, the second variant seems to have little to recommend it and it may therefore be useful to refer to a third method, although I do not believe that this was in the mind of the Japanese Government. Under this system, tankers would be attached to a series of single-point mooring buoys and would drift around the single points according to the tides and the winds. The vessels would thus be in one particular locale and, although we could possibly take exception to such an arrangement under Article 89 of ICNT which prohibits the subjection of any parts of the high seas to any state's sovereignty, this seems rather unlikely.

Otherwise there would seem to be no reason at all why states should not have a freedom to store oil in this way so long as, under Article 87(2) of ICNT, this freedom was exercised with due consideration for the freedoms of others. Mr. Miwa tells us that the area in question is situated away from the typhoon area and from regular shipping routes, but he does admit that the area includes a traditional fishing ground for bonita and tuna. This being so, I think it would be a question of weighing the degree of interference which would be caused with the fishing of other states in this area, and considering whether or not this use of the high seas was therefore being exercised without due consideration for the rights of other states. So much then for the high seas. If, on the other hand, the ships are to drift in the Japanese exclusive economic zone, there is less of a problem since, of course, the fishing rights of third parties would not be so closely involved--if at all. So, subject to compliance with Article 60 of the Informal Composite Negotiating Text, there is no reason why artificial structures could not be used to moor the vessels in these areas. One of the conditions to which they would be subject under Article 60 would be that there should be no interference with recognized shipping lanes.

So, I would conclude on this first paper that, although this is a fairly novel problem so far as the factual situation is concerned, it doesn't really raise any difficult international legal problems, and I think that the ICNT could accommodate arrangements of this type.

Turning next to Dr. Bardach's paper on the relation of ocean energy to ocean food, again I think it is fair to say that in general the ICNT and perhaps also the rules of general international law could be stretched to regulate the developments anticipated in his paper. I shall confine my remarks to two points raised in his paper. First, oil rigs and fishery management and, secondly, ocean thermal energy.

Almost by definition, fishery and fish farming developments associated with oil rigs will occur within the EEZ. The extent to which they should be permitted and subject to which rules are some things which will be determined by the coastal state under its EEZ jurisdiction; so this is really a question of sea-use planning--to anticipate what we are going to be discussing tomorrow.

Dr. Bardach mentions in his paper that redundant oil rigs or disused oil rigs must be removed under United States law. The position is the same under the ICNT, Article 80, but there would seem to be no reason why such structures or modification of such structures should not be retained as crowd stoppers or fish attracters under ICNT Article 60 which permits artificial structures to be created for, among other things, the exploitation of living resources of the sea.

Turning now to ocean thermal energy, let me deal first with the OTEC plants which will be "grazing" in the area beyond 200 miles from the coast. As I understand it, these grazers would be producing ammonia which would serve as a hydrogen carrier for a future power economy based on liquid hydrogen. Dr. Bardach speculates that such a process would raise problems for Committee I of UNCLOS III. I gather from Dr. Craven that it is very unlikely that these resources will be tapped for many years but some of us will not be too surprised if Committee I is still with us at that time!

The argument, in any event, was that such processes would raise problems for Committee I similar to those raised by mining of ocean minerals. Now, it is true that under Article 87, Paragraph 2 of ICNT, such plants would have to operate with due consideration for activities in the seabed "area," but unless all the products of the waters above the seabed are later to be claimed as the "common heritage of mankind" (again it would not altogether surprise me in the future) then the ammonia and hydrogen obtained in this way would not in my view be subject to ICNT, Part XI. This is so because Part XI deals with the seabed "area" which is defined in Article 1, Paragraph 1 of ICNT to exclude the superjacent waters. Thus, there is no reason why ammonia and hydrogen should not be exploited like any other common resource of the high seas.

Finally, on Dr. Bardach's paper, let me touch on another question raised by ocean thermal energy plants. If there is an upwelling in the high seas, creating favorable conditions for fish, the question might be raised whether the home state of the operator has exclusive or preferential rights in relation to fish which are so attracted and nourished. I would argue that such plants may be established on the high seas under Article 87(1)(d) which provides that the freedom of the high seas comprises inter alia freedom to construct artificial islands and other installations permitted under international law, subject to Part VI of ICNT. And I would say that a state would be entitled to have a reasonable safety zone around such installations (reading Article 87(1)(d) with Articles 60 and 80 which deal with artificial installations in the exclusive economic zone and the continental shelf, and around which we may have a reasonable safety zone). It may be then that, if we could have safety zones around such plants, the home state would be able at least to have exclusive rights in the fishery resources in those particular safety zones. Anything more than that would, I think, require an article similar to Article 77 of ICNT which gives the coastal state primary interest in the stocks originating in its rivers. The mind rather boggles at that.

This brings me to Mr. Keith's paper, and I am afraid that my commentary on this must be less precise and detailed than I would wish or his paper deserves, but unfortunately I received it only last night and I do not have the facilities here to follow up some of the questions which his paper has raised in my mind. May I, however, make a few observations?

Mr. Keith has inquired into the definition of ships, vessels and structures under American law. Now it is true that he has acknowledged that United States law provides only an example of the kind of characteristics which might attract international recognition, but it would have been useful if this account could have been supplemented by reference to, inter alia, the rules on islands and continental shelf installations in both the 1958 Geneva Conventions and the ICNT, as well as to the various conventions on oil pollution which define ships and installations. He might also have referred to the considerable amount of preparatory work which has been done on the legal status of ocean data acquisition systems. My own feeling is that the ICNT and these various other existing conventions already provide enough models on which to base the status of ocean platforms, though I recognize of course that this would not solve problems of status under American law or any other municipal law.

Turning to another aspect, I confess that I do not share Mr. Keith's enthusiasm for ocean city states. I do not believe that it would be in the interests of the public order of the oceans if we were to allow the proliferation of such ocean city states. They would raise almost insurmountable problems in relation to questions of responsibility and security (security in the sense of both their own need for defense and the threat they might pose to other states if they were to be used to provide facilities for third parties). I believe we have far too many mini-states in the world already. I would add that, so far as I know, no entity situated at sea beyond the limits of national jurisdiction has ever been granted recognition as an international person in the absence of naturally formed land. Atlantis, Abalonia, Minerva and Sealand are all interesting testimony to ingenuity, but never came anywhere near being recognized as persons in international law. Nor do I think that they will attract recognition in the future any more than did the sea-based "radio pirates" of the recent past.

In this connection, I wonder if Mr. Keith could perhaps tell us what his authority is for saying that a British Court has upheld the independent status of the Royal Principality of Sealand. In fact, the court simply said that the structure in question, being situated outside the territorial sea, was beyond the reach of the British courts in relation to the particular law involved. That of course is very different from recognizing the independent legal status of Sealand; I think this point would be brought out very forcibly if the United Kingdom were to extend its territorial sea to twelve miles. The structure would then most decidedly be within the jurisdiction of the English courts.

My third point is to take issue with Mr. Keith's suggestion that it appears that ocean thermal energy conversion could be regulated by the Seabed Authority. It seems to me that this may well be a Hawaiian interpretation of Article 133 of the ICNT, because Dr. Bardach refers to the same point in his paper! I have already referred to this in passing while commenting on Dr. Bardach's paper, but Mr. Keith's reasoning is that the jurisdiction of the Seabed Authority extends to "resources," defined in Article 133 of ICNT to include water, steam and hot water. As I read Article 133, however, it refers only to the resources off the "area," and the "area" defined in Article 1 does not include the waters above the seabed and subsoil. It follows that those waters are a common high seas resource, and would not fall within the jurisdiction of International Seabed Authority.

Finally, I would like to draw attention to the fact that Article 87(1)(d) of the ICNT would seem to permit the installation of floating platforms on the high seas. It would seem to me this is all the authority you require for installations of this kind. Mr. Keith has referred to the position under Article 60 where you have similar authority in the EEZ, but there is a very similar provision in 87(1)(d) which would allow any such installation to be set up and operated in the high seas.

So, to sum up, my feeling is that although these are fascinating topics from the scientific and factual point of view, by and large they do not in fact strain over much the rules which we find in the ICNT. New problems will undoubtedly arise if and when devices such as OTEC platforms come into operation, but, as you know, law tends to follow technology. Thus, I think that to expect ICNT to cover such issues in advance would be asking for too much.

DISCUSSION AND QUESTIONS

EDWARD MILES: I want to make some comments that lead me in an opposite direction from Dr. Brown's, and I want to deal with the political implications of what Kent Keith had to say in conjunction with the political implications of what Dave Ross had to say in his panel yesterday. Both papers I regard as being excellent and important; they can be made to speak to the future of what we call the global enclosure movement. Let me go through this argument. In the first place, we can reduce the dynamics of global ocean politics,as I have suggested elsewhere, to five major types. These seem to me, first, to be differences in capabilities between the players; these differences are critical because they imply differences in the distribution of income which have political implications. The second type I would call differences in bio-geophysical conditions. These have to do with resource endowments. The third difference is in the interests of the players. I would break these down into bureaus, states, multi-national corporations, and international organizations. The fourth type is the relationship of what I call pure to contaminated issues; pure issues have to do with only ocean-related activities. Contaminated issues are those which have components from the international system at large, unrelated to those ocean issues. Finally, the fifth type I would call the decisions, rules and procedures, and these have both internal and external dimensions. What is critical here is that there is a catalyst which starts and fuels the process. The important ones are technological advance and people's expectations about those technologies. The latter is more critical because human beings are capable of being generated by expectations which have almost nothing to do with observable activities in the external world.

Now, why do we have extensions of coastal state jurisdiction in the ocean since 1930? It seems to me there are three kinds of reasons. In the first place, we must focus on resources and the increase in the salience of those resources to governments. This was evident in 1929-1930 in the position of the Portugese government at the Hague Conference with respect to the territorial sea. Do you remember their initial claim for eighteen miles, scaled down eventually to twelve, mainly on account of fisheries over the continental shelf? The second reason is the ineffectiveness of international arrangements based on open access regimes; this ineffectiveness has two dimensions. First, there is lack of control; then there are the distributional inequities which flow from lack of control. These generate a lack of trust on the part of governments in international arrangements because he who cheats wins, and this stimulates a desire to extend national jurisdiction and control. There is a presumption here that may not be justified, to the effect that increased national jurisdiction will in fact increase effective control. I think that remains to be demonstrated.

Now one has to ask whether two-hundred-mile limits and two-hundred-mile economic zones are permanent or transient. The question arises whether these dynamics somehow come to rest at the magical number of two hundred. Quite clearly, it would be foolhardy to maintain that they do, so I agree completely with Kent Keith that the technologies involved in what he calls OFEP's (My God!) are potentially much greater than we appear to understand at this time.

Where are the likely sources of major destabilizing changes in the future, i.e., what I would call, the step-level changes to the new ocean regime? It seems to me they lie in the relationship between expectations and technological advance. The two most likely areas out of which they would come would seem to be these OFEP's and the seabed beyond national jurisdiction. While I agree with Dave Ross, it is not enough to say that the minerals in the deep-ocean floor are present in sufficient economic concentrations. All we have to do is look at the manganese nodules of 1967 and 1968. Again it does not really matter whether the stuff is there in economic concentration, to generate the kinds of expectations I am talking about. I think these expectations will remain high and, remaining at that level, will generate major political consequences. Now, will the combined effects of the expectations about controls of OFEP's and the expectations about controls over the resources in the deep seabed beyond national jurisdiction lead to greater or lesser expansions, i.e., will we see 500 mile zones, or will we see the rolling back from 200 miles? I can't answer that, and I don't know that anyone else can at this point, but I would be very interested in people's responses. What is likely to happen, and under what conditions? If the trend is toward greater expansions, then I think it will lead to even more severe restrictions on the conduct of scientific research, and therefore more restrictions on the rate of technological advance and diffusion in the directions that the panel was talking about.

JOHN CRAVEN: Thank you very much for that insightful intervention. I would like to turn to the panel and to the audience for response to it, but the response really is almost another session or a detailed commentary beyond the limits of time. So I am going to exert the Chairman's prerogative and call this session to a formal close. I would recommend that the topic of luncheon conversation be a debate between the Brown distillation and the Miles distillation of a product which has been so effectively presented here this morning. Thank you very much.

PART VII

MILITARY ISSUES IN THE LAW OF THE SEA

INTRODUCTORY REMARKS BY SESSION PROGRAM CHAIRMAN

H. Gary Knight
Louisiana State University

I welcome you to the session dealing with military issues in the law of the sea. My name is Gary Knight. I am a lawyer, but I am pleased to point out that among our speakers and commentators today we have the first and only session at the entire conference in which there are no lawyers.

Your response motivates me to follow in David Ross' footsteps and tell a very brief lawyer story. It concerns one of the Law of the Sea Institute's recent meetings at which there was the usual interdisciplinary cocktail party. A gentleman attending this meeting was a modern-day Diogenes with a quite simple problem--he wanted to know the answer to the sum of two and two.

He first approached a scientist--a physical oceanographer--and asked him, "Sir, what is the sum of two and two?" The scientist replied, "It is exactly 4.00." Our friend then went a bit further and found a marine economist and asked the economist, "Sir, what is the sum of two and two?" The economist thought for a moment and then replied, "It lies somewhere between three and five." Then, our seeker of truth went a bit further and found a lawyer. He said to the lawyer, "Sir, what is the sum of two and two?" The lawyer shuffled nervously for a second, looked about to see if he were being heard, and then whispered, "How much do you want it to be?" Now this has absolutely nothing to do with the program this afternoon, but I enjoy lawyer jokes and I had to let David Ross hear that one.

Our session this afternoon concerns military issues in the law of the sea. Like Paul Fye, I am intimidated by the setting and surroundings of our conference. One might conclude that it is in a way inappropriate in a setting imbued with peace and the values of peace to discuss military issues. After all, we are but a few blocks from the International Court of Justice; our host country has a well-deserved reputation as a seeker of peace among nations. We are in the home of Hugo Grotius, the father of international law whose advocacy, as Edgar Gold told us yesterday, led to the establishment of the doctrine of freedom of the sea.

But we must not forget that it was not by Grotius' efforts alone that the seas were kept free with the attendant values and virtues for trade, travel, and commerce. Indeed, during

Grotius' own time, nearly a century of warfare at sea ultimately was necessary to ensure that status. Thus, regardless of one's philosophical attitude toward the threat of or use of force, one must recognize that the existence of naval force remains a principal determinant in the evolution of international law and order at sea.

As I observed at the opening session, military issues have not, in my opinion, been neglected at the Law of the Sea Conference. They have been neglected in public analysis, although I am hopeful that our session today can begin to remedy that defect.

One final observation--it is too much, I think, to expect, and we cannot expect, any nation to disclose facts about its military machinery, strategy, or tactics that it deems essential to its national security. However, I believe there are sufficient facts available in public fora to permit considerable depth of analysis of these issues; I think that the public and the nations involved will benefit from that kind of analysis.

Our procedure this afternoon will be to hear a single principal paper followed by commentaries from three quite disparate sources and viewpoints. Our principal paper will be delivered by Professor Kenneth Booth. Professor Booth is presently a professor in the Department of International Politics at the University College of Wales in the United Kingdom. He has in the past been a visiting professor at the United States Naval War College. He has written widely on the subject of the role of navies and foreign policy and has published a most stimulating book entitled Navies and Foreign Policy. Professor Booth is therefore well qualified to discuss with us the implications of recent law of the sea developments on naval strategy.

THE MILITARY IMPLICATIONS OF THE CHANGING LAW OF THE SEA[1]

Kenneth Booth
University College of Wales
United Kingdom

There has always been a connection between naval strategy and the law of the sea, but never have the implications of the relationship been as complex as they promise to be in the foreseeable future, when the variables and issues which are the stuff of international politics promise to be more complicated and inter-related than ever before. It is against this unsettled and unavoidably dangerous background that we have to consider the possible relationships between the yet undefined future of the law of the sea and the even more speculative prospects for naval strategy.

As it happens there is a good deal of unanimity among western (British and American) writers about the military implications of the changing law of the sea. This consensus sees the impending changes in the law of the sea (summed up in the phrase "creeping jurisdiction") as an adverse trend--indeed a threat--to that traditional and useful instrument of policy, naval power. Essentially, it is feared that creeping jurisdiction will add legal inhibitions to the growing political and economic costs involved in the exercise of naval power. Because of restrictions on mobility and access, a further increment will be added to the cost side of the cost-benefit argument in naval strategy. As a result, the impending changes in the law of the sea promise a serious decline in the future usefulness of naval power, especially in circumstances short of all-out war. This widely accepted interpretation is not the thesis of this paper. On the contrary, it will be argued that prospective developments in the law of the sea, rather than threatening the usefulness of warships, in fact promise to rescue naval diplomacy from its ritualistic and less than fully effective habits of recent years.

It is not the opinion of this paper that we are on the brink of a new "golden age" for naval diplomacy. But what can be expected is that naval diplomacy will have the opportunity to become a more useful and important instrument of policy for a wide range of countries. The sea promises to be a more significant issue area in international politics than it was even

[1] I wish to record my appreciation of the invaluable assistance given by Jane Davis in the preparation of this paper.

in the past. In parallel with this, changing developments in the law of the sea will give the opportunity for an increase in the usefulness of warships and in the potential significance of naval diplomacy.

Introduction

Strategists and international lawyers generally make strange bedfellows. In areas where they have overlapping interests, such as the law of the sea, they tend either to ignore each other's area of expertise entirely, or embrace its conventional convictions with enthusiasm, and some relief. This means that even in an area as important as the future of the sea in international politics the general standard of commentary on the law/strategy interface is not as fruitful as it might be. The scope and character of the discussion has also been affected by bureaucratic perspectives and debates. Significantly, one does not have to read much on this subject to find oneself confronted by familiar material. There seem to be few complicated ideas. This first impression seems to suggest that only the surface of the subject has been touched.

Another first impression is that both sets of specialists at the law/strategy interface seem to have suffered from the "blindness of involvement" with their own body of expertise. Strategists tend to regard international law as inconsequential in the world of force, while lawyers (among others) still tend to regard strategy as being too serious to be left to anybody but the experts. These habits have resulted in highly compartmentalized knowledge: "specialist shall not speak unto specialist" seems to be a remarkably common operating principle in western academic life. This has obvious drawbacks. The world is full of problems which are made worse for the want of shared information and ideas. International history is full of it. In the study of maritime affairs one detects signs of the creeping jurisdiction of different disciplines which parallels that of the maritime policy of national governments, although while in the latter case politics and economics are the spur, in the former it seems to be a "fit of absent-mindedness." For those interested in policymaking it is important to avoid the tendency to compartmentalization. From the policymaking perspective one should be stressing the essential unity of international law and strategy, not their separateness. Both international law and strategy have their roots in and are concerned with politics. Both are concerned with creating order, dealing with disorder, and generally coping with the succession of problems which arises in the international marketplace of power and influence. In short, law, as well as war, is a continuation of politics.

In recent years the law of the sea has become one of those growth industries so characteristic of modern academic life. At first, such growths are reactions to events in the world of affairs, but after a time the writing and talking tends to expand to fill the time which their experts have to develop their ideas, which is usually a great deal. Despite this habit, on this occasion the naval aspects of the law of the sea problem have tended to be put to the sidelines, by academics if not by governmental insiders. Over the years most attention has generally been focused on the resource-allocation aspects of ocean affairs. This is partly because western naval strategists in the 1970's have been distracted by what they believed were more significant and immediate problems, notably the big fat Soviet challenge and the technical, political, and economic perplexities facing those interested in maintaining or enhancing the utility of naval forces in a much more hostile environment. While the naval strategists were for the most part otherwise engaged, the attention of the law of the sea community in general was dominated by the determined voices concerned with the commercial and resource problems relating to the management of the world's oceans. This general (although not universal) emphasis on resource rather than strategic questions not only matched the immediate concerns of most countries involved, but it also tended to confirm a growing belief that international affairs, including security affairs, are and should be more concerned with economic and social issues than with the military issues which have traditionally dominated national policies. The traditional military and security concerns remain at the forefront of national agendas, however, but economic and social questions have increasingly forced their way upwards to the pinnacle of "high" politics, making the lives of policymakers even more complicated. This paper reflects such a standpoint. There are undoubtedly some important and interesting military implications in law of the sea issues, but for most countries these are not nearly as significant as some of the economic implications. For almost all countries, strategy will not be the overriding factor in their policy on the law of the sea.

But, neither will developments in the law of the sea be the prime determinant in the evolution of naval strategy. The underlying point is that neither the law of the sea nor naval strategy is an independent variable. To a large extent the same factors that are shaping the evolution of the one are also shaping the evolution of the other. Naval strategy has and will be shaped more importantly and more directly by the profound political, economic, and technological changes taking place in this issue area than by any foreseeable international legal regime, which itself would be a manifestation of the same profound secular changes. Prospective changes in both naval strategy and the law of the sea therefore grow out of identical roots. It follows that in its broad outlines future naval strategy would have changed regardless of whether and how the international legal regime at sea changed. It would have to have adjusted to the objective conditions established by the underlying political, economic, and technological developments of the contemporary period. Within these broad limits, however, changes in the law of the sea will affect naval strategy, but it will be in terms of fine-tuning rather than in any fundamental way. In terms of a familiar analogy, naval strategy can be conceived as a canoe being propelled down-stream by an irresistible current, while law of the sea developments can be conceived as the paddle. The canoe has rationally to "go" with the current, but the paddle will enable it to veer marginally to one side or the other as usefully and successfully as the sense and strength of the occupant permits. No foreseeable international legal regime at sea will <u>fundamentally</u> affect the exercise of naval power. It will be seen that this view is at variance with those theologians of naval power who have asserted that the erosion of the traditional concept of the "freedom of seas" presages a radical change for naval strategy (by which they implicitly or explicitly mean superpower naval strategy).

In thinking about such a diverse and unsettled set of future inter-relationships, it is sensible to avoid attempts at highly pin-pointed prediction. Highly pin-pointed prediction more than a short time ahead (the time will vary with the subject) is an activity which cannot be taken very seriously. This paper makes no such attempt. Its aim is more modest: it is an exercise in conjecture or speculation, attempting to think ahead with what relevant evidence is available in order to identify types of developments and relationships which might arise out of likely trends in the legal and strategic developments affecting the maritime environment insofar as they might be shaped by the likely predispositions and capabilities of the relevant actors (Knorr and Morgenstern, 1968). This more modest exercise would seem entirely justified by the subject matter under discussion. Strategic doctrines that are thought "timeless" one year have dropped out of sight in the year following; weapons technology is as changeable as anything else in a throw-away era. Furthermore, some national policies on law of the sea issues have altered dramatically, in both speed and direction, while a number of maritime conflicts contain many inter-locking variables about which it is difficult if not impossible to predict the likely occurrence or timing of change, or the combination of their inter-relationships. So much will be dependent on the impact of the contingent and unforeseen and on the dynamic interaction of multiple unpredictable developments. Highly pin-pointed prediction is impossible. The sea is an uncertain medium in more ways than one.

The military implications to be discussed below will be subsumed within the phrase "naval power" or "naval strategy." However, it should go without saying that naval strategy no longer simply means warships. Not only has it become increasingly important to stress the interconnectedness of land, sea, and air forces, but more than ever "naval strategy" has come to be concerned with the projection of military power or force shore. The idea that warships exist simply to fight warships has had its day. The concept of naval strategy has had to be expanded to meet this change. The inter-connectedness of factors and the wide scope of meaning should be kept in mind when the term "naval strategy" or "naval power" is used below. Our concern is with the use of the sea insofar as it has military implications. These will be mainly but not exclusively naval.

When discussing the implications of particular developments, strategists are usually more comfortable when talking about the implications "on what?" rather than the implications "for whom?". This is because strategy is a peculiarly ethnocentric profession. "For whom?" can usually be taken as a given since it refers to their own countries. But the ethnocentrism goes further. Strategists have a long tradition of being incurious about other nations, including a poor record of being able to see how their own behavior appeared to others, and a poor record of being able to appreciate the hopes and fears of other nations. The literature which exists on the military implications of the law of the sea is dominated by western and especially U.S. hopes and fears. This paper attempts to show an awareness of different perspectives and at least to indicate some of the implications for medium and lesser navies. However, there is little material to help detailed speculation in this area. It is to be hoped that the inadequacies of this paper in this regard will encourage further work. While recognizing the variety of perspectives focusing on this problem, the emphasis will nevertheless be a western one. This is because the major military implications will most affect the major naval powers, which happen to belong to the industrialized world and, with one exception, all belong to the industrialized <u>western</u> world. But we should try to broaden our discussion away from the dominating United States-Soviet Union axis. In a world of better communications (but not necessarily better communication), increased interaction (but not necessarily understanding of it), and with the rise of new regional powers, it is more important than ever to think increasingly in terms of global implications.

These lengthy prefatory remarks have indicated the standpoints on which this paper has been developed. They are, to summarize: (i) discussion of the future military use(s) of the sea in view of impending changes in the law of the sea has tended to fall between two stools; only the surface of the problem has been dealt with; (ii) international law and strategy have common roots, and it is useful to conceive them as being unified by politics rather than being independent concerns; (iii) the dominance of resource issues over strategic issues in much of the discussion about the law of the sea is a fair reflection of their relative significance for most countries; (iv) in practice naval interests will probably impact more on the development of the law of the sea than will law of the sea developments impact on the changing character of naval affairs; (v) the military implications of prospective changes in the law of the sea are to be understood in terms of limited alterations of course rather than radical changes in direction; (vi) highly pin-pointed prediction in this issue area is unprofitable; (vii) naval strategy cannot be compartmentalized; warships no longer have exclusive proprietorship of naval strategy, and naval strategy is concerned with much more than the sea; and (viii) we should try to avoid the risk of seeing the implications of prospective changes exclusively in terms of western interests and preoccupations.

In tackling this multi-faceted subject, it is proposed to concentrate on the broader ramifications of the impending changes. There is little value in presenting another detailed analysis of the Informal Composite Negotiating Text (ICNT) or in commenting on the latest round of negotiations at the U.N. Conference on the Law of the Sea (UNCLOS). Indeed, such a worm's eye view will be deliberately neglected. At the risk of being too general, the paper stands well back from such matters of immediate attention.

The Main Questions

In line with these introductory remarks, the paper attempts to answer the following sets of questions:

1. What is the context of our discussion? What are the trends in the changing law of the sea? Where have we been, and where are we going?

2. What is the consensus about the military implications of foreseeable changes? What are the "first order" implications of creeping jurisdiction over the sea, especially in relation to the transit of warships along coasts, their passage through straits, and military uses of the seabed?

3. What are the "second order" implications of these trends for the future of naval diplomacy? In particular, what are their implications for (i) the "presence" role of warships, (ii) the basic assets of warships as instruments of diplomacy, and (iii) the evolving character of naval diplomacy?

4. What are the implications of creeping jurisdiction for intervention by sea? And is the enclosure of parts of the oceans a form of de facto arms control?

5. What are the regional military implications of the sources of dispute which might arise out of evolving law of the sea issues? What are the potential conflicts, and how serious might they be?

6. What are the implications of all these considerations for the future utility of navies? In particular, what old tasks are affected? What new tasks are created?

7. What are the implications of the foregoing discussion for naval policy, in terms of planning and operations, and on the technical requirements and the shape of navies?

8. Finally, what is the relationship likely to be between navies and the evolution of law and order (or disorder) at sea? What are the emerging patterns arising out of the interacting trends between law, force, and diplomacy at sea?

The Context

If we cannot agree about the context, we are unlikely to agree about the implications. At the outset, therefore, it is necessary to make some assumptions and assertions about trends, both past and present.

1. Where have we been?

Our views about the past will determine in important ways our assertions and speculation about the future. Getting this matter right (or at least agreed) is therefore a matter of some practical value.

As it happens, the history of the law of the sea is very much dominated by traditionalist, navalist Anglo-American viewpoint. This reflects the outlook of a more confident and less complex era, and, for the western powers, an era of great maritime supremacy. For many in the west this outlook has not changed. It is an axiom of historians, however, that we write about the past in the light of the present. All history is contemporary history. If we approach the evolution of the law of the sea in this light, then we might choose to emphasize a number of different points from those which form the backbone of standard treatments. The western perspective of the late 1970's happens to be one in which there are moral uncertainties, an eroding maritime supremacy, an increasingly complex world, a global inter-relationship of highly politicized issues, and a reduced ability to control events in a period in which there exists a persistent if presently tolerable level of conflict. In the light of this more defensive and uncertain outlook, one might choose to stress the following points about the history of the law of the sea rather than those emphasized in the standard authorities.

(a) The law of the sea has always been about politics. This fact of life was evident in the very origin of the modern concept of the "freedom of the seas." The *Mare Liberum* of Hugo Grotius was written in order to uphold the right of the

Dutch to navigation and commerce with the Indies in spite of the Portugese claims to monopoly. From the outset the freedom of the seas was conceived as an extension of politics. So it has remained.

In the nineteenth century the pax Britannica was characterized by a long and stable maritime regime, representing a remarkable example of international order. But it was not a regime which just gave order; it also helped to create the conditions in which British political and economic supremacy could be exercised over and recognized by the contemporary targets of great power foreign policy. At the present time, when the former targets have become independent and sovereign states in their own right, with their own ideas about security and prosperity and order and justice, it is well for the spokesmen of the former naval powers to accept the "freedom of the seas" for what it basically was, namely, a political instrument rather than a moral order. To accept this should not mean that one needs feel guilty about it. It is just a fact of life. Changing attitudes on such questions is always difficult. In the case of the British, it flies in the face of the traditional habit of investing any status quo with moral authority, of believing that support for the status quo is somehow "apolitical," and of seeing change as always being for the worse. The concept of the "freedom of the seas" has become cant, just as the concept of the "common heritage of mankind" will become, if it has not done so already.

(b) Ocean regime development has always followed a pendulum character. Historically speaking I am tempted to say that the more the law of the sea has changed, the more it has stayed the same. Against the image of an unchanging maritime order, so beloved by western navalists, the law of the sea has evolved in a pendulum fashion, swinging, albeit slowly, between enclosure on the one hand and freedom of navigation on the other. Consequently, this is not the first time we have been where we seem to be going. Extensive claims were made to the "Sovereignty of the Seas" by Norman Kings. Wardens were appcinted of the sea, as well as of the Cinque Ports and regional provinces. Responsibility for the maintenance of peace,rights and equity crept out from the land and extended out to sea (Laughton, 1866, pp. 721-25; Colombos, 1967, pp. 48-9). Again, centuries later, an extensive period of debate surrounded arguments for and against the freedom of the seas. The arguments were "strikingly similar" to those of today, while the whole debate was "suprisingly contemporary in its character" (O'Connell, 1978, p. 11).

The pendulum has swung according to the contemporary constellation of power and beliefs about the exhaustibility of the ocean's resources. From this perspective the "golden age" of the freedom of the seas, where both freedom and order were at a maximum, represents but one, admittedly long, period. It was a stage; it has not been the "norm" historically.

(c) The untidiness of law of the sea development. Those who would tend to regard the nineteenth century as a maritime golden age underestimate the extent to which the detailed character of the evolution of the law of the sea has been the subject of variable norms and overlook the fact that extensive formal agreement has been the exception rather than the rule. The famous freedom of the seas associated with the *pax Britannica* was a customary legal regime. It was not the outcome of a grand conference.

The society of states has never found it easy to codify a universally acceptable law of the sea. Leaving aside the present round of discussions, which began over ten years ago, we should note the "100 years of hullabaloo over innocent passage" (O'Connell, 1978, p. 17), the failure in 1930 to codify the law of the sea, the nine year preparation for the first U.N. Conference on the Law of the Sea at Geneva in 1958, the failures at Geneva in 1958 and 1960 over the territorial sea, and of the limited number of ratifications of the Conventions adopted. Parallel with the problem of codification was a growing trend towards "unilateralism" in maritime claims. This was instigated in the post-war period by the U.S. Government, the future opponent of unilateralism, in the issuing of the 1945 Truman Proclamation. It was quickly followed by the 200 mile claims of some South American states and subsequently by a proliferation of claims resulting in a variety of fish wars, resource claims, and disputes and conflicts over a wide range of interests in ocean space. During this period there were frequent reversals of national policy on law of the sea issues. If one takes a forty year perspective on the problem therefore (including the war years) one might approach the recent hullabaloo and foreseeable untidiness with a more philosophical attitude than that exemplified by some of the professional alarmists, who strew such words as "chaos" into the debate rather too indiscriminantly. Furthermore, the untidiness of these years should give some pause to those who either expect too much from UNCLOS (and underestimate the extent to which accords have been reached) and to those who may well equate a failure to produce a comprehensive treaty with the spread of turmoil at sea. If the future is not what it was, neither was the past.

The lessons to be drawn from these brief points are mainly relevant for the traditional naval powers. At the risk of oversimplifying, we can look at the past in two ways. Firstly, we could visualize it as a golden age now cracking up, a period of history which represented a remarkable degree of order in at least one area of international life. The alternative viewpoint, however, equates this old order with the era of British supremacy and the era of imperialism. From this perspective the golden age was at their expense. We are not therefore moving from a golden age into chaos, but instead we are attempting to move from a position of injustice to a more generally acceptable regime, one which is both more equitable and better suited to deal with the changed situation in world politics.

Both these outlooks point to the essential political character of the problem. To recognize the political nature of the law of the sea issue is important because what matters in practice is not satisfactory to important and/or numerous actors in the system, then the foundations for the development of the regime will be shaky. And the fact is that many governments see the old regime as a vestige of colonial domination, out of touch with the present needs and desires of the international community. It should also be added that the foundations will also be shaky if the most powerful do not accept the changing norms. When they think about this problem, however, it will be helpful if the representatives of the naval powers accept that the concept of the freedom of the seas has been a political instrument rather than a moral order. When self interest becomes mistaken for moral rectitude, trouble is bound to occur. In this case the freedom of the seas should not be mistaken for a universal moral good. Whether one sees the concept as theology or politics is important, for if one sees it as the former, one will tend to cling to attitudes with rather more determination than "objective interests" might dictate. Furthermore, other views will tend to be dismissed as illegitimate, and their holders seen as evil, rather than simply different. We are all merely fellow competitors in the games that nations play. Those who hold opinions contrary to those of the naval powers will certainly not see their own attitudes as illegitimate, and so it is important for the traditional naval powers to divest their thinking of theological overtones. This is easier said than done, for the mighty regularly dress up their security interests in ideological garb, as indeed do the meek. As long as it is invested with theological overtones, the concept of the freedom of the seas will continue to be what Sir Julian Corbett described it as over sixty years ago, namely, one of those "ringing phrases which haunts the ear and continues to confuse the judgement."

2. Where are we going?

Historically speaking, one might characterize the development of the law of the sea in terms of a pendulum. But there has been movement along another dimension as well. Important new developments give the present period some distinctive characteristics. Together these developments have connived to make Mahan's "wide common" a very troubled one indeed (Booth, 1977, pp. 274-281). The main new features are: (i) The spread of nationalism, which has filled out the world map with independent post-colonial nation-states. (ii) Rapid civilian technological innovation, which has made it easier to exploit the resources of the sea on an extensive scale. Parallel with this there have been far-reaching innovations in military technology which have increased the utility of submarine naval power, but decreased the potential of surface naval power. (iii) The rising significance of the sea as a factor in international politics, mainly, but not entirely, because of economic considerations. The resources of the sea are seen to be more important, more accessible, but at the same time no longer unlimited. When people cease to believe that there is enough for everyone in an unregulated situation, they tend to move towards unilateralism, a policy of every man for himself.

In theory there are four conceivable futures for the law of the sea. (i) No change. This is inconceivable, since the momentum for change has now progressed too far, and its supporting forces are too strong. (ii) A maritime "state of nature." For reasons which will become apparent later, a maritime struggle of "all against all" is not thought to be the likely situation operating at sea. (iii) A grand all-encompassing and detailed treaty, internationally enforced or nationally enforced and based on internationally accepted norms. History, as well as current clashes of interest, warn against such optimism. Furthermore, in terms of this paper, this outcome would represent such an unprecedented degree of community within international society as to make the discussion of military implications a technical rather than a strategic matter. (iv) The continuation of a troubled common, in which order generally prevails but in which the possibility of disorder is always present, in which there is some formal regulation but also some disagreement about norms and some areas of dispute and conflict. It is this last of these possible futures which provides the context for the subsequent discussion.

The future of the sea is facing pressure from the forces of disorder, as we see a major regime change, from one dominated by the traditional naval powers to one in which all states claim greater rights in the exploitation of ocean space (and correspondingly greater responsibility for its management). Even with the "best will" in the world (and how often is <u>that</u> present in international relations?) nobody is expecting the process to be easy or the outcome destined to be successful. UNCLOS has been the chief forum for the interplay of these contending interests; if its results have not been as successful as many hoped, neither have the proceedings been as acrimonious as some feared. The sessions have shown the new importance attached to maritime issues (albeit sometimes at the level of rhetoric rather than immediate interest), growing national sensitivity about maritime sovereignty (across a spectrum of states), the complexity of the issues (involving at least as much intra-governmental bargaining on the part of the developed states as inter-governmental bargaining between the national negotiators), the changeability of national policies (on the part of both developed and third world countries), and the persistence of the obstacles confronting those who had hoped to reach a comprehensive agreement. Interestingly, the proceedings have also shown how relatively easy and how relatively quickly it was sometimes possible for some well-established norms about the maritime regime to be changed, even in the face of the vested interests of the developed maritime powers.

Whatever else can be said about UNCLOS, at least it can be noted that "worst fears" have not materialized. The moods of UNCLOS watchers have fluctuated considerably. In thinking about the immediate future, Barry Buzan (1978, pp. 2-3) has provided us with an intelligent and succinct framework. His words are worth quoting at length:

> At worst it (LOSC III) may break up completely (though this seems unlikely) and at best it may produce some form of new law of the sea convention. Should such a document emerge, it will bear many scars of battle. Some political compromises will be marked by clauses so heavily qualified as to border on the meaningless, and issues on which no real agreement could be reached will be sign-posted by clauses with exceedingly vague or ambiguous wording. In other words, on a number of issues political acceptability will have to be bought at a cost of legal clarity. The convention will not so much resolve some disputes as contain them. It will not create order out of chaos, but rather define the terms of disorder. Possible outcomes of the Conference which fell short of a full convention would have much the same effect, for the many years' work of LOSC III, in conjunction with individual states' unilateral actions, have established a new framework for the law of the sea, regardless of whether any new convention comes into force. The essence of this new framework is the nearly universal acceptance that coastal states have substantial rights and interests in the resources and environment off their shores out to a distance of 200 miles. Thus, even if the Conference broke up or transformed itself into a semi-permanent, long-term negotiating body, the practical effect would still be one of continuing dispute within the bounds of a broadly legitimised framework.

One might add two further comments. Firstly, that legal clarity is not a value to pursue at any significant political cost. Too much definition can be a bad thing; we could rue the day when the chances for political compromise are sacrificed at the altar of legal clarity. Secondly, the image of a semi-permanent negotiating body would accord well with the needs of the times. In view of the complexities of the issues and their global implications, it would not be surprising if UNCLOS became, like UNCTAD and SALT, not so much a set of negotiations, but more a way of life (and strife).

Even if a comprehensive treaty does not materialize, it is not the view of most observers that the outcome will be "chaos and anarchy" at sea. There are some alarmists, of course, but they rarely seem to be convinced even by their own words. The alternative, and more moderate viewpoint, recognizes that the history of the law of the sea has been predominantly a history of the evolution of customary rules through state practice and expects that process to continue, even in the absence of an UNCLOS treaty (Knight, 1977, p. 34).

Although the strength of the forces for order at sea are sometimes overlooked, undoubtedly the immediate future promises more uncertainties than the immediate past. What finally emerges from the present process will be the result of hard bargaining and practice over a long period. Even a comprehensive treaty would be a beginning. The new regime is likely to be rather messy, but not necessarily unsatisfactory. It is likely to be full of disputes, but not extensive conflict. It is likely to be highly politicized, but not necessarily disorderly. Much is bound to emerge, as in the past, by customary development, and one can foresee a variety of unilateral claims, backed in some cases by force. However coherent or however cobbled the eventual outcome, few if any states will achieve all their objectives, and there will be ambiguities, omissions, and problems which will give rise to the possibility of later disputes and possibly conflict. Furthermore, partly because of the speed of change and the uncertainty of evaluations, the degree of international commitment to whatever norms are legitimized will not be evident for many years--some think a generation. The subject is enormous, the problems are complex, and the interests are extensive.

It is in the military sphere where some of the uncertainties are likely to last longest; this is because the issues involved are so important to some states, while the general problem is sensitive to all. It is an area in which the prospects for disagreement are strong and the prospects for legal clarity are weak. The way in which the ICNT has circumvented the issue is significant. It has adopted the tactic of silence, a silence within which are hidden a number of rights for navies: the right to conduct naval exercises within the EEZ of other states; the right to hold weapons tests there; the right to set up platforms for military use, and deploy non-nuclear weapons as long as there is no interference with the "exploration or exploitation of the economic resources" of the EEZ; furthermore, states also have the right to exclude themselves from having disputes concerning their military activities submitted to the dispute settlement machinery (Young, 1978, p. 200).

In sum, these "military exclusions" make Article 88 of the ICNT (the high seas shall be reserved for "peaceful purposes") a familiar piece of pious rhetoric, calculated to degrade respect for the document rather than legitimize new patterns of behavior.

The context we have to contend with, therefore, assuming no cataclysmic breakdown of international order or mind-boggling spread of international harmony, is the further development of the troubled common. This is an example of the "constant problem" aspect of the international ordering process in which, as Buzan has explained, "the achievement of higher levels of regulation and standardization does not necessarily bring problems to an end, but solves some lower-order problems at the expense of creating higher-order ones" (Buzan, 1978, p. 48). In short, as somebody once said about life in general, the evolution of the law of the sea will continue to be "one damned thing after another."

The Threat to Naval Strategy: Creeping Jurisdiction

The "damned thing" which is presently exercising the minds of those with extensive security interests in the use of the sea is all tied up, in one way or another, with the phenomenon of creeping jurisdiction over and under the ocean, in straits, coastal zones, the seabed and in what was formerly the high seas. The traditional international regime has been falling back before the advancement of national claims which have become increasingly legitimized on the international stage.

1. What is the problem?

In recent years there has been what has appeared to be an almost irrestible tendency for jurisdiction to creep beyond the existing three-mile territorial sea. At present the limit of the spreading jurisdiction is set by the 200-mile EEZ, which places about 30 percent of the oceans under some form of national administration. This is obviously a matter of great concern for those governments thinking about operating their warships in distant waters. They are obviously interested in both the extent of the creeping and the precise character of the controls given to national administrations. The details remain to be settled, by either convention or practice, but what is clear is the direction in which matters are moving. Together, technology, interest, and the will to govern seem set to fill out large chunks of the map of the sea with forms of national and international administration as inexorably as railways, the industrial revolution and nationalism spread government control throughout land masses in the last century.

"Creeping jurisdiction" is now a familiar term. The process has attracted other names. Neville Brown called it "parcellation" (1977, p. 145); others have described this trend to national determination of the extent of jurisdiction over the sea as "unilateralism." Gary Knight has given this idea more precision with his concept of "propertization," the idea that the ocean is becoming increasingly impregnated with all the characteristics of "real" property, namely boundary disputes, the granting of property rights, the imposition of regulations, the duty to avoid nuisance, and so on. Another term, extending this idea even further is "territorialization." This is the idea that national administration over the land is simply extending seawards in terms of rights and duties concerning good order, the exploitation of resources, and the exercise of sovereignty. Although international lawyers might quibble with the term because of its "dry land" connotations, "territoriality" is a politically relevant term in our present discussion, if we think of it in terms of ethology rather than law. In ethology "territoriality" refers to an area in which one group is dominant; it regards that area as its own private property and will resist intrusion by other groups. One small piece of evidence to support such usage occurred in the Anglo-Icelandic fisheries confrontation. Although British warships carefully refrained from intruding into Iceland's legally-defined territorial waters, the Icelandic Government nevertheless accused the British of "invasion" (New York Times, 1973, p. 3). This suggested that the zone claimed by Iceland had taken on a deeper meaning than that normally attached to areas of salt-water. What might hitherto have been called "intrusion" (or some such word) was now deemed tantamount to territorial invasion.

The substantive strategic point arising out of this discussion is that new uncertainties arise over the exact legal and political future of up to 30 percent of the ocean. Appropriately, the EEZ concept has been described as "a zone sui generis," since it is neither high sea nor territorial sea as normally understood. However, the validity of this conception has been challenged by some writers. D. P. O'Connell (1978, p. 16), for example, sees the EEZ's intruding into the high seas (one is tempted to say his high seas). This viewpoint is diametrically opposed to that of the coastal states, who see the EEZ's as simple extensions of national jurisdiction over adjacent sea areas. O'Connell's argument is that the matter has to be looked at "historically." But why this is so is not evident. Politically, it would seem more profitable to look at the matter in terms of present realities and future expectations. From the ethnocentric/navalist perspective it is claimed that the EEZ is essentially an area of high seas, which has now become subject to certain limited jurisdictional rights "which are in the nature of police rights rather than sovereignty"; it is "high seas, and superimposed on that you have certain coastal state rights with respect to (the) enjoyment and protection of marine resources." Thus, O'Connell concludes that the residual character of the zone is high seas. To those unschooled in the verities of Anglo-American navalism, however, this argument is not self-evident; it is not obvious why the zone should, in principle, have the "residual" character of high seas rather than the "emerging" character of territorial sea. This is a good illustration of the bureaucratic maxim "where you sit determines where you stand." O'Connell gives his own game away when he states that the "great fear" (presumably the Anglo-American navalist fear) is that of the self-fulfilling prophecy. If people go around saying (admitting?) that the zone is sui generis then it may well increasingly take on the characteristics of territorial sea. Depending upon one's viewpoint, this could be regarded as on the one hand an adverse trend in international order or, on the other, as a step towards progress in the international legitimation of national aspirations. Regardless of the precise legal rules, however, the political fact is that one man's distant water is another man's maritime backyard; all the signs are that states want a bigger say in what happens in their own backyards. Creeping jurisdiction is an idea whose time has come. As Knight has put it, there is "substantial evidence that this is a permanent and probably irreversible trend."

2. <u>How far can it go?</u>

The military implications which arise from these developments come from both the character and the extent of the burgeoning territorialization of the sea. Knight has identified four stages in the history of the law of the sea: "unrestricted freedom of the seas," "reasonable use of the seas," "regulated use," and what he has called the fourth and final stage, namely "property rights" in the ocean (Knight, 1977, pp. 33-34). But there is, theoretically at least, yet another stage. This would be the full enclosure of the ocean, a "genuinely global <u>mare clausum</u>, a regime providing government, law and order - including a monopoly of limited force - for the whole of the world's last common" (Young, 1974, p. 262). The present halt at 200 miles is not because of any inherent "logic" in the precise extent of that zone but rather because there is a mutual interest in giving the existing changes a chance to settle. However, it has already been asserted that the EEZ concept represents a minimum acceptable compromise for the African states, and that failing satisfaction they would follow a new and more radical approach to solving ocean problems (Njenga, 1974, pp. 87-105). If the recent history of the law of the sea suggests anything, it is that the only fault is in being overly conservative.

In answer to the question "how far can creeping jurisdiction go?" the ultimate answer is simple--"much further, and in theory all the way." Although it is true, as Buzan has argued, that the 200 mile zone "encloses most resources of interest" (Buzan, 1978, p. 8), one must accept that there will now be more interest in what is left unregulated. Furthermore, material interest is not the only spur. As Neville Brown (1977,

p. 146) has put it, "there is enough political momentum here to keep the process of parcellation going, irrespective of any objective necessity." If the "freedom of the seas" can represent blind dogma, so can its counter doctrines.

One would hesitate to envisage further creep if the rationale behind the 200 mile zone were stronger. However, this boundary has an arbitrariness which suggests that change will not be irresistible. The breadth of the EEZ had its origins in the claims of Chile, Ecuador and Peru in their 1952 Declaration of Santiago. A 200 mile zone happened to cover the productive fisheries areas off their coasts, related to the Humboldt current and nutrient-rich areas. This claim for exclusive jurisdiction for designated purposes came to be known as the "Patrimonial Sea," a phrase already suggesting a sense of territoriality much stronger than that of the neutral acronym EEZ. In words which have a very contemporary ring to them, the Santiago Declaration also recognized their seas as "irreplaceable sources of essential food and economic materials" necessary to further goals of economic development and independence. Once established and promoted by the Latin American states, 200 miles then became the magical figure for the 1970's; it was embraced with enthusiasm by African states when they discovered that the sea could be more than a medium for the transport of imperialist warships. But the arguments which led to the 200 mile zone could also be used for more distant horizons. The Humboldt current does not have the universality of the old three-mile cannon shot. In theory, another 25 miles of ocean might be desirable from a particular national viewpoint, but one hardly expects the next jump to be to 225 miles. Round figures and simple divisions have a strong pull. On this basis a mid-ocean EEZ is the next possibility. One of the principles behind the old three-mile limit, measured by the range of cannon shot, was that "the dominion of the land ends where the power of the arms ends" (Colombos, 1967, pp. 92-93). This limit persisted long after the range of weapons exceeded this distance. At its very inception the 200 mile limit fell short of the military reach of all countries with warplanes.

The further extension of zones may be a distant event. A more immediate possibility is an intensification of national regulation within the existing EEZ's. The "natural" tendency will be for governments (for no other ulterior motive than that of governing efficiently) to push out the regulations of the territorial sea into the EEZ. The naval powers can be expected to try to hold out against this. If they think such a possibility is illegitimate and unacceptable, it is salutary for them to be reminded that it is only a very short time since western opinion scoffed at the "bizarre" Latin American claims for jurisdiction out to 200 miles.

The trend is therefore one in which national jurisdiction seems destined to creep further, both in scope and intensity. We have seen growing claims by coastal states, followed by the crumbling of the opposition of the naval powers on all but security matters. During this process, as Mark Janis has pointed out, economic concerns were the major preoccupation for most states; however, once these issues have become more settled he argues that it is likely that national security issues will emerge to the fore. Already some third world spokesmen have claimed that the support of the naval powers for a narrow territorial sea represents not so much a defense of the internationality of the oceans but more a tactic by which they can legally place their warships as close as possible to the shores of coastal states (Janis, 1976, pp. 69-70).

Regardless of exact rights and duties, the fundamental problem boils down to the fact that the "blue water" of the naval powers is inevitably somebody else's maritime backyard, a backyard in which the coastal states have both greater interests and a greater desire to enjoy those interests for themselves. It is the interplay between these two sets of interests which provides the detailed military problems arising out of law of the sea, and it is to these we now turn.

First and Second Order Implications

It can be recognized at the outset that the military implications of the changing law of the sea will at the same time be both simple and complex. The former will be called "first order" implications. At this level there is broad agreement among the commentators about the main issues and their implications. Essentially, the problems arise from the threats to the mobility of warships implied by the process of creeping jurisdiction. But there is another level to the problem, what will be called the "second order" implications. This level is more complex, less discussed, and likely to be the cause of more disagreement. It is at this level, the implications of the implications, that the paper will concentrate. This mainly involves ways of overcoming the new problems and exploiting the new opportunities.

Straits and Archipelagoes

It has been the straits issue which has to date attracted most attention from those interested in the security aspects of the law of the sea. It is also a subject on which opinions have differed strongly between the naval powers and the relevant coastal states. In the last UNCLOS text, however, the position appeared to be satisfactory for the naval powers, assuaging their fears for the time being at least. The same was true for the problem of archipelagoes. Despite the obvious geographical differences between the two, the first order implications listed below are applicable, in principle, to both straits and archipelagoes.

1. <u>The nationalizing of strategic seaways.</u>

There is a general agreement that the extension of national control across international straits might have the following inter-related implications:

(a) Many international straits would be overlapped by territorial seas governed by rules of innocent passage. This would give the straits states important discretion over the passage of foreign warships (surface and submarine) and the overflight of foreign aircraft.

(b) A new regime would considerably enhance the strategic significance of those countries at the choke points of the most important straits. A small group of states would be given the opportunity for the exercise of greatly enhanced political leverage.

(c) An innocent passage regime would increase the possibility for disputes and conflict between the straits states and potential users. The definition of innocent passage allows plenty of scope for unilateral interpretation. The attempted redefinition in the ICNT is based on twelve specific considerations, most of which are open-ended and open to disagreement.

(d) With a new regime, the political and other costs of passage would potentially increase. Naval powers cannot assume the goodwill of straits states; thus the possibility of manipulation arises. In exchange for unimpeded access, a straits state (even an ally of a naval power) might demand a political, economic, or military price.

(e) With regulation, reaction time in crises may be affected. Restrictions placed on the passage of warships through straits might delay a build-up and weaken the force which could be deployed. More serious obstacles, ultimately physical resistance, would seriously raise the costs of passage. It would divert ships from their primary mission, and, if the costs could not be met, cause the naval power to look for an alternative (and longer) route, or call off the contemplated mission.

(f) A new regime would increase the problems of foreign policy for the naval power. States naturally try to minimize third-party opposition in crises. Any hostility by a straits state would result in a diversion of diplomatic effort, possibly a slower reaction time, the need to "buy off" the straits state, a diversion of route, or even cancellation.

(g) A new regime would strengthen the hands of potentially hostile straits states. Already the geography of straits does something to neutralize the military advantages of the mighty over the relatively weak. A new regime would legitimize the activities of a hostile straits state.

(h) Some types of restriction would increase the vulnerability of warships. If passage were to be restricted to particular traffic lanes, surveillance (and hence interdiction) by hostile forces is made easier.

(i) Under an innocent passage regime the invulnerability of submarines will be decreased. This is of particular importance for those engaged in strategic deterrence (SSBN's). Anything which detracts from their ability to move through and hide in the lengths and depths of the oceans detracts from their basic mission. If they are required to give prior notice of passage, or transit on the surface, it will be easier to track them.

(j) The threat of impeded (or costlier) access in time of crisis might reduce the significance of a naval presence in the eyes both of potential friends and potential enemies.

(k) As well as the transit of warships, distant military powers also have a strong interest in the overflight of straits, for resupply and more directly military purposes.

2. Living with new problems.

From the list above, a more restrictive regime would seem to be an unquestioned threat to the interests of the naval powers, and an obvious good for the straits states. But the picture is not as clear as that.

(a) The possibility that access may be impeded and made more costly should objectively have the effect of creating a politico-strategic "fail-safe" mechanism. This should be of significant advantage to all members of the international community in an era in which great power force is both less useable and more costly. Such a "fail-safe" mechanism should encourage rationality and discourage knee-jerk responses. Anything which helps to clarify the definition of superpower "vital interests" is presumably to be welcomed.

(b) Undoubtedly the nationalizing of straits would add many new problems for the naval powers, but it must be mentioned that the norms have already been changing behind the existing "freedoms." In tense situations, for example, transiting warships have sometimes had to make self-defensive precautions, as was the case with the Royal Navy task force passing through waters claimed by Indonesia in 1964.

(c) Any regime change would put a higher premium on the coordination of foreign policy and strategy, for diplomacy will become a more important factor in securing military access. This in turn increases the need for good communication between the political and naval arms of government, something which has often been notable by its absence. A particular responsibility is imposed on naval establishments to educate their political masters on the limitations as well as the requirements of naval forces as instruments of policy.

(d) The naval-related foreign policy implications of this discussion point in the direction of improving relations with those states which bestride the key straits, notably Bab el Mandeb, Dover, Gibraltar, Hormuz, and Malacca. Thus, it might seem that the naval tail might be wagging the foreign policy dog, but there is more to it than that. One only has to identify the states involved to appreciate that it should be an aim of a sensible foreign policy to attempt to be on good terms with the states concerned anyway, because of their regional significance. Furthermore, as it happens, the issues for which the straits might be used by the United States against the wishes of the coastal states are not likely to be "marginal." They are likely to be so important (the support of Israel in the case of Gibraltar, the securing of oil supplies in the case of Hormuz) that the hostile attitude of a straits state will not be the decisive factor. It would be a bad day for Israel, for example, if Morocco's disapproval of U.S. support were to be decisive in determining whether or not the U.S. dispatched warships.

Over the years some of the key straits and archipelagic states have had difficult relationships with one or both superpowers. These states as a group are characteristic of various trends and viewpoints in international politics and on "marginal" matters it may be perfectly sensible to harmonize with their preferences. For example, there is an evident sense of irritation in O'Connell's account (1975, pp. 110) of the potential (illegal) threat represented by the Philippines to Australian warships transiting to Vietnam. However, had the archipelagic claims been legitimized by international law, and hence allowed to tip the balance in the Australian debate on the issue, would Australia have suffered?

(e) Subtle diplomacy should be able to deal with the ambiguities of the definition of innocent passage to the satisfaction of any determined naval power. Furthermore, one can predict that in almost all circumstances almost all straits states will be content to back away in the face of a superior force. Indeed, they may well accrue prestige from so doing; being pushed around by the mighty is the only source of prestige for some countries. Third world states do not lose friends by being the "victims" of the policies of the superpowers. On its part, a naval power might not lose friends if it could appeal to a higher court than that of the law of the sea. The scope for diplomacy is wide. Resolution and bargaining should win the day. The effectiveness of U.S. arrangements with Indonesia is instructive in this case (Osgood, Hollick, Pearson, Orr, 1975, p. 69). Furthermore, while naval powers tend to dwell on the possibility of obstruction, there are occasions when straits states would support and legitimize a naval action, as would be the case of warships engaged in a U.N. blockade against the regime of the Republic of South Africa.

(f) The possibility must obviously be faced that things will go wrong from the viewpoint of the naval power. In this case resolution will be at a premium. Again, the Indonesian case may be pertinent; it suggests the local states will see the advantage of giving way. The exhibition of military power does not necessarily backfire. Vietnam encouraged glib, as well as deep, lessons for liberal democracies. Prestige and respect can sometimes accrue if the international community sees a state acting decisively in defense of its interests, as was illustrated by the blockade of Cuba and the sharp response to the capture of the *Mayaguez*. In any event, the taking of self-defensive precautions in the face of an innocent passage regime would be trifling as far as diplomatic "incidents" are concerned.

(g) A more restrictive regime would undoubtedly give the straits states a stronger sense of legitimacy in venting their hostility against a naval power, especially in time of crisis. This underscores the need for the naval power to have forces in sufficient quantity and with sufficient firepower to get its way without a fight - the true meaning of military *power*. This, for the foreseeable future suggests that they will need aircraft carriers, for their offensive and defensive potential.

(h) In concentrating on their own potentiality as targets, the naval powers tend to underestimate the degree to which the straits states will face new problems and occasionally feel themselves to be targets. In concentrating on the new costs they might have to face, the naval powers tend to ignore the sorts of costs straits states believe they might have to face if they impede a superpower on a matter the latter thinks is critical.

The implications of a regime change for the straits states are therefore more serious than might at first appear. Perceptibly, they would take on the role of potential *targets* as well as arbiters. They would have to face all the problems of power. They would have new authority, including duties and commitments they could formerly avoid. If they do not have commensurate power to discharge these tasks, they might be encouraged to develop their own naval power (thereby perhaps provoking a local arms race or encouraging external meddling for arms sales and influence), or they might be encouraged to seek the support of naval allies. However they reacted (and some no doubt would be inclined to do the minimum) their new situation could breed either responsibility (and a propensity to compromise) or the opposite. A more restricted regime would seriously increase the military and foreign policy problems of straits states. They would have more rights, but they would also have more duties and problems. They might find that they would have either to take tougher stands--putting their ships where previously they put only their rhetoric--or they would have to compromise, or they would have to be satisfied merely with the appearance of authority. In this latter case it is interesting to note that Morocco has claimed straits rights which it has not exercised.

(i) Although the naval powers could live with a new regime, the latter would appear to be in the security interests of the third world in general. Anything which is calculated to inconvenience the superpowers might be seen as being to their advantage. However, this attitude can smack of theology rather than a careful calculation of interests. Some third world countries might find good use for superpower military support. The superpowers are the major producers of order, and most states will have little interest in regional disorder.

(j) Acting with legitimacy is very important for the naval powers; indeed it is increasingly important in a world where interdependence is growing and the costs of using force are rising. If a particular foreign policy is seen to be legitimate, then associated actions will be seen to be legitimate by the international community, even if it means forcing straits. This is a matter of ensuring that foreign policy is made to work for naval strategy. The problem is to get the foreign policy right, and then acquiring the power to act. Making legitimacy work for one's strategy is very important (Fisher, 1971, pp. 185-6). And legitimacy in this area does not derive solely from the law of the sea. There are "higher" causes to which a state can appeal (the right of self-defense or collective self-defense for example). In addition, we can easily exaggerate the significance and sensitivity which states might feel about law of the sea questions in the total sum of things in an international crisis.

In a case where it was not possible for a naval power to secure international support for its actions, but it decided to proceed nonetheless (as in a particularly "vital" interest) the very fact that it showed the will to override legal inhibitions while appealing to some higher sense of justice would make its sense of purpose, and hence its credibility, all the more evident. Furthermore, if a superpower has to act and cannot gain the support of a large sector of the international community, does the hostility of an additional (albeit straits) state matter? If, for example, the United States undertook some naval action in support of Israel against the wishes of the whole Arab world, what would be the special significance of Moroccan disapproval? The outcome in such cases will depend upon the capability and will of the superpower concerned. As it happens, these are qualities whose future is open to discussion for reasons unrelated to any prospective changes in the law of the sea. The failure to attempt to keep open the Straits or Tiran in 1967 was a significant pointer in this respect.

(k) As far as local wars and crises are concerned, straits states might object to the passage of foreign warships, but they will only attempt to obstruct passage (assuming they have the capability) on the rare occasions when they are in fundamental opposition to the country concerned (Osgood, 1976, p. 15). In the main their interest will be to allow the vessels to go ahead (Buzan, 1978, p. 46). We need not therefore be alarmist about the risks of straits being closed merely because of any changes in the law of the sea. The Montreux regime is instructive. Despite limits on passage, in terms of prior notification and limited numbers, the western perception over the past ten years has not been that the Soviet squadron in the Mediterranean has lacked credibility in crises.

(l) Whereas one's first impression is that the threat of a more restricted passage would seriously affect the mobility of warships and therefore their essential instrumentality, when the problem has been examined on a mission-by-mission basis, commentators have concluded that the impact of a new regime would not be as drastic as first appears.

There has been much discussion of the impact on SSBN operations, and the arguments need not be rehearsed here. Although a new regime would require some readjustments (an inconvenience) the essential significance and utility of neither U.S. nor Soviet SSBN's would be affected, mainly because of the increased range of their missiles. Diplomacy can also be helpful. The United States, for example, managed to effect working arrangements for satisfactory SSBN transit through Indonesian-claimed waters (Osgood, 1976, p. 14). In war, of course, any legal restrictions would be almost irrelevant.

The problems that arise over straits are more complex in terms of conventional naval operations. The general view is that the threat of impeded access could seriously reduce the effectiveness of forces engaged in the naval presence mission. Particular attention has been drawn to the U.S. forces in the Mediterranean and in the Indian Ocean (Janis, 1976, pp. 6-7). This matter will be discussed at more length later, but several immediate comments are worthwhile. Firstly, the threat of a regime change is a relatively small one in comparison with the deep political, economic, and technical factors which will impact on the utility of forward deployment in the years to come. Secondly, the phrase "could reduce the effectiveness" of presence forces is a sleight of hand. Of course a new regime could reduce the effectiveness of presence forces. It need not. We need only examine the build-up and impact of Soviet naval forces in the Mediterranean since the mid-1960's. They have operated under the regime of the Montreux Convention, and through straits controlled by a country which has been both a historical enemy and a powerful member of a hostile alliance. Under these adverse conditions, an impressive military and diplomatic instrument has been built up. Thirdly, if a threat to access is seen as a threat to naval effectiveness, the implication to be drawn might not be withdrawal, but augmentation, to keep larger numbers of ships permanently on the "far" side of the straits concerned. This would obviously have foreign policy implications (bases, etc.) as well as the more obvious economic (opportunity cost) ones. Finally, if it is argued that reaction-time is such a decisive factor that any possibility of delay might tip the scales between the success and failure of a mission, it must be concluded that there is no alternative but to maintain full strength, permanently, in the likely trouble spots. If a hair-trigger response is so desirable, this is a reform which should be instituted independently of any law of the sea developments.

(m) As far as SSBN's are concerned, the first implication of creeping jurisdiction threatens their essential mobility. When this is examined further, one can see it merely as an inconvenience. But finally, one can see that this problem might raise the whole question of the future of SSBN's. Michael MccGwire (1975, pp. 1074-75) has questioned whether they are even needed in their present form. Might there not be cheaper and better alternatives?

(n) The two most significant naval cockpits affected by a changed straits regime would be the Mediterranean and the Indian Ocean. For reasons which will be discussed later, the logic of the situation for the naval powers points in the direction of a further exploration of naval arms limitation. This could give them the least worse of various more complex worlds.

(o) The concerns about naval access are also transferred to overflight. This is a significant problem, but a regime change would be unlikely to make a decisive difference. The straits states would be unlikely to obstruct passage, out of a mixture of diplomacy and capability (Osgood, 1976, p. 15). Not least of the safeguards of the country wanting to overfly nationalized straits would be the fact that aircraft cannot be impeded as conveniently as ships. Any attempt to "stop" aircraft would be a matter of the greatest concern. The resolution shown by major powers in face of hostility, e.g., the U.S. re-supply of Israel in 1973, is a lesson which is usually not lost on observers. Again, this problem seems to imply a need for a prudent naval power to have as many aircraft at sea as possible.

(p) Most of the arguments about straits suggest that the Soviet Navy would be more inconvenienced by a restrictive regime than the United States, because so many activities of the Soviet Navy depend upon access through straits controlled by unfriendly (if not always uncooperative) states. This suggests that the United States pay more attention to the possibility of a more variegated policy, defining its interests comparatively rather than dogmatically, thereby using the law of the sea more explicitly as an instrument of naval policy vis-a-vis the Soviet Union. There may be more to gain from harmonizing with the majority and putting the Soviet Union into the minority rather than harmonizing with the Soviet Union to defend some existing but expendable naval advantages.

3. The balance.

The problems of forward naval deployment have been growing in recent years because of economic burdens, new political complexities, and more powerful deterrents from potential targets. A changed straits regime at best, or worst, would add a noticeable but not radical impetus to this process.

The problem is evidently a serious one for the naval powers, and hence their resistance to regime change. But the impact is not uniform. The implications are more serious for U.S. general purpose forces and aircraft than for SSBN's, and are generally more serious for the Soviet Navy rather than the U.S. Navy. But if new problems are created for the naval powers, it is not apparent that increased national control is inevitably in the interests of the straits states, for they will be faced with new dilemmas and responsibilities for no more tangible benefit than the satisfaction of being given authority. Nor is it obvious that nationalizing straits is inevitably to the advantage of the international community at large. Is international order and justice assisted by, on the one hand, slightly adding to the problems of superpower military mobility or, on the other hand, slightly adding to the ability of individual states to interfere with that mobility? There is not a self-evident answer to any but the ideologically committed.

Not surprisingly, the difficulties of resolving these questions have inhibited any radical regime change, and for the immediate future the situation will meet the interests of the naval powers. Given the strength of superpower feeling on the problem, it is no more in the interests of straits states to resist them than it became for the developed countries to resist the 200-mile zone. Laws without norms are just words, and troublesome words at that. Be that as it may, the tendency for authority over straits and archipelagic waters to be claimed, and to creep, may well be evident in the years ahead, regardless of the outcome of UNCLOS. Disputes and minor conflicts may arise. If they do, they will only serve to highlight the importance of maritime access and the continuing military significance of warships. These conditions will also highlight some continuing truths about strategy and foreign policy. Although the problems of access are growing, a changed straits regime need not be an insurmountable obstacle for a country whose diplomacy is subtle, whose policy attempts to secure legitimacy in the eyes of the international community, whose force is impressive, and whose will is strong. The requirements are clear, but fulfilling them will be difficult, and more than ever the creature of domestic politics.

The Seabed

In 1970 it was resolved that the deep seabed should be "the common heritage of mankind." The character of the international administering authority has caused much dispute. It has proved only relatively easy to secure agreement on generalities, that an authority be established, and that the deep seabed be reserved exclusively for "peaceful purposes." Some have argued that the seabed is one of the most important areas of the subject with military implications. For this reason the complete demilitarization of the seabed has found some supporters; however, it has not been possible to go beyond the Seabed Treaty in this respect. This treaty, which entered into force in 1972, prohibits the emplacement of nuclear weapons and other weapons of mass destruction. So far, the agreement appears to have worked satisfactorily (Vayrynen, 1978). Looking beyond this, it is very difficult to discuss the military implications of prospective changes in the law of the sea, for this is metaphorically as well as literally a very dark area indeed. Those without access to secret scientific-military information are scarcely in any position to determine whether or not the implications in this area are "important" or not.

1. Hindrances and disputes.

There is a ready consensus about the first order implications of a changed seabed regime. The problems arise in the second order, in determining their relative importance.

(a) The exploitation of the deep seabed would interfere with sensors and navigation aids. This would degrade both one's own navigation and one's ability to track the vessels of other states.

(b) "Peaceful purposes" will be defined subjectively, in order to include seabed listening devices (this, in fact, is the not-surprising and not-unreasonable position of the U.S. Navy). This will be a source of dispute, especially on continental shelves. In its adherence to the Seabed Treaty in 1973 India announced that there could be no restriction of its sovereign right to verify, inspect, remove or destroy any weapon, device, structure, installation or facility which might be emplaced on or beneath its continental shelf by any other country. The position of the United States was that the rights of coastal states were restricted to purposes of exploration and exploitation of natural resources and therefore did not concern military equipment.

(c) There will be similar disputes in sensitive areas about what constitutes "scientific" research. If any law of the sea convention leaves any ambiguity over rights to conduct scientific research in areas of national jurisdiction, the possibility of disputes will obviously arise over what is "scientific" on the one hand and what is "military" or "commercial" on the other (Buzan, 1976, pp. 12-13).

(d) If an international regime is established, it could in time be seen to need relevant forces to support it against the possibility of illegal acts, e.g., mining in illegal areas; economic sanctions might not be enough.

(e) If an international regime is not established, the result may be a grab by companies from industrialized states, an action which will be seen as illegitimate by the majority of proponents of the common heritage of mankind doctrine. This could provoke a range of responses (from sabotage and covert attacks to commodity boycotts and diplomatic boycotts) (Buzan, 1976, p. 14), some of which would call for naval protection. In this regard Henry Kissinger has already pointed out that if there was no international regime the United States was well able to protect its companies by its navy.

(f) Apart from pressures from other states, seabed activities might in some areas become the target for terrorists, saboteurs and guerrillas.

2. Out of sight, out of mind.

If the principle of out of sight, out of mind is an apt one, then the seabed should not be a matter of significant military importance, although there is much scope for commercial disagreements. It would appear to be a problem involving inconveniences rather than serious effects on military behavior.

(a) The possibility of keeping foreign sensors and listening devices out of one's own maritime backyard by international agreement would be welcomed by all states. However, as long as mines and other actual weapons are not involved, the devices concerned are not direct "threats," and in most cases are probably relevant in the context of the United States-Soviet Union confrontation only.

(b) The threatened hindrance to tracking submarines raises the basic question of the desirability of tracking the adversary's SSBN's at all. If theories about maintaining invulnerable second-strike capabilities are valid, this suggests that states should be very solicitous about their adversary's retaliatory force. Attempting to track his SSBN's (which increases one's chances of destroying them) is, in the theory of deterrence, a potentially destabilizing activity.

(c) Other types of ASW are relevant to the problem of dealing with the threat to convoys, but this is an eventuality whose probability is thought to be very low. Before one can comment further, one needs to know about the relative efficacy of fixed as opposed to mobile ASW systems.

(d) As far as the emplacement of sensors for the tracking of all types of submarines is concerned, there would not appear to be many places in the U.S.-Soviet confrontation which were not either within the authority of an ally (and whose emplacement was presumably acceptable) or within the zone of the adversary (and therefore presumably already "fair game" for interference). The one potentially dangerous area of dispute over this problem is the Norwegian-Soviet boundary in the Barents Sea.

3. The balance.

After this brief examination, it is difficult to go along with those who have stressed the potential military significance of changes in the long-accepted legal regime for the seabed. If, as seems likely (Vayrynen, 1978, p. 240), there are no prospects for any sort of arms race on the seabed, the prospects for serious conflict are low (Spitzbergen apart). While there are potential sources for dispute elsewhere, limited capabilities on the part of non-naval powers will help encourage a compromising attitude. ASW could be affected by a very far-reaching regime, but it is impossible for those without access to secret information to know how significant the effect would be. The geographical character of one's alliance of one's alliance system is more important than the seabed regime. The future alignment of Iceland, for example, appears to be far more significant for the United States in this respect than does the future of UNCLOS. Again, the relative advantages lie with the United States. If, as seems possible, problems arising out of the future seabed regime cause very serious rifts in UNCLOS, the likelihood will be that these will be the result of economic rather than military considerations.

Creeping Jurisdiction and Naval Diplomacy

It is in the processes and meaning of naval diplomacy where the prospective changes in the law of the sea have the most interesting implications, in terms of the impact of creeping jurisdiction on the warships transiting through and demonstrating in areas which were formerly high seas and "free." It is also in this aspect of the subject where this paper departs furthest from the gathering consensus.

The military implications of creeping jurisdiction on naval diplomacy arise from the problem of access, which, as MccGwire (1975, pp. 1060-61) has explained, is the factor which gives the sea its essential strategic quality. In MccGwire's words,

> the strategic quality of a particular waterway will reflect some combination of the importance of the use to which it is put, the ease with which that use can be prevented, and the availability and cost of alternative routes.

The possibility of the denial of this access threatens to limit the utility of warships in their diplomatic roles.

The phrase "naval diplomacy" refers to the use of warships in support of foreign policy short of major violence. It, therefore, involves their use for signalling various intentions, negotiating from strength in a crisis, furnishing a general bargaining counter, providing influence-building options, and supportive and representational tasks of various kinds.

1. Limited access: limited usefulness?

There is general agreement on the first order implications of creeping jurisdiction on the diplomatic potential of warships.

(a) There would be "less sea-room for free transit."

(b) If the tendency to territoriality proves irresistible, one might expect countries to require prior notification before the passage of the naval vessels of other countries.

(c) Arising from the last point, naval presence operations would come to be at the discretion of the coastal states. Because general compliance cannot be expected, this would result in a "patchwork" character for naval operations.

(d) Because presence forces will have to operate at a longer distance from shore, they will not be as visible as formerly, and therefore will not have the same diplomatic impact.

(e) Coastal states will be particularly sensitive about the presence of foreign intelligence-gathering ships. If access is denied, the naval powers will be deprived of information which could affect their operational performance.

(f) If, in practice, the new regime turns out to be rather permissive insofar as its "military exclusions" are concerned, the sense of territoriality will nevertheless still exist in the maritime backyards of coastal states; one might therefore expect a mixture of complaints directed against foreign warships. Criticism might take the form of demands for "zones of peace," or complaints that naval activities are interfering with the economic rights of the coastal states concerned. Together the complaints might build up a strong sense of inhibition on the part of the naval power and lessen its willingness to deploy its warships.

(g) States will become more reluctant to allow foreign vessels to engage in scientific research in their coastal zones. Some "scientific" research will have military implications, and to the extent navies are deprived of this information, their performance will be affected.

(h) If warships are to move only in designated sea-lanes because of traffic and/or pollution and/or security restrictions, all countries will find them easier to track; this will increase their vulnerability in both peace and war.

(i) Deployment in crises will be hindered. If a patchwork pattern is imposed on naval operations, this will increase reaction-time in crises (if the possible political costs of intruding into unwelcome areas are to be avoided).

2. <u>The many facets of naval diplomacy.</u>

If these first-order implications are valid, the implications of a regime change are clearly serious. However, three cautionary remarks should be made before taking too sweeping a view of the impact of the law of the sea developments:
(i) The first order implications above are generally a form of worst-case analysis. They mainly refer to what <u>could</u> happen; this is based on an exaggeration of the extent to which foreign warships will be the targets of attention and the extent to which the interests of the coastal states will lead to an obstructionist policy. (ii) Major inhibitions on distant water naval activity have been growing and would continue to grow regardless of law of the sea developments. Any legal inhibitions would add an increment to a deteriorating trend.
(iii) Our immediate attention is drawn to the impact on naval diplomacy of the EEZ concept, in which warships have transit and other rights (by default rather than designation) but in which it can be expected that constraints will accumulate

because of territorial impulses on the part of the coastal powers, e.g., the extension of domestic legislation for traffic and pollution purposes, and the growing costs for the naval powers involved in maintaining forward deployments. Whatever the detailed character of any future international legal regime, creeping territorialization into about 30 percent of ocean space seems both irresistible and bound to have an effect on naval diplomacy. But the long-term implications are far from being as clear as the first-order implications might suggest.

(a) While the pushing out of the claims of coastal states implies less sea-room for transit, this is a trend which is already inherent in other developments. Already, because of pollution and security considerations (note the "zone of peace" proposals) some coastal states have demonstrated their sensitivity towards the passage of foreign warships. Of more immediate practical significance, tactics are pushing warships further from adjacent coasts. The need for dispersal tactics is prone to make "inconveniently large" the amount of sea space for the deployment of a sizeable and well-balanced task force (Brown, 1977, p. 179). A carrier task force is said to require a base of 200 square miles when deployed for action. "Moreover it is desirable to leave one or two hundred miles more between the task force perimeter and a hostile coastline and also to have several hundreds of miles extending in other directions to allow for tactical manoeuvre" (Brown, 1977, p. 179).

(b) If warships avoid zones in which they are unwelcome in time of crisis, it is correctly argued that this would affect the timeliness with which they could act. In practice, a number of considerations complicate this proposition. Although the political costs of a deployment would be increased by intrusion into an unwelcome zone for the purpose of a rapid transit, the precise costs can only be discussed in each case; one could argue that this is such a scenario-dependent problem that the general proposition is virtually meaningless. The problem cannot be fruitfully discussed without knowing the third parties involved, the time saved by intruding into their sea space, the political trouble caused, the importance of the incident concerned, the importance of timeliness, and so on. Few third parties are likely to have the power to stop a major naval task force, and may well keep quiet on that account. In most crises, by definition, "vital interests" are engaged, and this will mean less willingness to be solicitous of third party sensibilities (and in any case, the integrity of maritime frontiers will not be a vitally sensitive matter for most states).

These arguments raise a general point about the value of reactive naval deployments in crises. Criticism has been levelled against the posturing by U.S. naval forces after the Pueblo incident and during the 1971 Indo-Pakistan war. MccGwire's comments (1975, p. 1075) about the latter have a wider applicability:

> There is a suspicion that this type of deployment often represents action for its own sake and is an overly crude form of diplomatic signal. It also manages to combine the worst of two worlds. It lacks the type of influence that stems from the political commitment of a permanent presence, affords no possibility of precautionary deployments, and inevitably means a delay of several days before force can be brought to bear. Meanwhile, the high visibility of interocean deployment raises political expectations that are unlikely to be met. It can be argued that with regions as large as the Indian Ocean, one either maintains forces in the area or allows events to take their course, and that reactive (as opposed to periodic) deployments should only be ordered in exceptional circumstances.

In short, when we discuss the timeliness of warship reaction, we tend to concentrate on the instrument to the exclusion of the aim.

(c) The possibility that warships might be required to move in designated sea-lanes is said to increase their vulnerability. In fact, the opposite might well be true. The very predictability of normal behavior may well be an advantage in the abnormal conditions of crisis or the outbreak of war. Standard operating patterns might have the effect not of increasing the chances of interdiction, but of increasing the opportunities for taking the enemy by surprise. The more predictable one's behavior is believed to be by a potential enemy, the greater are one's chances of engineering a tactical surprise. The long history of intelligence failures attests to the extent organizations nurture their cognitive consistency. A lively navy might well be content with designated routes in peacetime, while keeping fresh ideas for diversion and surprise in the event of war. In any case, as already happens, naval forces transiting archipelagoes do tend to stay within predictable routes (Knight, 1977, p. 38).

(d) Although the problem of potential political costs cannot be ignored, it can be minimized. For example, it would be sensible for naval powers to begin to negotiate bilateral and multilateral treaties to establish their rights of navigation in advance of a crisis (Knight, 1977, p. 39). More heretically, there might be something to be said from a strategic if not legal viewpoint in letting navigation rights through some EEZ's lapse, in a de facto though not de jure sense. If one's warships are not regularly crossing the sea adjacent to a particular country, this will increase the meaning of any crossing which does take place. This might mean that the country concerned might be willing to accept such an event on the rare occasions when it proves necessary; it might make easier the drawing up of special crisis arrangements. It would establish the basis for a working compromise between the coastal state's sensitivity about its maritime backyard in general, and the naval power's urgent requirements for transit on rare occasions. There is evidence to suggest that such compromises are possible. When the carrier USS Enterprise and its accompanying ships passed through the Malacca Straits on its way to the Bay of Bengal in 1971 the Indonesian Government reaffirmed the right of the littoral states to control such passage but reconciled this right with the U.S. action by stating that the Command of the Seventh Fleet had given advance notice (Oliver, 1973, pp. 27-33). Subtle and quiet diplomacy should be able to make such arrangements common.

The last point is another reminder of the importance of diplomacy in naval strategy, which in turn calls for improved coordination between naval and foreign ministry establishments and a deeper comprehension of the relationship between the instrument and the aim.

(e) When discussing such matters there is a tendency, especially for academics, to put too high a price on the new (or old) law of the sea. The law of the sea is important, but it is certainly not the most important thing for policymakers to consider. Justice and legitimacy are important matters in foreign policy, and they do not necessarily involve pedantic adherence to the law of the sea. In contemplating an exercise in naval diplomacy, the legal dimensions are broader (or 'higher') than simply the law of the sea. There is body of universally accepted rights, as well as rules, relating to the conduct of civilized states. Among those rights are the right of self-defense (which may be exercised in anticipation of an act of aggression), the right of humanitarian intervention (to protect one's own nationals), and the right resulting from military necessity (which justifies the application of regulated force required to ensure the prompt submission of an enemy). In addition, there is the right of collective self-defense deriving from Article 51 of the U.N. Charter. If a dispute takes on a legal or moral character, therefore, there is far more to it than the law of the sea. Indeed, compared with these other rights, one's duties in terms of the law of the sea are relatively unimportant. If a state cannot justify a particular naval action on the basis of these other rights sufficient to satisfy a significant portion of the international community, we might conclude that the action probably is immoral or futile. On the other hand, if some individual states object very strongly, this suggests that they are acting with a degree of hostility that arises from more serious roots than their sense of property over a patch of water. In rare cases an action will have to be undertaken by a naval power in support of such an important matter of national interest that the requisite political costs will have to be paid. We often make mistakes because we underestimate the determination of states to have their way, even if it means paying a heavy price. The main point is that if the action at the destination is seen to be legitimate, then the accompanying naval action will be seen accordingly.

3. <u>The problems and opportunities for naval presence.</u>

The "presence" role of navies is the most difficult of all to write about. There is a vagueness at the very heart of the concept, which is its essence from a strategic point of view but its curse from that of an analyst. When the implications of the changing law of the sea have been discussed in relation to naval presence, few writers have given necessary credit to the great complexity of the mission. From the first-order implications enumerated earlier, it appeared that creeping jurisdiction threatened to undermine the future of the presence mission. The discussion below will suggest that this mission, which is under challenge from a variety of sources, can only be saved by the territorialization of the sea.

The traditional and well-understood concept of naval presence has been under challenge for a number of years. The U.S. Navy has had a troubled existence recently, while Admiral Gorshkov has deployed his limited literary skills to explain why a navy was needed by the Soviet Union for more than the limited purposes of the past. All find it difficult to assess the utility of naval presence. There are major problems in explaining and justifying the mission to inward-looking publics. There are problems in planning how presences should work in order to convey the appropriate signals. There are tactical and technical problems arising out of the new array of threats which can be thrown against them. There are problems arising out of their increased economic costs. And there are strategic problems arising out of the restricted useability of force in a more complex international environment. In some circumstances a naval presence may well represent "the best of a bad job," i.e., the unenviable lot of most armed services, but naval presence does not seem to offer the clear benefits of previous generations. Warships in forward deployment can still attempt many missions, but all the costs involved in discharging them are growing. All this suggests that the utility of the historic concept of naval presence is in decline.

Having recognized the changing cost-benefit relationship, it must also be recognized that superpowers will sometimes need to show a military interest in a distant region, and that they will sometimes wish to act. There will be issues on which they will not be dictated. As long as warships represent the most efficient method by which they can bring flexible firepower to bear in distant regions, warships will retain a major strategic role. The problem is how to make them useable and effective. Changes in the law of the sea will be of decisive assistance in this respect.

After ten or so years in which the currency of naval diplomacy has been depreciating, the changing law of the sea promises to revive it. It can revive it by making naval diplomacy more selective and more salient. This new significance arises out of the new sensitivity attached to EEZ's. The EEZ means a new boundary _to cross_, as well as to observe. Related to the new salience _will be_ a new selectivity in use. This is important because the market of naval diplomacy has been saturated in the past decade. Changes in the law of the sea will help alter that. The new inhibitions (the extra costs) involved in sending warships off unfriendly coasts will be a discouragement to the knee-jerk naval diplomacy so characteristic of much U.S. strategy in particular. They will discourage the ritualistic and inevitable responses of the recent past, which have tended to produce confused signals (the Indo-Pakistan war) or futile demonstrations of power which have reduced precious prestige and credibility (the _Pueblo_ affair). But if after calculation it is decided to deploy naval forces, the very fact that a new boundary has to be crossed will help make the action more salient. In the era of knee-jerk naval diplomacy, familiarity has tended to breed apathy. In contrast, the prospective changes in the law of the sea promise to make the exercise of naval diplomacy both more selective and more meaningful, because warships will have to intrude into waters over which the coastal state will have special and legitimized interests. For the first time since the western powers stopped wielding the big stick with some effect, the sailing of a group of warships in distant waters will approach the symbolism of tanks at Checkpoint Charlie or aircraft buzzing over Berlin.

The thesis just presented contradicts the first order implications discussed earlier and is at odds with current naval thinking as reflected in the open literature. The validity of this thesis will be brought out further when we examine in more detail some of the subtleties of naval presence.

(a) One of the assertions about the problem is that naval presence will lose its significance because, as it is sometimes put, "the flag will not be as visible." That fact is undeniable, for "The flag, after all, is considerably more difficult to see at 200 than at 3 or 12 miles" (Janis, 1976, p. 8). However, it is not as simple as that. There is more to strategy and diplomacy than optical truths. If one thinks of the presence mission in some of its complexities, the fallacy of this argument will be revealed.

(i) Distance might actually help naval diplomacy. Distance helps withdrawability, which recent history suggests is sometimes more of a problem for the mighty than becoming involved in the first place. As the costs of commitment grow, the advantages of potential withdrawability might appear to be more telling to policymakers than the advantages of timely involvement. There are advantages in a low profile. On the other hand, if a naval power wishes to make a hostile signal against a particular country, this can always be done by a mixture of declaratory and action policy; the latter can involve warships almost anywhere in contiguous seas. For the naval power, wanting the coastal country to feel unsettled but not intending to use force (e.g., the United States after the Pueblo incident) there is a positive advantage in keeping one's head well below the horizon, in case it decides to lose gracefully.

(ii) Distance assists not only the naval power but also the local country (and the general development of a moderate international system). The greater the distance from which the naval diplomacy is exercised the smaller will be the excalatory steps before a face-off. And if successful military power consists of achieving one's objectives without having to use force, such small steps are valuable. They make it easier for the target state to compromise, but also easier for the mightier power to accept a loss. The smallness of the steps means that important questions of face and prestige are not engaged so immediately. Without small steps, an immediate face-to-face confrontation can make it more difficult for the parties to back down. Some states might feel too weak to compromise and see a defiant gesture worth more than surrender. In such circumstances a warship might well be a tempting prize for a leader willing to take risks, or a leader seeking prestige and possessing gift-wrapped forces from a developed country. Actually seeing a hostile warship might tempt the will to hit it. From the shore, with binoculars, warships can look rather small, and hopelessly waterbound. Far out of sight warships can be just as threatening and just as politically visible, but at lesser political and physical risk. One wonders to what extent did the very availability of the Pueblo or the Maddox tempt their attackers?

(iii) Actual visibility is rarely the issue. What matters is the political visibility of warships. In this respect Knight (1977, pp. 35-56) has properly pointed out that:

> public perceptions of naval power are largely irrelevant in most Third World Nations because of their totalitarian forms of government. The head of state knows what vessels are situated where and probably has his copy of Jane's Fighting Ships (or a knowledgeable admiral) nearby to tell him the nature of the threat posed. Credibility

> of the threat becomes the critical factor at that stage, and whether the public can actually see the vessels would seem to be of relatively minor importance.

"Very minor importance" we might add, and also note that these comments are also pertinent to those countries which do not have totalitarian forms of government. Clearly, in naval presence, "the flag" does not _actually_ have to be seen. In the 1971 crisis in the Indian Ocean, for example, the main naval diplomacy took place well over 100 miles from the coast of India (Jackson, 1975, pp. 229-230; Zumwalt, 1976, pp. 367-68). On this occasion nobody could say that the Soviet and U.S. warships were not _politically_ visible. Indeed, they were embarassingly visible in the case of the United States. That the signals given by the deployment of the U.S. task force appeared confused was more a matter for the White House than the Chief of Naval Operations; it was a problem of vague aims rather than dimly visible ships.

(iv) In practice, therefore, naval diplomacy and naval presence rarely take place within sight of land. Some of our images are too strongly affected by the hey-day of gunboat diplomacy, kept alive by the fashion for Victorian prints of British gunboats off Chingwangtao, or of cruisers lying at anchor off west African towns. Port visits apart, it is a long time since naval diplomacy involved the parading of warships in sight of land.

The Mediterranean, which is both strategically important and physically confined, gives some illustrations of this. J. C. Wylie (1969, p. 56) (a former deputy commander in chief of U.S. Naval Forces in Europe) has related that in the Suez crisis of 1956 the Commander of the Sixth Fleet took his main force and "operated idly" mid-way between Suez and Cyprus (that is, over 100 miles from Suez, where the main action was). The Commander kept his destroyer screens out and his combat air patrols up, but "he took no action, even though he was obviously ready and everyone, on both sides, knew he was ready." One might note that in the intervening twenty years surveillance and communication systems have improved markedly, such that what could be seen then will be even more visible today. It was Wylie's verdict that this distant readiness of the Sixth Fleet exerted a stabilizing influence on the situation, as did the alerting of even more distant U.S. warships. He comments (1976, p. 56):

> a major stabilizing element in the international situation at this time was that, except for the ships in the eastern Mediterranean, _no one knew where the American fleets were_. It was only known that they had left their usual operating areas.

So much for the disadvantage of not seeing the flag! Diplomatic messages are various, and so are the types of naval signals.

The tendency for naval demonstrations to take place at some distance from the coast can be a matter of military as well as diplomatic tactics. The closer the warships are to the shore, the more vulnerable they will be to "bee-sting attacks" from the small, fast but powerfully-armed warships of coastal states and also to their shore-based aircraft. To be out of range of fighter-aircraft was the reason the U.S. Navy wanted to push the blockade of Cuba further out to sea than President Kennedy thought desirable from the point of view of giving Mr. Khrushchev time to stop and think. And it was similar reasoning which led Admiral Zuwalt to question Presidential orders relating to the stationing of Task Group 74 during the Indo-Pakistan war. In Admiral Zumwalt's words (1976, p. 368):

> The first orders to TG 74 had been to go on station in the Bay of Bengal, off the East Bengal coast. I argued against stationing the ships there. I felt it was taking an unnecessary risk to put a task group without a stated mission in precisely the place where harm was most likely to befall it. I won my argument, and the group was sent south of Ceylon, where the Russians, when they arrived, promptly began trailing it.

In view of the earlier comments about the ritualistic character of much contemporary naval diplomacy, we should not leave this episode without quoting some of Zumwalt's later remarks. For the first week or so of 1972, he records:

> the American and Russian ships circled around each other warily, much as their counterparts had been doing in the Mediterranean for years. Then, on 8 January, Task Group 74 was ordered out of the Indian Ocean as mysteriously as it had been ordered in.

In addition, those who fear that a regime change will significantly affect the timeliness of naval responses might note Zumwalt's observation that the U.S. task group was not formed until the outcome in East Bengal was already clear. Even in the recent past, timeliness has not been an important attribute of naval diplomacy.

(v) Naval diplomacy can serve to give many signals (Booth, 1977, Chapter 2). The signal one wants to transmit will affect the character of the naval deployment, in terms of location, force structure, behavior and so on. It was argued above that one can transmit involvement without actual visibility. It is to be expected, therefore, that one can transmit aloofness and non-commitment even more effectively by avoiding actual visibility off the crisis area coasts. The behavior of the Sixth Fleet during the Middle Eastern crisis of 1967 provides some useful illustrations (Wylie, 1969, pp. 58-59). On signals such as these, changing attitudes to the law of the sea will have no significant effect whatsoever.

In 1967 U.S. policy for the Middle East was to stand aloof from military involvement if possible, to play the military role in a very low key in order to give maximum scope for diplomatic manoeuvre, but at the same time to be within striking distance in case circumstances dictated commitment. A variety of naval activities were pursued in support of this posture. There were no premature departures of U.S. warships from any port. No scheduled visits to Mediterranean ports were interrupted or shortened. The amphibious forces were deliberately and visibly maintained in the central Mediterranean, between Naples and Malta. "This put them where everyone could see them and knew exactly where they were - a thousand miles away from the southeast corner of the Mediterranean. This signal...was promptly received and noted." Finally, the main body of the Sixth Fleet was purposefully retained south of Crete, and well clear of the crisis area. "They were well over three hundred miles from Suez and at least two hundred miles from Egypt's western desert." However, because of the role played by American newsmen and the presence of escorting Soviet ships, "American whereabouts and actions, or lack of action, were known to all interested parties." In these various ways, therefore, the move to readiness in the Arab-Israeli mobilization period had a variety of careful signals built into it, in which maintaining distance from the flash-point was a help in demonstrating the wish to keep aloof (Wylie, 1969, pp. 58-59). Indeed, one might conclude that in the prosecution of its diplomatic mission on such occasions, the presence of American newsmen and Soviet warships is more important in ensuring the <u>political</u> visibility of the U.S. warships than is any close contact with any local powers.

(b) One of the first-order implications discussed earlier was that the changing legal regime would inhibit the presence role because it would impose a patchwork character on deployment patterns. This might not be such a significant or adverse development as immediately appears. In the first place, some operations already take on a patchwork character, by choice, as is apparent in some of the operations described above. This pattern can make valid diplomatic points. Secondly, if the adoption of a patchwork deployment pattern means that the Sixth Fleet could operate in some sea areas (those of its allies) from which Soviet forces would be excluded (as perhaps in a more restrictive regime) then this would give sanctuaries from the continual presence of the shadower. Thirdly, if deployment in some zones is left to the discretion of local countries, this adds another quiver to the bow of naval diplomacy. Another boundary might inhibit, but it also adds another rung to the escalation ladder, and hence increases the flexibility of the instrument (warships) able to move up that ladder.

The potential patchwork character of naval diplomacy does not therefore have fundamental implications for naval diplomacy. It does lead one, however, to consider some potential advantages of naval arms control schemes; this will be discussed later.

(c) Some of the problems of naval reaction-time in crises were discussed earlier in relation to straits and transit along coasts. If reaction time is thought to be all-important, one wonders why more is not done now, regardless of any developments in the law of the sea. Reaction-time could be cut by keeping more forces deployed fully forward, thereby avoiding the type of delay in reinforcement which took place in the 1970 Jordanian crisis (Zumwalt, 1976, p. 298). Such an augmentation might seem unthinkable at present, because of economic and other constraints, but in a more troubled world (especially one where access to resources becomes more critical (Kemp, 1978, pp. 396-414)) perceptions of costs might quickly change. The oil crisis following 1973, the uncertainties of western economies, and the image of Soviet imperialism in the Third World have all served to make the late 1970's rather more hard-nosed in the west than seemed remotely possible in the "liberal" and affluent days which saw the decade begin.

(d) As was already mentioned in relation to straits, the territorialization of sea areas will help serve as a fail-safe device for naval powers; this should improve the rationality of naval diplomacy.

It can be argued that the diplomatic potential of warships has been threatened in recent years as a result of a variety of trends, both political and economic (Booth, 1978, pp. 12-20). Among the factors which have affected perceptions of the U.S. Navy, it could be argued that (i) warships have been used too much rather than too little and that consequently the diplomatic market has been saturated; (ii) the credibility of U.S. forces has been called into question by their deployment in "unuseable" situations; (iii) their prestige has been frittered away by futile gestures; and (iv) their employment has been ritualistic rather than relevant to the subtleties required by U.S. foreign policy. In the case of the United States their usage has sometimes appeared to be not so much a continuation of politics, but merely a knee-jerk reaction of a macho leadership, the have-gunship-will-travel syndrome (or, as President Ford put it after the Mayaguez incident, "To do something was at least an expression of effort" (Rowan, 1975, pp. 142-143)).

These habits are having a deleterious effect on the diplomatic potential of the U.S. Navy. This is of some importance for western security at this juncture of world politics;

despite the growing problems they face, warships still retain unique qualities in terms of furnishing the United States with flexible military options in distant areas. This puts a premium on selectivity and appropriateness of usage, in order to nurture credibility and prestige. The territorialization of the sea will assist this task by intruding a fail-safe mechanism into the decision-making process. It should encourage decision makers to stop-to-think, and clarify their interests and objectives before allowing the availability of the instrument to shape the will to find it employment.

The need for such deliberation should guard against two possible pitfalls. Firstly, as suggested, it should discourage the instrument from shaping the will. If a government has a powerful instrument on hand, there is always a tendency to use it, to let the instrument shape the will rather than let the aim determine the instrument (Booth, 1977, pp. 100-103). In this respect some of Admiral Zumwalt's criticisms of the White House in 1971-72 are very relevant (Zumwalt, 1976, pp. 367-68). As useful as warships are, they cannot do everything. They are no substitute for an intelligent foreign policy, nor can they compensate for a bad one. Secondly, more deliberation should discourage futile employment, which risks losing prestige, one of the main assets of any military service. Because of the new constraints on force, maintaining military credibility is more difficult than hitherto. In these circumstances each diplomatic "shot" must be made to count. The overall "game" is always bigger than the next small "play"; a navy's prestige should not be sacrificed on the altar (as Mr. Ford might have put it) of simply "expressing effort."[2] If the useability and credibility of superpower naval forces are being questioned, it makes it all the more important that their diplomatic potential be carefully nurtured. This should be stressed because there are some functions which warships alone can perform; it is therefore very important that they have impact and be seen as credible when their political masters _do_ really mean business. This calls for the exercise of some restraint on use in other circumstances.

The extra political significance given to bigger parcels of sea should give the naval powers more incentive to deliberate about what they are doing. From both a national and international point of view this additional inducement to rationality is surely a development to be welcomed.

---

[2]This point is not a criticism of the _Mayaguez_ affair. This affair is involved only because it was the occasion for President Ford to make a characteristic, revealing, and quotable sentence.

(e) Some of the problems with naval presence which might be complicated by law of the sea developments might be eased by prospective technical developments. Improvements in surveillance mean that the whereabouts of ships will be better known, however distant, and this should help signalling. Improvements in weapons range mean that it will not be necessary to operate near to shore in order to pose an offensive threat. Improvements in the speed of some types of warships may help reduce the problems of reaction-time, atleast where a small force will suffice.

(f) The patchwork pattern of maritime jurisdiction and the increased significance of that jurisdiction will give more scope for the naval forces of developed states, especially the superpowers, to be used to show their support of friendly countries, traditionally an important diplomatic usage of warships. Instead of merely symbolic visits, the new boundaries and the task of policing them will give supporting warships a practical as well as symbolic significance. The Guinea Patrol of Soviet warships is a harbinger of this possibility.

(g) When commentators discuss the visibility of the flag, the tendency is always to consider the naval flag. But states can show a maritime presence in other ways. Historically, the British merchent marine helped to show the British flag in many parts of the world and on a daily basis it was a more regular and visible symbol of British greatness than the Royal Navy. A similar argument could be put for the Soviet Union today. With our attention distracted by their rakish warships, there is a tendency to overlook the use and utility of the Soviet merchant marine as an instrument by which they attempt to win friends and influence people (MccGwire, 1973; MccGwire, Booth, McDonnell, 1975; MccGwire and McDonnell, 1977). The image of one's presence is built upon more than simply the ready availability of one's warships.

4. The changing law of the sea and its implications for the traditional assets of warships as diplomatic instruments.

Of all the military instruments, warships have often been thought to possess special and indeed unique qualities in terms of their diplomatic usefulness. Cromwell called a man-of-war his "best Ambassador." There are various ways of describing these qualities, but they can be summarized as follows (Booth, 1977, pp. 33-36): versatility (the ability to perform a variety of tasks), controllability (escalatory and de-escalatory potential), mobility (the ability to move between regions with relative ease and relative independence), projection ability (as efficient bulk carriers of manpower, firepower, and hardware), access potential ("The sea is one" as an old Admiralty maxim had it), symbolism (arising out of their being chunks of national sovereignty), and endurance (their staying power enables warships to be adjacent but removable, but also removed but committable). What do the prospective changes of the law of the sea imply for these qualities?

(a) Versatility. This will be unchanged. Of all the weapons systems in a country's inventory, warships are still the most mutable. If some tasks are now better performed by other instruments, e.g., by aircraft because of the need for instantaneous response as in Shaba Province, 1978, this is not a consequence of law of the sea developments.

(b) Controllability. For reasons discussed earlier, the escalatory aspects of naval diplomacy will be assisted by changes in the legal regime. Increased distance will assist withdrawability, while the new boundaries will add another rung in the escalation ladder, thereby adding to the flexibility of the instrument. To marry the phraseology of Francis Bacon and Thomas Schelling, warships will still be able to take as much or as little of the diplomacy of violence as they wish.

(c) Mobility. There are threats of restriction here, though in practice a mixture of diplomacy and resolution should overcome most problems at an acceptable price. Whatever the new inhibitions, warships will remain a unique instrument; they alone give governments the ability to project large amounts of pre-packaged firepower to distant regions within a relatively short time.

(d) Projection ability. When "vital interests" are engaged, the use of the sea becomes a matter of capability rather than law. In both peace and war the payload of warships enables naval powers to be relatively independent military powers outside their own regions.

(e) Access potential. Changes in the law of the sea affecting maritime access constitute the biggest threat to the traditional usefulness of warships. But if there are new challenges, obstacles, and potential inhibitions, it nevertheless remains true that the movement of sizeable armed forces across the sea is much easier than it is over land or in the air. Potentially, a country with a navy remains a military neighbor to all countries with coasts. Despite the new problems, those states wanting to be global or regional military actors across a spectrum of military power have little alternative but to provide themselves with the offensive and defensive potential which warships provide.

(f) Symbolism. The role of warships as visible signifiers and representatives of a country's intentions and commitments is likely to be enhanced by prospective changes in the law of the sea. These changes will make the sea an area in which matters of legitimacy will become more important, and hence the increased symbolic potential attaching to the movement of chunks of national sovereignty. In addition, in a more general sense, the symbolic use of military instruments has grown in inverse proportion to the costliness of using naked military force.

(g) Endurance. Technology has increased the potential endurance of warships; economic considerations on the other hand have tended to work in the opposite direction. The potential staying power of warships will remain one of their advantages, but to the extent a regime change increases distances from and complicates access to bases, to this extent it will diminish the efficiency of men and ships.

In summary, we can conclude that prospective changes in the law of the sea threaten some of the basic assets of warships but promise to enhance others. All the old liabilities of warships remain, but here again prospective changes have a two-edged effect. Some liabilities may be increased (e.g., the problem of timeliness) while others may be lessened (e.g., the responsiveness of potential targets to naval diplomacy might be increased as a result of the new significance of maritime affiars). As diplomatic instruments,warships continue to have valuable, indeed unique, assets. Problems of cost and useability are growing, but warships retain special characteristics which cannot be ignored by those states with the interest and economic capacity to use the sea in extensive ways. In this respect, the prospective changes in the law of the sea pose problems for navies but they also provide new opportunities.

5. The law of the sea and the revival of naval diplomacy.

In the last ten years a number of factors have converged to focus attention on naval diplomacy, notably the expansion of Soviet naval activity, the advantages of a "blue water" strategy in the light of the Nixon Doctrine, and the occurrence of a succession of regional problems tempting superpower attention short of war. The advantages of naval diplomacy have been evident, but at the same time the costs of exercising naval power in somebody else's maritime backyard have been growing. These costs were the result of deep trends in international politics and were evident before the problem of the law of the sea raised its head in the late 1960's. In most respects the prospective changes in the law of the sea have confirmed these trends, by threatening to increase the costs involved in the exercise of naval power. But in one important respect, that of naval diplomacy, the very fact of threatening to increase costs paradoxically promises to increase the usefulness of the instrument. Law of the sea developments pose new problems, but they also provide new challenges and opportunities for those who might wish to use warships for diplomatic purposes.

In light of the earlier discussion it is difficult to accept the view that any imminent changes in the law of the sea could threaten the basic nature of naval strategy, as opposed to complicating its execution. But two groups do tend to prophesy a fundamental effect: navalist alarmists who prophesy that a traditional and favored instrument is about to be blunted, and the anti-strategist wishful-thinkers, who see in the possible horning-in of warships a blow against the use of force in general. Those who make such claims do so partly because they pitch their argument at too high a level of generalization, apparently without considering what naval diplomacy can do and how it does it. Certainly the problems involved in the use and management of all kinds of military power are growing, but we still live in a troubled world of independent sovereign states, with multiple instabilities matched by, and sometimes caused by, a proliferation of modern weaponry and military manpower. Against this background the sea is becoming a more significant political arena. One would hardly think that there is any reason to believe that warships were about to go out of business therefore. The problem is, what exactly is that business to be? This question is putting severe demands on the intellectual and political resources of the major navies of the world, whether they are in-being or aspiring.

By concentrating on change we risk overlooking continuity. In thinking about the break-up of an old order at sea, based on "freedom" (for some) we risk overlooking the extent to which what will emerge will be permissive insofar as naval activity is concerned, at least in the short-run. Assuming that there are no radical developments in the immediate future, the emerging regime will allow free transit through international straits and accepts that "what is not forbidden is permitted" as far as military activities in the EEZ's are concerned (Young, 1978). There will therefore be plenty of scope for old-style naval diplomacy, within the constraints which have already changed its character from that of the hey-day of gunboat diplomacy. If the new opportunities for more selective and decisive demonstrations are grasped, naval diplomacy will be revived to an extent thought unimaginable by the recent critics of naval power.

Policymakers and naval establishments can therefore think about the trends in the law of the sea not so much as inhibitions on naval diplomacy, but as opportunities for maximizing its diplomatic potential. Deployments near to foreign coasts will have more meaning, whether of a supportive or coercive character, because of the greater symbolism invested in the seaward extension of the national entity. This outcome is the logical implication of the extension of national jurisdiction over areas that were formerly international. The question is not whether the opportunities exist, but whether governments will attempt to exploit them by supplying the necessary hardware and strategic guidance. We can take for granted that the occasion for supportive and coercive demonstrations will arise. The likelihood is that governments will exploit these opportunities. In the case of the superpowers this may be for no other reason than that they already possess impressive navies which need employment. As it happens, both major navies have continued to do well in appropriations in recent years. It is difficult to imagine major crises in the years ahead in coastal states which will not have some warship involvement by one or both superpowers, however minor. The territorialization of the sea will enhance the symbolism of their involvement. In addition to superpower navies, we must not allow the relative decline of the western European navies to obscure the emerging navalism of some regional powers elsewhere, and the general proliferation of modern maritime weapons systems to countries hitherto lacking any naval punch. Taken as a whole, this means that the opportunities for the exercise of power at sea are present, as is the hardware; the necessary, if not sufficient, conditions objectively exist for a significant era of naval diplomacy. The sufficient conditions will be completed by the peculiar characteristics of the disputes and conflicts which will inevitably arise in the Third World, and by the interplay of forces impinging on the decision-makers in Washington and Moscow.

Despite the forecast immediately above, it may happen that the political masters of naval power will not take advantage of the opportunities offered for a more selective and salient naval diplomacy. It may be, as some have argued, that the new boundaries will impose "psychological inhibitions" on the exercise of naval power. This is a point on which there is much scope for discussion, not least about the meaning of "psychological inhibition." Presumably what is meant is not an emotional reflex-action, but rather the weighing of costs by policymakers and the decision that in some cases it will not be worth intruding into the coastal zones of particular states. This already happens. It would not be unreasonable to expect it to happen more frequently. But when intrusion is thought necessary, perhaps in the maintenance of transit rights, the symbolism of the act will be significantly enhanced.

Elizabeth Young (1974, p. 262) has been a prominent prophet of the demise of naval diplomacy. In her view the likely tendency will be for presence operations to be performed:

> only in the territorial waters of already friendly and aligned states, others--members perhaps of a regional body like the Organisation of African States--being no more willing to welcome a naval contingent than Switzerland or Sweden would be to greet a regiment of Soviet tanks or a wing of B-52s.

This beguiling and much-quoted piece of writing, which implies the decreased usefulness of warships, is mistaken and misleading in a number of important ways: (i) While purporting to make an anti-presence point, the quotation nevertheless tacitly admits the continuing value of presence forces in supportive roles. This role, in fact, has been a notable one in recent years. We need only consider the Sixth Fleet, described by one prominent Israeli as Israel's strategic defense, and the various supportive deployments undertaken by Soviet warships in Egyptian and Guinean waters. We can certainly expect it to be a role for which there will be many calls in the years ahead, for as Inis Claude has pointed out, many of the present and future problems of the Third World arise out of weakness rather than strength, out of incapacity rather than power, and out of helplessness rather than arrogance. The weak, like the poor, are likely always to be with us, and both can either be exploited or helped. The ability to project military power at great distances is relevant for both these possibilities. (ii) The arguments in Young's doubts about the presence mission actually underline the very utility of the mission. If the supportive value of warships is accepted, it is logically implied that the supported nation has security problems (against somebody) for which friendly warships can offer some assistance. They are symbolic of a military or political commitment. If this is so it is impossible to give credit to the later assertion that presence forces may become a "mere folkloristic manifestation." Providing support to one's associates against potential adversaries is hardly a manifestation of an outworn belief; it is an activity at the very heart of high politics. (iii) The comment about the Organization of African Unity misleads by its generality and by its comparison with Sweden and Switzerland. Certainly the OAU might not "welcome" a naval contingent, but Guinea, or Angola or Ethiopia might. In fact they have. More recently Zaire welcomed an intervention by western airborne forces. The behavior of nations cannot be predicted (although it might be affected) by the rhetoric of organizations. Governments on the whole are far more practical. In addition, it is very misleading to compare the political and security interests and aspirations of the OAU in general and individual countries in particular with those of Sweden and Switzerland, the secure and archetypal European neutral states. (iv) There is a logical problem in the critique. If warships are carrying out supportive tasks in the waters of friendly and aligned states, this implies that they have already been welcomed. There is, therefore, no problem for this type of presence mission. If on the other hand warships are carrying out a presence mission in waters in which they are not welcomed, that was presumably the point of the demonstration, as a way of supporting an alternative position or making displeasure evident. In this case also, therefore, there is no problem about the useability of the presence mission. The problem in this case is how to ensure that the message will be effectively transmitted and understood (and as was argued above, trends in the law of the sea will assist in this respect). (v) Regional bodies like the OAU are by no means necessarily hostile to the naval forces of the superpowers. The South American states helped to legitimize what some regarded as the illegal U.S. blockade of Cuba in 1962 while the Arab states in 1967 and 1973 welcomed the naval support given them by the Soviet Union. And what of the OAU? Did it speak out against the Soviet warships helping Angola? And has it spoken out against the Soviet presence off Guinea? Would it speak out against a naval blockade of South Africa? It certainly welcomed the ill-fated British blockade of Beira. In short, the members of the OAU and other regional bodies will always be willing to welcome external support against their local adversaries. South Africas may come and go, but regional pariahs will go on for ever. (vi) The problems of naval presences have been growing regardless of the outcome of UNCLOS. Any further constraints arising out of UNCLOS, relating to legal costs, will not be the result of "psychological inhibitions" but of rational responsiveness to the changing conditions of the time. But it is evident that the new boundaries mean new opportunities as well as new constraints, and even if there is developing what Hedley Bull has called "a maritime territorial imperative" much closer to the feeling which nations have had previously only about their sovereignty over land (Bull, 1976, p. 8), the new boundaries out at sea will always be less clear, less immediately sensitive, and further from the national nerve-endings than those on land. It will therefore be that much easier both to play chicken and to swerve away without too much loss of prestige. It will encourage rationality and add another rung on the escalation ladder. It will allow a face-off, as at Checkpoint Charlie, but without the high drama and awful consequences of failure. It will help flexibility as well as face-offs. It will allow states to lose as well as win. All this is to be welcomed both by the possessors of naval power and the supporters of a moderate international system.

The Law of the Sea and the Utility of Warships

The general implication of the earlier discussion was that within a general trend in which there will be additional constraints on the exertion of large amounts of force by superpowers, the prospective changes in the law of the sea promise to help enhance the significance of navies as instruments of diplomacy. This verdict has obvious relevance to any discussion of the utility of warships, a regular debating point in western (and presumably Soviet) defense circles in recent years. The discussion which follows examines a number of additional areas relevant to this problem.

1. Maritime sources of conflict.

The sources of dispute arising out of a changed maritime regime have been thoroughly explored by a number of writers;

the details do not need to be repeated here (Buzan, 1976; Osgood, 1976). However, the general question of maritime disputes is obviously relevant, because they will all have potential military implications in terms of local arms races, missions, procurement patterns, and so on.

Potential maritime sources of conflict can be characterized in a variety of ways: (i) Regionally. A region-by-region survey of law of the sea disputes forms the bulk of Barry Buzan's A Sea of Troubles?. (ii) Issue areas. This approach was also adopted by Buzan; he classified the sources of dispute under four main headings (disputes over national boundaries, those over rights within national boundaries, those over rights in the ocean area beyond national jurisdiction, and those arising from non-ocean sources). Robert Osgood classified the main issue areas as economic zones, commercial boundaries, straits, security measures, superpower naval interests, and the deep seabed. (iii) Relevant actors. Rather than examine the sources of conflict regionally, Osgood (1976, pp. 12-14) has looked at the prospects for conflict in terms of possible contenders: Major Powers versus Major Powers, Big States versus Small States and Small States versus Small States.

Despite some alarmist views about the "chaos" which might arise out of a regime change, there is a fairly general agreement that the prospects for armed conflict are limited. This is a sensible conclusion. Although prospective changes in the law of the sea could be the source of significant disorder arising out of disputes over rights, Buzan has properly stressed a range of countervailing factors; crystallizing norms and limited capabilities; the issues involved will rarely carry politically important emotional appeal; the remoteness of the disputes will help the "encapsulation" of the problem and provide various options for settlement; and few of the disputes will have immediate and significant strategic implications for the countries concerned (Buzan, 1976, pp. 45-48). There are some exceptions, and these exceptions are important. Among the maritime disputes with serious strategic implications, those between the Soviet Union and Norway on the one hand and Japan on the other seem the most dangerous. Among the national confrontations which might take on a maritime dimension, the Greek-Turkish dispute over the Aegean is one of the most dangerous, and certainly one of the most complex. In these disputes, as in others, it can be argued that if the states concerned are rational, then they will use non-violent methods by which to solve their differences. It hardly needs adding that behavior in international politics is often determined by feelings rather than the rational calculation of interests.

It would be surprising if a regime change at sea failed to produce at least several crises, together with a slight increase in the thankfully low level of violence at sea. These possibilities increase the need for governments to show that at least they intend to defend their rights in what they regard as their own patches of sea, if not beyond. There is no more effective way of doing this than deploying warships. We cannot predict that particular disputes will take on a military character, but we would be very optimistic indeed if we believed that no clashes would occur. The ingredients are present in many areas, in terms of interest and capability; one only requires a triggering event. This is always the most difficult thing to predict, but there are many possibilities in a period of unstable international politics. "Pleikus are streetcars," McGeorge Bundy said in explaining how the Viet Cong attack had affected the U.S. decision to bomb North Vietnam. If you wait long enough, one will come along.

2. The arms control dimension.

Elizabeth Young (1974, p. 262) has described "One unavoidable side-effect" of UNCLOS as "substantial new constraints on military activity at sea," what she then termed "a kind of de facto arms control not specifically intended or designed as such." Hedley Bull (1976, p. 9) found this point "hard to deny," though he added the reservation that the idea might underestimate the determination of the great powers to protect their interests, by force if necessary, and that it overlooked the possibility that some regional powers might change their ideas about naval power when they acquired "blue water" fleets of their own.

On first sight, the tendency to confine military activities to particular areas, the "patchwork" implication of the law of the sea, does appear to be a form of arms control (i.e., restraint internationally exercised on deployment). However, the arms control dimension is not as simple as this suggests. It is necessary to make some reservations and consider some of the further implications of the arms control dimension:

(a) Although something described as "a kind of...arms control" might sound self-evidently a good thing, it should be noted that there has grown up a real uncertainty within the strategic community about the value and meaning of arms control. In comparison with the verities of the early 1960's, arms control is now regarded more skeptically, particularly in the light of SALT, which appears to many to have stimulated arms racing rather than the reverse. Arms control is easier to define than to recognize. To label something "arms control" often begs more questions than it answers.

(b) Some forms of arms control in the maritime environment are not self-evidently desirable. In criticizing the idea of a completely demilitarized seabed, Laurence Martin (p. 36) has argued that bottom-based sensors would be an important source confidence-building in any agreement designed to enhance seaborne deterrence by prohibiting the trailing of SSBN's. More generally, the possibility exists of arms control agreements in which one side might secure a unilateral advantage, or arms control negotiations in which both sides are tempted to engage in heavy arms racing in order to amass bargaining chips.

(c) Although a more patchwork character to naval deployments would tend to support the standard definition of arms control, this in no way diminishes the essential strategic utility of warships. The sea still uniquely provides large-scale military access to distant regions, and arms control is not a separate activity from strategy. Arms control is merely a continuation of strategy with some restraint on military means.

(d) As well as the law of the sea intruding into arms control, the opposite is sometimes the case. Some arms control treaties have implications for the law of the sea (for example, the Antarctica Treaty and the Latin American Nuclear Free Zone). The related concept of "zones of peace" has practical implications. It could affect some existing operational patterns if put into effect, although the increased range of SLBM's, together with the very limited significance of nuclear weapons outside the U.S.-Soviet context means that the establishment of zones of peace would be of limited strategic significance outside the Mediterranean and even there it would be marginal, given the reduced nuclear significance of the Sixth Fleet, as long as the agreement was restricted to nuclear weapons and did not include nuclear propulsion.

Arms control and the law of the sea can therefore overlap at various points; both can be conceived as extensions of naval strategy. The Mediterranean and the Indian Ocean have both been the objects of some (albeit limited) arms control attention in recent years. Several developments led the Carter Administration to worry that the Indian Ocean might become the scene of a costly and dangerous naval arms race. This led to some consideration of naval arms control in the region (Haass, 1978, pp. 50-57). If this fear were valid for the Indian Ocean, the logic pointed even more strongly in the direction of examining arms control for the Mediterranean. The advantages which an arms control agreement (superpower disengagement) would give to naval diplomacy in terms of providing a fail-safe mechanism, increasing the selectivity of usage, and enhancing the significance of those demonstrations which do take place are identical to the effects which were claimed earlier for the trends in the law of the sea (Booth, 1978, pp. 20-24). The situation in the Mediterranean suggests that rather than maintain the cold-war concept of presence, the United States should be thinking about a reduced presence (or a mutual withdrawal by treaty) for normal times, thereby permitting a surge in the event of crisis. This would help maintain the value of the capital of naval diplomacy and make up in political impact what it might lack in reaction time. In this conception, naval strategy, the law of the sea, and arms control usefully and effectively walk hand-in-hand.

3. Changing emphases for new navies.

Much of the discussion about the law of the sea suggests that prospective changes will promote a variety of new tasks as well as new laws for old navies. However, it can be argued that what is happening is changing emphases rather than new tasks, and that the changed emphasis would have happened regardless of UNCLOS. Indeed, it could be argued that rather than changing the emphasis in naval tasks, the new norms which have emerged as a result of UNCLOS have prevented these emphases going as far as they might otherwise have done.

The main focus of attention has been the policing or constabulary tasks in coastal waters. The rationale given to this task by law of the sea developments is readily apparent (note the "sovereignty flights" of Canadian aircraft) but pollution, economic exploitation and increased traffic would have pushed matters in this direction in any case; in fact, there might have been more emphasis on this task in an unregulated situation marked by determined unilateral claims. The need for good order in contiguous seas existed independently of any change in the law of the sea. If it can be argued that there would have been more trouble at sea in the absence of the EEZ concept, as a result of more disputes over rights, then it can be seen that some states will have fewer requirements for naval forces than they would otherwise have had. In short, the development of the law of the sea has let some states off the hook in a military sense.

Having said that, however, the changing regime obviously does affect political expectations and naval requirements. The creation of new rights and responsibilities over larger areas of sea creates an objective "need" which did not previously exist. Although this need does not necessarily have to be met, several factors will tend to mean that at least a token effort is made. There is the feeling behind the idea of the "maritime territorial imperative"; warships will become badges of sovereignty. The acquisition of these badges will be made easier by the superpowers and other developed countries looking for local supporters and outlets for naval armaments. At the same time the existence of so many regional security problems in many parts of the world might well provoke those states unable to cope to call for support in the shape of naval aid, equipment, advice, and even direct help. There will be plenty of scope for a maritime version of the assistance already extensively used in internal security and economic development. The trend towards jurisdictional fragmentation will also be further assisted by the immediate punch given by some types of coastal warship. Some countries will undoubtedly be too preoccupied by other matters to make more than the most token naval effort, but others will take it very seriously. Buzan (1976, 46-47) has drawn attention to a very important difference of perception in this respect between developed and less-developed states:

> whereas a developed state would tend to look upon enforcement as a technical problem, a less-developed state may not have that option. Where it is physically unable to police its zone adequately, its government may have to resort intermittently to more drastic political or military action in order to influence violators. One might therefore expect that developing countries would tend more towards extreme actions, such as violent seizures of vessels or disruptions of political and economic relations, than would more powerful developed states.

If the conclusion to be drawn is that naval power encourages maritime responsibility, the practical implication is that the proliferation of modern naval vessels to less-developed countries is an act of international responsibility.

Some pressures are therefore encouraging some coastal defense forces to become more like "real" navies (some EEZ's cover considerable amounts of ocean). On the other hand, some wider pressures have constrained some former great navies to become more like coastguards. These wider pressures mainly arise out of the sheer cost of maintaining sizeable "blue water" navies, together with a decreasing need for distant water operations as a result of withdrawals from empire. While this process was taking place, the new needs in coastal areas were building up. These same pressures were present but by no means as strong for the superpowers. On the one hand they had the will, interest, and capability to contemplate extensive global efforts, while on the other hand they already maintained impressive coastal forces for their rather different reasons. New attention was naturally drawn to the constabulary role, but the superpowers could not avoid having the basic shape of their naval forces fixed by general war requirements, although this difficult and improbable scenario has caused much discussion among naval establishments and their critics alike. For some reason naval forces have come under particularly heavy criticism for their alleged lack of usefulness at the highest levels of violence in major war. This is a strange criticism, but one which is badly dealt with by naval establishments. Certainly warships will find it extraordinarily difficult to carry out their missions in general war, but are they any different in this respect from tanks or infantrymen or aircraft once nuclear weapons start flying? In general war, all the traditional military missions become a nightmare. The law of the sea is essentially irrelevant at such levels of violence except to the extent that any peacetime inhibitions on ASW, oceanography, or geographical familiarization will degrade operational capabilities and skills.

The debate about major navies in recent years has often been shaped by arguments about the "hi-lo mix." The bulk of discussion suggests that law of the sea developments are likely to confirm the trends of the "lo" end of the spectrum. On the other hand, it was argued earlier that the legitimizing of coastal rights by international agreement will tend to reduce any sense of urgency in this respect (for most countries) while continuing general war requirements (together with some fairly bad scenarios regarding threats to sea lines of communication) will continue to draw much attention to the "hi" end of the spectrum for the superpowers. Running just beneath these "hi" needs, there are such considerations as the new navalism in several parts of the world, regional problems, and increased opportunities for naval diplomacy. This suggests that the ships conceived for the "hi" end of the spectrum should also have built-in flexibility for the middle levels. This inevitably seems to suggest a continuing need for aircraft carriers or at least some means of getting air power to sea.

By pushing out the naval interests of new states, by promising to enhance naval diplomacy, and by helping to create some maritime-based disputes, the main implications of the changing law of the sea in terms of naval tasks lead in a variety of directions. They add complications to almost all tasks; they let some countries off the hook; they add renewed emphasis to existing trends at the lower end of the spectrum; they have no effect on the higher end; and finally, most interestingly, they promise to draw more attention to the "middle" or "grey" part of the spectrum in the "hi-lo" debate.

4. Intervention from the sea.

One of the traditional primary tasks of warships has been that of projecting military power ashore in the form of amphibious operations. If this activity is classified as belonging to the (upper) middle of the spectrum of force, then this would appear to be one area where prospective law of the sea changes have negative rather than positive implications.

There has been an extensive literature in the last 10-15 years about the declining utility of great power intervention (Knorr, 1966). Expressed simply, the argument is that the political, economic, and military costs have risen, while the purposes for which intervention frequently proved useful in the past are no longer relevant for the foreign policies of the superpowers. Prospective changes in the law of the sea appear to add another weight to the cost side of this argument.

Running parallel with the general trend against great power intervention, there are a number of particular maritime developments. MccGwire (1977, pp. 3-25) has listed these as follows: (i) Advances in weapons technology. As the specialized demands of naval war have grown, so have warships become less flexible. (ii) The proliferation of modern weaponry. Medium-sized fleets are proliferating. (iii) The Soviet Navy. This adds new complications for the United States. (iv) Maritime rights. Creeping jurisdiction complicates naval planning and increases potential costs. As the latest of these factors on the scene we can conclude that developments in the law of the sea are confirming existing trends against intervention.

From an international viewpoint, inhibitions on intervention are generally thoughtto be desirable, and therefore whatever further inhibitions are added by legal rules are to be welcomed. This is not a self-evident truth, however. It is easily possible to envisage occasions when justice as well as order might be served by military intervention, and occasions when maintaining the balance of power by intervention will be seen as more important than sticking to the letter of international law (Bull, 1977, pp. 142-45).

Developments in the law of the sea promise to compound the growing costs which have to be faced when intervention is considered. However, we should not forget the extent to which we still live in an "anarchical society." We should not therefore underestimate "the menacing interaction of trends" in the years ahead (Brown, 1977, Chapter 21); "the spectre of a new mercantalism" (Bull, 1976, p. 3; Kemp, 1978); the determination and will of superpowers to "go it alone" if necessary (Kissinger, 1978, pp. 5-10); the absence of a "recognised and respected structure for conflict management" (Strategic Survey, 1978, p. 4); the many sources of instability, and the many opportunities where the intrustion of external force will be to somebody's advantage. In addition, one can exaggerate the extent to which "the great equaliser" has arrived in the shape of midget navies with giant punches (Howard, 1976, p. 6). International politics are always changing, but more kaleidoscopically than in a linear direction. "Intervention is dead" proclaimed the war in Vietnam. "Long live intervention" proclaimed individual African states in 1978, despite the rhetoric of the OAU. Colonialism had gone; a form of taut neo-colonialism seems to have arrived. Interventions will still take place, if not as frequently as in the age of imperialism. Whether or not they intervene, or whether it be by land, sea, or air, the fundamental decision of governments will principally be determined by factors other than international law, including the law of the sea.

5. The changing utility of warships.

Some of the well-established answers about the utility of warships have been under scrutiny in recent years (Booth, 1977, Chapter 9). The business of adjusting military means to political interests has been particularly disturbing for the traditional naval powers. Technological, political, and economic changes affecting the maritime environment have left the old answers about the utility of navies in a state of flux. However, this breast-beating uncertainty has almost exclusively been a concern of the western maritime nations. Any uncertainties in the Soviet Union have not been overt, while the increasing potential of the middle and smaller navies seems so adequately to meet their needs in using the sea that there is little questioning of costs and benefits. The turning point for the former monopolist naval powers occurred because some of the foreign policy goals for which navies had always played an essential supporting role either changed or disappeared. This brought into question the character of naval needs. Additional complications have arisen because of the improbability of general war and the uncertainties entailed in the proposition that in the modern world,naval strategy, like other forms of strategy, is less concerned with contributing to victory in war than with furthering national interests short of war.

An important distinction must therefore be made between those few states wishing to use their navies in support of foreign policy in distant seas, and the majority interested in exercising naval power only within their own coastal waters. There is little evidence that the many small-navy countries are dissatisfied with the return they receive from the money they invest in ships. But Third World countries are facing problems of naval adjustment because of law of the sea developments, although in no way comparable to the major adjustments forced on the former naval giants because of earlier drastic shifts in their international position. Law of the sea developments pull in two ways. On the one hand they encourage a form of mini-navalism. There are EEZ's to be patrolled, there is good order to be maintained, and there is the badge of maritime sovereignty to be fashioned. On the other hand, these same developments pull in the opposite direction; the new norms discourage others from trampling on new-found rights and therefore tend to alleviate some naval concerns. This increase in the feeling of security is presumably in the interest of all.

Whatever type of state we are considering, the cost of all forms of military power is increasing. Governments tend to be more aware of a wider range of alternative instruments. However, military power is certainly not without utility. For one thing, the rising cost of war enhances the use of military power for deterrence. Consequently, the non-acquisitive utility would seem to have declined, however, although it should be added that between smaller countries there are many fewer of the military inhibitions which have come to characterize relations between the great powers. War at sea still has a future, but it will be written by the naval historians of such countries as India, Iran, Israel, and Brazil. For the major naval powers the deployment of power at sea will be more a matter of deterrence and diplomacy rather than brute force. On the other hand, the navies of all types of states will have increased utility for constabulary purposes (a feature which parallels the increased utility of armed forces generally in the domestic setting). Regardless of developments in the law of the sea, therefore, it could be argued that navies would still have had decreasing utility for the great naval powers in an acquisitive sense, but that they would have additional utility for all states in enhancing the non-acquisitive functions of military power. This is simply illustrated by the case of old-style military intervention. One of the reasons for its declining utility on the part of the great powers is directly related to the increasing utility of the defensive military potential of smaller countries. Although it has been rather limited, developments in the law of the sea have had some impact on the question of utility. They have served to enhance the significance and hence the utility of warships for constabulary functions of all types of states, and they will give new opportunities for the diplomatic usage of warships for the great naval powers and for the newer naval powers which are challenging existing perceptions about naval balances either globally (as is the case with the Soviet Union) or regionally (as is the case with Iran). Since most states are satisfied with using their navies for constabulary functions and non-acquisitive roles in regional seas, this suggests that their warships have no need to fear for future employment.

Despite their growing problems, the major naval nations (the producers rather than the consumers of international order at sea) cannot escape from their military responsibilities without facing significant risks. As far as their navies are concerned, this means that there will always be a pressure for them to modernize as long as they have interests in using the sea, and especially if they wish to support policy in distant regions. While many states will be interested in a practical sense only in what happens immediately off their shores, perhaps up to twelve miles, many others will be interested in what happens beyond, up to 200 miles. Whatever a particular state's attitude to the ongoing regime at sea, whether it wants to challenge it, suffer it, defer to it, or enjoy it, its ability to threaten and use force at sea will have some bearing on the responsiveness of other states to its diplomacy on maritime-related matters.

The Implications for Naval Policy

In addition to the general implications discussed earlier, law of the sea developments have also been thought to have implications of a more detailed and practical character for naval policy, particularly in terms of technical requirements and operations.

1. The technical requirements of lawships.

If the emphasis is to be on non-acquisitive uses, and on deterrence and demonstration in particular, it can be assumed that this will have implications for the shape of maritime forces. However, when we examine the problem we can see that the shape of maritime forces will not be significantly changed as a result of law of the sea developments. All that can be said is that these developments have crystallized thinking and helped accentuate some particular qualities.

Richard Hill (1972, pp. 178-79) has discussed the character of future maritime law-keeping forces according to their operational reach.

(a) All nations with coasts have the requirement of maintaining good order in the territorial sea. At the bottom end of the scale, therefore, they require at least a few patrol craft. This will build up with the "size, importance, and maritime bias" of the country concerned. At its biggest it will be an organization as comprehensive as the U.S. Coast Guard. The needs of such forces are the ability to apply carefully graduated force, to keep the sea, to move rapidly when required, to gather information, and to communicate. Aircraft and helicopters will be essential for some, useful for all.

(b) Nations with deep sea interests (fishing) may require vessels for administrative support, and perhaps to support their regulation. Sea keeping and endurance would be their primary needs.

(c) Nations wishing to employ maritime forces in the protection of their legal interests on a world-wide basis require vessels capable of operating independently in conditions of minimal threat, with some backing force capable of taking a tactical initiative. Combat aircraft will be necessary in some situations, submarines less so. The nearer the ships are to an area of dispute, the more essential will be the ability to deploy graduated force. This means guns, some self-defense, good data acquisition and communications, and command and control facilities. Higher quality forces, including fleet submarines and combat aircraft, will act as deterrents to higher levels of action.

Hill's conclusion is that:

> It so happens that such forces are not very different from the shape of many modern navies. If there are differences, the law-keeping requirement tends to weight the balance away from general war-fighting ability towards the capacity for low-level confrontation.

If this is so for most navies, the superpowers, and to a lesser extent their most capable allies, have to build for the "worst case," which is as far removed from law-keeping operations as we can get. This means that the shape of their naval forces is primarily determined by general war tasks. However, while the "unthinkable" must be given attention, this should not be to the exclusion of the probable, and here the earlier discussion pointed to the importance of flexibility in the middle of the spectrum. This implies that warships should not become so specialized and valuable in order to be of some use against the ultimate threat that they cannot be used at lower levels, since a convergence of trends (regional conflicts, law of the sea disputes, the increasing importance of maritime affairs, the new navalism of local powers, superpower interests, problems of access to resources) suggests that this is a level at which attention will be focussed on whatever comes in the way of confrontations at sea. The requirements are a technical matter, but clearly there will be a need for offensive and defensive capabilities; endurance may be more important than speed; good reconaissance capabilities will be needed, but also the ability to communicate with enemies as well as friends; and it may well mean a decision to accept some loss of quality in return for greater quantity and risk-taking potential (Eberle, 1976, pp. 29-32). Despite their costs and their vulnerability, this seems to point to the continuing need for aircraft carriers, particularly as modern combat aircraft as well as mini-navies are proliferating in many parts of the world. Easily mobile airfields, which provide a range of defensive and offensive potential, can, as yet, be provided only in one (unavoidably costly) way.

Some of these requirements cannot be easily met. When this is added to the wide range of different interests in using the sea, it is apparent that although the gap between the small and the mighty navies may decrease slightly, it will not decrease by much. A more significant reduction will come between the emerging naval powers of the second rank and the mighty in the area of usable force in the middle of the spectrum. This would have happened regardless of law of the sea developments, although some aspects of this new pattern will be given some shape and salience by the burgeoning of jurisdictional fragmentation.

2. Operations.

The complications and opportunities produced by law of the sea developments discussed earlier were seen to have implications for operations in a strategic sense. However, they will also have implications below that level, in terms of the planning, tactics, and techniques of operations. Among the main implications which have been talked about are the following.

(a) The need for pre-crisis planning (Knight, 1977, pp. 38-39). This will be the more important for states which believe that the law of the sea has developed in an adverse fashion. Steps to be taken might include the negotiation of bilateral and multilateral treaties to serve naval interests, the threat or use of force to prevent claims which threaten naval missions, and the employment of covert operations, e.g., emplanting ASW devices on continental shelves.

(b) Tactics. International law affects the exercise of naval power in a wider sense than the narrow law of the sea as interpreted in this paper. A variety of rules affect the use of weapons systems, the rights of neutrals, rules of engagement, and so on. Because these exist, and because they exist in an increasingly complex environment (including one where the war/peace distinction is less clear), it behooves naval staffs to become better equipped to handle the legal aspects of naval planning, whether it is in the drafting of rules of engagement or in their interpretation (O'Connell, p. 189; McCoy, 1977).

(c) Coordination in planning. The convergence of problems at the intersection of developments in naval strategy, foreign policy, and international law calls for the coordination at a policymaking level of specialists in each field; it is important for each specialist, in turn, to attempt to become literate in the language and concepts of the others.

(d) Enforcement procedures. There is a particular requirement to work out enforcement procedures, in order to assist naval officers in carrying out their duties, and in order to minimize misunderstandings from those being dealt with.

(e) The need for effective two-way communication. If law, strategy, and diplomacy are to work effectively and with minimum violence in the unsettled period ahead, it is important that those involved can communicate quickly and effectively with each other. The Mayaguez incident was interesting for many reasons, but one of the problems it revealed was the poverty of communications between the United States and Cambodia. At one critical stage the U.S. President could only communicate quickly to Phnom Penh through the press! (Rowan, 1975, pp. 204-205). If it be glibly assumed that this is a matter mainly for the naval power concerned, it should be added that the matter was of even more importance to the local country. After all, the Cambodians suffered most from the confusion.

There are other possibilities which could be discussed, but all the detailed implications in the area of naval operations have one thing in common. They all relate to one of the central concerns of strategy, namely, the attempt to ensure a proper relationship between instrument and aim, between power and purpose, and between context and capability. This requires generalists as well as specialists, and intellectuals as well as technicians. Shared knowledge can sometimes prevent avoidable errors. George Walker (1978, p. 99) has written:

> Not many military commanders can or should make policy or practice law; not many lawyers can or should make policy or make war; not many policy scientists or decision theorists wage war or practice law. All three disciplines, and other professions as well can, however, learn from the processes of others and appreciate the multifaceted issues of seapower and ocean law...

Conclusion: Navies and the Developing Law of the Sea

In the years ahead we can undoubtedly expect to see more friction at sea than we have been accustomed to in the post-war period. In large part this is because in the recent past we have become accustomed to expect so little. As new as well as old forces of order and disorder develop and rub against each other, disputes are bound to occur, but widespread and violent conflict need not be assumed, short of some extreme possibilities which are thinkable, but not presently predictable. In approaching this changing maritime environment, nations will be subject to a wide variety of pressures. They will also have at their disposal a wide range of instruments. If the sea is no longer "one," neither are the ways of dealing with it. The conclusions below are either summaries of what was discussed earlier, or extrapolations.

1. <u>The influence of navies on international legal development.</u>

- Navies will have a role in the regime change, regardless of the character of the regime or the nature of the change.

- Naval power and naval interests will help determine whose norms survive.

- The less the likelihood of a satisfactory agreement, the greater will be the propensity for dispute and conflict; this will give more scope for the naval support of diplomacy.

- To date, naval interests have had a significant impact on the evolution of law of the sea developments. They have certainly not wrecked the prospects for securing a treaty, but some problems could always become the occasion for major disputes.

2. The influence of international legal developments on navies.

- The character and stability of whatever regime emerges will affect naval strategy and policy in a variety of noteworthy but not fundamental ways.

- At the lower end of the spectrum of force, foreseeable developments will accentuate some trends but may limit the naval needs of some coastal states.

- At the highest end of the spectrum of force, the law of the sea is almost irrelevant. It will slightly degrade performance, but this is likely to be of limited concern to all except those professionally involved. For the rest, general war is a nightmare to be avoided rather than a mission to be accomplished.

- In the middle levels, law of the sea developments will complicate almost all naval operations, but at the same time it will provide some new opportunities for the exercise of naval diplomacy, making it both more selective and salient as an instrument of policy. Naval diplomacy is a potentially valuable instrument of policy, and more careful usage will nurture its credibility and prestige.

- The increasing significance of naval diplomacy arises out of the changing character of strategy in this historical period, which emphasizes the manipulation of threats and symbols in an environment in which force is less usable by the great powers. Parallel with this,a number of regional powers recognize the usability and utility of force in traditional ways.

- The convergence of trends suggests that naval forces should optimize for flexibility in terms of probable usage rather than for specialization for the improbable. The main impact of this proposition is on the balancing of quantity and quality.

- Law of the sea developments pose challenges to naval forces, but also new opportunities. This places new intellectual demands on naval establishments comparable with those of the last century. Whereas the problem then was one of technology, it is now a more complicated mixture of technology, politics, economics and law.

- The new regime does not mean a basic change in the nature of naval strategy; it is more a shift in style. It is no more an end to naval diplomacy than the shift from close to distant blockade represented the end of blockade.

- The increasing complexity of issues will require the orchestration of a greater mix of expertise, with the result that thinking about naval strategy will be less narrowly focussed, and will also continue to move from the periphery of strategic studies.

3. Law and politics.

- States will use the law of the sea as a continuation of political, economic and strategic interests.

- In addition to naval operations being complicated by legal developments, naval strategy (the particular interests of particular navies) can also be furthered by the changing rules of the law of the sea.

- The western naval powers will have to decide between going all the way with the Third World on the naval aspects of the law of the sea problem, or standing on the traditionalist viewpoint, as represented by the Soviet Union.

- The western states have less to fear from restrictive changes than the Soviet Union, or rather the Soviet Navy. The interests of Soviet foreign policy and the interests of the Soviet Navy are not necessarily identical.

- Law of the sea positions often seem to be determined more by national styles than the careful articulation of interests. There is Third World rhetoric, American absolutism, Soviet insecurity, British traditionalism, and French national sensitivity. Behind these styles there has been exhibited a willingness to change positions and adopt moderate positions on some issues.

- Attitudes to the law of the sea can appear to be based on irrational impulses, but the law of the sea can also be rational and instrumental, assisting naval strategy, discouraging potential adversaries, providing the opportunity to harmonize policies (or secure unilateral advantages) helping to avoid having to take some military steps, and even helping to save some countries from their bad habits.

4. Forces for order and disorder.

- Order at sea has been the norm in the modern period. The pattern has been stable and flexible, and has generally adjusted peacefully to challenges. It may have been untidy, but it has worked.

- A good deal of sense has been shown in UNCLOS. There has been a greater willingness to look for agreement between the major and minor actors in both practice and rhetoric than has been evident in some of the other episodes of conference diplomacy in the post-war period. It is not true that "whatever the subject, the conference is just the same."

- The ability of diplomacy and commerce to adjust to change is often overlooked; this adds an urgency to the desire to maintain the well-established status quo.

- Many worst cases are conceivable, but it is easy to exaggerate the change which is immediately likely, just as one can underestimate the strength of continuities in international politics. If rationality and economic and functional factors favor the continuation of order, this suggests that most trouble will result from inefficiency and irrationalities rather than as the continuation of carefully worked-out policies.

- The tendency of the naval powers to worry about the problems which smaller powers can cause results in their overlooking the extent to which they have the power to threaten the others, and the extent to which the superpowers in particular are perceived to be able to go it alone.

- Maritime affairs are likely to be a few degrees more dangerous, at least until new norms settle. But everything else seems destined to be at least a few degrees more dangerous.

5. <u>The future regime.</u>

- The sea will continue as a troubled common, with a steady growth of national jurisdiction into coastal zones.

- Whatever the character of the treaty which emerges, many issues will still be left to be settled by customary development. In this situation, order will be more a creature of bilateral relations, which in turn places a premium on diplomacy.

- Naval interests have so far been met by developments at UNCLOS. The seabed and straits are not seen to be problems at present, while military activities within EEZ's may continue (by silence rather than designation).

- The idea of reserving the high seas for "peaceful uses" and the growth of conflicting uses of ocean space within EEZ's suggests that the present generally satisfactory position will not be indefinite. These are signposts to a future which promises to increase the growing costs of exercising naval power in distant seas.

- Law will play a part if the oceans are to be governed by order, but stability requires that the law be supported by generally agreed norms and backed by politically visible policemen.

- If the maritime regime is to develop in an orderly fashion, the expectations of the participants will be a significant factor. The more trouble is expected, the more it is likely to arise. Whether or not pessimism is valid in an objective sense, optimism must be the operating principle for practical politics. A positive and optimistic attitude to the future of the law of the sea should help bring about that future. A negative and pessimistic attitude may have a self-fulfilling effect in the opposite direction. Since it would be difficult to predict in detail and hence avoid the manifestations of the latter, it makes sense to embrace the attitude that is least likely to produce such troubles in the first place.

6. The wider meaning of security.

- The development of order in international life seems destined to depend upon a more generally acceptable distribution of wealth and an increase in the satisfaction of national self-images.

- It is necessary for states to formulate their goals and try to structure the "game" so that it accords with their preferences. For the developed states this means law instead of violence. It requires the formulation of acceptable goals, and then the shaping of instruments and tactics accordingly, to encourage others to act in such a way as to strengthen the norms we support. Navies have a role in this, used either forcefully or with restraint, depending on circumstances.

- For the naval powers to equate "security interests" with naval interests is to assert what remains to be proved. Security is finally taking on a wider meaning among strategic thinkers than merely the manipulation of the instruments of force. "Better security" might come from harmonizing policies with the majority rather than ensuring an easier life for what is only one instrument of policy, albeit an important one.

7. A moderate international society.

- Law of the sea developments in general promise to impose complications on naval operations while at the same time offering some hope of a slight increase in the sense of security of that large body of states which was historically the victim of gunboat diplomacy.

- If the possession of maritime capability discourages extremism and encourages responsibility within EEZ's (leading to enforcement being treated as a technical matter) then the proliferation of some kinds of naval weaponry can be conceived as an act of international responsibility.

- Law of the sea developments help the evolution of a moderate international society by encouraging rationality, giving more flexibility in escalation strategies, assisting the tactics of diplomacy (especially withdrawal), channelling attention to an area where sensitivities are not as great as on land, and enhancing the symbolic use of warships.

- Law of the sea developments run parallel with some arms control proposals (especially superpower disengagement) which might have healthy effects on the regions concerned.

- Some law of the sea developments point in the direction of moderation rather than chaos at sea. Disputes are bound to occur, but they might take place within a regulated and orderly framework of customary and conventional rules. The troubled common may well become a notable area of stability in comparison with the world's chronically troubled continents.

REFERENCES

Booth, K. Navies and Foreign Policy. London: Croom Helm, 1977.

Booth, Ken. U. S. Naval strategy: problems of survivability, usability, and credibility. Naval War College Review, Summer 1978.

Brown, Neville. The Future Global Challenge. London: The Royal United Services Institute, 1977.

Bull, Hedley. Sea power and political influence. In Power at Sea I. The New Environment, Aldephi Papers No. 122, Spring 1976.

Bull, Hedley. The Anarchical Society. A Study of Order in World Politics. London: The Macmillan Press, 1977.

Buzan, Barry. A Sea of Troubles? Sources of Dispute in the New Ocean Regime, Adelphi Papers No. 143, Spring 1978.

Colombos, C. John. The International Law of the Sea, 6th Ed. London: Longmans, 1967.

Eberle, Rear-Admiral J.H.F., RN. Designing a modern navy: A workshop discussion. Power at Sea II. Super-Powers and Navies, Adelphi Papers No. 123, Spring 1976.

Fisher, Roger. Basic Negotiating Strategy. London: Allen Lane, The Penguin Press, 1971.

Haass, Richard. Naval arms limitation in the Indian Ocean. Survival, March/April 1978.

Hill, Captain J. R., RN. The Role of Law at Sea (thesis). Department of Laws, University of London, King's College, 1972.

Howard, Michael. Order and conflict at sea in the 1980s. In Power at Sea III. Competition and Conflict, Adelphi Papers No. 124, Spring 1976.

Jackson, Robert. South Asian Crisis. India-Pakistan-Bangladesh. London: Chatto and Windus, 1975.

Kemp, Geoffrey. Scarcity and strategy. Foreign Affairs, January 1978, 56(2).

Kissinger, Henry A. The Admiral Raymond A. Spruance Lecture, March 8, 1978. Naval War College Review, Summer 1978.

Knight, H. Gary. The law of the sea and naval missions. USNIP, June 1977.

Knorr, Klaus. On the Uses of Military Power in the Nuclear Age. Princeton, NJ: Princeton University Press, 1966.

Knorr, Klaus and Morgenstern, Oskar. Political Conjecture in Military Planning. Princeton University, Policy Memorandum No. 35, November 1968.

Laughton, J. K. The sovereignty of the sea. Fortnightly Review, May 15-August 1, 1866, V.

Martin, Laurence. The role of force in the ocean. In Osgood, Perspectives on Ocean Policy.

McCoy, Dennis F., Crd. USN, International Law and Naval Operations. Center for Advanced Research, Naval War College, 1977.

MccGwire, Michael (Ed.). Soviet Naval Developments: Context and Capability. New York: Praeger, 1973.

MccGwire, Michael. The geopolitical importance of strategic waterways in the Asian Pacific region. Orbis, Fall 1975, 19(3).

MccGwire, Michael. Changing naval operations and military intervention. Naval War College Review, Spring 1977.

MccGwire, Michael, Booth, Ken, McDonnell, John (Eds.). Soviet Naval Policy: Objectives and Constraints. New York: Praeger, 1975.

MccGwire, Michael and McDonnell, John. Soviet Naval Influence: Domestic and Foreign Dimensions. New York, Praeger, 1977.

New York Times, May 22, 1973. Quoted by Mark Janis in Sea Power and the Law of the Sea. Lexington, MA: Lexington Books/D. C. Heath & Co., 1976.

Njenga, Francis X. Africa. In R. E. Osgood, et. al, Perspectives on Ocean Policy. Conference on Conflict and Order in Ocean Relations October 21-24, 1974. Washington, DC: The Johns Hopkins University, 1975.

O'Connell, D. P. The Influence of Law on Sea Power. Manchester: Manchester University Press, 1975.

O'Connell, D. P. Transit rights and maritime strategy. RUSI (Journal of the Royal United Services Institute for Defence Studies), June 1978.

Oliver, Captain Edward F. Malacca: dire straits. USNIP, June 1973.

Osgood, Robert. Military implications of the new ocean politics. In Power at Sea I. The New Environment, Adelphi Papers No. 122, Spring 1976.

Osgood, R. E., Hollick, A. L., Pearson, C. S., Orr, J. C. Toward a National Ocean Policy: 1976 and Beyond, Ocean Policy Project, The Johns Hopkins University. Washington, DC: USGPO, 1975.

Rowan, Roy. The Four Days of Mayaguez. New York: W. W. Norton and Co., 1975.

Strategic Survey 1977. London:IISS, 1978.

Vayrynen, Raimo. The sea-bed treaty reviewed. World Today, June 1978.

Walker, George K. Sea power and the law of the sea: the need for a contextual approach. Naval War College Review, Spring 1978.

Wylie, J. C. The Sixth Fleet and American diplomacy. In J. C. Hurewitz (Ed.), Soviet-American Rivalry in the Middle East. New York: Praeger, 1969.

Young, Elizabeth. New laws for old navies: military implications of the law of the sea. Survival, November/December 1974.

Young, Elizabeth. Jurisdiction at sea. World Today, June 1978.

Zumwalt, Elmo R. On Watch. New York: Quadrangle/The New York Times Book Co., 1976.

COMMENTARY

Frank L. Fraser
Chief Hydrographer to the Government of India

I would like to congratulate Professor Booth on his very exhaustive paper on the military implications of the changing law of the sea. The document we have before us has enlarged the horizons of the military implications of sea law in a measure which hitherto I certainly had not perceived. The depth of research undertaken by the author of this excellent thesis presents a scenario of military and maritime interests vis-a-vis the law of the sea that has certainly saved me the time and effort of plunging into the large amount of literature that has grown all around the subject. However, with such a formidable paper before me, I venture with some trepidation to offer a few preliminary comments as it was only a few days ago that I received the paper in India.

In the first place, I would like to make it clear that I am neither a lawyer nor a professor nor a naval strategist nor a naval policy maker nor a foreign policy maker. I am the Chief Hydrographer as you have just mentioned and responsible for charting and defense oceanography at home. My comments, however, are my personal views resulting from my continued association with the Law of the Sea Conference since its Sea-Bed Committee days in 1973, during which I covered second committee matters in my delegation. I make these comments also as a member of the entire international team of negotiators and draftees attending the Law of the Sea Conference who have been the authors of the provisions contained in the ICNT. My comments would naturally be influenced by the experience of the negotiating process at the Conference of the Law of the Sea, by the tensions and pressures which characterize the intense negotiations that resulted in package compromise proposals which we hope offer the most promising solutions for a consensus, and the awareness of the complicated political and security interests involved in the negotiations.

A harsh sense of realism was essential in order to arrive at the best balance among the multitude of competing interests of the developed and the developing states and the regional and interest groups. But I would not venture to say that this realism was always present in the negotiations at the Conference. The changing attitudes of developed and developing states, both of which exhibited a degree of unpredictability and uncertainty of their positions with regard to some of the so-called hardcore issues that still plague the negotiations, also have to be borne in mind.

It is important to remember that the Law of the Sea Conference functions by consensus. It has so far not voted on a single article or amendment, even on an indicative basis. The consensus procedure is considered necessary so that wide spread agreement could be achieved on what can truly be regarded as universal law. It is this procedure of consensus which has made the negotiating process difficult and complicated, but nevertheless an essential device if a generally acceptable regime respected by all is to emerge.

Professor Booth has forcefully brought out that the law of the sea is a matter of foreign policy and international relations rather than mere legalities. He has highlighted the essential political character of the problems and said that to recognize the political nature of the law of the sea issues is important because what matters in practice is not so much the law as the underlying norms.

He has also made the point that while there are undoubtedly important and interesting military implications in the law of the sea issues, for most countries these are not really as significant as some of the economic implications. In his introductory portion of the paper, he has pointed out that for almost all countries, strategy will not be an overriding factor in the policy of the law of the sea itself. Professor Booth has also warned that if a regime is not satisfactory to important and/or numerous actors in the system, then the foundations for the development of the regime will be shaky.

On these points, I am in full accord with Professor Booth. And I would even go to the extent of saying that he has reflected the mood of the Conference as realistically as could be appreciated from a distance. However, it is my understanding from reading the paper by Professor Booth that his thesis on the military implications of the law of the sea stems from the premise that there is a trend for the exclusive economic zone to become territorialized, judging from his discussion on creeping jurisdiction under the heading "How Far Can It Go?". I find it difficult to agree that at this stage of the ICNT such a trend exists. The implications of territorialization have been clearly brought out by the author. I would not hesitate to agree with him, if in fact this were so. However, the negotiations as they have proceeded, I believe, do not point to the existence of this trend.

The allegation of creeping jurisdiction has been hurled at the sponsors of the concept of the exclusive economic zone from the time it was first proposed during the early Sea-Bed Committee days. The vices and virtues of creeping jurisdiction should be weighed against the exercise of distant water freedoms so that we can get our perspectives right.

Except for a few maritime powers, the nature and characteristics of the legal status of the 200 mile exclusive economic zone has now been universally recognized and accepted as described in the ICNT. The existing provisions describing the regime for the exclusive economic zone is an extremely sensitively balanced text and part of an overall package incorporating the application of the compatible high seas provisions. The so-called creeping jurisdiction of territorialist states has therefore been balanced against the traditional freedom of the seas concept favored by the maritime powers. The concept has been an implicit sui generis nature and character of the exclusive economic zone that it is neither high seas nor territorial seas and having a specific legal regime.

Most of the high seas freedoms are preserved, as mentioned by Professor Booth in the section entitled "Where Are We Going?", however stating that the ICNT has adopted the tactic of silence within which is hidden a number of rights for navies. He quoted these rights as the right to conduct naval exercises within the EEZ of other states, the right to hold weapon tests there, the right to set up platforms for military use, and to deploy non-nuclear weapons.

While agreeing with the first two of these rights, I cannot agree that the regime for the EEZ allows for the other two remaining rights, owing to the nature and characteristics of the EEZ being implicitly a sui generis zone having a specific legal regime.[1]

Some writers may at once point a finger at me that this would be creeping jurisdiction. My answer to them is that they must adapt to the changed circumstances eminently brought out by Ken Booth, and that is what the law of the sea is all about. Such are the realities, subtleties and nuances of the ICNT, so designed, that the interests of coastal states on the one hand and the interests of maritime powers on the other are carefully balanced. The military and maritime interests have had their impact on the EEZ since these have been taken into account by the group of coastal states at the time of drafting this portion of the regime. The rights and duties of coastal states and the rights and duties of other states have also been clearly spelled out.

The provision for the freedom of navigation and other internationally lawful uses of the sea related to this freedom, such

---

[1]The use of the Seabed for military purposes is being considered under the Seabed Arms Control Treaty provisions which prohibit the emplacement of nuclear weapons and other weapons of mass destruction on the Seabed beyond 12 nautical miles from the coast.

as those associated with the operation of ships and aircraft, were accepted by the coastal states' group in 1977 after very hard negotiations, accordingly redrafting the 1976 RSNT provisions for the EEZ and the definition of the high seas. Hence, it would be incorrect on my part if I were to agree that the military sphere has been circumvented in the ICNT as stated by Professor Booth. The same applies to his remarks that warships have transit and other rights by default rather than by designation. In fact, it is the other way around.

Article 60 of the ICNT, which deals with installations and structures on the seabed in the EEZ, does not explicitly preclude the installation of military devices, but does so implicitly as records of the seventh session of the Conference will show. It would be unrealistic to be explicit about what can be done and what cannot be done in the military sphere in the EEZ as it would only tend to provoke either side.

So it was necessary not to have any provocative provisions if agreement was to be reached. For instance, one has Peru's proposal to make it explicit that military installations on the seabed are prohibited. Other examples are the Soviet proposal for the no sovereignty clause to be included in the definition of the EEZ and the group of coastal states' amendment to clearly define the legal status of the EEZ as neither high seas nor territorial sea. None of these was accepted by the Conference at its recently concluded seventh session since each disturbs the extremely delicate balance of the ICNT. The legal status of the EEZ has reached a stage in the ICNT where there is no more room for compromise without blowing up the whole issue again.

The only area of dispute that could arise in the regime would emanate from the exercise of residual rights that would in any case be required to be resolved under the provisions of Article 59 of the EEZ regime, notwithstanding Article 297's exempting disputes concerning military activities from compulsory procedures. I believe, therefore, that the use of naval diplomacy as practiced today within or without the EEZ does not impinge upon the rights or jurisdiction of coastal states and in my view should not create apprehensions of a legal nature inhibiting the exercise of naval diplomacy in these zones. The apprehensions would be relevant only in their political and economic consequences, which at any rate would be appreciated by the maritime power concerned.

For as long as international disputes or tensions continue, areas of potential intervention will always be speculated about where the maritime powers would like to exercise naval diplomacy by a seen or unseen presence and influenced by their own political compulsions, especially if the area is one of rivalry between the two super powers. Similarly, regarding straits used for international navigation and the regime for archipelagoes the realities of military implications in the law of the sea have been fully taken into account by devising a liberal regime wherein the right of transit passage through these areas for all ships without specifying the type of ship (whether military or civil, surface or submarine) has been provided. Hence, mobility for fleets would remain unaffected. In fact, the provisions for both straits and archipelagoes regarding unimpeded transit passage have been accepted over the last two years as given in the ICNT during which time no amendment of any significance has been adopted by the Conference.

In fact, in the case of archipelagic states that decide to designate sea lanes, there is a duty to allow for a width of as much as 50 nautical miles for these sea lanes. A task force, for instance, spread 50 miles across and 40 miles in depth would be accommodated in such a sea lane. I would say the military interest has been generously accommodated. After all, a 50 mile wide sea lane is not required for the safe passage of a lone merchant ship.

Regarding the continental shelf, agreement on this issue has not yet been reached and no compromise has emerged which would command the substantial support likely to lead to consensus. This is one of the few hard-core issues still remaining to be resolved before the Conference; the military implications have begun to manifest themselves more than ever before on this issue and are creating difficulties to finding a solution.

The use of the seabed for military purposes pertaining to underwater listening devices, if not for emplacement of weapons, it may be reasonable to suppose, appears to be a matter of serious concern to the Soviet Union who opposes any extension of national jurisdiction over the continental shelf beyond 300 nautical miles. It would, therefore, appear that national jurisdiction over the continental shelf rather than the international area of the deep seabed could be of greater significance to military interests.

In conclusion, I would be inclined to agree with some of the conclusions drawn by Professor Booth in his exhaustive paper. However, I would also like to say that far from complicating almost all naval operations, there would be a further set of "do's and don'ts" to guide navies in general, besides the generally accepted rules of international law such as the IMCO regulations for the prevention of collisions at sea. A new law of the sea treaty would introduce a better order into the conduct of naval operations, as planners and operational staff would be more confident in their knowledge of what could or could not be done.

However, much of what is presently involved will undoubtedly continue. At the same time, some of it will also become unnecessary. A new world order for the sea would necessarily be a compromise between the interests of Third World countries and the industrialized countries, more on the economic aspects of the law of the sea than on the naval aspects. Western naval powers would have to go along with the compromise contained within an overall package rather than any extremist viewpoint.

I would like to end my comments with a note of cautious optimism about the chances for a new political and economic order for the seas, within which a more rational and confident naval policy could be applied by all maritime countries, developed or developing. Such a new order is likely to emerge in the near future once the few remaining hard-core issues are resolved. The new world order would reduce existing maritime disputes and tensions in the world rather than escalate them.

COMMENTARY

Shannon D. Cramer, Jr.
United States Navy

I feel like the admiral who died and went to heaven. When he arrived at the gates, St. Peter met him personally. He looked over and saw a large group of clergymen, clerics, priests, and rabbis standing over there, but St. Peter personally escorted him in his sleek limousine to his quarters. And sure enough, the others were made to walk along side the road. As he went into a beautiful villa, he passed the small cell-like rooms where the other members who had passed away and gone to heaven were in dingy cells eating bread and water, and he sat down to a huge repast served to him by beautiful angels overlooking a beautiful picture window of heaven. He turned to St. Peter and he said, "I'm very embarrassed because I don't understand why I'm getting this treatment." St. Peter said, "Well, you realize how seldom it is we get an admiral up here."

I tried to weave that joke into lawyers versus clergy and St. Peter said, "No, they're all busy on the law of the sea, so they're not up here either." And we didn't discuss the price of the admiral's brains, Dave, but they're scarce too, I assume.

But I am delighted to be here. I was called out of retirement and just signed on board last Friday. I am flattered to be in such distinguished company with a group of people that have worked for several years on structuring what I think is a forward step for all seafaring men, mariners, naval types, anyone who goes to sea in ships. And I think that you have done a tremendous job.

I appreciate the opportunity to comment. When Bill Browe called me even before I signed on board, he apologized and he sent his respects to this group. He is involved in an exercise which has taken a lot more of his time than he anticipated. I am sure that he would prefer to be here in this scenic setting and talking to you in my place.

It is a pleasure to be on the same rostrum and podium with my good friend Admiral Fraser because we made supreme sacrifices for our countries about a year ago and attended the International Hydrographic Organization meeting for two weeks in Monaco.

To get to the purpose of being here, I would say it is almost impossible in the short time available to give a meaningful critique to the many complex interrelated issues which Ken has so ably presented for our consideration. And at the risk of oversimplification, it appears to me that the thrust of Ken's paper is that no foreseeable international regime at sea (and I emphasize foreseeable) will fundamentally affect the exercise of naval power.

Ken would like to assure me and my fellow naval officers that whether or not we view changing ocean law as eroding the traditional concept of the freedoms of the sea, the evolving law does not forecast a radical change for naval strategy. He suggests that the regime which appears to be emerging from the law of the sea negotiations may in fact enhance the use of naval power as a political instrument. This reflects an assessment with which I agree, that the qualitative nature of the regime suggested by the ICNT regarding navigation remains unchanged. Ken has presented a very convincing case. I concur with the general thrust. But I do not want to leave the impression that any sweeping changes suddenly appearing in the ICNT could be acceptable to the military.

Everyone knows in today's world of advanced and advancing technology and with the increasing interdependence of states that the body of law governing two-thirds of the world's surface will change. Military uses of the ocean, or if you will the broader category, navigational uses of the sea, are but one of the many issues of ocean law which states are studying in great detail.

For many, like the United States, who are dependent upon sea lines of communication, navigational issues rank among the most important considerations, if not the most important, in formulating an oceans policy. For most states, however, issues related to ocean resource development are more significant. It is these resource and resource-related issues which motivated the world community presently to focus its attention on the law of the sea. As Ken has noted, the traditional law of the sea, at least as it is related to navigation, worked quite well in that there was a remarkable degree of order in this area of international life. As Edgar Gold pointed out yesterday, it was during the Dark Ages when there was really no law of the sea that the pirates *et al.* enjoyed freedom to the detriment of those who wanted law and order.

If changes, however, are inevitable, we must consider structuring these changes in an orderly manner to serve best the interests of the international community. This brings me to the point of questioning what, if any, purpose is served in amending ocean law relating to navigational freedoms which has historically worked so well.

I do want to make clear that I am not of the school that believes some changes in the law of the sea, for example, resource jurisdiction, will necessarily affect the rules governing navigation nor result in radical change for naval strategy. Those theologians of naval power who view that any erosion of traditional freedom of the seas could result in fundamental changes for military operations are looking at the worst case situations, and these cases certainly merit study. The concept which they are generally studying is that of the phenomenon of creeping jurisdiction. Although scenarios can easily be conceived which would have significant impact upon the exercise of naval power, not every change in the ocean law will doom its effective utilization.

Today we are speaking, however, in the context of what appears to be emerging from the ongoing law of the sea negotiations; I address the foreseeable future. For its part, the Department of Defense has taken the position that a comprehensive treaty which, one, preserves the freedom of navigation and overflight of the high seas; two, which permits unimpeded passage through, under and over the straits used for international navigation; and three, which preserves other traditional high seas freedoms in a reasonably defined economic zone, except those connected with resources, would satisfy U.S. navigational interests. You have heard these many times. Some would say that this is no more than a restatement of our traditional views. These perhaps do not represent radical changes in ocean law pertaining to navigation but nonetheless, when analyzed in the context of rights and duties of all participants in ocean affairs, the changes are significant; they are a departure from the traditional norm.

It appears at the present time that an ocean regime containing these elements will emerge in the near future. These principles are supported by those most interested in navigation; apparent consensus is emerging from the law of the sea negotiations on this point. On the one hand, as pointed out by Ken, naval interests will probably impact more on the development of the law of the sea than will law of the sea developments impact on the changing character of naval affairs. Any regime that would emerge in the absence of a treaty, albeit less stable and uniform, would probably retain most of the above principles affecting military activities.

I should mention at this point that the Department of the Navy and Department of Defense strongly believe that conclusion of a widely supported comprehensive law of the sea treaty is in the best interest of all. We will continue to strive toward that goal, and I hope to see it done before I retire again.

I agree with Ken that the character and stability of whatever regime emerges will have some effect on naval strategy and policy in a variety of noteworthy ways. Law of the sea developments need not, however, unduly complicate naval operations. I anticipate the use of naval diplomacy as an instrument of policy will be tailored to suit the times, as it has in the past.

The assertion that Western powers must choose between going all the way with the Third World on the naval aspects of the law of the sea challenges and standing on a traditionalist viewpoint disturbs me. I must note that not all the Third World is like minded. I frankly do not see the necessity of naval powers making such a choice.

Law of the sea negotiations seem to indicate that the legitimate interests of the Third World can be accommodated even though this necessitates significant change from a traditionalist viewpoint. This accommodation is possible because many Third World states recognize that retaining traditional views on navigation insofar as possible will not adversely affect them and in many instances will be beneficial to them.

This also leads me to believe that seas need not necessarily continue to be a troubled common, as Ken has stated. He used the word "troubled common." I like Mahan's definition of place of wide common. But I am an optimist and I try to shy away from trouble.

In summary, significant change in many aspects of the law of the sea need not fundamentally change naval strategy. We all recognize there are many difficult issues to be resolved before a comprehensive treaty emerges from the law of the sea negotiations. On the other hand, many difficult issues have already been resolved. The sentiment of many delegations is that the time has arrived to conclude these negotiations. I am optimistic that the world community will decide to develop the maritime regime in an orderly fashion. I am confident that naval power will continue to be a valuable instrument of policy. I believe that naval strategy can be adapted to the maritime regime which is foreseen in the years ahead as it has been in years past.

COMMENTARY

Michael MccGwire
Dalhousie University
Halifax, N.S., Canada

Ken's paper was an excellent review of the subject, and my disagreements are mainly ones of emphasis. Meanwhile, Gary asked me to focus my comments on the Soviet Union's interests in the military use of the sea and to compare these with U.S. interests.

Let me start by making two points which help in understanding Soviet policy. First of all, the Russian navy has traditionally been seen as an expensive necessity, rather than as a preferred instrument of policy, as was and is the case in the West. Traditionally, the main threat to Russia has come from land, but navies were necessary to prevent maritime powers such as Britain and France from dictating the outcome of events in sea areas adjacent to Russia. And, of course, there are four of these sea areas, all widely separated, each requiring its own fleet to defend it.

The second point concerns the Soviet Union's perception of the threat from the West. Although it no longer expects a premeditated attack, it considers that the possibility of nuclear war is inherent in the present situation. It does not want such a war; indeed, the avoidance of such a war is a primary objective of Soviet foreign policy, but if such a war is forced upon them, they are prepared to fight and win it. The fact that they think the problem through in this way, and make plans to cover such a contingency, is important to understanding their interests. The Soviets define "world war" as a fight to the finish between two social systems. Victory is synonymous with survival, defeat with extirpation. It is the catastrophic consequences of defeat that explain the relative priority given to planning to fight a world war, despite the admittedly low probability of having to do so.

The concept of war fighting brings with it a requirement for strategic reserves, which lends a new importance to sea-based nuclear delivery systems, such as missile submarines and strike carriers. These can be held back from the initial exchange with a fair certainty of survival. They therefore acquire a particular importance as components of the national strategic reserve. Remember that the military leadership is dominated by ground forces; hence the governing concepts will be those of the land battle.

With that as background, let us now look at the Soviet navy's two main missions in the event of war with the West, as stated by their Commander in Chief, Admiral Gorshkov. The first mission is to carry out strikes against targets on land, and the second mission is to counter the enemy's sea-based strategic strike capability.

What are the implications of the first mission? The Soviet SSBN force has three overlapping functions, inter-continental strike, intra-theatre strike, and being held back as part of the strategic reserve. In other words, you do not know exactly when these missiles will be used, but the security of the SSBN force must be ensured meanwhile. The Soviets are seriously concerned for the security of their SSBN force, and not without reason. During the Congressional appropriation hearings in 1967-68, it was clearly stated that the U.S. intended to develop two new classes of submarine, one very fast and the other very silent, which would be designed to deal with Soviet SSBN.

To protect themselves against this threat, the Soviets have adopted the concept of defended bastions. In the Pacific area you will see that the Sea of Okhotsk has a useful deep, located behind the defensive barrier of the Kuril chain of islands. In the Northern Fleet area, there is the Barents Sea, but that tends to be shallow, and probably the best area is the deep at the top of the Greenland Basin, i.e., to the West of Norway.

These bastions are part of a wider concept of area defense which is fundamental to Soviet naval strategy. Area defense is based on two zones, an inner one, where they expect to have command of the sea, and an outer zone, where command is contested. The greater part of Soviet naval policy over the last 50 years can be explained in terms of pushing out this inner zone of effective command to natural defensive barriers such as the Baltic and Black Sea exits.

In the Northern Fleet area, the natural defensive perimeter would run from North Cape, up through Bear Island and Svalbard; one can assume that at the onset of war the Soviets would attempt to seize these islands and the intervening Norwegian coastline. However, with the new requirement for SSBN bastions at the head of the Greenland Sea, the defense perimeter would have to be moved forward to the 70°N parallel, at the very least, and preferably it should now lie across the Iceland/Faeroes Gap.

This of course brings Soviet military interests into direct conflict with the Norwegian economic zone, and I suspect that this explains partly why the Soviets are so concerned about excluding any implication of sovereignty from the definition of the EEZ. This conflict is present in peacetime, since the Soviets have to develop the capability to defend their bastions.

The second mission is to counter western sea-based strategic delivery systems. I do not think that this has any serious implications in law of the sea terms. It is of course conceivable that U.S. ballistic missile units might wish to operate in another country's economic zone, as for example in the Mediterranean, and that the Soviet Union might bring pressure on the coastal state to deny such use and even to authorize Soviet units to act on its behalf. But this does not seem very likely, since the same arguments could be used against the Soviet Union in the Norwegian Sea. Meanwhile, the new Trident system will take U.S. forces further out into the deep ocean. The Soviets are placing increased reliance on space-based detection systems.

So much for war with the West; the key factor here is the Soviet Union's vital interest in the Norwegian Sea, i.e., Norway's EEZ, as a defense zone shielding its SSBN bastions.

The next problem is war with China which has a lower calamity factor but a higher probability factor, and must therefore be covered in contingency plans. Law of the sea implications stem from the requirement to supply the Far Eastern front by sea, on the assumption (which is shared by both the Russians and the Chinese) that the trans-Siberian railway will be taken out in the early days of war. There are two main ways of supply by sea, across the Arctic and across the Indian Ocean.

Finn Sollie tells me that the Soviets made an Arctic transit in 18 days last year. But this was an experimental passage, north of the Arctic islands, and I would not have thought that you could write this route into your war plans at this stage. It could, however, become important in the longer run. This would have implications in terms of their jurisdictional aspirations in the Arctic.

The more certain and more likely route is across the Indian Ocean, shipping supplies across Iran if the Suez Canal is blocked. This means that the Soviet Union has a vital interest in unimpeded passage through the Indonesian archipelagic barrier, because the supplies must get through to the Far Eastern front before the stockpiles run out. This time-critical interest is unique to the Soviet Union. Japanese concern for the free flow of oil and raw materials can be met by diversion around Australia, which (in 1975) would have raised their cost of living by about 1%. American SSBN can also take the long way round; carrier deployments, which could be time-critical, serve a different order of interests to those engaged in a Sino-Soviet conflict.

Turning to the U.S., we can see that their war-related requirements do not depend on the law of the sea in the same way. This is partly because the Western alliance is better provided with water-front real estate, partly because the interests are so different, and partly because most of the missions do not require permanent deployment in peacetime.

Let us now move on to the employment of naval forces in peacetime and particularly to the projection of traditional force. Once again I will start with the Soviets and make a couple of background points. First, there are different perceptions of the status quo and how it shapes the attitude towards military intervention. The Soviets see the status quo as a dynamic process of change, driven by historical inevitability. This predisposes them to a policy of opportunistic exploitation, only intervening where the situation is already moving their way. In the West we see the status quo as being static, which prompts us to a series of rearguard actions and fire-fighting operations. In consequence, the West tends to have a much more active policy in terms of overseas intervention, with their navies playing a major role.

The second point is that the Soviet Union is Mackinder-land but in a way which Mackinder could not have foreseen because the aircraft was not then available. Eighty-five percent of the world's population lives within 3,000 miles of Soviet territory, a mere trans-Atlantic air flight. It is true that China runs along 4,500 miles of the southern frontier, but only Southeast Asia is truly in balk to Russia by air. Europe, North Africa, the Middle East, and Indian subcontinent are all within 2,000 miles. In other words, we are talking of an alternative means of access.

The strategic qualities of the sea derive from the access it provides to nonadjacent areas. For centuries, this was a unique form of access,and it still is for the sustained shipment of large quantities of supplies. But in other circumstances the air now offers an attractive alternative, particularly when fast reaction is required. So the Soviets have an advantage here. And there is a basic asymmentry between American and Soviet requirements for seaborne intervention, because of Russia's classical Mackinder posture.

Bearing in mind these two points, let us look at the Soviet Union's involvement overseas, military involvement overseas. Between 1955 and 1965 their primary instrument of policy was arms supply and training. They were raising the cost of western imperialistic intervention. The more weapons they put in,the harder it became for the West to interfere with the "course of history." Sometimes, this policy also served broader strategic interests, as for example, the supply of naval arms to Indonesia, which drew the British strike carriers east of Suez away from the NATO area.

From 1965 to the present, you have the emergence of a more assertive policy and the evolution of a doctrine concerning the role of a Soviet "military presence" in the pursuit of overseas objectives. This was the result of a series of convergent, and I think, coincidental developments, such as the availability of a projection capability which had originally been acquired for general war purposes; change in threat perception and in the balance of risk and opportunities; and the rising competition for China. The final decisions were precipitated by the Arab/Israeli war of attrition which started up in 1969-1970 and forced the Russians to make up their minds about deploying forces overseas.

I think that this was the subject of a wide-ranging argument between 1969 and 1973, the result of which was the decision that the Russians would provide training, arms and equipment, and logistics instruction, including battlefield logistic support. But the combat role or direct involvement would be delegated to the forces of "revolutionary states." You saw that happen, first of all, in the Arab/Israeli war in 1973, and subsequently in Angola and Ethiopia.

What are the primary instruments of Soviet policy in this type of situation, the projection of force? The primary instruments are Soviet arms and training, supplied by the merchant fleet and by airlift. What, then, is the role of the navy? It is basically supportive, both in a logistic and a military sense. We have seen it being used to deter attacks by local states on Soviet-provided logistic support. This can be seen, for example, with the Israelis against the Arabs, the Somalis against the shipment of supplies from Aden to Ethiopia. But in my judgment, and I must emphasize this can only be a judgment, despite its avowed mission of countering imperialistic aggression, the Soviet navy would not protect a client state against direct American intervention. In other words, the Soviets have a rather different approach to the whole question of using naval power in peacetime, from the traditional Western approach.

So far, the Soviets have been involved only in supportive intervention, and it is important to emphasize the distinction between supportive and coercive intervention. Ken Booth did mention the distinction, but tended to talk more generally about "naval diplomacy" as a blanket category. It is important to keep the two categories distinct because they have important differences.

First of all, the type of intervention determines the type of capability you need to carry out such an intervention. Second, the cost benefit calculus is quite different for the two different types of interventions. Supportive intervention only requires the provision of sufficient additional capability to shift the balance of power. It assumes the availability of facilities within the state, either ports or airfields, and some measure of political support. Supportive intervention has a pretty good record of success since 1945. And, I would argue, it has continuing utility.

But coercive intervention, whether actual or threatened, not only requires more effort, but also has a fairly bad record. But here again we need to distinguish between different categories of coercive intervention, not only because they differ in effectiveness, but also because they generate very different requirements in terms of military capability.

At the bottom of the scale of coercive intervention we have the coup-de-main, which relies upon surprise and shock to achieve success. At the high end of the scale we have military invasion, where we actually occupy a country. In the middle lies a very broad range of operations involving the threat or use of force, where coercion takes the form of punishment. For example, you can punish with a carrier air strike or with a punitive raid by marines.

There are widespread doubts about the effectiveness of this middle range of coercive operations. The Brookings study was skeptical about its political effectiveness, and in general it has a poor record of success. It can be argued that, except within the national security zones of the major powers, where power gradients and political justification are both high, this type of coercive intervention has been counter-productive.

These strictures do not apply to the two ends of the spectrum of coercive intervention. The coup-de-main, the short, sharp, rectifying operation, still has utility. At the other end of the scale, there is no evidence to suggest that a properly planned invasion by a superior power, mobilized for war, would not succeed. All that has been argued is that the broad middle range of coercive intervention is no longer politically effective.

The conclusion is important because it is this broad middle range of intervention operation which has provided a primary justification for the peacetime deployment of naval forces. If we drop the middle range of coercive intervention from our policies and plans, it has an immediate effect on naval requirements. Supportive intervention can be provided by air lift and merchant ship, as the Soviets have demonstrated to some effect. The coup-de-main can often be done by air, as the Israelis demonstrated at Entebbe. Of course the maritime invasion requires naval forces, but this is a carefully thought out operation, where reaction time is not critical, and the build-up may take six months or even a year.

By foreshortening the argument in this way I have had to ignore all sorts of factors, but it does get across the main points. Namely, supportive intervention has a continuing role, but navies are not necessarily the best way of meeting this requirement. Coercive intervention has lost much of its political utility, particularly in the broad middle range, which used to provide the bread and butter of peacetime naval operations. The significance of these developments is that even if the law of the sea negotiations go sour, or if we end up with a more restrictive regime in the EEZ than we would like, then for two reasons the situation will not be as disadvantageous to maritime powers as we are inclined to think. First, the utility of coercive intervention has waned; and second, there are now means of gaining access other than with naval forces.

Let me close this part of my discussion by saying that I am generally skeptical of naval posturing as a means of coercing other states. As an example, I would cite the deployment of the carrier Enterprise to the Indian Ocean during the Indo/Pakistan War in December 1971 which achieved nothing at the time, aroused intense hostility in Delhi, and ensured Indian support for a Soviet naval presence in the Indian Ocean. This leads on to Ken's argument that the advent of the economic zone, rather than limiting the utility of naval forces, will increase their utility by providing an additional frontier which can be flouted as a diplomatic signal. This may be so in theory, but in practice I find it rather far fetched. The impact of naval forces stems from their latent power and the ability to bring it to bear if required. In bringing such power within range, I doubt if it makes much difference whether or not the national jurisdiction represented by the EEZ is flouted. This brings me to another point of disagreement with Ken's paper, where he argues that, because the use of coercive force is increasingly constrained, therefore the role of navies as symbols is increasingly important. To my mind, this is a fallacy. The value of naval forces as a symbol stems from the beholder's appreciation that they can and will be used to support national interests if the need arises. To the extent that their use is constrained, so too is their value as a symbol.

Finally, we must ask ourselves whether or not the U.S. role of "world gendarme" (as the Soviets term it) is as important as some claim. Is the U.S. navy important to the maintenance of "good order" at sea, a role taken over from the British?

We tend to assume that America and the West have some special interest in the use of the sea, which leads them to be more concerned for orderly navigation and freedom of the seas. But this is largely a myth. When we look more closely, or objectively, we see that all states in the world have a purposive interest in the use of the sea for maritime trade and that a very large number have a greater interest in the use of the sea for that purpose than does the United States. The latter's special interest in the use of the sea turns out to be strategic, to be able to project force by sea. And of course that is something very different. And we find that when we talk about freedom of the sea, and freedom of navigation, what we are really talking about is freedom to project force by sea.

Now, just as all states in the world have a purposive interest in the use of the sea for maritime trade, so do <u>all</u> states have a <u>preventive</u> interest in its use to project coercive force against their own territory. Consequently, there is a commonality of interest in the use of the sea, purposive for goods and people, preventive for projection of force, and only a handful of states have a purposive interest in projecting coercive force overseas. The latter must therefore be wary of claiming their special interest as being of benefit to the world at large.

I suggest that this commonality of interests in the free use of the sea for commerce is being reinforced by the proliferation of national shipping lanes and by the interdependence of maritime trade. The spread of maritime weapon systems among coastal states should allow them to promote order in their adjacent sea areas, to secure their use for the conveyance of goods and people, and prevent their use for the projection of force by external powers. This seems to me a very healthy development. We are all too prone to talk about "responsibility" when what we really mean is "Western interests" and to claim that developing nations are "irresponsible" when what we mean is that they pursue their own. It is time the traditional maritime powers stopped thinking in terms of "policing the world oceans," and handed over the task to the coastal states, who have as great, if not a greater, interest in maritime trade and orderly navigation in their adjacent waters.

So I conclude that developments in law of the sea will not have a significant impact on the traditional use of naval force in peacetime. This is mainly because that use is already being constrained by other developments such as advances in the technology of maritime weapon systems, by attitudes towards the use of coercive force in the international system, and by the spread of nation states. I foresee that developments in the law of the sea will lead to a more orderly use of military force at sea, which I think is eminently desirable. And the conflicts which do arise will be constrained and framed by the evolving law of the sea and on the whole will not be provoked by these new developments.

DISCUSSION AND QUESTIONS

KENNETH BOOTH: Each commentator, I think, misunderstood what I had to say in one respect. I would just quickly like to get these out of the way to correct any wrong impressions.

I was unsure at the start about using the word "territoriality" among a group of international lawyers. I was using "territoriality" in the sense that writers about animal behavior use the word. Territoriality in this sense does not mean the spread of actual sovereignty into the EEZ. I was talking about a _feeling_ of property over a patch of water. So, I think I led Admiral Fraser astray if I gave him the impression that the EEZ was about to become an area of sovereign territory.

Admiral Cramer said I was advocating "going all the way with the Third World." That goes further than what I implied. What I was trying to say was that if it were decided for foreign policy reasons that the industrialized western world should harmonize with the Third World, then there was nothing in naval strategy which should be allowed to present an insurmountable obstacle.

In answer to Professor MccGwire, I think I said quite a lot about the distinction between "supportive" and "coercive" intervention in my talk; I agree with him entirely in his views about that because I have just been putting them forward.

On his second point about symbolism and non-use, I think Professor MccGwire has extrapolated what I said beyond that which makes sense, or accords with the real world. What I was saying was because states do not want to suffer the rising costs of using force, they have come to rely more on the symbolic uses of military force. That is not the same as saying major powers will not ever use military force or that the potential targets will cease to worry about the possibility that hurt might be done to them. I am not saying on the one hand you have got the traditional use of force and on the other hand you have now got exclusive symbolism (whatever that means).

DANIEL CHEEVER: I am most grateful for a very stimulating session and particularly for the first paper by Professor Booth. But I am a little bit puzzled about what may be a problem of asymmetry. Is the notion that there is a new opportunity for naval diplomacy perceived in the same way by both sides in a world which quite obviously is still bipolar in a naval sense? That is, are we to assume that in the paper you are constructing a general theory about naval diplomacy applicable to today's world? Or, was it rather an analysis that is useful for geographic reasons for _one_ of the two super powers or _one_ of the two military alliances? Will Soviet leaders conclude there are increasing opportunities for naval diplomacy as readily as NATO leaders can be expected to?

KENNETH BOOTH: I was talking about what you call the general theory. I think the points I was making would in theory be equally valid for both sides. There are lots of asymmetries in the way the two super powers use the sea, and perceive their naval interests, missions, and so on. But in theory what I was saying was intended to be valid for both.

THOMAS CLINGAN: I first want to congratulate the major speaker and the panel for a series of very, very interesting papers that I am sure will stimulate a great deal of discussion. I have three or four comments to make.

First of all, I have not had the opportunity to read Professor Booth's paper but I am looking forward to it. I did detect in his presentation a slightly different treatment, for example, between the economic zone and international straits. I think he is entirely correct in his observation that the developing littoral states (particularly developing littoral states in straits) gain a political advantage from a less restrictive straits regime. It enables them to avoid being put into an awkward position where they may have to, on a given occasion, choose between major maritime powers or even decide whether to favor or not favor a single major maritime power in the question of transit through straits. When transit is free, that choice does not have to be made and that is a political advantage to the littoral state.

In that regard, by the way, any discussions that the United States may have had with Indonesia with regard to Malacca, for example, were not over rights but how those rights should be exercised. I think that is a perfect example of the kind of thing he is talking about. When you have a clear regime for transit that everybody understands, then it is not necessary even to have conversations of that nature so it relieves a developing state of that burden.

I may have misunderstood him with regard to the economic zone, but it seems to me the same kinds of political considerations might apply there as well. I am not talking, as I think he did, about a naval power putting vessels into the zone to demonstrate a point vis-a-vis that coastal state. I am posing the situation where that power may like to transit the economic zone of a coastal state in order to make a demonstration in the economic zone of its neighbor. It would seem to me that the degree to which you liberalize the navigation regime in the economic zone again, you might relieve that coastal state through whose zone they wish to transit of the embarrassment of making decisions that might not favor a neighbor with whom they want to preserve neutrality. I agree with Admiral Fraser and

Admiral Cramer about the status of the economic zone articles in that regard.

With regard to what you mentioned concerning naval disengagement, you made your point well, Professor Booth. Naval disengagement does allow more flexibility in the use of naval forces if they have been withdrawn. You may deal with this in your paper. I just point out there are political consequences as well. Once having engaged, the disengagement of one naval power, if it is a unilateral disengagement, may signal the abandonment of political goals that were otherwise sought by that power in that area.

Now with regard to Frank Fraser, I would like to address Article 60 for a minute. As I understood you, Frank, you were talking about an implication regarding military installations on the shelf under Article 60. I prefer to look at Article 60 in another way. Article 60 gives the coastal state exclusive jurisdiction over installations; and it gives three special categories. It gives it jurisdiction over artificial islands, over installations provided for in Article 56 (and of course they are talking about economic installations there), and installations which interfere with the exercise of rights of the coastal state. Now, the way I would approach the problem is to say that any installation, be it military or non-military, that falls into one of those three categories would be prohibited. Any installation which does not fall in those categories would not be prohibited. I would draw that kind of distinction rather than a military/non-military distinction.

Professor MccGwire mentioned the Soviet insistence upon a "no sovereignty" clause, which is true. The United States had supported the Soviet Union on the "no sovereignty" clause. I just wanted to point out, however, that from my own personal view it is nonsense. It is not needed. Taken together of Articles 56, 58 and 86, and incorporated with Article 88, makes it legally clear that there is no sovereignty and, therefore, makes such a clause totally unnecessary.

KENNETH BOOTH: I shall just say something about the possibility of super power naval disengagements in the Mediterranean. My interest in the subject, in fact, arose from the possibility that the United States' Sixth Fleet might withdraw unilaterally as a tenet of anti-American feeling in Europe or some decision of Congress and so on. The idea of super power disengagement is not my own. There have been many ideas for super power naval disengagements in the past. But my belief that it is an idea worth supporting derives from the possibility that only one super power navy might be there in the future. Given this possibility, I am suggesting that it would be better if both left, and under controlled conditions.

FRANK FRASER: Tom Clingan has made a reference to Article 60 and explained that installations which are not covered in the provisions, then the EE zone regime does not apply. There was a test case about this in the negotiations in Geneva. In fact, we did not want to rock the boat about it. Peru was suggesting removing the purely resource-related provisions which are present in Article 60, and to do so specifically or explicitly, and to remove any right of a third state to place structures or installations on the seabed in another state's EEZ. The Conference did not, however, adopt this amendment.

This is where I would say that the subtleties have come into the text. When we were negotiating these provisions last year in New York, we were doing so after office hours when we had left the conference halls and would assemble in someone's mission.

Nevertheless, it was understood by those who were trying to find a balance and at the same time retain the sui generis nature of the exclusive economic zone, that it would not involve what Tom Clingan has just said, that third states would have these kind of rights. In leaving Article 55 as it was and by rewording Article 86 on the high seas, it was understood among all of us that these installations will not be permitted in the EEZ.

RODERICK OGLEY: Ken Booth distinguished in the use of naval force between the physical visibility of a traditional deployment and the political visibility which was now required which would entail the greater employment of reporters and the lesser employment, as I understood it, of ships. Now I am no naval economist, but I would guess that a reasonably sophisticated reporter would come rather cheaper than even a small warship. Would I be right then in predicting that we can look forward to reductions in defense expenditures as a result of this technological advance?

EDGAR GOLD: I have a very general question for the panel which is based on my own expereince as a mariner during the U.S. blockade of Cuban waters. At that time the U.S. navy controlled all approaches to Cuba and required full information from foreign vessels on the high seas on innocent passage to and from the Panama Canal. The most direct route passes, of course, quite close to the east coast of Cuba, Ships were regularly ordered, in no uncertain terms, to alter course and proceed via another passage east of the Dominican Republic. This caused considerable extra expense due to loss of time. Of course, the U.S. navy acted clearly in contravention of acceptable international law. Ken Booth in his excellent presentation, and Mike MccGwire in his comments, both appear to point to the moral of this story, that the military will not alter its operations significantly because of the law of the sea--for them it will be business as usual! Am I mistaken or simplistic in such as assumption?

FRANK FRASER: Naval staff are not well educated in law of the sea issues; generally we find there is a weakness among the navy. We have a legal department headed by the judge advocate general. When the naval staff want to know what they can do and what they cannot do, they refer matters to him. This is because of the existing uncertainty that prevails since the 1958 Geneva Convention. There are numerous national laws pertaining to the movement of warships in territorial seas and so on. All this would become uniform once there is a regime which is generally applicable to all. This would be placed on the desks of the naval staff, so they can better understand once we do have a treaty.

SHANNON CRAMER: Well, I think that is a worst case scenario that you leaped on. It was thoroughly agonized over in many long hours at the Oval Office before the Navy policy or the strategy was implemented in that particular case. I am mindful of the story that the Chairman of the Joint Chiefs told once at lunch when I happened to be present when he was questioning an Air Force aviator. They were trying to determine how many seats they should have in a newly designed aircraft. He was trying to talk to a pilot. The Chairman said, "Why do you feel you need an additional seat? Do you need a bombardier? Do you need a co-pilot? Do you need a communications expert?" He said "No, I need a legal advisor for the rules. I can't sort them out and keep on top of them." Now, I believe that any law of the sea treaty that is recognized as clear and does not require legal expertise on a ship or an aircraft would be a good step forward!

I also wanted to make a brief comment on the connotation that we "mill around" as navy ships or we bumble along in our activities. Ironically I am here today rather than Admiral Crowe because we war game, we do study the worst case scenarios. We feel that we are responsible. Ken made the statement that what you do at the far end of a transit is the important thing and justifies what you do enroute. Well, I feel very strongly that I would like, as always, and as I have tried to do, so I can be an admiral in heaven, have a pure heart, and do it in a legal fashion. And I think most naval officers feel this way either both in planning their operations or carrying them out.

I have found these sessions extremely beneficial--far from being in a group of brass, if you will, that sit around and look for ways to build ships, the "have enterprise, will tow" concept. No, I am not going to go back and say we need a mini-task force now to defend those icebergs that are towed. When we moved into the Indian Ocean, for instance, we were exercising the right of the freedom of seas that existed at that time; it was done in a legal fashion. I would like to think rather than just "milling around in the Mediterranean or the Indian Ocean" that certainly the military are the <u>last ones</u> that want a confrontation or a war. Having been there, we are the ones who get shot at. We are not pushing to have a confrontation. But, by following the policy of our country, our prime mission, as opposed to projecting our forces, which Michael mentioned, is deterrence and keeping the sea lines of communication open. I would like to leave that with this audience because all of us feel very strongly that those are our prime missions.

GARY KNIGHT: I would like to thank all of the panel, Professors Booth and MccGwire and Admirals Fraser and Cramer, and all of you for your questions and comments. We owe Professor Booth a special debt of gratitude for his time and effort in preparing our principal paper and helping to focus public attention on some of these issues.

PART VIII

SEA-USE PLANNING IN THE NORTH SEA

INTRODUCTORY REMARKS BY SESSION PROGRAM CHAIRMAN

Albert W. Koers
Institute of International Law of the University of Utrecht

On Monday morning when this Conference started I made some introductory remarks on the subject of sea-use planning. Those remarks were focused on the reasons we had for including this subject in this Conference. I will not repeat those remarks except by saying that I summarized my observations on Monday by stating that sea-use planning in the North Sea is not so much a reality as a necessity. Considerable innovative and creative thinking will be required if this necessity is to become reality.

Today I would like to add one more thing. In many ways this session is unique. The other sessions focused on particular resources, or on particular areas or activities. This session, on the other hand, is concerned not so much with individual activities or individual resources as with the interaction between resources. The essence of what we are going to talk about this morning, sea-use planning, is precisely this: the interaction between activities and between resources.

Before we hear the first paper, I would like to introduce the people who have agreed to contribute to this panel. We will start this morning with Dr. D. Eisma who is with the Netherlands Institute of Sea Research. He is an active marine geologist and he has been involved with various groups in this country that are concerned with the use, and in some cases the abuse, of the North Sea. Dr. Eisma will discuss the need for sea-use planning in the North Sea.

Then we will have Professor E. D. Brown, who is Director of the Center for Marine Law and Policy of the University of Wales. He is a specialist in international law and has published widely on the law of the sea and I might add that contrary to what was said yesterday, he is one of the people who has published on the military aspects of the law of the sea. Professor Brown will examine the legal framework of sea-use planning in the North Sea. When I read his paper I realized that he was given a task which is almost too difficult for anyone to deal with in one paper.

These two presentations will be followed by three commentaries.

THE NEED FOR SEA-USE PLANNING IN THE NORTH SEA

D. Eisma
Netherlands Institute for Sea Research, Texel

As has been pointed out on the first day of this conference, sea-use planning, or more specifically North Sea use planning, is considered by many a necessity. Before going into this question, however, I would like to make some introductory remarks on the North Sea itself.

Figure I gives the general distribution of water depth in the North Sea. Apart from some exceptions it is a shallow sea which,on the basis of depth and general bottom characteristics can be divided into the Southern North Sea (south of Doggerbank) with maximum depth slightly more than 50 meters, the Central North Sea with depths down to 100 meters, the Northern North Sea with depths down to nearly 200 meters, and the Norwegian Channel, which has a minimum depth of about 225 meters off Stavanger and a maximum depth of slightly more than 700 meters in the Skagerrak. The well-known division of the North Sea into jurisdictional sectors belonging to the surrounding coastal states does not allow for this natural division. The jurisdictional boundaries intersect the natural sea floor boundaries. This is also true for the sub-bottom, and some of the oil and gas-bearing structures in the middle of the North Sea are situated partly in the Norwegian sector, partly in the British sector.

Figure II gives the distribution of the different water masses in the North Sea as based on differences in salinity and chemical composition. These water masses are formed (a) by mixing of ocean water flowing in from the Atlantic and from the Channel with river water and with brackish water from the Baltic, and (b) by gradual changes in composition, especially in the content of phosphate, nitrate and silicate, which take place when the water moves through the North Sea. The boundaries between the different water masses are not sharp; there is continuous movement of water across these boundaries. There is a general counter-clockwise circulation in the North Sea, with water from the Atlantic Ocean flowing in from the northwest around Scotland and Shetland and water from the Channel flowing in through the Strait of Dover, while the outflow into the Atlantic Ocean is concentrated in the northeast along the Norwegian coast. This circulation actually is very complicated and tends to be variable, being strongly influenced by meteorological conditions and by differences in density of the water, as well as by the tides. It takes in the order of

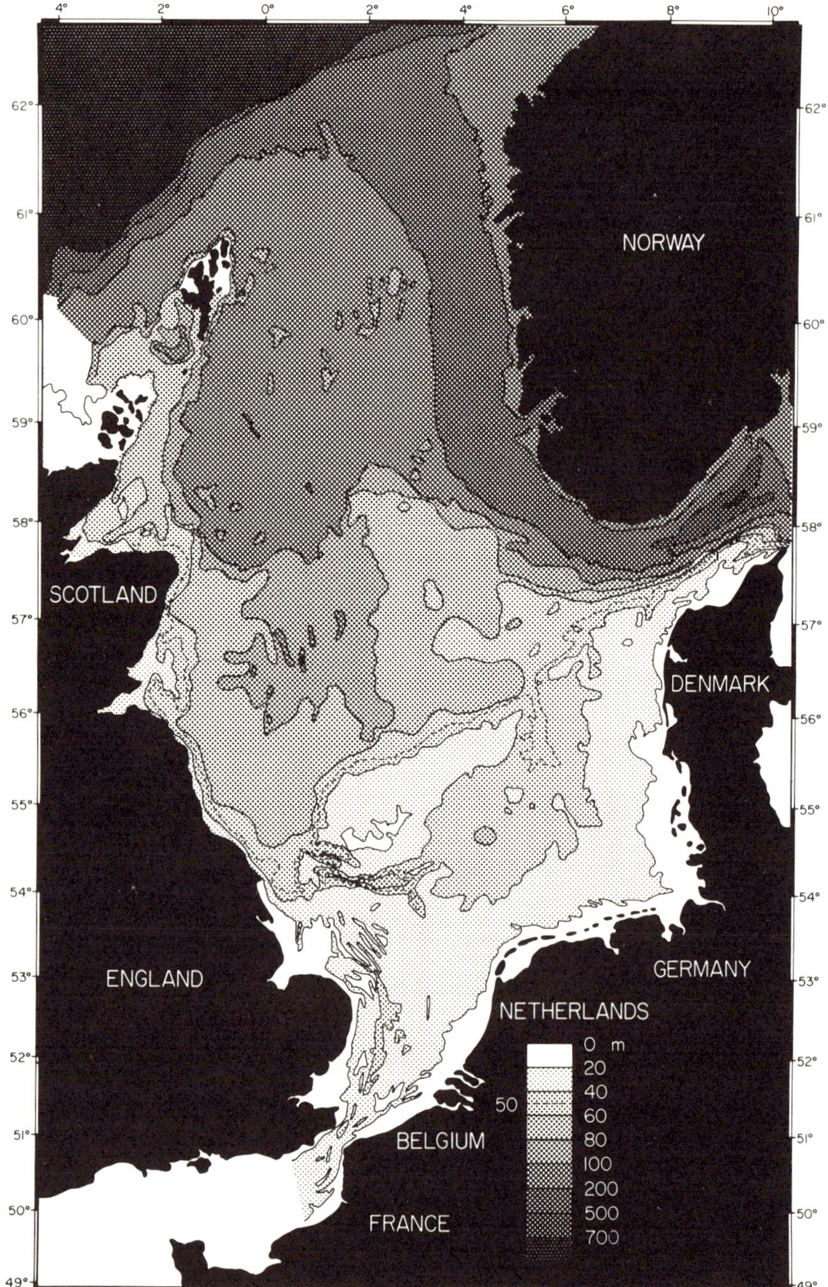

FIGURE I

Depth Chart of the North Sea

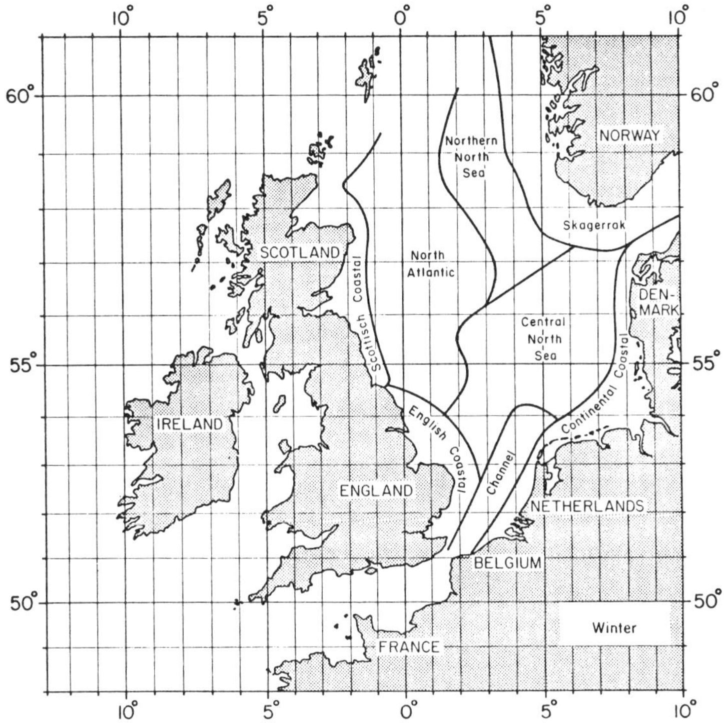

FIGURE 11

Watermasses of the North Sea
(Goldberg, 1973)

one to two years to renew the waters of the North Sea. The division into jurisdictional sectors also does not allow for the natural boundaries between the water masses; the same applies to the eastern limit of the North Sea between Norway and Denmark, as fixed in 1951 in the Laws and Regulations on the Regime of the High Seas. This limit is drawn from the Lindesnaes Lighthouse on the Norwegian coast to the northwest point of Denmark (Hanstholm Lighthouse) and cuts the Skagerrak off from the North Sea. Topographically and structurally, however, the Skagerrak and the Norwegian Channel belong to the same unit; also, hydrographically, the Skagerrak is part of the North Sea. Water from the Southern North Sea flows along the north coast of Denmark into the Skagerrak and also water from the Atlantic Ocean, flowing into the North Sea around Shetland and following the western side of the Norwegian Channel, reaches the Skagerrak. Here the waters from the Southern North Sea and the Atlantic are mixed and outflow from the Baltic is added. This mixture, called the Skagerrak-water, goes northward along the Norwegian coast and flows out into the Atlantic Ocean. The natural limit of the North Sea in this area is therefore formed by the coastlines of Norway, Sweden and Denmark and by a line across the Kattegat, from Cape Skagen to Sweden.

In the north the natural limit of the North Sea lies somewhere near a line from Shetland to Cape Stad on the Norwegian coast slightly north of 62°N, instead of along the 61st degree of latitude, which was fixed as the northern limit in 1951. It follows from the above that when thinking about sea-use planning in the North Sea, we have to take into account that the natural boundaries, as well as the natural limits in the east and north, are very different from the jurisdictional ones.

In the North Sea the traditional activities, fisheries, merchant shipping and warfare, go back in time at least as far as the Roman period. All countries bordering the North Sea have a long seafaring tradition. The way these activities are carried out has changed very much during history. Industrial developments since the beginning of the 19th century profoundly changed their character and increased their scale. The number of ships, their size and speed are larger than ever. There have been important shifts towards different types of ships and cargo as well as to different techniques of fishing and treatment of catches.

In the North Sea, merchant shipping is concentrated in Strait Dover and in the Southern Bight, which is the southern part of the southern North Sea between England on the western side and France, Belgium and the Netherlands on the eastern side. At present annual transport of oil through Strait Dover is in the order of 220 million tons of which two-thirds go to Rotterdam and Antwerp and the remainder chiefly to north German ports further east in the Southern North Sea. On the average, about 300 merchants ships pass Strait Dover daily, again mainly for ports in the southern North Sea. Also there is a considerable amount of fishing going on in this area.

Besides traditional activities, other activities have been developed or are planned in the North Sea, including oil and gas exploration and production, extraction of gravel and sand, dumping of waste and the construction of artificial islands. Some of these activities hinder or harm other activities; some are mutually exclusive. Thus, deep-draught shipping needs traffic lanes which cannot be obstructed by offshore constructions, the upkeep of marine life as it is today is incompatible with pollution from oil and other waste; fisheries are hampered by pipelines and by the extraction of gravel and sand from the seafloor. Pipelines are hampered by fishing gear. The future of the North Sea as a buffer zone between areas of important coastal development is diminished by industrial developments within the sea. Artificial islands involve permanent occupation and bring problems concerning site location, provision of building materials, transportation, waste disposal and interference with other marine activities. Last but not least, the development of these activities in the North Sea has a profound impact on the coastal areas as well as significant social consequences.

It is perhaps not surprising that the Netherlands is among the countries where sea-use planning is a serious proposition and is considered a necessity. There is by now a considerable amount of experience here with land planning in a densely populated and intensively used country. There is also a long maritime tradition and a lasting experience with expansion into the coastal sea. Moreover, since the late 1960's, the North Sea, and especially the shallow Southern Bight, became increasingly regarded as a probable solution to all kinds of problems on land. The dumping or discharging of waste into the North Sea, including city sewage and chemical waste, increased. All kinds of proposals were made for placing industries of other activities that are too noisy, too dirty or too dangerous, on artificial islands in the North Sea. Thus, plans were put forward by government agencies as well as by private initiative to locate a large international airport on a fixed or floating island off the Dutch coast, to build a large industrial center for the treatment of waste materials in the middle of the Southern Bight, to construct an offshore deepwater port that would be able to receive the biggest ships, and to place nuclear reactors as well as a terminal for liquid natural gas on an artificial island. Similar proposals for the emplacement of nuclear reactors in the sea were made in Belgium and also have been considered in Britain. Plans for the construction of a floating power station in the German Bight, using locally produced natural gas, are in an advanced stage.

The most comprehensive proposal so far has been made by a group of industries for an industrial complex to be placed on an artificial island either in the Dutch sector off Rotterdam or northwest of the Dutch Wadden Sea or in the British sector off Great Yarmouth. It would involve a large island with a cluster of industries including oil refineries and petrochemical industries, ferrous and non-ferrous industries, storage and transshipment of bulk cargo (in particular of dangerous cargo), an emergency harbor, a terminal for liquid natural gas, power plants and waste treatment facilities.

In Figure III the extension of all present and planned activities in the Southern Bight is shown, except fisheries, since fishing as well as the spawning areas of commercial fish species cover almost the whole area. Indicated are shipping lanes, military training areas, dumping areas, areas where waste is being burned from ships, larger natural gas fields, as well as platforms and drilled holes, pipelines for natural gas and two short ones for waste disposal, telephone cables, concession areas for the extraction of sand and gravel, and locations proposed for artificial islands and a windpower station. This picture is somewhat misleading in that activities can take place on the seafloor that do not affect activities at the surface, but it conveys the scale of activities in the southern North Sea.

Existing developments and future plans will have a profound impact on the North Sea and the coastal areas, as has already been the case in Scotland, Shetland and Norway because of North Sea oil and gas developments. Coastal states therefore should anticipate and decide at an early stage on the desirability of certain developments and should plan early for the inevitable effects of offshore developments. Especially in an area like the southern North Sea, where the increasing activities involve more and more space, plans are being made for very complex changes with increasing interaction between marine activities. There is a strong need for some kind of sea-use planning. I use here the word planning and not management, although there is no generally accepted definition of what sea-use planning is or should be. There probably is no sharp distinction between planning and management. Management, if it is done well, will involve a lot of planning. I use the word planning here because it conveys the development of a broad framework and of general concepts, because it involves the expression of what you want with the North Sea or with certain parts of it, and because it stresses the interrelation between activities. Whereas management tends to be more concerned with a number of separate activities that have to be managed.

At present, sea-use planning, so far as it is done, is carried out by government agencies on an ad-hoc basis for separate activities, although in the Netherlands some study is

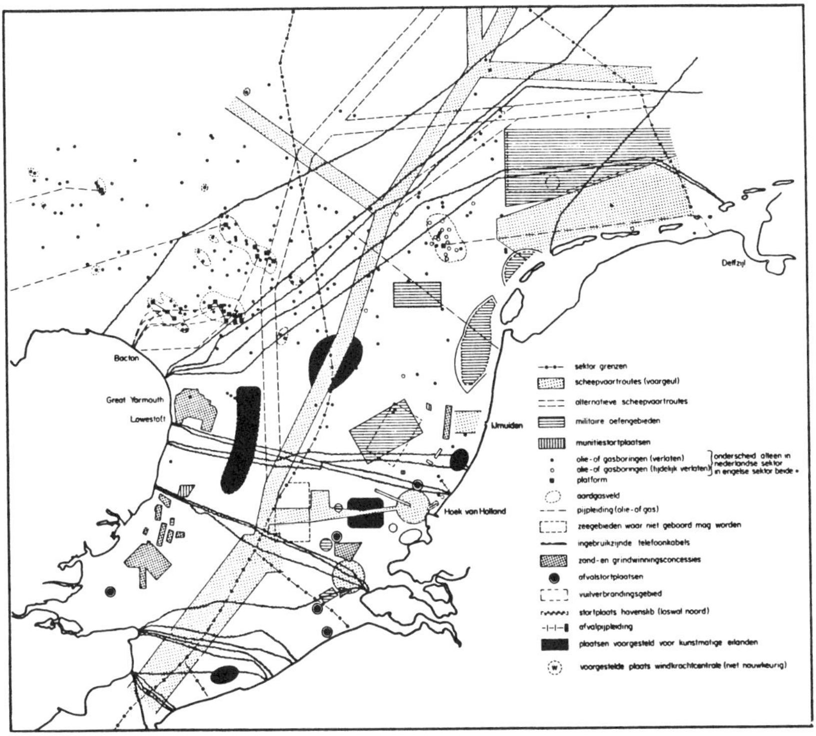

FIGURE III

Distribution of Actual and Planned Activities in the Southern Bight of the North Sea

being done on a wider scale. This is done by the Civil Planning Group of the Technical University at Delft and by at least two government study groups, one concerned with, among other things, the feasibility of sea-use planning, the other one concerned with the consequences of the construction of one or more artificial islands in the Dutch sector of the North Sea. During discussions in the Dutch Parliament on the budget of 1977 the lack of adequate planning law for the North Sea was recognized by various representatives as well as by the government. The then minister for housing and physical planning indicated that he would explore the possibilities for a study on the legal aspects of a possible North Sea planning law. It was observed that at present provincial and local government as well as the population in general do not take part in decisions concerning the North Sea except at a very late stage; whereas for land planning there are extensive procedures for preliminary consultation and discussion. Also, it was recognized that there is no adequate framework for coordination of all the aspects of North Sea use that are now regulated separately. I may mention briefly that some discussion on sea use planning is going on in Britain, that coastal zone planning is being developed in France and that in the United States there is a movement towards more extensive planning of activities in the offshore waters.

In the Netherlands planning on land is done on the level of municipalities and regions, while the main lines are laid down in nationwide plans and structural outlines. At the local level it has been pushed towards great detail, but even compared to nationwide planning, sea-use planning has to be done on a larger scale than planning on land, as is indicated by, e.g., the width of shipping lanes, the size of fishing grounds, the areas needed for gravel extraction and the area polluted after a serious tanker accident. Sea-use planning therefore does not have to go into much detail but it has to be done internationally. It should also allow for the different character of a sea area as compared with a land area since in the sea activities can be simultaneously carried out at the surface of the water, in the water and on the seafloor (as well as in the air and in the subsoil). Also, boundaries in the sea are fluid-like in the air, instead of fixed as on land or on the seafloor.

With regard to classifying the separate activities, several kinds of subdivisions can be made, such as those based on mobility (fixed, moving along fixed routes, or moving along variable routes) and on the basis of the relation with the mainland. Some activities (fishing, oil and gas production) are primarily done at sea with certain consequences for the mainland. For other activities (shipping) there is primarily interaction between the activity on land and in the sea, and some activities (extraction of sand and gravel, waste dumping and artificial islands) are the direct consequence of developments on the mainland. Sea-use planning should allow for these different categories to the extent that some problems at sea may be solved more by a different policy on land than by sea-use planning.

The planning activity should work towards some kind of consensus on what the future of the North Sea should be. As pointed out in a report on North Sea planning by van Hoorn and de Jong (1977) the North Sea has basically seven functions. It is a very large natural area. It is an open space and acts as a buffer between highly developed areas. It is used for activities like shipping and recreation that do not exclude future use. It is used for the extraction of limited resources of minerals, including gravel, oil and natural gas, and is used for dumping and discharging waste substances. Finally, the North Sea is considered to be a suitable area for activities that on the mainland for some reason or another lead to difficulties. The interaction between these functions leads to spatial and environmental conflicts. Sea-use planning, like all planning, therefore involves making choices directed towards one or more of these functions.

In an attempt to establish a conceptual framework for North Sea planning van Hoorn and de Jong (1977) proposed four models:

- the North Sea remains exclusively a nature reserve, an open space and a buffer zone between developing coastal areas. This is an extreme case, implying that important activities that have already been developed in the North Sea should be stopped.

- the North Sea remains as much as possible a natural area, and is used for activities that do not exclude future use, as well as for exploitation of limited resources and for discharging and dumping waste. In this model the present situation is continued.

- the North Sea remains a natural area and is used only for activities that leave room for future use. This corresponds more to a policy of conservation of resources and of preservation of the North Sea for use by future generations.

- the North Sea is used primarily for exploitation of resources, for discharging waste, and for activities that cause serious problems on land. This is another extreme with full exploitation without regard for future use or for other functions or qualities of the North Sea.

The planning measures that are needed differ for each model, but considering that realization of both extremes is not realistic or desirable, we arrive at concepts wherein either conservation is given more emphasis or short term exploitation. For both types of concepts a planning policy can be worked out in four levels, as proposed by Wiggerts (1976):

- on the first level, international coordination and formulation of guiding principles on the use of the North Sea.

- on the second level, the drafting of structural outlines, particularly for those activities that cover the entire North Sea, like oil and gas production, merchant shipping, fisheries and military use of the sea.

- on the third level, the drafting of regional structural outlines and zoning in specific areas such as parts of the Southern Bight and the Scottish coast.

- on the fourth level, the drafting of project plans which have a strong technical character, for projects like pipelines, artificial islands or natural gas terminals.

I have yet to mention the feasibility of sea-use planning in the North Sea which is largely a question of appreciation. It would not do, I think, to aim at more bureaucracy, such as establishing a new ministry or department or a broad committee for coordination of government activities. A government agency with broad possibilities for cooperation with all kinds of specialists and for international cooperation will do. The main difficulty is probably the complexity of the problems involved. Also, the problems tend to come to the surface piecemeal so that it is difficult to obtain a good overview. To overcome this, some effort and much creative thinking will be necessary as well as great flexibility in approach. The latter will also be necessary when short-term decisions will have to be made and when sea-use planning has to be directed towards regional plans and towards planning of certain large projects like an artificial island. Nevertheless North Sea planning should involve primarily the whole of the North Sea and should work towards an international basis in the form of a general agreement among the bordering states on the use of the North Sea.

REFERENCES

Chapman, K. North Sea oil and gas, a geographical perspective. In R. Lawton (Ed.). Problems in Modern Geography. David and Charles, Inc., 1976.

Goldberg, E.D. (Ed.). North Sea Science. Cambridge, MA, 1973.

van Hoorn, H. and de Jong, A. Naar een planning van de Noordzee. Rapport werkgroep Planologie van de POOL. 1977.

Sibthorp, M.M. (Ed.). The North Sea, Challenge and Opportunity. Europa Publications, 1975.

Wiggerts, H. Naar een planologie van(uit) de Noordzee : blue heart megalopolis. Plan 3. 1976.

SEA-USE PLANNING IN THE NORTH SEA: THE LEGAL FRAMEWORK

E. D. Brown
Professor of International Law, University of Wales
Director, Centre for Marine Law and Policy
UWIST, Cardiff

The subject on which the writer was invited to prepare this paper is the legal framework for sea-use planning, with particular emphasis on the North Sea. It was intended that it should present, in analytical terms, the national and international law problems associated with sea-use planning. "Sea-use planning" is not of course a term of art, and no generally recognized definition of the concept seems to exist. Since, however, it is obviously impossible to examine the legal framework for sea-use planning unless the meaning and scope of the term is reasonably clear, the purpose of the first part of this paper must be to provide a working definition.

I. The Meaning and Scope of Sea-Use Planning

"Sea-use planning" is a term which has become fashionable in the past few years, but it has been used with a variety of meanings. In some contexts it is used interchangeably with "coastal zone management," whereas in others it refers to sea space more generally.

Commentators in the United Kingdom have been interested in sea-use planning mainly as a function of national government and have not concerned themselves too much with the scope of the term. Thus, in a Fabian pamphlet, the purpose of which was to insert the phrase into the British political vocabulary (Young and Fricke, 1975, p. 3) and which spoke of sea-use planning as "a necessary function of government" (Young and Fricke, 1975, p. 1) and "a necessary intellectual tool," Elizabeth Young decided not "to define the concept, which is new but rather to draw attention to the consequences of its absence as a mode of thinking about off-shore developments" (Young and Fricke, 1975, p. 3).

Replying to a subsequent debate on sea-use planning in the House of Lords (February 1976, Col. 557), Baroness Birk, while denying the existence of "any real definition," nevertheless came close to providing one in saying that:

> Primarily, I understand it to mean that what we do on, in, or under the sea should be done by design, in accordance with a positive and cohesive approach, rather than dictated solely by the accident of immediate

> pressures. Further, our decisions about the use of the sea should be based on consideration of all the relevant factors and forward projections in order to take ample account of future developments. I also understand it to mean that, in our relations with other countries, we should be guided by a balanced appreciation of all our various interests in the seas.
>
> In other words, we have to have an international as well as a national approach. The fundamental question which has been raised tonight is whether the Government has the body of information, including information about future developments, and the necessary machinery of co-ordination between different Government Departments, to enable them to achieve these objectives.

The "key question" for her was "whether our administrative machinery is really adequate to cope with this dimension of our society" (Debate, February 1976, Col. 559).

It is clear from the debate in the House of Lords that the analogous concept of land-use planning has been a major formative influence on the thinking of many of the advocates of sea-use planning. It would appear that in most cases the influence has been more or less subconscious and that the validity of the analogy has been accepted without much thought. It is perhaps useful therefore to an inquiry into the meaning and scope of the concept of sea-use planning to make explicit the kind of model of planning which is probably implicit in the very use of the term 'sea-use planning.'

The model will of course vary in detail from state to state but may be illustrated by reference to the British variant. It is easy to forget that even in a highly developed, densely populated country like the United Kingdom, the "need for co-ordination and central control over the use of land became generally recognized (only) in the present century. Before then it had been thought that free and untrammelled enterprise was necessary for national prosperity; any extension of Government activity beyond what was considered its proper sphere would have been looked upon as an encroachment on personal liberty and likely to handicap initiative" (Town and Country, 1975, p. 1). The result was urban congestion and a suburban sprawl on good farming land and over rich mineral deposits. This laissez-faire philosophy thus resulted in the sterilization of some of the country's most valuable natural resources, in addition to creating serious social difficulties. It was a belated appreciation of the results of this policy which led to the passing of the Housing, Town and Country Planning Act 1909, the forerunner of the much more comprehensive legislation which now operates in the United Kingdom. The basic purpose of the system of land-use planning has been described as being "to ensure, as far as possible, that land is used in the best interests of the nation as a whole, rather than being simply subject to market forces" (Town and Country, 1978, p. 1).

Under current planning legislation, the local planning authorities prepare a planning survey which takes into account the main physical and economic characteristics of the area and provides details of, inter alia, land use, population, and transport. This planning survey serves as a basis for the development plan which consists of two parts, a structure plan and one or more local plans. The structure plan requires ministerial approval and consists of a written statement, illustrated diagrammatically and setting out and justifying policies and general proposals for development and other use of land. The local plan, which must conform to the structure plan, consists of a written statement and a map showing the nature and location of future development and other land use in the area. All development requires planning permission and, in considering applications, the local planning authority must have regard to the provisions of the development plan. Planning permission is normally granted (or refused) by the local authority but the Minister may "call in" controversial applications and there is in any event a right of appeal to the Minister. Extensive provision is made, as an essential part of these procedures for, publicity for, and public discussion of, development plans and planning applications, and an important role is played by independent inspectors and public local inquiries (Town and Country, 1975; Heap, 1978).

The analogy is certainly a tempting one, given the fear that the mismanagement of what a Government Minister recently referred to as the second industrial revolution, based on the sea (Birk, February 1976, Col. 559), might, like the first, provide for the needs of powerful sectoral interests in a piecemeal, uncoordinated manner, at the expense of the broader interest of the community at large. Nor is it difficult to sympathize with the type of ideal scenario to which thinking along these lines tends to lead. Would it not be a fine thing if we could draw a Rawlsian veil of ignorance[1] over our eyes and, innocent of present maritime boundaries and the distribution of rights and resources, conduct a planning survey of the

[1]A procedure advocated by John Rawls in his A Theory of Justice, Oxford U.P., 1972, whereby the jurist attempts to work out the principles of justice from a hypothetical original position, that is, the position revealed when the "veil of ignorance" excludes from the jurist's thinking the knowledge of those contingencies of natural fortune or social circumstances which set men at odds and allow them to be guided by their prejudices.

North Sea and, in the light of it, draw up a North Sea community "structural" plan and national "local" plans designed in accordance with agreed North Sea Community criteria?

The question is how useful is such thinking? The "realist" might well say that, while it may be obvious that there is a need for a degree of sea-use planning, it is equally obvious that sea-use planning already takes place on several levels, even though the process may not be so described. He would point out that land-use planning in a national context is a very different process from sea-use planning in an international context, so different, indeed, that it is questionable whether the analogy has any validity except in the most general sense. Different levels of integration are involved. Land-use planning is to a large extent concerned with the rational exploitation of an area under the exclusive domestic jurisdiction of only one state. Planning decisions can be made and conflicts between competing users resolved in accordance with locally agreed development plans reflecting a national scale of socio-economic priorities. Sea-use planning may also of course be concerned with sea areas under the exclusive jurisdiction of a coastal state. Typically, however, it will refer to a number of maritime jurisdictional zones in which competition rationae materiae (fish versus oil for example) is aggravated by competition ratione personae (French versus British nationals for example) and in which decisions on use of the sea are made and conflicts resolved by a variety of national and public international institutions, as well as, in the case of the North Sea, by the institutions of the European Economic Community (EEC). Moreover, in the light of the difficulties of coordinating policies even between the present nine states of the EEC, there is room for no easy assumptions about closer integration in the years ahead among the member states of an enlarged European Community.

To sum up these preliminary thoughts:

(1) Advocates of the need for sea-use planning in the North Sea are aware that there is much law and regulation of maritime activities and many institutions concerned with maritime affairs on the national, international, and European Community levels. Their complaint is that the problems tend to be dealt with piecemeal and in isolation rather than as integral parts of an overall coordinated policy for the rational exploitation of the sea. The need, it is argued, is not for more government but for more coordination in government.

(2) It can thus be said that the demand for sea-use planning is essentially a plea for the provision of institutions and procedures capable of ensuring the rational, coordinated exploitation of the sea in the interests of the community at large and in the light of adequate information, and the

resolution of conflicts between competing interests in accordance with agreed upon criteria.

(3) In considering how best to respond to this plea, it should be borne in mind that planning models developed for the rational exploitation of land in areas subject to the exclusive jurisdiction of one state are not necessarily suitable for transplantation to a marine environment subject to a multiplicity of jurisdictions.

II. The Legal Framework

Having arrived at a rough working definition of sea-use planning, the next task is to provide an understanding of the present legal framework within which proposals for sea-use planning would have to be developed.

For the purpose of this analysis, the definition of the North Sea used in the Convention for Regulating the Police of the North Sea Fisheries, 1882, has been adopted.[2] The North Sea is thus bordered by the coasts of seven states, the United

---

[2] Laws and Regulations on the Regime of the High Seas, Vol. 1, United Nations Legislative Series, ST/LEG/SER.B/1, 1951, p. 179. Article IV fixes the limits of the North Sea as follows:

1. On the north by the parallel of the 61st degree of latitude;
2. On the east and south:
   (1) By the coasts of Norway between the parallel of the 61st degree of latitude and Lindenaes Lighthouse (Norway);
   (2) By a straight line drawn from Lindenaes Lighthouse (Norway) to Hanstholm Lighthouse (Denmark);
   (3) By the coasts of Denmark, Germany, the Netherlands, Belgium, and France, as far as Gris Nex Lighthouse;
3. On the west:
   (1) By a straight line drawn from Gris Nex Lighthouse (France) to the easternmost lighthouse at South Foreland (England);
   (2) By the eastern coasts of England and Scotland;
   (3) By a straight line joining Duncansby Head (Scotland) and the southern point of South Ronaldsha (Orkney Islands);
   (4) By the eastern coasts of the Orkney Islands;
   (5) By a straight line joining North Ronaldsha Lighthouse (Orkney Islands) and Sumburgh Head Lighthouse (Shetland Islands);
   (6) By the eastern coasts of the Shetland Islands;
   (7) By the meridian of North Unst Lighthouse (Shetland Islands) as far as the parallel of the 61st degree of

Kingdom, France, Belgium, the Netherlands, Germany, Denmark, and Norway. Of those seven states, only Norway is not a member of the EEC. It must also be borne in mind that the North Sea is extensively used by non-North Sea states for a variety of purposes. The term "North Sea" is taken to include not only the whole water column, but also the subjacent seabed and subsoil and the superjacent airspace. As so defined, the North Sea provides a number of valuable uses. Without attempting an exhaustive enumeration, the interests involved include navigation, fishing, exploitation of inanimate natural resources (oil, gas and gravel for example), cable and pipe laying, the establishment and use of artificial islands, installations and structures, the production of energy from water, currents and winds, scientific research, environmental conservation, military uses, recreational uses and overflight.

In considering the planning of these uses of the North Sea, the politician tends to think of sea-use planning as a process of national government; the international lawyer tends to place emphasis on the jurisdictional framework created by international law within which sea-use planning must take place; and the EEC official has a marked tendency to regard it as a basic tenet of natural law that the role of planner-in-chief should fall to Brussels. It is more useful, however, to view the situation objectively from outside the three systems of law and it can be said that:

(1) Some maritime affairs are within the exclusive domestic jurisdiction of the coastal state and planning in relation to such affairs is therefore an exclusive function of national government.

(2) In a second category of maritime affairs, the sovereignty of the coastal state is limited by rules of European Community law and planning in relation to such affairs is a function of both national government and of the institutions of the European Community.

(3) In a third area of maritime affairs, the sovereignty of the coastal state is limited not only by rules of European Community law but also by rules of public international law. In relation to these matters, a multiplicity of institutions may have a role to play in sea-use planning: national governments, the institutions of the EEC and a variety of public international institutions.

---

latitude.
The same definition is adopted for the purposes of the Convention respecting the Liquor Traffic in the North Sea, 1887 (ibid, p. 262, Article 1).

(4) Finally, there are maritime affairs in relation to which the sovereignty of the coastal state is limited by rules of public international law alone and the planning function may thus be shared by national governments and public international institutions.

An understanding of this fundamental part of the framework of sea-use planning may be assisted by the diagram in Figure 1.

Since the regulation of marine affairs is taking place on three different levels, the first and most important question to ask is whether sea-use planning is a recognized function of the institutions operating on these three levels and, if so, have they been given the necessary powers to undertake effective and efficient sea-use planning.

1. Sea-Use Planning as a Function of National Government

It is beyond the scope of this paper to make a comparative study of the provision made within each of the North Sea states for sea-use planning. All that will be attempted here is a short, illustrative account of the position in the United Kingdom and an even more brief reference to recent developments in Sweden.

In the United Kingdom, a review of the arrangements for coordination of government responsibilities for marine affairs was made in 1976. On June 8, 1976, the Prime Minister stated that it had shown no need to introduce fundamental changes in existing ministerial responsibilities (*Marine Activities*, 1977, p. 1). The Lord Privy Seal was, however, given the responsibility for coordination of policy in matters connected with the law of the sea, and the use of the sea and seabed, as well as continuing to perform the role of coordinating measures for the protection of British offshore and other maritime interests. In a further statement made on July 30, 1976, the Prime Minister announced the establishment of a new Interdepartmental Committee on Marine Safety (ICMS) to coordinate the development and implementation of policy relating to safety at sea (*Marine Activities*, 1977, p. 1). Following the *Amoco Cadiz* and *Eleni V* disasters earlier this year (1978), the Prime Minister again declined to accept the view that the setting up of a new Department of Marine Affairs would add to departmental coordination in relation to oil tanker disasters (*The Times*, June 23, 1978). He did, however, arrange for an inquiry into the effectiveness of the procedures used in dealing with the *Amoco Cadiz* and *Eleni V* incidents (*The Times*, June 1, 1978). As a result, the Government announced on August 2, 1978 that a small Contingencies Planning and Operations Unit was to be established, based in the Department of Trade but with strong support from the Navy.[3]

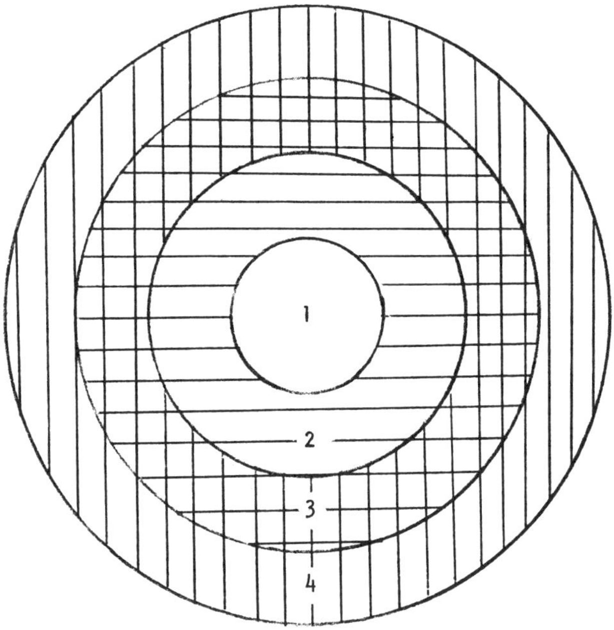

1. Exclusive domestic jurisdiction of coastal State. Planning authority: national government.

2. Sovereignty of coastal State limited by EEC law. Planning authority: national government and EEC institutions.

3. Sovereignty of coastal State limited by EEC and international law. Planning authority: national government, EEC institution, and international institutions.

4. Sovereignty of coastal State limited by international law. Planning authority: national government and international institutions.

FIGURE 1
Planning Jurisdiction on Different Levels of Integration

Guide to the responsibilities of Government Departments

Subject	Policy Authority	Legislation	Administering Authority	Comments
Ships and navigation				
(a) Construction and Repair-Onshore and Offshore (i) methods and materials, etc	DoT/Mar	MS Acts	DoT/Mar	
(ii) occupational health and safety	HSC	FA 1961 HSW Act 1974	HSE	Excludes officers and crew
(b) Officers and Crew (i) qualifications	DoT/Mar	MS Acts	DoT/Mar	
(ii) occupational safety and health	DoT/Mar	MS Acts	DoT/Mar	
(c) Loading and Unloading (i) docks	HSC	FA 1961	HSE	
(ii) offshore – in territorial waters and designated areas of the continental shelf	HSC	HSW Act 1974	HSE	
(iii) other	DoT/Mar	MS Acts	DoT/Mar	
(d) Safety of ships and navigation	DoT/Mar	MS Acts CP Act 1949	DoT/Mar	IMCO recommendations apply to United Kingdom registered vessels
(i) lighthouses etc	DoT/Mar	MS Acts	General Lighthouse Authorities	
(ii) pilotage	DoT/Mar	PA 1913	Local Pilotage Authorities	
Offshore oil and gas – general				
(a) Exploration and exploitation	DEn	PP Act 1934 CS Act 1964 MW(OI) Act 1971 and P and SP Act 1975	DEn	General policy, eg designation of areas, licensing, development etc
Offshore installations				
(a) Structural Integrity	DEn	MW(OI) Act 1971	DEn	
(i) construction onshore and offshore (materials and certificate of fitness)	DEn	MW(OI) Act 1971	DoT	Certificates of fitness issued by Certifying Authorities
(ii) construction onshore and offshore (occupational health and safety)	HSC	FA 1961 HSW Act 1974	HSE	Construction work in territorial waters and designated areas of the Continental Shelf
(b) Production Risks eg Blowouts	DEn	MW(OI) Act 1971	DEn	
(c) Siting and Navigational Hazards	DEn DoT/Mar	CS Act 1964 CP Act 1949	DEn DoT/Mar	Liaison between two Depts with DoT/Mar consent on markings eg lighting, buoyage etc
(d) Occupational Health and Safety	HSC	HSW Act 1974	DEn	Administration by Agency Agreement
(e) Tow out to permanent location by United Kingdom Registered and other ships from United Kingdom ports	DoT/Mar	MS Acts	DoT/Mar	Also includes United Kingdom registered ships in tow out from foreign ports
(f) Control of Marine Operations in Designated Sea Areas	SO	OPD(s) Act 1975	SO	Regulations and Licensing procedures under the Act
Diving				
(a) From offshore installations	HSC	HSW Act 1974 MW(OI) Act 1971	DEn	
(b) In connection with pipelines	HSC	HSW Act 1974 P and SP Act 1975	DEn	
(c) Other diving within territorial waters and waters of Great Britain	HSC	HSW Act 1974	HSE	
(d) From United Kingdom registered ships outside the territorial waters of Great Britain	DoT/Mar	MS Acts	DoT/Mar	

Submarine pipelines and pipelaying operations (a) Route, capacity and structural integrity	DEn	P and SP Act 1975	DEn	
(b) Occupational Health and Safety (Including Construction from Component Parts)	HSC	HSW Act 1974	HSE	Excludes crew members in normal manning of ships
Fisheries (a) Fishing limits	MAFF, DAFS, DANI	UKFL Acts 1964 to 1976 SF Act 1968	MAFF, DAFS, DANI	
(b) Conservation of stocks	MAFF, DAFS, DANI	SF(C) Act 1967 SF(S) Act 1967 SF Act 1968	MAFF, DAFS, DANI	
Aggregate Recovery	DOE Crown Estate Commissioners	CP Act 1949	Crown Estate Commissioners	
Submarine cables	DOI	ST Act 1885	Post Office	
Pollution – marine (a) Discharges from land	DOE, SDD, WO, DOE(NI)	R(POP) Acts at present Part II of the COP Act 1974 when brought into force W Act (NI) 1972	Regional Water Authorities River Purification Boards and Islands Councils DOE(NI)	
(b) Discharges of or containing oil (i) from land	DOE, SDD, WO, DOE(NI)	POP 1971	DOE, SDD, WO, DOE(NI)	
(ii) from offshore installations into waters within the 3 mile limit	DOE, SDD, WO, DOE(NI)	POP Act 1971	DOE, SDD, WO, DOE(NI)	
(iii) from offshore installations into waters outside the 3 mile limit	DEn	POP Act 1971	DEn	
(c) Oil from UK Registered Ships	DoT/Mar	POP Act 1971	DoT/Mar	Includes foreign ships in United Kingdom territorial waters
(d) Dumping of Substances and Articles from land-based sources	MAFF, DAFS, DOE(NI)	DS Act 1974	MAFF, DAFS, DOE(NI)	
(e) Radioactive Waste	DOE, MAFF, WO, SDD, DOE(NI)	DS Act 1974 RS Act 1960	DOE, MAFF, WO, SDD, (HMIPI), DOE(NI)	Joint consultation and liaison
Search and rescue	DoT/Mar	MS Acts	HM Coastguard (DoT/Mar)	
Relations with foreign countries	FCO	Various Conventions and Agreements	FCO	Co-ordination of Depts on Law of the Sea matters
Hydrographic surveys	MOD		MOD	

Key:
DEn – Department of Energy
DOE – Department of the Environment
DOI – Department of Industry
DoT – Department of Trade
FCO – Foreign and Commonwealth Office
HSC – Health and Safety Commission
HSE – Health and Safety Executive
MAFF – Ministry of Agriculture, Fisheries and Food
MOD – Ministry of Defence
DAFS – Department of Agriculture and Fisheries for Scotland
DANI – Department of Agriculture for Northern Ireland
WO – Welsh Office
DOE(NI) – Department of the Environment (Northern Ireland)
SDD – Scottish Development Department
SDD (HMIPI) – HM Industrial Pollution Inspectorate for Scotland
SO – Scottish Office
COP Act 1974 – Control of Pollution Act 1974
CP Act 1949 – Coast Protection Act 1949
CS Act 1964 – Continental Shelf Act 1964
DS Act 1974 – Dumping at Sea Act 1974
FA 1961 – Factories Act 1961.
HSW Act 1974 – Health and Safety at Work etc Act 1974
MS Acts – Merchant Shipping Acts
MW(OI) Act 1971 – Mineral Workings (Offshore Installations) Act 1971
PA 1913 – Pilotage Act 1913
P and SP Act 1975 – Petroleum and Submarine Pipelines Act 1975
PP Act 1934 – Petroleum Production Act 1934
OPD(S) Act 1975 – Offshore Petroleum Development (Scotland) Act 1975.
UKFL Acts 1964 & 1976 – United Kingdom Fishery Limits Acts 1964 to 1976
SF(C) Act 1967 – Sea Fish (Conservation) Act 1976
SF Act 1968 – Sea Fisheries Act 1968
SF(S) Act 1967 – Sea Fish (Shellfish) Act 1967
ST Act 1885 – Submarine Telegraph Act 1885
W Act (NI) 1972 – Water Act (Northern Ireland) 1972

FIGURE 2

One of the fruits of the debate on sea-use planning in the United Kingdom and of the consequent establishment of the ICMS has been the publication in 1977 of a 49-page booklet, prepared by ICMS, on Marine activities. Guide to the responsibilities of Government Departments and Agencies. The table in Figure 2, reproduced from this publication, provides a bird's eye view of the current situation, though it must be added that the position becomes even more complex when the fine detail is added.[4]

It is difficult for the outsider to assess the efficacy of the changes in government structure which have been introduced other than by observing results over the medium term. It may not be wishful thinking, however, to discern a change in the Government's attitude. Speaking in the House of Lords debate in February 1976 (Col. 520), Lady White regretted that "There is no one whose job it is to take a synoptic view." Perhaps it is more than a coincidence that the inquiry ordered by the Prime Minister into the effectiveness of oil pollution emergency procedures, was described by Whitehall "...as designed to take a synoptic view of all the departmental, local authority and international interests involved" (The Times, June 1, 1978).

Commentators in the United Kingdom have in the main adopted a rather broad, general approach to the question of sea-use planning. They have drawn attention to the need for more coordination in policy making, on the basis of better information, more widely disseminated. They too have made general proposals for the creation of new Departments or the allocation of a coordinating role to an existing Minister and the adoption of planning procedures suggested by the analogy with land use planning. Relatively little attention has been focused, however, on what is usually called "coastal zone management." The extent of this zone is loosely defined, but the term is usually intended to refer to the foreshore and a narrow strip of adjoining land, together with the more landward of the sea areas lying within the limits of national jurisdiction. That this area has attracted relatively little comment is not surprising, for only the specialist can hope to unravel this legislative ball of knots. Fortunately, one of the writer's colleagues in the Centre for Marine Law and Policy, John Gibson, has made a start on this

---

[3] Written answer by Secretary of State for Trade to a Commons Question. The report on the basis of which the decision was made has been published as Accidents at Sea Causing Oil Pollution. Review of Contingency Measures, Department of Trade, H.M.S.O. 1978.

[4] See also the informative description of "Government responsibilities for maritime safety" given by J. Archer, Under Secretary, Marine Division, Department of Trade, in Trade and Industry, April 18, 1975, pp. 130-134.

work, and reference to a few of his observations may serve to illuminate this somewhat neglected aspect of the overall problem of sea-use planning.

Commenting on the fact that no attempt has yet been made to integrate the corpus of law regulating the performance of numerous interconnected activities of a commercial, administrative or recreational character pursued within the same coastal region, Mr. Gibson (p. 1) observes that:

> The difficulty is due partly to obsolete jurisdictional distinctions between terra firma, foreshore and sea, whereby rules have developed in comparative isolation and without reference to the relationship of adjoining areas. Secondly, the survival of anachronistic principles of common law alongside statutory provisions of more recent origin has produced an unhappy marriage of antithetical doctrines that inhibits the implementation of new policies. Thirdly, piecemeal powers are distributed among a wide variety of governmental institutions and official bodies, whose insular traditions have created a complex and uncoordinated structure of overlapping constraints.
>
> The depth of these problems has escaped popular attention, because they are frequently rooted in local legislation and practice that have been omitted from presentations of public general law.

Mr. Gibson's researches have led him to the conclusion that:

> Many of the problems afflicting the coastal zone are aggravated by the inaccessibility of the local Acts and Orders under which it is governed. Not only are these often excessively old, but they are mostly omitted from the annual volumes of public legislation, and there are wide discrepancies in official procedure...
>
> The general result is that individual institutions are largely unaware of each other's powers and responsibilities, and do not always possess all the statutory materials describing their own functions. This defect could best be remedied by a programme of legislative consolidation, similar to that which is now being undertaken by county councils (Local Government Act 1972, s. 262 (9)).
>
> It is fashionable to assert that a solution to the difficulties of the maritime environment would be found in the imposition of centralized ministerial direction. Such claims ignore the extreme complexity

> and inconsistency of the legal framework within which a supervisory department would have to operate. There is a danger that a further tier of bureaucratic constraints would merely inhibit the performance of subordinate duties, unless the law itself has first been thoroughly overhauled. Hitherto, the failings of the existing system have been obscured by administrative compromise, but that palliative is no longer adequate to satisfy the new demands upon marine resources. Laws that depend for their acceptance on the ignorance of those who implement them do not deserve to be retained (Local Government Act 1972, pp. 21-22).

If this brief account of the position in the United Kingdom has any relevance for a wider study of sea-use planning, it is that one must beware of oversimplifying the problem, of solving complex legislative problems by a simple restructuring of departmental responsibilities, of the careless borrowing of analogies from different environments and different countries, with their quite different historical backgrounds. While such government restructuring may be helpful and such analogies fruitful, they are no substitute for a thorough review of what will frequently turn out to be a complex tangle of uncoordinated laws and regulations, ancient and modern.

It rather follows from this conclusion that it would be rash of the writer to venture to comment upon the position in other North Sea states, especially in the presence of colleagues from these states. It may, however, be of interest, by way of comparison, to refer in the most general terms to recent developments in Sweden.[5]

The question of sea-use planning has been under consideration in Sweden for some years, the Commission on Oceanic Resources having proposed the establishment of a "Special Delegation for Oceanic Resources" as long ago as in its report of 1972.[6] The Government was unwilling to act on these proposals

---

[5]Norway introduced a measure of governmental restructuring even earlier with the appointment of Mr. Jens Evensen as the first Norwegian Minister for Law of the Sea Questions in 1974. It would, however, appear from reports on his activities that his Ministry's main function is in the area of international relations, particularly the coordination of fishery negotiations.

[6]Swedish Ministry of Industry report on Samordning Av Havsresursverksamheten (Industridepartementet 1977-06-30; Ds. I 1977 : 5) Stockholm 1977, English summary, pp. 111-118, at p. 111. The writer is grateful to R. Churchill for drawing his attention to this report.

at that time and a new commission was set up in 1975 as a result of Parliamentary pressure on the Government.[7] The Commission's report, published in 1977, makes familiar reading for the student of British marine affairs. The following passage will perhaps serve to convey the flavor of the report:

> Ten ministries are more or less deeply engaged on matters of oceanic resources...[8]
>
> Although the work on oceanic resources is dispersed in many ways, some sectorial coordination exists and some efforts are being made to achieve united and more efficient work in the field as a whole.
>
> Within the ministries concerned the work of the different sectors is coordinated in the normal way. On certain issues, e.g., the establishment of heavily polluting industrial plants in coastal areas, the matter must be dealt with jointly by a number of ministries...[9]
>
> The various specialized agencies also have the natural responsibility as coordinators in their own branches. Many authorities are explicitly assigned the responsibility for coordination. Increased coordination has recently started within the Physical National Planning Department of the Ministry of Housing. During the autumn of 1976 a special working group, the Marine Environment Group, was established. It consists of representatives of most of the authorities dealing with oceanic resources. The group's work forms part of physical national planning, which aims at achieving the best possible use of land and water resources in the country.[10]
>
> Naturally there are great difficulties in coordinating the work on oceanic resources. The ministries dealing with this field represent and plan for their special sectors and act in relation to these plans. The work on oceanic resources is not considered a special sector, and the ministries do not issue directives for the total work on oceanic resources. For the time

---

[7] Ibid.

[8] Ibid., p. 112.

[9] Ibid., p. 114.

[10] Ibid., p. 114-115.

> being, there is no overall programme for the total work on oceanic resources.
>
> Within government agencies and separate sectors different activities are of course jointly planned. But there are no administrative means for joint planning of activities in several sectors. As it is, the authorities try to attain the best possible results within their special sectors, but it is by no means certain that acceptable results for the total work on oceanic resources can be achieved. There is also a great risk that personnel and technical equipment will be inefficiently used within different organizations if looked upon from the viewpoint of the total work on oceanic resources.[11]

The Commission recommended that "a delegation for oceanic resources" should be set up:

> It should work as the Government's advisory body and as far as possible independently of sectorial interests. The delegation should be responsible for the establishment and continuous development of an overall programme for work on oceanic resources. It should promote Swedish oceanic research. It should advise specialised agencies on the allocation of grants for oceanic activities and work for more efficient use of personnel and technical equipment in all fields. Furthermore the delegation should be an organ for cooperation between government authorities and industry and should mediate information and contacts in the field of oceanic resources.[12]

It was recommended that the delegation should consist of 11 members served by an eight-man secretariat and that it should be subordinate to and housed in the Ministry of Housing[13] a Ministry which, as noted above, already has marine planning functions.

In a White Paper published on March 16, 1978 (Prop. 1977/78: 167), the Government accepted the Commission's recommendations and proposed that:

> A body should be set up to coordinate Swedish marine resources activity. The functions of this body shall

---

[11] Ibid., p. 116.

[12] Ibid., p. 117.

[13] Ibid., pp. 117-118.

> include the establishment and development of a comprehensive programme for the exploitation of the sea and the protection of the environment together with research and development concerning the sea. It shall promote marine resource activities and work for effective achievements in this area.

It would seem then that the Governments of the North Sea states are gradually becoming aware of two needs, each the result of the intensified use of the sea. First, there is a need to ensure that the left hand of government knows what the right hand is doing and that some agency should be given the responsibility to supervise and coordinate the marine policies of the various departments of government. Secondly, there is a need to review the corpus of law which has grown up piecemeal over the centuries to regulate activities in the coastal zone. Comparative studies in this area are, however, of only limited value in view of the peculiarities of the structures of government in different states.

2. Sea-Use Planning as a Function of the European Economic Community

The extent to which the EEC can play a role in sea-use planning in the North Sea depends upon the material scope of the Community's jurisdiction (over what uses of the North Sea does it have jurisdiction?); its geographical scope (does it extend to all the waters of the North Sea?); and its personal scope (does it have jurisdiction over all states and other persons using the North Sea?).

(1) The material scope of the Community's jurisdiction.

The material scope of the Community's jurisdiction is determined in the first place by Article 2 of the EEC Treaty, which describes the "task" or "purposes" of the Community:

Article 2

> The Community shall have as its task, by establishing a common market and progressively approximating the economic policies of Member States, to promote throughout the Community a harmonious development of economic activities, a continuous and balanced expansion, an increase in stability, an accelerated raising of the standard of living and closer relations between the States belonging to it.

It is complemented by Article 3 which provides that:

Article 3

For the purpose set out in Article 2, the activities of the Community shall include, as provided in this Treaty and in accordance with the timetable set out therein:

(a) the elimination as between Member States, of customs duties and of quantitative restrictions on the import and export of goods, and of all other measures having equivalent effect;

(b) the establishment of a common customs tariff and of a common commercial policy towards third countries;

(c) the abolition, as between Member States, of obstacles to freedom of movement for persons, services and capital;

(d) the adoption of a common policy in the sphere of agriculture;

(e) the adoption of a common policy in the sphere of transport;

(f) the institution of a system ensuring that competition in the common market is not distorted;

(g) the application of procedures by which the economic policies of Member States can be coordinated and disequilibria in their balances of payments remedied;

(h) the approximation of the laws of Member States to the extent required for the proper functioning of the common market;

(i) the creation of the European Social Fund in order to improve employment opportunities for workers and to contribute to the raising of their standard of living;

(j) the establishment of a European Investment Bank to facilitate the economic expansion of the Community by opening up fresh resources;

(k) the association of the overseas countries and territories in order to increase trade and to promote jointly economic and social development.

It will be noted that it is said merely that the Community's activities shall "include" those specified, thus indicating that this is not necessarily an exhaustive enumeration. If, moreover, additional powers are required for the attainment of the Community's objectives, resort may be had to Article 235:

> <u>Article 235</u>
>
> If action by the Community should prove necessary to attain, in the course of the operation of the common market, one of the objectives of the Community and this Treaty has not provided the necessary powers, the Council shall, acting unanimously on a proposal from the Commission and after consulting the Assembly, take the appropriate measures.

In considering the material scope of the EEC's maritime jurisdiction, it is helpful to draw attention to the distinction between the relatively narrow, specific "activities" referred to in Article 3 and the more general matters which this article also includes among the EEC's activities. The adoption of common policies on agriculture and transport[14] are two of the specific activities which clearly have a maritime dimension, and of course the Common Fisheries Policy (CFP) is being developed under the former head. It is also important, however, to be fully aware that the more general activities referred to in Article 3 may also provide a basis for Community intervention in the maritime arena. The need to abolish obstacles to freedom of movement for persons, services and capital, to institute a system ensuring that competition in the common market is not distorted, and to approximate the laws of Member States to the extent required for the proper functioning of the common market, may all, from time to time, require Community action in relation to the uses of the North Sea. It is indeed in reliance on these provision that the Community has been able to develop its environmental policy.

Since the CFP and the environmental policy are the two most important of the Community's maritime policies at the present time, it may be helpful to consider in a little more detail the basis of the Community's powers in these fields and the use which has been made of them by the Community. It is also instructive to refer to the Community's powers in relation

---

[14]See, however, EEC Treaty, Article 84, under which it is for the Council, acting unanimously, to decide whether, to what extent and by what procedure appropriate provisions may be laid down for sea and air transport. On the scope for application of this and other provisions of the EEC Treaty to sea transport, see D. Rizzi, "The EEC Treaty and the Merchant Fleets of the Member States," <u>Marine Policy</u>, October 1978, <u>2</u>(4), pp. 268-274.

to the exploitation of the North Sea continental shelf. As will be seen, despite the Commission's acknowledgment of the sovereign powers of the coastal state over continental shelf resources, the material scope of the Community's jurisdiction is not static, and the development of an efficient Community energy policy is bound to place limitations upon the powers of national administrations.

(i) The Common Fisheries Policy. Under Article 3(d) of the EEC Treaty, the adoption of a common policy in the sphere of agriculture is one of the recognized activities of the Community. That this common policy should embrace fisheries is made clear by Article 38 which includes "fisheries" in its definition of "agricultural products." It is by virtue of these provisions that the CFP has been developed through Regulations 2141/70 and 2142/70 (O J, 1976, pp. 1, 19), Articles 98-103 or the Act of Accession, 1972 (Sweet and Maxwell, 1977) and the Hague Resolutions of November 3, 1976 (Bull. EC 10-1976, pp. 23-24).

As the Court of Justice made clear in the Kramer case:

> It follows from these provisions taken as a whole that the Community has at its disposal, on the internal level, the power to take any measures for the conservation of the biological resources of the sea, measures which include the fixing of catch quotas and their allocation between the different member-States.[15]

A brief review of the progress made by the Community, pursuant to these powers, provides a fair account of the Community's sea-use planning role in relation to the North Sea fisheries and at the same time emphasizes the frustrations placed upon that role by the decision-making process of the EEC.

Article 1 of Regulation No. 101/76 provides that:

> Common rules shall be laid down for fishing in maritime waters and specific measures shall be adopted for appropriate action and the coordination of structural policies of Member States for the fishing industry to promote harmonious and balanced development of this industry within the general economy and to encourage rational use of the biological resources of the sea and of inland waters.

---

[15]Officier van Justitie v. Kramer and Others, Joined Cases Nos. 3, 4, and 6/76, Preliminary ruling of July 14, 1976, 2 C.M.L.R. 440, at 469, Para. 14. The reference was to EEC Treaty Articles 29, 40 and 43, Regulations 2141/70 and 2142/70 and Article 10 of the Act of Accession.

Article 2(1) adds that the:

> Rules applied by each Member State in respect of fishing in the maritime waters coming under its sovereignty or within its jurisdiction shall not lead to difference in treatment of other Member States.
>
> Member States shall ensure in particular equal conditions of access to and use of the fishing grounds situated in the waters referred to in the preceding subparagraph...for all fishing vessels flying the flag of a Member State and registered in Community territory.

These provisions are complemented by Article 4, which empowers the Council, "acting in accordance with the procedure provided for in Article 43(2) of the EEC Treaty, to "adopt the necessary conservation measures," if a stock of fish in the waters subject to the sovereignty or jurisdiction of a Member State is in danger of being over-fished. Finally, mention should be made of Article 102 of the Act of Accession which provides that:

> From the sixth year after accession at the latest, the Council, acting on a proposal from the Commission, shall determine conditions for fishing with a view to ensuring protection of the fishing grounds and conservation of the biological resources of the sea.

At first sight, these articles would seem to make adequate provision for the orderly development by the Community of a CFP. Unfortunately, this picture is drastically altered when it is added that far-reaching derogations from the equal access principle were written into the Act of Accession as a sine qua non of the United Kingdom's membership. These derogations were due to be reviewed in 1982. This review would have been extremely difficult in any event. Given the detrimental effect on the British fishing industry of the widespread extension of North Sea fishery limits to 200 miles, the renegotiation of the CFP looks like being well-nigh impossible without a change of heart by either the United Kingdom or her Community partners. The fact that the Luxembourg Accords of January 1966 would seem to give the United Kingdom a virtual right of veto in these negotiations scarcely eases the task (Brown, 1972, pp. 37-73).

The continuing difficulties are reflected in the lack of progress made since the Council adopted the Hague Resolutions on November 3, 1976. In accordance with these resolutions, the Member States extended their fishery limits to 200 miles from January 1, 1977, and agreed that the exploitation of fishery resources in those zones by fishing vessels of third states should be governed by agreements concluded between the Community and those third states. The Council also approved a statement (Annex VI) to the effect that, pending the implementation of Community measures for the conservation of resources, Member States would not adopt unilateral measures. If, however, no agreement was reached in the fishery Commissions for 1977 and no Community measures could be adopted immediately, the Member States were authorized to adopt "as an interim measure and in a form which avoids discrimination appropriate measures to ensure protection of the resources situated in the fishing zones off their coasts." Such measures must not prejudice the future guidelines for Community conservation provisions and the Member States must, before adopting such measures, seek the approval of the Commission which must be consulted at all stages.

Since the Hague Resolutions were adopted, the Council has been unable to secure agreement because of the firm opposition of the United Kingdom to the various proposals prepared by the Commission. The consequent freedom of action for Member States has been reconfirmed by the Court of Justice in Case 61/77, brought by the Commission against Ireland.[16] Having reiterated its finding in the Kramer case that the Community had the capacity "to take conservation measures both independently and in the form of contractual commitments with non-member States or under the auspices of international organisations,"[17] the Court confirmed that "In so far as this power has been exercised by the Community the provisions adopted by it preclude any conflicting provisions by the member-States."[18] It went on to add, however, that:

> On the other hand, so long as the transitional period laid down in Article 102 of the Act of Accession has not expired and the Community has not yet fully exercised its power in the matter, the member-States are entitled, within their own jurisdiction, to take appropriate conservation measures without prejudice, however, to the obligation to cooperate imposed upon them by the Treaty, in particular Article 5 thereof.[19]

It followed, of course, that Ireland was entitled to adopt conservation measures unilaterally, in view of the Council's failure to reach agreement. It was only because the measures

---

[16] Re Sea Fishery Restrictions: E.C. Commission v. Ireland, Case No. 61/77, Judgment of February 16, 1978, 2 C.M.L.R. 466.

[17] Ibid., at 515 (63).

[18] Ibid., at 515 (64).

[19] Ibid., at 515 (65).

actually adopted, being discriminatory, did not conform to the requirements of Community law, that they were held by the Court to be illegal.

(ii) The Community's Environmental Policy. According to the preamble of the EEC Treaty, "the essential objective" of the efforts of the Member States is "the constant improvement of the living and working conditions of their peoples." Moreover, as has been seen, Article 2 includes "an accelerated raising of the standard of living" among the purposes of the Community. Since the improvement of the quality of life is an essential part of raising living standards and producing better living and working conditions, the tasks of the Community would seem to include environmental protection generally and the control and prevention of marine pollution in particular. The need for community action is further underlined by the provisions of Article 3, Paragraphs (e), (f), and (h) of the EEC Treaty.

Paragraph (f), which calls for the institution of a system ensuring that competition in the common market is not distorted, is relevant because the uncoordinated imposition of anti-pollution measures by Member States might well distort competition by placing unequal burdens on the same industries in different countries.

Paragraph (e) provides a further foundation for Community action in relation to marine pollution since the imposition of anti-pollution measures on shipping is a matter which would have to be considered in relation to the adoption of a common transport policy.

Finally, the Community has a role to play under Paragraph (h), which calls for the approximation of the laws of the Member States to the extent required for the proper functioning of the common market.

The European Communities Action Programs on the Environment,[20] through which the Community is discharging its obligations in this field, laid stress on "the paramount importance to Western Europe that effective action be taken against the dangers inherent in the carriage of hydrocarbons, including the threat of serious pollution of coastal areas from accidents on the high seas" and specified that protection of marine waters to ensure that ecological balances are preserved is a priority task (Council Resolution of June 26, 1978).

The Community has responded to the need to protect the marine environment on two levels. On one level, it has

---

[20] O J No. C 112, 20.12.1972, p. 1 and O J No. C 139, 13.6.1977, p. 1.

cooperated with other international institutions which are active in this field and has signed and ratified the following conventions:[21]

(i) the Paris Convention for the Prevention of Marine Pollution from Land-Based Sources (1974);[22]

(ii) the Barcelona Convention for the Protection of the Marine Environment against Pollution in the Mediterranean (1976);[23] and

(iii) the Bonn Convention on the Protection of the Rhine against Chemical Pollution (1976).[24]

On a second level, the Community has more recently adopted a resolution establishing an action program on the control and reduction of pollution caused by oil spills at sea.[25] Under this action program, the Commission is to undertake studies and submit early proposals to the Council on the following matters:

1. Computer processing of the existing data, or data still to be collected, on ways of dealing with marine pollution by hydrocarbons with a view to the immediate use of such data in the event of accidental pollution.

2. The availability for the Member States of relevant data on tankers liable to pollute the waters around the Community and the coasts of the Member States and on offshore structures under the jurisdiction of the Member States.

---

[21] On June 26, 1978 the Council adopted a Recommendation (O J L 194, 19.7.1978) concerning the ratification of further international conventions on safety of shipping. Council also noted that, following the action of its Member States, the group of North Sea States--to which Norway and Sweden also belonged--had invited Italy and Ireland to accede to the Memorandum of Understanding between the North Sea countries on the maintenance of standards on merchant ships (Bull. EC 6-1978, point 2.1.62).

[22] International Legal Materials, 1974, 13, p. 352.

[23] Ibid., 1976, 15, p. 285.

[24] Ibid., 1977, 16, p. 242.

[25] Council Resolution of June 26, 1978 setting up an action program of the European Communities on the control and reduction of pollution caused by hydrocarbon discharged at sea (O J No. C 162, 8.7.1978). The program was put before the Council by the Commission on April 27, 1978 (Bull. EC 4-1978, point 1.4. 8) and approved in its broad outlines on May 30, 1978 (Bull. EC 5-1978, point 2.1.53).

3. The need for measures to enhance the cooperation and effectiveness of the emergency teams which have been or which are to be set up in the Member States.

4. A possible Community contribution to the design and development of clean-up vessels to which may be fitted the equipment needed for the effective treatment of discharged hydrocarbons.

5. The amendments and improvements which may have to be made to the legal rules on insurance against the risks of accidental pollution from hydrocarbons.

6. Establishment of a proposal for a research program on chemical and mechanical means of combating the pollution due to hydrocarbons discharged at sea, on the subsequent history of such hydrocarbons and on their effects on marine flora and fauna.[26]

(iii) <u>The Community role in relation to the exploitation of the North Sea continental shelf</u>. The resources of the continental shelf are, for the most part, static and inanimate, whereas those of the North Sea fisheries are mobile and animate. Whether these distinguishing features justify in law the establishment of a common-resource, equal-access regime for fish, while preserving a regime of national sovereign rights over oil and gas is at least debatable (Brown, 1972, pp. 53-54; Churchill, 1977, pp. 26-36; Fleischer, 1971, p. 148; Winkel, 1977, pp. 329-337). In any event, at first sight, the status of the resources of the continental shelf and the relatively narrow scope of the Community's jurisdiction in relation to them appeared to have been firmly established by the Commission's Written Answer of March 12, 1974 to a Written Question put to it by Lord O'Hagan.[27] The following points emerge from the Answer:

1. In the view of the Commission, the provisions of the Treaty and of Community acts under the Treaty clearly specify the sovereign rights enjoyed by Member States over economic activities on the continental shelf and in particular over the exploitation and exploration of oil resources. It follows that these natural resources belong entirely to the Member States concerned which may therefore derive the full economic advantages from them (for example, dues, taxation and balance of payments benefits).

[26] <u>Ibid</u>.

[27] Answer to Written Question No. 489/73, O J No. C 49, 27.4.1974, p. 3.

2. The EEC Treaty does apply to the continental shelves of Member States. Accordingly, in exploiting continental shelf resources, Member States must take into account the various provisions of the Treaty which apply to different aspects of industrial and commercial activity, particularly those governing the principles of freedom of movement of goods and of establishment, although these rules do not diminish the benefits to the Member States concerned already referred to.

3. The Treaty does not exclude the possibility of nationalization by a Member State of any sector of economic activity, although nationalized industries are of course also subject to the provisions of the Treaty.

Unfortunately, when one descends from this level of generality and seeks answers to more specific policy questions, it becomes clear that the views of the Commission and the British Government are quite different. For example, the British Government considers that it follows from their sovereign rights over the continental shelf, as recognized by the Commission, that the Government is entitled to control the development of its continental shelf oil resources and in particular to determine the rate of depletion. Since, however, Community finance has been made available to British firms for oil development in the North Sea as part of the Community's energy policy, the Commission and other Member States consider that the Government's discretion is no longer unlimited. There appears to be some difference of opinion over pricing policy as well, the Commission holding that hydrocarbons offered for sale to consumers in other Community states should be offered without discrimination in terms of price or quantity, whereas the British Government seeks to maintain a pricing policy designed to favor the British industrial consumer. There would seem to be little doubt that, though the process will be long and difficult, the Community's role in this area must expand; Community sea-use planning will thus acquire a new dimension.

(iv) <u>Vertical and horizontal planning roles</u>. The EEC Treaty has a vertical structure, in the sense that it deals with different areas of European economic and social affairs in separate, relatively self-contained sections. Moreover, this vertical approach is reflected in the structure and practice of Community institutions. There is therefore a built-in tendency to develop common policies in, for example, fishing or transport, without considering the relationship which such policies may have with other areas of Community concern. It is of course true that the close relationship between the energy and environmental policies has been recognized and, similarly, the Commission's marine pollution proposals, referred to above, were considered by three sessions of the Council so that their environmental, shipping and international implications could be examined by the appropriate sets of ministers. However, there would seem to be no reason why a greater degree of horizontal planning should not be introduced into Community practice. There are of course difficulties in coordinating the Community's maritime policies which do not exist within national administrations. As the above brief survey of some of these policies has indicated, the material scope of the Community's maritime jurisdiction is by no means comprehensive. Nevertheless, the horizontal functions of preventing or resolving conflicts between competing users and of rationalizing the enforcement of separate common policies should be as much a Community interest as a national one. Perhaps the habit of consultation and cooperation in law of the sea matters, encouraged by participation in UNCLOS III, is pushing the Community in this direction in any event.

(2) The geographical scope of the Community's jurisdiction.

It is sometimes argued (Fleischer, 1971, p. 151) that Article 227 of the EEC Treaty, which declares the Treaty to be applicable to the Member States, restricts the authority of the Community to the territories of those States. The result of this interpretation would be, inter alia, that the Community's fisheries policy and its marine environmental policy would have no validity beyond the territorial sea. There is little merit in this argument (Koers, 1977, pp. 269-301). Where it was the intention to limit the Community's authority to the territory of Member States, specific provision to this effect has been included in the Treaty--in Articles 48 (free movement of workers) and 53 (the right of establishment) for instance. Moreover, in the Kramer case, the Court has ruled quite explicitly in relation to the CFP that the rule-making authority of the Community ratione materiae also extends, insofar as the Member States have similar authority under public international law, to fishing on the high seas (supra footnote 15 at p. 469, Para. 14). It seems likely that the Court would take a similar view of the Community's authority in relation to other maritime activities over which it has jurisdiction and that potentially, therefore, the whole of the North Sea lies within the geographical scope of the Community's planning powers.

(3) The personal scope of the Community's maritime jurisdiction and the question of the Community's external capacity.

In any consideration of the potential role of the Community in sea-use planning in the North Sea, it has to be borne in mind that the North Sea is not the private pond of EEC Member States. Norway is also a riparian State, and of course other States are heavy users of the North Sea for a variety of purposes. The rule-making authority of the Community, however, extends ratione personae only to the Member States of the Community. It follows that the EEC's marine policies can only be fully effective in the North Sea if they can somehow be extended to bind non-Member States. Such states cannot of course be bound by Community-made rules without their consent. Since, however, the Community has far-reaching and, in some cases, exclusive treaty-making powers, it is frequently in a strong negotiating position and thus able to ensure through agreements with non-Member States that Community policies will be effective. It is the purpose of this section to provide a brief account of this external capacity of the EEC as reflected in the jurisprudence of the Court of Justice.

(i) The ERTA case.[28] This case was concerned with the treaty-making powers of the Community in relation to international transport and the Court held that, in the absence of specific treaty provisions, it was necessary to turn to the "general system of Community law relating to agreements with non-member States." It went on to say that the incorporation of Article 210, stating that "the Community shall have legal personality," in Part VI of the Treaty, devoted to "General and Final Provisions," "means that in its external relations the Community enjoys the capacity to establish contractual links with non-member States over the whole extent of the field of objectives defined in Part One of the Treaty, with which Part Six must be read together."[29]

A general treaty-making capacity is not of course the same as a power to enter into treaty relations on particular subjects. On this question too, however, the Court explained the need to take into account "the whole scheme of the Treaty no less than...its specific provisions" and found that "such authority may arise not only from an explicit grant by the Treaty, as is the case with Articles 113 and 114 for tariff and commercial agreements and with Article 238 for association agreements, but may equally flow from other provisions of the Treaty add from steps taken within the framework of these provisions, by the Community institutions."[30] The Court went on to say that:

> In particular, each time the Community, with a view to implementing a common policy envisaged by the Treaty, lays down common rules, whatever form these may take, the member-States no longer have the right, acting individually or even collectively, to contract

---

[28] Re The European Road Transport Agreement: E.C. Commission v. E.C. Council, Case no. 22/70 (1971) C.M.L.R. 335.

[29] Ibid., Paras. 12-14.

[30] Ibid., Paras. 15 and 16.

> obligations towards non-member States affecting these rules.
>
> To the extent that such common rules come into being, the Community alone is in a position to assume and carry out contractual obligations towards non-member States affecting the whole sphere of application of the Community legal system.
>
> One cannot, therefore, in implementing the provisions of the Treaty, separate the category of measures internal to the Community from that of external relations.[31]

Summing up, where there is no express attribution to the Community of a treaty-making power, an exclusive treaty-making power may nevertheless arise from the adoption by the Community of common internal rules in implementation of a common policy envisaged by the Treaty. In such a situation the rule is that "internal leads to external."

(ii) The OECD case.[32] This case was concerned with the external powers of the Community in the area of commercial policy, in relation to which an express treaty-making power is accorded to the Community in Article 113 of the EEC Treaty. The Court held that the exercise of external powers in this area need not be preceded by the adoption of internal measures:

> A commercial policy is in fact made up by the combination and interaction of internal and external measures, without priority being taken by one over the others. Sometimes agreements are concluded in execution of a policy fixed in advance, sometimes that policy is defined by the agreements themselves.[33]

It went on to hold that the Community's treaty-making power was exclusive in this area since the exercise by Member States of a concurrent power would "call into question the mutual trust within the Community and prevent the latter from fulfilling its task in the defence of the common interest."[34]

(iii) Kramer Case.[35] This case was concerned with the external powers of the Community in relation to the CFP.

---

[31] Ibid., Paras. 17-19.

[32] Re The OECD Understanding on a Local Cost Standard (Opinion 1/75) (1976) 1 C.M.L.R. 85.

[33] Ibid., Para. 23.

[34] Ibid., Para. 32.

[35] Supra footnote 15.

Having examined Articles 39, 40 and 43 of the EEC Treaty, Regulations 2141/70 and 2142/70 and Article 102 of the Act of Accession, the Court held that:

> It follows from these provisions taken as a whole that the Community has at its disposal, on the internal level, the power to take any measures for the conservation of the biological resources of the sea, measures which include the fixing of catch quotas and their allocation between the different member States.[36]

It held, moreover, that this rule-making authority extended, insofar as the member states had similar authority under public international law, to fishing on the high seas.

It followed of course from the principle laid down in the ERTA case that the adoption of common rules in implementation powers in relation to the CFP. Since, however, the Community had not yet fully exercised its internal powers for the conservation of fish stocks, the Court held that member states retained the power to assume treaty obligations (in this case under the North-East Atlantic Fisheries Convention) and ensure their application. It was stressed, however, that this power was of a transitional nature and that member states were bound by Community obligations (especially EEC Treaty Articles 5 and 116[37]) in such negotiations. Moreover, under Article 102 of the Act of Accession, this transitional power of Member States would come to an end once the Council adopted conservation

---

[36] Ibid., Para. 14.

[37]

Article 5

Member States shall take all appropriate measures whether general or particular, to ensure fulfillment of the obligations arising out of this Treaty or resulting from action taken by institutions of the Community. They shall facilitate the achievement of the Community's tasks.

They shall abstain from any measure which could jeopardise the attainment of the objectives of this Treaty.

Article 116

From the end of the transitional period onwards, Member States shall, in respect of all matters of particular interest to the common market, proceed within the framework of international organisations of an economic character only by common action. To this end, the Commission shall submit to the Council, which shall act by a qualified majority, proposals concerning the scope and implementation of such common action.

During the transitional period, Member States shall consult each other for the purpose of concerting the action they take and adopting as far as possible a uniform attitude.

measures; it was envisaged in the Article that this would happen "from the sixth year after Accession at the latest," that is, from the end of 1978.[38]

In commenting on this case, Dr. Koers (1977, p. 297) has described the Court as having adhered "to the doctrine of the ERTA decision that, if there is no express conferment of authority under the Treaty, the Community must first adopt common rules before it has external authority--a doctrine which implies a certain sequence in time." The protracted and continuing failure of the Community to finalize its common internal rules has not, however, prevented Member States from agreeing to the Commission's proposal that all negotiations with third states should be conducted by the Community, and a first bilateral agreement was concluded between the Community and the United States in 1977.[39] Nevertheless, the absence of common internal rules and, therefore, in accordance with the ERTA rule, of exclusive Community treaty-making powers, has given the United Kingdom an argument for blocking approval by the Council of framework agreements with a number of non-Member States, including, most recently, Spain (The Times, September 26, 1978).

A basis for the exclusivity of the Community's treaty-making powers (prior to the adoption of common rules internally) may, however, be provided by the decision in a later case, the Rhine case,[40] which was concerned with the treaty-making powers of the Community in relation to inland waterway transport.

The Rhine Case. The position in this case was that the EEC Treaty provided no express treaty-making power, nor had relevant internal rules been adopted. The Court found that Articles 3 and 75 provided the legal basis for the establishment of a European laying-up fund for inland waterways vessels but that the system proposed could not be fully attained through the adoption of common rules since the participation of Switzerland, a non-Member State, was also required. The Court held that the Community possessed the necessary treaty-making powers, arguing that:

---

[38]The Treaty of Accession entered into force on January 1, 1973, in terms of its Article 2.

[39]The Commission's proposal was accepted by the Council on November 3, 1976 (Bull. EC 10 - 1976, Paras. 1501-1505). The first bilateral Treaty, an Agreement concerning Fisheries off the Coasts of the United States, was concluded between the Community and the United States on February 15, 1977 (International Legal Materials, 1977, 16, p. 257.

[40]Re The Draft Agreement Establishing a European Laying-up Fund for Inland Waterway Vessels, Opinion 1/76 (1977) E.C.R. 741.

> whenever Community law has created for the institutions of the Community powers within its internal system for the purpose of attaining a specific objective, the Community has authority to enter into the international commitments necessary for the attainment of that objective even in the absence of an express provision in that connexion.[41]

This was particularly so "in all cases in which internal power has already been used in order to adopt measures which come with the attainment of common policies," but it is "not limited to that eventuality."[42] This dictum would certainly seem to be applicable also in relation to fisheries, for it is the case here too that the attainment of the objectives of the CFP require the conclusion of agreements with non-Member States.

In the Rhine case, the concurrent participation of the Member States in the treaty-making process was held to be justified only because it was necessary to provide for the modification of earlier agreements but it was made clear that such participation "must be considered as being solely for this purpose and not as necessary for the attainment of other features of the system."[43]

It would seem fair to conclude, therefore, reading the judgments in the Kramer and Rhine cases together, that even in the absence of express treaty-making powers or of common rules adopted internally, the Community will have exclusive treaty-making powers whenever it has internal powers to attain a specific objective and the conclusion of an agreement with a third party is necessary for the attainment of that objective. Member States will retain only such external powers as may be necessary to enable them to effect modification of earlier incompatible treaties.

(4) The overlap of Community law and public international law.

As was noted above (Part II, at Fig. 1), there is an area of maritime affairs in which the sovereignty of the coastal state is limited not only by rules of Community law but also by those of public international law. The legal framework of sea-use planning is particularly complex in relation to such areas. Where the third states concerned are prepared to enter into treaty relations with the Community and the Community is itself

---

[41] Ibid., Para. 3.

[42] Ibid., Para. 4.

[43] Ibid., Para. 7.

in a position to conclude an agreement, the task of dovetailing community law and international law will not normally present any great difficulties.[44]

Where, however, the third states concerned decline to accept the Community as a negotiating partner, or where, as is the case in UNCLOS III, the negotiations embrace both questions within the competence of the Community and others which are not, the position is more difficult. The question is perhaps best clarified by viewing it first in the context of Community law and then in the context of international law.

The position in Community law has arisen in three of the cases mentioned above, the ERTA case, the Kramer case and the Rhine case. In the ERTA case, although the Court recognized the exclusive competence of the Community in relation to the subject matter of the treaty negotiations, it took into account the fact that most of the negotiations had taken place prior to the attribution of exclusive powers to the Community. It held therefore that the Council was entitled to adopt a negotiating procedure involving joint action by Member States since any other procedure "might well have jeopardised the successful outcome of the negotiations."[45] Thus, even where the Community has an exclusive treaty-making power under Community law, there may still be a role for the Member States, acting jointly with the Community or even alone but on behalf of the Community, where this is necessary to overcome practical or political obstacles such as the refusal of third states to recognize the international personality of the Community.

In the Kramer case, the Court was concerned with the transitional power to negotiate conservation agreements which the

---

[44]Problems can arise, however, as to the applicable law and as to which tribunals have jurisdiction over disputes arising from such an agreement. Since the agreement is clearly a treaty, international law applies in the relations between the parties to it but, since the International Court of Justice has contentious jurisdiction over only inter-state disputes, it would not be competent to adjudicate in such cases. The European Court of Justice has, however, accepted that a Tribunal may be established by the agreement (The Rhine Case, supra footnote 40 at Para. 21). It is also of course the case that a treaty between the Community and a third State is "an act of one of the institutions of the Community" Second Haegeman case - Case No. 181/73 (1975) 1 C.M.L.R. 530, and that the European Court is thus competent to accede to requests for interpretation under Article 177 of the EEC Treaty. Such rulings would not however bind the third state concerned.

[45]ERTA case, supra footnote 28, at pp. 361-362.

Member States retained pending the exercise by the Community of its powers in this field. As has been seen, the Court emphasized that, in their negotiations, Member States were bound by Community obligations, especially under Articles 5 and 116 of the EEC Treaty.[46] Moreover, after noting that this transitional power was destined to terminate shortly under Article 102 of the Act of Accession, the Court said that:

> ...member-States participating in the Convention (i.e., in this case NEAFC) and in other similar agreements are now not only under a duty not to enter into any commitment within the framework of those conventions which could hinder the Community in carrying out the tasks entrusted to it by Article 102 of the Act of Accession, but also under a duty to proceed by common action within the Fisheries Commission.[47]

Furthermore,

> ...as soon as the Community institutions have initiated the procedure for implementing the provisions of the said Article 102, and at the latest within the period laid down by that Article, those institutions and the member-States will be under a duty to use all the political and legal means at their disposal in order to ensure the participation of the Community in the Convention and in other similar agreements.[48]

Finally, in the Rhine case, the Court, having found that the Community had power to conclude an agreement with Switzerland, held that the participation of the Member States with the Community to conclude this agreement was justified in the circumstances since it was necessary to provide for the modification of earlier agreements. However, the participation was to be "solely for this purpose and not as necessary for the attainment of other features of the system."[49]

This case is also important in confirming that the treaty-making powers of the Community entitled it to secure the attainment of its objectives by cooperating with third states in establishing a public international institution. It was stressed, however, that its composition must not "result in weakening the institutions of the Community" or surrender "the bases of a common policy even for a specific and limited objective."[50]

---

[46] Supra, footnote 37.

[47] Supra, footnote 15 Para. 21.

[48] Ibid.

[49] Supra, footnote 40, Para. 7.

[50] Ibid., Para. 14.

Applying these dicta to the status of the Community in the UNCLOS III negotiations, it can thus be said that:

(a) the Community has the power to take part in the negotiations in relation to matters falling within the material scope of the Community's jurisdiction;

(b) the Community may participate in the establishment of international institutions, subject to the provisions laid down in the Rhine case;

(c) if, for any reason, third states decline to recognize the Community in the UNCLOS context, the Council would be entitled to adopt a negotiating procedure involving joint action by the Member States (ERTA case);

(d) where Member States participate in the negotiations on matters falling within the scope of the Community's jurisdiction, whether exclusively or not, they are bound by Community obligations (see Kramer case), including the obligation to use all political and legal means to ensure the participation of the Community in the convention.

In fact, steps have been taken to ensure that the Community should be permitted to become a party to the convention simultaneously with Member States. In September 1976, the Chairman of the Netherlands delegation to UNCLOS III wrote to the Chairman of UNCLOS III on behalf of the EEC Council, explaining the need for the Community to become a party to the convention and suggesting the following clause for incorporation in the convention:

> Customs unions, communities and other regional economic groupings exercising powers in the areas covered by this Convention may be parties to this Convention (UNCLOS III Official Records, Doc. A/CONF. 62/48).

It was pointed out that, since the Community was now exclusively competent in relation to some of the matters covered by the convention, it must become a party to the future convention simultaneously with its Member States. It was only in this way, it was claimed, that third parties would have "a legal guarantee that they had before them partners capable of honouring in their regard the totality of obligations envisaged by the Convention"(UNCLOS III Official Records, Doc. A/CONF. 62/48).

It is also necessary, if the Community Member States are to become parties to the convention, that steps should be taken to ensure recognition of the special status of the Community maritime zone under which Member States enjoy preferential rights. It was accordingly proposed in the letter to the

UNCLOS III Chairman that a clause should be inserted in the Convention to the effect that nothing in the Convention would prevent EEC Member States from implementing Community provisions for "the mutual granting to the nationals of such states of national treatment or any other special treatment." As it was put in the letter, "The transposition to the Community level of the responsibility to apply the convention, or certain provisions thereof, would leave to internal law of the Community the task of regulating relations between member States in the areas concerned."

These are questions which have still to be resolved by the Conference and, until they are resolved, it is not possible to determine what limitations the convention will place upon the scope of the EEC's planning powers in the marine arena. In view of the many legal and political problems raised by the Community's proposals, it may well be that UNCLOS III will decline to permit it to become a party to the convention but will recognize its special status by providing for derogations from certain provisions of the convention in favor of the Community and other similar regional bodies.[51] The onus would then be left with Member States to ensure that common Community policies would permit them to honor their international commitments under the convention to the extent that derogations were not provided for. They could also of course arrange for common Community policies to be pursued through the agency of Member States in UNCLOS III and in any institutions set up under the new convention.

3. Sea-Use Planning as a Function of International Law and Institutions

As the above review of the roles of national government and the EEC has shown, sea-use planning in the North Sea is difficult enough within the framework of national and Community laws and institutions. The North Sea is not a closed regional system, however, and, in planning its use, account has also to be taken of the rules and institutions of public international law, particularly in relation to the rights in the North Sea of non-Members of the EEC and in relation to uses of the North Sea which do not fall within the material scope of the Community's jurisdiction. It was suggested above that sea-use planning

---

[51] See further UNCLOS III Doc. A/CONF.62/L.13, July 26, 1976 (Draft alternative texts of the preamble and final clauses prepared by the Secretary-General), Doc. A/CONF.62/48, p. 125. See also Report drawn up on behalf of the Legal Affairs Committee of the European Parliament on the Conference on the Law of the Sea as it affects the European Community (European Parliament Working Documents 1977-78, Document 82/77, May 9, 1977).

means the provision of institutions and procedures capable of ensuring the rational, coordinated exploitation of the sea in the interest of the community at large and in the light of adequate information, and the resolution of conflicts between competing interests in accordance with agreed criteria. Looking at the role of international law and institutions in the light of this definition, it will be appreciated that this is a vast subject in itself and it is hardly feasible to do more than consider it in outline in a relatively short paper.

It is to public international law that one looks for the rules on such fundamental questions as the division of the seas into various jurisdictional zones, the determination of the rights of states to use these zones for different purposes, and the provision of procedures for the settlement of disputes concerning such matters. Leaving the labors of UNCLOS III on one side for a moment, it is fair to say that the "institutions and procedures" which have created these basic rules are simply the law-creating processes of public international law. Thus, for example, the scope and status of the various jurisdictional zones are the combined product of international customary law, based on state practice, and treaties, negotiated at ad hoc conferences such as UNCLOS I (1958). Similarly, the allocation to states of rights to use these zones for various purposes has been effected in the same way. Finally, only the relatively primitive provisions of general international law for the settlement of disputes have been available for the resolution of conflicts concerning such questions.

Within the framework of these basic rules, a large number of public international institutions have grown up to supervise the implementation of treaty rules (again usually the product of ad hoc conferences) on such matters as the allocation and management of fish stocks, the protection of the marine environment, and safety of shipping. On the universalist level, they include the FAO, IMCO, WHO, WMO, UNEP, UNESCO, UNCTAD and ESCAP. On the North Sea regional level, they include the NEAFC and regional pollution agencies.

Turning next to UNCLOS III, the long-awaited Caracas Convention, if it ever materializes, will introduce fundamental changes in the basic framework described above, new jurisdictional zones, a revised allocation of rights of user in these zones, new criteria for the resolution of conflicts and new institutions for the settlement of disputes.

In their future planning in relation to the North Sea, national governments and Community institutions will therefore have to take into account: (a) the framework of jurisdictional zones created by UNCLOS III (or, possibly, by customary law); (b) the rules created by UNCLOS III concerning the allocation of uses within these zones, to the extent that they have not been modified by derogations in favor of the Community; (c) the new institutions created by UNCLOS III and the procedures established for the settlement of disputes; (d) the network of universalist and regional institutions referred to above and the conventions which they administer; and (3) rights which states may still enjoy under international customary law.

It is beyond the scope of this paper to consider all the aspects of this complex international framework in depth. It is hoped, however, that concentration on the following two aspects will facilitate an understanding of the international legal dimension of sea-use planning. The first aspect is the need for coordination among international institutions. The second is the international jurisdictional framework within which conflicts may occur in the North Sea.

(1) Coordination among international institutions.

The difficulty of coordination between the EEC and UNCLOS III and the problems raised by the proposal to permit the Community to become a party to the Caracas Convention have already been alluded to, and of course the same problems will have to be overcome in relation to other universalist institutions. There is, however, another problem of coordination, that caused by the co-existence of a large number of universalist institutions with a maritime role.

Fortunately, the problem has been recognized and steps have already been taken to ensure the efficient coordination of their potentially overlapping activities. The need to coordinate the work of universalist institutions in the maritime field is only a part of the wider need for consultation and coordination of activities among United Nations agencies. One of the principal means of coordination on the more general level is provided by the Administrative Committee on Coordination (ACC). Made up of the Secretary-General and the administrative heads of the U.N. agencies, the ACC "can review the whole field of operations of the various organizations in the light of the need for coordination, fixing priorities and enabling a concentration of efforts and resources" (Bowett, 1975, p. 62).

The ACC operates directly and through sub-committees. One of these sub-committees, the Sub-Committee on Marine Science and its Applications, met recently for the first time under a new name, the Sub-Committee on Marine Affairs, and new terms of reference and is now charged with wider responsibilities in the coordination of all ocean affairs within the U.N. system (UNESCO, March 1978, pp. 1, 8). The Sub-Committee deals with inter alia the implications of, and developments in, science and technology related to the use of the sea, interaction between uses of the sea as reflected in the functions of the United Nations organizations, examination of the implications of major decisions and resolutions of the United Nations organizations as they affect marine affairs (UNESCO, March 1978, p. 1). In the course of its eighteenth session in February 1978, the Sub-Committee agreed that member organizations would contribute to a study on "uses of the sea" to be prepared by the U.N. Ocean Economics and Technology Office for submission to the U.N. Economic and Social Council in 1979 (UNESCO, March 1978, p. 8). This study will deal with the trends towards regionalization and 200 mile national resource zones. A separate study is also to be made on regionalization in marine affairs, with the Inter-governmental Oceanographic Commission acting as lead agency (UNESCO, March 1978).

A further indication of the growing awareness in the United Nations of the need for institutional reform is provided by the progress made since 1978 towards a restructuring of the economic and social sectors of the United Nations system, "so as to make it more fully capable of dealing with problems of international economic cooperation and development in a comprehensive and effective manner...and to make it more responsive to the requirements of the provisions of the Declaration and the Programme of Action on the Establishment of the New International Economic Order as well as those of the Charter of Economic Rights and Duties of States" (UN General Assembly Resolution A/RES/32/197). Following the report of an ad hoc Committee set up to examine the question, the General Assembly endorsed its recommendations for a fundamental restructuring, including the creation of the post of Director-General for Development and International Economic Co-operation (Resolution A/RES/32/197, p. 236). The new Director-General has responsibility for:

> (a) Ensuring the provision of effective leadership to the various components of the United Nations system in the field of development and international economic cooperation and in exercising over-all coordination within the system in order to ensure a multidisciplinary approach to the problems of development on a system-wide basis;
>
> (b) Ensuring, within the United Nations, the coherence, coordination and efficient management of all activities in the economic and social fields financed by the regular budget or by extrabudgetary resources (Resolution A/RES/32/197, p. 236).

It may be useful to bear this development in mind in the context of the proposal tabled recently by a group of 19 states in UNCLOS III for a "declaration or resolution on international institutional arrangements in ocean affairs" (Doc. A/CONF. 2/L.30). It was proposed inter alia that an ad hoc study group should be established to:

(i) review and identify gaps in the present institutional arrangements in the field of international ocean affairs;

(ii) evaluate the institutional implications resulting from the implementation of the (expected Caracas) Convention;

(iii) formulate alternative proposals aimed at improving, where appropriate, the effectiveness of the United Nations System in the sector of ocean affairs and on its gradual adjustment to the functions referred to in the Convention (Doc. A/CONF.62/L.30, Para. 2(b)).

There is always the danger that the result of such reviews will be the application of Parkinson's law to the area in question, i.e., the addition of yet another costly layer to the existing bureaucracy. Nevertheless, a thorough review of the functions of the various maritime agencies, global and regional, and of the provision made for their coordination would seem to be a useful exercise.

(2) The international jurisdictional framework within which conflicts may occur in the North Sea.

In constructing this framework, it is useful to consider where the conflicts may arise (their scope ratione loci); about what uses of the sea they may arise (their scope ratione materiae); and between whom they may arise (their scope ratione personae).

(i) <u>Conflicts ratione loci</u>. In relation to any inquiry into the international legal regime governing the uses of the sea, the basic framework is provided by the division of the sea into a number of jurisdictional zones. Pending the successful conclusion of UNCLOS III, or the development of a stable regime in international customary law, it is impossible to state with any certainty how many jurisdictional zones there are, where their limits lie or what their precise jurisdictional natures are. It will suffice for present purposes, however, to assume that the sea may be divided horizontally into the jurisdictional zones shown in Figure 3.

It is, however, necessary to bear in mind a number of points which the diagram helps to make clear. First, at the present time, France is the only North Sea state which has claimed a 200 mile exclusive economic zone (EEZ), although, of course, this is of little practical consequence in the North Sea, given France's situation in the southern North Sea. Looking to the future, however, others may well follow suit. Until they do, the basic residual status of the 200 mile exclusive fishing zone (EFZ) will remain that of the high seas. Once an

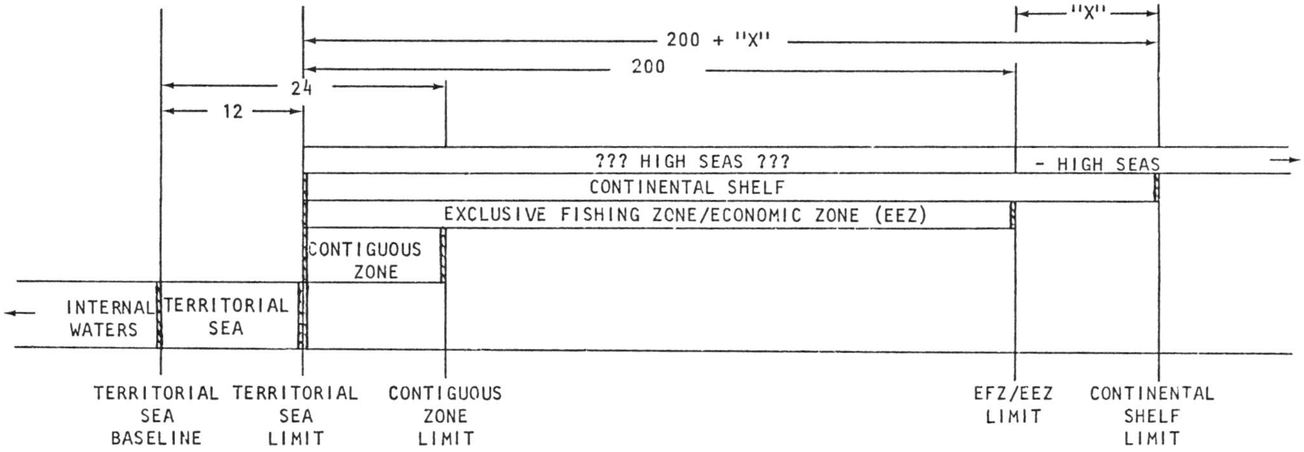

FIGURE 3 - Maritime Jurisdictional Zones (Horizontal)

EEZ is proclaimed, however, the status of the zone will be sui generis. Secondly, some of these zones overlap. Thus, the waters of the 24-mile contiguous zone also fall within the 200 mile EFZ/EEZ and the seabed and subsoil of the EEZ will coincide with those of the continental shelf out to the 200 mile limit.

To obtain a more accurate jurisdictional zone framework, it is necessary to divide the sea not only horizontally but vertically as well. It is then possible to identify the 28 jurisdictional zones indicated in Figure 4.

(ii) Conflicts ratione materiae. Having determined where the conflicts may arise, the next question is what conflicts are likely to arise. The answer is that a conflict may arise whenever there is competition between two or more parties to use the same space for the same purpose or for different but incompatible purposes.

(iii) Conflicts ratione personae. Conflicts may take place between persons of different nationalities, and the juridical nature of the conflict depends not only on the jurisdictional zone in which it occurs, but also on the nationalities of the persons involved. Thus, in the North Sea area, it will be material to determine whether the dispute is one between two or more persons having the same nationality or between persons of different nationalities. It must also be known whether the parties have the nationality of an EEC member state or a non-EEC state.

(iv) Jurisdiction over conflicts. Any of the potential conflicts identified in section (ii) above, between any of the persons referred to in section (iii) may take place in any of the zones identified in section (i). The authority having jurisdiction over any conflict and the law applicable to it will depend upon the precise permutation of these three factors in the case concerned. To obtain a comprehensive, detailed picture of the authorities and legal systems governing all the uses of the North Sea--this is to gain an understanding of the legal framework of sea-use planning in the North Sea--it would thus be necessary to draw up a statement for each jurisdictional zone of (1) who has jurisdiction (2) under which law (3) over every conceivable use of the sea (4) for any person or persons. Such an exhaustive account is beyond the scope of this paper, but the method may be illustrated by considering an example (Brown, 1977, pp. 325-350). If attention is focused on fishing in the United Kingdom's zone (IVB, for example) it would be necessary to look at the United Kingdom's fishery laws and regulations, the acts of the EEC adopted pursuant to its CFP and the rules of public international law, be they derived from international customary law, bilateral or multilateral fishery agreements or from a new UNCLOS convention. Precisely which "mix" of those

	Internal Waters	Territorial Sea	Contiguous Zone	Exclusive Fishery Zone	Exclusive Economic Zone	Continental Shelf	High Seas
Airspace	I A	II A	III A	IV A	V A	VI A	VII A
Water	I B	II B	III B	IV B	V B	VI B	VII B
Seabed	I C	II C	III C	IV C	V C	VI C	VII C
Subsoil	I D	II D	III D	IV D	V D	VI D	VII D

FIGURE 4 - Maritime Jurisdictional Zones (Horizontal and Vertical)

rules would be applicable to the dispute in question would of course depend upon the nationality of the persons involved.

III. Conclusion

The overall picture which emerges from the above survey is one of considerable complexity. The North Sea is used intensively for a variety of purposes by the nationals of both North Sea states and other states outside the region. Their activities are regulated by several systems of national law, by European Community law and by public international law. The division of responsibilities between the institutions on these three levels of integration is not always clear and on all three levels; the law is at present in a highly fluid state. Given this complexity, the writer is inclined to share the view expressed by Mr. William Ogden (1978, p. 2), writing about the management of the coastal lands of the English Channel and southern North Sea:

> ...complex systems cannot be planned : they cannot be comprehended well enough; neither is it possible to establish agreed objectives with the many interacting organisations either now, or in definable futures. But complex systems can be managed.

"Planning" in this context may be considered to be a relatively static process essentially concerned with arranging things in advance and prescribing criteria in advance for the resolution of conflict. Planning in this sense is exemplified by the system of land-use planning described earlier in this paper. "Management," on the other hand, is, relatively, a more dynamic process, the aim of which "is to achieve a negotiated order in changing contextual and transactional relationships, using conflict when it arises constructively, and as a stimulus to political and social innovation" (Ogden, 1978, p. 1). Management, in this sense, is less concerned with arranging things in advance than with providing institutions and procedures for the continuing arrangement of things. There is of course a continuum between planning and management; it is a matter of where the emphasis lies.

It is suggested that in relation to "sea-use planning" in the North Sea, the emphasis ought to be on management in this sense rather than planning. From this point of view, the land-use planning analogy is not helpful. The degree of integration achieved on the European Community and international levels falls far short of that required to sustain such a system, conceived and reared in a developed system of municipal law.

Given that the objective is "management," what changes are required in the present system? The main need, it is suggested, is in the field of education. The legislator, the administrator and the judge must be taught that if the North Sea is to be exploited equitably, economically and with due regard for the marine environment, they must understand the sea as an area in which there is a continual interaction between a number of competing uses and users. They must appreciate that decisions concerning one use will frequently affect others. They must have an understanding of the three kinds of law operating in the North Sea and of the relationships among them and the institutions which serve them. They must be taught to realize that there are no recognized formulae or criteria by reference to which conflicts may be simply resolved. More often than not it will be a question of determining the value in socio-economic terms of the benefits which the conflicting users might be expected to derive from their conflicting activities, weighing them in the balance and considering what equity requires (Brown, 1977, pp. 338-346).

If more of the decision-makers were to receive this kind of training, the need would be less pressing for the establishment of institutions or procedures to ensure that particular decisions are taken in awareness of the general maritime context. Given the likelihood that the need for such training will continue to be ignored, it is important that further progress should be made in providing or improving the kind of coordinating machinery referred to earlier in national government, in the institutions of the EEC and the United Nations.

Whether this be the way ahead or not, it is hoped that the above analysis will have provided a useful outline of the legal framework within which any form of sea-use planning will have to be established and operated.

REFERENCES

Birk (Lady). Debate on Sea Use Planning. House of Lords Hansard, February 1976.

Bowett, D. W. The Law of International Institutions, 3rd ed. London: Stevens, 1975.

Brown, E. D. British fisheries and the Common Market. Current Legal Problems, 1972, 25.

Brown, E. D. The exclusive economic zone: criteria and machinery for the resolution of international conflicts between different users of the EEZ. Maritime Policy and Management, 1977, 4(6).

Churchill, R. The EEC fisheries policy. Towards a revision. Marine Policy, 1977, 1.

Fleischer, C. A. L'Accès aux lieux de peche et le traité de Rome. Revue du Marché Commun, 1971, 14.

Gibson, J. The law of coastal zone management in the Severn Estuary and the Bristol Channel. (Typescript kindly made available to the writer.)

Heap, Sir Desmond. An Outline of Planning Law, 7th ed. London: Sweet & Maxwell, 1978.

Koers, A. W. The external authority of the EEC in regard to marine fisheries. Common Market Law Review, 1977, 14.

Marine Activities. Guide to the Responsibilities of Government Departments and Agencies, Dept. of Trade, H.M.S.O., 1977.

Ogden, W. The Study of the Management of the Coastal Lands of the English Channel and Southern North Sea. A Conceptual Analysis of the Theme of the Study: A Discussion Paper. 1978.

Sweet & Maxwell. European Community Treaties, 3rd ed., 1977.

Town and Country Planning in Britain. Central Office of Information Reference Pamphlet 9, H.M.S.O., 1975.

UNESCO, International Marine Science Newsletter, 1978, No. 18.

Winkel, K. Equal access of Community fishermen to member state fishing grounds. Common Market Law Review, 1977, 14.

Young, E. and Fricke, P. (Eds.) Sea Use Planning. Fabian Tract 437, Fabian Society, London, 1975.

COMMENTARY

O. Wattne
Deputy Director
Norwegian Ministry for Petroleum and Energy

We see today that activities such as shipping, fishing, oil and gas exploration and exploitation, and naval warfare are taking place to such an extent that they affect each other, sometimes negatively, and frequently, one activity actually prevents the other. A typical example of this is oil installations with their safety zones which preclude fishing and any other activity in the area covered by the safety zone.

An activity which has been briefly mentioned by Dr. Eisma is recreation and sports along the coast. It occupies more and more space. It is the basis of a large industry. Manufacturers of all kinds of equipment depend on this and for millions of people the coastal resort areas are a must for their vacations. Any other sea activity which affects this activity will therefore also affect land activity and this, of course, goes for all the other sea activities which have been mentioned. I think it is a very important general point that we should underline. The way the sea activities interact very often has an important social and economic impact on land based activity.

In order to get a clearer view of the problem we are discussing, the two previous speakers have made many important distinctions and subdivisions in categories of jurisdictional and geographical areas. We have been shown horizontal distinctions and been reminded that more than on land we are operating with a three dimensional perspective.

I think a good illustration of this is a film recently shown on Norwegian television. It was taken by a fisherman who upon seeing that the trawl had a very heavy catch started his camera only to have the net come up with a Russian submarine. This also illustrates another point which is extremely important, that is, sea-use planning is difficult enough for the normal activities and their interactions, but it is even more difficult for abnormal situations. This of course could occur in connection with any of the activities taking place, but may be seen especially in connection with transport of large quantities of oil and oil exploration and exploitation.

Let me take a few examples from two activities with which I am particularly familiar which Norway has come to face in a relatively short period. Fishing existed a long time ago. By adding the oil activity in the same waters, we have more and more frequently seen the interactions and often negative results from having fishing and oil in the same area.

Let me give you some figures about the oil activity. There are many ways to measure this, but by the beginning of this year nearly 2,000 wells have been drilled in the North Sea, in all of the North Sea. There were 104 fixed installations in place. In addition, there are nearly 3,000 kilometers of pipeline. The pipelines go from the installations to the shores and also between installations.

Total fishing activity is more difficult to quantify, but I have indications that the fishing activity which most often could interact with the oil activity is the industrial trawlers and they have increased in numbers over the last year.

How did this problem start and how could we have planned to avoid the negative effects? Of course, the first platform, the first oil platform, was a mobile platform in place for a short time to drill. It did not cause any big uproar, but as the number of platforms increases suddenly we have a major problem. This was first recognized as the physical space with the safety zone preventing fishing in the area, but later we started getting reports that the fishing was obstructed by pollution of the seabed. Partly, this was due to wellheads not being properly removed after drilling and partly to debris from empty barrels.

Now, if we had been able to have foreseen the right legislation and administrative bodies to prevent this, of course, we would not have the next problem which occurs, i.e., how to regulate this abnormal situation of the pollution of the seabed. Before I go into the problems of mending the conflict which has taken place between fishing and oil, I think we have data which show that fishing has been obstructed. The catch of fish by Norwegian fishermen has been estimated to have been reduced in three years time by about 30-40%. This was measured by looking at industry trawlers, the numbers of them, motor sizes, effectiveness, etc. At the same time the Maritime Institute was asked to see if there were any reduction in the fish population which could cause this reduction in catch; they could not point out any such reduction. So, a fairly safe conclusion is that it was oil activity and especially the pollution of the seabed that was an important factor in causing reductions.

Now, if we had had adequate legislation to compensate the fishermen, they would at least have not been harmed in economic terms. But nobody owns the fish. So in terms of normal liability, practice and legislation nobody has had a loss. It makes planning extremely difficult because even if you should allow the confrontation and the problems for the fisheries, you see the problems in adequate compensation.

Another example of the abnormal situation and the difficulty of planning for it is the effect of a large blow out. We know that it may occur from time to time and that the risk has increased along with oil exploration and exploitation. We may take the responsibility for not having had better contingency equipment and plans in connection with oil exploration and exploitation. I feel, however, it is very strange, since obviously the risk with bulk transport of oil is so great, that so little has been done.

Let me give another example of how difficult it is to plan. We know that the supply vessels cross from the land to the installations and back fairly regularly and in relatively stable lanes. At the same time we may have fishing nets standing still for several days out there. Now, would not it be a good idea to establish specific lanes so that the fishermen knew where they should not set their nets in order not to have them destroyed? However, since the mackerel run is not stable, the fishermen did not know where their nets would be positioned.

Let us move a bit from the North Sea to see what lessons result. We are planning activity north of the 62nd parallel which basically takes you out of the North Sea. We have had a lot of experience which we should be able to learn from; in fact, there is proof that we have learned something. We have been in close contact with the fishing industry. We are looking at the effects of sea-based activity on the coastline and on the activity on land. One very practical result of this planning is that for the starting period we are operating with drilling seasons in order to avoid the fishing seasons.

We have got adequate proof that it is very difficult to regulate and plan when you have many institutions involved, many countries involved, etc. Fortunately, in this area we do not have that in Norway. I think that is an advantage.

Another point which I would like to mention in connection with this is the necessity of coordination and centralization so that you know what is taking place and have one responsible authority. When the oil activity started in Norway there was one division responsible for almost everything. This situation persisted for some years. In fact, until only five years ago you had several distinct activities, e.g., geological mapping and control, concessions, economic conditions for the licenses, safety of installations and control and supervision in that connection, contingency planning, oil spill questions, labor related matters, telecommunications and air traffic related to the oil activity, all gathered in one division. Today these activities are distributed among seven different bodies, ministries, directorates, and the national oil company.

This change resulted not from the need to give better planning, but to avoid letting the horse watch the sack of corn. The latest administrative change was to separate the safety control division from the Ministry of Petroleum and Energy and move it to the Ministry for Municipal Affairs. This was because of the feeling that concessions would be granted too quickly with too little regard for safety.

Is my conclusion then that we should go on with ad hoc decisions taking all relevant factors into account and then go on from there? Would effective planning have been possible given the rapidly changing circumstances? Would we have been able to make sensible plans even if we had had the will, the administrative power and the legislation to do so? I would respond in the affirmative. Planning can be made such that it takes changing circumstances into consideration to implement new developments. I think that the most important factor in planning would be to assure that all interested groups have a possibility to influence developments. I think that with planning we can deal with long term problems and can help avoid irrevocable situations which very often occur when you have the all-too-familiar piecemeal planning and ad hoc decisions.

Are not there also dangers involved in planning, apart from the fact that it is difficult? Yes, you can say that in many ways, I guess, if you have very thorough planning and a system which looks far ahead, things may go a little bit slower. I feel that even if the development of the North Sea in many respects went a bit slower, the North Sea would still be there and what we do now may affect the situation for such a long time that we should afford cautious behavior.

COMMENTARY

D. Tromp
Secretary, the Oslo Commission

I wish to approach the subject from the experience of the Oslo Commission during the last couple of years. As an introduction, I should say that I am Secretary of the Oslo Commission, a commission between Western European coastal states endeavoring to prevent marine pollution from dumping from ships and aircraft. The second convention under which we operate, the Paris Convention, also deals with marine pollution, specifically with the marine pollution from land-based sources.

The Oslo Convention has been in force since 1974; the Paris Convention came into force in 1978. The aims of both conventions, of course, are the prevention of marine pollution; however, they deal with different subjects and different methods.

These two conventions touch marine pollution from two sources. The area in which we work goes west to Greenland and includes the whole sea area. The activities of the Commission include regulation of certain uses of the sea, some of which are exclusive. For example, if you have dumping areas, you cannot, at the same time at least, fish there in the same area. Incineration areas will clash with shipping lanes requiring regulations.

If I had looked then at what happened during the last years in both Commissions, I must say that the procedures of taking this issue and the time which this involved is very long indeed. It is difficult to reach a decision with this structure. This is due to the large amount of manpower involved in the different countries and because of the need for coordination with the country.

There is also an international factor which makes this kind of decision difficult. Professor Brown touched it and he touched it in a certain example. You must not have the illusion in our North Sea area that we are dealing with a number of countries all of which have the same interests, the same priorities and the same goals. That certainly is not the case. The example Professor Brown mentioned is the common fishery policy which should be agreed upon in the framework of the European Community. He showed very clearly the many difficulties involved in trying to develop a common fishery policy.

But problems are not limited to fisheries. Comparable divergencies exist in the use of the sea environment, approaches to the dumping of waste and approaches to incineration of waste at sea. There are large differences of opinion in each of these areas. As an example, some countries are very clearly of the opinion that the sea can be used to discharge waste, so long as you monitor it correctly and thoroughly and understand what you are doing. This is reflected in the national laws of the United Kingdom.

On the end of the scale, you have the Nordic countries like Norway, Sweden, where national law prohibits dumping waste into the sea. Such different approaches make the process of decision making quite lengthy and difficult.

All the difficulties which I just mentioned will increase in the future. I think the level of effort needed in these countries is simply insufficient. Coordination nationally is certainly one of the most important things which has to be dealt with.

I shall now turn to the content of the papers. Mr. Eisma contends that sea-use planning must begin with agreement among the bordering countries on the development and the management of the North Sea. He stresses the need of planning in advance. Professor Brown, on the other hand, expresses his favor not so much for planning but for management, general agreement of what the future of the North Sea should be.

I am afraid if we try to tackle sea-use planning on an international basis and begin with trying to get an agreement on the future of the North Sea, we shall encounter such difficulties that agreement will take a very long time. I am much more in favor of trying to be a little more careful, perhaps proceed somewhat more slowly, but at least to do something in the near future. I am certainly not saying then we should go on as we used to, taking ad hoc decisions without much coordination on a national or international basis.

If you asked me how these matters should be tackled, I think you should not ask that question of somebody who is presently responsible for the function of an inter-governmental body. I would add that I hope in the future sea-use planning will not be dealt with by a number of small organizations all dealing with one aspect of the subject. I hope it is possible in the future to coordinate these activities in one organization.

At the beginning of the 1970's, the North Sea area was a little ahead of the other areas in Europe or in the world, having concluded conventions like the Oslo and Paris Conventions dealing with a single subject, prevention of marine pollution of a certain source. I think now the North Sea area is a little behind the Baltic and the Mediterranean Seas. We have tackled the matter, at least the matter of the pollution of the environment, somewhat more comprehensively. In the convention dealing with these areas, not only dumping is regulated but also pollution from land based sources. Regional coordination of the implementation of worldwide conventions like the IMCO Convention, dealing with prevention of marine pollution by ships, is dealt with in the convention; pollution from offshore operations also is covered.

COMMENTARY

John M. Armstrong
University of Michigan

I am indeed honored to be before this body. I have participated in some of the Institute meetings before but have not had the honor recently to speak before you. I shall try to be brief since I am the last commentator. I do not know whether that is good or bad because some of what I wanted to say has been touched on by the other gentlemen. Like a previous speaker said yesterday, I feel slightly uncomfortable with all of you lawyers here. But over the years I have learned to live with this--some of my best friends are lawyers, as the saying goes.

I also feel uncomfortable in commenting on papers that address the North Sea in terms of sea zone management, much in the same sense that other speakers here might feel uncomfortable coming to the United States, listening to one or two papers, and then to comment on our ocean programs in the U.S. But fortunately some of the comments I was going to make have also been made by people who are from Europe and so I will not be alone in some of these ideas.

I thought the two papers that were given were excellent. I learned a considerable amount from them and that is to be expected at a prestigious meeting as this. I think the subject of sea-use management, sea-use planning (and I would like to talk a little bit about semantics) is a very important one. I think the analogy here at this meeting is that we are somewhat like the winemaker who sent his sons into a vineyard to dig for buried treasure. They did not find any but their digging vastly improved the soil. I think that is what is happening here, and, if I may say so, that is an invaluable, necessary process.

It is very important for people who are interested in law of the sea negotiations and related research to be interested in the subject of sea zone planning and sea zone management. I looked at the agenda here today and it seemed that perhaps some people might think this subject to be out of place in a society of people primarily interested in the processes of international ocean law. I think there are several reasons that many of us have thought about which make this subject very important to those involved in law of the sea.

There is a tremendous amount of interest (as we have heard here today) in the North Sea, in the U.S. and elsewhere around the world in the concept of ocean management or sea-use management and a good deal of that has been brought about exactly because of the law of the sea negotiations.

I believe that we have to begin to realize that as law of the sea negotiations go forward we are providing a "forcing function" on the governments that are participating, particularly the coastal states, a responsibility that at least some of them are now recognizing. The various LOS concepts and agreements will have the result of forcing states to come up with new approaches, new institutions, new ideas about managing at least their own territorial seas. And of course, those territorial seas may expand. The concept of the extended economic zone is fairly common. The management of that zone, and it is a mixed zone, is going to require new concepts and policies, new institutions and new arrangements that do not exist today. We have certainly heard about one approach here today, a very logical approach.

So, I think some of the problems that arise from this "forcing function" are going to have to be faced by the units of government. That is, the linking of existing management problems and programs in the territorial sea, and also outside the territorial sea in the high seas. In the case of the United States, we have 30 coastal states, all of which have their own idea about what should be done not only in the territorial sea but in many cases in the ocean in general, some more and some less. So I believe that we will see a trend towards more formal rule making, more complex management procedures, more openness, more data required, more enforcement, more communication required among the various decision makers, etc.

A question arises then, that I think has to be addressed by those of us involved, or those of you involved in law of the sea research, support and negotiations--can the coastal states indeed do this? Can they indeed meet the challenge of increased resource management responsibility that LOS implies? I do not have the answer to that but I think it is something that is most important and precisely why we are talking about sea zone managementhere today at a law of the sea conference.

The process of answering the question of whether the coastal states can actually do resource management in their coastal waters and elsewhere should relate directly to LOS. We would have liked to have this question much more clearly perceived before we ever went to the law of the sea. I know that is the feeling I have about the United States. I wish we had an ocean policy, an integrated ocean management concept for our own "domestic waters," if I might use the term, at least so that we would have a better idea of where we stand in terms of "domestic" ocean management. At the present time we are still evolving this as it goes on. Of course, this is an idealistic wish when one considers the reality and scope of ocean politics and international relationships.

So, my interest here today is in management of the sea as the problem of management of a natural resource system. I would like to get away somewhat from what agency should do what and what formal institutions we might need. I think first we need to address the problem as a resource management problem. Now, I think there is some importance to distinguishing between planning and management. I do not want to get hung up on semantics. The idea of planning to me implies wishful thinking and there is many a slip twixt cup and tongue when it comes to what we do with plans and what we do in actual management, where the word manage means controlling something, influencing the course of action by decision making, but we could argue all day about semantics.

Comment has been made about the analogy between land use management and sea use planning. There was also the counter comment that perhaps the analogy is not so useful. My own belief is that there is no real or useful analogy between land use planning and ocean planning, management in the sense that there are too many disparities between the natural, economic and political systems that make up the ocean and those of the lands we try to manage.

I think the analogy or the value of the transfer of land management experience is that we have had a long history of managing large public resources, called lands, forests, rivers and lakes in the world. When we then recognize that the oceans are also large, complex "public" resources and probably should or could be subjected to public management, I think we have exhausted the usefulness of the analogy.

We wish somehow that we could better understand how to manage large public resources such as our lands and oceans. It seems to me that from time to time what we really have done is to learn to ask questions about managing large public resources; from time to time we have formulated potential approaches for managing large public resource systems; and from time to time we have established some principles that we try to adhere to when we manage our public lands.

Now, let me say immediately that every country is different. I am impressed with the land planning capabilities of the Netherlands and Great Britain. We certainly do not have that in the United States; I know many other countries do not either. So, even if the analogy were valid, we do not have very much knowledge to transfer from land management to sea management.

Another problem in terms of the analogy of that concept to ocean management is that we have had centuries of living in and on the land and the forests and in a sense the rivers, so we have had the benefit of that long history, that time of "immersion," if you will pardon the pun, so that there has been a strong thread of associative development in terms of the way we think about large land resource systems. In spite of this history, and I am sure John Craven will disagree, we do not have a similar sense or experience in living in the ocean like we have in the lands. We have not been surrounded by the oceans physically like we have the lands and I think there is something to that in the way our perception of how to manage those lands has developed.

I do not want to give the impression that there has not been much said about ocean management or sea-use management or "policy." There has been an enormous amount of material written under the rubric of ocean planning, ocean management or policy, and so on. Unfortunately, almost none of it has dealt with the problem of <u>management</u> of the ocean as a system. We can categorize this body of literature into three categories. First, much of it has been concerned with one way or another of examining the need to do marine research and how to get more money for more research. Secondly, a lot of it has dealt with the subject that we are expert at, the law of the sea negotiations, which in many cases I claim does not address management per se, although it is certainly intertwined and inseparable. And, three, we see a lot of writing, particularly in the United States, about <u>who</u> should do ocean management, sea zone management, which agency should get which part of the turf. This of course has really not very much to do with the problem of managing the natural oceans.

Part of our difficulty in understanding how to do sea use management is a lack of understanding of how the ocean really works. I am sure Dave Ross would support that as a marine scientist. We do not really understand very much at all about how the ocean responds to different pressures and uses and how its various systems and subsystems interrelate.

Well, I could talk a long time about how we view management of the oceans from some of the work we have done in the United States but I do not think I have very much time to do that. One of the things we have had to grapple with is defining what management means in the sense of "degree of control." I see management of the oceans as a spectrum of possible control where we mean control as either enhancing actions that occur in the ocean or restricting them in some general way. Now, the spectrum of control might run all the way from what we might call comprehensive, integrated, total management of the oceans. This would be one end of the management spectrum. The other end of it might be the programs and ideas that <u>influence</u> our use of the oceans but do not really directly control them. We could call that management but it would be arguable.

And, of course, there are all the classical functions that one could talk about in a management program: research, information gathering, enforcement, and all of the components that make up management. I will not get into defining all of these. I think however there are one or two points to be made about sea use planning with respect to the question of "boundaries," the definitions of the management boundaries that one considers when we talk about sea use management.

The first one would be the natural ocean system itself including two parts, the resources of the ocean, the fish, the minerals and so on, and then the idea of ocean space. The actual, volumetric space of the ocean in light of management objectives. This of course gets into the business of controlling the traffic, allocating the space, zoning, etc. Then, secondly, there are the ocean users themselves that need control or management and their activities. Third, we still have to learn how to manage our management programs. How do we put together and manage the groupings of laws, programs, agencies, and institutions that we want to control with?

After we recognize these components in a management context we can begin to discuss rationally how to use natural resource management ideas and principles to manage the oceans. We can begin to talk about multiple-purpose programs, optimal yield, use zoning in the ocean and other tools, e.g., suitability, capability, impact analysis, critical areas, unique value protection, etc.

I think there are two other important problems that we face in evolving ocean management. I know in our country we are facing this problem and I am sure others are too. One is that we must be sure that when we talk about ocean management we do not forget that there are many other national functions to be performed that go far beyond the oceans. For example, such things as: food policy, energy policy, environmental policy, etc. Those of us who tend to be advocates of the ocean always think that the oceans are the most important things in the world, when indeed the constituency is often smaller than it is in other categories. This affects the way in which we can gain support for ocean management efforts.

Secondly (and this I do not think is unique to the U.S. and it may bear upon the two talks given here) is that when we talk about designing and implementing a new ocean management approach, we are implying that we know something about how to measure how bad the old approach was, whatever it was. In other words, we have in the U.S. (and I am sure in many other countries) something that you could describe by drawing a circle around it as a management "system." It varies from country to country, but it is there and it exists and when one says we must have a new approach, one implies that there is a measure that tells us that if we have a new approach, it is better than the old one. I maintain that this is almost an impossible problem.

It is like saying, for example, if one could measure something called "the gross ocean product" and it was X billions of dollars under the old system or the existing system, and one evolved a new ocean management system with a new gross ocean product of Y, then the question is, is X less than or greater than Y? This observation is of particular importance if LOS creates the apparent need to carry out different or expanded "ocean management" on the part of the coastal states.

There are two other matters I would like to address. The first is the need for what I would call in increased use-assessment capability. I maintain that regardless of the approach or the method of ocean management or sea-zone management selected that what we really need is a way in which we can assess the consequences of various ocean resource development proposals before they are implemented. This is a need but not very many people do this. We need the capability of assessing the consequences of proposed developments in the ocean. I would maintain as an hypothesis that if we had such a capability (presumably done by the government) and if this capability were made available to all of the parties involved in ocean development, we would have gone a long way towards improving our ability to control the oceans.

The second factor which is obviously related to the assessment idea is the information itself, management information. If we really want to do something called sea use management, what information do we need to make decisions? Of course this implies knowing what decisions we need to make. We have to do a good deal more work on that problem as well! In the United States and in many countries our lack of information about what is happening out in the oceans is becoming increasingly unacceptable. I do not mean necessarily just <u>research</u> information about currents, diffusion, dispersion, biological water quality factors, etc. I mean the ocean-use <u>activities</u>, the ocean users and uses and what they are doing in "ocean space." I suggest that we need some sort of a dynamic "ocean use atlas," I suppose one could call it that, which will allow us to at least visualize from time to time if not more often what is going on out in the ocean and how things change as we take management action. A comprehensive system that would depict all the traffic, energy extraction, mining, fishing, and other on-going and planned activities.

DISCUSSION AND QUESTIONS

LEWIS ALEXANDER: I guess my question will be addressed to the two gentlemen who wrote the original papers. In the United States for about the last decade we have become very much enamored with the idea of coastal zone management, and so I was wondering how would coastal zone mix into the type of management you are talking about here?

E. D. BROWN: Coastal zone management to me is management of the foreshore and a narrow strip of adjoining land, together with the more landward of the sea areas lying within the limits of national jurisdiction. It was to this area that I was referring when I said that one of the needs which was very evident in the United Kingdom was for a thorough look at the statute book so far as the use of that area was concerned. This to me is a question, not entirely, but predominantly within the exclusive jurisdiction of the coastal state. You do not have quite the same difficulties of having to contend with community interests and with international interests in that area. It is an ill-defined zone and of course it is going to become even more ill-defined. If you had asked me this question a few years ago, we could simply have said that it was the area out to the outer limit of the territorial sea. Of course, now that the bounds of national jurisdiction extend to 200 miles, it is no longer possible to define the geographical scope of coastal zone management in a way which would be valid for all coastal states. It is a question of seeing what arrangements each state makes within this limit.

D. EISMA: I agree. In the Netherlands, no coastal zone management exists. There has been none developed in that direction. The coastal zone is supposed to extend in the North Sea. I wouldn't know where to let it end.

PAUL ADAM: I want to comment briefly on what I feel has been a neglected issue. Although the resources from the sea have been mentioned by almost every speaker, I think there is some misunderstanding about their economic meaning. It looks as if they are considered as something exploited at a given cost and sold at a somewhat higher value, allowing a profit margin rewarding the ability of the producer.

Unfortunately, this is never so for the resources of the sea. If you happen to know a river where you can find sturgeons, your profit margin will multiply your cost by about 100; consequently, you will no longer find sturgeon in the surrounding waters. We might still be in a position where there are more salmon in the North Sea, or coming to the North Sea, than there are fishermen for salmon. If you could increase the number of salmon, the number of fishermen would certainly immediately increase and at a faster rate. In these circumstances the economists immediately ask for regulation, that is to say for the help of lawyers, in the expectation that they will contribute to the preservation of the resources.

The nodules have been mentioned at length, but the two economic problems that they present have not been clarified. It is economically impossible to schedule the sharing of resources for which nobody knows the economic and commercial conditions of exploitation. Only the second problem can be answered, i.e., to guarantee a return on the money resource which is to be invested into the potential sea resources.

If you look at the krill business, the real resource is not the krill which is only a potential resource. The actual resources are boats. Nobody knows what to do with superfluous whalers and trawlers, so why not use them to catch krill? All this means that the resource problem confronting the lawyers is not only the usual problem of sharing a resource. It is a much wider problem because the absence of a law of the sea or a given law of the sea can create imaginary resources or destroy actual resources. In that sense the law can be considered as an integral part of the economic game.

I have no conclusion because it has already been put forward by Professor Brown. Certainly, the problem of sea-use planning is important and urgent; but for the time being, it is so intricate and obscure that we are perhaps still at the stage of being educated and seeking information.

D. EISMA: Again, the question of difficulty has been mentioned. Almost all speakers, myself included, have mentioned the difficulties of planning in the sea. There are two types of difficulties, solving conflicts between conflicting activities and solving conflicts between conflicting states. As far as conflicting activities go, I do not see much difference between land planning and sea planning. If you are familiar with land planning in a densely populated and intensively used area like Holland, you are aware that it is at least as difficult to plan on land, especially big operations, as it is to plan in the sea. For instance, I can cite the question of a new international airfield in Holland, which is a big problem. It has also international ramifications which have to be discussed with Belgium and Germany. At the local level, the planning process is very complicated. The local councils have to consult at least 25 government agencies and institutions; when they are wise, they consult another 20 more, so that it takes sometimes years to get plans completed.

So, I do not think that this type of difficulty in the sea is essentially different from difficulties on land. Then you have the difficulties between states, and I think that is a question of appreciation. When you look, for instance, at cooperation in fisheries or at the cooperation between Norway and Britain on the gas and oil exploitation along the median line and on the transport of oil and gas towards the shore, or at the question of pollution in the North Sea which follows the water transport paths crossing jurisdictional boundaries, cooperation is forced on the countries concerned because the natural conditions necessitate it. Therefore, I think then it is much wiser to anticipate these problems by sea use planning than to wait until the conflicts arise.

JOHN BARDACH; My question is to Dr. Eisma and to Dr. Brown. My former colleague, John Armstrong, has mentioned the very complex nature of systems planning and management. It is apparent that this complexity, while perhaps recognized by government, cannot at present be dealt with by existing organizations. One might assume also that it is easier to deal with this on the data taking, data interpretation, advisory level, than in applied and university research organizations.

I would like to know the trend in organizations and institutions that deal with sea-use planning and management in the EEC towards coping with the truly multi-disciplinary nature of the problem with which you are dealing.

E. D. BROWN: I think we might allow the chairman to say something about this because he has in fact been closer to the practice of the EEC than I have been. I can only repeat what I said in my paper that I do not think in fact that they are aware of or have taken into account the interaction between the various uses of the sea. My complaint was that they have a vertical structure and a vertical practice. They deal with things like fisheries and the environment and transport in separate boxes. My plea was that we should have some kind of agency for coordinating activities and being aware of interaction between them. I do not know whether there is any informal structure in EEC practice which does take care of this problem but certainly I am not aware of it.

ALBERT KOERS: I could say a few words about your question, Professor Bardach. Of course, my experience is limited to the Commission only and, in general, I would agree with the remarks made by Professor Brown. The Commission is organized vertically which means that there is very little coordination on a horizontal level. The experience with the law of the sea negotiations illustrates that the decision-making process of the Community is set up in a vertical fashion. There are coordination groups dealing with pollution, fisheries, shipping, etc. Now, of course, this is all supposed to come together at a higher level. But even there discussion is restricted to the major political questions to the exclusion of certain practical questions relating to particular activities and coordination. Thus, I think that statements made by Professor Brown in his paper are quite accurate. However, the staff of the Commission is becoming aware of these problems. We have now several groups that operate rather informally attempting to arrive at some level of coordination on a horizontal level, but this is still at a very formative stage.

JORGE VARGAS: What I would like to do is to give a different dimension to this discussion. I consider that sea-use planning or coastal zone management is a very important area of the law of the sea. However, my impression is that the coordination aspects are essential for sea-use planning and these aspects have been rather neglected by the Law of the Sea Conference.

Most developing countries have no experience in sea-use planning or coastal zone management. Because of that, they are running the risk of undertaking a massive exploitation of marine resources with a very substantial cost, negative cost, to the resources themselves and also to the natural environment. So, for developing countries it is of paramount importance to know about coordination in planning these types of activities.

On the other hand, most developing countries have good ecological conditions; the natural environments are clean and unpolluted. However, these countries are not concerned with the application of sea-use planning policies, but rather interested in achieving a fast economic development regardless of its cost. Consequently, this is a good opportunity to transfer knowledge to developing countries in this area, where international organizations have a leading role to play. These organizations should improve the coordination among themselves in order to transfer this knowledge to developing countries. As far as I know, the Intergovernmental Oceanographic Commission has indicated a strong interest in this area. Other agencies such as FAO, UNEP, IMCO, etc., are not as active as IOC.

Developing countries should be aware of the importance of sea-use planning now and try to develop an integrated or at least a coordinated approach to the multiplicity of coastal uses so they would get the most benefit out of this emerging area of the law of the sea.

JOHN ARMSTRONG: Well, I just will say, and I think Mr. Vargas knows already, that there has been a small amount of work by the United Nations. There was a seminar in Berlin two years ago jointly sponsored by the U.N. and the German Foundation for International Development where the subject was a two week workshop on developing nations and coastal zone management. There were about 35 countries there. I was fortunate enough to be there for it, and it was successful enough that there should be a follow up to that and I think perhaps Mr. Vargas knows more about a follow up conference to be held next year somewhere I believe in Mexico. So, there is an effort underway and I think anything that a group like this can do to support it is very important.

At the Berlin Conference, I was struck by the fact that almost without exception everyone at that conference, from each of the developing nations, had what seemed to be a very strong desire to do something about coastal resource management, to have a balanced approach. That concern seemed to be independent of the particular political structures of the countries present. Everybody seemed to have a general agreement that regardless of how you ran the country, whether it was democratic, socialistic, or whatever, there were certain basic things that needed to be done, certain information needed to make decisions, and to me it was encouraging in that sense. So, I would support what Mr. Vargas has recommended here.

J. C. KREFFER: I would like to make a few remarks, being quite involved in different matters in the North Sea. I made two notes from the speakers which I want to quote here. The first was Professor Brown saying that the left hand should know what the right hand has done. I heard Professor Armstrong saying that it is very important to manage the management.

Now, these two things I think are very relevant to what is going on. At this moment, we ask ourselves is it really such a mess that we think it is. Well, we do not know. There is a commission and an interdepartmental commission, in which most of the departments in the Netherlands are represented, which is making a list of various activities concerning what ministries, commissions, committees, working groups, institutions, etc., are working on the continental shelf of the North Sea. We might well discover that there are hundreds of these.

Now, I come back to Professor Armstrong's words, how are we going to manage this kind of management? Is it absolutely necessary to reduce the number of entities involved? Is that really necessary or are we able to handle all these different institutions and commissions which are at work? We simply do not know yet. It may be a bit late, but I am pleased we are at least addressing the problem.

JOHN ARMSTRONG: I am in complete agreement. The point of my comment was indeed that many times there is no dependable way to tell whether we should do something different than the present approach. I am glad to see you are wrestling with it. We in the United States also have the same debate about whether something new is needed in the sense of ocean management and whether or not the collection of agencies and programs and policies that exist now is not as good as could be done some other way. It is not a problem with an easy or obvious answer.

PATRICIA BIRNIE: I just wanted to follow up the last remark and to ask Professor Brown and Mr. Tromp in particular whether they thought any new institutions were needed in the North Sea? We do have a very large number of institutions, the Oslo Commission, the Paris Commission, and several others. Professor Brown did say at the end of his talk that he thought we should devote our attention to new procedures and institutions. Mr. Tromp said that the models of the Baltic Convention and of the Barcelona Convention might be considered for the North Sea since in one sense they were better, being more comprehensive. I am wondering, and I think this is a rather crucial question, whether we should accept the suggestion made by many that we need an overall commission in the North Sea. Do we really, or would this merely add another level of complexity?

E. D. BROWN: I entirely agree with you. I do not think we need more institutions. This would be yet another level of bureaucracy and would merely clog up the working of the system. My plea for more institutions and procedures was rather within the existing systems. I think, for example, that we need a better system at the national level. The example I gave was the United Kingdom, where we have a Minister who is supposed to have a coordinating function but in fact has neither a staff nor any muscle in relation to the other departments. This is the kind of coordinating institutional procedure I meant there. On the Community level, I think we also require not a new institution but simply a new procedure to formalize the initial coordinating efforts to which Professor Koers referred. On the public international level, again I am looking not for new institutions with comprehensive functions but a greater degree of coordination among existing organizations. Responding to the question which Mr. Vargas put, there is I think a much greater degree of coordination on this level than his question seemed to suggest. I will not repeat myself here, but I have referred in my paper to the steps which have been taken to coordinate the work of universalist organizations in the maritime field.

O. WATTNE: I think it is very important to underline the necessity of identifying where we have interference and where we have the problems. To establish means to observe those, and to listen to the problems in relation to other activity. A good example is fishermen's complaints which at first were dismissed as having no relationship to offshore activities and said to be caused only by old shipwrecks and the result of navigation for 50 years. Relatively complicated systems were developed later consisting of ocean bed going vessels combined with side-scanning sonar and videotape recording to prove beyond doubt that it in fact was the offshore activity that caused more of the problems than anything else. Then you could start discussing the problem, but not earlier because nobody believed there was a real problem.

PART IX

CONCLUDING SESSION

REMARKS BY
CONFERENCE PROGRAM CHAIRMAN

John King Gamble, Jr.
The Pennsylvania State University

In putting together a program for this Conference, I thought it desirable to impose upon a couple individuals, asking them to synthesize and analyze what we have been doing for the last four days. I also asked them to be provocative; knowing them as I do, that will be the least of our worries.

The two principals for this session are Barry Buzan, a political scientist from the University of Warwick, and Douglas Johnston, a lawyer from Dalhousie University. This is Barry's first time on a Law of the Sea Institute program. Doug has been on the program of most Law of the Sea Institute events for the past decade. He came to this meeting expecting to maintain a low profile--I have prevailed upon him on very short notice to give us the benefit of his analysis of these meetings. I am sure we shall all benefit from Doug's reverting to his customary, active role.

COMMENTARY

Barry Buzan
University of Warwick
United Kingdom

My mandate, and I would just like to read it to you, is that I am supposed to provide a "provocative hard-hitting analysis of what this conference has done and failed to do." This seems to me as a political scientist to put me under some strain here between being provocative and being polite, and I'll try to tread this boundary as carefully as I can. But I will ask for your indulgence beforehand if I appear to trespass on the side of outrageousness every so often.

The necessity for synthesis is, as I am sure you can all appreciate, rather difficult at this stage, and indeed a number of you have whispered in my ear "I'm glad that you're doing this and not me, ha, ha."

Now what I am going to try to do here by way of creating some sort of synthesis is to revisit the conference theme of neglect. What I would like to do is survey it briefly in the light of the four days of meetings and work that we have done here, and try to draw some conclusions about the theme for the future work of the Law of the Sea Institute. I hope that is not too pretentious a task for me to undertake since I am not a member of that body. So, the question I want to ask is how useful has the concept of neglect been in tying together the various subjects that we have looked at? I am going to give a rather personal view of this.

First of all, let me say that neglect as a concept, as was pointed out in the keynote address, tends to have pejorative connotations. It is all very well to look at its dictionary definitions and say that it does not, but in common usage it does have a negative connotation. The dereliction of duty aspect of it, I think, stands out, and I think this may have been unhelpful in relation to the way in which we have looked at some of these issues.

To some extent it may have turned us slightly too much towards the rather easy game of placing blame, and fault finding, in relation to the work of the Law of the Sea Conference. In another respect, it may have led us to elevate perhaps to an unwarranted status certain fringe and peripheral issues. The question has been raised in various indiscrete corridor conversations as to whether we have been scraping the bottom of the barrel for something new and exciting; this is maybe something that neglect pushes one towards. It seems to me that if one were to take neglect as a pursuit, there are no limits to the kinds of abstract problems one could dredge up. Why, for instance, has the Law of the Sea Conference not dealt with the disruptive effects of continental drift on boundary delimitation agreements between various opposite states! I mean, you could go on and on like this, dredging up various kinds of unimportant problems.

Now, it seems important to make clear that the idea of neglect does not stand alone. It is part of the spectrum which relates to the act of choice. In other words, it has a positive counterpart and that counterpart is selection, the reasoned choice, defining a manageable set of tasks if you will, in the light of your interests, your priorities and your capabilities. Neglect in its pejorative sense covers only half of this spectrum. The other half covers, as I said, this respectable activity of making reasoned choices. And I think it is important to keep this balance in mind when one throws around a concept like neglect. So having said that, let me give then some personal assessment of the subjects that we have covered, and see how the concept of neglect applies to them.

I am going to do this under three heads. First of all, I am going to look at subjects which in my assessment have not been neglected by the Law of the Sea Conference. I would then like to look rather briefly at subjects which some people think should have been neglected. In other words, it would have been somehow advantageous for them to have suffered some neglect. And finally, I will make a few comments about what I think perhaps are genuinely neglected issues to which we might turn future attention.

So, first of all, the subjects which I do not think have been neglected, and these include most of the subjects that we have in fact covered during the past week. By saying that I do not think they have been neglected I mean that the concept of neglect is an inappropriate or misleading way in which to approach analysis of them.

I think that some of these subjects, on the basis of the discussion that we have had about them, appear to be quite adequately covered by the work of the Law of the Sea Conference, given the kind of available information we have, the levels of interest that pertain, and the kinds of urgency which these issues seem to imply. I think it is perhaps worth stating as a warning here, a cautionary note, that a number of people have said that Committee I was a good example of over-negotiating, of pushing the law or trying to push the law too far in advance of practice, and that perhaps this same warning could be applied to some of these other issues.

So let me go through them briefly. First of all is non-nodule resources. This, it seems to me in the light of the discussion we had, has been covered perfectly adequately in the

ICNT; in Section XI there are plenty of references to the resources of the area and these references seem to be adequately defined. This issue has not been neglected. Indeed, one would have the conceptual problem here on the basis of papers presented as to whether it is possible to neglect something that is not there? I suggest that we turn that one over to our underemployed colleagues in philosophy departments!

A second category of things, I am going to coin a new acronym for this, I have called LFO's, or large floating objects. I toyed with the idea of calling them FOLI's for "floating objects of large importance," but thought that was stretching the art of the acronym a bit too far. This includes, OFEP's, OTEC's, drifting super tankers and icebergs, and it seems to me that none of these has been neglected in the sense of not having been given attention appropriate to its importance.

As Professor Brown indicated in his very useful intervention on this, the general provisions on navigation and resources seem to cover most of the problems pertaining to these quite well. This is particularly so in relation to these things needing to await development until we know a bit more clearly exactly what they are about, but they clearly do not fall wholly outside the spectrum of the kind of legal framework that the ICNT gives us.

Again, I point to this analogy of Committee I and the danger of trying to legislate too far in advance of some kinds of development. For those of you who read science fiction, you will be aware of the delights, and of the dangers, of becoming too obsessed with any particular fantasy of the scenario spinners. On the question of air space, this seems also to have been quite adequately covered. It seems to me that this is not really a law of the sea issue anyway, and that there are appropriate things said about air space in the ICNT. A minor ambiguity seems to exist in relation to the economic zone, but perhaps this is more a problem for those fora which deal with air space matters, such as the ICAO, than it is a problem of law of the sea.

On the question of shipping, I do not think anybody who has followed the Law of the Sea Conference could in all honesty say that shipping has been neglected as a question. The shipping interest might have been defeated but that is quite a different thing from being neglected. The reasons for its defeat are controversial, as was indicated in the discussion. But nonetheless I do not think that neglect is an appropriate way to deal with this.

Finally, on regional and area issues, the polar regions and the North Sea, there are burgeoning literatures on these areas; experts are available in droves. These are not symptoms of neglected issues. Indeed, nobody could say that the Canadian or Norwegian Arctic issues have been neglected. Several people in this room , including me, have built their careers, on aspects of this. Clearly there has been no neglect!

Antarctica and the North Sea strike me as being things that should be addressed as regional matters, and not law of the sea matters, although there is clearly a lot of scope for examining the issue linkages between law of the sea and the particular problems emanating from these regions. But this is not something that has been neglected by the Law of the Sea Conference. This is an <u>outcome</u> of the Law of the Sea Conference's work, a rather different matter. The present uncertainty of outcome of the Law of the Sea Conference clearly causes difficulties in regional affairs. These need to be looked at as linkage problems, for instance problems of delimitation, but this uncertainty again is not neglect. It is a different thing.

I'll move onto my second category here, that of subjects which might have benefited from some neglect. Here I am simply gleaning opinions that were heard in corridors, at dinner parties, etc., probably lubricated by too much alcohol and therefore incautious, but I think they do represent a certain body of feeling in this room.

There has been a considerable expression of opinion one way or another that scientific research and manganese nodule mining would have been better off if they had suffered a bit of neglect in the Law of the Sea Conference. In other words, neglect and attention here appear as a two-edged sword. There may have been insufficient emphasis given in this gathering to the problems of something suffering too much attention as opposed to suffering neglect. Various people said in one form or another that in Committee I the problem has been over-negotiated. It is led to incomprehensible, unworkable, and self-destructive outcomes of one sort or another. Scientific research and perhaps also shipping seemed to have suffered the same fate; they have been pushed too hard, paid too much attention to, and the outcome has been not particularly desirable.

If these interpretations are accepted and clearly some of you accept them, then over-attention may be a larger problem at the Law of the Sea Conference than neglect. Finally, the things that have been in my opinion genuinely neglected; these are things which I see as having emerged from the discussion that we have had here. I am not making a more general survey. There seem to me to be three points of neglect. One is very specific. Two are rather general.

The first point of neglect is the status of ice. This seems to me to link a number of issues we have had. It has relevance to both of the polar regions and also to the dreaded problem of towing icebergs! Now there is only one article in the ICNT that deals with ice, Article 235, and this covers only a very small aspect, that which meets the particular Canadian problem of pollution control and regulation. In other words, something put in there to justify the Arctic Waters Pollution Prevention Act, and it seems to me that the problem of ice is a genuine conceptual dilemma which bears very strongly on the law of the sea which has not been adequately confronted either in this forum or in others. Ice is not land. Ice is not water. What is it? It clearly occurs at the interface between the two and clearly as more and more use is made of the Arctic, ice is going to have an increasingly direct and immediate relevance to law of the sea matters. I think this has been inadequately dealt with.

The second genuinely neglected issue is one I am going to lift almost completely from Ken Booth's paper. I think he made a number of excellent points there which bear repeating. I think he identified rightly that there is an important link between strategic interests and the law of the sea and that that link has not been adequately dealt with. Not so much by the Law of the Sea Conference because it is sort of understood there, but in this kind of gathering. In intellectual communities there is a deficiency of understanding about the relationships between these two things. Some very basic questions arise here as Ken brought up as to the nature of law. Is law merely an expression of a civilized community seeking to regulate its own affairs or is it in some sense a vehicle for preserving the interests of dominant groups? Is it in other words a rather polite substitute for the use of force?

Ken also points out the cause for this neglect, i.e., the disinclination of strategists and lawyers to consider each other's work in sufficient depth. Partly this disinclination arises because of the rather theological differences of approach which these two groups have, and one may be said to be a theology of power, the other a tehology of common interests. It is difficult to put these together. They are naturally incompatible; it is matter and anti-matter, if you will. It seems to me that there is a case here for a substantial program of intellectual bridge-building. This is the kind of task which is very well suited to this kind of gathering. It also seems to be a task that is necessary to any proper understanding of the political dynamics of the Law of the Sea Conference.

Finally, the third neglected issue in my particular list (and I think this is an interesting one because it does seem to me to tie together most of the very varied and disparate components of our agenda this past week) is how can the advantages of a fixed law of the sea convention be combined with the necessary flexibility to adapt to new developments? Most of the things we have talked about have been in the nature of new developments, things happening on the side, things happening in the future; there is a problem of how these fit into the law of the sea. It strikes me as being a perpetual tension between the desire to set up some sort of fixed body of law and the problem of keeping that body of law contemporary and relevant and appropriate to practice.

Now, it seems to me that much of what has been gathered here under the heading of neglect really reflects this problem of adaptation of, and update to, the central work of the Law of the Sea Conference. This raises a lot of issues. At what stage in the emergence of a new issue as a collective problem is it appropriate to move towards some kind of legislation? Should legislation, in other words, be anticipatory or reactive and how detailed should legislation be in relation to new issues where the actual needs of the users are not yet clear? There are all sorts of difficult questions that arise there.

This is not a new problem. It has been with us throughout the Law of the Sea Conference. I have argued elsewhere the pace, if you like, of the evolution of issues is frequently faster than the progress towards agreement in the negotiations. Because of this, we may indeed never get a fixed convention. If we did get a fixed convention, the problem would still not disappear. We would still have this problem of new issues arising and the necessity of finding ways of continuing to evolve law to meet them. I think this may be in part what Ed Miles was getting at in his very useful intervention yesterday.

This strikes me as being an issue of basic procedure and as such it is perhaps more important than all of the particular substantive problems that we have been looking at this week. I am not saying that one doesn't need to look at particular substantive problems but the question is basic procedure: how one approaches creating a living body of law. It seems to me to be more basic.

I think that tackling this problem is perhaps a worthy task for the Law of the Sea Institute, given that it also is going to face a need to adapt itself to a working environment in which the Law of the Sea Conference is ceasing, one way or another, to be the dominant focus of interest. UNCLOS has provided a common umbrella for us all over at least a decade and has clearly greatly facilitated the Law of the Sea Institute's task of combining the wisdom of disparate interests and disparate disciplines. It strikes me, and I may be putting this a little extremely in order to be provocative, that there may be some present danger of disorientation and fragmentation as the Law of the Sea Conference winds down. This may lead to an over-emphasis on peripheral issues and on the flashier items of technological speculation.

As a central institution in creative thinking about ocean issues, the Law of the Sea Institute, it seems to me, needs to cultivate a very clear sense of direction and a larger understanding in which we can put regional and technological and other component interests into their proper perspectives. I am not convinced that the concept of neglect as used in this session provides that necessary guidance.

COMMENTARY

Douglas M. Johnston
Dalhousie University
Halifax, N.S., Canada

Like Dr. Buzan, I would like to take the mandate of the chairman literally and be as provocative as possible. In my case, I hope it is not too provocative to choose, as I do, to look at the impact of neglect on the new law of the sea from the point of view of legal development. I realize, of course, that legal development is not the only aspect of the Law of the Sea Conference. Indeed it may not even be the most important single aspect. Legal development is, I suppose, a sort of political development, and political development for that matter is only an aspect of social development, but as a lawyer it is my natural inclination to adopt the legal development point of view.

To me the interesting thing about UNCLOS III from the juridical point of view is that, beginning as it did in the 1960's, it represents the first major departure from the classical tradition of legal development: that is, the first major departure from the classical tradition of lawmaking through codification. We are now in transition from the classical to the romantic approach to legal development - if I may borrow metaphors from the history of art. During this transition we may find some difficulty, intellectually, in separating ourselves from all the characteristics of "good" scientific legal development which we have inherited, each of us, from the classical tradition.

UNCLOS III has often been described quite wrongly, as this conference brings out, as a comprehensive and systematic approach to the development of the new law of the sea. That is precisely what UNCLOS III is not. It is not comprehensive and it is not systematic. It is "non-scientific" in the classical sense. It owes little to the concept of reason, and even less to that of what is natural.

Our classical expectations come from the Romans. The classical approach began essentially with the decision by the Emperor Justinian to engage jurors to codify the Roman law. For the next fifteen hundred years or so all attempts to codify and develop law on the large scale were but variants of the Roman model. This Roman tradition continued into the late 20th century, both at the international and national levels. It is reflected in the Charter of the United Nations in references to codification and progressive development of international law. More important, the classical tradition is reflected in the establishment of the International Law Commission to prepare treaty drafts intended to serve these purposes. The International Law Commission is the 20th century counterpart of the jurists of Justinian, designed to pursue the neo-classical approach to the development of international law.

It was only in the 1960's that the United Nations first realized that the really important problems of policy-making and legal development under U.N. auspices were incapable of solution in any single exercise. These "meta-problems," the major problems, facing the world community in the late 20th century are just too large, too complex, and too controversial to be dealt with in the simple, direct, and rather dispassionate tradition of classical legal development. Yet those, "meta-problems" are what most "law-making" or policy-making conferences of the U.N. system are about.

It was in the late 1960's in preparation for one of the first of the great "meta-problem" conferences of the world - the Stockholm Conference on the Human Environment - that it was discovered that the neo-classical mechanism of the International Law Commission was simply not appropriate. It should be evident now that law-making in the late 20th century has to be carried out in the Sturm und Drang of conference diplomacy. Indeed, I would suggest that we are now in the high romantic period of the history of international law, and that we still have to learn how to modify the excesses of romanticism in law-making. Our grandchildren might finally get to the end of that line. We are just dimly perceiving the enormous intellectual and institutional problems that have to be met before we can retain the best of the romantic tradition that is upon us without losing all the advantages and virtues of the classical tradition.

How do we start down that path? How do we get relatively scientific, reasonably structured, internally coherent, comprehensively conceived, conceptually consistent law out of the Sturm und Drang of conference diplomacy? Do we have to accept the common view that there can be no preparation for a modern law-making conference that deals essentially with a "meta-problem" of the world community? Is there no alternative to the open-ended system of the present age of romance?

There is a paradox here, because the convening of UNCLOS III was at the urging of Arvid Pardo, whose proposal for a charter of the ocean was motivated by a Bentham-like vision of how you proceed scientifically into legal development. It was a vision that was not acceptable to the world of conference diplomacy. Pardo had a systematic view. He had a conceptual framework in which an overriding principle was to be predominant, that of the common heritage of mankind. He envisaged a universally valued and centrally organized structure for all uses of the sea. That is the irony. The history of UNCLOS III has been exactly the opposite.

It is true, of course, that the conference draws upon a lengthy agenda of interrelated issues. But these are dealt with in the most unsystematic manner conceivable, in ad hoc response to the wills of national state governments. The arena is designed for a contest of wills and passions, not an exercise in human reason. This is not to say that a great deal of logical thought has not been given to the problems, but the structure, the framework of discourse, is the object of passion, not of reason.

I have two suggestions to make. One is that in discarding the International Law Commission, and therefore discarding the classical "scientific" approach to legal development, we might find a substitute that would be free of some of the criticisms that are directed at the I.L.C. as a mechanism for preparing certain kinds of law-making conferences. The suggestion is this, that there might be a role for the United Nations Secretariat, not in the preparation of draft articles in the manner of the International Law Commission, but rather in the preparation of a "framework agenda" which would be conceived from the point of view of legal development. To the extent we are concerned about the problem of neglect in legal development, we might expect that in this way the worst kinds of neglect would be avoided. Prior thought would be given by the Secretariat to the logical sequence and the interrelationships among the various subjects. I am not, of course, suggesting that the Secretariat should be asked to write any content under the rubrics listed in the "framework agenda." That would remain the task of the delegations.

If this seems strange to you - preparing a table of contents before writing the book - remember that we do it all the time in the academic community. In the supervision of doctoral candidates it is normal, at least in North America, to suggest at an early stage, long before the candidate has gone far into his research and acquired his personal opinions, that he provide an outline of his dissertation. He is asked to begin with a structural approach, one which admittedly may have to be modified as a result of the inquiry to be undertaken.

Admittedly, if this proposal were acceptable, it would only be because the U.N. Secretariat itself is able to overcome its traditional reluctance to say anything at all that might be construed as politically offensive. It would require delegations of the United Nations to grant them this role. The Secretariat would have to be encouraged to overcome its reluctance to seem to be anticipating the wishes of the delegations. But, in any event, the "framework agenda" would be subject to discussion and amendment by the delegations when they first convene.

So that's my first suggestion how, in the late 20th century, we might get away from the worst excesses of disorderly legal development in the period of high romance: by having this modest approach taken prior to a "meta-problematic" law-making conference by the U.N. Secretariat. But then inevitably, as long as we have the prevailing principle of universal participatory democracy, which I support very strongly, as the governing principle of international organization, we shall have to live with the *Sturm und Drang* of conference diplomacy. This means, I fear, that we are going to have to live with seriously flawed conventions in the next several decades - seriously flawed by any intellectual or scientific criterion. Therefore, the question is even if the proposal for agenda preparation by the Secretariat were acceptable, how do we remedy these expected textual deficiencies after the event of the *Sturm und Drang*?

My proposal here would be that we might have something to learn from the past, admitting that the past is the classical past. In the past, what they did was encourage individual jurists, called glossators, to superimpose on the legal code their own personal "gloss" or interpretation. There emerged in the Middle Ages a community of scholars who, not cooperatively but by individual study and commentary, provided the famous glosses of the great codes of the world.

Now, is there anything at all in that tradition that might be useful for the late 20th century to remedy the deficiencies of major international conventions that are seriously flawed through one kind of neglect or another? Can we mount some kind of modern "neo-glossatory" mechanism to remedy such texts that are incomplete, inadequate, lacking a conceptual framework, internally incoherent, or otherwise the victim of neglect? Such a mechanism today could hardly take the form of individual jurists in university libraries. For one thing, most of the problem areas we are talking about, such as ocean management, are much too complex to be left to lawyers. They are nothing if not problems of common interest to several departments of human knowledge. So we have to be thinking about a multi-disciplinary mechanism. Nor could it work if it consisted merely of a variety of undirected individuals. It would have to be some kind of task force or commission. Moreover, the composition of the task force would have to vary with the subject matter of the convention. Each would require a different mix of knowledge to perform a useful task. So, what I have in mind is a mechanism that would be established by the United Nations, perhaps with a permanent staff but involving commissioners who would be drawn from the various areas of knowledge most relevant to the subject matter of the convention. Ten or 20 years after the conclusion of a seriously flawed convention, such a commission or task force could be appointed ad hoc to produce ideas about how the convention could be improved, without going through the tiresome business of another treaty-making conference and all the current difficulties of the Sturm und Drang world of conference diplomacy.

It may be that by the expiry of the ten or 20 year period the nation states and international agencies will have accumulated a catalogue of criticisms of the flawed convention arising from confusion, ambiguity and conflict engendered by it. If so, the first job of the task force would be to collect all these critical thoughts, to establish (if possible) a pattern of interpretations and applications reflected in national legislation and practice around the world. Then, with this evidence before them, the task force would be able to compose nothing so grand as a revised treaty but perhaps a series of "understandings," which could then be referred to the Sixth Committee of the General Assembly. From there to the General Assembly itself the text would proceed, suitably amended. At best, such a procedure could result in guidelines accepted by resolution of the General Assembly which would be officially supported (and even sanctioned, in appropriate circumstances).

To my mind, it makes little difference that such a resolution of the General Assembly might not be deemed to be technically binding under the strict law of treaties. This seems very nearly irrelevant. It is more important that the "understandings," guidelines or recommendations in the resolution should be construed as the opinion of the world community, with whatever moral suasion that might carry, so that at least any nation or agency wishing to go in a different direction under the flawed convention would know it is doing so with the disapproval at least of most other states making up the membership of the United Nations.

I admit that there would be problems both in the initiation and in the implementation of these proposals. Yet they might be worthy of critical consideration as an effort to establish some kind of bridgehead between the classical period of treaty law, which died 12 years ago, and the romantic world of the late 20th century.

DISCUSSION AND QUESTIONS

BARRY BUZAN: Well, I must confess right away that Doug and I have a conspiracy afoot here as to sequencing of these events.

By and large, I agree with what he says. I think if there is a common thread between what he says and what I have said, it is that we both agree on the particular need to examine the process of the further evolution of international law and its development in the face of continuing rapidly unfolding new issues. Perhaps we also both agree that there is an important goal here for the Law of the Sea Institute, I am not sure.

I have a wish to prey yet further upon the indulgence of our hosts and make some more provocative comments on a slightly different topic. This I am doing partly at my own instigation, partly at the instigation of others, and partly in line, of course, with my mandate to speak to what the conference had failed to do.

I want to speak to the particular way in which these meetings have been held. I think one of the things the conference has failed to do is to stimulate (I have picked that word very carefully) - has failed to stimulate many of the participants as much as they had a right to expect. This is not because of any lack of interest in the topic, not because of any deficiency in preparation by the presenters. It seems to me there is a structural problem in a meeting of this sort which it might be useful to consider.

There are two deficiencies I would like to address. I think first of all that the ratio of discussion to presentation has been exceedingly poor - and you may note that I make this statement after having made my own presentation - and learning theory tells us that there is a disastrous drop-off in attention and retention in any long listening exercise, and this is despite the best will and highest interest that the listener may have. He simply cannot cope with that much input, and it strikes me also that we do not need to travel such large distances at such great costs to hear verbatim presentations. We can read these things at home. The purpose of meeting should be to <u>discuss</u> the questions and to <u>exchange</u> views and I think we have had an insufficient quota of this at this meeting.

This leads me to a second point, that is to say what do you do about it? Well, either you give fewer papers which seems to be a bad solution, or you make the papers available beforehand. You take the papers as read, the presenters summarize them briefly, and the emphasis is put on discussion.

I am fully aware as a past participant and sometime organizer of such events, that it is extraordinarily difficult to do this in many respects. Time factors become a problem. It costs money. There is the usual campaign of passive resistance by authors who insist on penning their works on the plane, etc. But it seems to me that despite these difficulties the benefit of having the papers available beforehand - and I do not necessarily mean mailed out to all the participants, but here when we get here, so that they can be purchased and read - improves the quality of the discussion immensely. By an interactive effect it also tends over time to improve the quality of the papers. If people know that they are simply giving a paper off the top of their heads which nobody is going to have read or very few people will have read, then they can be fairly guaranteed that the quality of the questions is on the whole not going to be tremendously incisive because people just simply have not had that much time to think about what they've said.

If, on the other hand, presenters come knowing that everybody or a large number of people will have read what they are going to say, their incentives are higher to say something more profound. So I think that having the papers available encourages more active participation, and it also allows more time for it, and I think it would be very useful if this gathering could in some way give its sense or its opinion on this question. Since there are going to be other meetings like this - and if as I say, this is an opinion which I am reflecting not just of my own but an opinion which has been discussed with a number of people and seems to have at least some support in the room - if it has widespread support, then it may be of interest to our hosts and organizers.

DOUGLAS JOHNSTON: It was a conspiracy, ladies and gentlemen; we only justify ourselves on the grounds that we were asked to be provocative and outrageous. Considering in particular the problems I suggested that lie in the world of conference diplomacy, there is a need for a circuit to be created, a circuit of interested and informed people who would be interested in all aspects of ocean management. These people would be aware of the deficiencies in law-making in politics and diplomacy, would have the trust of government and international agency officials, and would perform a remedial function. This circuit could produce ideas and recommendations, albeit in an unofficial manner.

If you think of the role of the circuit, of which Law of the Sea Institute surely is an important member, how should such organizations prepare their own conferences? It is all very well for me to criticize the way that the United Nations organizes its official law-making conference, but probably we should look to our own circuit.

There are, of course, problems of cost as Dr. Buzan has

said. This creates the need for fund raising on a scale that would be commensurate with the role that I believe the circuit ought to be playing. I feel some difficulty as a former member of the Board and, indeed, as the chairman of the last conference of the Law of the Sea Institute. I recognize there are serious constraints, (particularly cost constraints); but these constraints are no more difficult and severe than face other organizations and can be overcome with the assistance of our global constituency.

The important role that should be played could begin, at least in part, if the Law of the Sea Institute could experiment with an improved format. I am not sure it is necessary to jump to the opposite extreme and insist, as a matter of policy, that all papers be written months in advance and circulated in a package weeks before the conference convenes. For one thing, many of these areas are of interest precisely because they are topical and in such interesting flux. One might defeat some important objectives and take away some of the topicality and immediacy by having to read a lot of three month old papers. I am not sure that the scientific method of running conferences is necessarily the best one; but an experiment might be carried out with some of the sessions of the program organized in this particular manner. These would be areas of the program that are regarded by the Board to be relatively stable so that the papers could be produced weeks before the conference begins.

There may be another class of panels that could not be done so far in advance with the papers available for pickup on arrival at the conference. We might consider two or three roundtable discussions where no papers would be given, presumably in the later stages of the conference after people have overcome jet lag and other kinds of problems associated with sudden adjustment.

The participants at a Law of the Sea Institute conference speak about 20 different languages. By some cruel chance of fate, most of these people have to talk and listen in a foreign language. I never cease to marvel at the facility and brilliance of these linguists; but the people running conferences should recognize that it must be difficult for non-native speakers of English to attend a four-day conference without the benefit of papers available in advance. It may be too much to ask that they be run off in several different languages. It may be sufficient that they be in English so long as enough time is provided for proper consideration of these papers.

JOHN GAMBLE: Before opening this session up for questions, I should like to comment briefly on some of the interesting points raised by Barry Buzan and Doug Johnston. I feel they have done the Law of the Sea Institute a great service providing us, among other things, with enough work to occupy us for at least a decade. I appreciate Barry Buzan's comments about operational changes in Law of the Sea Institute conferences. I agree with the intent of all his remarks. But if we tried to implement such suggestions, I am afraid the cure would be worse than the disease. Insisting that all the papers prepared for this conference be ready three weeks before the meeting would have, in my judgemnt, made fully half the participants unwilling to take on the task. No doubt other people could be found who would guarantee to meet an earlier deadline. But would the papers be of as high quality! Barry's line of reasoning assumes that if papers are available in advance, everyone will have the time to read and analyze the papers. Those of us who teach realize that, while this is a laudable goal, it is often unrealistic. In my opinion, Institute conferences can be viewed at a first iteration, the final version of which is the published proceedings containing all the papers, questions, and discussions.

DOROTHY ALLAN: I want to comment on, or rather ask for clarification on a point that Mr. Buzan made. As I understood it, he said he felt that a couple of the major participants at the LOS Conference were noted for their "theological differences," one of power, one of common interest. To me that sounded quite a bit like the "good guys" versus the "bad guys" that we are so familiar with in the U.S. in our cowboy movies. It also denoted the sort of black and white psychology that one usually abandons on leaving the 20's. Maybe you have not yet left the 20's. But I just wondered it you would like to elaborate a bit.

BARRY BUZAN: I don't know whether at my age that's a compliment or an insult! However, I'm not going to entertain you with my age.

I agree I am speaking partly for effect here. One of the reasons why this came out perhaps overstated, other than my following the mandate, was because I spent much of last week locked into a completely fruitless dialogue with a distinguished international jurist about this very issue, about the strategic aspects of law of the sea and the influence of strategic thinking and strategic interests on law. In this equation I come out as a strategist; I suppose that is my primary interest and training. I was seeking ways to follow up Ken Booth's point that there were theological elements to this debate. I rather grossly characterized them as being those who are mostly concerned with power on the one hand, and see the world through such a filter that one assumes that power is the major operative motive for human action. In contrast there are those who see the world through other kinds of lenses and look more for rational collective interests. It seems to me that Ken Booth suggested that these kinds of theological differences in approach prevented more communication between these two groups. This seemed to me to be a very salient point, as I say, underscored by my extensive discussions with this jurist which reached this particular dilemma. Now, it could be that my experience is unrepresentative, and in fact lawyers and strategists are talking to each other with no difficulty. But I do feel there is something in this, that these two groups are like matter, anti-matter type groups that find it very difficult to get together and do something creative without causing an explosion. That was the thrust of my point. I thought that there was an intellectual gap here, which since this is primarily an intellectual forum, was particularly appropriate for discussion.

THOMAS CLINGAN: Professor Johnston has very appropriately identified the fact that given the number of articles in this very complex document and the method by which it is being developed, there are bound to be defects or flaws that would need to be adjusted. I just wanted to mention that some thought, at least, is being given to this very subject. There have been a couple of suggestions. I have one here from last April, a proposal by Peru, and I shall read a couple of paragraphs. The operative paragraph says "There is hereby established the International Commission on the Law of the Sea as an intergovernmental body responsible for the examination of problems which may arise in connection with the application of the provisions of the present convention as well as some situations not covered by it." The proposal goes on with eleven different specifics. I suppose the most appropriate one to mention here is that it suggests suitable methods of making good ambiguities, inconsistencies, gaps, anachronisms or overcoming other difficulties encountered in the provisions of this convention which are not covered by any of the procedures for settlement of disputes. I thought I would bring that to the attention of this assembly, and for those who are interested the document number on this is A/Conf 62/1.22.

LEWIS ALEXANDER: In Doug Johnston's "seriously flawed" convention, there are several issues that I think if not neglected were deliberately left vague, perhaps this was so to achieve some sort of a treaty. Three of them have come to my mind.

First is the limitation of maritime boundaries between opposite and/or adjacent states. The way the text reads both for boundaries on the continental shelf and boundaries between economic zones, this is an extremely vaguely worded provision that has, as you probably know, been in a Negotiating Group trying to operate at the Seventh Session to work out some better text. But it has been absolutely impossible to do. So, I think this is an issue that is going to be left vague because countries will not agree to anything more stringent.

A second thing is the definition of regions and sub-regions or regional agreements. Frequently through the text there runs the term "appropriate global or regional," and in the case of fisheries, even of "sub-regional" arrangements or groups. And they even speak of regions as geographic areas when referring to the land-locked and the geographically disadvantaged states. This is a very vague term the way it is used in the ICNT.

A third point is the "geographically disadvantaged states" themselves. If you think of the various criteria almost any state in the world is geographically disadvantaged one way or another, except perhaps the United States. I think the joke is just about over on the GDS's because too many of them got into the act.

A fourth point, and this does bother me a good deal, is the definition of the outer edge of the continental shelf. How that will be worked out I do not know. Perhaps like the other terms I've referred to, it is deliberately kept vague, this being the only way general agreement can be reached.

JOHN CRAVEN: The justification for the topic of this conference of the neglected issues was aptly demonstrated by the quality and constructive nature of the epilogue of Barry Buzan and Doug Johnston. The way this topic elicited their constructive response demonstrates, I believe, that the topic was an effective one.

I would also point out that Barry distilled three neglected issued from this conference. Considering all of the issues that have been discussed in the past, almost a decade of conferences on the law of the sea, to distill three issues that have been neglected would be a worthy achievement.

But more important things were highlighted by these speakers, for example the dichotomy and the paradox that we face when bringing together a collection of lawyers, scientists, and social scientists, etc. The lawyer's task is the codification of a document which appropriately and adequately addresses all the issues. Yesterday we saw this dichotomy fully demonstrated in the summary by Ed Brown and the response by Ed Miles. One half of the dichotomy is the lawyer, who in determining whether the issue has been neglected or not, quite correctly goes to all the texts to see whether these issues have been covered in the codification. The other half is the scientist and the political scientist who, correctly prophesying change, examine these texts in the context of whether they are adequate and appropriate in the years to come.

This debate is appropriate and continuing. Doug Johnston highlighted the fact that there must be a structuring of these two inputs to the changing law of the sea.

I think we should recognize that the changes are a part of the process of legitimate growth. Many of us remember the first couple Law of the Sea Institute Conferences at which time it was very difficult to persuade ourselves and the world that the law of the sea was an important and all-embracing subject. We have now come to the Twelfth Conference of the Law of the Sea Institute. As a result of this long process we have developed a worldwide community of scholars who need a more effective, better programmed and better structured way of interacting so that their deliberations will be more fruitful and more productive. I particularly appreciate Doug Johnston's remarks in which he made some suggestions as to how this might come about.

As the same time, this gives me an opportunity to indicate that this conference itself is a healthy and welcomed and to me a very rewarding sign of growth of this community of scholars and of this Institute. This is the first conference to take place outside the United States. Future conferences will certainly do so and must do so. I also welcome the suggestions that more adequate preparation should be done, although this does not take away from the preparation that has taken place.

JOHN GAMBLE: I have been asked if someone from the audience would care to comment on recent developments at the United Nations' Conference. I should like to prevail on Ed Miles to undertake this task.

EDWARD MILES: I was afraid of that! In my view this was perhaps the least productive session of the Conference, second only to the second session in 1976. There was one major difference, however, in that the session was not as contentious, the confrontation was not as intense, as it had been in the second session of 1976.

In terms of substantive work, the most important work done, in my opinion, was done in Negotiating Group 2 on financial arrangements concerning the sea-bed, the group chaired by Ambassador Tommy Koh of Singapore. The issues here are very technical, very difficult, but in particular in response to a Norwegian initiative, the paper introduced by Minister Evensen, this led to the only significant exchange that could have been witnessed in the session.

Within Negotiating Group 1 on the system of exploration and

exploitation, essentially it seemed to me that we marked time. We marked time by going through yet another reading of most of Annex II, in which particular problems developed with respect to paragraph 5 concerning the selection of applicants. It also seemed that there were no substantive negotiations on the system of exploitation in part because of the response of the United States and the EEC countries to what had been done in Geneva in the paper put out as NG1/10/ Rev. 1, and the feeling on the part of the Group of 77, and a number of other countries, that the developed countries had in effect gone back on compromises made in Geneva and that there was no point to continuing substantive negotiations. The spectre of unilateral action by the United States hung over the Conference as well and this generated the fear that perhaps the Conference would be preempted.

Within Negotiating Group 3 concerned with the organs of the Authority, it was agreed to leave off discussion of a major contentious issue, in particular decision-making within the Council and the relationship of the Council to the Assembly, and instead to focus on the subsidiary organs of the Council. One could be charitable and say that this work was very useful. I didn't particularly think so. It seemed to me another way of marking time.

With respect to Committee II, there seemed to be the situation in which the work done in Negotiating Group 4 on the landlocked and geographically-disadvantaged states in Geneva was about as far as the Coastal States Group and others were prepared to go and that, in effect, the Group of Landlocked and Geographically Disadvantaged States could expect no further concessions. In fact, this point had been made quite clearly by Ambassador Castaneda speaking for the Coastal States Group at the end of the Geneva session. Therefore it would have been possible to wrap up the work in Negotiating Group 4 if the work in Negotiating Group 6 on the margin had been completed, but since there is a link between those two, at least in the eyes and minds of the landlocked and GDS group, it was not possible to conclude that work. The work on the margin remains very important. The confrontation, if you would call it that, between essentially the Soviets on the one hand and increasing numbers of states on the other, continued.

There was a new proposal by the Seychelles, supported by the African Group, with respect to the revenue-sharing provisions for the continental margin beyond 200 miles and the aim was for increasing the revenue sharing provisions from 7% to 10%. It seems to me the assumption was that the African Group was not prepared to show its support for the Irish formula for free, as it were, that it would cost the large margin states something and that something would be in the form of increased payment on the revenue-sharing provision.

With respect to the other groups in Committee II, Group 5 on dispute settlement did not meet. I didn't, from my own idiosyncratic point of view, find what went on in Group 7 on delimitation very useful. In fact, I found it rather painful. There remained the same old conflict between equitable principles and the median line. As a whole, however, it is important to mention that Committee II completed another reading of its portion of the ICNT.

In Committee II, some very useful work was done on pollution and it seems to me this is virtually completed, though the Committee has not formally completed its work and there has been a new proposal introduced by Tanzania. On scientific research, there was a new paper put in by the United States. This generated a variety of responses from harsh to helpful. There may have been attempts as well to seek agreement on the sub-package within Committee II, but it wasn't possible to do this because it appeared that different people had different views on what should be in the package.

So that when, by the last two weeks, it seemed that there was very little movement, the emphasis of the Conference shifted to a concern for whether or not, when and where it should meet and for how long, and whether or not a deadline should be written into the Resolution from the General Assembly authorizing the 8th and 9th sessions of the Conference. This was significant, at least to me, because it seemed that there was considerable support within the Latin American and the African Groups for writing in a termination date to the Conference proceedings, i.e., not to go beyond 1979. This was not supported by a number of other countries, the United States, Norway, a number of others, who claimed that it wouldn't be wise. The Soviet Union and the entire Socialist Bloc argued that writing in a termination date would in effect be a guillotine and would be tantamount to admitting failure. As you know, the eventual compromise was that there would be an 8th session in the Spring of 1979 in Geneva. At the end of the 8th session, the Conference would decide whether sufficient progress had been made to enable a second session to be held in 1979.

As part of the Latin American proposal, (it didn't seem that the Africans were going that far), there was a specific request for formalization at the end of the 8th session, that is the Spring session in Geneva. This meant that by the end of the 8th session there would be a revised ICNT and that this revised ICNT would be formalized; that means we would move to voting. The Latin American Group argued that unless this was done there would be no point in holding a second session in 1979.

The sentiment is growing that the Conference has just about reached the end of the road. I don't think that it will be easy to ignore it a second time. It was expected, as you know, that there would be legislation from the U.S. Congress authorizing sea-bed mining on an interim basis. At the last moment this proved not to be possible. I don't think that it's possible to delay this legislation indefinitely; it will be introduced again the next session of Congress. Perhaps then it will pass.

So maybe 1979 willy-nilly is the critical year for the Conference. Whether or not it would prove possible to resolve the remaining problems between Committee I and the rest of the Conference remains to be seen. As most of you know, I seem to be a congenital pessimist. There are a number of others in this room who may be congenital optimists who would have a different point of view. But I didn't expect to be called on, Mr. Chairman, to do this kind of work, and that is all I have to say.

BANQUET ADDRESS

BANQUET ADDRESS

Jens Evensen
Norwegian Minister for Law of the Sea

Allow me at the outset to express my great pleasure in being able to attend this conference of the Law of the Sea Institute of the University of Hawaii co-sponsored by the Institute of International Law of the University of Utrecht, and in being allowed to address this illustrious banquet. This occasion has also given me the opportunity to meet many friends, some of whom I have not seen for years, such as our chairman, Richard Young. Many years ago we had the privilege of working together for one of the giants of international law, Professor Manly Otmar Hudson. I have many warm and cherished memories from that period for which I am very grateful to Judge Hudson and to you.

I have been asked to make a key-note address on some of the main outstanding issues with which the U.N. Conference on the Law of the Sea is confronted. I wish to take as my starting point the fundamental changes and development in regard to ocean space, technologically, economically, politically and also legally, especially after the Second World War. These developments have been so fundamental and so rapid, and they have to such an extent changed conditions and concepts of the international community, that it is reasonably correct to describe them as revolutionary. Fortunately until now, with the exception of certain minor incidents, it has been a peaceful revolution, but an international revolution nevertheless.

Over the last three decades the gap between the increasing importance and the new or changed uses of the oceans and the ocean floors on the one side and the traditional concepts and principles of international law and foreign policy on the other have become unbridgeable. All the elements of a major international confrontation were thus present. I believe that future historians will admit that such a confrontation has been avoided through the tireless efforts of the United Nations mainly through the U.N. Law of the Sea Conference and its preparatory committee but also through the work of other U.N. fora.

In order to understand the true nature and scope of the U.N. Law of the Sea Conference, the problems with which it is faced, and the time it consumes in a seemingly endless series of sessions, it must be realized that with the law of the Sea Conference as its medium the international community is in the midst of a gigantic attempt to create a modern international constitution for the world oceans. It is in all probability the most significant and the most comprehensive legislative attempt ever made in the annals of international law. It is certainly the most comprehensive legislative work undertaken by the United Nations in its thirty-three years of existence.

Through extensive preparatory work and during seven sessions of the Conference proper we have succeeded in drawing up a first informal draft of such a constitution, the so-called Informal Composite Negotiating Text (U.N. Doc. A/CONF.62/WP10 of July 15, 1977). It is a vast, modern code which is now slowly being shaped, a document consisting of hundreds of articles, paragraphs and sub-paragraphs and a number of annexes. It is an impressive work of law. It is equally impressive as a pioneering work in the field of foreign policy, economic planning with an overall and deep-rooted concern for the environmental aspects of ocean space.

The established rules and principles of the law of the sea and the traditional doctrines of international relations pertaining to the oceans with which we have lived for centuries obviously contained and contain governing principles that are of basic value today as well, principles such as the freedom of the seas, the freedom of navigation and fishing and the right of passage through straits. But we must bear in mind that this traditional legal system and the underlying principles of foreign policy were mainly formed over the centuries by world powers and other economically advanced powers of Europe, later also including the U.S.A. and Japan. At least some of the main principles of this governing system met first and foremost the special interests of these powers.

At the same time these traditional doctrines and freedoms reflected an innocent and a rather primitive stage of economic, technological and political realities which became increasingly outdated at the turn of this century. After the technological revolution and the complete upheaval of the existing international order following in the wake of two world wars, this system and this age of innocence became hopelessly antiquated and thus doomed.

The factors contributing to the downfall of the system are many and varied including:

1. The overall technological revolution especially after the Second World War, including the advent of the nuclear age.

2. The fundamental breakthrough of a marine technology and science which opened up the oceans and the ocean beds for a mode and rate of exploitation both of the living and non-living resources heretofore unimaginable.

3. At the same time this new technology exposed the marine areas to abuse and overexploitation both of the living resources and the mineral resources to an extent mankind had never dreamt of.

4. Another new factor was the abolition of colonialism and the emergence of some hundred new states. This event totally changed the fabric of the international community. These new states entered the international community with their own dreams and aspirations anchored in concepts that are different from those of the industrialized and Westernized countries.

Here we are in our Conference experiencing but also benefiting from a clash of ideologies and cultural concepts which obviously has caused international strains and which we must overcome through new and flexible compromise solutions on many important issues.

A serious problem to the industrialized world and to a lesser degree also to the developing world is the fact that mankind has exhausted or is rapidly exhausting many invaluable mineral resources on land, including petroleum. This results from centuries of use and unfortunately also centuries of abuse of the landbased resources. The loss of colonies has dramatized this situation for certain countries and their "multinational" corporations.

One pressure which is especially felt by small coastal states like my own Norway is the increased strategic importance of the oceans and the ocean floors. The emergence of two superpowers, that are being both divided and linked by the oceans, has polarized and accentuated this enhanced strategic importance of the oceans.

The terror balance that the world powers have established in the weird and perhaps justified hope that it will maintain world peace, is to a great extent hinged on the new strategic dimension of the oceans. Norway is one of the countries that feels this special dimension most acutely. It is well known that those parts of the Arctic Ocean and the Barents Sea washing the coasts of Norway contain vast food resources for Europe and the world. It gives us tremendous responsibilities with regard to management and conservation. Our management and conservation policies are not made easier by the possibly enormous oil potentials of the Norwegian continental shelves in these areas. We have the same possibilities and responsibilities in the North Sea, almost half of which is part of the Norwegian continental shelf and economic zone.

One glance at the world map suffices to show the strategic importance of the Barents Sea and the Arctic Ocean in the nuclear age. The increased strategic importance given to the Murmansk area by the Soviet Union is well known. It has enhanced the importance of the Barents Sea as a strategic lung for the Soviet Union. Two world wars have also in their tragic ways emphasized the importance of the North Sea in the strategic picture.

It follows that the enormously increased and changed importance of the oceans both for peaceful purposes and strategic uses, coupled with the new doctrines of international law and of foreign relations, has given Norway perhaps more than most other coastal states, new and changed dimensions in the world picture. It has given us new possibilities and potentials but it has also given us vastly added responsibilities and burdens. I shall refrain from an overall assessment. But I may assure you that our people and our authorities are aware of these circumstances. We are trying to meet them with appropriate policies and measures. We certainly need time as does everyone. But I believe that we are helped by the fact that these seas have been an integral part of our nature and our lives for thousands of years.

Let me now proceed to another question. What is the present status of the Law of the Sea Conference, and what are its chances of success? We have had seven sessions of the Conference. During the Sixth Session of the conference which convened in New York from May to July 1977, the President jointly with the Chairmen of the three main committees was able to prepare the so-called Informal Composite Negotiating Text, covering most aspects of the Conference. This is undoubtedly a rather strange title for a document entailing a novel approach to U.N. negotiations. The document is (as it states) a negotiating text, but as such in principle purely a procedural device in order to make it possible for delegations and the conference to have an orderly document before them during negotiations. It is in principle an intermediary stage in the search for consensus. It has not been voted on. Any delegation may suggest revisions, informal revisions. We avoid the term amendments because we have not reached such a formal stage yet. The document is not a draft text, let alone a draft convention. Nothing in it has been adopted by consensus.

Still, in my humble opinion, it is a document with considerable legal and political implications. It has started leading an independent life of its own. International lawyers refer to it. Politicians and governments refer to it. There are a great number of areas in which the Informal Composite Negotiating Text expresses the tentative consensus of the Conference.

Thus the document should not be underestimated. It will obviously serve as a main stepping stone towards the finalization of a draft convention. And if against all hopes and expectations our Law of the Sea Conference should fail it would be a major source in years to come of the world order of the oceans, or we may perhaps call it a source for a modern customary law of the sea. The trends here are clear and irreversible.

This document emerged, as I said, from the Sixth Session The purpose of the Seventh Session was to revise and formalize this document on the road to a draft convention adopted by consensus. The Seventh Session was not entirely successful in reaching these aims. But it was surely not a failure. The Seventh Session had two meetings. The first meeting was held in Geneva from March to May of 1978. Then we had a four-week resumed session in New York in August/September of 1978. Unfortunately the Seventh Session started out with a bitter procedural fight on the presidency which almost proved disastrous to the Conference. Hopefully this issue is now settled, although a certain danger exists that the issue may be raised again either during the present General Assembly or during our Eighth Session. The forthcoming Eighth Session will convene in Geneva on March 19, 1979, and last till the end of April. This session may possibly continue later in the summer if the first meeting is sufficiently successful.

It is our hope that during the March/April session we shall be able to agree on a compromise package deal on the main outstanding issues. If successful, this may again make it possible to continue our work in July/August to have a decision-making session in order to arrive at a more formalized draft text. The aim is to arrive at such a text by consensus on all main issues, and thus leave the procedure of amendments and voting to minor questions of drafting and editing. This may sound optimistic, but not unrealistic. The stakes are too high both for the Conference, the United Nations and the world as a whole, for the Conference to founder, so we must persevere.

There are of course some crucial issues still outstanding. But the greater number of issues have found modern and realistic solutions. But even within these issues there are certain crucial unsolved points which may prove disastrous if they remain unsolved. The issues on where we have arrived at broad general solutions (I may perhaps say consensus) are many and significant. I believe that it would be correct to say that some 90% of the Informal Composite Negotiating Text commends such agreement. But the remaining issues are so crucial that it would certainly prove disastrous to the Conference, if we were not able to find solutions to them.

The items on which we have found the general solutions are:

a. The territorial sea, extent, uses and delimitation.

b. The contiguous zones.

c. The status of and passage through international straits.

d. The questions of archipelagic states and the passage through archipelagic waters.

e. The establishment and uses of the Exclusive Economic Zone of 200 miles.

f. The status of the continental shelf.

g. The high seas, status, uses and management and conservation of the resources.

h. The regime of islands.

We have likewise succeeded in drawing up generally acceptable proposals on:

i. The protection and preservation of the marine environment including ice-covered areas, and

j. Marine scientific research.

Especially on these last two items the Seventh Session proved highly useful. Compromise formulations were reached on a number of important outstanding issues commending general consensus. On other provisions formulations were arrived at which offer a substantially improved prospect of consensus. These results were reached mainly through the untiring efforts of the Chairman of the Third Committee, Ambassador Yankov of Bulgaria, and the Chairman of the Informal Working Group, Ambassador Vallarta of Mexico.

Two interesting documents emerged from the Seventh Session in this respect. The first is a report emerging from the Geneva meetings of the Seventh Session from the Chairman of the Third Committee. It is included in the report of May 19, 1978 from the Geneva session. The other document is a report from the Chairman of the Third Committee dated September 13, 1978, emerging from the resumed New York session.

On the other hand we shall have some outstanding issues of extreme importance which the Seventh Session left unsolved. Among these issues are:

a. Issues pertaining to the exploitation of the mineral resources of the deep ocean floor, the so-called international area. Among these are the access to the area, production ceilings, and the organization and power of the Authority especially the composition of the Council, the financial arrangements, and transfer of technology.

b. Certain formulations concerning the legal status of the seas of the economic zone seem to have gained importance.

c. The outer limit of the continental shelf. Especially the so-called Irish formula versus a 200 mile distance criterion or a Soviet proposal of a 300 mile distance criterion.

d. The rights of landlocked and geographically disadvantaged states.

e. Certain aspects concerning the settlement of disputes pertaining to obligatory arbitration.

f. Aspects traditionally belonging to the chapter final clauses. Among such are:

   (i) the number and nature of ratifications needed for the entering into force of the Convention--a very delicate issue especially because of the contemplated special composition of the Council of the International Authority.

   (ii) Reservations to the convention, and

   (iii) The question of the preliminary entering into force of the convention or other special temporary arrangements for an interim period.

   (iv) Duration of the convention and revision clauses.

To many <u>the</u> main outstanding issue is the question of the exploitation of the mineral resources of the area. Here we are in a race against time. The exploitation of the rich layers of nodule deposits on the deep ocean floor is now technologically and economically feasible. At least one main participant in the Conference, the United States, is proposing unilateral national legislation which again makes it urgent to find internationally acceptable solutions before it is too late. Fortunately the U.S. Congress has now adjourned without having passed the bill. This gives us at least a temporary respite.

We have made great strides towards a compromise solution of this complex issue during both the Sixth and Seventh Sessions. I believe that a compromise is within reach both with regard to the access to the area and to the question concerning production ceilings. Similarly, a solution of the question of the composition of the Council is within reach.

In regard to the question of the financial arrangement a significant development took place during the New York meetings of the Seventh Session. The questions hidden under the term "Financial Arrangements" are highly volatile. They are, in short, what shall the international corporations or state corporations pay for the privilege of exploiting the nodules? Until the resumed session, the Conference seemed to shy away from proposing concrete figures. During the very last days of the session, the chairman of Informal Working Group, Ambassador Tommy Koh of Singapore, made such concrete proposals. He proposed a composite system of three types of charges:

a. First, a processing fee of $500,000 per application. Any part of this fee not used for processing the application shall be refunded to the applicant.

b. An annual fixed fee of $1 million per concession area. Such annual fee shall be deducted from the production charge.

c. Finally, the third type of payment is a production charge. Two alternative systems of production charges are proposed.

A single system consisting of the payment of a higher production charge only. From year one through six of the commercial production, the production charge shall be 7.5% of the value of the processed metal.

In years seven through twelve of commercial production the production charge is 10%; in years thirteen through twenty it is 14%.

A contractor may, however, choose a mixed system consisting of production charge plus a share of the net proceeds. Under this system the production charge would be:

In years 1-6 of the commercial production	2%
In years 7-12 of the commercial production	4%
In years 13-20 of the commercial production	6%

In addition, the authority shall have a share of the so-called attributable net proceeds in the following percentages:

In years 1-6 of the commercial production	40% of A.N.P.
In years 7-12 of the commercial production	70% of A.N.P.
In years 13-20 of the commercial production	80% of A.N.P.

Ambassador Koh's proposal also contains certain safety clauses which shall protect the contractor against exaggerated payments.

The response to Ambassador Koh's proposal was rather negative, at least on the part of some of the main industrialized countries. One reason why the problems of the First Committee on the exploitation of the International Seabed area have been so controversial and difficult to solve is the clear clash of ideologies and systems. Among the 15 basic seabed principles adopted on December 17, 1970 by the 25th General Assembly was the principle contained in Section 1 of that resolution to the effect that:

> The Deep sea-bed and the ocean floor outside the continental shelves of coastal states are <u>the common heritage of mankind</u> together with all the resources on and in this sea-bed.

This concept of "the common heritage of mankind" is in many ways a new and revolutionary doctrine both in international law and in foreign policy. The concept taken from the outer space resolutions was included on the insistence of the developing world assisted by a few progressive industrialized countries. The "common heritage of mankind," wherever we meet this principle, will bestow upon us as mankind enormous rights and possibilities but also obvious obligations even outside the sphere of law and politics. It should be given a philosophical content that accepts and materializes our obligations toward and interdependence with our surroundings in their entirety be they living or organic entities or non-organic matter and even the importance of and our interdependence with space and time.

This main principle is a cornerstone in Chapter XI of the Informal Composite Negotiating Text dealing with the International Area and the system to be adopted for the exploitation of the area. Article 136 provides that:

> "The area and its resources are the common heritage of mankind."

This principle and its implications are closely linked to the doctrine of a new international economic order.

I shall merely mention its implied realization of the interdependence between peoples and nations in today's world with the ensuing need for close and harmonious relationship and cooperation among states, bilaterally as well as multilaterally, in international organizations which in the future must be endowed with supranational authority in many fields.

One of the main difficulties hampering the work of the First Committee is that in some respects its work is the first major example of making the new economic order a political and legal reality in an area which both in geographic extent and in political and economic importance is a very significant part of our globe.

I have frequently been asked the question whether I believe that the Conference will succeed. My answer has always been in the affirmative. We have a good chance of success for many reasons. One reason is that there is an increasing understanding among all countries and delegates that it is essential that we succeed. The new problems which we face are of such magnitude that unless we are able to find solutions to them we might enter into an era of unrest and severe international tension. Secondly, the United Nations, as such, has invested so much in terms of economic efforts, expertise and prestige in this Conference that it would be a severe blow to the United Nations, as the world organization, if the Conference were a failure.

On the other hand, if we should meet obstacles of such a magnitude that we are faced with a prolonged impasse, where do we then stand? Even in such an unlikely event, the Conference has made enormous contributions to the development of a modern law of the oceans, both legally and politically.

I believe that the question of the twelve mile territorial sea must now be considered as an established principle of international law. I believe that the concept of the continental shelf has been further strengthened and enlightened by discussions during the Law of the Sea Conference. I also believe that the concept of two hundred mile economic zones has already acquired the force of international law. The legal reasoning behind this assumption may be somewhat unorthodox. Has the concept of economic zones acquired the force of customary international law? Under traditional concepts of international law obviously not. On the other hand a number of elements have played a role in the law-making process. The urgency of the situation and the need for new approaches have been overwhelming. Thus the provisions on economic zones may to some extent have their base in an emergency law concept. Technology has been running wild to such an extent that it is an absolute necessity for coastal states to protect the living resources in their coastal seas to defend themselves against over-exploitation or even extinction of important marine species. Additionally, the concept of the economic zone has inherent elements of natural law. Furtherfore, during the Conference a consensus has developed to make it reasonable to maintain that this concept of the economic zone has acquired the status of international law by consensus. State practice has likewise developed to such an extent during the last several years that it would be politically naive to assume that states would be willing to give up the concept of 200 mile economic zones and to accept again the antiquated concepts of international law which gave no effective protection to the endangered species in the oceans. Too much has been invested by coastal states in legislative efforts and in efforts to establish effective supervision over fisheries, in establishing effective coastal patrols and coast guards for these purposes to expect that the clock could be turned back. Consequently, it is reasonable to assume economic zones are here to stay with or without a successful outcome of the Law of the Sea Conference.

The situation is probably entirely different with regard to the mineral exploitation of the deep ocean floor. It would be impossible to assume that an international organization, or international organ, with supra-national powers would automatically be created under international law on the basis of the preliminary draft we have worked out. On the other hand, I believe that the fifteen principles adopted by the 25th General Assembly in 1970 on the mineral resources of the deep ocean floor have acquired the status of international law; one example is the principle that the riches of the deep ocean floor are the common heritage of mankind and that they cannot be subjected to expropriation or annexation by states or persons. But these are general legal principles which need further elaboration to make them effective. Consequently we certainly need, in addition to these principles, the detailed provisions now emerging from the Law of the Sea Conference on First Committee matters. We shall never be able to elaborate a modern system for the exploitation of the mineral resources of the deep ocean floor without a basis in treaty provisions. The success of the Law of the Sea Conference is also essential for this reason.

It is likewise essential with regard to landlocked and geographically disadvantaged countries, with regard to the questions of passage through straits and passage through waters of archipelagic states. The question of the extent and delimitation of coastal waters and continental shelves to establish clear treaty language in order to avoid unnecessary international tension is also vital.

As far as Third Committee matters are concerned, both the broad principles laid down on pollution and the principles contained in the Composite Negotiating Text on scientific research are essential for a modern approach to a regulation of ocean space. Some of these principles may already have acquired the force of valid international law. But a convention would be essential for the effective implementation of a modern system both on marine pollution and on scientific research.

Mr. Chairman, I have exhausted the time at my disposal, and I thank you for the occasion to make this address. I wish the Law of the Sea Institute and the Institute of International Law of the University of Utrecht success in their future work with law of the sea questions.

PARTICIPANTS
LIST

Paul Adam
OECD
Paris, France

Lewis Alexander
University of Rhode Island
Kingston, RI, U.S.A.

Dorothy W. Allan
Washington, DC, U.S.A.

Scott Allen
Law of the Sea Institute
Honolulu, HI, U.S.A.

John M. Armstrong
Coastal Zone Laboratory
University of Michigan
Ann Arbor, MI, U.S.A.

J. Arnst
Ministry of Economic Affairs
Mining Department
The Hague, The Netherlands

H.A.H. Audretsch
Institute of European Law
Utrecht, The Netherlands

M. Balkenstein
Ministry of Transport and Water Management
The Hague, The Netherlands

John E. Bardach
East-West Center
Honolulu, HI, U.S.A.

L.A.N.M. Barnhoorn
T.M.C. Asser Institute
The Hague, The Netherlands

P.B. Beazley
United Kingdom Hydrographer
Surrey, U.K.

M.F.M. Bertels
Ministry of Transport and Water Management
The Hague, The Netherlands

Jean-Pierre Beurier
Faculty of Law
Brest, France

Patricia Birnie
University of Edinburgh
Department of Public International Law
Edinburgh, U.K.

W. Bogaard
Institute of Public International Law
Amsterdam, The Netherlands

Gerlinde Boks
University of Utrecht
Utrecht, The Netherlands

K. Booth
University College of Wales
Department of International Politics
Aberystwyth, Dyfed, U.K.

M. Box
Institute of International Law
University of Utrecht
Utrecht, The Netherlands

Leo J. Bouchez
Institute of International Law
University of Utrecht
Utrecht, The Netherlands

Robert Bowen
Institute of Marine and Coastal Studies
University of Southern California
Los Angeles, CA, U.S.A.

S.W.P.C. Braunius
Royal Netherlands Navy
The Hague, The Netherlands

E.D. Brown
University of Wales
St. Fagans, Cardiff, U.K.

PARTICIPANTS LIST

Hans Butselaar
University of Utrecht
Utrecht, The Netherlands

Barry Buzan
Department of International Studies
University of Warwick
Coventry, U.K.

Daniel S. Cheever
Editor, Ocean Development and International Law Journal
GSPIA, University of Pittsburgh
Pittsburgh, PA, U.S.A.

Gordon A. Christenson
Naval War College
Newport, RI, U.S.A.

Carl Q. Christol
University of Southern California
Los Angeles, CA, U.S.A.

Thomas A. Clingan, Jr.
University of Miami
Coral Gables, FL, U.S.A.

Shannon D. Cramer, Jr.
Department of Defense
Washington, DC, U.S.A.

John P. Craven
Law of the Sea Institute
University of Hawaii
Honolulu, HI, U.S.A.

A.Y.M. Delissen
University of Nijmegen
Nijmegen, The Netherlands

J. Demmink
Ministry of Defense
The Hague, The Netherlands

Brigitte Deniaux
National Centre for Scientific Research
Olivet, France

Isabella Diederiks-Verschoor
Institute of Public International Law
University of Utrecht
Utrecht, The Netherlands

P. van Dijk
University of Utrecht
Utrecht, The Netherlands

P.A. Fijn van Draat
Ministry of Transport, Water Management, and Public Works
The Hague, The Netherlands

John Drapeau
United States Navy
Alexandria, VA, U.S.A.

M.H. Dubbeldam
Netherlands Maritime Institute
Rotterdam, The Netherlands

A. van Eden
Ministry of Transport, Water Management, and Public Works
The Hague, The Netherlands

D. Eisma
Netherlands Institute for Sea Research
Texel, The Netherlands

Adam Englund
Cambridge University
Trinity Hall
Cambridge, U.K.

Curt Epperson
University of Washington
Seattle, WA, U.S.A.

Jens Evensen
Minister for Law of the Sea
Norway

David Fairbairn
Australian Ambassador
The Hague, The Netherlands

Frank L. Fraser
Naval Hydrographic Office
Dehra Dun, India

Gunter Freericks
Chlodwigstr. 4
Federal Republic of Germany

Robert Friedheim
University of Southern California
Institute for Marine and Coastal Studies
Los Angeles, CA, U.S.A.

Alan Friedman
Office of the Secretary of Defense
The Pentagon
Washington, DC, U.S.A.

Paul M. Fye
Woods Hole Oceanographic Institution
Woods Hole, MA, U.S.A.

John King Gamble, Jr.
The Behrend College
Pennsylvania State University
Erie, PA, U.S.A.

R. van Ginkel
Ministry of Transport, Water Management, and Public Works
The Hague, The Netherlands

Thor Gislesen
Royal Norwegian Embassy
The Hague, The Netherlands

A.L. Goedhart
Ministry of Education and Sciences
Nieuwe Uitleg 1
The Hague, The Netherlands

W.M. Goedhart
Netherlands Maritime Institute
Hofpleinig
Rotterdam, The Netherlands

Daniel Goedhuis
International Law Association
Newark, U.K.

Jochen Goetz
Am/Buchel 53b
Federal Republic of Germany

Edgar Gold
Faculty of Law
Dalhousie University
Halifax, N.S., Canada

Gerald Graham
Graduate Institute of International Studies
Geneva, Switzerland

T.F. Groustra-de Kat
Ministry of Education and Sciences
The Hague, The Netherlands

K. Hailbronner
University of Heidelberg
Heidelberg, Federal Republic of Germany

Michael Hardy
Commission of the European Communities
Brussels, Belgium

R.H. Hartog
Ministry of Transport, Water Management, and Public Works
The Hague, The Netherlands

W.P. Heere
Institute of International Law
University of Utrecht
Utrecht, The Netherlands

Paul Heller
University of Auckland
Auckland, New Zealand

Kazuya Hirobe
Seikei University
Tokyo, Japan

PARTICIPANTS LIST

T. van 't Hof
Ministry of Education and Sciences
The Hague, The Netherlands

Ann L. Hollick
Johns Hopkins University
Washington, DC, U.S.A.

J.P. Honig
Civil Aviation Department
The Hague, The Netherlands

H. van Hoorn
North Sea Working Group
Harlingen, The Netherlands

G. Gallandat Huet
Industrial Council for Oceanology
Haarlem, The Netherlands

Howard Hume
Petro-Canada
Calgary, Alberta, Canada

Robert C. Huston
United States Department of State
Washington, DC, U.S.A.

Vladimir Ibler
Faculty of Law
University Zagreb
Zagreb, Yugoslavia

Douglas M. Johnston
Faculty of Law
Dalhousie University
Halifax, N.S., Canada

M. de Jong
Netherlands Maritime Institute
Haarlem, The Netherlands

P.J.S. de Jong
Chairman Industrial Council for Oceanology
The Hague, The Netherlands

Kent M. Keith
Cades Schutte Fleming & Wright
Honolulu, HI, U.S.A.

Judith Kildow
Massachusetts Institute of Technology
Cambridge, MA, U.S.A.

J.R. Kluyver
University of Utrecht
Utrecht, The Netherlands

Gary Knight
Louisiana State University Law Center
Baton Rouge, LA, U.S.A.

J. Koehorst
Industrial Council for Oceanology
Delft, The Netherlands

Albert W. Koers
Institute of International Law
University of Utrecht
Utrecht, The Netherlands

J.C. Kreffer
Director of Hydrography
The Hague, The Netherlands

Robert B. Krueger
Nossaman, Krueger and March
Los Angeles, CA, U.S.A.

L. Kuyper
Ministry of Economic Affairs
The Hague, The Netherlands

C. Laban
National Geological Service
Haarlem, The Netherlands

Rainer Lagoni
Institute for International Law
University of Kiel
Kiel, Federal Republic of Germany

J.A. Lamers
Civil Aviation Service
Rijswijk, The Netherlands

W. Langeraar
Netherlands Maritime Institute
Rotterdam, The Netherlands

David L. Larson
University of New Hampshire
Department of Political Science
Durham, NH, U.S.A.

Finn Laursen
European University Institute
San Domenico di Fiesole, Italy

C. Leenders
University of Amsterdam
Bussum, The Netherlands

Michael Lehane
Lawyer
Baltimore, MD, U.S.A.

Po-lun Liu
Sun Yat-sen Center
The Hague, The Netherlands

Tony Loftas
Editor, Marine Policy
Oxon, U.K.

Curt Marshall
House Merchant Marine Sub-Committee on Oceanography and Fisheries Commission
Washington, DC, U.S.A.

Michael MccGwire
Dalhousie University
Halifax, N.S., Canada

Sandra McMahan
San Diego Law Review
San Diego, CA, U.S.A.

T. van Meerbeke-Hendriksz
Lawyer
The Hague, The Netherlands

Edward Miles
Institute for Marine Studies
University of Washington
Seattle, WA, U.S.A.

Barbara Mitchell
International Institute for Environment and Development
London, U.K.

Yoshihiko Miwa
Reporter
Hunabashi City, Japan

L.M. Moerings
Dutch Board of the Faculty of Law
Utrecht, The Netherlands

A. Moll
Ministry of Transport
Rijswijk, The Netherlands

W. Patrick Morris
House of Representatives
Merchant Marine and Fisheries Committee
Washington, DC, U.S.A.

L.B.J. Movig
Royal Netherlands Navy
Den Helder, The Netherlands

Roderick C. Ogley
University of Sussex
Brighton, U.K.

Willy Østreng
Fridtjof Nansen Foundation
Lysaker, Norway

Choon-ho Park
Culture Learning Institute
East-West Center
Honolulu, HI, U.S.A.

Walter Parker
Federal/State Land Use Planning Commission for Alaska
Anchorage, AK, U.S.A.

Carlos Parra
Institute for the New Chile
Rotterdam, The Netherlands

A.M. Peeters
Ghent University
Gent, Belgium

N.P. Pellenbarg
Rykswaterstaat
The Netherlands

Paul Peters
Shell Int. Petr. Mij.
The Hague, The Netherlands

Donat Pharand
University of Ottawa
Ottawa, Canada

Renate Platzoder
Stiftung Wissenschaft und Politik
Haus Eggenberg, Germany F.R.

Norbert J. Prill
Institute of International Law
University of Bonn
Bonn, Federal Republic of Germany

Walter Roy Quanstrom
Ocean Minerals Company
Chicago, IL, U.S.A.

H. Rombach
Netherlands Hydrographic Department
The Hague, The Netherlands

David A. Ross
Department of Geology and Geophysics
Woods Hole Oceanographic Institution
Woods Hole, MA, U.S.A.

R.H.H. Rutten
Ministry of Defence
Oestgeest, The Netherlands

A. Schmeink
Journalist
Amsterdam, The Netherlands

T.C. Schweif
Ministry of Transport, Water Management and Public Works
The Hague, The Netherlands

Ko Swan Sik
T.M.C. Asser Institute
The Hague, The Netherlands

P.J. Slot
Ministry of Transport, Water Management and Public Works
The Hague, The Netherlands

Robert W. Smith
United States Department of State
Office of The Geographer
Washington, DC, U.S.A.

Finn Sollie
Fridtjof Nansen Foundation
Lysaker, Norway

Eddy Somers
Ghent University
Gent, Belgium

H.H.M. Sondaal
Ministry for Foreign Affairs
The Hague, The Netherlands

W. Spans
University of Utrecht
Department of Public Relations
Utrecht, The Netherlands

A. van Strijen
Ministry of Transport, Water Management and Public Works
Zoetermeer, The Netherlands

William L. Sullivan, Jr.
Director, Office of Marine Sciences and Technology Affairs
United States Department of State
Washington, DC, U.S.A.

George Taft
United States Department of State
Office of the Law of the Sea Negotiations
Washington, DC, U.S.A.

Hideo Takabayashi
Ryukoku University
Faculty of Law
Kyoto, Japan

H.J. Tausk
Billiton International Metals
The Hague, The Netherlands

L.N. Tekstra
Civil Aviation Department
Lisse, The Netherlands

Dr. A.A. Thiadens
Aerdenhout, The Netherlands

A. Thurmer
International Fisheries Expert
Voorburg, The Netherlands

William J. Trainor, Jr.
United States Department of State
Washington, DC, U.S.A.

Tullio Treves
University of Torino
Milano, Italy

D. Tromp
Secretary
The Oslo Commission

Dirk G. Troost
Intergovernmental Oceanographic Commission, UNESCO
Paris, France

D.S. Tuijnman
Minister of Transport and Public Works
The Netherlands

R. Vaessen
Royal Netherlands Navy
The Hague, The Netherlands

K.F. Valken
Ministry of Transport, Water Management and Public Works
The Hague, The Netherlands

Jorge A. Vargas
Center of Economic and Social Studies for the Third World (CEESTEM)
Mexico, D.F., Mexico

O.C.W. van der Veen
Ministry of Transport, Water Management, and Public Works
Rijswijk, The Netherlands

J.E. Vorbach
United States Department of Transportation
Washington, DC, U.S.A.

Marie-Eleonore, F.T. Vossen
Lawyer
The Hague, The Netherlands

J.A. Walkate
Foreign Affairs
Oestgeest, The Netherlands

Ola Wattne
Ministry of Oil and Energy
Norway

H.W. Wefers Bettink
University of Utrecht
Utrecht, The Netherlands

Per Magnus Wijkman
Marine Policy Program
Woods Hole Oceanographic Institution
Woods Hole, MA, U.S.A.

C. Ruediger Wolfrum
Institute of International Law
Bonn, Federal Republic of Germany

Elizabeth Young
Greenwich Forum
London, U.K.

Richard Young
Lawyer
Van Hornesville, NY, U.S.A.

Roger D. Wiegley
Law of the Sea Institute
Aiea, HI, U.S.A.

John W. Zerolis
United States Department
of State
Washington, DC, U.S.A.